Joseph Stalin

Significant Figures in World History

Charles Darwin: A Reference Guide to His Life and Works,
by J. David Archibald, 2019.

Leonardo da Vinci: A Reference Guide to His Life and Works,
by Allison Lee Palmer, 2019.

Michelangelo: A Reference Guide to His Life and Works,
by Lilian H. Zirpolo, 2020.

Robert E. Lee: A Reference Guide to His Life and Works,
by James I. Robertson Jr., 2019.

John F. Kennedy: A Reference Guide to His Life and Works,
by Ian James Bickerton, 2019.

Florence Nightingale: A Reference Guide to Her Life and Works,
by Lynn McDonald, 2019.

Napoléon Bonaparte: A Reference Guide to His Life and Works,
by Joshua Meeks, 2019.

Nelson Mandela: A Reference Guide to His Life and Works,
by Aran S. MacKinnon, 2020.

Winston Churchill: A Reference Guide to His Life and Works,
by Christopher Catherwood, 2020.

Catherine the Great: A Reference Guide to Her Life and Works,
by Alexander Kamenskii, 2020.

Golda Meir: A Reference Guide to Her Life and Works,
by Meron Medzini, 2020.

Karl Marx: A Reference Guide to His Life and Works,
by Frank Elwell, Brian Andrews, and Kenneth S. Hicks, 2020.

Eva Perón: A Reference Guide to Her Life and Works,
by María Belén Rabadán Vega and Mirna Vohnsen, 2021.

Adolf Hitler: A Reference Guide to His Life and Works,
by Steven P. Remy, 2021.

Sigmund Freud: A Reference Guide to His Life and Works,
by Alistair Ross, 2022.

Henry VIII: A Reference Guide to His Life and Works,
by Clayton Drees, 2022.

Harriet Tubman: A Reference Guide to Her Life and Works,
by Kate Clifford Larson, 2022.

Joseph Stalin: A Reference Guide to His Life and Works,
by David R. Marples and Alla Hurska, 2022.

Joseph Stalin

A Reference Guide to His Life and Works

David R. Marples
Alla Hurska

ROWMAN & LITTLEFIELD
Lanham • Boulder • New York • London

Published by Rowman & Littlefield
An imprint of The Rowman & Littlefield Publishing Group, Inc.
4501 Forbes Boulevard, Suite 200, Lanham, Maryland 20706
www.rowman.com

86-90 Paul Street, London EC2A 4NE, United Kingdom

Copyright © 2022 by David R. Marples and Alla Hurska

All rights reserved. No part of this book may be reproduced in any form or by any electronic or mechanical means, including information storage and retrieval systems, without written permission from the publisher, except by a reviewer who may quote passages in a review.

British Library Cataloguing in Publication Information Available

Library of Congress Cataloging-in-Publication Data
Names: Marples, David R., author. | Hurska, Alla, author.
Title: Joseph Stalin : a reference guide to his life and works / David R. Marples, Alla Hurska.
Description: Lanham : Rowman & Littlefield, [2022] | Series: Significant figures in world history | Includes bibliographical references and index. | Summary: "Joseph Stalin: A Reference Guide to His Life and Works" captures his life, and legacy. It features a chronology, an introduction offers a brief account of his life, a dictionary section lists entries on Stalin's associates from the period of the Russian Empire in the late 19th century to the leader's death in 1953, and beyond"—Provided by publisher.
Identifiers: LCCN 2022012838 (print) | LCCN 2022012839 (ebook) | ISBN 9781538133606 (cloth) | ISBN 9781538197653 (paper) | ISBN 9781538133613 (epub)
Subjects: LCSH: Stalin, Joseph, 1878–1953—Encyclopedias. | Stalin, Joseph, 1878–1953—Friends and associates—Encyclopedias. | Statesmen—Soviet Union—Biography—Encyclopedias. | Soviet Union—Politics and government—Encyclopedias.
Classification: LCC DK268.S8 M32 2022 (print) | LCC DK268.S8 (ebook) | DDC 947.084/2092 [B]—dc23/eng/20220429
LC record available at https://lccn.loc.gov/2022012838
LC ebook record available at https://lccn.loc.gov/2022012839

To my wonderful husband Sergey Sukhankin and my sons Borys and Liam, who have always been supportive and who always inspire me. And to the millions of those (including my family members) who lived and suffered under Communist rule in the USSR, who were arrested, tortured, killed, dispatched to labor camps, exiled to remote territories, and starved to death. Let us hope this never happens again.
—*Alla Hurska*

For Lyuba Pervushina (1960–2021), scholar, musician, and friend.
—*David R. Marples*

Contents

Acknowledgments	xi
List of Acronyms	xiii
Maps	xv
Chronology	xvii
Introduction	1
THE DICTIONARY	11
Bibliography	275
Index	281
About the Authors	289

Acknowledgments

The authors would like to acknowledge assistance from the Faculty of Arts, University of Alberta, Distinguished Professors Fund. We are also grateful to Jon Woronoff for commissioning the project and for his patience and guidance throughout the process. April Snider of Rowman & Littlefield always responded promptly to queries about presentation of the text. Alla's acknowledgment of her family appears as a dedication to this book. David would add his own appreciation for the patience of his family during its writing, and particularly to his wife—Aya Fujiwara—and his young children—Akiko and Kaella—during the COVID-19 pandemic of 2020–2022.

List of Acronyms

CC CPSU	Central Committee of the CPSU
Cheka	Extraordinary Committee to Combat Sabotage and Counter-Revolution
Comintern	Communist International
CPSU	Communist Party of the Soviet Union
CPU	Communist Party of Ukraine
GKO	State Defense Committee
Glavkomtrud	Main Committee on General Labor Conscription
GUGB	Chief Administration of State Security
Narkomvneshtorg	People's Commissariat for Foreign Trade
NKVD	People's Commissariat of Internal Affairs
OGPU	Joint State Political Directorate
Orgburo	Organizational Bureau of the CC CPSU
Rabkrin	People's Commissariat of Workers' and Peasants' Inspection
RCP(b)	Russian Communist Party (Bolshevik)
RSDWP	Russian Social Democratic Workers' Party
RSFSR	Russian Soviet Federative Socialist Republic
SMERSH	Chief Administration of Counter-Intelligence
Sovnarkom	Council of People's Commissars (Soviet government)
VGIK	All-Russian State Institute of Cinematography
VOKhR	Military Tribunal of the Internal Security Troops of the NKVD of the Republic
VTsIK	All-Russian Central Executive Committee

Maps

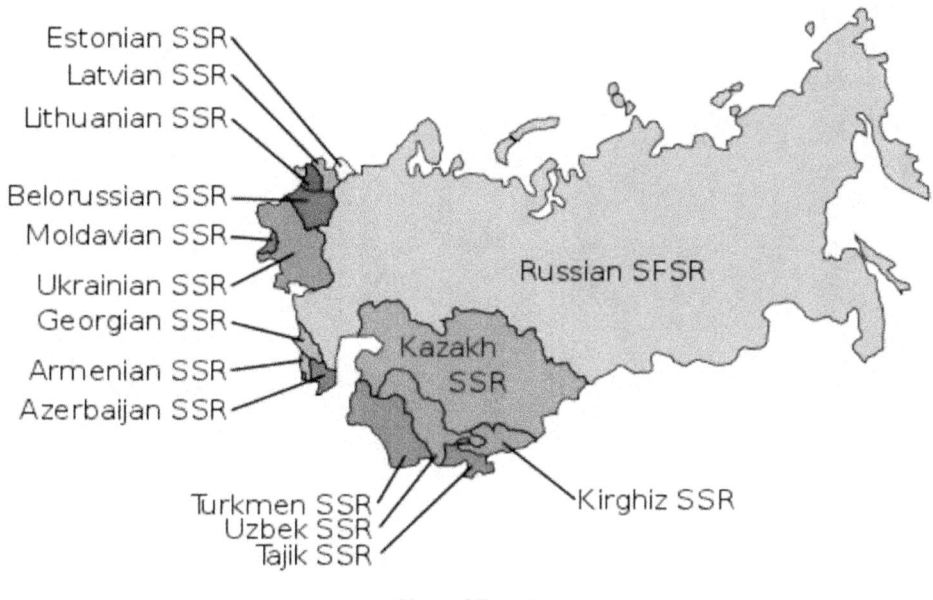

Map of Russia

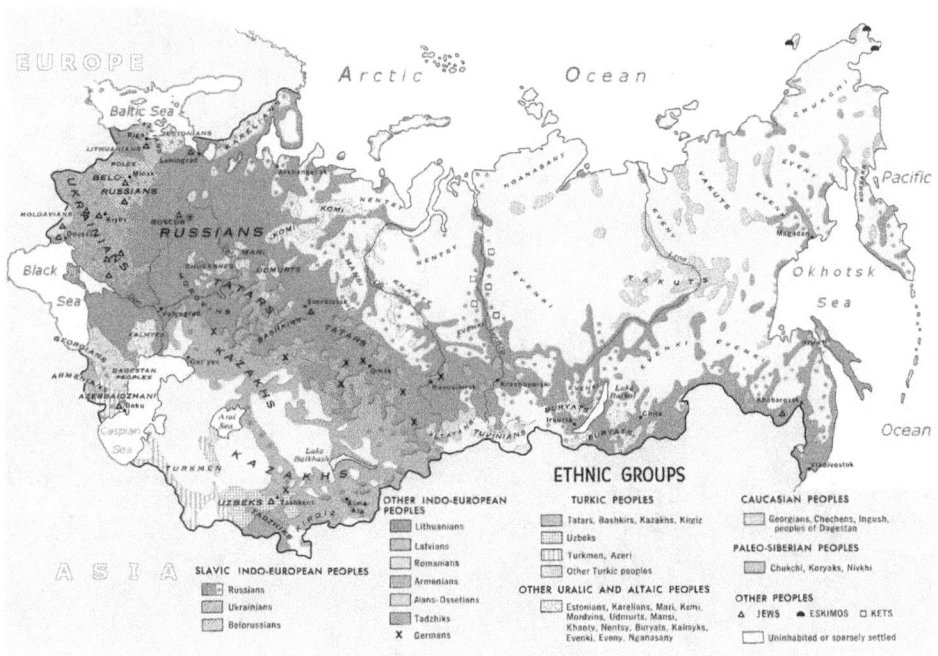

Map of ethnic groups

Chronology

1878 December 18: Stalin is born in Gori, Georgia, Russian Empire. (His official birthday, used throughout his lifetime, is December 21, 1879.) **December 29:** He is baptized.

1884 Stalin contracts smallpox, which leaves marks on his face for life.

1885 Stalin is injured after being hit by a phaeton. Subsequently, his left arm does not fully unbend at the elbow and therefore seems shorter than his right arm.

1886–1888 At the request of his mother, the children of the priest Christopher Charkviani teach him the Russian language.

1888–1894 Stalin studies at the Gori Church School.

1890 For the second time Stalin is hit by a phaeton. His leg is badly injured.

1894–1899 Stalin studies at Tiflis Theological Seminary.

Beginning of 1895 Stalin establishes contact with Russian underground revolutionary Marxist groups expelled by the tsarist government to Transcaucasia.

1896–1898 Stalin leads an illegal Marxist circle of students at the Tiflis Theological Seminary.

1898 August: Stalin joins the Mesame Dasi group—the first social-democratic party in the Caucasus, based in Tbilisi, Georgia.

1898–1899 Stalin leads a revolutionary circle in the railway depot.

1899 May 29: Stalin is expelled from the seminary. The official reason is "for not showing up at exams for an unknown reason," but in fact this decision is a result of his propagation of Marxism among seminarians and workers of railway workshops. **June 30:** Stalin meets Mikhail Kalinin, a member of the St. Petersburg League of Struggle for the Emancipation of the Working Class. He is exiled to the Caucasus and starts to work as a turner in the main workshops of the Transcaucasian Railway.

1900 August: Stalin, with the active participation of M. Kalinin, prepares and conducts a grand strike, in which up to four thousand workers of railway workshops and depots take part.

1901 March 21: Police conduct a search at Stalin's apartment and receive orders to arrest him; at the time of the search, he is not present at the apartment. **April 22:** Stalin leads the May Day demonstration in Tiflis, which is attended by about two thousand workers. Lenin's *Iskra* newspaper assesses this demonstration as an event of historical significance for the entire Caucasus. Summer: Stalin becomes a close acquaintance of the legendary "Kamo": Simon Arshaki Ter-Petrosian. **November 11:** Stalin is elected to the first Tiflis committee of the RSDWP (Leninist–"Iskra" course). **December 2:** Stalin is sent to Batum to conduct propaganda work.

CHRONOLOGY

1902 January: Stalin creates an illegal printing house in Batum, writes leaflets, and arranges the printing and distribution of proclamations.

April 5, 1902–January 5, 1904 The first arrest of Stalin, his imprisonment (first in Batumi, then in the Kutaisi prison and again in the Batumi prison) and exile to Siberia (the village of Novaia Uda, Balagansky district, Irkutsk region). In total, he spends fifteen months in prison and two months in exile. While in Kutaisi prison, on **July 27, 1903**, Stalin organizes a riot of prisoners. He makes his first contact with Lenin through correspondence.

1904 January 5: Stalin escapes from exile. **January:** In Tiflis Stalin meets Sergei Alliluev, the worker who would later become his father-in-law. **February:** Stalin heads the work of the Caucasian Union Committee of the RSDWP and writes the program document "Credo," dedicated to internal party differences and organizational tasks of the party. **Spring:** Due to his illness, Stalin stays with his mother in Gori. **December 13–31:** Under the leadership of Stalin and P. A. Dzhaparidze, a strike of oil workers takes place in Baku. It ends with the conclusion of the first collective agreement in the history of the workers' movement in Russia between workers and industrialists. The Baku strike serves as a signal for the January–February demonstrations throughout the Russian Empire.

1905 May: Stalin's brochure "Briefly on Party Disagreements" is published. **End of November 1905:** Stalin supervises the work of the fourth Bolshevik conference held by the Caucasian Union of the RSDWP.

1906 January 7: Stalin's pamphlet *Two Struggles* is published. **April 10–25:** Fourth (unification) congress of the RSDWP in Stockholm. During the congress, Stalin (under the pseudonym "Ivanovich," in honor of his paternal grandfather) opposes the Mensheviks and supports the Bolsheviks' revolutionary tactics. **June–November:** Stalin leads the organization of the first professional union of printing workers in Tiflis. **July 15:** Stalin's wedding with Iekaterina (Kato) Svanidze, daughter of the social democrat Semen Svanidze is officiated by Khristiy Tkhinvaleli (Stalin's former classmate at the seminary).

1907 March 18: Stalin's son Iakov is born. **April 24–28:** On his first trip abroad, Stalin meets with Lenin in Berlin. **April 30–May 19:** Participation of Stalin, a delegate from the Tiflis organization, in the work of the fifth congress of the RSDWP in London. **June 20:** The first issue of the illegal Bolshevik newspaper *Baku Proletarian*, edited by Stalin, is published. **August 12:** On Stalin's initiative, the first legal Bolshevik newspaper *Gudok* is published. **September–October:** Stalin participates in the election campaign for the third State Duma. **October 25:** Stalin is elected a member of the Baku Committee of the RSDWP. **November 22:** Stalin's wife, Ekaterina (Kato) Svanidze, dies.

1908 January–February: Baku Committee of the RSDWP under Stalin's leadership organizes workers' strikes in Baku, as well as the partisan "Self-Defense Headquarters." **March 25:** The second arrest and imprisonment of Stalin in the Bayil prison (Baku), where he spends eight months. While in prison, Stalin establishes contact with the Baku Bolshevik organization and writes articles for the newspapers *Baku Proletarian* and *Gudok*. **November 9:** Stalin is exiled to the town of Solvychegodsk (Vologda province) under police supervision for two years. **June 24:** After seven months of exile, Stalin escapes from Solvychegodsk. For nine months, he lives illegally and is engaged in revolutionary activities.

1910 Stalin is appointed the party's Central Committee commissioner for the Caucasus ("agent of the Central Committee"). **March 23:** The third arrest of Stalin (under the name of Zakhary Melikiants) and imprisonment in Baku. **October 29:** Stalin is exiled to Solvychegodsk.

1911 December 14: Stalin is exiled for three years under police supervision to Vologda.

CHRONOLOGY

1912 February 29: Stalin escapes from Vologda, and after transit through Baku, Tiflis, and Moscow (in Moscow he meets with Sergo Ordzhonikidze), he moves to St. Petersburg. **April 22:** Stalin is arrested again. **July 24:** Stalin is exiled to Narym. **September 1:** He escapes, lives underground, and is engaged in revolutionary activities. **September 12:** Stalin illegally moves to St. Petersburg.

1913 February 23: Stalin is arrested. **July 2:** Stalin is exiled for four years to the Turukhansky Krai. In 1914, Ia. Sverdlov and Stalin are transferred to Kureika, Krasnoiarsk Krai (north of the Arctic Circle).

1917 March 8: Stalin and a group of political exiles leave Achinsk for Petrograd. **March 12:** Stalin, liberated by the February Revolution from the Turukhansk exile, arrives in Petrograd ahead of Lenin, L. Trotsky, N. Bukharin, and G. Zinoviev and stays at Alliluev's house. **March 13:** The Bureau of the Central Committee introduces Stalin to the editorial board of *Pravda*. **March 15:** Stalin is elected to the presidium of the Bureau of the Central Committee of the party. **April 3:** Stalin welcomes Lenin when he returns from emigration to Petrograd on the "sealed train." **April 24–29:** At the seventh (April) All-Russian Conference of the RSDWP(b) in Petrograd, Stalin supports Lenin's course toward the socialist revolution (April Theses). He also presents a report on the national question, in which he promotes the idea of "a single proletarian party in the multinational Russian state." During this conference, the Central Committee of the party is elected. It consists of Lenin, Stalin, Sverdlov, Zinoviev, Kamenev, Nogin, Smilga, and Fedorov. **May:** Stalin is included in a newly created Politburo of the Central Committee of the Bolshevik Party. **October 24–25:** Lenin, together with Trotsky, Stalin, and others, leads the armed uprising in Petrograd (October Revolution). **October 25–26:** Lenin and Stalin head the work of the second multiparty All-Russian Congress of Soviets of Workers' and Soldiers' Deputies in Petrograd. Stalin is elected a member of the All-Russian Central Executive Committee and is appointed people's commissar for nationalities. He keeps this post until 1923. **November 2:** The Council of People's Commissars promulgates the "The Declaration of the Rights of the Peoples of Russia," written by Stalin. **December 18:** Lenin and Stalin sign the decree of the Council of People's Commissars on the state independence of Finland. **December 21:** Lenin and Stalin take part in the first meeting of the All-Russian Collegium on the Organization of the Red Army.

1918 January 28: Lenin and Stalin send a telegram to the Soviet peace delegation in Brest-Litovsk demanding that peace with Germany be concluded immediately. New style (Gregorian) calendar. **March 10–11:** Stalin, along with other members of the Soviet government, moves from Petrograd to Moscow.

1919 March 24: Registration of marriage of Stalin with Nadezhda Allilueva. **March 25:** The plenum of the Central Committee of the RCP(b) approves Stalin as a member of the Politburo and the Organizing Bureau of the Central Committee of the RCP(b). **March 30:** By a resolution of the All-Russian Central Executive Committee, Stalin is appointed the people's commissar of the State Audit Office. **July 5:** Stalin is appointed a member of the Revolutionary Military Council of the Western Front. **September 27:** Stalin is appointed a member of the Revolutionary Military Council of the Southern Front. **November 16:** At Stalin's suggestion, the Revolutionary Military Council of the Southern Front decides to create the Cavalry Army. **November 27:** Stalin is awarded the Order of the Red Banner.

1921 March 16: The plenum of the Central Committee of the RCP(b) elects Stalin a member of the Politburo and the Organizational Bureau (Orgburo) of the Central Committee. **August 22:** The Central Committee of the RCP(b) entrusts Stalin with leadership of the Agitation and Propaganda Department of the Central Committee. **November 18:** Stalin becomes one of the editors of the journal of the Central Committee of the RCP(b): *Vestnik agitatsii i propagandy* (*Bulletin of Agitation* and *Propaganda*). **December 28:** The ninth All-Russian Congress of Soviets elects Stalin a member of the All-Russian Central Executive Committee.

1922 April 3: The plenum of the Central Committee of the party (at Lenin's suggestion) elects Stalin the general secretary of the Central Committee of the RCP(b). Stalin would remain in this post until his death. **December 5–16:** Stalin writes the draft of the "Declaration on the Formation of the Union of Soviet Socialist Republics."

1924 May 23–31: Stalin leads the work of the thirteenth congress of the RCP(b), the first party congress after the death of Lenin. **June 17–July 8:** Stalin participates in the work of the fifth congress of the Communist International. He is elected a member of the presidium of the congress and a member of the commission for the development of a resolution on Leninism. He is also elected chairman of the Polish commission. **August 4:** Stalin speaks on the development of the Pioneer movement.

1925 September: The triumvirate Stalin–Zinoviev–Kamenev disintegrates.

1926 January 1: At the plenum of the Central Committee, Stalin is elected a member of the Politburo and Orgburo, is elected secretariat of the Central Committee of the party, and is approved as general secretary of the Central Committee of the All-Union Communist Party (b). **February 27:** Stalin's collection of works *Questions of Leninism* is published. **April 30:** Stalin writes a letter to the members of the Central Committee of the CPSU in which he exposes the alleged factional activities of Zinoviev.

1927 January 23: The Society for the Assistance of Defense, Aircraft, and Chemical Construction (abbreviated as Osoaviakhim), the predecessor of Volunteer Society for Cooperation with the Army, Aviation, and Navy (DOSAAF), is created on Stalin's initiative. **November 23:** Stalin speaks at the sixteenth Moscow Provincial Party Conference on "The Party and the Opposition."

1928 January: Initiation of an emergency policy of requisition of surplus bread in the villages. **May–June:** Shakhty Trial—the first important Soviet show trial.

October 1928–December 1932 The first Stalin Five-Year Plan for the development of the national economy of the USSR.

1929 November 10–17: Stalin heads the plenum of the Central Committee, which decides to remove Bukharin from the Politburo. **December 21:** Nationwide celebration of the official fiftieth birthday of Stalin.

1930 January 5: Stalin signs the decree of the Central Committee of the All-Union Communist Party "On the Rate of Collectivization and Measures of State Assistance to Collective Farm Development." **February 13:** Stalin is awarded his second Order of Labor Red Banner.

March 2: Stalin's article "Dizzy with Success: Concerning Questions of the Collective-Farm Movement" is published in *Pravda*. **November 25–December 7:** The Industrial Party Trial—the first post-NEP show trial. A group of Soviet scientists and technical intelligentsia is accused of creating an anti-Soviet underground organization for the purpose of sabotage in industry and transport and plotting a coup against the government of the Soviet Union. **December 24:** Stalin is approved as a member of the Labor and Defense Council.

1931–1933 Construction of the Stalin White Sea–Baltic Sea Canal, the first construction site using prison labor.

1932 Spring: M. Riutin, the former secretary of the Party Committee of Krasnopresnensky District of Moscow, writes an anti-Stalin manifesto, "Stalin and the Crisis of the Proletarian Dictatorship." September: Arrest of members of Riutin's organization, and introduction of passport regime and registration system in the

USSR. **November 9:** Stalin's wife, N. Allilueva, commits suicide. **December 31:** Introduction of the passport system in the USSR.

1933 January 19: The inclusion of grain procurements in the mandatory state-established tax. **May 8:** Stalin and V. Molotov send instructions to all local party and Soviet organizations demanding the end of acute forms of repression.

1934 May 15: Stalin signs the decree of the Central Committee and the Council of People's Commissars of the Soviet Union "On the Teaching of Soviet History in the Schools of the USSR." **December 1:** Murder of Sergei Kirov. A resolution of the presidium of the Central Executive Committee of the USSR "On the Procedures for Handling Cases on Preparation or Commitment of Terrorist Acts" is adopted. Beginning of "Great Terror."

1935 January 5–16: The first Moscow trial—the trial of the "The Case of the Trotskyite-Zinovievite Terrorist Center." **Summer:** The "Kremlin case"—a criminal investigation on charges of high treason. A number of Kremlin employees, employees of the Kremlin commandant's office, and military personnel are accused of creating an illegal anti-Soviet organization and preparing an attempt on Stalin's life. **August 31:** The start of the Stakhanovite movement.

1936 January: The beginning of new purges in the Party. **June 11:** Stalin's speech at a meeting of the presidium of the Central Executive Committee of the Soviet Union with a report on the draft constitution of the USSR. **September 29:** Stalin holds a Politburo meeting on assisting the Spanish government. According to this plan, between 1936 and 1938, 648 aircraft, 347 tanks, 120 armored vehicles, 1,186 guns, 20,500 machine guns, about 500,000 rifles, and a lot of ammunition are delivered from the USSR to Spain. Also, 584 Soviet military advisers and instructors, 772 pilots, 354 tankmen, about 100 artillerymen, 77 sailors, 166 signalmen, 140 military engineers and technicians, and 204 translators arrive in Spain to assist the Republican government against military rebels. **September 30:** Removal of Genrik Iagoda and appointment of Nikolai Iezhov as people's commissar of internal affairs. Under Iezhov, the repressions in the USSR reach their maximum scope. **October:** Purges in the NKVD apparatus. The arrests of "Trotskyists" Piatakov, Radek, Sokolnikov, and Serebriakov and some senior workers in the coal industry and transport. **December 5:** Stalin's constitution is adopted.

1937 The period of Iezhovshchina—mass repressions take place throughout Soviet society. **January 23–20:** Second Moscow Show Trial—the case of the "Parallel Anti-Soviet Trotskyist Center" (Piatakov, Radek, Sokolnikov, and Serebriakov). **February 18:** Suicide of Grigory (Sergo) Ordzhonikidze. **March 17:** Introduction of restrictions on migration of the rural population. **May 10:** Stalin establishes the Institute of Military Commissars in the army and navy. **May:** Mass arrests in the Red Army—Tukhachevsky, Iakir, Uborevich, Putna, Kork, Eideman, and Primakov.

1938 January: N. S. Khrushchev is sent to Ukraine to lead the Communist Party of the Republic. **March 12–13:** Third Moscow Show Trial—the case of the Anti-Soviet "Bloc of Rightists and Trotskyites" results in the prosecution of twenty-one senior officials (Bukharin, Rykov, Rakovsky, Ikramov, Iagoda, and others). **March 25:** Large-scale purges in the army in the Kyiv Special Military District. **December 8:** Dismissal of Iezhov from office and appointment of L. Beria as people's commissar of internal affairs.

1939 January 17: The All-Union Population Census is held in the USSR. **March 10–21:** Eighteenth congress of the All-Union Communist Party (Bolsheviks). A course toward the completion of socialist construction and a gradual transition from socialism to communism in the USSR is announced. **May 3:** V. Molotov is appointed people's commissar for foreign affairs, replacing M. Litvinov. **May 10:** P. A. Sudoplatov is appointed deputy chief of foreign intelligence of the NKVD of the USSR and responsible for the preparation of Operation "Duck" (Utka) (liquidation of L. Trotsky). **August 23:** The conclusion of a ten-year Soviet–German Non-Aggression Pact—the "Molotov–Ribbentrop Pact"—with a secret protocol to divide occupied lands into spheres of interest. **September 17:** The Red Army invades eastern Poland. **September 19:** Military units of the Red Army occupy Vilnius. Soviet ships blockade the coast of Estonia. **September 28:** The signing of the Soviet–German Treaty of Friendship and Border between the USSR and Germany. **November 30, 1939–March 12, 1940:** Soviet–Finnish war (the Winter War). **December 20:** By the decree of the presidium of the Supreme Soviet of the USSR, in connection with Stalin's sixtieth anniversary, he is awarded the title of hero of socialist labor for exceptional services in the organization of the Bolshevik Party, the creation of the Soviet state, the building of a socialist society in the USSR, and the strengthening of friendship between the peoples of the Soviet Union.

1940 August 20: Assassination of L. Trotsky in Mexico.

1941 April 13: Signing of the Soviet–Japanese Neutrality Pact. **May 6:** Stalin is appointed chairman of the Council of People's Commissars of the USSR. **June 22:** The beginning of the Great Patriotic War—Nazi Germany invades the USSR. **June 24:** Stalin signs the decree of the Central Committee of the CPSU and the Council of People's Commissars of the USSR "On the Creation and Tasks of the Soviet Information Bureau." **June 30:** M. Kalinin and Stalin issue the Resolution of the Presidium of the Supreme Soviet of the USSR, Council of People's Commissars of the USSR, and the CC CPSU on the creation of the State Defense Committee (GKO) composed of Stalin (chairman), V. Molotov, K. Voroshilov, G. Malenkov, and L. Beria. **July 3:** Stalin's historic radio address to the citizens of the Soviet Union: "Comrades, Citizens, Brothers and Sisters, Soldiers of Our Army and Navy!" **July 12:** Signing of the agreement between the USSR and Great Britain on joint actions in the war against Germany. **July 19:** Decree of the presidium of the Supreme Soviet appoints Stalin people's commissar of defense of the USSR. **July 30:** On Stalin's behalf, Soviet ambassador to London I. Maisky concludes with the Polish government-in-exile an agreement on mutual assistance in the war against Germany and on the establishment of Polish military units from POWs in the Russian army under the command of General Wladyslaw Anders to participate in hostilities against Germany. **August 8:** By a decree of the presidium of the Supreme Soviet of the USSR, Stalin is appointed supreme commander-in-chief of the Armed Forces of the USSR. **September 29–October 1:** Stalin takes part in a conference of representatives of the USSR, Great Britain, and the United States in Moscow. The three allied states sign a protocol on mutual military supplies. **November 7:** Historical parade marking the anniversary of the October Revolution as Soviet soldiers march through the Red Square to the front lines.

1942 July 28: Order No. 227—"Not a Step Backward!" **September 5:** Stalin issues an order "On the Tasks of the Partisan Movement."

1943 October 19–30: Moscow Conference of Foreign Ministers of the USSR, UK, and the United States. **October 1943–June 1944:** Mass deportations of the Crimean Tatars, Chechens, Ingushetians, Kalmyks, Karachays, and Balkars to Siberia, Central Asia, and Kazakhstan for alleged collaboration with the invaders in accordance with the decree of the presidium of the Supreme Council and Council of People's Commissars of the USSR. **November 5:** Stalin approves the sketch of the Order "Victory." **November 28–December 1:** The Tehran Conference. Stalin signs the "Declaration of the Three Powers."

1944 July: Stalin is awarded the first order of "Victory" no. 3 (no. 1 was awarded to Georgy Zhukov, no. 2 to Aleksandr Vasilevsky).

1945 February 4–12: Stalin and Molotov participate in the Crimean conference of the leaders of the three allied powers: the Soviet

Union, the United States of America, and the United Kingdom. **May 9:** Stalin in a radio address congratulates the Soviet people on the victorious end of the Great Patriotic War. **May 24:** At a reception in the Kremlin, Stalin delivers his "Victory Speech" to the commanders of the Red Army. **June 24:** Stalin attends the historic Victory Parade on Red Square in Moscow. **June 26:** Stalin is awarded his second order of "Victory." **June 27:** The supreme commander-in-chief of all the armed forces of the USSR, Stalin, is awarded the new and highest military rank—generalissimus of the Soviet Union. **July 17–August 2:** Potsdam Conference of the three allied leaders in Berlin. **August 20:** Stalin signs the State Defense Committee Decree No. 9887, in which the coordination of all research work in the USSR on the creation of the atomic bomb is entrusted to L. Beria. **Between October 10–15:** Stalin's first micro-stroke occurs.

1946 February 25: Generalissimus of the Soviet Union Stalin, by decree of the presidium of the Supreme Soviet of the USSR, is appointed the people's commissar of the armed forces and supreme commander-in-chief of the armed forces of the USSR. **March 19:** The first session of the Supreme Soviet of the USSR approves Stalin as chairman of the Council of Ministers and minister of the armed forces of the USSR.

1948 May 14: With the active support of Stalin, the independent state of Israel is created. **June 17, 1948–May 23, 1949:** The Berlin blockade attempts to isolate West Berlin from western Germany. **November 20:** The dissolution of the Jewish Anti-Fascist Committee.

1949 January 5–8: During the economic meeting of representatives of the USSR, Bulgaria, Poland, and Czechoslovakia, the Council for Mutual Economic Assistance (CMEA) is created. **January 1949:** The start of the anti-cosmopolitan campaign. **August 29:** The first Soviet atomic bomb is tested in the USSR (Semipalatinsk).

1952 May–June: Trial of the Jewish Anti-Fascist Committee. **December:** Arrests of "saboteur doctors"—the Doctors' Plot. **December 16:** The arrest of the head of Stalin's security, General N. Vlasik.

1953 February 17: Stalin holds his last meetings in his Kremlin office. **March 5:** Death of Stalin. **March 9:** Stalin's funeral, during which a number of people are crushed and trampled to death.

Introduction

The figure of Stalin continues to intrigue, fascinate, and repel historians into the 21st century, while in the Russian Federation, he has returned to the status of a figure to be respected, principally as the leader who led his country through industrialization and militarization, enabling it to defeat Nazi Germany in the Second World War, thereby saving Europe and much of the world from the "brown plague" of fascism. In the Western world, Stalin is also the subject of numerous biographies that continue to appear even though it would seem that nothing further could be written about his life.[1] He presided over some of the most cataclysmic events of the 20th century, of some of which he was the architect: collectivization of agriculture, famine, the Purges, and the Second World War.

Before providing outlines of the careers of those around Stalin—the chief purpose of this book—it is worthwhile to describe the main events of his life, one that began in the late Russian Empire in Georgia during the reign of Aleksandr II, the "reforming tsar" who abolished serfdom but was later assassinated, and ended in Moscow with Stalin's death in March 1953, a time of the Cold War, when the Soviet Union had detonated its own atomic bomb and encouraged North Korea's leader Kim Il Sung to attack the south and start a bloody conflict that has not been resolved almost seventy years later.

By the Western calendar adopted by Soviet Russia in 1918, Stalin was born on December 18, 1878, but his official birthdate, and the one used throughout his time as Soviet leader, was December 21, 1879. His birthplace was the city of Gori, in Tiflis gubernia, in the Russian Empire. He was the leader (1924–1928 might perhaps be described most accurately as the period of co-leadership) of the Soviet state, from January 21, 1924, to March 5, 1953. Among his most notable titles were those of general secretary of the Central Committee, Communist Party of the Soviet Union (1922–1953); marshal of the Soviet Union, 1943; and generalissimo of the Soviet Union, 1945.

From 1895 at the age of 15, he took part in the underground revolutionary movement, leading Marxist propaganda among students in the Tiflis seminary and at factories. In 1900, he took part in organizing a workers' strike. In 1901, he joined the RSDWP, and after it split into two branches in 1903, he sided with Lenin and the Bolsheviks. In 1902, Stalin was arrested, and the following year he was sent for three years of exile to Irkutsk gubernia in Siberia, but he managed to escape in January 1904, returning to the Caucasus. In March 1903, at the first congress of the Caucasus Social Democratic organization, he was elected unanimously as a member of the Caucasus Union Committee of the RSDWP. At this time, his main task as a revolutionary was to lead the strike movement and promote the Bolshevik wing of the party.

In 1904, he was one of the organizers of a great bank robbery in Baku, which provided funds used for party work. At the end of 1905, a tempestuous year in Russia that had seen a revolution following a catastrophic defeat in the Russo-Japanese War, Stalin traveled to Tammerfors, Finland, as a delegate representing

Bolsheviks of the Caucasus at the First All-Russian Bolshevik Conference. He met Lenin for the first time here and also visited Stockholm to attend the fourth united congress of the RSDWP. He was also a delegate at the fifth congress, which was held in London in 1907. During this period, Stalin married his first wife, the Georgian Ekaterine (Kato) Svanidze, who he had met after being invited to live with her family by her brother Aleksandr (Aliosha), a fellow member of the RSDWP. The marriage took place in the summer of 1906 in a church near their place of residence in the early hours of the morning. Stalin was already known to the secret police, and his wife had a brief jail sentence while allowing another revolutionary to stay at the house. On March 18, 1907, Kato gave birth to a son, Iakob. The family moved to Baku after Stalin's role in a Tiflis bank robbery, and she suffered from the intense heat there. She died on November 22, 1907, possibly of typhus. Stalin was genuinely disconsolate at her passing, but during the Purge period, the family that had hosted him was not spared. Aliosha and his wife were both executed. Stalin was notably unaffectionate with Iakob, who lived with him from 1921.

In the summer of 1907, Stalin was helping to produce some socialist newspapers in the Caucasus region, including *Bakinsky proletary* and *Bakinsky rabochy*. In March 1908, he was again arrested and given a two-year sentence to be spent in Vologodsk gubernia, but after fourteen months there, he escaped and returned to Baku. He also started his career as a publicist, contributing several articles to the regional Bolshevik newspapers in the Caucasus. In March 1910, the authorities caught up with him in Baku and gave him an eighteen-month prison sentence, followed by exile in Solvychegodsk (Arkhangelsk region) in the Russian Arctic.

At the Plenum of the Central Committee of the RSDWP in January 1912, Stalin was appointed in absentia as a member of the CC as well as the CC of the Russian Bureau. The following month, he broke free from his exile and returned to St. Petersburg, where he found work on the Bolshevik newspapers *Zvezda* and *Pravda*. In April, he was once again detained and dispatched for three years of exile in Narymsky (currently Tomsk region). However, the exile lasted only five months before he once again turned up in the Russian capital, this time joining the editorial board of the Bolshevik Party newspaper *Pravda*. He spent the final two months of the year in Krakow, at a conference of the party's Central Committee and rank-and-file party members. In this same period and into 1913, Stalin wrote the pamphlet *Marxism and the National Question*, his first venture into party theory and one that defined *nationalism* as based on the historical formation of a group of people with a common territory, language, territory, and economic life. The pamphlet was written in support of Lenin's belief in the primacy of a centralized country that would include smaller nationalities. The pamphlet appeared to have been edited quite heavily by Lenin (and perhaps Bukharin) but nonetheless established Stalin's pedigree as an expert on the nationalities question.

In February 1913, the tsarist authorities once again arrested Stalin in St. Petersburg and sent him into exile in Turukhansk region (Krasnoiarsk), where he resided from 1914 to 1916. He was mobilized into the tsarist army briefly in December 1916, taking part in engagements in Krasnoiarsk and Achinsk, but the outbreak of revolution in Petrograd in February (March) 1917 brought a rapid end to his service. Stalin returned to Petrograd, where he was elected into the Central Committee of the Bolsheviks and rejoined the editorial board of *Pravda*. Two months after the revolution, which brought to power a provisional government to replace the monarchy, and a system of power sharing with the Petrograd Soviet, the RSDWP(b) held its seventh conference. Stalin presented a speech on the national question and was elected to the Central Committee of the party. He retained that position at the party's sixth congress, which took place in July and August, following the uprising of the July Days, a failed attempt to take power that resulted in Lenin's flight to Finland and the arrest of Trotsky.

At the congress and subsequently, Stalin remained faithful to Lenin, communicating his instructions to the party leadership and preparing for the October takeover of power through an armed uprising as advocated by his leader. Though Stalin was not at the center of the October events,[2] he had established himself as an important figure in the Bolshevik Party, and after the victory in Petrograd, he was elected as a member of the All-Russian Central Executive Committee and as the commissar for nationalities in the fledgling Soviet government. He retained his position in the Central Committee of the RCP(b) at the seventh congress of the party in March 1918.

Stalin was a prominent figure in the ranks of the Bolsheviks during the period of Civil War and foreign intervention, occupying the years 1918–1921 (and partially into 1922 in some areas). He was a member of the regional military Soviets on the Western, Southwestern, and Southern fronts. His most notable service was in Tsaritsyn, the future Stalingrad, on the Volga, where together with A. G. Shliapnikov, he was given the role of plenipotentiary for ensuring the food supply in a city encircled by anti-Bolshevik Cossacks. Stalin wrote to Lenin asking for enhancement of his authority. In almost all instances, Stalin avoided writing to his enemy Trotsky, his nominal superior, writing directly to the head of the Soviet government. He especially distrusted former tsarist officers, accusing them of cowardice and having no qualms about arresting—and even executing—those deemed guilty of treachery. The situation at Tsaritsyn improved after the arrival of Red forces, and the campaigns there acquired a legendary status during the later Stalin regime. After helping to defeat the White Army of General Anton Denikin and taking a prominent part in the defense of Petrograd, Stalin received the Order of the Red Banner on November 27, 1919.

Stalin's star was rising, but he had differences with Lenin over the makeup of the Soviet state and its national republics. As the commissar for nationalities, Stalin was given a prime role in the formation of a permanent state structure but rejected the idea of a union of equal powers for a more centralized approach with the nationalities subordinate to a Russian state. Ultimately, Lenin prevailed. Still, the Soviet leader's approach to Stalin seemed ambivalent, perhaps as a consequence of his deteriorating health and mental capacity. Thus, on April 3, 1922, he appointed Stalin as general secretary of the Central Committee of the party, a position he would retain until his death thirty-one years later. Lenin himself led largely as a result of his personality and leadership, but Stalin but would use the new post as the foundations of a future autocracy. All future leaders were elected to this same position by the Politburo (Khrushchev would use the more modest first secretary).

As his illness worsened, Lenin made assessments of potential successors in rather unflattering terms. His biggest concern seemed to be Stalin. In his testament, which he penned as a "Letter to the Congress" on December 25, 1922, he noted that Stalin had acquired enormous powers and could not be trusted to use them carefully enough. The power over the Secretariat meant that Stalin could dictate entrance and departure from the party: he had control over party cadres and was creating a solid contingent of Communists who owed their loyalty to him alone. He did not have the same reservations about Trotsky, whom he considered the "most capable" of the leaders, distracted at times by minutiae and his personal arrogance. On January 4, 1923, Lenin added a postscript advocating Stalin's removal and his replacement by someone who had a better personality, more loyalty, and who would pay more attention to other comrades. The testament would remain in the background during the inner-party conflicts of the 1920s that followed the death of Lenin, but it did not turn out to be a decisive factor because of the loyalty shown to Stalin or to party unity by other leading figures at that time.

After Lenin's death on January 21, 1924, it was Stalin who took charge of the funeral arrangements, as well as the eulogy, written in Biblical format, while Lenin's old comrades G. Zinoviev and L. Kamenev turned the loss of a leader into a new cult of Lenin, including the preservation of his body in the mausoleum on Red Square. Already, the leadership of the country, over which Lenin had debated so carefully, was transformed into a triumvirate against Trotsky, ostensibly led by Zinoviev and Kamenev, with Stalin as third partner, somewhat in the background, seemingly calm and reasonable, and distanced from the petty squabbles around him. At the same time, Stalin was taking steps to give status to a new reputation as a party theorist. In 1924, he wrote the pamphlet *The Basics of Leninism*, to be followed up in November of the same year with *Trotskyism or Leninism?* In December, he penned yet another: *The October Revolution and the Tactics of Russian Communists*.

Stalin used Lenin as the infallible source of party dogmatism, whose statements could not be questioned, and on which basis the party should build socialism in the Soviet Union. But the party's economic program at least was far from static. In March 1921, at the tenth party congress, Lenin had switched from the harsh policy of War Communism, involving grain requisitions from the peasants and nationalization of most industry to the New Economic Policy (NEP), which replaced requisitions with a flat tax, after which the peasants were free to sell goods on the open market. Privatization of smaller companies was encouraged. Soviet society began a period of recovery from the constant years of warfare. Stalin was not the chief advocate of the NEP—this was N. Bukharin—but he was content to support it as long as Trotsky was advocating a rapid switch to industrialization and the collectivization of agriculture.

The struggle with Trotsky continued until the later 1920s, though he began to lose his bases of power not long after Lenin's death. Stalin had to deal with Trotsky's attempts to aggrandize his own role in the October Revolution, on which he wrote a pamphlet called *The Lessons of October*, which emphasized that Zinoviev and Kamenev had not supported the uprising and his theory of Permanent Revolution. The latter was standard Marxism, namely that the mainly rural Russia could not hope to achieve a successful workers' revolution in isolation, but depended on the success of revolutions abroad. Stalin, together with Bukharin, countered with the view that Russia could achieve socialism alone, through its own efforts, or "Socialism in One Country," a slogan that had instant appeal and was at the same time patriotic. Stalin made an effort to harness Lenin's writings, by taking as an example some isolated sentences the former leader had written back in 1915.

As Zinoviev and Kamenev began to recognize Stalin's growing authority, they formed an alliance with the isolated Trotsky, dubbed by historians as the "United Opposition" and by Stalinists as the Trotskyite-Zinovievite bloc. Using the powerful party machine and a bloated bureaucracy filled with his own supporters, Stalin ruthlessly demoted his rivals from their main positions: Zinoviev lost his position as Leningrad party leader and control over the Comintern; Kamenev lost his post as the Moscow party boss; Trotsky had earlier been deprived of his key position of commissar for war, which had given him control over the Red Army. But the demotions were gradual, leaving the hope that the rivals could recant their views and return to the fold, and always using the words of Lenin as the decisive factor. Once the victory was complete, Stalin's views on economic policy began to change, and he turned instead on the so-called rightists and supporters of the NEP (also known as the Right or Rightist Opposition and consisting inter alia of Bukharin, M. Tomsky, and A. Rykov) as a prelude to the launching of his own campaign for crash industrialization and coercive collectivization of agriculture. Bukharin's "wager on the peasants" was transformed into a policy of "liquidation of the kulaks as a class."

The upheaval in the countryside was Stalin's biggest gamble, and it caused dissension within the higher party ranks as well. It destroyed the alliance with the peasantry that had been enunciated early in Soviet rule and developed during NEP and emphasized the primacy of the working class. For many ideological Bolsheviks, it was the natural policy to follow, and it was in line with Socialism in One Country. The kulaks, or richer peasants, were never clearly defined, and in fact those subject to expropriation, exile, or outright execution as criminals far exceeded the estimated 5 percent of the peasant population. Those in the rank of middle peasants (*seredniaky*) all too easily could find themselves categorized as kulaks, as could any household that opposed joining the new collective farms. Many peasants destroyed (and often ate) their own livestock rather than have them confiscated, with the result that mass shortages of food were soon in evidence. The collective farms were subject to grain procurements—a restoration of the methods in place during War Communism—and the peasants had few resources with which to subsist or resist.

The combination of grain procurements, weakly organized farms, and ruthlessness from the authorities—at both the central and local levels—resulted in mass famine by 1932, which reached catastrophic proportions in Ukraine, the North Caucasus, and the Volga region by early 1933, when mass deaths could be counted in the millions. Passports were introduced for urban residents at this time but not for rural dwellers, so the peasants who were flooding to the towns had to return home. Moreover, the Soviet leaders never acknowledged the mass starvation. It was reported mainly by Western journalists, often freelance ones who were bold enough to travel to the affected areas. Stalin, through his letters to V. Molotov and L. Kaganovich, his closest subordinates in the campaign to dekulakize and enforce grain quotas, expressed his fears of nationalist sentiment in Ukraine and interference from Poland, a country with which the Soviets had fought a largely unsuccessful war in 1919–1920.

In turn, the collective farms were intended to support new industries, and the country embarked on its First Five-Year Plan in 1929–1933 with the goal of catching up with the industrialized West in development. The plan called for the expansion of industries beyond the Ural Mountains, with a focus on machine-building, metallurgy, hydroelectric stations, and iron and steel. The combined plans changed the country, though initially the targets of the plans proved far too ambitious. The chaos in the countryside also provoked some serious disaffection, and the allegations that saboteurs and wreckers were hindering industrial development in mines and factories prompted the emergence of the Riutin Platform in 1932, which called for Stalin's replacement. Already by this time, there were some ominous events.

From his official fiftieth birthday in December 1929, not only had Stalin been recognized as the key leader in the country, outranking all rivals, but also a personality cult was being officially nurtured. Whereas in the 1920s Soviet propaganda emphasized the hegemony of the Communist Party, guided by the teaching of Lenin, the 1930s heralded campaigns to raise the status of Stalin to unprecedented levels. Gradually, he replaced the party as the key element of Soviet rule. While Stalin affected a modest disposition, and his speeches were given almost in a whisper, one can only assume that the cult was to his liking. It contrasted with an unhappy family life that saw the death of his second wife (Nadezhda Alleluieva) in 1932, most likely through self-inflicted wounds from a shotgun after an argument with Stalin during a social gathering.

The 17th party congress of 1934, which took place from January 26 to February 10, was a watershed of sorts. Called "The Congress of Victors," it represented in theory the triumph of Stalin over adversity and over his designated enemies on the left and right. Collectivization was almost completed, kulaks had been removed from the villages, and the First Five-Year Plan had ended. The tumultuous nature of the process, however, had alienated many party members, and Stalin never appeared comfortable with the status quo. On December 1, his friend and close ally Sergei Kirov, the party leader in the city of Leningrad, was assassinated in the headquarters of the city NKVD office by Leonid Nikolaev, a former party member. Nikolaev was well known to the NKVD since he had been detained in the same building six weeks earlier after a revolver was found in his suitcase. On the second occasion, however, he was not detained, and he fired from almost point-blank range with Kirov's security officials nowhere to be seen.

The circumstances of the assassination have led to much speculation that the deed had been ordered by Stalin. No hard evidence has ever been found, and it seems more likely that Stalin was genuinely shocked by the event. He immediately left for Leningrad, and a draconian law was passed on the detention and execution of suspects without trial. The death of Kirov has been seen as the start of the purges and the beginning of Stalin's paranoia about enemies in his own camp. An investigation supervised by Aleksandr Iakovlev, one of the chief officials in the administration of Mikhail Gorbachev, and conducted in 1989–1991, concluded that neither Stalin nor the NKVD appeared to be implicated in the murder. By this time, the KGB and Supreme Court had released documents that allowed for this conclusion, which was pursued most rigorously by Alla Kirilina, who had been a curator of the Kirov Museum in Leningrad. The conclusion refuted those of earlier examiners such as Amy Knight.

There is little question, however, that Stalin used the death of his friend as a means to destroy the careers of Zinoviev and Kamenev, as well as many others who were caught up in the web of accusations. The years 1935 and 1936 marked the first stage of the purges, sometimes known as the Great Terror. It resulted in the deaths of tens of thousands of people, beginning with the higher party personnel, particularly those who had been members of the Bolshevik Party from its earliest stages. Stalin and his associates then proceeded to decimate the Red Army and finally turned on the NKVD itself. In addition, it encompassed several million peasants and workers, many of whom were tried in troikas rather than a court. The top leaders were tried in three great show trials held in Moscow, presided over by the formidable prosecutor-general Andrei Vyshinsky, who was later one of the chief Soviet judges at the Nuremberg Trials of 1945–1946. Victims were forced to confess as a result of torture and sleep deprivation in NKVD prison cells, as well as to inculpate as many of their colleagues as possible. Stalin listened to some of the trials from the upper balcony of the House of Unions.

The reasons for the purges have been the subject of many debates but without any definitive conclusions. Were they a result of Stalin's personality, his suspiciousness and paranoia? Was there any real method to them, or were they a web of intrigue that spiraled as they penetrated society? Clearly they required a significant body of personnel at all levels, people prepared to arrest people without cause, often based on lists of numbers rather than any specific belief of plots, links to Trotsky, or foreign powers. The accusations also covered up economic weaknesses and flaws in the planning system since virtually any failure could be attributed to wrecking, flooding coal mines, poisoning livestock to undermine collective farms, and others. The purges only ended after one of Stalin's most ruthless subordinates, Lavrenty Beria, replaced Iezhov at the head of the NKVD in 1938, but they took on a new life as the Soviet Union expanded westward as a result of the pact with Hitler's Germany, signed on August 23, 1939, which effectively started the Second World War.

Stalin's career was approaching its apex by this stage. His sixtieth birthday was the cause for more outpouring of adulation, while his fear of external enemies prompted a rapid military buildup that was anticipated to be completed by 1943. The sudden German invasion was another crisis point in Stalin's career. He had several warnings that it was about to happen. And eleven days passed before he made a personal announcement. Still, the stories of Stalin having a nervous breakdown and retreating to his dacha may be questioned. He was most frequently at one of his dachas, and perhaps he did fear being overthrown because of his lack of preparation. Much of the border air force was destroyed on the ground by the Luftwaffe, and the three German armies advanced rapidly into Soviet territory, amassing a huge number of prisoners. Some eight hours after the invasion, the voice of Molotov was heard on the radio, vowing vengeance on the "treacherous" enemy, the sort of message that one might make to a friend who suddenly betrayed one's confidence.

If Stalin did lose his nerve at the start of the Nazi-Soviet conflict, he soon recovered. His subordinates proved loyal, possibly because they had no idea what to do. But it took several months before the Soviet side was able to offer much resistance. Stalin's initial response was to arrest those officers who had retreated or surrendered and to rely on political commissars for vital information. After the successful defense of Moscow, led by G.

Zhukov, Stalin came more into the picture, replacing party rule with a State Defense Committee that could make rapid decisions, and allowing his commanders more initiative in the field. Yet it was only after the prolonged battle of Stalingrad and Soviet victory there that Stalin once again showed his public face. By that time, the conflict had been transformed into a Great Patriotic War, churches had been opened, and Russians were defending their homeland, along with other nationalities. Partisans harassed the occupiers in the lands of the Belarusian SSR and northern Ukraine, and massive Soviet armies were prepared to fight to the death to defeat a merciless foe.

It had become Stalin's war, and his name adorned tanks as the Soviet forces advanced westward in 1943–1944. Iconic generals such as Zhukov, I. Konev, and K. Rokossovsky led the armies of the Ukrainian and Belarusian fronts, which eventually destroyed the German Army Group Center that had occupied Minsk, Smolensk, and other cities en route to Moscow. The siege of Leningrad, which had lasted nearly three years and had seen the deaths of about 2 million people, was lifted, and in the south, tough battles took place to regain cities like Belgorod, Kharkiv, Kyiv, and Sevastopol. Losses were truly catastrophic, partly because of the tactics deployed by Zhukov and others of attacking in waves that would overwhelm the invader but necessitated the sacrifice of the initial waves. The losses also emphasized the fact that the bulk of the German army was being defeated on the Eastern Front.

The war also brought conciliation with traditional enemies, and the alliance with Britain and the United States was decisive. The trio of Stalin, F. Roosevelt, and W. Churchill was reminiscent of the alliance that destroyed Napoleon more than a century earlier, and the three held summits in **Tehran** and pivotally at the Livadia Palace in Ialta in January and February 1945 to decide the fate of the world. The two key figures were Stalin and Roosevelt, Symbolically, Churchill, the British imperialist, was relegated to the minor player, as the British Empire had exhausted its resources. Roosevelt, in turn, was determined to show Stalin that the English speakers would not form an alliance against him. That Ialta was on Soviet territory, and recently reoccupied, was a signal advantage. The NKVD bugged Roosevelt's rooms at the Livadia Palace, which was probably not needed. Roosevelt was prepared to accept Soviet influence over much of eastern Europe. As for Britain, its raison d'etre for joining the war—to maintain the integrity of the Polish state—could not be achieved, as Stalin had already set up a committee of Polish Communists in Lublin to take over the postwar Polish state.

Stalin was now a world statesman, on a par with the U.S. president, and an arbiter of the world's destiny. The initiator of mass purges against his own people, which saw millions of them in gulag camps by the 1930s, could now make decisions on the fate of much of the planet. But the fear of communism that permeated western European thinking in the interwar period spread to the United States after the death of Roosevelt in April 1945. The Soviet Union, based on its agreement with its two allies, violated its nonaggression treaty with Japan three months after the war ended and sent its armies into Manchuria against the remnants of the once-powerful Imperial Japanese Army. But it was not allowed to determine the fate of Japan. The Pacific War remained the domain of the United States, as did Japan's future, which was decided mainly by General Douglas MacArthur. The Western Allies also were concerned about the spread of communism into Europe. Several countries appeared vulnerable, including Greece, where a civil war was taking place, but also Italy and even France.

At the end of the European war, a parade was held in Moscow on June 24, with Stalin presiding but leaving the physical participation of riding horses and leading the parade to Zhukov and Rokossovsky. Alongside the pomp was the reality of a country almost destroyed. About 36 million had died, including at home and in German labor camps. Much of agriculture and industry was destroyed. Stalin's reaction, now as one of the most powerful figures in the world, was very much along the lines of his fears and suspicions of the 1930s. As the Cold War began, the fear that the Americans might remain in Europe became a reality. The warm relationship with President Roosevelt was replaced by a frosty one with President Harry Truman, particularly after he initiated his doctrine that promised to halt the spread of communism. Stalin regarded this, as well as the U.S. Marshall Plan, as betrayals of the promises of Ialta. But even his allies could not be trusted. He demonstrated an ambivalence toward the victory of Communists in China and chose to treat Mao as a subservient figure, reliant on Soviet aid and expertise to survive.

The final years of Stalin were a grim time. More plots were uncovered, in Leningrad, among Soviet doctors, and the emergence of the State of Israel, initially welcomed, evoked more fear. The final years of the dictator were marked by anti-Semitism, the dismantling of the Jewish Anti-Fascist League, and the deaths of its leaders, one of whom (Solomon Mikhoels) was murdered on a Minsk street. The western borderlands, reannexed at the end of the war, saw sustained guerrilla resistance, which was overcome largely by Soviet security forces, deportations, a police campaign in alliance with Poland and Czechoslovakia, and mass collectivization, once more enforced over angry resistance. The gulags filled with Ukrainians and citizens of the Baltic States. Returning troops who had spent years of the war abroad, either in labor camps or as part of the victorious army, also fell under suspicion. Zhukov soon lost his former eminence and was removed as minister of defense. Stalin kept his cronies close as earlier, but none had much real power other than perhaps Beria, a sinister figure but a regular visitor at Stalin's dachas. The cult of Stalin reached epic proportions; indeed, he was almost a deity, but he was increasingly remote and seen in public less and less often. When he died of a stroke on March 5, 1953, he was left alone for hours on the floor of his bedroom. He recovered briefly, a moment captured in the darkly humorous movie *The Death of Stalin*, but his subordinates were left to pick up the pieces and embark on a new struggle for power.

The Soviet Union in many ways remained Stalin's state. His mark on it was deep because of the epic struggles of the 1930s and the terrible conflict that affected every citizen. His eventual successor, N. Khrushchev, tried to distance himself from his former mentor and denounced some of his crimes such as the excesses of collectivization, the purges of innocent people, and his lack of readiness for the Nazi assault in his secret speech at the twentieth party congress in February 1956. But Khrushchev was erratic and overcome by his rash policies of experiments and Cold War bravado such as installing nuclear missiles on Cuba and then backing down when the United States imposed a quarantine. He was removed in 1964 and replaced by a collective leadership from which L. Brezhnev had emerged as the main figure by 1970. Brezhnev attempted a return to veneration of Stalin but could only go so far. Few wanted a return to the 1930s. Instead, Brezhnev's period offered relative stability and a somewhat-better economic life. Always, the Communist Party was the key factor in public life. The war became the main event in national identity and the quest for legitimacy, but the country gradually became quite corrupt and its leadership limited to issuing ritualistic platitudes about successes and triumphs.

The party had lost its dynamism, and by the 1970s, the personality cult of Brezhnev was a source of humor and jokes, as an ailing figure, bloated from drugs and increasingly immobile, who gave long speeches that meant nothing, was awarded medals for things he had not done, and even won the Lenin Prize for literature for his endless and monotonous volumes of party laws that made a mockery of some of Lenin's calls to action fifty years earlier. The country could never really replace Stalin, a leader who had defeated the so-called Brown Plague of the Nazis and in the Soviet narrative had single-handedly rescued Europe. Nor could it revert to democracy or Western-style governance, or resolve the failure of its collective-farm system.

The same war-based narrative prevails in the 21st century, almost eight decades on, in President Vladimir Putin's Russia. Stalin is once again a figure to be honored rather than held in opprobrium like his nemesis Hitler. Putin has also restored the Great Patriotic War as the main event of the 20th century and pivotal to the formation of modern Russian identity. In so doing, Stalin once again has emerged as the principal figure in the victory over the forces of fascism. The war is a symbol of the greatness of an evil man, his astuteness as a politician, and his skill in outwitting enemies. And yet he made many fundamental errors, particularly in his later years, when he overplayed his hand in Berlin and Korea, and failed to foresee the resilience of the West. There were opportunities for change: for freeing gulag prisoners, for allowing the states of eastern Europe to develop their own ways to socialism, and taking a broader and more progressive role on the world stage. Stalin was too narrow in his vision to take them, and he overestimated his own influence. But his impact remains on Russian society, for better or worse.

NOTES

1. See, for example, Deutscher, Tucker, Volkogonov, Sebag Montefiore, Suny, and Kotkin.
2. Stalin became very sensitive about his relatively minor role during the armed uprising of October 2017. According to Volkogonov, "he was pathologically sensitive to anything getting into print that might obliterate his more than modest part in October or exaggerate Trotsky's." Dmitri Volkogonov, *Stalin: Triumph and Tragedy* (London: Weidenfeld & Nicolson), 32.

The Dictionary

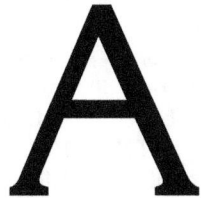

ABAKUMOV, VIKTOR SEMENOVICH (1908–1954). Born in Moscow to the son of a stoker, he was educated to the fourth grade before taking on a number of jobs as a manual laborer in the city. In 1930, he joined the Communist Party of the Soviet Union (CPSU), and his first position of note was as secretary of the Komsomol cell in the stamp factory "press." In 1932, he was moved to the OGPU at a time of purges, and as a result was able to rise rapidly in his career. In 1934, he was exposed for using his work headquarters for liaisons with women and demoted to work in the gulag camps as part of his work for the Third Section of the Economic Administration of the NKVD (the OGPU had been renamed in that same year). In 1937–1938, he worked for the Fourth (secret political) Section of the Chief Administration of State Security (GUGB) within the NKVD, and took on a number of similar positions in the NKVD thereafter. Once **L. P. Beria** became the leader of the NKVD in 1938, Abakumov was elevated to the head of the NKVD in Rostov Oblast in December of this year. He then led mass repressions in that region and gained a reputation for extreme cruelty. Trusted by Stalin, he was subsequently appointed deputy people's commissar, people's commissar, and minister. Possessed of great physical strength, Abakumov was known for personally beating prisoners.

During the third year of the **Great Patriotic War**, on April 19, 1943, the special sections were removed from the NKVD, and Abakumov was put in command of the newly created Chief Administration of Counter-Intelligence (acronym SMERSH, literally: death to spies). Additionally, Abakumov took on the role of deputy commissar of defense. SMERSH focused on counterintelligence in the army and fleet and the exposure of hostile elements in the newly liberated territories of the USSR. It was on his orders that the Swedish diplomat Raoul Wallenberg, who had saved thousands of Jews from the Nazis, was arrested in Budapest. In 1944, he took part in the deportation of people from the North Caucasus, for which he received the Order of Kutuzov and the Order of the Red Banner. In January through June 1945, he was the chief NKVD official on the 3rd Belarusian Front as the Soviet armies moved into the eastern regions of Germany.

In 1946, Abakumov was elected a deputy of the Supreme Soviet of the USSR, and on May 4 of that year, he replaced **V. N. Merkulov** as the minister of state security of the USSR, with SMERSH merged into the ministry as part of the Third Directorate. In 1946–1951, he was also a member of the Politburo Commission for legal affairs. In 1950–1951, he initiated and led the so-called Leningrad Affair, one of the final major purges under Stalin, which resulted in numerous arrests and executions, especially of the party elite in Leningrad. During this period, his career reached its peak, and he became a major rival to L. P. Beria within the Stalin leadership. In 1948, he authorized the assassination in Minsk of **S. M. Mikhoels**, leader of the Jewish Anti-Fascist Committee at the start of the "anti-cosmopolitan" affair against Soviet Jews. It was a result of alleged lack of vigilance in the related **Doctors' Plot** that he was removed from his post in July 1951.

After the death of Stalin, Beria was arrested after a few weeks as the leading figure in the country, and Abakumov remained interned. His case was heard by the Leningrad Military

Court on December 12–19, 1954. He was accused of fabricating many cases, including the Leningrad Affair and named as a member of "Beria's band." Abakumov responded that he was merely following the orders of Stalin, but he was found guilty of acts of terrorism and participation in "counterrevolutionary" organizations and sentenced to death. Though one of the more odious figures in the Stalin administration, he was known as a man who loved social life: dancing the foxtrot, playing football, and eating "shashlyki," which he had delivered to him by a local restaurant.

AGRICULTURE. *See* NEW ECONOMIC POLICY, FIVE-YEAR PLANS, WAR COMMUNISM.

ALLILUEV, FEDOR SERGEEVICH (1898–1955). A Russian revolutionary, he was Stalin's secretary and the brother of Stalin's second wife, **Nadezhda Allilueva** (Stalina).

Fedor Alliluev was born at the Mikhailovo station (now the town of Khashuri, Georgia), where his father (Sergei Iakovlevich Alliluev) worked as an assistant driver at a railway transport hub. In his youth he was very skillful student and showed unique abilities in mathematics, physics, and chemistry. In 1914, he graduated from gymnasium (high school) with a gold medal and entered navigational school. In 1917, he joined the RCP(b) and at the same time enrolled as a student of the Mathematical Faculty of Petrograd University. After the February Revolution (1917), he was drafted into the army. Later, he voluntarily joined the Red Army and participated in the Civil War. From April 1918, Fedor, together with his sister Nadezhda, worked as Stalin's secretary. During the German offensive against Petrograd, he fought in the Pskov direction, then took part in the defense of Tsaritsyn, and in 1919 he again defended Petrograd.

In 1920, Fedor fell ill with typhus. After recovery, he ended up in a special assignment unit under the command of **S. Ter-Petrosian**, known as Kamo. During his service, he underwent mental trauma and remained disabled for the rest of his life. Until Stalin's death, he continued to work as his secretary. He received a personal pension and later lived in Moscow in a one-room apartment. He died in 1955 and was buried at the cemetery next to his parents, brother, and sister.

ALLILUEV, SERGEI IAKOVLEVICH (1866–1945). Best known as Stalin's father-in-law, Alliluev was born into a peasant family in Voronezh region, and from 1890 he worked as a locksmith in Tiflis (Tblisi). From 1896, he was a member of the RSDWP in the city and became a leader of revolutionary activities, operating in Tiflis, Baku, Moscow, and Rostov-on-the-Don. He evidently met Stalin for the first time in 1903, when the two men were helping to move a printer from Baku to Tiflis. He was frequently arrested, and on two occasions given punishments. From 1907 to 1918, he worked in St. Petersburg (Petrograd) at a printing house and at an electric power station. He continued his revolutionary activities from 1912, and in 1917, he was elected a member of the power station's party committee. It is cited often that Lenin hid in Alliluev's apartment during the period of the July Uprising under the provisional government of 1917. In the civil war period, Alliluev was a leader of underground activity in Ukraine and in the Crimea. In 1921, he was a leader of the revolutionary committee in Ialta, and subsequently took up leadership posts for the Bolsheviks in Moscow, Leningrad, and Ukraine. There was never any overt animosity between Stalin and his father-in-law, who would be a frequent visitor to Stalin's dacha, along with the senior figures of the Politburo, taking part in discussions, but more frequently reminiscing about the past. He died after the end of the German–Soviet war, on July 27, 1945.

ALLILUEVA, NADEZHDA SERGEEVNA (1901–1932). Stalin's second wife, she was born in Baku, but her family moved frequently (see **Sergei Alliluev** above), and after 1907 she remained in St. Petersburg. She met Stalin again as an adult—he had known her as a child—in July 1917, and the two married in the spring of 1919, when Stalin, a widower with one son, was forty years of age, twenty-two years her senior. According to Volkogonov (*Stalin*, p. 148), she was well balanced and took an avid interest in Stalin's work in the Commissariat of Nationalities. Clearly seeking a defined role of her own, she became part of Lenin's secretariat in Gorky. Their first child, **Vasily**, was born in 1921, and the second, **Svetlana**, in 1926. **Iakov Stalin**, who was born to Stalin's first wife, **Iekaterina Svanidze (Kato)**, in 1907, also came to live with the family from 1921, as did Nadezhda's parents.

In 1921, she was briefly expelled from the party, reportedly because Stalin preferred her to be at home, but she was restored by 1924. Several accounts suggest that the marriage was tempestuous, with frequent arguments. In 1932, she was on Lenin's Mausoleum in Red Square for the 15th anniversary of the October Revolution, and attended a large party at Voroshilov's apartment in the Kremlin, attended by Stalin and others the following evening. On November 9, she committed suicide with her own pistol. Montefiore maintains that during the dinner, she and Stalin had an argument, perhaps prompted by his flirtations and that he had thrown a crust of bread at her.[1] Volkogonov attributes her death to Stalin's callousness and lack of attention.[2] Stalin never remarried, and though he had not attended Nadezhda's funeral, he began to speak more favorably of her in his later life.

ALLILUEVA, SVETLANA IOSIFOVNA (NÈE STALINA [DZHUGASHVILI], LANA PETERS IN EMIGRATION) (1926–2011).

Stalin's daughter through his marriage to his second wife, Nadezhda Allilueva, she was a Soviet translator, philologist, candidate of philological sciences (PhD), and memoirist.

Svetlana Allilueva was born in Moscow. She was six years old (in 1932) when her mother, **Nadezhda Allilueva**, committed suicide (see above). Only many years later did Svetlana learn what had happened to her mother. After her mother's death, she was very lonely. She studied at Moscow exemplary school no. 25, situated near the Kremlin. She was taken to school by a personal driver, while at home she was surrounded by numerous governesses but strictly forbidden to communicate with her classmates, play with neighbors' children, or enter into conversations with strangers. During her leisure time she studied English and watched Soviet films on a home cinema projector. Her nanny, Aleksandra Andreevna—who previously worked in the family of the Russian director, dramatist, and theater practitioner Nikolai Evreinov—was entrusted with the upbringing of Stalin's children, Svetlana and Vasily. She influenced Svetlana's decision about her future career: from her childhood she wanted to become a philologist. Svetlana's relationship with her father was very difficult. She was his favorite child. But later, his daughter began to annoy him. In 1943, Allilueva graduated with honors from school.

After graduation, Svetlana wanted to enter the Literary Institute in Leningrad, but since Stalin considered writing an unworthy occupation for his daughter, he insisted that she enter the Faculty of History at Moscow State University. In 1944, she married Grigory Morozov, a classmate of her brother, Vasily. Subsequently, the marriage was dissolved. Her son from this marriage, Iosif Alliluev (1945–2008), became a cardiologist and doctor of medical sciences. In 1949, she graduated from Moscow State University and married Iury Zhdanov, who adopted Svetlana's son. In 1950, Svetlana gave birth to their daughter, Ekaterina. In 1954, she defended her dissertation at the Academy of Social Sciences of the Central Committee of the CPSU and became a candidate of philological sciences (PhD). After Stalin's death (1953), Svetlana inherited 900 rubles. Between 1956 and 1967, she worked at the Institute of World Literature. In 1957, she married Ivan Svanidze. However, in two years they were divorced. In May 1962, she and her children were baptized in Moscow.

On December 20, 1966, Svetlana traveled to India, accompanying the ashes of her civil partner, Brajesh Singh. On March 6, 1967, she asked the Soviet ambassador, Ivan Aleksandrovich Benediktov, to allow her to stay in India, but he insisted that she return to Moscow. On March 8, she went to the U.S. embassy in Delhi with her passport and luggage and asked for political asylum. She was taken to Italy, then to Switzerland, and from there she moved to the United States. Her escape to the West and subsequent publication of a book, *Twenty Letters to a Friend* (1967), in which Allilueva described her Kremlin life with her father, caused a worldwide sensation.

In 1984, unexpectedly, Svetlana Allilueva decided to return to her homeland. In the USSR, she was warmly greeted and provided with housing, a private car with a driver, and a pension (the KGB did not want to let her out of sight). To escape KGB surveillance, she moved to her father's homeland in Georgia, where she was also provided with luxurious living conditions. But the following two years brought her neither happiness nor tranquility, and she decided to return to the United States, with the assistance of the new Soviet leader, Mikhail Gorbachev. She renounced her Soviet citizenship at this same time. Under the name Lana Peters, she settled in a nursing home in Madison, Wisconsin. On November 22, 2011, Svetlana died in Richland Center from complications arising from colon cancer.

ANDREEV, ANDREI ANDREEVICH (1895–1971). Born into a peasant family in Smolensk region, he joined the Bolshevik Party in 1914 and between 1915 and 1917 was a member of the Petrograd Committee and was one of the organizers of the Union of Metal Workers while working in the Putilov arms factory. He was one of the organizers of the strikes of early 1917 that helped to bring down the Russian monarchy. Between 1917 and 1919, he was a trade union leader in the Urals and Ukraine. On all key questions, he demonstrated his loyalty to Lenin, and he was appointed the leader of the Union of Railway Workers, a position he held between 1922 and 1927. From 1924, he was a secretary of the Central Committee of the party and loyal to Stalin in his conflict with **Trotsky**. He joined the Politburo as a candidate member in 1926 and became a full member in 1932. The years 1928–1930 saw him in the role of first secretary of the North Caucasus party committee with responsibility for introducing collectivization, which was imposed harshly, resulting in a rebellion that was forcibly repressed. He was a chairman of the Central Control Commission of the CPSU from 1930 to 1931 and 1939–1952. During the war, his role was to ensure the passage of agricultural supplies to the front as the commissar of agriculture, and his tenure in the position extended into 1946. By this time, he was one of Stalin's trusted associates and held the position of deputy chairman of the Council of Ministers of the USSR from 1946 to Stalin's death in 1953.

After being brought into the Orgburo in 1935, he was given responsibility for presiding over its sessions and, together with **Nikolai Iezhov**, for establishing its agenda. Andreev played a prominent role in Stalin's **Purges of 1937–1938**, particularly in rooting out alleged Trotskyists and in the trial of the Right Opposition leaders, **Bukharin** and **Rykov**, and the later removal of **Pavel Postyshev**, then in Kuibyshev at the January 1938 party plenum. Postyshev, who was one of the architects of the harsh famine in Ukraine in 1933, had complained that Kuibyshev's party leadership had been paralyzed by the consequences of the purge and was no longer operating because of lack of members. In turn, all the major party leaders then blamed Postyshev for the state of affairs, with Andreev among the most prominent accusers. Andreev was among the few prominent party leaders to survive the purges unscathed.

NOTES

1. Simon Sebag Montefiore, *Stalin: The Court of the Red Tsar* (London: Weidenfeld & Nicolson, 2003), 14.
2. Dmitri Volkogonov, *Stalin: Triumph and Tragedy* (London: Weidenfeld & Nicolson, 1991), 154.

B

BAZHANOV, BORIS GEORGIEVICH (1900–1982). Stalin's personal secretary for four years, between 1923 and 1927, Bazhanov was born on August 9, 1900, in Mogilev-Podolsky, Podolsky gubernia, in the Russian Empire, into a doctor's family. After completing school, he studied physics and mathematics at Kyiv University, but the institution shut down before he could complete his studies. He was seriously wounded in the demonstrations that followed the closure of the university. He joined the Bolshevik Party in the following year and was employed in writing speeches for Stalin's close associate, **L. Kaganovich**. From 1923, he was also a member of the Organizational Bureau (Orgburo) of the Central Committee of the CPSU. In August of that year, he was appointed as Stalin's assistant and a secretary of the Politburo CC CPSU. The work entailed regular attendance at Politburo meetings, recording debates, and adding information when needed.

In 1926, he was appointed editor of the newspaper *Finansovaia Gazeta* and employed by the Ministry of Finance. Bazhanov was accused of being a supporter of **G. Zinoviev**, former head of the Comintern and close friend of V. I. Lenin, but an enemy of Stalin from 1927 onward. In his own memoirs, he maintains he had become disillusioned with communism, and consequently crossed the border into Iran on January 1, 1928. When the USSR received permission to extradite him, he moved to India and finally to France, where he spent the rest of his life. He died on December 30, 1982, in Paris. He is perhaps most significant for the memoirs he wrote about life in the Soviet Union, and particularly Stalin as a dictator. His memoirs appeared in Russian for the first time in 1980, though they were published only in France. They later reappeared in Russia after the demise of the Soviet Union, in several editions in both St. Petersburg and Moscow between 1990 and 2017.

BERIA, LAVRENTY PAVLOVICH (1899–1953). Beria was a Soviet politician, marshal of the Soviet Union, and state security administrator, as well as chief of Soviet security and secret police apparatus (NKVD) during the Second World War. Beria gained a reputation as one of the most sinister and ruthless of Stalin's associates. Of Mingrelian background, he was born in the village Merkheuli, in Sukhum district of Tiflis gubernia, Georgia, on March 29, 1899, and educated in Russian-ruled Azerbaijan at the Baku Polytechnic for Mechanical Construction, which focused on oil production, graduating in 1919. He joined the RSDWP in March 1917. From June to September 1917, he served in the army as a technician. In 1918–1920, he worked in the Baku Council Secretariat as a factory clerk and at Baku customs house.

During the Civil War, between April and May 1920, he was a commissioner of the registry section of the Caucasus Front with the Military Revolutionary Council of the 11th Army. For a time, he reportedly worked with the anti-Bolshevik Muslim Mussavatists, and he was arrested in June 1920 when the Reds captured the region. Possibly at the behest of **S. M. Kirov**, however, he was freed. By

1921, he had been assigned the role of deputy to the head of the new Cheka, Mir Dzhafar Bagirov, in Baku. In 1921, the Bolsheviks in Georgia staged a revolt against Menshevik rule in the republic, resulting in a takeover by the Red Army. Beria, at this time, played a prominent role in uniting Georgia under Bolshevik rule by suppressing rival factions, particularly the national communists, who sought autonomy from rule by Moscow. In 1922–1924, he headed a secret-operational section in the Georgian Cheka, and from 1924 to 1927, he was in charge of the political section of the Transcaucasian OGPU.

In December 1926, Beria was appointed chairman of the GPU of the Georgian SSR. Five years later, he was appointed first secretary of the Central Committee of the Communist Party of Georgia, and in the following year his authority was extended to the whole of Transcaucasia. He also became known as the author of the book *On the Question about the History of the Bolshevik Organizations of Transcaucasia*, which inflated the role of Stalin in the revolutionary movement. In this same year, he was introduced to Stalin personally by **Sergo Ordzhonikdze**. By February 1934, he was a member of the CC CPSU. In 1936–1938, he was responsible for conducting the purges in Transcaucasia. In the latter year, he moved to Moscow as deputy chairman of internal affairs of the USSR, then under the leadership of **N. Iezhov**, who was leading the purges nationwide, and instituted a complete cleansing of the party leadership at all levels of the USSR. When Iezhov was removed in November 1938, Beria became the head of the NKVD and promptly began to purge Iezhov's associates, replacing them with his own protégés from Georgia.

With Beria as head of the NKVD, purges in the central regions eased, and over 100,000 prisoners were released. After September 1939, however, when the Soviet Union extended its territory by annexing eastern Poland, followed by annexing the Baltic States and the Bukovynian and Bessarabian regions of Romania in 1940, the purges were renewed, with arrests and mass deportations of about 200,000 people to Siberia and other regions. In 1939, Beria was promoted to candidate member of the ruling Politburo. He had emerged as one of Stalin's most trusted associates. In 1940, Beria gave the order to execute about 22,000 Polish prisoners held by the Soviet forces in Katyn, Kalinin, and Kharkiv camps. In October of that year, he was appointed deputy chairman of the Council of People's Commissars (the name was changed to the Council of Ministers in 1946). Thus, by the start of the German–Soviet war in June 1941, he was one of the most powerful figures in the Soviet Union, controlling both the secret police and government.

During the war, Beria demonstrated his organizational abilities, particularly in organizing the evacuation of factories and materiel, especially military goods, eastward, as the German army advanced rapidly eastward into the USSR in the summer and fall of 1941. This remarkable transfer permitted the Soviet Union to restore its military capabilities by the summer of 1942. He was also appointed a member of the **State Defense Committee** (GKO), which ran the country under Stalin's leadership until the end of the war. On May 10, 1944, he recommended to Stalin that the Tatars should be deported from Crimea, and subsequently supervised the removal of other nationalities to the east: Chechens, Ingushetians, Germans, and Meshketian Turks.

Beria's responsibilities were soon extended further. He organized weapons production in the growing gulag camp system of Corrective Labor Colonies. Stalin also entrusted him with leading the effort to produce an atomic bomb from December 1944. Beria worked diligently, using his intelligence networks and scientists, who worked in secrecy east of the Urals, resulting in the detonation of the first Soviet bomb in August 1949, some years before the Western powers had anticipated. He also attended the **Ialta Conference** in February 1945, which resolved the fate of eastern Europe after the war. Beria was a key figure in the subjugation of east European countries and the imposition of communist rule, which continued throughout the Cold War until late 1989.

By the end of the war, he had amassed significant power through several different positions. In 1946, he became a full member of the Politburo. In Stalin's later years, the Soviet leader encouraged infighting among his subordinates, and evidence suggests he promoted **Andrei Zhdanov** at the expense of Beria and **Georgy Malenkov**. In addition, Beria stepped down as NKVD leader in 1946, and his main fiefdom thereafter was the police and intelligence apparatus of the Ministry of Internal Affairs (MVD). His replacement as head of the NKVD, Sergey Kruglov, and the new head of the Ministry of State Security (MGB), **Viktor Abakumov,** began to remove Beria's associates from these organizations. Until Zhdanov died in 1948, Beria's position looked uncertain. Abakumov's attack on the Jewish Anti-Fascist Committee in 1948 targeted an organization that Beria had founded and patronized. Beria and Malenkov responded with an attack on Zhdanov's empire in the so-called Leningrad Affair, resulting in the executions of several leading figures headed by **Nikolai Voznesensky** (head of the State Planning Commission), **Aleksei Kuznetsov** (Zhdanov's former deputy), and **Mikhail Rodionov** (premier of the Russian Republic).

After Stalin's death in March 1953, Beria's position appeared to be the most powerful among the five leaders who might have replaced him: **Malenkov, Khrushchev, Molotov,** and **Kaganovich** were the others. His first steps appeared to be a complete reversal of Stalin's policies. He curtailed several investigations that would have resulted in major purges, such as the **Doctors' Plot,** initiated armistice talks in the Korean War, issued a May 9 amnesty (in advance) for the release of 1.1 million prisoners, and demanded more local rights for Soviet republics, such as appointing indigenous personnel to the leading positions. He spoke in favor of restoring relations with Yugoslavia (severed when Stalin broke with **Tito** in 1948) and opposed the creation of the German Democratic Republic (GDR), arguing that western and eastern Germany should be reunited. He also spoke out against "incorrect" Russification policies and illegal repressions.

These proposals confuse the general picture of Beria as a cynical manipulator and mass executioner who had also gained a reputation as a serial rapist and sexual predator. Were they a means to remove himself from the past or a reflection of his genuine views? Some of the policies emanated from an earlier proposal of Malenkov to begin a gradual de-Stalinization of society and were later encapsulated in Khrushchev's speech at the twentieth party congress in 1956. Suffice it to say that they do little to remove the general impression of Beria gained from his earlier activities. In the power struggle that ensued, Khrushchev managed to combine forces with Malenkov (formerly Beria's ally), **Zhukov,** and others to have Beria arrested and removed from all his posts on June 26, 1953. At the plenum of the CC CPSU in July 1953, he was excluded from the Presidium (former Politburo) and the Central Committee, and expelled from the party. The case against him alleged that he was a British spy, seeking the restoration of capitalism and the return of the bourgeoisie, statements as ludicrous as any of the accusations of the 1937–1938 peak of the purges. A special session of the Supreme Court of the USSR in December 1953 sentenced him to execution, which was carried out by General P. F. Batitsky. He was survived by his wife, Nina Teymurazovna Gegechkori (1905–1991), the niece of a former cellmate in Baku, whom he had met in 1920.

Beria (seated, second right) with (L to R) Khrushchev, Voroshilov, Kaganovich and Nestor Lakoba

BERMAN, BORIS DAVYDOVICH (1901–1939). Boris was the second of the Berman brothers (a third, younger brother—Solomon— was also employed by the NKVD, though he did not achieve the prominence of his elder siblings), born in the village Andrianovka of Chita district of the Zabaikal Oblast to the owner of a Jewish brickyard enterprise. He rose to become a leading member of the state security organs. He received a fourth-grade education in the city school and subsequently worked in a store in Chita before joining the Red Army in May 1918. In 1919, he was posted along the Chinese Eastern Railroad but returned to Chita in December 1920. In February 1921, he joined the Cheka, working in the Economic Section. In August 1923, he joined the Bolshevik branch of the Russian Communist Party. From February 1928, he was the head of the counterintelligence section of the OGPU in central Asia. Three years later, he was posted abroad as the resident Soviet intelligence agent undercover in Germany. In 1934–1935, he became the first deputy chairman of the Foreign Section of the Chief Administration of State Security (GUGB) of the NKVD.

After a term as deputy chief of the Secret-Political (Fourth) Section of the GUGB, Berman was appointed the minister (people's commissar) of internal affairs of the Belarusian SSR and head of the special section of the Belarusian Military District (March 1937) as the purges were reaching a peak in this republic. In 1937–1938, he supervised mass arrests and executions in the republic, including the shooting of over one hundred writers and poets executed on the night of October 29–30, as well as thousands of "kulaks" and former party leaders. In May 1938, he was transferred to Moscow, where he led the Third Section of the NKVD USSR dealing with transport and communications. In this period, he was involved in the arrest of the prominent Bolshevik theoretician **N. I. Bukharin**. After the fall of **N. I. Iezhov**, Berman was arrested and accused of association with the Right Opposition—ironically, given his role in the arrest of the leader of this faction. He declared himself guilty of espionage on behalf of Hitler's Germany and was executed on February 23, 1939.

BERMAN, MATVEI DAVYDOVICH (1898–1939). The older brother of **Boris Berman**, Matvei was also born in the village of Andrianovka in Zabaikal Oblast, but he is better known for his leadership of the gulag camps during the height of the Stalin Purges. He was educated at Chita Commercial Institute, graduating in 1916, and Irkutsk Military Institution, completing his studies in October 1917 and becoming a cadet in the 25th Reserve Infantry Regiment, headquartered in Tomsk. In June 1917, he joined the RSDWP. In 1918, he was recruited by the Cheka, heading its branch in the town of Glazov in the Udmurt Republic. Matvei had a reputation for debauched behavior and was even dismissed briefly for drunkenness in September 1918. After 1919, he occupied leading posts in the local organs of the Cheka in Ekaterinburg, Tomsk, and the Far Eastern Republic. Between 1921 and 1923, he took on more prominent positions in distant outposts of the Cheka in Irkutsk and the Buryat-Mongolia sections before becoming the deputy chairman of the GPU in Central Asia and head of its secret-operations section. In 1927–1928, he was head of the GPU of Uzbekistan SSR, after which he took on the same position in Vladivostok.

He helped to create the gulag labor camps in the summer of 1930 and became the deputy chief of the administration. He became the head of the gulag camps under the control of the OGPU (later the NKVD) from June 1932, retaining the post for the next five years. He is best known for creating the ambitious industrial projects carried out by prisoners, such as the Moscow-Volga Canal. In July–October 1936, he also held the position of deputy chairman of the NKVD. He was elected a deputy of the Supreme Soviet of the USSR in 1937. His demise, like that of his brother, came quickly after **Iezhov**'s fall from power. He was arrested on December 24, 1938, and sentenced to death by the Military Collegium of the Supreme Soviet. The sentence was carried out on March 7, 1939, twelve days after that of his brother Boris.

BLIUKHER, VASILY KONSTANTINOVICH (1889–1938). A Soviet military commander, he was born in the village Barshchinka near Rybinska (Iaroslavl region, north of Moscow) into a peasant family. In his early career, he worked as a locksmith in Mytishchin factory, and in 1910 he was arrested for calling for a strike and sentenced to two years and eight months in prison. He joined the Russian Army as a noncommissioned officer in 1914 but was wounded and demobilized the following year. Subsequently, he worked in mechanical factories in Nizhny Novgorod and Kazan. He joined the RSDWP in 1916, returning to the army the following year as head of a strategic committee in Samara. In October 1917, he led the Military-Revolutionary Committee (MRC) in Samara. In November, the party dispatched him to Cheliabinsk as head of the MRC and leader of the Red Guard. In the Civil War, he was deployed as commander of the eastern section fighting against the White Armies in the Orenburg region from March 1918. By August, he was commander of the partisan Ural armies that carried out a raid over a wide front stretching from Orenburg to the Urals, a campaign for which he received an Order of the Red Banner. In 1920, as the Civil War turned in the Reds' favor, he led attacks on Perekop and Crimea against the last White Army leader, Baron Piotr Wrangel, which resulted in heavy casualties but was ultimately successful, resulting in further awards. In total, Bliukher received five Orders of the Red Banner.

Between July 1921 and 1922, Bliukher was the war minister and commander of the People's Revolutionary Army of the Far Eastern Republic, helping to consolidate Bolshevik power along the Amur River. From 1922 to 1924 he returned to European Russia as commander of the Petrograd Military District. He was soon to return to the Far East as the Soviet military adviser to China—he took the name Galen during this time—working with Sun Yat-Sen and Chiang Kai-shek. He was largely responsible for the creation of the Chinese Army, which mounted a northern expedition to unify China under the Kuomintang. Between 1927 and 1929, as Stalin was consolidating his power, Bliukher took over the leadership of the Ukraine Military District. In 1929, he was given the prestigious position of commander of the far eastern armies, which he held until 1938. In 1935, he was promoted to marshal of the Soviet Union. Effectively, he was dictator of the Soviet Far East.

The position kept him far away from Stalin's initial purges, though he was recalled as chairman of the Military Tribunal that imposed the death sentence on Marshal **Mikhail Tukhachevsky** and other leading offices of the Red Army in 1937. Thereafter, back at his post in Khabarovsk, he became engaged in several skirmishes with the Imperial Japanese armies (July–August 1938) around the Khasan Lake on the border with Korea, then under Japanese occupation. These were costly and consequential, with over 2,500 Soviet casualties.

Bliukher became embroiled in the purges after the NKVD head in his region, Genrikh Lushkov, fled to Japan, but it may also have been a result of his failure to defeat Japanese forces or the purging of those responsible for the court-martialing of Tukhachevsky and others. In August 1938, he was relieved of his command, and on October 22, he was arrested during a visit to Moscow. Refusing to confess to any association with Japanese spies, he was beaten to death in his jail cell. In 1956, he was rehabilitated.

BLOKHIN, VASILY MIKHAILOVICH (1895–1955). A Soviet major-general who served as the chief executioner of the Stalinist NKVD under the administrations of **Genrikh Iagoda**, **Nikolai Iezhov**, and **Lavrenty Beria** during the Great Purge and the Second World War (**Great Patriotic War**). In 1937–1938, he participated in the most high-profile executions. He directed the execution of Marshal **Mikhail Tukhachevsky** and other high-ranking military personnel. Thousands of victims (according to some sources, nearly 20,000 people) were executed personally by his hand, including about 7,000 Polish prisoners of war during the Katyn massacre in spring 1940.

He was born on January 7, 1895, into the family of a poor peasant in the village of Gavrilovskoe, Vladimir province. He worked as a shepherd in the village of Turovo, Iaroslavl province (1905–1910), and as a mason in Moscow (1910–1915). In 1915, upon reaching draft age, he was drafted for active military duty and was sent to the 82nd Infantry Reserve Regiment. During the First World War he rose to the rank of senior noncommissioned officer. After the February Revolution, he was elected as a chairman of the Army Committees of the 218th Infantry Regiment. In December 1917 he returned to his native village to help his father with the housework. In October 1918 he joined the Workers' and Peasants' Red Army and in April 1921 became a member of the RCP(b).

In May 1921, Blokhin was transferred to the Republic Internal Security Forces (VOKhR). Further, he continued his career in state security agencies: the Joint State Political Directorate (OGPU), the People's Commissariat for Internal Affairs (NKVD), and the Ministry for State Security (MGB). After winning the favor of Stalin, in 1927 and until his retirement in 1953, he had a permanent position as the NKVD's chief executioner and was in charge of what Stalin defined as *chernaia rabota* (black work): intimidations, tortures, and murders. He personally participated in all of the individual high-profile executions during Stalin's Terror, including the executions of the Old Bolsheviks convicted at the Moscow Show Trials, Marshal Tukhachevsky, **Iona Iakir**, **Ieronim Uborevich**, and executions of two former NKVD chiefs (**Genrikh Iagoda** in 1938 and **Nikolai Iezhov** in 1940) whom he had previously served. In 1933, without quitting his job, he graduated from the Moscow Institute of Architecture and Civil Engineering. He was awarded the Badge of Honor for his service in 1937.

In 1939, when Beria did his best to cleanse the NKVD of Iezhov's cadres, he received information that the commandant Blokhin was too close to former NKVD secretary Bulanov and Iagoda. So Beria wanted to arrest Blokhin, but according to Beria himself, Stalin did not concur with his decision, saying that "such people are needed for dirty work." After that, the question of Blokhin's arrest was never raised again.

The culmination of Blokhin's professional career was the shooting in May 1940 of a group of Polish military and police officers interned in the Ostashkov (now Tver region) prisoner of war camp in the Katyn forest. While some of the executions were carried out by senior lieutenant of state security Andrei Rubanov, Blokhin was the principal executioner. He initially decided on a quota of three hundred executions per night but was able to kill only 250 people per night. He worked without pause for ten hours each night, executing an average of one prisoner every three minutes. He shot 7,000 individuals in twenty-eight days. In 2010, he was listed in the Guinness World Records as "Most Prolific Executioner." Blokhin had his own special uniform, consisting of a leather cap, long leather apron, and elbow-length gloves. He never used anyone else's tools for killings and had a briefcase filled with his own personal Walther PPK pistols.

After Stalin's death in March 1953, Blokhin was forcibly retired and during Khrushchev's de-Stalinization campaigns was deprived of the rank of major general. He died on February 3, 1955.

BREZHNEV, LEONID ILICH (1906–1982). Best known as the longtime leader of the Soviet Union as general secretary of the CC CPSU from 1964 to his death in November 1982, Brezhnev's career was largely made during the Stalin era. He was born in Kamenskoe (Kamianske, formerly Dniprodzerzhynsk) in the Russian Empire—today part of the Dnipropetrovsk Region of Ukraine—into a workers' family. He was educated at Kursk Technical School for Land Improvement, graduating in 1927, and Dniprodzerzhynsk Metallurgical Institute. As deputy chairman of the Urals Oblast Land Administration, he took part in the collectivization of this region in 1928–1930, including in the mass arrests and "liquidation of the kulaks as a class." He formally joined the Communist Party in 1931 and worked as an engineer in the 1930s in the Dzerzhinsky Metallurgical Factory in his home city.

Brezhnev began to rise to prominence by the late 1930s, prompted in part by the evisceration of the party leadership as a result of the purges. By 1939, he was a secretary of the Dnipropetrovsk Oblast Committee of the party. Likewise, his activities during the war, which were highly exaggerated in accounts during his leadership, resulted in elevation as officers fell. Starting as a political commissar in 1941, he had risen to the rank of major general by 1944, despite reports about his "weak military knowledge." After the war, he became the party leader of Zaporizhzhia region and, from November 1947, of Dnipropetrovsk Oblast Committee, one of the most important industrial regions of Ukraine. From 1950, he was a deputy of the Supreme Soviet of the USSR. In July 1950, Brezhnev was appointed first party secretary of Moldova, and by the final years of Stalin, he was a secretary of the CC CPSU, a member of the Central Committee, and a candidate member of the ruling Presidium. He lost all his posts temporarily after the death of Stalin but returned as a candidate member of the Presidium in 1956, and full membership in 1957, after Khrushchev consolidated his position and removed the more hardline Stalinist rivals **Molotov**, **Malenkov**, and **Kaganovich**. Still, Brezhnev experienced more turbulence in his political career and was demoted to the ceremonial position of chairman of the Supreme Soviet in May 1960, before returning to Presidium in 1963.

He was closely involved in the KGB plot to remove Khrushchev in 1964 and took over subsequently with the title of secretary in a triad of power with **Aleksei Kosygin** as premier and **Nikolai Podgorny** as chairman of the Supreme Soviet. Once in power more firmly by 1966, when he adopted the position of general secretary, Brezhnev began a partial rehabilitation of Stalin, suggesting his deep-seated opposition to the reforms conducted by Khrushchev. Though his time in the highest office brought stability, it later became known as the "era of stagnation," a phrase widely disseminated by Mikhail Gorbachev, the final Soviet leader, in 1985–1991.

BRIUKHANOV, NIKOLAI PAVLOVICH (1878–1938). A Soviet statesman, member of the Central Executive Committee of the USSR of the first through second and fourth through sixth convocations, one of the organizers of the mass requisition of grain from the peasants, people's commissar of finance (1926–1930), and a candidate member of the Central Committee of the CPSU(b) in 1927–1934, Nikolai Briukhanov was born into a Russian family in Simbirsk (today Ulianovsk, Russia). His father was a land surveyor, and his grandfather (N. P. Briukhanov) served as a gardener at the Tsarskoe Selo Palace. In 1889, he entered the Simbirsk classical gymnasium. At age 13–14, he openly abandoned religion (his father was a religious person) and declared himself an "atheist." During studies at the gymnasium, Nikolai considered himself a "Marxist." In 1897, after being discovered reading illegal books (by D. Pisarev, N. Dobroliubov, and N. Chernyshevsky), Nikolai was not admitted to the final exam. In 1898, however, he was able to pass the exam and received his school diploma. From 1899 to 1901, Briukhanov studied at the Faculty of History and Philology of Moscow University, from which he was expelled for his political activities and participation in student riots. He then continued his studies at the Faculty of Philology of Kazan University. In Kazan, Briukhanov again became involved in revolutionary activities.

In 1902, he became a member of the RSDWP, which led to his expulsion from the university once more. On June 23, 1903, he was arrested and exiled to Vologda. In 1904, Briukhanov joined the Bolshevik faction of the party. In 1905, due to amnesty, he was released from exile, and the party sent him to work in Ufa. Until July 1906, he was a member of the Ufa Committee. In August 1906 he returned to Simbirsk and worked there as a member of the Simbirsk RSDWP group. In 1907, he was a Bolshevik delegate to the RSDWP congress in London. The same year, he moved permanently to Ufa. In 1912, he was nominated as a candidate from the Social-Democrats (Bolsheviks) to the city's fourth State Duma, but was once again arrested and imprisoned for three months. After the Russian Revolution, he became the head of the Bolshevik committee in Ufa and the commissioner for food in the Ufa province.

In 1918, Briukhanov was transferred to Moscow and was appointed deputy people's commissar with responsibilities for food supplies in the Moscow region. Simultaneously he worked as chairman of the Special Supplies Commission of the Eastern Front. From 1921 to 1924, he served as people's commissar of food of the RSFSR, a member of the Council of Labor and Defense of the USSR, and a head of the Main Directorate for the food supply of the Red Army and Navy. At the meeting of Russian food supply organizations (December 30, 1918–January 6, 1919), he presented a draft decree on the introduction of *prodrazverstka* (food apportionment), a policy and campaign of confiscation of grain and other agricultural products from peasants. Briukhanov became one of the organizers of the mass requisition of grain from the peasants and directed operations of food detachments. In 1921–1922, he was a member of the Pomgol (Relief for Starving) Central Commission.

In December 1922, Briukhanov became the head of the People's Commissariat of Supplies of the USSR. From 1924 to 1926, he was deputy people's commissar of finance. In 1926, **Grigory Sokolnikov**, the head of the Finance Commissariat, who decided to support **Zinoviev** and **Kamenev** in their unsuccessful opposition to Stalin, was replaced by Briukhanov. He kept this position until October 1930, when Briukhanov—together with **Georgy Piatakov**, the chairman of the State Bank—was held responsible for surging inflation and fired from his post. In April 1931, Briukhanov was appointed deputy people's commissar of supplies of the USSR. From 1933 to 1937, he served as deputy chairman of the Sovnarkom's Central Commission on grain yields. In February 1938, during Stalin's Great Purge, he was arrested and sentenced to death. On September 1, 1938, Briukhanov was executed. In 1956 he was rehabilitated.

BUBNOV, ANDREI SERGEEVICH (1883–1938). One of the seven members of the first Politburo, he was born in Ivanovo-Voznesensk (after 1932, Ivanovo), about 250 kilometers southeast of Moscow into the family of a shopkeeper. In 1903, he joined the Bolshevik wing of the RSDWP. His term of study at the Moscow Agricultural Institute was terminated because of his revolutionary activities. He was active during the 1905 Revolution in Russia as a member of the Ivanovo-Voznesensk committee of the party. After the revolution he took part in the Moscow committee. Active after 1910 in various cities, he was arrested several times. After his late-1916 arrest, the tsarist authorities sent him to Siberia, but he returned to Moscow after the February Revolution. Bubnov was quite prominent in the October Revolution period, as the chairman of the party's Central Committee in Petrograd and as a member of the Military Revolutionary Committee that organized the uprising to overthrow the provisional government. Afterward, he was a member of the first Bolshevik government as commissar of railways. By December, he held the same position in the south. Bubnov spoke out against the Treaty of Brest-Litovsk, by which Russia withdrew from the First World War, ceding its industrial heartland to the German Empire. His next major role was during the Civil War, when he was posted to Ukraine, working in underground party organizations in Kyiv, and by March 1919, he was a member of the Politburo of the Central Committee of the Communist Party of Ukraine. Subsequently, he was posted to the North Caucasus.

With the Civil War over, Bubnov joined the Moscow party committee, taking part in the suppression of the Kronstadt Uprising of sailors in March 1921. His political allegiances were not static, and for a brief period, he was part of the Left Opposition and close to **Trotsky**. By 1924, however, he had switched to the side of Stalin and took over responsibility for political control over the Red Army and serving as a member of the Military Revolutionary Council of the USSR. At the same time, he was editor-in-chief of the Red Army newspaper, *Krasnaia Zvezda*. In 1929, he was appointed people's commissar of education of the RSFSR, introducing communist ideology into Russian schools and focusing on skills needed for industrial enterprises. His term contrasted with that of his progressive predecessor, Anatoly Lunacharsky. Bubnov was arrested on October 17, 1937, on charges of espionage and anti-Soviet activities (mainly contacts with the Right Opposition of **N. Bukharin** and **A. Rykov**) and sentenced to death and executed (on the same day) on August 1, 1938. He was rehabilitated in February 1956.

BUDENNY, SEMEN MIKHAILOVICH (1883–1973). Marshal of the Soviet Union (1935) and a close political ally of Stalin, Budenny was born in the hamlet of Koziurin, Salsk District of the Don Region (today part of the Rostov Oblast), into a family of poor peasants, Budenny is best known as one of the last cavalry officers. He joined the tsarist army in 1903, was posted to the Far East, and took part in the Russo–Japanese War in 1904–1905. He was next active in the First World War. In the summer of 1917, he led his cavalry division into Minsk, where he was elected chair of the Regimental Committee and deputy chairman of the Divisional Committee. He returned to his home area after the October Revolution and in 1918 he formed a cavalry unit to fight against the White Guards, which was eventually expanded into a full division. Under Budenny's command, the division was sent to Tsaritsyn (Volgograd), and early in 1919 it carried out a successful raid to the rear of White Army leader General P. A. Krasnov. By November of this year, his unit had been transformed into the First Cavalry Army. Budenny, a striking, mustachioed figure, was decorated for his actions during the Civil War with an Order of the Red Banner. He received this award twice more in 1923 and 1930. By October 1923, after the end of the period of warfare, Budenny led the Cavalry Section of the Red Army and was a member of the Military Revolutionary Council of the USSR. Between 1924 and 1937, he was inspector of the cavalry of the Red Army. In the early 1930s he also acquired his first formal education at the "Frunze" Military Academy. After graduating in 1934, he was made a marshal of the Soviet Union in the following year.

In 1937–1938, Budenny, by then military commander of the Moscow District, was among the most outspoken critics of those former leaders put on trial for alleged crimes against the USSR and Soviet leadership, particularly in the case of **Nikolai Bukharin** and **A. I Rykov**, urging execution for both. He played a similar role once the purges were extended to military leaders **M. N. Tukhachevsky** and **Ia. E. Rudzutaks**. Budenny owed his late prominence to the purges of army leaders as well as to historical narratives that portrayed him as one of the major figures during the civil war. As a result, in Soviet military thinking, the cavalry enjoyed an extended honeymoon into the early years of the war at the expense of more advanced tactics. The fallibility of such thinking was soon uncovered once war broke out. Budenny became a member of the Soviet military command (Stavka) with responsibility for armies of the southwest once war began (July–September 1941). Allowing his army to be encircled, he suffered two major defeats at the battles of Uman and Kyiv but was allowed to maintain strong influence. In August 1942, he commanded the North Caucasus Front, but he was removed from leadership as the Germans approached.

Despite his incompetence during the **Great Patriotic War**, he continued to be well regarded, remained in the Central Committee, and took on the role of deputy minister of agriculture. He retired with honor in 1954, and after his death nineteen years later was buried in the Kremlin Wall.

Semen Budenny

BUKHARIN, NIKOLAI IVANOVICH (1888–1939). A Bolshevik revolutionary, Soviet

Union politician, and author on revolutionary theory, Bukharin had a short but fascinating career that has long provided interest for historians because he does not seem to fit the mold of the gangster-type leader around Stalin, perhaps epitomized by **Kaganovich** and **Beria**, but appears rather as a mild intellectual, disinterested in factional struggles. He came from a middle-class family of schoolteachers in Moscow, and the family moved to Kishinev when he was five, when his father acquired the position of tax inspector.

Bukharin joined the RSDWP in 1906 after the failed revolution of the previous year, and as a member of the Bolshevik faction. He was a leader of party work in trade unions and the editor of the journal *Golos zhizni* (*The Voice of Life*). He attended the Law Faculty of Moscow University, where he studied in the Economics Department, but he was expelled in 1911 for revolutionary activities. In this same year, in June, he was arrested and sent into exile in the northern Arkhangelsk region, but within weeks he had escaped and fled abroad, initially to Hanover, Germany. In this period, he traveled to Krakow, where he met Lenin for the first time. His time in Europe was also marked by arrest by the Austro-Hungarian authorities on suspicion of spying, and in 1914 he was living in London before moving on to Stockholm the following year. He left that city in April 1916, moving to Denmark and then to the United States from October 1916. There, he became editor of the journal *Novy Mir*, and one of his coeditors shortly afterward was another new arrival in New York City, **L. D. Trotsky**.

During his period of exile, Bukharin authored several books that established him as a theoretician of the party. He returned to Russia in May 1917, traveling via Japan, and was elected a member of the RSDWP's Central Committee and based in Moscow, where he drafted the decrees of the Moscow Soviet. Between 1918 and 1929, he was the chief editor of the party newspaper *Pravda*. In the early post-revolution period, Bukharin was regarded as a "left" Communist and initially opposed the Treaty of Brest with the Central Powers, advocating instead a revolutionary war against them. Ultimately, however, he accepted Lenin's decision to sign the treaty, extricating Russia from the First World War.

Bukharin continued to write prolifically: together with **Ievgeny Preobrazhensky**, he authored *The ABC of Communism*, and he was the single author of *Economics of the Transitional Period* (1920), which focused on the transformation from a capitalist to a socialist economy. At the same time, he gradually advanced through the party hierarchy. From March 3, 1919, he was a candidate member of the Politburo of the CC RKP(b), and from September 9, 1923, he was a candidate member of the Orgburo of the Central Committee. He became a full member of the Politburo after the death of Lenin when the leadership engaged in intrafactional struggles over the succession question. Bukharin became associated with two other figures, **A. Rykov** and **M. Tomsky**, who were later to be designated as the Right Opposition. For some time, however, Bukharin remained close to Stalin and a key supporter in his struggle with Trotsky.

As an economist, despite his earlier radical enthusiasms, Bukharin had a practical side and recognized the necessity—as had Lenin—of attaining the economic recovery of the country after the lengthy years of warfare. In March 1921, Lenin had introduced the **New Economic Policy**, which was enthusiastically endorsed by Bukharin. After Lenin's death, Bukharin was a key supporter of Stalin in his conflict with Trotsky, and later with his earlier allies, **Zinoviev** and **Kamenev**. Yet Bukharin was not partisan and could not comprehend the depth of the enmity. He valued most the teachings of Lenin and the need for collective decision-making and party unity. Together with Rykov, he placed emphasis on the alliance between the workers and peasants and the need to incorporate the peasants into the Bolshevik system. He thought this would be best achieved by a gradualist approach to industrialization, while allowing the farms a chance to recover from the disastrous years of war and famine through the NEP. There is no doubt, however, that Bukharin was an important figure in enabling Stalin's victory over the "Left Opposition" of Trotsky, Zinoviev, and Kamenev.

Subsequently, Stalin's plan to industrialize the country rapidly, which demanded the introduction of harsh measures of collectivization, prompted Bukharin to write his pamphlet *Notes of an Economist* in September 1927, criticizing the speed of the process. Together with Rykov and Tomsky, he was denounced as part of a "Right Opposition" and lost his major positions: as a full member of the Politburo, head of the Comintern since 1926, and editor of *Pravda*. His fall was gradual, however, because he recanted his views, gaining a position as a presidium member of the Supreme Economic Council and as a leader in the Commissariat of Heavy Industry. Even though his influence was diminishing, he spent his later years, 1934–1936, as editor of the government newspaper *Izvestiya* and took part in the writing of what was to be termed the "**Stalin Constitution**" of 1936.

Once the Show Trials began in 1936, Bukharin became caught up in the attacks on the "anti-Soviet bloc of Rightists and Trotskyites," though only two years later was he brought to the court, likely because of the difficulties of coercing his confession. Officially, he was the leading figure in the "Trial of 21" in Moscow in March 1938 and accused of treason and counterrevolutionary activities. He may have confessed to save his twenty-two-year-old second wife, Larina, and their baby son, Iury, born that year. He was executed after the trial. Bukharin was perhaps the most genuinely popular of the Bolshevik leaders with wide personal friendships, including with cultural figures such as Boris Pasternak and André Malraux. Mikhail Gorbachev rehabilitated him in 1988.

BULANOV, PAVEL PETROVICH (1895–1938). An NKVD officer and one of the defendants in the Case of the Anti-Soviet "Bloc of Rights and Trotskyites," he was secretary to **Genrikh Iagoda**. He was born in Penza gubernia and educated in the Penza Land Surveying Institute. He served for a brief time in the Russian army in the First World War. In August 1918, he joined the Bolshevik Party and was recruited by the Cheka in August 1921 and elevated to the central apparatus of the OGPU by the end of the year. Once the NKVD was established, replacing the OGPU, Bulanov became a secretary of the People's Commissariat. He was a loyal and entrusted assistant to Iagoda, who was appointed leader of the security agency in July 1934. He lost his position once Iagoda was replaced by **Nikolai Iezhov**, and was arrested on March 29, 1937. He was part of the last great Show Trial in Moscow on March 2, 1938, designated as the affair of the "Anti-Soviet Right-Trotskyite bloc," and executed on March 15. In 1988, he was rehabilitated posthumously and restored to party membership.

BULGANIN, NIKOLAI ALEKSANDROVICH (1895–1975). Bulganin was a Soviet politician, marshal of the Soviet Union (1947, deprived of this title in 1958), hero of socialist labor (1955), and a full member of the party's Central Committee (1937–1961), who served as a minister of the armed forces of the USSR (March 1947–March 1949), minister of war of the USSR (March 1953), USSR minister of defense (March 1953–February 1955), and premier of the Soviet Union/chairman of the Council of Ministers of the USSR (1955–1958). He gained a reputation as a faceless apparatchik who obediently carried out the orders of Stalin and **N. Khrushchev**, and as an alcoholic who admired ballerinas.

Of Russian background, he was born in Nizhny Novgorod into a family of an office worker. In 1917 he graduated from a technical school and worked as apprentice to an electrician and later as a clerk. In March 1917, Bulganin joined the RSDWP(b). In 1918 he was recruited into the All-Russian Extraordinary Commission (VChK) and served there until 1922. After the end of the Civil War, he worked in the Supreme Council of the National Economy (1922–1927). In 1927, he was appointed director of the Moscow Electric Lamp Plant. In 1930, the plant, the first among the industrial enterprises of the USSR, was awarded the Order of Lenin (type 2), and Bulganin became one of the first cavaliers of the Order of Lenin in the USSR. Acquaintance with Nikita Khrushchev played a fateful role in Bulganin's career. They met in 1930, when

Bulganin was then the director of the electrical factory, and Khrushchev was a member of the commission that checked the party organization of this enterprise. Bulganin earned a reputation as a successful manager and a practical administrator and was promoted to the position of chairman of Moscow Soviet of People's Deputies. He served in that position from 1931 to 1937 and energetically devoted himself to Moscow's rapid growth (including the construction of the city's famous subway system, named after **Kaganovich**).

A loyal Stalinist, he was also able to successfully build his party career. In 1934, the 17th congress of the CC CPSU elected Bulganin a candidate member of the Central Committee. In 1937–1938, his career took off rapidly, as other leaders fell victim to Stalin's Great Purge. The mass terror of the 1930s paved the way for the next generation of Soviet political leaders, including Bulganin. In 1937, he was elected to the Supreme Soviet of the USSR. He later became prime minister of the Russian Republic (1937–1938), chairman of the State Bank of the USSR (1938–1941), deputy prime minister of the Soviet Union (1938–1941), and a full member of the Central Committee of the Communist Party (1939). Simultaneously, from January 1938, he served as chairman of the Foreign Affairs Commission of the Council of Nationalities. On August 1, 1939, as chairman of the Board of the State Bank of the USSR, he created the collection (encashment) service at the State Bank.

During the **Great Patriotic War** (1941–1945), Bulganin played a leading role in the Soviet government and in the Red Army, although he never served in the army and did not have a military education. He was a member of the Western Military Council (July 1941–December 1943), the 2nd Baltic Front (December 1943–April 1944), and the 1st Belarusian Front (May–November 1944), and served as Stalin's principal agent in the High Command of the Red Army. An unofficial function of the members of military councils was to supervise the front commanders. Reports about military leaders were submitted directly to Stalin. Great zeal in the performance of this function was highly encouraged. Since Bulganin's position had never been shaken during the whole war, apparently, he provided exemplary service.

In 1942, he was promoted to the rank of lieutenant-general. Later, he was promoted to colonel-general (1944) and army-general (1944). He also replaced **Kliment Voroshilov** as a member of the **State Defense Committee** (GKO) (November 21, 1944–September 4, 1945). From November 20, 1944, he served as deputy people's commissar of defense of the USSR. In February 1945, he was included in the Stavka of the Soviet Armed Forces (the headquarters of the Main Command of the Armed Forces of the USSR). In March 1946, he became the first deputy minister of the armed forces of the USSR.

After Bulganin was approved as a candidate member of the Politburo of the CC CPSU (March 18, 1946–February 18, 1948) and a member of the Organizational Bureau (Orgburo) of the Central Committee of the CPSU(b) (March 18, 1946–October 5, 1952), his influence in the party leadership increased dramatically. According to **Georgy Zhukov**, who first became acquainted with Bulganin in 1941, he was a typical party functionary and understood nothing of military affairs and operational-strategic issues. But he was cunning and was able to gain the party's confidence. Stalin knew that Bulganin would fulfill any task asked of him. This attitude became the decisive factor in the subsequent appointment of Bulganin as minister of war in 1947 and deputy chairman of the Council of Ministers of the USSR (March 5, 1947–April 7, 1950). On November 3, 1947, he was promoted to the highest army rank: marshal of the Soviet Union. The appointment of a civilian politician who never commanded troops to the post of head of the military department could be explained by Stalin's desire to maintain control of the army in the postwar period and to avoid strengthening the military leaders, who gained popularity during the war.

On February 18, 1948, Bulganin became a member of Politburo of the CC CPSU (February 18, 1948–October 5, 1952) and first deputy chairman of the Council of Ministers of the USSR (April 7, 1950–February 8, 1955).

He was approved by Stalin as a member of the Presidium of the Central Committee of the CPSU (October 16, 1952–September 5, 1958) and a member of the Bureau of the Presidium of the Central Committee. After the 19th congress of the Communist Party of the Soviet Union, at Stalin's suggestion, the "leading five" was created as part of the Presidium. According to Khrushchev's memoirs,[1] in the last years of his life, Stalin named Bulganin as his possible successor. In March 1953, after the death of Stalin, Bulganin benefited from the division of power after Stalin's death. Having retained the post of the first deputy chairman of the Soviet government, Bulganin was appointed minister of war of the USSR on March 5, 1953, a post he held for just ten days, and minister of defense of the USSR (March 15, 1953–February 9, 1955).

In February 1955, during the struggle between the party and state branches of power in the immediate post-Stalin period, **Georgy Malenkov** was removed from the post of the chairman of the Council of Ministers of the USSR. He was replaced by Bulganin, a less divisive figure. In this post, Bulganin became the closest ally of Khrushchev. As head of the USSR government, Bulganin (along with Khrushchev) made a number of important official visits: to Yugoslavia (where the Soviet leadership reconciled with Josip Broz Tito), India, and the UK. In 1956, together with the prime minister of Japan, I. Hatoyama, he signed a Soviet–Japanese Joint Declaration, ending the wartime conflict between the two countries, in Moscow.

In 1957, he was linked with the so-called Anti-Party Group of Molotov–Kaganovich–Malenkov. The group rejected both Khrushchev's liberalization of Soviet society and his denunciation of Stalin. Bulganin's disloyalty cost him the post of head of government. Khrushchev was appointed to this position in his place. Bulganin returned to work as chairman of the Board of the State Bank of the USSR (March 31–August 15, 1958), but his political fate was sealed. The plenum of the Central Committee relieved him of his duties as a member of the Presidium of the CC CPSU that same year. He was demoted to colonel-general (November 26, 1958) and was appointed chairman of the Stavropol *Sovnarkhoz* or Economic Soviet from August 1959 until his retirement in February 1960.

Bulganin (center) with Mao (left) and Stalin (right)

NOTES

1. "Memuary Nikity Sergeevicha Khrushcheva," *Voprosy istory*, no. 2 (1995): 78–79.

CHEKA (All-Russian Extraordinary Commission). Founded on December 5, 1917, after the October Revolution, the All-Russian Extraordinary Commission to Combat Sabotage and Counter-Revolution, the Cheka gradually expanded into a formidable secret police organization that carried out mass arrests of real and alleged enemies, followed by imprisonment, torture, and often execution. Its original leader was **Feliks Dzerzhinsky**, until his death in 1926. The Cheka underwent several metamorphoses during the period of Stalin's life. In 1922, it was replaced by the GPU (State Political Directorate), generally regarded as a less severe organ as the Bolshevik state became more consolidated, and the period of occupation and civil war ended. From 1917 to 1922, the secret police's mandate was for the territory of the RSFSR, but in 1923, its area of control was extended to the Soviet Union as a whole, under the name Joint State Political Directorate (OGPU). From 1934, it became known as the people's commissariat of internal affairs (NKVD) and was responsible for the purges of the 1930s, and especially in 1937–1938 (the Great Purge or Terror) under the leadership of **G. Iagoda** and **N. Iezhov**, and from November 1938, **L. Beria**. Under Iagoda and Iezhov, it was used to eliminate perceived enemies of the regime, including supporters of the so-called Left Opposition and Right Opposition, alleged spies, kulaks, members of the bourgeoisie, and priests, with executions running into the tens of thousands. After Stalin's death, many of its victims were rehabilitated, especially under Khrushchev (after 1956) and Gorbachev (1987–1991). After the war, its functions were divided between the Ministry of State Security (MGB) and the Ministry of Internal Affairs (MVD). From 1954 to 1991, it was known as the Committee for State Security (KGB).

CHERNIAKHOVSKY, IVAN DANILOVICH (1906–1945). The youngest-ever Soviet general of the army and one of the foremost Soviet commanders in the Second World War, he was a double recipient of the title Hero of the Soviet Union.

He was born on June 16, 1906, in the small Ukrainian village Oksanyna, Uman County, Kyiv Gubernia, in the Russian Empire (today part of Ukraine) into a Jewish Ukrainian family. His father was a switchman on the railways. Cherniakhovsky was eight years old when the First World War broke out and his father was sent to the front. A year later, his father returned, wounded. Due to the lack of work, the family moved to the village of Verbovo, currently in the Vynnytsia region of Ukraine. In spring 1919 both Cherniakhovsky's parents died from the typhus plague that spread throughout the neighborhood. Cherniakhovsky and his five siblings were left orphans, and he had to interrupt his studies (in 1919 he graduated from the fifth grade of an elementary railway school at Vapniarka station). In May 1920, he took on a position as a repair worker and a mechanic's assistant at Vapniarka station. Ivan constantly self-educated, and in May 1921, he successfully passed all exams at the junior high school. In the same year, he was elected Komsomol cell secretary in the village of Verbovo. In 1921, his Komsomol cell was assigned to the Tulchinsky battalion of special forces (CHON). Under Cherniakhovsky's command, the cell participated in the defeat of anti-Soviet forces in local forests.

In 1924, he joined the Red Army. In 1924–1925, he was a cadet of the Odesa Infantry School. In 1925, he was transferred to the Kyiv artillery school and graduated with distinction in 1928. In this same year, he became a member of the CPSU and served in the 17th Corps Artillery Regiment in the Ukrainian military district (the regiment was stationed in Vynnytsia). In 1929, he became the assistant commander of the battery, then the head of the topographical detachment, and commander of the training battery. In 1931, he entered the Military Technical Academy named after F. E. Dzerzhinsky in Leningrad. In 1932, he was transferred to the newly created Military Academy of Mechanization and Motorization of the Red Army. He graduated from the academy with honors in 1936 with the rank of senior lieutenant. During training at the academy, there were some rumors that Cherniakhovsky had concealed his social origins. An important role in the fate of the young commander was played by the intervention of Maria Ilinichna Ulianova, head of the Joint Complaints Bureau of the People's Commissariat of the RKI (Workers' and Peasants' Inspectorate) of the USSR and the People's Commissariat of the RKI of the RSFSR.

After graduation, Cheriyakhovsky rapidly rose in rank. In 1938, he became commander of the 9th Light Tank Brigade. By March 1941, he was commander of the 28th Panzer Division in the Baltic Military District. During the **Great Patriotic War**, he commanded the 28th Panzer Division (in December 1941 it was reorganized into the 241st Infantry Division) and participated in defensive battles southwest of Šiauliai, on the Western Dvina, near Soltsy and Novgorod. In the first months of the war, he was awarded the military rank of colonel. The reputation of the young, aggressive officer quickly grew. Rokossovsky regarded Cherniakhovsky as his "most capable fighting commander."[1] On February 14, 1943, he was promoted to the rank of lieutenant-general.

From July 1942 until April 1944, he assumed command of the 60th Army, which took part in the Voronezh-Kastornensky operation, the Battle of Kursk, crossing the Desna and Dnepr rivers, and operations in Kyiv, Zhytomyr-Berdychiv, Rivne-Lutsk, and Proskurovsk-Chernivtsi. After the liberation of the city of Voronezh, he was awarded the Order of the Red Banner. Cherniakhovsky's army played a decisive role in the rapid reoccupation of Kursk, delivering an unexpected deep flank strike. On October 17, 1943, by a decree of the Presidium of the Supreme Soviet of the USSR, for high organizational abilities during the crossing the Dnieper River and for personal heroism, Chernyakhovsky was awarded the title Hero of the Soviet Union.

Within three war years, he was promoted from the rank of colonel to four-star general, becoming the youngest ever Soviet army general and from April 1944 the commander of the 3rd Belarusian Front. The front under his command successfully participated in the Belarusian, Vilnius, Kaunas, Memel, Gumbinnen-Goldap, and East Prussian operations. In 1944, for the successful actions of his troops during the liberation of Vitebsk, Minsk, and Vilnius, he was awarded his second Gold Star medal. In 1945, Cherniakhovsky launched the Soviet East Prussian Offensive, and from January 1945 until his death, he served as the Soviet supreme commander of East Prussia. On February 18, 1945, while inspecting the combat readiness of units of the Red Army located in the rear, Cherniakhovsky was mortally wounded by a fragment of an artillery shell and died the same day.

CHERNOV, MIKHAIL ALEKSANDROVICH (1891–1938). A Russian political leader and people's commissariat for agriculture (Narkomzem), he was born on November 8, 1891, in the village of Tezino, Kostroma province (since 1925, it has been part of the town of Vichuga in Ivanovo Oblast), to a family of weavers. In 1909, he joined the Mensheviks. In 1911, he graduated from gymnasium in Kostroma. In 1913–1917, he studied at the Mathematics Department of the Physics and Mathematics Faculty of Moscow University, but did not graduate. During his studies, he became close friends with Dmitry Furmanov, a Russian writer, revolutionary, and military officer who studied at the same university in 1912–1914. In 1919, he became a member of the RSDRP (internationalists), and in 1920, he joined the Russian Communist Party (Bolshevik). From 1920, he worked as the head of the Ivanovo-Voznesensky provincial department of state control and the head of the provincial department of public education. On March 8–16, 1921, Chernov was a delegate at the tenth congress of the RCP(b) from Ivanovo-Voznesensky province, with the casting vote. In 1921, he was appointed as a secretary of Ivanovo-Voznesensky Regional Committee of the RCP(b). During 1922–1923, he chaired the Executive Committee of Ivanovo-Voznesensky Provincial Council (Ispolkom).

In 1923–1925, he was transferred to the Ukrainian SSR, where he was chairman of the Executive Committee of the Donetsk Provincial Council in Artemovsk. From June 15, 1925, to 1928, he served as people's commissar of internal trade of the Ukrainian SSR. In 1928–1930, he was a member of the board of the people's commissariat of trade of the USSR. In 1930, he led the association Soiuzkhleb (Bread Union). In 1930–1932, he was deputy people's commissar of the supply of the USSR. From 1932 to April 1933, he chaired the Committee on Agricultural Products in Soviet government (KomzagotSTO). From January 26 to February 10, 1934, he was a delegate of the 17th congress of the CPSU from KomzagotSTO. From February 10, 1934, to December 8, 1937, Chernov was a member of the CC CPSU. From April 10, 1934, to October 29, 1937, he was people's commissar of agriculture of the USSR. He was one of the key figures in implementing collectivization, which resulted in the deterioration of the economic situation of the peasantry and famine in the grain-growing regions of the country. On February 17, 1935, Chernov articulated a proposal of the commission to organize an Exhibition of Achievements of National Economy in 1937. Due to the organizational and political circumstances (the onset of the peak of the purges), the opening of the exhibition was first postponed to 1938, and then to 1939.

On November 7, 1937, Chernov was arrested. His wife and children were arrested shortly afterward. He became one of the defendants in the Trial of the Twenty-One, the last of Stalin's Show Trials. On March 13, 1938, the Military Collegium of the Supreme Court of the Soviet Union sentenced Chernov (along with **Bukharin**, **Rykov**, and others) to be shot. All his personal property was confiscated. On March 15, 1938, he was executed and buried at Kommunarka (Moscow Region). His daughter, Maria (age 23), was sentenced and executed on April 21, 1938. His son, Mikhail, died in 1942 in the Magadan gulag camp. On February 4, 1988, Chernov (together with Bukharin, Rykov, and others) was rehabilitated.

CHICHERIN, GEORGY VASILYEVICH (1872–1936). A Marxist revolutionary and Soviet diplomat of noble background. Chicherin was the nephew of the famous jurist Boris Chicherin and a distant relative of the great Russian poet Aleksandr Sergeevich Pushkin. He served as people's commissar of foreign affairs in the Soviet government from March 1918 to 1930. In 1918, he was among those who signed the Treaty of Brest-Litovsk and as the head of the Soviet delegation took part in the Genoa Conference and signed the Rapallo Treaty with Germany. He was also a musicologist and author of a book about Mozart. He was a member of the Central Executive Committee of the Soviet Union of the USSR (first through fifth convocations) and a member of the CC CPSU (1925–1930).

Chicherin was born on November 12, 1872, into an old noble family that owned the estate in the village of Karaul, Kirsanovsky district of the Tambov province. His father, Vasily N. Chicherin, was a diplomat in the service of the Russian Empire and a brother of Boris Chicherin, Russian jurist and political philosopher, who elaborated a theory that Russia needed a strong, authoritarian government to persevere with liberal reforms. His mother, Baroness Zhorzhina Meyendorf, an ethnic German, was a granddaughter, niece, and cousin of famous Russian diplomats from the Meyendorf family. Chicherin's parents belonged to the Pietists movement, founded in Russia by Lord Redstock. The family very often read prayers and the Bible, and sang religious hymns.

In 1884, Chicherin entered the Tambov gymnasium, then studied at the gymnasium in St. Petersburg. In 1891, he was admitted to the St. Petersburg University's Department of History and Philology, where he studied until 1896. From an early age, Chicherin was a polyglot (he knew several European languages), was an accomplished pianist, and had a phenomenal memory. He was fond of European modernism and actively propagated the music of Wagner and Mozart, and the writings of Nietzsche in Russia. In 1897, upon graduation from university, Chicherin started his career at the archive of the Ministry of Foreign Affairs, where his father was also an employee. This was also a time when his passion for left-wing political ideas started.

In 1904, Chicherin joined the Menshevik wing of the RSDWP. The same year he inherited the estate of his uncle, Boris Chicherin, and became very wealthy. He used his wealth to support revolutionary activities on the eve of the Russian Revolution of 1905. Because of his revolutionary activities, he was forced to flee to Germany to avoid arrest. According to the testimony of his cousin Baron Aleksandr Meyendorf,[2] there, in parallel with revolutionary activity, Chicherin sought treatment for his homosexual tendencies. In 1905, he became a member of the Menshevik branch of the RSDWP, and in 1907, he was elected secretary of its Foreign Central Bureau. At this time, he also collaborated with the group "Voice of the Social Democrat."

At the end of 1907, Chicherin was arrested in Berlin for using fake documents. Later, he moved to the town of Leiben, not far from Dresden. In 1908, he was forced to leave Germany and moved to Paris. There, he participated in the work of the French Socialist Party of Jean Jaurès. In 1914, Chicherin lived in Belgium. With the outbreak of the First World War, Chicherin adopted the position of defeatism widespread among the Bolsheviks, and moved to London, where he became a member of the British Socialist Party. He was one of the organizers of the Russian Political Prisoners' Assistance Committee. His main associate was the radical suffragist Mary Bridges-Adams. Gradually, the committee turned into a political body and began to conduct systematic campaigns against the Russian government. After the February Revolution in Russia, Chicherin began to help to send political emigrants to their homeland. On August 22, 1917, he was arrested by the British police for his antiwar writings and imprisoned in Brixton prison, where he spent several months. After the October Revolution 1917, at the request of the Soviet government, Leon Trotsky, people's commissar of foreign affairs, secured Chicherin's release and safe passage to Russia in exchange for George Buchanan, the British ambassador, and some other British citizens held in Russia. On January 19, 1918, he arrived in Petrograd and joined the RSDWP(b) (from March 1918, it was known as the Russian Communist Party).

On January 21, 1918, he was appointed deputy people's commissar of foreign affairs under Trotsky and participated in the negotiations that led to the Treaty of Brest-Litovsk. On March 3, 1918, he signed the treaty. On May 30, 1918, Chicherin was appointed people's commissar of foreign affairs. He made significant efforts to end Soviet Russia's international isolation. On March 2, 1919, he was one of five men chairing the first congress of the **Comintern**. In 1920, on behalf of Soviet Russia, he signed a peace treaty with Estonia, and in 1921 concluded agreements with Turkey, Iran, and Afghanistan. In April 1922, he headed the Soviet delegation at the Genoa Conference, during which he signed the Rapallo Treaty with Walther Rathenau, the German foreign minister.

In 1923, he represented the Soviet delegation at the Lausanne Conference, where the postwar status of the Turkish Straits was determined. He also signed the USSR's treaties with Turkey (1925) and Iran (1927). In 1925, he was appointed a member of the CC CPSU. From 1928, due to health issues and a progressive mental disorder, he could no longer perform the duties of people's commissar and was replaced by **M. M. Litvinov** (although

Chicherin himself wanted to see **V. V. Kuibyshev** as his successor) on July 21, 1930. After retirement, he was removed from the Central Committee. In his political testament, he wrote that the party's purges, public work, squabbles, hijackings, and denunciations interfered with the normal functioning of the people's commissar. He died on July 7, 1936, and was buried in Moscow.

CHUBAR, VLAS IAKOVLEVICH (FEBRUARY 22, 1891–FEBRUARY 26, 1939). A Ukrainian Bolshevik revolutionary and Soviet statesman, Chubar was the longtime chairman of the original Soviet government, the Council of People's Commissars of the USSR. He participated in the revolution of 1905, and both the February and October revolutions of 1917. He was the first Ukrainian to be elected to the all-Union Politburo of the CC CPSU. Chubar was an economic administrator and the top Communist Party official in Ukraine during the 1932–1933 famine (Holodomor). In 2010, the Ukrainian Supreme Court found him guilty of participation in this tragedy.

He was born into a Ukrainian peasant family in Fedorovka, Iekaterinoslav Governorate, Russian Empire (now Polohy Raion, Zaporizhzhia Oblast, Ukraine). He had seven siblings. In 1904–1911, he studied at the Aleksandrovsky mechanical technical vocational college. He became a Marxist revolutionary when he was a teenager. His brother Pavel, who later died on the barricades during the Russian Revolution of 1905, introduced him to the ideas of the Bolshevik organization. Chubar also took part in the First Russian Revolution and participated in clashes with the police in 1905. In 1907, he joined the RSDWP.

After graduation, he worked at factories in Kramatorsk, Mariupol, Moscow, and Petrograd. He was repeatedly prosecuted by the authorities for his revolutionary activity. In 1915, he was mobilized into the Russian Imperial army, but at the beginning of 1916 was seconded to the Petrograd Gun Plant and worked as turner. After the February Revolution of 1917, he became the chairman and later a member of the factory committee. Also, he became a deputy of the Petrograd Soviet. After the October Revolution, he was appointed a commissar of the Military Revolutionary Committee in the Main Artillery Directorate in Petrograd and then held a number of administrative positions in Russia. In 1921, he became a member of the Central Committee of the Soviet Communist Party.

In January 1920, Chubar chaired the Organizing Bureau for the Reconstruction of Industry in Ukraine and the Supreme Council of the National Economy of the Ukrainian SSR, and he was also a member of the All-Ukrainian Revolutionary Committee. From January 1922 to July 1923, he led the Central Administration of the Coal Industry in the Donets Basin. After the formation of the USSR, he promoted the interests of Ukraine in relations between the center and republican bodies. In 1923, for example, defending the idea of Ukrainization, he opposed the theory of D. Lebed, second secretary of the Central Committee of the Communist Party (b), about the "struggle of two cultures," which advocated the leading role of Russian culture associated with the city and working class, over "backward" Ukrainian peasant culture. From July 1923 to April 1934, Chubar was chairman of the Sovnarkom (head of government) of the Ukrainian SSR. At the same time, from July 1923 to May 1925, he was a deputy chairman of the Council of People's Commissars of the USSR.

In 1924, he headed the commission for the supervision of the electrification of the Dnieper (Dnipro) River. In January 1925 at the plenum of the CC CPSU, he proposed to reduce the single agricultural tax imposed on peasants at the start of the **New Economic Policy** in 1921, and to consistently pursue a policy of "union with the middle class." In 1925, Chubar also headed the Committee for Ukrainization. He proved to be a talented manager in Ukraine, but as an obedient member of the Bolshevik Party, he pursued the adventurist policy of crash industrialization. The accelerated pace of industrial development, which Chubar implemented, led to a substantial impoverishment of the majority of the Ukrainian population. In October 1932, he was responsible for grain procurements in the Dnipropetrovsk region. During the Famine of 1932–1933, he took an active part in requisitioning and used repressive forms and methods of confiscation of bread from collective farmers and individual farmers. On November 18, 1932, he signed a resolution of the CC CPSU, developed by V. Molotov in accordance with Stalin's instructions, which established in-kind fines for "debtors" in grain procurement. At the same time, in June 1932, he asked Stalin to reduce the plan for food procurement in Ukraine and to provide food aid to the republic.

His vacillating policies satisfied no one, and Stalin criticized him for opportunism and inability to rule the republic. In 1934, he was recalled from Ukraine and transferred to Moscow, where he became deputy chairman of the National Council of People's Commissars and deputy chairman of the USSR Council of Labor and Defense. In February 1935, his career recovered, and he was made a full member of the Politburo. Between August 16, 1937, and January 19, 1938, he served as the people's commissar of finance. On July 4, 1938, however, the NKVD arrested Chubar. He was accused of being an agent of German intelligence and a member of an anti-Soviet terrorist sabotage organization. On February 26, 1939, the Military Collegium of the Supreme Court of the USSR (composed of **V. V. Ulrich**, Dmitriev,[3] and A. G. Suslin) sentenced him to death. He was executed the same day. In 1955, during the first wave of de-Stalinization, the Soviet government cleared Chubar of all charges.

CHUIKOV, VASILY IVANOVICH (FEBRUARY 12, 1900–MARCH 18, 1982). A marshal of the Soviet Union (1955), twice Hero of the Soviet Union (1944, 1945), and Red Army commander during the **Great Patriotic War**. He commanded the defense at the **Battle of Stalingrad**. He was commander-in-chief of the Group of Soviet Forces in Germany (1949–1953), commander of the Kyiv Military District (1953–1960), commander-in-chief of the ground forces of the USSR, deputy minister of defense of the USSR (1960–1964), chief of Civil Defense Forces of the USSR (1961–1972), and a member of the Central Committee of the CPSU (1961–1982). Chuikov had several nicknames: "The Man of Iron Will," "The Stone," and "General Assault (Storm)."

Chuikov was born into a Russian peasant family in the village of Serebrianie Prudy in the Tula region south of Moscow. He had eight brothers and four sisters. His father, Ivan Ionovich Chuikov (1865–1958), a peasant from the village of Serebrianie Prudy, was a groom at the wedding of Count Sheremetev and was known as a good fist fighter. His mother, Elizaveta Fiodorovna, was a religious person and for many years was the head of St. Nikolai Church. In 1937 the church was closed and scheduled to be destroyed, but she went on foot to Moscow in protest, resulting in its survival. Vasily Chuikov believed that he inherited firmness, determination, and self-confidence from his mother. From his father he inherited physical strength and cockiness. All these traits helped Vasily later to quickly advance in the military service.

Chuikov finished four classes of a parish school (1907–1911), and at the age of 12 he left school. He went to St. Petersburg to earn his living in a factory. In 1917, he served as cabin boy in the miners' detachment in Kronstadt. In April 1918, he joined the Red Army and became a cadet of the First Moscow Military Instructor Courses. In July 1918, he participated in the suppression of the rebellion of the Left Socialist Revolutionaries in Moscow. During the Civil War, he was assistant commander of a rifle company. On May 4, 1919, he became a member of the RSDWP(b). In May 1919, the 19-year-old Chuikov replaced the wounded commander on the battlefield, and from that day until the end of 1921, he commanded the 43rd Regiment of the 5th Infantry Division (until 1919 the 40th Regiment of the 28th Infantry Division of the 2nd Army). He fought on the Southern, Eastern, and Western fronts. His record of service during the Civil War was distinguished—he was awarded two orders of the Red Banner, nominal gold watches, and gold weapons. During the Civil War, Chuikov was wounded four times (he bore one of this war wounds for the rest of his life) but did not leave the front. His troops ousted White leader Admiral Aleksandr Kolchak from the villages of Vozdvizhenka and Voskresenskoye. Near the village of Allaki, he defeated a White Guard Regiment and occupied the villages of Karabolka and Kuyash.

After the war (from July 1921 to January 1922), he first became the head of Combat Unit No. 4 and later the head of the garrison of the city of Velizh in Smolensk Oblast. From January 1922, he was again the commander of the regiment. In 1925, he graduated from the Frunze Military Academy. After graduation and because of his excellent academic achievements, he was allowed to continue his studies at the academy, where he learned the Chinese language and history in the Oriental Studies Department. During his studies, Chuikov joined a Soviet diplomatic delegation that visited Harbin, Changchun, Port Arthur, Dalian, Tianjin, and Beijing, cities in northeastern and northern China. According to Chuikov himself, during this trip he became fluent in Mandarin and successfully fulfilled the tasks of a military diplomat-adviser.

In July 1927, after graduation from this program, Chuikov became a military adviser in China. In 1929, after the Soviet Union broke off diplomatic relations with the Republic of China (after the Sino-Soviet conflict), he was forced to leave this country. In September 1929, he was appointed chief of staff of the Intelligence Division of the Special Red Banner Far Eastern Army under the command of **Vasily Bliukher**. In August 1932, he led advanced training courses for intelligence personnel of the Red Army Headquarters. In 1936, he graduated from academic courses at the Stalin Military Academy of Mechanization and Motorization of the Worker-Peasant Red Army. Stalin's purges of 1937–1938 in the Red Army indirectly contributed to Chuikov's ascent. From December 1936, he was the commander of a mechanized brigade (military unit Kiselevichi in Babruisk), from April 1938 he was the commander of the 5th Rifle Corps, and from June 1938, he commanded the Babruisk Army Group in the Belarusian Military District.

In September 1939, the army group was transformed into the 4th Army, which under Chuikov's command participated in the Soviet invasion of Poland. Before this campaign, on October 7, 1938, he was approved as a member of the Military Council with the People's Commissariat of Defense of the USSR. In December 1939, he became a commander of the 9th Army, which fought in northern Karelia during the Soviet–Finnish War of 1939–1940. From March to December 1940, he once again commanded the 4th Army of the Western Special Military District. From December 1940 to 1942, Chuikov returned to China as military attaché and chief military adviser of the commander-in-chief of the Chinese army, Chiang Kai-shek. At this time, China waged war against the Japanese invaders, who were able to capture the central regions of the country, Manchuria, and a number of Chinese cities. During this period, a number of military operations were carried out against the Japanese army. Chuikov reportedly played a prominent role in ending the hostile military confrontation between Chiang Kai-shek and Mao Zedong with the goal of creating a united front against the Japanese invaders.

With the outbreak of the Great Patriotic War, Chuikov repeatedly asked the command to withdraw him from China and send him to the front. After his return to the USSR, he was assigned to Tula, where an army was formed to be sent to Stalingrad. In May 1942, he was sent to the front as a commander of the 1st Reserve (from July—the 64th) Army. In September 1942, he commanded the 62nd Army. The High Command ordered Chuikov to defend Stalingrad at all costs. Subsequently, he led the heroic six-month defense of **Stalingrad** against the German 6th Army, commanded by General Friedrich von Paulus. His soldiers took part in the street battles in a completely destroyed city. In September 1942 alone, despite the numerical superiority of the enemy in manpower, tanks, and aircraft, units of the 62nd Army killed up to 20,000 German soldiers and officers. Chuikov's headquarters were situated almost at the forefront of the defense line during the most critical moments of the battle. Toward the end of the defensive operation, his troops held the area north of the Stalingrad Tractor Plant, the Barricades plant, some parts of the Red October plant, and several blocks in the city center.

At Stalingrad, Chuikov developed hand-to-hand combat tactics.[4] Soviet and Nazi trenches were located within throwing distance of grenades, which complicated the task of German aviation and artillery (they were afraid to hit their own troops). Once, when Chuikov wanted to check the positions of the enemy and flew over Stalingrad, his plane was shot down by the German Junkers and literally split in half. The commander miraculously survived this attack. The appearance of special "assault groups" is also associated with the name of Chuikov. Such groups moved very quickly and attacked unexpectedly. These groups included trained "specialists": snipers, engineers, sappers, and chemists. Such tactics proved to be very successful. Later, this experience was useful during the Battle of Berlin (April 16–May 2, 1945). For the unprecedented mass heroism and resilience of the personnel in April 1943, the 62nd Army was redesignated the Soviet 8th Guards Army. For the defense of Stalingrad, Chuikov was awarded the Order of Suvorov of the first degree.

After the Battle of Stalingrad, from April 1943 to May 1945, with the 8th Guards Army, he participated in the liberation of Ukraine, Belarus, and Poland. His army successfully fought in the Izyum-Barvenkovo and Donbas operations, in the battle of the Dnepr, Nikopol-Kryvyi Rih, Bereznegovato-Snegirevskaia, Odesa, Belarusian, Warsaw-Poznan, and Berlin operations. For the liberation of the territory of Right-Bank Ukraine and successes in the Vistula-Oder offensive operation (January 12–February 3, 1945) and for the Battle of Poznan (February 23, 1945), Chuikov was twice decorated as a Hero of the Soviet Union.

After the Second World War until July 1946, Chuikov continued to command the 8th Guards Army, which was stationed in Germany. At the same time, he was the head of the Soviet military administration in Thuringia. In July 1946, he was appointed the deputy, and later the first deputy commander-in-chief, of the group of Soviet forces in Germany and deputy head of the Soviet Military Administration in Germany. In March 1949, he was the commander-in-chief of the group of Soviet forces in Germany. Simultaneously (until October 1949), he was the commander-in-chief of the Soviet Military Administration in Germany, which directly controlled the Soviet zone of occupation of Germany. From October 1949, Chuikov was appointed chairman of the Soviet Control Commission, which controlled the territory of the German Democratic Republic, formed from the Soviet occupation zone at the end of the war. In this post, he played one of the key roles in resolving the Berlin crisis of 1948–1949, which began after the Soviet side cut off access to West Berlin from the Western occupation zones by rail, land, and water. In total, he served in various positions in Germany for eight years.

In 1953, after Stalin's death, he was transferred from Germany and, from May 26, 1953, to April 1960, commanded the troops of the Kyiv Military District. On March 11, 1955, while serving in that post, he was promoted to Marshal of the Soviet Union. In 1960, Chuikov became commander-in-chief of the ground forces of the USSR and later the deputy minister of defense of the USSR, the highest position that he held over the years of his service. Simultaneously, from August 1961, Chuikov was the first chief of the newly created Civil Defense of the USSR. He identified the main tasks and set of measures of civil defense in peace time. On Chuikov's initiative, the Moscow Military School of Civil Defense was created. This was the first university in the USSR to train civil defense specialists. In 1962, Chuikov was one of the organizers of the Operation Anadyr—the secret operation to deploy ballistic missiles, medium-range bombers, and a division of mechanized infantry to Cuba to create an army group that would be able to prevent an invasion of the island by U.S. forces. In June 1964, during **N. Khrushchev**'s army reform, due to the liquidation of the post of the High Command of the Ground Forces, Chuikov was dismissed from his duties as commander-in-chief of the ground forces of the USSR. Until 1972, he remained head of the Civil Defense of the USSR.

From 1952, Chuikov was a candidate member of the Presidium of the CC CPSU. From 1961 until the end of his life, he was a member of the CC CPSU. He was also a deputy of the Supreme Soviet of the USSR from 1946 until the end of his life. He was an honorary citizen of the city of Berlin from May 8, 1965, to September 29, 1992. On May 4, 1970, for the defense of the city during the Battle of Stalingrad, Chuikov was awarded the title "Honorary Citizen of the Hero City of Volgograd." He was a major consultant for the design of the Stalingrad battle memorial on Mamaev Kurgan.

Chuikov died on March 18, 1982. According to his will, he was buried in Volgograd on the Mamaev Kurgan at the foot of the Motherland monument, next to the soldiers of his army who died in the major battle of the Second World War. After his death, while sorting through his father's belongings, his son found a small piece of paper with a prayer in Chuikov's party ticket (*partbilet*). It was the guardian prayer, a blessing that his illiterate mother had dictated to him before he went to the front.

COMINTERN (COMMUNIST INTERNATIONAL). Founded in 1919, the Comintern, sometimes referred to as the Third International, sought to expand the Bolshevik (October Revolution) to a world level by overthrowing the international bourgeoisie and establishing a Soviet republic. Since the first workers' state had been founded in Soviet Russia, that state led the movement, and subsequently it was controlled by the Soviet Union. It arose from the serious differences among socialist parties across Europe in their attitude to the First World War, and was solidified by Lenin and **L. Trotsky**'s fear that standing alone, the Soviet state would be unable to withstand imperialist capitalist states and be overthrown. The first congress, held in Moscow in March 1919, included representatives of thirty-four socialist parties and elected **G. Zinoviev** as the chairman of the executive. Zinoviev remained at the helm until his clash with Stalin, which resulted in his removal in 1926. He was replaced by **N. Bukharin**, but he too fell out of favor with Stalin in 1928, when he was associated with the Right Opposition supporters of the **New Economic** Policy. He was replaced in turn by the Bulgarian Communist **G. Dimitrov**, who remained at the helm until the dissolution of the Comintern in May 1943. The Comintern held seven world congresses between 1919 and 1935. It evolved from an organization closely controlled by Lenin and devoted to world revolution to one linked even more firmly to Stalin, who emphasized the need to protect the Soviet state in line with his policy of **Socialism in One Country**. The seventh congress was arguably the most significant, at which time delegates were asked to support popular fronts and alliances with bourgeois parties against the threat of National Socialism (Germany) and Fascism (Italy).

NOTES

1. Konstantin Rokossovsky, *Soldatsky dolg* (Moscow: Olma-Press, 2002), 274.
2. Baron Aleksandr Meyendorff, "My Cousin, Foreign Commissar Chicherin," *The Russian Review* 30, no. 2 (1971): 178n.
3. No initials were included on the original document. There were two Dmitrievs in the Military Collegium of the Supreme Court of the USSR (Leonid Dmitrievich and Iakov Petrovich), but in Chubar's documents, there is no information which one was in his case.
4. This was a type of urban warfare. Chuikov had to introduce new tactics of urban fighting. One of them was the close-combat tactics (to "hug the enemy"), when the front edge of the defense lines was as close as possible to the enemy, forcing him to abandon the use of aviation (the Wehrmacht Stuka dive bombers). Another of Chuikov's innovations was the creation of small sabotage groups (assault groups numbering one or two platoons, which were the first to suddenly burst into houses and eliminate enemy's soldiers. Their main weapons were bayonets, grenades, and shovels. Such groups have shown high efficiency in urban warfare. Later, during urban fights in the German capital, such tactics turned out to be invaluable. Subsequently, Chuikov received the nickname "General Assault" (general-*shturm*).

D

DEKANOZOV, VLADIMIR GEORGIEVICH (DEKANOZISHVILI) (1898–1953). A Soviet statesman, one of the leaders of the Soviet State Security, and one of the active participants in the Stalinist repressions (Great Terror) of the 1930s, Dekanozov was also a diplomat and USSR ambassador to Germany before the start of the **Great Patriotic War**. He belonged to the inner circle of **L. P. Beria**.

Dekanozov (real name Dekanozishvili), was born in 1898 in Baku (now capital of Azerbaijan) into a Georgian family. His father, Georgi Dekanozishvili, who was from a noble Georgian family belonging to the Georgian Orthodox Church, was the controller of an oil company and a founder of the Party of Georgian Social-Federalists. Dekanozov was well educated. He studied at the gymnasia in Baku (1914) and Tiflis (1916). Later, he studied at the medical faculties of the Saratov and Baku universities. He took part in the revolutionary movement in Transcaucasia. In 1918, during the civil war, he joined the Red Army and in 1920 became a member of the RCP(b). From 1921 to 1931, he worked in the Extraordinary Commission (Cheka) in the Azerbaijan SSR and Georgian SSR. There he became acquainted with Lavrenty Beria, who would later become his patron and who subsequently supported Dekanozov. In 1931 when Beria became the first secretary of the CC CP(b) of Georgia, Dekanozov was appointed the secretary in charge of transportation and supplies of Georgia. In 1934, he became the head of the Central Committee's Department of the Georgian SSR. In October 1936, he was transferred to the Council of People's Commissars of Georgia, with the position of people's commissar of the food industry. From 1936 until 1938, he was appointed minister of food industry of the Georgian SSR. Simultaneously, during 1937–1938, he was chairman of Gosplan of Georgia and a deputy chairman of the Georgian government.

In December 1938, when Beria was appointed people's commissar of internal affairs of the USSR, Dekanozov was transferred to Moscow. On December 2, 1938, he became the head of the Fifth Department (foreign intelligence), and simultaneously, Beria appointed him head of the Third Department (counterespionage) and deputy head of the Main Directorate of State Security (GUGB) of the NKVD of the USSR. During Stalin's purges, he became the main assistant to Beria. In 1939, he was one of the chief organizers of further repressions in the Red Army. In March 1939, he was elected a candidate member of CC CPSU(b). Two months later, he was transferred to the People's Commissariat of Foreign Affairs and became deputy commissar of foreign affairs of the USSR.

In the summer of 1940, he was active in Lithuania, where he coordinated efforts to force Lithuania to join the Soviet Union. He also headed a campaign of arrests of "anti-Soviet elements" there. On November 24, 1940, Dekanozov was appointed Soviet ambassador to Germany. He remained in that position until June 22, 1941, when Nazi Germany invaded the USSR. A few days before June 22, Dekanozov made his last attempt to establish a dialogue with the German top authorities and to get permission to meet with Hitler. He sent a "note verbale" to the Reich foreign minister, Ribbentrop, which indicated violations of the Soviet borders by German aviation between April 19 and June 19, 1941 (180 German aircraft invasions into Soviet airspace). On June 22, 1941, at 4 a.m., Dekanozov was summoned by Ribbentrop, who read out a formal note to the Soviet government declaring war. After the beginning of the Great Patriotic War, Ambassador Dekanozov was interned along with the embassy staff and exchanged for the German ambassador to the USSR, Friedrich-Werner Graf von der Schulenburg, and German diplomats on the USSR-Turkey border.

From 1941 to 1952, Dekanozov was a member of the CC CPSU. In May 1945, he was appointed deputy commissar of foreign affairs of the USSR. In March 1947, Dekanozov was removed from the Ministry of Foreign Affairs and transferred to the Main Directorate of Soviet Overseas Property. In 1949, he again lost his position and remained without any portfolio until 1952, when he was appointed a member of the Committee of the Radio Broadcasting. In April 1953, after Stalin's death, he became minister of the interior of the Georgian SSR. On June 30, 1953, after **L. Beria**'s arrest, Dekanozov was removed from his post and arrested as "a member of Beria's gang." In June 1953 he was sentenced to death and shot in December of the same year. On May 29, 2000, the Military Collegium of the Supreme Court of the Russian Federation refused his rehabilitation.

DIMITROV, GEORGY MIHAILOVICH (1882–1949). A Bulgarian communist politician and the first communist leader of Bulgaria (1946–1949), Dimitrov was a general secretary of the **Comintern** from 1934 to 1943. He was called the "Bulgarian Lenin" and the leader of the Bulgarian people. After his death, a Lenin-like mausoleum was built in Sofia, where his body remained until the end of the Communist period in 1990.

Dimitrov was born on June 18, 1882, in the village of Kovachevtsi, Pernik District, Bulgaria, into a family of a craftsman. He had seven younger siblings. In 1894, he worked as an apprentice typesetter. In 1901, he was the secretary of the Union of Printers in Sofia. The following year, he became a member of the Bulgarian Workers' Social Democratic Party, and in 1903 he joined the Bulgarian Social Democratic Workers' Party (called the Narrow Party). In 1919, the party was renamed as the Bulgarian Communist Party (Narrow Socialists, BCP-NS). From 1909 to 1923, Dimitrov was the secretary of the General Workers' Union. He actively took part in party activities, including the organization of strikes. In 1906 and 1911, he was one of the leaders of the strike of the coal miners in Pernik. In 1909, he participated in the strikes of the match factory workers in Kostenec and in 1919–1920 in the railwaymen's strikes. From 1913 to 1923, Dimitrov became a member of the Bulgarian Parliament. During the Balkan Wars in 1912–1913, he condemned Bulgarian expansionist policies and promoted pacifism. For these activities, he was constantly persecuted. In 1921, he participated in the third congress of the Comintern (the Communist International), where he met Vladimir Lenin, and in the same year he was elected a member of the Central Council of the Profintern (the Red International of Labor Unions—an international body established by the Communist International). In September 1923, Dimitrov was one of the leaders of the armed uprising against Aleksander Tsolov Tsankov's government in Bulgaria. After the failure to seize power, together with Vasil Kolarov (another Bulgarian communist political leader and leading functionary in the Communist International), and other agents of the Comintern, he first fled to Yugoslavia, then to the USSR. For his participation in the armed rebellion, the Bulgarian authorities sentenced Dimitrov to death in absentia.

During his exile, Dimitrov was a member of the foreign bureau of the BCP-NS and continued his work in the Executive Committee of the Communist International and the executive bureau of the Profintern. He also was the secretary of the Balkan Communist Federation. In the fall of 1929, he moved to Germany. He lived in Berlin incognito and actively participated in the activities of the Comintern;

in particular, he led communist propaganda outside the Soviet Union. During this period, he used the code name "Diamond." After the Reichstag (German Parliament) fire of February 27, 1933, a month after Adolf Hitler was appointed Chancellor of Germany, Dimitrov was arrested by the Nazis on charges of arson, but he provided an alibi and was acquitted during the Leipzig trial in September–December 1933. During the trial, Dimitrov built his defense in such a way as to adopt the role of prosecutor against the Nazi regime. Since Dimitrov was fluent in German, his speeches during the trial were later used widely in anti-Nazi propaganda and served as a model for other communists on trial. For example, the same strategies were used by Toivo Antikainen, who was called "the Northern Dimitrov" in Finland, Nikos Beloyanis in Greece, and Brahma Fishar in South Africa. After the trial, Dimitrov and his comrades-in-arms, Popov and Tanev, were granted Soviet citizenship, and the USSR demanded their extradition.

On February 27, 1934, Dimitrov returned to the USSR. He became part of Stalin's inner circle, and immediately after arrival he was elected deputy of the Leningrad City Council. At the end of April 1934, he was elected a member of the Political Commission of the Executive Committee of the Comintern (ECCI) and was appointed the head of the Comintern's Central European Secretariat. Along with Ernst Thälmann and Dolores Ibárruri, he became one of the leaders of the international communist movement. At the seventh congress of the Comintern (1935), Dimitrov was entrusted to offer the keynote address about the rise of fascism. During his speech, he highlighted the role of the Comintern in the struggle against the Nazi threat, encouraged the formation of popular-front movements in Europe, and represented Soviet ideology as a mainstream anti-fascism. After the congress, the Comintern proclaimed a course for a broad anti-fascist coalition.

From 1935 until the dissolution of the Comintern in 1943, Dimitrov served as its secretary general. During Stalin's repressions of 1937–1938, the influence of the Comintern decreased. Unlike some leaders of the Communist parties of Eastern Europe, Dimitrov was not repressed. On the contrary, he received a promotion. From 1937 to 1945, he became a member of the Supreme Soviet of the USSR. On June 22, 1941, he was also appointed as the head of the "leading three" of the ECCI and headed all ECCI's activities. In 1942, Dimitrov took the lead in founding and leading the Fatherland Front of Bulgaria, which was created under Moscow's control. This organization played an essential role in rallying the Bulgarian popular masses in the struggle against fascism and carrying out the Bulgarian coup d'état of 1944. Shortly after the dissolution of the Comintern, in June 1943, Dimitrov was appointed head of the International Policy Department of the CC CPSU, which became the de facto successor of the ECCI. The newly created department supervised the Soviet Party's relationships with foreign communist parties and with international communist front organizations.

In November 1945, after a pro-Soviet regime was established in Bulgaria, Dimitrov returned to his country. The same year, the Presidium of the Supreme Soviet of the USSR awarded Dimitrov the Order of Lenin. On November 6, 1946, he was appointed chairman of the Council of Ministers. From December 1948 until his death, he held the post of secretary general of the Central Committee of the BCP. In the era of Dimitrov, Bulgaria maintained close relations with the USSR and was sometimes called the "17th republic of the Soviet Union" (from 1940 to 1956, the Karelian-Finnish SSR was the 16th republic). At the same time, Dimitrov actively supported the idea to create a Bulgarian–Yugoslav Federation. But the plans of Yugoslav's (and Dimitrov's) leader, **I. Broz Tito**, were an obstacle to Stalin's aspirations for total control over the new Eastern Bloc. After the breakdown of relations between Stalin and Tito in 1948, Dimitrov's ideas caused great discontent among the Soviet leadership. Also, despite the fact that Dimitrov spoke in support of the Yugoslav leader, he and Tito had serious disagreements on the Macedonian question. Tito insisted on the recognition of the Macedonians as an independent nation, and Dimitrov considered them a sub-ethnos of the Bulgarian people. As the result, the ideas of a Balkan Federation and a united Macedonia were abandoned.

In April 1949, Dimitrov came to Moscow for medical treatment. He suffered from cirrhosis of the liver, diabetes mellitus, and chronic prostatitis. Two weeks later, his health condition deteriorated sharply. On July 2, 1949, Dimitrov died in Barvikha near Moscow. Soviet doctors diagnosed heart failure. His body was returned to Sofia and embalmed. The sarcophagus with Dimitrov's body was placed on display in Sofia's Georgi Dimitrov Mausoleum. After the fall of the Communist regime in Bulgaria, in 1990, the BSP party (the former Bulgarian Communist Party), at the request of relatives (according to the official version) decided to bury the body. The mausoleum was torn down in 1999.

According to some sources, Peter Gylybov, who was an employee of the Bulgarian mausoleum group from 1949 to 1990, managed to take some hair samples from Dimitrov during the interment and, together with his colleagues, conduct an examination of the existing remains. Studies found a high mercury content in the samples. Nevertheless, the theory that he was poisoned never acquired much credibility.

DOCTORS' PLOT (1948–1953). Also known as the case of saboteur doctors or poisoning/killer doctors, in the investigation materials it was named as the case of a Zionist conspiracy in the Ministry of State Security, and the case of **Abakumov**. It was a criminal case against a group of prominent Soviet doctors accused of conspiracy and intent to murder a number of Soviet leaders, including Stalin.

The Doctors' Plot was caused by the intensified struggle for power at the end of Stalin's life and largely influenced the course of the struggle for his inheritance. Even though the first arrests occurred in 1951, the origins of the campaign date back to 1948. Two main events became forerunners of the Doctors' Plot. Firstly, in 1948, a campaign against cosmopolitanism was already underway in the USSR. Since the role of the so-called "rootless cosmopolitans" most often turned out to be people with Jewish surnames, this campaign took on anti-Semitic forms. There were unspoken instructions not to allow Jews into important key posts. Secondly, in 1948, a cardiologist, L. Timashuk, sent several letters to the Soviet official bodies (including to the Ministry of State Security) about the improper treatment of a member of the Politburo of the Central Committee of the All-Union Communist Party of Bolsheviks, **Andrei Zhdanov**, who died shortly thereafter. The statement was ignored.

But in 1951, the topic of saboteur doctors began to develop in connection with the campaign against the "cosmopolitans." The campaign was used in the struggle of groups of party functionaries and leaders of the Ministry of Internal Affairs led by **G. Malenkov** in the fight against the minister of state security, V. Abakumov. In 1951, M. Riumin, a security officer of the Soviet MGB (the Ministry of State Security of the USSR), decided to make accusations against his boss (Abakumov) and enlisted the support of Malenkov. Riumin sent a letter to Stalin, in which he wrote that Abakumov prohibited him to investigate the terrorist activities of the therapist professor Ia. G. Etinger, who was arrested on November 18, 1950. According to Riumin, Etinger "confessed" that in 1945, while being a consultant to the Kremlin's Medical and Sanitary Directorate, by "sabotage treatment" he contributed to the death of A. Shcherbakov (a member of the Central Committee of the CPSU and first secretary of the Moscow Regional Committee of the CPSU).

Abakumov was arrested, and within the framework of the "Abakumov case," the Etinger case began to be intensively developed and finally grew into the "Doctors' Plot." Timashuk's letters came in handy. She was awarded the Order of Lenin. All doctors involved in the treatment of Shcherbakov and Zhdanov, including professors P. Egorov, V. Vinogradov, and doctors M. Vovsy, M. Pevzner, I. Lembergsky, N. Shereshevsky, B. Levin, S. Karpai, and V. Vasilenko, were arrested. Members of their families and some ordinary health workers were also arrested: in total thirty-seven people. Riumin and S. Ignatiev, the curator of the case appointed by Malenkov, sought evidence of deliberate sabotage. So-called "marathon" interrogations and beatings were used extensively. Dimitrov was added to the list of persons killed by doctors. But Stalin was declared to be the main target.

On January 13, 1953, the party newspaper *Pravda* published a TASS report "The Arrest of a Group of Saboteur Doctors." It stated that the Soviet security organs had uncovered the terrorist activities of a group of doctors who sought "to reduce the lives of Party leaders of the Soviet Union by means of destructive treatment." The report also linked the saboteur doctors with the "international Jewish bourgeois-nationalist organization Joint." Stalin's long-term secretary, **A. Poskrebyshev**, and a devoted security guard, **N. Vlasik**, were also arrested. Stalin found himself isolated and without sufficiently qualified medical assistance. After he had a stroke on March 2, he was left without medical and other assistance for several hours. On March 5, Stalin died, and the new minister of internal affairs, **L. Beria**, approved the decision to terminate the criminal prosecution of all those under investigation.

DYBENKO, PAVEL EFIMOVICH (1889–1938). A Soviet revolutionary, political and military leader, the first people's commissar of maritime affairs of the RSFSR, and member of the Supreme Soviet of the USSR, the Military Revolutionary Committee of the USSR, the Central Executive Committee of the USSR, and the Leningrad military district commander (1937), Dybenko was the husband of **Aleksandra Kollontai**.

He was born in the village of Liudkovo, Chernihiv province (now the city of Novozybkov, Briansk region, Russia), into a large Ukrainian peasant family. He received his primary education at a public school. From 1899 to 1903, he studied at the Novozybkovsky city school. Due to the low social status and difficult financial situation of the family, he was unable to continue his education. In 1907, Dybenko took part in the work of the Bolshevik circle and became an active revolutionary. He helped to distribute revolutionary anti-tsarist literature throughout the Novozbykov region. Because of these activities, he came under secret police surveillance.

In 1908, Dybenko left for Riga, where he worked as a laborer, port loader, and an apprentice electrician. In 1911, Dybenko was arrested for his failure to appear at the recruiting station and forcibly placed in the Baltic Fleet. He served on the training vessel *Dvina*, graduated from a mine school, and was promoted to noncommissioned officer. In December 1912, he was transferred to the battleship *Emperor Paul I* in Helsingfors (Helsinki) and served as the ship's electrician until the end of October 1915. In 1912, Dybenko also formally joined the Bolshevik Party and became a member of the underground Bolshevik group on the battleship. With the outbreak of the First World War, he participated in the military campaigns of the squadron in the Baltic Sea. In 1915, he was one of the organizers and leaders of the anti-war mutiny on the battleship, after which he was arrested and imprisoned for six months. In 1916, after his release, he was sent to the front with the infantry, where he was again arrested for antiwar propaganda and imprisoned for two months. Subsequently, he returned to the Baltic.

In 1917, during the February Revolution, Dybenko took part in the armed uprising in Petrograd. In March 1917, he became a member of the Helsingfors Soviet, and in April 1917, he became chairman of the Central Committee of the Baltic Fleet. In July 1917, Dybenko became a member of the Petrograd Military Revolutionary Committee and took an active part in an anti-government demonstration. He also actively participated in the preparation of the October armed uprising. On July 5, he was arrested and imprisoned until September 5, 1917. During the October Revolution, Dybenko supervised the formation and dispatch of the detachments of revolutionary sailors and warships in Petrograd. He also commanded the red detachments in Gatchina and Krasnoe Selo and personally arrested General Piotr Krasnov. During the Second All-Russian Congress of Soviets of Workers' and Soldiers' Deputies, he joined the new government as a member of the Committee on

Military and Naval Affairs. In November 1917, he was elected a deputy of the All-Russian Constituent Assembly from the Baltic Fleet. In addition, until March 1918, he served people's commissar of maritime affairs.

In February 1918, when the German offensive on Petrograd began, the Bolshevik government sent Dybenko to defend Petrograd by deploying the Baltic Fleet. But after a short battle in Narva, Dybenko and a group of sailors fled the battlefield, allowing the Imperial German Army to move 100 kilometers inland into Russian territory. According to some historians, the defeat at Narva caused the Bolshevik to sign the Treaty of Brest-Litovsk with the Central Powers. Lenin's government issued an order to arrest Dybenko and expel him from the party (he was reinstated only in 1922, after the Civil War). On March 16, 1918, Dybenko was removed from all his posts and arrested. On March 25, he was released on bail before the trial, but he fled to Samara. In May, he was returned to Moscow and was put on trial. The Revolutionary Tribunal declared him innocent. According to some sources, the intervention of Kollontai, people's commissar of social affairs, played a huge role in this decision.

In the summer of 1918, Dybenko was sent for underground work to Odesa. In August 1918, while in Sevastopol, he was arrested by the Crimean authorities and kept in a Sevastopol prison. But in October he was exchanged for captured German officers. In November 1918, Dybenko commanded the 1st Zadniprovsky Ukrainian Soviet Division, which included detachments of famous Ukrainian atamans: Nikifor Grigoriev and Nestor Makhno. Dybenko did not gain popularity among the soldiers. Throughout his military career, he always preferred "the Iron Fist method." He regularly used executions as the only method of elimination of discontent in the army and ordered the execution of soldiers even for critical remarks against him. In April 1919, Ukrainian Soviet troops under Dybenko's command occupied Crimea (with the exception of Kerch). This "Crimean operation" was conducted in violation of the order of the commander of the Ukrainian Front. According to this order, Dybenko had to move his forces into eastern Ukraine (Donbas) to protect this area from the White Army. As a result of this maneuver, the White army occupied Donbas, and later, from August to December 1919, conquered all of Ukraine. Dybenko then created the independent "Crimean Soviet Army" and established the Crimean Soviet Socialist Republic. This regime combined banditry and anarchism, as Dybenko's troops robbed the local population and terrorized national minorities.

From June to September 1919, Dybenko's troops took part in the suppression of "Grigorievschina" (literally, the phenomenon of Grigoriev) and "Makhnovshchina" (phenomenon of Makhno) in Northern Tavria. Dybenko's Crimean "kingdom" did not last long. On June 20, 1919, the Soviet authorities and the Red Army fled from Crimea to Kherson. After Crimea was reoccupied by White Army leader Anton Denikin, Dybenko left for Moscow. In October 1919, he enrolled as a student of the General Staff Academy of the Red Army, but after one month of study, he was appointed commander of the Division No. 37. In 1919–1920, he commanded formations that fought the White Army near Tsaritsyn (currently Volgograd), Tula, and later in the Caucasus. Dybenko was one of the leaders who captured Tsaritsyn, well known as the center of Stalin's activities in the Civil War, and defeated Denikin's army. In 1921, under the command of **M. N. Tukhachevsky**, Dybenko led the suppression of the Kronstadt Uprising. During its suppression, he used "barrier troops"—special anti-retreat forces. In April 1921, he participated in the suppression of the peasant rebellion in Tambov province. The crisis and chaos in the country, together with dealing with peasant uprisings against the Bolsheviks, represented the peak of Dybenko's career. For these operations he was awarded two orders of the Red Banner (later he received a third one).

In 1922, after only one year of studies in Military Academy, Dybenko graduated as an external "especially talented" student. The years 1922–1926 were a time of relative freedom for the Communists and foreign travels of party members. During this period, Stalin allowed Dybenko to travel to Norway for "medical treatment." In October 1928, he became a commander of the Red Banner Central Asian Military District, and in 1933 he was transferred to the Volga Military District. In December 1930, together with a large group of Soviet generals, Dybenko was sent for a five-month stay in a German military academy, where the "red commanders" were supposed to familiarize themselves with the achievements of European military science and technology. For many, including Dybenko, this trip turned out to be fatal. In the late 1930s during Stalin's terror, the trip became the main evidence of their "cooperation with German intelligence."

In 1937, Dybenko personally assisted the NKVD in arresting his own deputy, Ivan Semenovich Kutiakov (who was shot the same year), and helped to prepare M. N. Tukhachevsky's arrest. He acted as a prosecutor at a trial where the officers, led by Tukhachevsky, appeared before a military court. For a short time, Dybenko became one of the seven members of the Special Judicial Presence of the Supreme Court of the USSR. As a result, on June 11, 1937, eight senior military leaders, including Tukhachevsky, I. P. Uborevich, and I. E. Iakir, were sentenced to death (all were shot on June 12, 1937). The same year, Dybenko became a member of the Supreme Soviet of the USSR, was promoted to komandarm second class, and transferred to the Leningrad Military District. Under his leadership, purges were carried out in the district.

A few months later, Dybenko was present at a meeting of the Politburo of the Central Committee of the party and was accused of being a German and American spy. At the end of 1937, he was removed from his post as commander of the Leningrad Military District. On January 25, 1938, Stalin and Molotov signed a special decree concerning "Dybenko's betrayal," and on February 26, 1938, he was arrested. During the investigation, he was brutally beaten and tortured. He pleaded guilty to participating in the anti-Soviet Trotskyist fascist conspiracy and testified against "fellow conspirator" **Budenny**. On July 29, 1938, Dybenko was shot. In 1956, he was one of the first victims of the Stalinist purges to be rehabilitated.

DZERZHINSKY, FELIKS EDMUNDOVICH (1877–1926). "Iron Feliks" was a Bolshevik revolutionary and official, the founder of the Soviet security services, and the first chairman of the **Cheka**.

Dzerzhinsky, the son of a Polish nobleman and landowner, was born on September 11, 1877, at the Dzerzhinovo family estate near Minsk, Russian Empire (now Belarus). His father, Edmund Dzerzhinsky, belonged to a Polish gentry family—bearers of the Sulima coat of arms (Sulima was used by several noble [*szlachta*] families in the Kingdom of Poland and the Polish–Lithuanian Commonwealth). Feliks's mother, Helena Ignatieva, was a daughter of Ignatiy Januszewski, a Polish professor at Saint Petersburg University. Dzerzhinsky had eight siblings (one of his elder brothers died in infancy). In 1882, his father died from tuberculosis. As a child, he dreamed of becoming a priest and intended to enter a Roman Catholic theological seminary. From 1887 to 1895, he attended the Wilno gymnasium. Józef Piłsudski, Dzerzhinsky's future archenemy, was also a student at this gymnasium. Felix became fluent in four languages: Polish, Russian, Yiddish, and Latin. But his school documents showed that he was not a successful student. He attended his first year in school twice, and he was not able to finish his eighth year of studies. While in the gymnasium, he started his first "revolutionary activities."

In 1895, Dzerzhinsky joined a Marxist group, the Lithuanian Social Democratic Organization. In 1896–1897, he participated in the first and second congress of the Lithuanian Social Democratic Party (LSDP). In March 1897, he was sent to Kaunas and conducted agitation among the city's workers. In July 1897, as an organizer of a shoemakers' strike, he was arrested and imprisoned in the Coven prison (Kaunas), where he spent almost a year. In 1898, he was deported to Viatka province (the city of Nolinsk) for three years under police supervision. In Nolinsk, he continued to conduct propaganda among the workers. For these activities, he was exiled five hundred miles north of Nolinsk to the village of Kaygorodskoye. In August 1899, he fled from the village and made his way first to Vilna, then to Warsaw. In Warsaw, Dzerzhinsky became a professional revolutionary. He was a supporter of the merging of the Lithuanian Social Democratic Party with the Russian Social Democratic Labor Party and a follower of Rosa Luxemburg on the national question. In Warsaw, Dzerzhinsky also became one of the founders of the Social Democracy of the Kingdom of Poland and Lithuania (SDKPiL).

In January 1900, he was arrested and imprisoned first in the Warsaw Citadel and later at the Siedlce Prison. In January 1902, Dzerzhinsky was sent to the Siberian town of Viliusk for the next five years, but due to illness he had been left in Verkholensk, about 3,500 kms to the south. In June 1902, he was able to escape and returned to Warsaw. During the SDKPiL conference in Berlin, Dzerzhinsky was elected secretary of the party's foreign committee. He also worked in Switzerland for some time. In Berlin, he organized publication of the newspaper *Czerwony Sztandar* (Red Banner) and transportation of illegal literature from Krakow to the Kingdom of Poland (Congress Poland or Russian Poland). In July 1903, during the fourth congress of SDKPiL, he was elected a member of its General Board.

In 1905, during the Russian Revolution, Dzerzhinsky led the May Day demonstration and participated in a military revolutionary organization. In July 1905, he was arrested in Warsaw but released three months later through an amnesty. From July to September 1906, he lived in St. Petersburg, before moving again to Warsaw, where he was arrested in December 1906. In June 1907, Dzerzhinsky was released on bail. The same year, at the fifth congress of the Russian Social Democratic Labour Party (RSDWP), he was in absentia elected a member of the Central Committee. In April 1908, he was once again arrested in Warsaw, and in 1909 he was exiled to Siberia (first to the village of Belskoe, then Sukhovo and Taseevo, located in the Kansky district of the Ienisei province). In November 1909, he managed to escape to Capri, Italy, where he met Maksim Gorky. In 1910, Dzerzhinsky relocated to Krakow, from where he made frequent illegal trips to the Russian part of Poland. He was appointed secretary and treasurer of the party's main board in Krakow. He actively opposed the idea of giving the party's activity a legal and peaceful character and supported Lenin's politics. In Krakow, he married Zofia Muszkat, an RSDWP party member, who was arrested one month after their marriage. In Warsaw, in Pawiak prison, she gave birth to their son, Janek. In 1911, she was exiled permanently to Siberia.

On January 1912, Dzerzhinsky was arrested in Warsaw, and in April 1914 he was sentenced to three years of hard labor. After the outbreak of the First World War, he was transferred to Orel prison, and in 1916 he was moved to Butyrskaia prison in Moscow for an additional six years of imprisonment. After the February Revolution, on March 1, 1917, he was released. Together with his party, he joined the RSDWP(b). Dzerzhinsky was elected a member of the Moscow Committee of the RSDWP and a member of the Executive Committee of the Moscow Council. On April 7, during the All-Russian Conference of the RSDWP(b), he opposed the right of nations to self-determination. At the sixth congress of the RSDWP(b), Dzerzhinsky was elected to the Central Committee and its Secretariat.

Dzerzhinsky led the active preparations for the October Revolution and organized the Red Guard detachments in Moscow. In October 1917, he participated in a meeting of the Central Committee of the RSDWP(b), which approved the armed seizure of power in Petrograd. Dzerzhinsky became a member of the Military Revolutionary Committee and was actively engaged in organizing the coup. He participated in the Second All-Russian Congress of Soviets of Workers' and Soldiers' Deputies and was elected a member of the All-Russian Central Executive Committee and its Presidium. On October 21, 1917, he was also elected a member of the Executive Committee of the Petrograd Soviet. He opposed the agreement with the All-Russian Executive Committee of the Union of Railwaymen (Vikzhel). During the October Revolution, he led the seizure of the Main Post Office and Telegraph.

After the October Revolution, Lenin, who considered Dzerzhinsky a revolutionary hero, appointed him commissar of internal affairs and, from December 1917, head of the All-Russian Extraordinary Commission for Combating Counter-Revolution and Sabotage (Cheka). The organization turned into a vast enterprise that conducted mass executions of state enemies (real and imagined). Together with other leaders, Dzerzhinsky was entrusted with the task of organizing punitive measures against political opponents. He also initiated the infamous system of concentration camps in Russia and conducted a terrifying campaign against the peasantry. The Cheka was directly connected to almost all political repressions in the USSR, and Dzerzhinsky, as the head of this institution, was a key figure in the Bolshevik Red Terror. As a left-wing communist, Dzerzhinsky opposed the signing of the Brest Peace Treaty, but since he considered a split within the party unacceptable, he abstained during the vote on February 23, 1918. According to Stalin, Dzerzhinsky was initially an active Trotskyist, but subsequently he changed his point of view and actively fought against Trotsky.

In January 1919, together with Stalin, Dzerzhinsky formed a commission of the Central Committee and the Defense Council, which was responsible for investigating the reasons for the Red Army's defeats in the Perm region. From March 1919 to July 1923, he was simultaneously the people's commissar of internal affairs and the chairman of the Military Council of the Internal Troops (VOKhR). He also led the fight against the insurgent movement in Ukraine. In 1919–1920, during the Russo–Polish War, Dzerzhinsky was appointed to the Polish revolutionary committee that was intended to become the Bolshevik government of Poland. After the Russian retreat, he focused on Russian affairs.

From April 14, 1921, to July 6, 1923, Dzerzhinsky became people's commissar of railways of the RSFSR. From July 6, 1923, to February 2, 1924, he was appointed to the same position at the all-Union level. He led the restoration of the railway infrastructure and fought against corruption and bribery. In 1922–1923, Dzerzhinsky became chairman of the State Political Directorate (GPU or OGPU), the successor organ to the Cheka. On April 18, 1923, on his initiative, the Dynamo Sports Club was created. From September 1923, he was chairman of the OGPU at the Council of People's Commissars of the Soviet Union. In early 1923, he headed a Central Committee commission, which investigated the conflict between the Transcaucasian Krai and Georgian nationalist-communists. Together with Stalin, he supported the neutral line of the Krai and its chairman, **Ordzhonikidze**.

In 1924, after he had become a firm supporter of Stalin, Dzerzhinsky became head of the Supreme Economic Council and was also elected a candidate member of the Politburo. The leading figure in the economic structure, he was also the chairman of a commission to combat child homelessness. Dzerzhinsky initiated a vast orphanage construction program and organized a system of children's institutions, such as reception centers for temporary stays, orphanages, "communes," and children's "towns." In these institutions, thousands of homeless children received medical care, education, nutrition, and most importantly, the possibility of further self-realization, such as workshops and crafts. In 1924, after Lenin's death, Dzerzhinsky organized the embalming of his body.

On July 20, 1926, after a two-hour-long speech to the Bolshevik Central Committee, Dzerzhinsky collapsed and died of a heart attack.

E

EIKHE, HEINRICH (1893–1968). A Soviet military leader, military historian, the first commander-in-chief of the People's Revolutionary Army of the Far Eastern Republic, and cousin of Robert Eikhe, Heinrich Eikhe was born in Riga, Latvia. In 1914, he graduated from the Riga Commercial Academy. Heinrich had a passion for music and was enrolled into a composition correspondence course in the Berlin Conservatory. But due to the outbreak of World War I, he was drafted into the Russian Imperial Army and sent to the Petergof School of Warrant Officers. In 1915, after graduation, he was sent to the front, where he commanded a squadron and was a staff captain. After the February Revolution of 1917, he was elected a member of the regimental committee. In October 1917, he became chairman of the Military Revolutionary Committee of an infantry regiment. In November 1917, he was elected a member of the Council of Soldiers' Deputies of the 10th Army, and at the same time he was a member of the board for the formation of the Red Guard. He took part in the suppression of the rebellion of the Polish corps of General Józef Dowbor-Muśnicki in 1918.

In March 1918, Heinrich Eikhe voluntarily joined the Red Army. In 1918–1919 he commanded a rifle regiment, a brigade, and the 26th rifle division on the Eastern Front. From November 1919, he was a commander of the 5th Army, which participated in the Novonikolaevsk and Krasnoiarsk operations on the Eastern Front, which completed the defeat of Kolchak's troops. From March 1920 to April 1921, he was a commander-in-chief of the People's Revolutionary Army of the Far Eastern Republic. Under his command, the army made a big contribution to the formation of units of the regular Red Army from scattered partisan detachments. Also all large White Guard groups in the Far East were eliminated, and the Japanese troops occupying the Far East were forced to leave the Trans-Baikal, Amur, and Primorye regions.

In 1921, Eikhe became the commander of the troops in Belarusia and led the struggle against sabotage bands and white partisan detachments. The task was completed by the spring of 1922. For successful completion of the assigned tasks, he was awarded the diploma of the All-Russian Central Executive Committee. In March 1922, he was transferred to Central Asia to fight the Basmachi as commander of the troops of the Fergana region. After 1924, he held leading positions in the People's Commissariat for Foreign Trade of the USSR (Narkomvneshtorg).

In May 1938, Heinrich Eikhe was arrested by the NKVD's Counterintelligence Department on charges of "involvement in a Latvian counterrevolutionary organization" and sentenced to death. After the verdict, he was first put in the NKVD prison in Lefortovo in Moscow, where he was beaten and tortured during interrogations, and then he served time in gulags. After his release from the camps, he was exiled to the far north. From 1948 to 1949 he worked as an accountant at the Kamenka (not far from Pechora) *soukhoz*.

He was finally rehabilitated after sixteen years. In April 1954, the Military Collegium of the Supreme Court of the USSR overturned the decision of the NKVD Counterintelligence Department and dismissed the case for lack of evidence of a crime. He returned to Moscow and actively worked as a military historian. He also was a member of the Council of the Military Scientific Society at the Central Museum of the Soviet Army. He wrote several works on the history of the civil war in Siberia and the Far East.

Eikhe passed away on July 25, 1968. During his lifetime, he was awarded the Order of Lenin, two Orders of the Red Banner, and several medals.

EIKHE, ROBERT INDRIKOVICH (1890–1940). A Latvian Bolshevik who was a high functionary of the CPSU and one of the organizers of the 1930s repressions, Eikhe was elected several times to the CC and was a candidate member of the Politburo (1934). He was the first secretary of the Siberian territorial communist party during the forced collectivization of agriculture. He was also a member of NKVD troika (special commissions made up of three officials who issued sentences to people after simplified, speedy investigations and without a public and fair trial). He was a cousin of **H. Eikhe**, the Soviet military leader.

Eikhe was born on August 12, 1890, on the Avotiņu estate in Dobele District, Courland Province (modern-day Latvia), into a family of farm laborers. In 1904, he graduated from the Doblensky two-year specialized school. In 1906, he moved to Mitava (now Jelgava), where he worked as an apprentice in Weinberg's blacksmith workshop. In 1905, he joined the Latvian Social Democrat Party (LSDP, aligned with the Russian Social-Democratic Workers' Party). In August 1907, he was arrested, but after two months in prison, he was released because of lack of evidence of wrongdoing. This same year, he was elected to the district committee of the Latvian Social Democrat Party, and in 1908 he became a member of the Mitava Committee of the LSDP. In February, together with eighteen comrades, he was arrested during an illegal meeting. After six months in prison, he was released under police supervision.

At the end of 1908, he emigrated to the United Kingdom. He took a position as a stoker on a steamboat on long voyages. He also worked as a coal miner in Scotland and a zinc smelter in West Hartlepool. In 1911, he returned to Riga. He joined the trade union "Hammer," the society "Education," and the cooperative society "Product." In 1914, he became a member of the Central Committee of the Latvian Social Democrat party. In 1915, he was arrested and exiled to the Chereviansky volost, Kansky district, in Ienisei province. He was able to escape and fled to Irkutsk. He lived in Achinsky district under a false name and worked at an oil factory in the village of Krutoiarka.

After the February Revolution of 1917, Eikhe returned to Riga and was elected a member of the Presidium of the Riga Soviet. During the German occupation in the summer of 1917, he was engaged in underground work. In January 1918, he was arrested by the Germans, but in July, he escaped and fled to Moscow. In 1919, Eikhe became commissar of food in the short-lived Latvian Soviet Republic. After the fall of soviet power in Latvia, he was sent to Cheliabinsk province and lived in Siberia for the next eighteen years. In 1919, he was a deputy of Cheliabinsk People's Commissariat for Foodstuffs and deputy chairman of the Cheliabinsk Provincial Executive Committee. In 1921, he was a delegate to the third congress of the **Comintern**. Until 1924, he was chairman of the Siberian Food Committee. In this same year, 1924, Eikhe became a deputy chairman of the Siberian Revolutionary Committee (*Sibrevkom*), and on December 4, 1925, he was appointed chairman of the Siberian Regional Executive Committee. In 1925, Eikhe was a candidate member of the CC CPSU. In July 1930, he became a full member and in February 1935, a candidate member of the ruling Politburo.

In 1929, as a trustworthy supporter of Stalin, Eikhe was appointed first secretary of the Siberian Krai Executive Committee of the CPSU and, in 1930, the West Siberian Krai Committee of the CPSU. He was one of the organizers of collectivization and dispossession in the region and a member of the Politburo

Commission (January 1930), chaired by **Molotov**, which drafted instructions on eliminating private farms. In 1934, in the course of grain procurements, Eikhe demanded from the Politburo the right to sanction the death penalty from September 19 to November 15. In March 1935, he was awarded the Order of Lenin.

During the Great Purge, Eikhe led mass repressions in Siberia, eliminating anyone who came under suspicion. On June 28, 1937, he became a member of one of the early NKVD troikas, which repressed 34,782 people. At the end of October 1937, he was appointed people's commissar of agriculture of the USSR.

On April 29, 1938, Eikhe was arrested and accused of creating a "Latvian fascist organization." He was brutally tortured by NKVD officer Zinovy Ushakov. On February 2, 1940, Eikhe was sentenced to death and executed the same day. Eikhe's torture and execution were mentioned in the famous secret speech "On the Cult of Personality and Its Consequences" that Stalin's successor Nikita Khrushchev delivered at the twentieth party congress of the CC CPSU in 1956.

On March 14, 1956, Eikhe was rehabilitated by the Military Collegium of the Supreme Court of the USSR.

EISENSTEIN, SERGEI MIKHAILOVICH (1898–1948). A famous Soviet film and theater director, artist, screenwriter, art theorist, teacher, and honored artist of the RSFSR (1935), professor of All-Union State Institute of Cinematography (VGIK), doctor of arts (1939), laureate of two Stalin prizes of the first degree (1941, 1946), one of the most famous and significant directors in the world, and the author of fundamental works on the theory of cinema. His most famous works include the three film classics *Battleship Potemkin* (1925), *Aleksandr Nevsky* (1938), and *Ivan the Terrible* (released in two parts, 1944 and 1958).

Eisenstein was born on January 22, 1898, in Riga, Latvia (then part of the Russian Empire) into a wealthy Jewish family of urban architect Mikhail Osipovich Eisenstein. Since his mother, Iulya Ivanovna Konetskaia, the daughter of a prosperous merchant, was from a Russian Orthodox family, the family had converted to the Russian Orthodox Church. Sergei was baptized on February 2, 1898. In 1907, after the First Russian Revolution, the family left for Paris. Upon his return, Sergei entered the Riga Specialized School. In addition to basic education, he had lessons in playing the piano and riding. He learned English, German, and French and was fond of drawing comics and caricatures. In 1909, his parents divorced. By court order, Sergei was left with his father.

In 1915, Eisenstein entered the Petrograd State University of Architecture and Civil Engineering, where he studied architecture and engineering. After the October Revolution 1917, he became impoverished and was cut off from his wealthy parents and relatives. He was seriously interested in art, in particular the architecture of the theater. On March 18, 1918, Sergei joined the Red Army. For two years he traveled and lived in propaganda trains. In 1920, during the Soviet-Polish war, while on the Minsk Front, Eisenstein met a Japanese-language teacher and started to learn Japanese. He liked the new language, and after the peace treaty with Poland was signed, Eisenstein traveled to Moscow with the intention of entering the General Staff Academy to become a translator.

Shortly, Eisenstein gave up studying Japanese and got a job as a decorator in the First Workers' Theater of the Proletkult (an experimental Soviet artistic institution). He became a supporter of the ideas of the destruction of the old art and tried to "revolutionize" the theater, to create a revolutionary working-class aesthetic. In 1921, while continuing working in Proletkult, Eisenstein entered the State Higher Director's Studios, headed by Vsevolod Meyerhold. Meyerhold became a big influence on Eisenstein. In 1923, he wrote his first theoretical work, "The Montage of Attractions." The cinema attracted his full attention, and in 1925 Eisenstein produced his first full-length feature film *Stachka* (Strike). The picture contained various innovative elements—in particular, unusual camera angles and film metaphors—and received mixed reviews from both the press and the audience. It was called revolutionary and innovative but at the same time criticized for the complexity of its cinema language. In

1925, Eisenstein produced his famous film *Battleship Potemkin*, considered widely to be one of the greatest films of all time. The film was ordered by the Central Executive Committee of the USSR to commemorate the Revolution of 1905. In 1927, Eisenstein made the movie *October*, in which Lenin was depicted for the first time in a feature film.

In October 1928, Eisenstein, along with his film crew, which included Grigory Aleksandrov and cameraman Eduard Tisse, traveled abroad to study Western experience. It was an official trip, the purpose of which was to enable Eisenstein and his film crew to learn more about sound cinema, as well as personally to introduce famous Soviet artists to the capitalist West. For the next two years, Eisenstein traveled frequently and performed on Berlin Radio; lectured in Hamburg, Berlin, London, Cambridge University, Antwerp, and Amsterdam; and made a report titled "Intelligent Installation" at Brussels University.

After returning to the USSR in 1932, Eisenstein engaged in research and teaching activities. He became the head of the directing department of the State Institute of Cinematography, and in 1935 he received the title of honored artist of the RSFSR. Eisenstein wrote articles and drafted a program on the theory and practice of directing. In 1938, Eisenstein wrote the script for the historical and patriotic film *Aleksandr Nevsky*. He was awarded a doctorate in art history (without defending a dissertation). Music for the film was composed by Sergei Prokofiev. Eisenstein received for this film both the Order of Lenin and the Stalin Prize. In 1941–1945, he started to work on the film *Ivan the Terrible*, about the 16th-century Russian tsar Ivan IV, whom Stalin admired. The first part of the film won a Stalin Prize. The second part, released in 1946, however, was banned on the instructions of the CC CPSU on the grounds that it was "ahistorical." It was released belatedly in 1958.

On February 2, 1946, Eisenstein suffered a heart attack, and on February 11, 1948, he had a second one and died at the age of 50.

F

FARBMAN, RAFAIL BORISOVICH (1893–1966). A Russian-Jewish revolutionary and a Bolshevik, Farbman was in charge of the Information and Communication Party Department, a member of Orgburo of the Communist Party of Ukraine (CPU) and a member of the Central Committee of the Ukrainian Communist Party. He also served as a secretary of the Central Committee in the absence of its leader, **Stanislav Kosior**. In 1933, he was excluded from the party for alleged Trotskyism.

He was born into a Jewish family in Kursk (according to some sources, he was born in Kharkiv). He graduated from a two-year primary city vocational school and worked as a tailor in Kharkiv. In 1910, he became a member of the RSDWP(b). He conducted underground revolutionary activities in Kyiv during the late tsarist period. In 1914, Farbman was arrested and exiled to Tobolsk gubernia. After the February Revolution in 1917, he returned to Kyiv and was elected a member of the Kyiv Committee of the RSDWP(b). That same year, he became chairman of the Kyiv Council of Trade Unions. In 1918, he was a candidate member of the All-Ukrainian Bureau for Leadership of the Insurgent Struggle against the German Invaders (*Vseukrainskoe biuro dlia rukovodstva povstancheskoi borboi protiv nemetskikh okkupantov*).

In June 1918, Farbman became deputy chairman of the Extraordinary Military Revolutionary Tribunal of the 8th, 13th, and 14th armies of the Southern Front. At the first congress of the CPU, he was elected a member of the Central Committee, but in September he resigned and left Kharkiv for a job in Moscow. Several months later, he returned and became a member of the Kharkiv Provincial Executive Committee. Between June and August 1919, he was a member of the Emergency Military Revolutionary Tribunal of the Donets Basin. In 1919, Farbman also was in charge of the Information and Communication Department of the Frontlines Bureau of the CC CPU. Later, he was elected a member of the Orgburo and deputy secretary of the CC CPU. From January to March 1920, in the absence of Kosior, he took over as Ukrainian party leader. In 1920–1921, he was a supporter of the "democratic centralist" group. Later in 1920, Farbman again moved to Moscow, where he headed the Department of Public Education of the Krasnopresnensky district of the city. In 1922, he returned to Ukraine as the deputy head of the Agitation and Propaganda Department (Agitprop). The same year he moved back to Moscow and until 1924 worked as head of the Department of Public Education of the Mossovet (Moscow Soviet). From May 1924 until 1927, he was appointed chairman of the Arbitration Committee of Moscow and the Moscow Province.

In 1927, he became an active member of the "United Opposition," led by Lenin's old comrades **Trotsky**, **Zinoviev**, and **Kamenev**. Because of this activity, on December 18, 1927, he was expelled from the CPSU. On December 31, 1927, he was deported to Siberia for three years as an active Trotskyist. In May 1930, Farbman withdrew from the opposition and submitted a request to the CC CPSU to be reinstated. On June 23, 1930, he was prematurely released from exile and returned to Moscow. On June 27, 1932, his party membership was restored, but in February 1933 he once again was expelled from the party. On January 14, 1933, as a member of the "underground Trotskyist group of Smirnov," Farbman was arrested and sentenced to three years in prison. He served his sentence in the Verkhneuralsky detention center of the Joint State Political Directorate (OGPU). In 1935, he received a life sentence, but after Stalin's death in 1956, he was released. He retired and lived in Moscow until his death in 1966. On January 16, 1989, he was rehabilitated (posthumously) by a decree of the Presidium of the Supreme Soviet of the USSR.

FIVE-YEAR PLANS. A method of centralized economic planning, which aimed to achieve rapid economic development of the USSR. Five-year plans were developed by a specially created state body—the State Planning Committee (Gosplan) of the USSR, under the leadership of the CPSU. The First Five-Year Plan began in 1928. In total, there were twelve five-year plans in the USSR (one of them was a seven-year plan), including five in the Stalin era.

After the revolution of 1917, Soviet Russia, and its successor state, the USSR, sought an economic model for the further development of the country. From 1918 to 1921, the RSFSR went through a period of **War Communism**, which was characterized by a large-scale nationalization of industry, centralization of management, and surplus appropriation. After the Civil War, the authorities began to pursue a **New Economic Policy (NEP)**. *Prodrazverstka*, the Bolsheviks' policy of confiscation of agricultural products from peasants at nominal fixed prices, was replaced by *prodnalog* (the "tax in kind" or tax on food production). Also, some elements of market relations and private entrepreneurship were restored.

In the mid-1920s, it became clear to the Soviet authorities that the pace of industrial development under the NEP did not allow them to catch up with Western countries. Moreover, the industrial gap continued to widen, and unemployment in the cities rose dramatically. In addition, a "scissors crisis" developed with high prices militating for industrial products against a direct exchange with low-priced agricultural goods. Discussions began among economists and party functionaries about the ways to further and accelerate the country's development. As a result, Stalin, who had adhered to the NEP hitherto, supported those specialists who advocated an increased volume of production, future structural changes, and strict discipline. The Soviet authorities decided to take the five-year economic development planning as a basis.

In December 1927, the 15th congress of the All-Union Communist Party was held in Moscow. At this congress, directives for the preparation of the First Five-Year Plan for the development of the Soviet national economy were adopted. The plan (1928–1933) was developed by Gosplan and the Supreme Economic Council as a program of rapid industrialization and collectivization of agriculture. The main funds were to be directed to the development of heavy industry, to the "production of means of production." Most researchers include three five-year plans (the first from 1928 to 1932, the second from 1933 to 1937, and the third beginning in 1938) to the period of industrialization. There was enough manpower to implement the ideas of industrialization. The party and the Komsomol successfully carried out a propaganda campaign. Many people left the countryside for the sake of a better quality of life. That is why the first five-year plan was associated with rapid urbanization.

But in order to implement the plans, the Soviet government was forced to seek the help of foreign specialists. With the assistance of the *Amtorg* Trading Corporation (the first trade representation of the Soviet Union in the United States, established in New York in 1924), the Soviet government chose the American firm Albert Kahn Inc. From 1929 to 1932, an American firm designed and organized the construction of more than five hundred industrial facilities in the USSR, including tractor plants in Stalingrad, Cheliabinsk, and Kharkiv; automobile plants in Moscow and Nizhny Novgorod; mechanical shops in Cheliabinsk,

Liubertsy, Podolsk, Stalingrad, and Sverdlovsk; steel workshops and rolling mills in Kamenskoe, Kolomna, Kuznetsk, Magnitogorsk, Nizhny Tagil, Verkhny Tagil, and Sormov; and so on. Also, during the first and second five-year plans, DneproGES, Turksib, Dneproges, Uralmash, GAZ, metallurgical and tractor plants, as well as many other strategically important industrial facilities were built. In 1932, however, Albert Kahn's activities in the Soviet Union were terminated, and the contract with the firm was not renewed. Instead, renowned companies such as Siemens-Schuckertwerke AG and General Electric supplied modern equipment to the USSR. In the United States, it was announced that there were about 12,000 job vacancies in Soviet Russia. Also, a domestic system of higher engineering and technical education was urgently created in the USSR. In 1930, universal primary education was introduced. In 1930, the elimination of unemployment in the USSR was announced.

At the end of 1932, the successful and early implementation of the First Five-Year Plan in four years and three months was announced. Summing up its results, Stalin said that heavy industry had fulfilled the plan by 108 percent. Between October 1, 1928, and January 1, 1933, the production of fixed assets of heavy industry increased 2.7 times. At the same time, in 1932, famine broke out in the USSR. Despite widespread hunger and death of millions of people, Stalin's government continued export-import operations with capitalist countries, including Germany. Also, during the First Five-Year Plan, the first purges were initiated, targeting many people from Gosplan. The Great Terror also led to industrial disruptions. Repressions in industries were officially explained by sabotage. Fulfillment of the plan at any cost led to the displacement of many talented leaders.

The Second Five-Year Plan, adopted in February 1934 at the 17th congress of the CC CPSU, was supposed to ensure the start of production at the enterprises built during 1929–1933. Financing of production of consumer goods was somewhat improved, and pressure on agriculture was weakened. The plan was to double industrial production. The need for competent personnel stimulated the implementation of mass educational programs of the "cultural revolution." Despite the introduction of machines, manual labor continued to predominate even in industry. In order to increase labor productivity, socialist competition and the **Stakhanovite Movement** were introduced. Following the results of the first two five-year plans, the production of iron and steel in the USSR quadrupled, coal output increased by 3.5 times, oil by 2.5 times, and electricity by 7 times. From 1928 to 1940, the Soviet Union's GDP grew, according to various estimates, at a rate of 3–6.3 percent per year. The average annual growth rate of industrial production reached 16 percent. In terms of production volume, the USSR took second place in the world after the United States. But the quality of the products was not taken into account. Also, the desire to hide negative aspects and numbers led to an overestimation of statistics. Numerous falsifications of statistical data were not uncommon. In 1937, it was proclaimed that socialism had "almost" been built in the USSR.

The fulfillment of the Third Five-Year Plan (1938–1942) was disrupted by the beginning of the **Great Patriotic War** of 1941–1945. Before the start of the war, the main feature of the five-year plan was the increase in defense spending, which reached one-third of the overall Soviet budget.

The Fourth Five-Year Plan (1946–1950) became a plan for restoration and development of the Soviet national economy after the Great Patriotic War. The goal of the plan was to preserve the eastern industrial base, formed during the evacuation of industries in 1941–1942, and to restore industry in the territories affected by the war. Thus, it was planned not only to restore but also to significantly exceed the prewar economic potential. It was planned to increase the prewar level of industrial production by 48 percent, ferrous metallurgy by 35 percent, electricity by 70 percent, coal mining by 51 percent, and oil by 14 percent. Thanks to the enthusiasm of the workers, who sought to overcome the postwar devastation as soon as possible, as well as the organizational talent of the postwar generation of leaders, it became possible to completely restore the main industrial enterprises, including the Dneproges, the Stalingrad Tractor Plant, the Kirov Plant in Leningrad, and others. In 1949, the industrial production of the USSR exceeded prewar levels. Agriculture, however, remained in the doldrums. In 1946–1947, a drought caused a severe famine in the Ukrainian SSR, and agriculture failed to reach its 1940 output levels by the end of the plan.

The Fifth Five-Year Plan for 1951–1955 was adopted at the 19th congress of the CPSU, the last congress of the Stalin era and the first to be held for thirteen years. The plan differed from the previous ones by establishing approximately equal growth rates for heavy and light industries. A "peaceful competition with capitalism" was supported by Soviet authorities. The main goals for domestic development were the growth of industrial production by 70 percent, the growth of production by 80 percent, the output of consumer goods by 65 percent, doubling the capacity of power plants, and raising production of mechanical engineering.

In agriculture, the tasks were to raise mechanization, increase productivity, increase the private livestock population with a simultaneous significant increase in its productivity, and increase gross output of agriculture and animal husbandry. Over the five-year period, according to official data, national income grew by 71 percent, the volume of industrial production by 85 percent, and agricultural production by 21 percent. Mass electrification of railways was attained, the Volga-Don Canal was built, and the development of Virgin Lands, a program introduced by new party leader **Nikita Khrushchev** for grain-growing in remote area of Central Asia, started.

FRUNZE, MIKHAIL VASILIEVICH (1885–1925). A Bolshevik leader during the Russian Revolution of 1917, a Soviet army officer, one of the most successful Red Army commanders during the civil war of 1917–1923, and a military theorist, Mikhail Frunze was born on January 21, 1885, in Pishpek, Semirechye Region, Turkestan, Russian Empire (today Bishkek, Kyrgyzstan). His father, Vasily Frunze, was a Moldovan paramedic and his mother, Marfa, was a Russian peasant. Mikhail's father died when he was only twelve years old, and his mother had to work very hard to earn a living. Frunze graduated from the Pishpek town school and entered the gymnasium in the town of Verny (now Almaty, Kazakhstan). During his studies in the gymnasium, Frunze became familiar with revolutionary ideas.

In 1904, after graduation from the gymnasium with a gold medal, Frunze entered the Polytechnic University in St. Petersburg, where he became a member of the RSDWP(b). In 1904, he was arrested for his revolutionary activities and expelled from St. Petersburg. He participated in a demonstration near the Winter Palace during the Bloody Sunday events (January 9, 1905) and was wounded in the arm. Later, Frunze confessed that this particular event led him to the "generals of the revolution." During the revolution of 1905–1907, Frunze, as a member of the RSDWP committee, led party work in Moscow, Ivanovo-Voznesensk, and Shuia. During this period, he was known under the pseudonym "Comrade Arseny." In May–July 1905, he was one of the leaders of the Ivanovo-Voznesensk general strike of textile workers. As the head of the fighting squad of the Ivano-Voznesensk and Shuia workers, he participated in the Moscow uprising of December 1905. In 1906, Frunze was a delegate of the fourth congress of the RSDWP that took place in Stockholm, Sweden, where he met with V. I. Lenin.

In 1907, Frunze was elected a delegate to the fifth congress of the RSDWP in London, but he was arrested and sentenced to four years of hard labor in a forced-labor camp. In 1909, he was sentenced to death for attempted murder, but under pressure from public opinion his sentence was commuted to six years in Siberia in a forced-labor camp. While in exile, Frunze founded a military club for sentenced revolutionaries called the "War Academy" (*Voennaia Akademia*), where he advocated self-education and propagated revolutionary ideas. In March 1914, he was sent to an external settlement in the village of Manzurka in the Irkutsk province. In August 1915, he fled to Chita, where he lived under the name V. G.

Vasilenko and found employment in the statistical department of the resettlement administration and in the editorial office of the weekly newspaper *Zabaykalskoe Obozrenie*. In 1916, he first moved to Moscow, and then in early April on a fake passport bearing the name of Mikhail Aleksandrovich Mikhailov, he was sent to Belarus. On March 4, 1917, by order of the civil commandant of the city of Minsk, "Mikhailov"-Frunze was appointed interim chief of the All-Russian Zemstvo Union for Law Enforcement police in the city of Minsk. This date is now denoted in Belarus as the day of the creation of the Belarusian police.

The February Revolution marked a turning point in Frunze's life. On the night of March 4–5, 1917, detachments of worker fighting teams led by Frunze, along with the soldiers of the Minsk garrison, disarmed the city police, seized the city police department, as well as the archival and detective offices, and secured the most important state institutions. By summer 1917, Frunze (Mikhailov) was appointed leader of the Minsk Civilian Militia and chairman of the Executive Committee of the Council of Peasant Deputies of the Minsk and Vilenskaia provinces. He also worked as an editor of the Bolshevik newspaper *Zviazda*, was an organizer and member of the Minsk City Committee of the RSDWP, and was a member of the Soldiers' Committee of the Western Front and the Executive Committee of the Minsk Council of Workers' and Soldiers' Deputies. Mikhailov served in Minsk until September 1917, after which the party transferred him to the city of Shuia. Frunze was responsible for the creation of the underground party cells in the 3rd and 10th armies of the Western Front.

During the October Revolution (1917), the 2,000-strong Red Army squad, formed and led by Mikhail Frunze, fought the White Guard royalists in Moscow. He also participated in the skirmishes near the Metropol Hotel and showed himself to be a capable commander. After the revolution, in 1918 he was appointed chairman of the Ivanovo-Voznesensky Provincial Committee of the RCP(b), the Provincial Executive Committee, the Provincial Administration, and military commissar of the Ivanovo-Voznesensk province. In August 1918, he became military commissar of the Iaroslavl Military District. From February until May 1919, he was the commander of the 4th Army in the Red Army. Under his command, the 4th Army defeated the Whites during the spring offensive. In May–June 1919, Frunze commanded the Turkestan army and the Southern Group of Forces of the Eastern Front. From July 19 until August 15, he served as a commander on the Eastern Front. After carrying out successful offensive operations against the main forces of Admiral A. V. Kolchak, he was awarded the Order of the Red Banner. From August 15, 1919, to September 10, 1920, Frunze served as a commander of the Turkestan Front. In August–September 1920, he supported the "organization" of the revolution in the Bukhara emirate, drove out Basmachi insurgents, and led the assault on Bukhara (the Bukhara Operation).

From September 27, he commanded the Southern Front, which led to the defeat of Piotr Wrangel, the last major White general, in Northern Tavria and Crimea. Frunze fought against Wrangel together with Nestor Makhno and his Revolutionary Insurrectionary Army of Ukraine. Later, Frunze also turned against Makhno and played a key role in destroying his anarchist movement in Ukraine. On December 3, 1920, Frunze was appointed commissioner of the Revolutionary Military Council in Ukraine and the commander of the armed forces of Ukraine and Crimea. At the same time, he was elected a member of the Politburo of the Central Committee of the Communist Party of Ukraine (b).

In November 1921, Frunze headed the Extraordinary Soviet Embassy in Ankara. His task was to establish relations with Turkey and to hold negotiations with Turkish leader Mustafa Kemal Ataturk, an ally and friend. From February 1922, Frunze served as deputy chairman of the Council of People's Commissars of the Ukrainian SSR. In 1924, he was awarded his second Order of the Red Banner. In March of this year, Frunze became deputy chairman of the Revolutionary Military Council of the USSR and the people's commissar of military and naval affairs. In April 1924, he was appointed chief of staff of the Red Army and the head of the Military Academy of the Red Army. In January 1925, Frunze became the chairman of the Revolutionary Military Council of the USSR and the people's commissar of military and naval affairs.

Frunze led the military reform that was carried out in the Soviet Union in 1924–1925. His huge military and command experience allowed him to summarize his experience in the First World War and the civil war, and write theoretical works on Russian military art and science. He also produced the Unitary Military Doctrine, which was based on the application of Marxism to military theory. In this doctrine, Frunze defined the fundamental principles by which the military forces of the USSR guided their actions in support of state objectives.

For nearly twenty years, Frunze suffered from a chronic stomach ulcer. On October 31, 1925, he was hospitalized and died during what was expected to be routine surgery. Immediately after Frunze's death, rumors started to circulate around Moscow that Trotsky or Stalin had secretly ordered his death, evidence for which is inconclusive. On November 3, 1925, Frunze was buried in Red Square, Moscow.

G

GERASIMOV, SERGEI APOLLINARIEVICH (1906–1985). Gerasimov was a Soviet film director, actor, screenwriter, playwright, professor at VGIK (now the Gerasimov Institute of Cinematography), People's Artist of the USSR (1948), triple laureate of the Stalin Prize (1941, 1949, 1951), laureate of the Lenin Komsomol Prize (1970) and State Prize of the USSR (1971), hero of socialist labor (1974), Academician (1978), laureate of the Lenin Prize (1984), and cavalier of the Four Orders of Lenin (1961, 1966, 1974, 1981).

Gerasimov was born in the village of Kundravy, Orenburg Governorate (now Cheliabinsk region), in the Urals area of the Russian Empire, in 1906. His father, Apollinary Alekseevich Gerasimov (1863–1909), was a process engineer. In 1888, he was exiled to the Ienisei province for four years for organizing RSDWP circles at the Putilov factory in St. Petersburg. Gerasimov's mother, Iudif Estrovich, was from a Jewish merchant family. Sergei had four siblings. When he was three, his father died tragically on the Lozva River during a geological expedition.

At the age of eight, Gerasimov became enamored with the theater after watching the opera *Eugene Onegin*. In 1923–1925, he studied at the Leningrad Art College. He started his film career in 1924 as an actor. Later he became an assistant director, director, and screenwriter. In 1930, he was appointed director of the Sovkino film factory (after 1934—Lenfilm). He also taught acting classes at Lenfilm. His first sound movie, *Seven Brave Men* (1936), was a success. During the **Great Patriotic War**, Gerasimov took part in the creation of *Battle Movie Collection No. 1* (1941). Together with Mikhail Kalatozov, he also directed the films *Invincible* (1942) and *The Ural Front* (1944). In 1943, Gerasimov became a member of the CPSU. In 1944–1946, he led the Central Studio of Documentary Films. In February 1945, he headed the crew that filmed the newsreel of the Ialta Conference. Gerasimov also directed the June 24, 1945, victory parade in Moscow's Red Square.

After the war, Gerasimov worked as a director, actor, and screenwriter. He also taught at VGIK. Together with his wife, the well-known actress Tamara Makarova, he prepared several generations of Soviet actors. In 1959, 1965, 1969, and 1985, he was president of the jury at the Moscow International Film Festival.

Sergei Gerasimov died on November 26, 1985, in Moscow after heart surgery. He was buried at Novodevichy Cemetery.

GOLIKOV, FILIPP IVANOVICH (1900–1980). A Soviet military commander and marshal of the Soviet Union (1961), Golikov was born into a Russian peasant family in Borisova, in the Perm Governorate of the Russian Empire. His father, Ivan Golikov, served as a medical assistant in the garrison infirmary in Tobolsk. In April 1918, Filipp and his father joined the Communist Party. In May 1918, Golikov enlisted in the Red Army as a volunteer and took part in the Civil War. On July 4, 1918, Golikov was engaged in the suppression of the anti-Bolshevik uprising of peasants in the village of Tamakulsky. In October 1918, he worked as a correspondent for the newspapers *Okopnaia Pravda* and *Krasny Nabat*. In 1919, Golikov enrolled in a two-month military propaganda course in Petrograd. He became a political commissar and served in this role through most of the Russian Civil War and for eleven years afterward. He participated in the suppression of "kulak" rebellions in the Ufa province during the period of War Communism. In March 1921, he was appointed head of the political secretariat of the provincial military commissariat. From May 1922, he was first an instructor and later the leader of the political department of the Volga-Ural Military District. In June 1922, he was appointed an assistant chief and head of the agitation and propaganda department of the political department of the West Siberian Military District.

In 1929, Golikov graduated from the Advanced Training Courses of the highest commanding staff of the Red Army (KUVNAS). In 1933, he graduated from the M. V. Frunze Military Academy. In October 1933, he became the commander of the 61st Infantry Division of the Volga Military District. In September 1936, he was appointed the commander of the 8th Separate Mechanized Brigade and, in July 1937, commander of the 45th Mechanized Corps of the Kyiv Military District. In January 1938, he was transferred to the Belarusian SSR and appointed a member of the Military Council of the Belarusian Military District. According to some sources, he was sent there to supervise purges in the Red Army. From June 18, 1938, until 1940, he was a member of the Bureau of the Central Committee of the Communist Party of the Belarusian SSR (CC CPB). Interestingly, in 1938, he was suddenly dismissed from the Red Army. But K. E. Voroshilov refused to sign a warrant for the arrest of Golikov, and the latter was again called up for military service. In November 1938, he was appointed the commander of the Vinnytsia Army Group of the Kyiv Special Military District. On September 28, 1939, the Army Group was transformed into the 6th Army. Golikov, as its commander, participated in the Soviet invasion of eastern Poland.

On July 26, 1940, Golikov was appointed deputy chief of the general staff of the Red Army and head of Main Intelligence Directorate (GRU). Since five of his predecessors had been shot or were about to be shot, Golikov preferred to provide the leadership of the country only with the instructions of Stalin. Despite the fact that various Soviet agents reported about the possibility of war with Germany, information about the preparation and timing of the German attack on the USSR was often submitted as unconfirmed or not trustworthy. Even after receiving the information that a significant number of German troops were concentrated near the borders of the USSR and that Leningrad, Moscow and Kyiv were the main targets of enemy attacks, Golikov forecast that Germany's next military operations would be against the UK, in Gibraltar, North Africa, and the Near East. The result was an unexpectedly powerful enemy attack that caused the enormous losses of Soviet troops at the first stage of the **Great Patriotic War**.

During the first days of the war, Golikov was removed from the post of head of the Main Intelligence Directorate of the Red Army and was appointed head of the Soviet military mission to Britain and the United States. In this position, he led negotiations regarding military supplies for the USSR and the opening of a second front.

In October 1941, he returned to the USSR and was appointed commander of the 10th Army (Penza Region). Later, the army was redeployed to the Riazan region. In February 1942, he became commander of the 4th Shock Army on the Kalinin Front. From April 1942, Golikov was the commander of the troops of the Briansk Front. In July 1942, he was appointed commander of the Voronezh Front. In June–July 1942, he led the army during the unsuccessful Voronezh-Voroshilovgrad operation. During this operation, the Germans and their allies managed to break through to Voronezh, reach the Middle Don, and occupy a favorable line for attacking Stalingrad.

In August 1942, Golikov was appointed commander of the 1st Guards Army on the Southeastern and Stalingrad Fronts, and participated in defensive battles on the outskirts of Stalingrad. The following month, he became deputy commander of the Stalingrad Front.

In October 1942, he was transferred to the northern section of the Soviet–German front and was appointed commander of the troops of the Northwestern Front. A few days later, he was recalled to Moscow and reappointed head of the Main Intelligence Directorate of the Red Army.

Shortly afterward, he returned to command the troops of the Voronezh Front, leading three major operations. During the Ostrogozhsk-Rossoshanskoy campaign (January 13–27, 1943), his front troops defeated the main forces of the 2nd Hungarian army, the Italian Alpine Corps, and the 24th German Panzer Corps. According to Soviet data, up to 86,000 prisoners were captured. During the Voronezh-Kastornen operation (from January 24 to February 17, 1943), the 2nd Hungarian Corps and part of the forces of the 2nd German Army were surrounded and defeated. In the Kharkiv offensive operation (February 2–March 2, 1943), Soviet troops managed to advance more than one hundred kilometers and liberate Kharkiv. However, during the fourth operation, the Kharkiv defensive operation (March 2–25, 1943), the enemy managed to deliver severe blows to the troops of the Voronezh Front, exploiting a gap up to thirty kilometers along the front and entering the communications of the Soviet troops. Golikov greatly overestimated his initial successes and did not take into account the exhaustion and casualties among his own troops. In order to save the situation, **G. K. Zhukov** was urgently sent to the Voronezh Front and took direct command of the troops. Later Zhukov insisted that Golikov be dismissed.

In March 1943, Golikov was sent to Moscow and never returned to the front. In April 1943, he was appointed deputy people's commissar of defense of the USSR for personnel (later the position was renamed head of the Main Directorate of Personnel of the Ministry of Defense of the USSR). On October 23, Golikov headed the Administration of the Plenipotentiary of the Soviet of People's Commissars for the Affairs of Repatriation of USSR Citizens from Germany and the Countries Under Occupation. This department, with the help of the NKVD, created a powerful infrastructure network, based on NKVD screening and filtration camps, of which about two hundred were deployed only outside the USSR. In June 1946, Golikov presented a detailed case against Zhukov at a special session of the Military Council. In 1949–1950, he also contributed to the gathering of information to inculpate people in the Leningrad affair.

In September 1950, Golikov was appointed commander of the Special Mechanized Army. Three years after the death of Stalin, on May 17, 1956, he headed the Military Armored Forces Academy of the Soviet Army. By January 1958, he was head of the Main Political Directorate of the Soviet Army and Navy (the most important organ of the party leadership of the Armed Forces of the USSR). Unofficially, the head of the Main Political Directorate (*GlavPUR*) was considered the second person in the Ministry of Defense of the USSR. But since *GlavPUR* was a member of the Central Committee of the CPSU, he was subordinated primarily to the highest party authorities and only formally to the minister of defense. Golikov was also a member of the Supreme Soviet of the USSR in the periods 1938–1946 and 1954–1965.

In May 1962, Golikov was forced into retirement, officially for health reasons. In June 1962, he was appointed to a sinecure position for retired officials, inspector general of the USSR Ministry of Defense. He lived in Moscow during his final years and died on July 29, 1980.

GORKY, MAKSIM (ALEKSEI MAKSIMOVICH PESHKOV) (1868–1936). Gorky was a noted Russian and Soviet writer, poet, short-story writer, novelist, playwright, a founder of the socialist realism literary method, a political activist, initiator of the creation of the Union of Writers of the USSR and the first chairman of the board of this union, and a five-time nominee for the Nobel Prize in literature.

Aleksei Maksimovich Peshkov was born in 1868 in Nizhny Novgorod. His father, Maksim Savvatevich Peshkov (1840–1871), according to different sources, was either a carpenter or the manager of the Astrakhan shipping company. Aleksei was baptized into the Orthodox church. At the age of three, he developed cholera but survived. Unfortunately, he infected his father, who died on July 29, 1871, in Astrakhan. Aleksei's mother, Varvara Vasilievna (1842–1879), was from a bourgeois family. After the death of Maksim Peshkov, his mother remarried. She taught Aleksei to read, and his grandfather taught him the basics of church literacy. Aleksei briefly studied at the parish school but never graduated from secondary school. Nevertheless, he had a strong will to learn and an impressive memory.

On August 5, 1879, his mother died from phthisis, and Aleksei returned to Nizhny Novgorod to live with his maternal grandparents, who brought him up after the death of his parents. His grandfather treated the boy harshly. The only kindness he experienced as a child he received from his grandmother, Akulina Ivanovna. When his grandfather's business went bankrupt, Aleksei was left to his own resources. He worked as an assistant in a shoemaker's shop, as an errand boy for an icon painter, in a canteen on a steamer, and as a baker. The bitterness of these difficult experiences later (in 1892) led him to choose the pseudonym Gorky (literally "bitter").

In 1884, Aleksei Peshkov moved to Kazan and tried to enter Kazan University but failed. In that year, the university sharply reduced the number of places for people from the poorest strata, and Peshkov did not have a certificate of secondary education. He read a lot, studied, and quoted idealist philosophers such as Friedrich Nietzsche, Karl Robert Eduard von Hartmann, Arthur Schopenhauer, Elme Marie Caro, and James Sully. Yet, even the age of 30, Aleksei's writing was semiliterate, with a lot of spelling and punctuation errors, which his wife Ekaterina, a professional editor, corrected. In Kazan, he worked at the shipyard, where he began to attend gatherings of revolutionary-minded youth. He became acquainted with Marxist literature and propaganda work. In 1887, he worked in the bakery of the Narodnik Andrei Stepanovich Derenkov (1858–1953). In the same year, his grandparents passed away.

On December 12, 1887, in Kazan, the 19-year-old Peshkov attempted suicide, but the bullet got stuck in his lung. The wound was not fatal, but it served as an impetus for a long-term weakness of his respiratory organs. Peshkov was sent to the Zemstvo hospital, where he had a successful operation. A few days later, he repeated the suicide attempt in the hospital. For attempted suicide and refusal to repent, he was excommunicated from the Orthodox Church for four years.

During 1888–1891, Peshkov traveled around Russia in search of work and gathered impressions used later in his writing. He visited the Volga region, the Don, Ukraine, Crimea, southern Bessarabia, and the Caucasus. At the same time, he managed to make contacts in a creative environment, participated in clashes with the police, and earned a reputation as an "unreliable" citizen, as far as the authorities were concerned. During these years, he was also arrested for the first time for connections with the circle of N. E. Fedoseiev (a pioneer of Marxism in Russia). After the arrest, he was under constant monitoring by the police.

In 1892, *Makar Chudra*, Gorky's first story, was published. The following year, he returned to Nizhny Novgorod, where he met with the writer V. G. Korolenko who would play a huge role in the fate of the novice writer. In 1898, A. M. Gorky was already a famous writer. His books were distributed in thousands of copies, and his fame spread beyond Russian borders. Many focused on the wretched life of the urban proletariat. At the end of 1898, Gorky was hired by the Marxist journal *Life*. In 1901, the writer began to openly express his sympathy for the revolutionary movement, which provoked a negative reaction from the government. He participated in Marxist circles among workers in Nizhny Novgorod, Sormov, and St. Petersburg and wrote a proclamation calling for the struggle against autocracy. As a result, he was arrested and deported from Nizhny Novgorod. Subsequently, he was repeatedly arrested and persecuted.

In 1901, Maksim Gorky became the head of the publishing house Znanie and began to publish authors such as Ivan Bunin, Leonid Andreiev, Aleksandr Kuprin, Vikenty Veresaiev, and Aleksandr Serafimovich. During the winter of 1901 and the spring of 1902, Gorky wrote his famous play *The Lower Depths*. In 1902, it was staged at the Moscow Art Theater by Konstantin Stanislavsky. Stanislavsky, Vasily Kachalov, Ivan Moskvin, and Olga Knipper-Chekhova starred in the performances. Also, in 1902, the Imperial Academy of Sciences elected him an honorary academician. However, the election was canceled by the government, as the newly elected academician "was under police surveillance." In response, the famous Russian writers Chekhov and Korolenko renounced their membership in the academy. Gorky became the founder of the trend of "social realism" and the legislator of literary fashion. In the literary environment, it became prestigious to become friends with Gorky and show solidarity with him.

In 1905, Gorky joined the RSDWP and met Vladimir Lenin. The writer took an active part in the revolutionary events of 1905 and provided financial support for the revolution. The same year he was imprisoned in the Peter and Paul Fortress, but later he was released under pressure from the world literary community. In 1906, Gorky traveled to Europe and America. From the United States, he moved to Italy (Capri) and stayed there until 1913. After the announcement of a general amnesty on the occasion of the 300th anniversary of the Romanov dynasty (which concerned primarily political writers), Gorky returned to Russia. In St. Petersburg, he collaborated with the Bolshevik newspapers *Zvezda* and *Pravda*. After the October Revolution of 1917, Gorky was actively involved in social activities and participated in the creation of the publishing house World Literature. In 1918, he headed an expert commission for identification, collection, and study of nationalized works of art, antiques, and luxury goods.

In September 1921, due to his health issues (tuberculosis), Gorky left Russia for Berlin. From 1924, he lived in Italy. In exile, Gorky spoke out more against the policies pursued by the Soviet authorities. In 1928, at the invitation of the Soviet government and Stalin personally, he visited the USSR. In 1928 and 1931, Gorky traveled across Russia. During these trips, he visited the Solovki special camp. He later described this trip in his essay "Solovki." In 1932, Gorky was practically forced to return to the USSR. His return from Fascist Italy had not only cultural but also political meaning. The Soviet authorities used it for propaganda purposes. It was perceived as a complete recognition of the Soviet power by a world-famous Russian writer.

In the 1920s–1930s, Gorky was actively involved in the creation of the Union of Soviet Writers. In 1934, he headed the Union of Writers of the USSR and held the 1st All-Union Congress of Soviet Writers. On June 18, 1936, he died in Gorky, the former Nizhnyi Novgorod, which had been renamed in his honor four years earlier at the request of Stalin (it retained this name until 1990). His ashes were placed in the Kremlin wall in Moscow.

GREAT PATRIOTIC WAR (1941–1945). One of the defining events of the Soviet Union, the war has become part of the contemporary Russian narrative and one of the foundation stones of contemporary Russian national identity. The term applies only to the period from June 22, 1941, following the German invasion of the Soviet Union, and not to the period of Soviet–German cooperation between August 1939 and June 1941. The German invasion saw 3.2 million troops cross the border between German-occupied Europe and the Soviet Union, using three army groups: Army Group North, Army Group Center, and Army Group South. Early progress was spectacular, for several reasons. First, Stalin chose to ignore several warnings from his own secret agents and foreign leaders that an invasion was imminent. Second, the Germans attacked suddenly, without a declaration of war, and the element of surprise proved decisive in destroying much of the Soviet air force on the ground. Third, the border regions, annexed by the Soviet Union in 1939–1940, had suffered a number of depradations, including arrests, prison massacres, and deportations that alienated much of the non-Russian populations, especially in Ukraine and the Baltic States.

Though the German Wehrmacht advanced rapidly, changes of plans and Hitler's personal interventions in decision-making slowed the pace of the army. The onset of an early winter also proved problematic, making the prime target, the capture of Moscow, particularly difficult. In the north, Leningrad was subjected to a lengthy siege that saw about a third of its population starve to death. In the south, the capture of Kyiv was achieved by September, but as the Germans moved eastward, they faced more difficulties.

The leadership of the Soviet war effort was invested in a **State Defense Committee**, led by Stalin and including most of his most trusted personnel. Stalin and others appealed to Russian patriotism to resist the invader. Cultural figures also used creative achievements in rallying the people—music, literature, and art. The Russian Orthodox Church was also allowed to reopen many churches that had been closed during the Soviet period. Stalin's own role was fairly muted until the August 1942–February 1943 Battle of Stalingrad, the first major German defeat in the Second World War. At Stalingrad, Friedrich Von Paulus' 6th Army, together with the 4th Panzer Division, was ultimately surrounded by three great armies under the overall leadership of **G. Zhukov**, **N. Chuikov**, and **K. Rokossovsky**, which targeted allied troops of Romanians and Italians on the flanks.

Thereafter, Stalin's role became much more publicized, and his photograph appeared regularly in newspapers. He allowed prominent roles to his best generals, and after the Battle of Kursk, a major tank battle in July–August 1943, the German Army had begun to retreat on all fronts. Stalin received significant aid from the Western Allies, particularly the United States, with trucks and food, but he was frustrated by the failure of the West to form a Second Front by landing forces in continental Europe. By 1944, in Operation Bagration, the Red Army destroyed Army Group Center and reoccupied Belarus. In the south, the reoccupation of Soviet territory was completed by the summer of 1944. The siege of Leningrad was finally lifted on January 27, 1944. There was a six-month delay at the gates of Warsaw, as Zhukov's Army halted, ostensibly because of German resistance on the northern flank. There has long been speculation that the Warsaw uprising was encouraged by the Soviets, who then allowed the Germans to destroy it before finally crossing the Vistula in January 1945. In this way, the loss of so many Polish leaders allowed Stalin to select a new government from his Lublin Committee, made up of pro-Soviet Polish Communists. The battle for Berlin ended by May 8. Hitler committed suicide on April 30 in his Berlin bunker. In August 1945, in accordance with the agreement made at Ialta, three Soviet armies invaded Manchuria and quickly defeated Japanese forces. Together with United States and the United Kingdom, the Soviet Union took part in the founding of the United Nations and control over conquered Germany.

The war devastated the Soviet Union, with about 8.6 million military losses and a further 19 million losses of civilian population through military actions, executions, famine, and disease. Losses in certain republics were very high: about 25 percent in Belarus, 16 percent in Ukraine, and about 12 percent in Russia. Losses in Belarus and Ukraine included over 1 million Jews in the Holocaust on Soviet territory. On June 24, Zhukov led a military parade in Moscow, attended by Stalin and others, and the date of May 9 was coopted as the official Victory Day, coinciding with the surrender of German forces in Prague. Though Stalin did not use the war for propaganda purposes, commemoration began on the twentieth anniversary of the war's end, when **L. Brezhnev** became the general secretary of the CC CPSU. The war victory may be regarded as Stalin's greatest achievement: the defeat of Nazi Germany, Soviet westward expansion, and the birth of an empire that included much of eastern Europe. But it also led to a lengthy Cold War with the Western powers, mutual suspicion, and the threat of a future nuclear war after the detonation of the atom bomb in 1949. *See also* STALINGRAD, BATTLE OF; STATE DEFENSE COMMITTEE.

GREAT PURGE OF 1937–1938 (IEZHOVSHCHINA). The large-scale political repressions carried out by extrajudicial bodies in the USSR in 1937–1938. In the people's memory, it retained the name Iezhovshchina (after the Stalinist people's commissar of state security, **Nikolai Iezhov**).

The beginning of the mass terror started with Stalin's instruction given to Iezhov on July 20, 1937, to prepare an order for the arrest of all Germans who worked at defense enterprises. On July 25, the Politburo of the Central Committee of the All-Union Communist Party approved the operational orders of the NKVD No. 00439 (so-called "German Operation"). Apart from this, on July 30, 1937, a secret NKVD order No. 00447 was signed (the so-called "Kulak Operation"). This order targeted peasants, priests, former nobles, national minorities (this was explained by the authorities as the need to eliminate a potential "fifth column" in the conditions of impending world war), intelligentsia, as well as people suspected of having contacts with representatives of the White movement or opposition political parties.

On August 11, NKVD Order No. 00485 started the so-called "Polish Operation," which targeted Poles living in the border regions of the Ukrainian and Belarusian SSRs. On September 20, Order No. 00593 was approved (targeting the so-called anti "Harbinians" Operation—Soviet citizens who had returned to the USSR after the sale of the Chinese-Eastern Railway in 1935, who were considered potential agents of Japan). During the next few months, further NKVD orders expanded repressions against national minorities (November 30: repression against Latvians; December 11: repression against Greeks; December 14 and 16: repressions against "defectors, Finns, Estonians, Lithuanians, Bulgarians"; on January 29, 1938: repression against Iranians, etc.).

Between 1937 and 1938, approximately 1.7 million "enemies of the people," "counter-revolutionaries," "saboteurs," "spies," as well as their relatives ("family members of traitors to the Motherland") and friends were arrested in the USSR, and almost 700,000 were executed. During this year, every month about 100,000 people were arrested, of whom more than 40,000 were executed. For comparison, in the Russian Empire between 1875 and 1912, no more than 6,000 people were executed for all corpus delicti, including serious criminal offenses, as well as on the verdicts of military field and military district courts of the period of the first Russian revolution. During the Great Terror, those sentenced to capital punishment were not only shot. For example, in the Vologda region NKVD, Major of State Security Sergei Zhupakhin, nicknamed "the axman of Vologda," who would himself soon follow his victims, carried out executions with an ax. In the Kuibyshev region of the NKVD, out of almost 2,000 executed in 1937–1938, about 600 people were strangled with ropes. In Barnaul, convicts were killed with crowbars. In Altai and the Novosibirsk region, women were sexually abused before being shot. In the Novosibirsk prison of the NKVD, officers competed to see who would kill a prisoner with one blow to the groin.

According to numerous archival documents, the Great Purge was not chaotic. It was planned in the same way as everything else in the Soviet system. The same state plans were drawn up and approved for the murder of people as for the production of steel or children's toys. The documents show two uneven parts in the Great Terror. The first, comparatively insignificant, was the destruction of the party elites (the "nomenklatura" and the Old Bolsheviks)—for example, the Moscow open trials against Zinoviev, Kamenev, Bukharin, Rykov, and other prominent party members. Other trials were carried out through ordinary courts, which received direct instructions from the country's top leadership about the sentence (execution or imprisonment in a camp). There are 383 lists of arrests and executions of 40,000 Soviet leaders, approved by Stalin and his associates. The second part of the Great Terror consisted of the so-called "mass operations," during which more than 1 million "ordinary people" were prosecuted. This second part of the terror merits the adjectives *great* or *mass*.

The decision to conduct mass repressions was made by the country's leadership (more precisely, by Stalin). The main idea of the Great Terror was to liquidate physically or isolate in the camps those groups of the population that the Stalinist regime considered potentially dangerous: former "kulaks," former officers of the Tsarist and White armies, clergymen, former members of Socialist-Revolutionaries and Menshevik parties, and many other "suspicious" elements. For many years, the Soviet state security agencies kept records of such "hostile" citizens. December 1, 1934, is often called the starting point of Great Purge. On that day, the head of the Leningrad party organization, the secretary of the Central Committee, **Sergei Kirov**, was killed. In the summer of 1937, it was decided to completely eliminate the hostile factions. All repressed "anti-Soviet elements," according to the NKVD order No. 00447, were divided into two categories: the first was subject to immediate arrest and execution; the second was subject to imprisonment in a camp or prison for a term of eight to ten years. For each Soviet region, territory, and republic, plans for repression for each of the two categories were developed. Also, this NKVD order had special provisions that actually incited local leaders and security officers to escalate terror. Local leaders received the right to ask Moscow for additional quotas for arrests and executions. Under the Stalinist system, such a "right" actually meant an obligation.

For the prosecution of arrested "enemies of the people," special extrajudicial bodies called "troikas" ("a group of three") were created on at the state, republican, and regional levels. NKVD Commissar Iezhov and chief state prosecutor **Andrei Vyshinsky**, or their deputies, made up the two-man "dvoika" for prosecution of those arrested along national lines. As a rule, troikas included the people's commissar or the head of the NKVD department, the secretary of the party organization of the corresponding regional level, and the prosecutor of the republic, region, or territory. Troikas received unlimited extrajudicial rights and issued sentences after simplified, speedy investigations and gave orders for immediate execution without the right to appeal. During such "trials," the norms of the Criminal Code and the Criminal Procedure Code were violated, and mass falsification of charges was carried out. There are known cases of organizing "socialist competition" among troikas. With the help of brutal tortures, the arrested were forced to testify about their participation in "anti-Soviet organizations."

These "confessions" also provided names for the next arrests. The newly arrested, under torture, provided more names. Such a mechanism could function indefinitely.

Historians associate the Great Purge with the emerging threat of war. Indeed, one can note the synchronous development of repressions in the USSR and the aggravation of the international situation: the remilitarization of the Rhine zone, the Spanish Civil War, and the gradual expansion of Hitler's Germany and rolling back the stipulations of the Treaty of Versailles after the end of the First World War. The threat from internal enemies in the event of war was much talked about in 1937–1938. The content of the orders regulating mass operations also demonstrated the desire of the Stalinist leadership to eliminate the imaginary "fifth column." But there is no definitive consensus on the causes of the Terror.

GRECHKO, ANDREI ANTONOVICH (1903–1976). Grechko was a Soviet general, marshal of the Soviet Union, hero of Czechoslovakia (1969), minister of defense of the USSR (1967–1976), member of the Central Committee of the CPSU (1961–1976), member of the Politburo of the Central Committee of the CPSU (1973–1976), twice Hero of the Soviet Union (February 1, 1958, and October 16, 1973) and recipient of six Orders of Lenin (December 1942, 1945, February 1958, October 1963, February 1968, and October 1973).

Andrei Grechko was born on October 17, 1903, in the Golodaevka settlement (now the village of Kuibyshevo, Kuibyshevsky district, Rostov region, Russian Federation) into the Ukrainian family of a rural blacksmith. He was the thirteenth child in the family. In December 1919, he voluntarily joined the Red Army and as a part of the "Budenny Cavalry" participated in the Russian Civil War. He fought on the South and Caucasian fronts and fought against the troops of generals A. I. Denikin and P. N. Wrangel, and detachments of N. I. Makhno. He also participated in the elimination of political and criminal banditry.

From September 1921 to July 1922, he served in a special purpose battalion (*ChON*) in Taganrog. After the Civil War, Grechko studied in the 6th Cavalry College in the city of Taganrog, from which he graduated in August 1923. Immediately after graduation, Grechko was sent to study at the Taganrog Cavalry School of the North Caucasian Military District. In September 1924, he was transferred to the North Caucasian Mountain Nationalities Cavalry School (Krasnodar). During his studies, he was the foreman of the squadron, and in 1925 he took part in military operations against "bandit formations" in Chechnia and Dagestan. In 1926, he graduated from the school. In 1926 he joined the CPSU(b).

From September 1926 to April 1932, he served in the 61st Cavalry Regiment of the 1st Separate Cavalry Brigade of the Moscow Military District. In 1936, Grechko graduated from the Frunze Military Academy of the Red Army. After graduation, he served in the Stalin Special Red Banner Cavalry Division of the Moscow Military District, and was then transferred to the Belarusian Special Military District. In May 1938, he was appointed assistant chief of staff, and in October 1938, he became chief of staff of the division. In this position, he participated in the campaign of the Red Army campaign in the ethnically Belarusian part of Poland in September 1939. In 1941, Grechko attended the Soviet General Staff Academy K. E. Voroshilov, from which he graduated just a few weeks before the beginning of Operation Barbarossa.

From the first days of the **Great Patriotic War**, Lieutenant Colonel Grechko served in the general staff of the Red Army. In July 1941, he commanded the 34th Cavalry Division, which was formed on the Southwestern Front near the city of Priluki and which entered into battle with the Nazi invaders in the first half of August during the Kyiv defensive operation. In January 1942, he was appointed the commander of the 5th Cavalry Corps, which took part in the Barvenkovo-Lozovskaia offensive. In March 1942, Grechko became commander of the Operational Group of Forces of the Southern Front, which operated in the Donbas. In April 1942, he was commander of the 12th Army of the Southern Front and defended the Voroshilovgrad direction. From July, Grechko took part in the battle for the Caucasus. In September 1942, he became commander of the 47th Army and commander of the Novorossisk defense region. From October 19, 1942, he commanded the 18th Army of the Black Sea Group of Forces of the Transcaucasian Front. On January 5, 1943, Grechko was appointed commander of the 56th Army of the Transcaucasian Front. From October 16, 1943, he became deputy commander of the Voronezh (from October 20 known as the 1st Ukrainian) Front. He participated in the battle for the Dnepr, in the Kyiv offensive, and in the Kyiv defensive operations. From December 1943 until the end of the war, he was the commander of the 1st Guards Army, which participated in the Zhytomyr-Berdichev, Proskurovo-Chernivtsi, Lviv-Sandomierz, West Carpathian, Moravian-Ostravian, and Prague operations. He led his 1st Guards in a number of offensive operations, in particular in Hungary and Austria. On May 9, 1945 (Victory Day), his army was east of Prague.

After the end of the war in Europe, from July 1945, Grechko commanded the troops of the Kyiv Military District. On May 26, 1953, he was appointed commander-in-chief of the Group of Soviet Occupation Forces in East Germany (after 1954, the Group of Soviet Forces in East Germany). In this position, he participated in the suppression of the June 1953 uprising in the German Democratic Republic (GDR). On March 11, 1955, Grechko was promoted to the rank of marshal of the Soviet Union. On November 12, 1957, he became first deputy minister of defense of the USSR and commander-in-chief of the Land Forces of the USSR. In the period 1960–1967, he was the commander-in-chief of the Warsaw Pact Forces. From April 1967 and until his death in 1976, he served as minister of defense of the USSR. Grechko was one of the organizers of the Warsaw Pact invasion of Czechoslovakia in 1968. He was an active member in the Communist Party. From 1967 to 1976, he was a member of the Central Committee of the CPSU, and from 1973 to 1976, he was a member of the Politburo, CC CPSU. From 1973, he was editor-in-chief of the twelve-volume encyclopedic publication on the *History of the Second World War 1939–1945*.

Grechko died on April 26, 1976. He was buried in Red Square, Moscow.

GRINKO, GRIGORY FEDOROVICH (HRYNKO, HRYHORII FEDOROVYCH) (1890–1938). One of the leaders of the Borotbists (Fighters: a left-nationalist political party in Ukraine in 1918–1920), a Soviet Ukrainian leader who held high office in the government of the Soviet Union, member of the Central Executive Committee of the USSR of the second, sixth, and seventh convocations, candidate member, CC CPSU (1934–1937), and people's commissar of finance of the USSR (1930–1937).

Grigory Grinko was born into a Ukrainian family. His father was an employee of the zemstvo executive board (*zemskaya uprava*) in the village of Shtepovka (Kharkiv province, today in Ukraine). He studied at the history and philology departments of Moscow and Kharkiv universities but did not graduate. From 1906 to 1912, Grinko was a member of the Socialist-Revolutionary Party of Ukraine. In 1913–1917, he served in the tsarist army. During the First World War, he was a junior officer of the 1st (Emperor Aleksandr) Lifeguards Grenadiers Regiment.

In August 1919, Grinko became one of the organizers and leaders of the Ukrainian Party of Socialist-Revolutionaries (Borotbists). The Borotbists recognized the socialist character of the October Revolution and the dictatorship of the proletariat. Simultaneously, the Borotbists' leaders came out with their own theory of the "Ukrainian revolution" and "Ukrainian communism." It focused on the resolution of national problems (the organization of the Ukrainian national army, the independent management of the Ukrainian national economy, and the enforcement of Ukrainization). In August and November 1919, the Borotbists' leaders made two unsuccessful attempts to join the Communist International. On March 20, 1920, the All-Ukrainian Conference of the Borotbists decided to dissolve their party and merge with the CP(b) of Ukraine through individual admission of members. However, out of 15,000 Borotbists, only 4,000 joined the ranks of the Bolshevik Party. Among those 4,000 was Grinko. From 1920, he became a member of the RCP(b).

In 1919–1920, Grinko was a member of the All-Ukrainian Revolutionary Committee and participated in the elimination of White Army and rebel detachments in Ukraine. In 1920–1922, he served as the people's commissar of education of Ukraine and actively participated in party and economic work in Ukraine. From 1922 to 1923 and 1925–1926 he was appointed chairman of the State Planning Committee of the Ukrainian SSR. As a former member and leader of the Borotbists, seen by the Bolsheviks as a Ukrainian pro-independence party, Grinko was purged in 1922 for "nationalist deviation." He was able to regain party leaders' favor during the campaign for Ukrainization. In 1925, he once again served as Ukrainian commissar of state planning. In 1923–1925, he chaired the Kyiv Provincial Executive Committee and Kyiv City Council, and in 1926–1929, he was appointed deputy chairman of the USSR State Planning Committee. In 1929–1930, Grinko also served as the deputy people's commissar of agriculture of the USSR.

In October 18, 1930, Grinko was transferred to Moscow and was appointed the people's commissar of finance of the USSR (finance minister of the Soviet Union). He replaced Nikolai Briukhanov in this position. On August 13, 1937, he was removed and expelled from the CPSU as a supporter of Trotsky. On August 17, he was arrested and imprisoned in the Lefortovo prison. During interrogations, he pleaded guilty. Grinko was among those accused at the Third Moscow Trial, the last of the three public Moscow Trials, also known as the "Case of the Anti-Soviet Bloc of Rightists and Trotskyites" or the "Trial of the Twenty-One." Grinko was accused of "Trotskyism, cooperation with German, Italian, Japanese and American intelligence services, and preparation of the assassination of Stalin and Iezhov and other members of the government." Grinko was shot on March 15, 1938, at the Kommunarka training ground. On June 15, 1959, he was rehabilitated and reinstated in the CPSU.

Interestingly, while Grinko held the post of people's commissar of finance, banknotes of one, three, and five rubles contained his signature. After Grinko's arrest in 1937, the circulation of money with the signature of an "enemy of the people" was inadmissible from a political point of view. In this regard, it was decided to issue banknotes of the same denominations, but without Grinko's signature. In order to avoid a repetition of such a situation in the future, it was decided to print paper money without the image of any signatures. The decision turned out to be fortunate since Grinko's successor, **Vlas Chubar**, was also arrested and shot.

GROMYKO, ANDREI ANDREEVICH (1909–1989).

Gromyko was a Soviet diplomat, minister of foreign affairs of the USSR (1957–1985), chairman of the Presidium of the Supreme Soviet of the USSR (1985–1988), and doctor of economics (1956) who was known among his Western colleagues as "Mr. Nyet" ("Mr. No"). Gromyko, first as a member and then as head of the USSR state delegations, took part in twenty-two sessions of the UN General Assembly. The motto of all Gromyko's diplomatic activities was "Better 10 years of negotiations than one day of war."

Andrei Gromyko was born on July 18, 1909, in a poor "semi-peasant, semi-worker" Belarusian family (although in the official biography of a member of the CC CPSU Gromyko was listed as Russian). His family lived in the village of Starye Gromyki, Rechkovskaia volost, Gomel district, Mogilev province, near Gomel (now Homiel region, Belarus).

In 1904–1905, during the Russo-Japanese War, Andrei's father, Andrei Matveevich, fought in Manchuria, and in 1914 during the First World War in the southwestern sector of the Russo-German front. From childhood, Andrei helped his father to earn money. Already in his early years, the future minister was an avid reader. Until his death, he spoke with a Belarusian accent. After graduating from a seven-year school, he entered a vocational school in Gomel, and then a technical school in Borisov. In the vocational school, Gromyko headed the Komsomol cell, and in the technical school, shortly after joining the CPSU in 1931, he became the secretary of the party organization.

In 1931, Gromyko entered the Belarusian State Institute of National Economy, where he met his future wife Lidia Dmitrievna Grinevich.

In 1932, their son, Anatoly was born and in 1937 a daughter, Emilia. After completing two courses, Gromyko was appointed as a principal of the Kamensk rural school (in the village Kamenka, Dzerzhinsky district, Minsk region) and had to continue his studies at the institute as a part time student. On the recommendation of the Central Committee of the Communist Party of Belarus, Gromyko, along with several other comrades, was admitted to the Graduate School at the Academy of Sciences of the BSSR. At the end of 1934, Gromyko was transferred to Moscow.

In 1936, after defending his candidate of sciences dissertation (PhD thesis) on U.S. agriculture, Gromyko was sent as a senior researcher to the Research Institute of Lenin All-Union Academy of Agricultural Sciences. During his postgraduate studies and work on his dissertation, Gromyko studied English very comprehensively. At the end of 1938, he became the scientific secretary of the Institute of Economics of the Academy of Sciences of the USSR. Simultaneously, he gave lectures on political economy at the Moscow Institute of Municipal Construction Engineering. Gromyko also engaged in self-education. He was fond of reading Soviet and foreign publications on economy and continued studying English. He also gave lectures to workers and collective farmers. He tried to enter an aviation school to become a military pilot but was not accepted because of his youth.

Early in 1939, Gromyko was summoned to a Central Committee Commission chaired by **V. Molotov and G. Malenkov**. Stalin's repressions of the 1930s caused a shortage of personnel in the apparatus of the People's Commissariat for Foreign Affairs. The commission had to find new personnel to work in diplomacy. There were two main requirements for candidates: peasant-proletarian origin and at least some knowledge of a foreign language. Gromyko was the perfect candidate. He spoke and read English fluently. His height (185 cm) also played an important role in the party's decision to make him a diplomat.

In May 1939, Gromyko was appointed head of the Department of American Countries of the People's Commissariat for Foreign

Affairs. Six months later, Gromyko was requested to meet Stalin, who appointed him as an adviser at the Embassy (later the plenipotentiary) of the USSR in the United States. Lieutenant General Aleksandr Vasiliev—the head of the Foreign Relations Department of the general staff of the USSR Armed Forces, an employee of the Main Intelligence Directorate, Stalin's personal secretary-assistant on military-diplomatic cooperation with the USSR's allies in the **Great Patriotic War**, and the USSR representative in the UN Military Staff Committee—became Gromyko's informal mentor in the diplomatic sphere. When at the beginning of 1943, **Maksim Litvinov**, then the Soviet ambassador to the United States, was recalled to Moscow, Gromyko succeeded him as ambassador to the United States. He held this post until 1946. In 1943, when the USSR established diplomatic relations with Cuba, Gromyko also became the Soviet ambassador to that country as well.

During the Second World War, Gromyko was actively involved in the preparation of the **Tehran, Ialta,** and **Potsdam conferences**. In the latter two meetings, held in 1945, Gromyko was a Soviet delegate. From 1946 to 1948, Gromyko was appointed Permanent Representative of the Soviet Union to the United Nations (UN). He was the first Soviet diplomat to hold this post. All in all, Gromyko participated in twenty-two sessions of the UN General Assembly. As a head of the Soviet delegation, he often used the Soviet veto power, acquiring the nickname Mr. Nyet, literally meaning "Mr. No."

From 1946 to 1949, he served as deputy minister of foreign affairs of the USSR, and from 1949 to June 1952, he was appointed first deputy minister of foreign affairs of the USSR. In this capacity, in February 1950, Gromyko made a mistake (unusual for him). Without consulting the Kremlin and under pressure from the State Planning Commission and the Ministry of Finance, he signed an interstate agreement on the exchange rate of the ruble and the yuan with the People's Republic of China. This displeased Stalin, who personally controlled economic ties with China. Two years later, Stalin removed Gromyko from the post of first deputy minister and appointed him USSR ambassador to Great Britain. Gromyko held this post from June 1952 to April 1953. In 1951, Gromyko led the Soviet delegation at the San Francisco Peace Conference.

After Stalin's death, when Molotov once again became the foreign minister of the USSR, he recalled Gromyko from London. From March 1953 to February 1957, he served as first deputy minister of foreign affairs of the USSR. Under Molotov, Gromyko also became chairman of the Information Committee under of the Ministry of Foreign Affairs, a body created to analyze and develop recommendations on various aspects of the world situation, which included representatives of the Ministry of Foreign Affairs, the KGB, and the Ministry of Defense. In spring 1954, Gromyko took part in drafting and submitting an application for USSR membership in NATO. At the same time, Gromyko actively participated in the preparation of the draft of the Soviet project of the pan-European treaty on collective security. On March 31, 1954, an official note with a petition from the Soviet government for membership in NATO was sent to the governments of the United States, Great Britain and France. The West, expectedly, refused the request, which was likely submitted for propaganda purposes.

When **Nikita Khrushchev** came to power after the death of Stalin, he entered into a confrontation with Molotov. Khrushchev chose Gromyko as his favorite in the Ministry of Foreign Affairs. Gromyko accompanied Khrushchev on an important trip to India and during a "conciliatory" visit to Yugoslavia (Molotov remained in Moscow), reversing the policies of Stalin toward the latter country. In 1956, at the twentieth congress of the CPSU at which Khrushchev denounced Stalin, Gromyko became a member of the Central Committee.

From 1957 to 1985, Gromyko served as USSR minister of foreign affairs. Under Khrushchev, who independently shaped the country's foreign policy, Gromyko, as the head of the Ministry of Foreign Affairs, had no freedom of action and played the role of a loyal executor. Most of the key steps in the foreign policy of the USSR at that time—a break with China and reconciliation with Yugoslavia, proposals in the UN on granting independence to colonial countries and peoples, and on general and complete disarmament, disruption of the summit meeting of the leaders of the USSR, United States, Britain, and France in 1960—were the consequences of Khrushchev's personal intervention. Gromyko did not always share these initiatives. For example, in October 1962, during the Cuban missile crisis, Gromyko was initially skeptical about Khrushchev's intention to deploy Soviet missiles in Cuba and predicted "political explosion" in the United States. The foreign secretary was personally involved in negotiations with U.S. president John F. Kennedy. Subsequently, he recalled that these were the most difficult negotiations in his diplomatic career. Then, as during the Berlin Crisis of 1961, diplomatic efforts played a key role in resolving the tense situation.

In 1964, when Leonid Brezhnev became the general secretary of the CC CPSU, Gromyko quickly found a common language with him. Brezhnev, especially in the early years of his leadership of the country, willingly listened to an experienced diplomat. During his twenty-eight years as minister of foreign affairs of the USSR, Gromyko advanced the idea that no significant international agreement could be reached without the Soviet Union's involvement. On August 12, 1970, due to Gromyko's contribution, the Treaty of Moscow was signed between the Soviet Union and West Germany. From the Soviet side, the treaty was signed by Aleksei Kosygin and Andrei Gromyko. The treaty marked the high point of Detente, reversing the high tension of the postwar years.

In early 1970s, the relationship between the USSR and the United States improved. In 1972, Brezhnev and Gromyko held negotiations with U.S. president Richard Nixon and secretary of state Henry Kissinger in Moscow, and in 1973, there were follow-up talks in Washington. As a result, a number of important documents, including the document "On the Foundations of Relations between the Union of Soviet Socialist Republics and the United States of America" (a kind of code for the peaceful coexistence of the two superpowers) and the Agreement on the Prevention of Nuclear War, were signed. Gromyko also contributed greatly to the negotiation process on the arms control. During Gromyko's term in office, the Treaty on the Non-Proliferation of Nuclear Weapons (July 1, 1968), the Anti-Ballistic Missile Treaty (1972), the Strategic Arms Limitation Talks Agreement (SALT I treaties, 1972), and the Agreement on the Prevention of Nuclear War in 1973 were signed. Most of the signed documents, from the Soviet side, were prepared by Gromyko. Also, the Helsinki Final Act (also known as Helsinki Accords or Helsinki Declaration), which was signed during the Conference on Security and Cooperation in Europe in Helsinki (1975), was administered by Gromyko and his employees. In 1971, Gromyko signed the Treaty of Peace, Friendship and Cooperation between the USSR and India during Brezhnev's visit to this country. In 1973, together with Iu. Andropov and A. Grechko, Gromyko joined the Politburo of the CC CPSU.

In the late 1970s and early 1980s, when Brezhnev's health deteriorated sharply, and he gradually began to withdraw from state affairs, Gromyko almost single-handedly determined the vector of the USSR's foreign policy. The minister's intransigence and his suspicion of foreign policy initiatives that did not come from the Foreign Ministry had a negative impact on the international relations of the USSR. The country's foreign policy activity noticeably decreased. After the start of the Soviet–Afghan War (1979–1989), Soviet–American relations deteriorated rapidly. Many achievements of previous years were nullified: the United States refused to ratify the SALT II treaty, and the atmosphere of the "cold war" was reestablished in the dialogue between two states. Gromyko's statements about the United States in the early 1980s were harsh. In relations with the countries of the Warsaw Pact, as well as with China, Gromyko showed little flexibility.

Gromyko was one of those who actively contributed to Mikhail Gorbachev's rise to power. At the plenum of the Central Committee of the CPSU, he supported Gorbachev's candidacy. In July 1985, Gromyko resigned from the post of minister of foreign affairs of the USSR. Gromyko's new post was the post of chairman of the Presidium of the Supreme Soviet of the USSR, a ceremonial presidency. In 1989, the former foreign minister retired and died a few months later. Gromyko was buried at the Novodevichy cemetery in Moscow.

GUSEV, SERGEI IVANOVICH (NÈE IAKOV DAVIDOVICH DRABKIN) (1874–1933). Gusev was a Russian revolutionary and a founding member (since 1896) of the Bolshevik faction of the Russian Social Democratic Workers' Party (RSDWP), Soviet party leader, candidate member of Central Control Commission of the Communist Party of the Soviet Union (1920–1922), member of the Central Control Commission (1923–1930), member of the Presidium of the Central Control Commission (1923–1925), and secretary of the Central Control Commission (1923, 1925).

Iakov Drabkin was born on January 1, 1874, in Sapozhok (Riazan Governorate) into a Jewish family. His father was a schoolteacher. Iakov spent his childhood in the city of Borisoglebsk. In 1884–1886, he lived in Serdobsk. In 1887, he moved to Rostov-on-Don, where he entered the third grade of an artisan vocational school, from which he graduated in 1892. While studying in Rostov, he became involved in the revolutionary movement. In 1893, he tried to enter the St. Petersburg State Institute of Technology but was not accepted. He finally entered it in 1896.

At the university he joined the League of Struggle for the Emancipation of the Working Class. On March 21, 1897, after participating in a student demonstration (March 4), he was arrested. In 1899, Gusev was exiled to Orenburg, and then to Rostov-on-Don, under the public supervision of the police. He was a close associate of **Grigory Zinoviev**, one of Stalin's key enemies in the late 1920s and early 1930s. In 1925, Gusev traveled to the United States as a representative of the **Comintern**. He died after falling ill in Crimea in 1933.

I

IAGODA, GENRIKH GRIGOREVICH (NÈE IENOKH GERSHEVICH IEGUDA) (1891–1938). Iagoda was one of the main leaders of the Soviet state security bodies (Cheka, GPU, OGPU, and NKVD), people's commissar of internal affairs of the USSR (1934–1936), the first "general commissar of state security" (corresponded to the military rank "marshal of the Soviet Union"), and one of the main organizers of political repression and the gulag.

He was born Ienokh Gershevich Ieguda in Rybinsk (about 260 kilometers northeast of Moscow) into a large Jewish family. His father worked as a jeweler and goldsmith. As a family of a retired soldier, his grandfather's family was allowed to live outside the Pale of Settlement, and they became the first Jewish family to settle in Rybinsk. Iagoda's father was a cousin of Mikhail Sverdlov, the father of **Iakov Sverdlov**, who lived in Nizhny Novgorod. Iagoda studied at gymnasiums in Simbirsk and Nizhny Novgorod, where his family moved later. While living in Nizhny Novgorod, Iagoda met Iakov Sverdlov. Through Sverdlov's family, he met **Maksim Gorky**, with whom he maintained friendly relations during all his life. After completing his secondary education, Iagoda worked as a statistician.

In 1904, Iagoda's father hid an underground printing house of the Nizhny Novgorod Committee of the RSDWP(b) in their apartment. The 13-year-old Ienokh was involved in the work of this underground printing house. In December 1905, during the December armed uprising in Sormovo, Ienokh's elder brother, 15-year-old Mikhail, was killed. In 1907, as a 15-year-old teenager, Iagoda joined a group of Nizhny Novgorod anarchists and took part in planning bank robberies.

In the summer of 1912, Iagoda, who had moved to Moscow, was arrested for contacts with revolutionaries. He was exiled to Simbirsk for two years, but in 1913, he was amnestied on the Romanov Tercentenary (300 years of the Romanovs dynasty in Russia). To obtain the right to settle in St. Petersburg (outside the Pale of Settlement), Iagoda formally converted from Judaism to Orthodoxy. From 1913, he worked at the Putilov armaments factory. In 1915, he was drafted into the Russian Imperial Army and sent to the front. In the fall of 1916, he was wounded and was soon demobilized.

Iagoda returned to Petrograd and in the summer of 1917 joined the Bolsheviks. He participated in the October Revolution of 1917. From the end of 1917 to April 1918, he worked as executive editor of the newspaper *Derevenskaia Bednota* (*Village Poor*). From 1918, he worked in the Petrograd Cheka (the All-Russian Extraordinary Commission). In 1918–1919, he was an employee of the Supreme Military Inspectorate of the Workers' and Peasants' Red Army. In 1919, he was transferred to Moscow and, in 1919–1920, became a member of the board of the People's Commissariat of Foreign Trade. Simultaneously, from the end of 1919 till the end of 1920, he worked as a chief executive officer of the Special Department of the Cheka. In 1920, he became a member of the Presidium of the Cheka, and later a member of the board of the State Political Directorate (GPU). In September

1923, Iagoda was appointed second deputy chairman of the Joint State Political Directorate (OGPU).

In July 1926, **V. Menzhinsky** became the head of the OGPU, with Iagoda as his deputy. By the late 1920s, Menzhinsky developed a serious illness, and in practice, Iagoda already headed this institution. During the 1920s internal party struggle that followed Lenin's deterioration and death, Iagoda supported Stalin. In October 1927, he supervised the dispersal of anti-Stalinist demonstrations. In 1927 and 1930, he was awarded the Order of the Red Banner. During collectivization, Iagoda mercilessly suppressed peasant uprisings and exiled "kulaks" to Siberia. He also took an active part in the creation of the gulag. In the early 1930s, Iagoda supervised the construction of the White Sea–Baltic Canal, which was mainly carried out by prisoners of the gulag. For the coverage of this construction site, thirty-six prominent writers, headed by Gorky, were recruited. A thirty-meter five-pointed star with a huge bronze bust of Iagoda inside was erected at the last lock of the White Sea Canal. In 1932, he was awarded the Order of the Red Banner of Labor. In 1930, Iagoda became a candidate member of the Central Committee and, from 1934, a full member of the CC CPSU. On August 4, 1933, Iagoda was awarded the Order of Lenin (for the construction of the White Sea Canal).

In early 1933, Iagoda took part in the falsification of cases on sabotage in the system of the People's Commissariat of Agriculture and the People's Commissariat of State Farms of the USSR, and on espionage and sabotage cases of people allegedly working for Japan. About one hundred agricultural specialists were arrested in consequence, forty of whom were executed. Out of twenty-three arrested persons in the espionage case, all but two were executed. Convicted deputies of the people's commissar of agriculture wrote to Stalin from the camps that Iagoda was using illegal methods of conducting investigations. A Politburo commission (consisting of **Kaganovich**, **Kuibyshev**, and I. Akulov) formed on September 15, 1934, concluded that the statements were true. In addition, this commission identified other cases of law violation by the OGPU and NKVD, such as tortures of arrested persons and fabrication of cases. The commission prepared a draft decree, which called for the elimination of illegal methods of investigation and punishment of guilty officials. But **S. Kirov**'s assassination prevented the adoption of this decree.

In July 1934, the OGPU was transformed into the Main Directorate of State Security and became part of a more extensive new structure called the People's Commissariat for Internal Affairs (NKVD). Iagoda simultaneously headed both the NKVD and the Main Directorate. In 1935, he was appointed the general commissioner of State Security. In 1934–1936, under Stalin's pressure, Iagoda participated in organizing trials on dubious evidence for the murder of Kirov, the "Kremlin conspiracy," and in arranging a trial against **G. Zinoviev** and **L. Kamenev**. However, Iagoda acted extremely reluctantly against the party elite, and Stalin knew this. In the internal party struggle, Iagoda took a position close to that of **N. Bukharin** and **A. Rykov**. It was incautious, since Stalin considered these two latter figures as very dangerous for himself.

In September 1936, Iagoda was removed from the post of people's commissar of internal affairs and was replaced by the main "hero" of the Great Terror, **N. Iezhov**. Iagoda was appointed commissar of communications, but in January of the following year he was removed from this post. In March 1937, he was expelled from the party and arrested. He was accused of having connections with Trotsky, Bukharin, and Rykov, and of the "murder" of Gorky.

Iagoda (right) with Maksim Gorky

During a search of Iagoda's house, many pornographic objects, women's clothing, and even a rubber phallus were found. In 1938, he became one of the main defendants in the "Trial of the Bloc of Rightists and Trotskyites." At this trial, Iagoda pleaded guilty in part. During his speech, he turned to Stalin with a request for mercy. His request was rejected.

On March 15, 1938, Iagoda was executed in the Lubianka prison of the NKVD. In 1988, all the defendants who went through this trial, except for Iagoda, were rehabilitated. On April 2, 2015, the Supreme Court of the Russian Federation made an official decision to deny Iagoda's rehabilitation.

IAKOVLEV, ALEKSANDR SERGEEVICH (1906–1989). Iakovlev was a Soviet scientist, aeronautical engineer, academician of the USSR Academy of Sciences, colonel general, designer of the Iakovlev military aircraft, founder of the Light Aviation Design Bureau, general designer of the Iakovlev Design Bureau, deputy people's commissar of the aviation industry, twice hero of socialist labor, Lenin Prize laureate and laureate of six Stalin prizes, and deputy of the Supreme Soviet of the USSR.

Aleksandr Iakovlev was born in Moscow. His father, Sergei Iakovlev, was head of the transport department of the Nobel Brothers Oil Company. His mother, Nina Vladimirovna Iakovleva, was a housewife. Iakovlev's family came from the serfs of Count Dmitriev-Mamonov. The grandfather of Aleksandr Sergeevich, Vasily Afanasevich, kept a candle shop in Moscow and had a contract with the Bolshoi Theater.

Iakovlev graduated from the Aleksandrovskoe Commercial School, but from childhood he was fond of aviation and aeronautics. While still at school, he started to attend a school club, where he built his first model airplane. He even tried to build a perpetual motion machine and attended the school radio club, where he constructed a radio receiver.

In 1924, Iakovlev built his first aircraft, the AVF-10 glider, which was awarded a prize as one of the best Soviet gliders at all-Union competitions. For technical advice, he turned to S. Iliushin, then a student of the Zhukovsky Air Force Engineering Academy. The designer and his assistants were given a prize of two hundred rubles. But despite his award, he was not accepted (since he did not serve in the Red Army) into the Zhukovsky Air Force Military Engineering Academy—at that time the only higher educational institution in aviation. In March 1924, with the help of Iliushin, Iakovlev found a job in the workshops of the academy. Two years later, he was transferred to the flight detachment, where he worked as a mechanic. In this same year, he was admitted to the academy.

On May 12, 1927, the first flight of the light aircraft AIR-1 designed by Iakovlev took place. The aircraft successfully took off and made several circles over the airfield. Later the plane with the designer on board made a sports flight on the route Moscow-Kharkiv-Sevastopol-Moscow. In total, over the years of study at the academy, he designed four original aircraft.

After graduation in 1931, Iakovlev worked as an engineer at the aircraft plant, where in August 1932 he organized a group of light aviation. On January 15, 1934, Iakovlev became the head of the production and design bureau of the Aviation Industry *Spetsaviatrest*. Between 1935 and 1956, he was the chief designer. In 1934–1935, he designed the airplanes AIR-9, AIR-9 bis, and AIR-10. AIR-9 was recognized as the best in its class at the Paris Aviation Exhibition. Iakovlev not only created his own aircraft but also gained knowledge from famous designers of that time. In 1930s, he made numerous trips abroad, including to Italy, France, England, and Germany. In Germany, Iakovlev met with the famous aircraft designer Messerschmitt, and in 1940, he attended a reception with Adolf Hitler.

In 1938, Iakovlev became a member of the CPSU. In 1939, after a meeting in the Kremlin on the development of Soviet aviation, the Iakovlev Design Bureau began to create military aircraft. In 1939, a short-range bomber, the BB, was constructed. Stalin became interested in Iakovlev's engineering works and began to summon him to discuss aviation problems and for personal conversations. After Stalin's death, these close relations provoked attacks on Iakovlev from the side of some of his colleagues who had suffered from repression.

In 1940, Iakovlev created the first high-speed fighter aircraft, I-26, which in serial production was renamed Iak-1. Later, during the **Great Patriotic War**, the Iakovlev Design Bureau improved the aerodynamics of the Iak-1 aircraft. Also during the war years, the Iak-3 and Iak-9 fighter aircraft were constructed. In total, over 40,000 Iak fighter aircraft of various models were built during the war.

After the war, the Iakovlev Design Bureau began working on a new generation of aircrafts with a turbojet engine, the Iak-15 jet fighter. In April 1946, the first test flights of the new aircraft were carried out. And in May 1947, the Iak-15 became the first Soviet jet aircraft that passed state tests with a positive assessment and was put into service. Until July 1946, Iakovlev, apart from managing his design bureau, also worked as deputy people's commissar of the aviation industry for experimental aircraft construction and science. In March 1946, he was appointed deputy minister of the aviation industry. But in July 1946, due to the heavy workload and employment in the design bureau, he left this position at his own request.

Until his retirement in 1984, Iakovlev held the post of general designer at the Iakovlev Design Bureau. Iakovlev and his design bureau became famous not only for constructing military aircraft but also for creating, in total, over two hundred types and modifications of aircraft.

Iakovlev died in Moscow on August 22, 1989.

IALTA CONFERENCE. The second conference during the Second World War involving the leaders of the Allied forces (USSR, United States, and Great Britain, but minus France) took place at the Livadia Palace in Ialta in Crimea between February 4 and 11, 1945. The initiative for the holding of the conference came from U.S. president Franklin D. Roosevelt, but it was held on Soviet territory, ostensibly because of Stalin's fear of flying but more likely because it provided him with some advantages. The choice of the Livadia Palace rather than one of the others was in deference to the American delegation, as it was the temporary residence of Roosevelt upon his arrival. Further to Stalin's advantage was the bugging of the American rooms beforehand, and the fact that Soviet forces already occupied much of the territory under discussion (essentially central Europe) and were only forty miles from Berlin. By this time also, Stalin had helped to establish an alternative Polish government, the so-called Lublin Committee, made up of pro-Soviet Communists, and in defiance of the Polish Government-in-Exile in London. The purpose of the summit was to determine the composition and structure of postwar Europe, as by this date, the defeat of German forces was imminent. The three leaders (Winston Churchill led the British delegation) agreed on the full disarmament of Germany and its payment of reparations for war damages; the establishment of the United Nations after the war; and a Soviet commitment to invade Manchuria against Japanese forces three months after the war ended in Europe. After discussion, the Western partners assented to the Curzon Line as the Soviet-Polish border, thereby allowing the Soviet Union to retain the territories annexed as a result of the **Nazi-Soviet Pact**. Poland would, in compensation, receive German Silesia, West Prussia, and Pomerania, while the USSR would gain the northern part of East Prussia, including the port of Koenigsberg (which would be renamed Kaliningrad). Lastly, the three leaders agreed that after the end of the war, democratic governments would be formed in eastern Europe that were friendly toward the USSR. This latter agreement has remained contentious. In retrospect, the two Western Allies and the USSR approached the terms quite differently, as Stalin had no intention of allowing a "bourgeois" government to be formed in Poland or other eastern European states. On the other hand, the Western leaders took into consideration the sacrifices of the Soviet forces during the war. Roosevelt was already seriously ill by the time of the conference and died two months later. Churchill's position was much weaker than at the start of the war, and the British were dependent on their American partner for Lend-Lease arrangements. They had also lost much of their far-eastern empire during the war as a result of the attacks by Imperial Japan. Further, Roosevelt approached the meeting as one in which he and Stalin were the main arbiters of the future world, with the British reduced to a medium power.

IEGOROV, ALEKSANDER ILICH (1883–1939). Iegorov was a Soviet military leader, one of the most prominent commanders of the Russian Civil War, a Red Army commander during the Polish-Soviet War (in this campaign he worked closely with Stalin), and one of the first marshals of the Soviet Union (1935)

Aleksandr Iegorov was born in the city of Buzuluk, Samara Governorate (now Orenburg Oblast, Russia), into a large burgher family (*meshchane*). In 1901, he graduated from the Samara Classical Gymnasium and entered the army as a volunteer. In 1905, after graduating from the Kazan infantry cadet school, he received the rank of officer. He served in Baku and Tiflis. In January 1906, he took part in the suppression of the rebellion in the city of Gori. He also guarded the Transcaucasian railways. With the outbreak of the First World War, he commanded a company of the 3rd Army of the Southwestern Front. He participated in many battles and was wounded five times. In August 1916, he showed courage in the battle near Busk. For his bravery, he was awarded the St. George's weapon. In 1917, he was made a colonel and commanded an infantry regiment.

After the February Revolution of 1917, Iegorov joined the Right Socialist Revolutionaries. During this period, he called Lenin an "adventurer" and a "German spy." But in December 1917, he started to cooperate with the Bolsheviks. He became a commander in the Red Army and headed the attestation commission for the selection of officers for the formation of the Red Army. In July 1918, he joined the RCP(b). During the Civil War, he commanded different armies and fronts. He fought on the Don River and near Tsaritsyn against the White leader, General P. Krasnov. There, near Tsaritsyn, he met Stalin and **K. Voroshilov**. From that time, he became a close associate of Stalin. During the Tsaritsyn offensive, he used large cavalry formations for the first time to defeat the enemy. In 1919, he was seriously wounded. As commander of the Southern Front, together with Stalin, he developed and implemented the plan to defeat the armies of Denikin. In November 1919, he received his first honorary award: the Order of the Red Banner. In January–December 1920, during the Polish-Soviet war, he commanded the Southwestern Front and successfully carried out the Kyiv, Novograd-Volynsk, Rivne, and Lviv operations.

After the Civil War, from 1922, Iegorov frequently commanded the troops of the Kyiv and Petrograd military districts, the Western Front, the Caucasian Red Banner Army, and the troops of the Ukrainian Military District. He took an active part in the implementation of the military reform of 1924–1925. In November 1925, he was appointed military attaché in China. In March 1926, he became deputy chairman of the Military-Industrial Directorate and a member of the Collegium of the Supreme Council of the National Economy of the USSR, and in October, he also became a member of the Board of the Standing Meeting at the Revolutionary Military Council of the USSR. In May 1927, he headed the troops of the Belarusian Military District at the start of the collectivization campaign. In 1929, Iegorov "locked" the border with Poland, and it became impossible to get out to the west across the Polish border. Those who tried to do so were killed on the spot. For "successes" in collectivization, in 1931, he was made the chief of staff (from 1935 of the general staff) of the Red Army. In February 1934, at the 17th congress of the CC CPSU, Iegorov was elected a candidate member of the Central Committee. On November 20, 1935, he was made marshal of the Soviet Union. On May 11, 1937, he was given the position of deputy people's commissar of defense of the USSR. Iegorov was one of the initiators of the reorganization of the Soviet Army and Navy and a supporter of the creation of a powerful army, air force, and the country's air defense system. He also took an active part in the development of the theory of Soviet military art.

In June 1937, Iegorov was officially included in the list of the judges at Tukhachevsky's trial. But in January 1938, he was made commander of the Transcaucasian Military District. On March 2, 1938, Iegorov was removed from the list of candidates for membership in the CC CPSU. In March 1938, he was arrested on charges of "espionage, preparation of terrorist attacks, and participation in a counterrevolutionary organization." On February 22, 1939, the Military Collegium of the Supreme Court of the USSR sentenced him to death on charges of espionage and belonging to a military conspiracy. He was executed on February 23, 1939, on Soviet Army Day. He was rehabilitated in 1956.

IENUKIDZE, AVEL SAFRONOVICH (1877–1937). A member of the CPSU, member of the All-Russian Central Executive Committee, secretary of the Central Executive Committee of the USSR, and godfather of **Nadezhda Alliueva**, Avel Ienukidze was born in the village of Tskhadisi, Kutaisi Governorate (now in Georgia), into a Georgian peasant family. He studied at a rural school. In 1893, he moved to Tiflis, where in 1897 he graduated from the Tiflis Technical College. After graduation he worked at the Tiflis railway workshops. In 1898, he was transferred to Baku. In the same year, he joined the RSDWP (after the split, he joined the Bolshevik faction). In 1900, Ienukidze became one of the founders of the Social Democratic organization in Baku and a member of the Baku Committee of the RSDWP. At the beginning of 1901, he resigned from his job and became a professional revolutionary. He organized the underground printing house "Nina," where he worked until 1906. From 1902, he was repeatedly arrested. From 1906, he participated in party underground activities in Transcaucasia, Rostov-on-Don, Moscow, and St. Petersburg. During his stay in Transcaucasia, he became acquainted with Stalin. In October 1914, he was arrested and exiled to the Turukhansk region. At the end of 1916, he was drafted into the Russian Army.

In February 1917, Ienukidze was sent to the front. On the way to the front, his regiment arrived in Petrograd. It coincided with the first day of the February Revolution. Ienukidze actively participated in revolutionary activities. In April 1917, he was elected to the Central Executive Committee of the Soviets. In June 1917, he became a member of the Petrograd Soviet. He was an active participant of the October armed uprising. Until the fall of 1918, Ienukidze oversaw the Military Department of the All-Russian Central Executive Committee, where he was responsible for forced mobilization of officers and specialists from the Russian army (*voienspetzy*) into the Red Army.

From November 1917 to the fall of 1918, Ienukidze headed the Military Department of the All-Russian Central Executive Committee. He was one of the authors of the resolution of the All-Russian Central Executive Committee, signed on September 5, 1918, that initiated the Red Terror. He also supported the decisions to use forced labor of prisoners and on food expropriation from the peasants. From October 1918, he became a member of the Presidium and secretary of the All-Russian Central Executive Committee. In 1922, Ienukidze organized so-called "Philosophers' ships," which transported intellectuals expelled from Soviet Russia back to their homeland. From December 31, 1922, to March 3, 1935, he was appointed secretary of the Central Executive Committee of the USSR. After Lenin's death (January 1924), he was appointed to the Commission for the Organization of Lenin's Funeral. From 1924, he was also a member of the Central Control Commission of the CPSU. In 1922–1935, he headed the Government Commission for the Management of the Bolshoi and Art Theaters. In 1925–1927, he headed the Commission for Control over the daily operations of the Academy of Sciences. The commission was created by the decision of the CC CPSU. Ienukidze was engaged in political supervision of scientists' work. Under his supervision, many scientists were repressed. In 1927, Ienukidze was elected a member of the Presidium of the Central Control Commission.

On December 1, 1934, Ienukidze signed the Resolution of the Central Executive Committee of the USSR, written by Stalin and approved by Kalinin, on "accelerated proceedings" in "political" cases. Ienukidze supported

Stalin in the struggle against the United Opposition (**Trotsky**, **Zinoviev**, and **Kamenev**) and against **Bukharin**'s supporters. At the same time, he also played his own political game: he began to recruit supporters from the Kremlin apparatus, the Council of People's Commissars, and the Central Committee of the party. In 1935, the "Kremlin affair" started. A number of Kremlin employees, employees of the Kremlin commandant's office, and military personnel were accused of creating an illegal anti-Soviet organization and preparing Stalin's assassination. According to some historians, this case was directed primarily against Ienukidze. In June 1935, he was expelled from the CPSU "for political and domestic corruption" and was appointed director of the Kharkiv Regional Automobile Trust. In February 1937, he was arrested, and on October 29 he was sentenced to death "for active participation in the anti-Soviet Rightist-Trotskyist center." He was the only Soviet leader of this level officially accused of systematic seduction of young girls. On October 30, he was executed. In November 1959, he was posthumously rehabilitated.

IEREMENKO, ANDREI IVANOVICH (1892–1970). Soviet commander during the **Great Patriotic War**, Hero of the Soviet Union (1944), marshal of the Soviet Union (1955), and Hero of the Czechoslovak Socialist Republic (1970), Andrei Ieremenko was born in Markivka in Kharkiv Governorate (today Luhansk Oblast, Ukraine) into a large Ukrainian peasant family. In November 1913, he was drafted into the Russian Imperial Army. Ieremenko served as a private in the 168th Mirgorod Infantry Regiment. After the outbreak of the First World War, he fought on the Southwestern and Romanian fronts and took part in the Battle of Galicia (1914). In February 1915, he was transferred as a corporal to the Velikolutsk 12th Infantry Regiment of the 3rd Infantry Division of the same front and participated in the siege and capture of Przemysl. In 1917, he was promoted to noncommissioned officer and transferred to the cavalry reconnaissance regiment.

After the October Revolution of 1917, Ieremenko returned home, and in January 1918 organized a Markivka partisan detachment to fight against the German-Austrian intervention in the Luhansk region. His detachment later joined the Red Army. After the Germans left in January 1919, he was appointed deputy chairman of the Markov (Markiv) Revolutionary Committee and district military commissar. In 1919, he participated in the Luhansk defense.

In June 1919, Ieremenko officially joined the Red Army. He was enlisted in the 14th Cavalry Division of **Budenny**'s First Cavalry Army. In September 1919, he was made a platoon commander of the 34th Cavalry Regiment. In December 1919, he headed reconnaissance of the 1st Cavalry Brigade. In August 1920, Ieremenko was made chief of staff of the 79th Cavalry Regiment in the 14th Cavalry Division. He fought against the armies of Denikin, Pilsudski, Wrangel, and Makhno's troops.

After the Civil War, Ieremenko continued to serve as chief of staff of the regiment. In 1923, he graduated from the Leningrad Higher Cavalry School. In 1924–1925, he studied at the Leningrad Cavalry School. In October 1925, Ieremenko was appointed chief of staff and from December 1929, he became commander of the 79th (then 55th) Cavalry Regiment of the 14th Cavalry Division. In 1935, he graduated from the Frunze Military Academy. In June 1938, he headed the 6th Cavalry Corps, which in 1939 participated in the Red Army campaign in eastern Poland. In June 1940, he was made commander of the 3rd Mechanized Corps of the Belarusian Special Military District. In December 1940, he headed the troops of the North Caucasian Military District. In January 1941, Ieremenko led the 1st Red Banner Separate Army in the Far East.

In June 1941, just before German invasion into the USSR, Ieremenko was appointed commander of the 16th Army of the Transbaikal Military District. On June 30, he was transferred and headed the Western Front. In August–October 1941, he commanded the Briansk Front. In October he was seriously wounded and transported to Moscow. He was treated in a hospital in Moscow where Stalin personally visited him. In December, Ieremenko headed the 4th Shock Army of the Northwestern Front. In January 1942, he was wounded again. After recovery, from August 1942, he commanded the Southeastern Front (after September 28, it was called the Stalingrad Front). In 1942–1943, together with N. Khrushchev, he organized defensive operations during the Battle of Stalingrad. For almost four months, Ieremenko's troops restrained the enemy's offensive around the city. Under his leadership, the tactics of street battles were developed, including deployment of new methods of fighting inside buildings and widespread use of snipers. During Operation "Uranus" in November 1942, Ieremenko's troops broke through the enemy's defensive lines south of Stalingrad and joined forces with troops of General N. Vatutin, thus closing the encirclement ring around the 6th Army of General Friedrich Paulus. On January 1, 1943, the Stalingrad Front was renamed the Southern Front. The troops of the front advanced in the direction of Rostov-on-Don.

On February 2, the day the Germans surrendered at Stalingrad, Ieremenko was removed from his post of commander for health reasons and recalled to Moscow. He was treated in a hospital in the Georgian SSR. In April, he was appointed commander of the Kalinin Front. On August 27, 1943, he was made general of the army. In early October 1943, Ieremenko conducted a small but successful offensive in the Nevel area. From October 20, 1943, he commanded the armies of the 1st Baltic Front. On February 4, 1944, Ieremenko was once again transferred to the south, where he headed the Separate Primorsky Army, which took part in the Crimean operation. On April 18, 1944, he was made commander of the 2nd Baltic Front. During the summer strategic offensive in 1944, his front troops successfully conducted Rezhitsko-Dvinskuiu offensive operation. The enemy's losses in killed and captured amounted to over 30,000 people. For this operation, Ieremenko was awarded the title of Hero of the Soviet Union. In August, he performed the Madona operation (in Latvia). Ieremenko's troops recaptured the city of Riga, Latvia.

On March 26, 1945, Ieremenko was transferred to the post of commander of the 4th Ukrainian Front, where he remained until the end of the war. His troops operated in eastern Czechoslovakia and conducted the Moravia-Ostrava operation. When the German Instrument of Surrender was signed, his troops were in the eastern suburbs of Prague.

After the war, Ieremenko held numerous command positions. Between 1945 and 1946, he was the commander of the Carpathian Military District, in 1946–1953, he commanded the West Siberian Military District and in 1953–1958, he headed the North Caucasian Military District. On March 11, 1955, Ieremenko, along with five other Soviet military leaders, was made a Marshal of the Soviet Union. From 1956 and into the 1970s, he was a candidate member of the CC CPSU. In 1958, he was appointed inspector general of the Group of Inspectors General of the Ministry of Defense of the USSR.

Ieremenko died on November 19, 1970. The urn with his ashes was buried in the Kremlin wall on Red Square.

IEZHOV, NIKOLAI IVANOVICH (1895–1940). Iezhov was a chairman of the Party Control Commission under the Central Committee of the CPSU (1935–1939), member of the Orgburo of the Central Committee of the CPSU (b) (1934–1939), secretary of the CC CPSU (1935–1939), candidate member of the Politburo of the CC CPSU (1937–1939), people's commissar of internal affairs of the USSR (1936–1938), general commissar of state security (January 28, 1937), people's commissar of water transport of the USSR (1938–1939), and one of the main organizers of the mass repressions of 1937–1938, known as the Great Terror.

Information about Nikolai Iezhov's place of birth and parents is contradictory. In his party questionnaires and autobiographies, Iezhov claimed that he was born in St. Petersburg into the family of a Russian worker. But according to other sources, his father, Ivan Iezhov, served in Lithuania in the musical team of the 111th Don Infantry Regiment, stationed in the city of Kovno (Kaunas, Lithuania). After serving the due time, he stayed there, married a local Lithuanian girl, and took a position as a zemstvo guard (police). Nikolai was most likely born in the village of Veyvery, Mariampole district (Lithuania). In 1903, Nikolai studied at the Mariampol Primary School, but he did not finish it. In 1906, he was sent to his relatives in St. Petersburg, where he was a tailor's apprentice. In 1909, Nikolai returned to his parents and traveled a lot in Lithuania and Poland. After the outbreak of the First World War, he returned to Petrograd and started to work in a factory.

Iezhov was not subject to conscription because he was too short (only 151 cm) and had a frail body. Nevertheless, in June 1915, he became an army volunteer and, after training in the 76th Infantry Reserve Battalion stationed in Tula, he was enlisted in 172nd Lida Infantry Regiment of the 43rd Infantry Division. As part of the regiment, he took part in the battles on the Northwestern Front. On August 14, Iezhov was hospitalized, and upon recovery, he received a six-month leave. Subsequently, he served in the 3rd Reserve Infantry Regiment (in New Peterhof), first in the command of non-combatants and, later, as a worker in the artillery workshop no. 5 of the Northern Front in Vitebsk. During the February Revolution, he was in Vitebsk.

On August 3, 1917, Iezhov joined the RSDWP and henceforth was actively involved in political activities. He headed the Bolshevik cell in his workshop. When the Bolsheviks seized power in October 1917, Iezhov was appointed first assistant commissar, and then commissar of the Vitebsk railway station. In January 1918, he moved to Petrograd, but since he was unable to find any job, in August he went to his parents in Vyshny Volochek. There he started to work at the Bolotin glass factory, and, as a party member, he became a member of the factory committee and of the board of the Vyshnevolotsk trade union. Soon, he became the leader of the factory communist club.

In April 1919, Iezhov joined the Red Army, but he was not sent to the front. Instead, he was dispatched to the radio formation in Saratov. In August 1919, he was transferred to Kazan to the second base of radiotelegraph formations. He served there first as a *politruk*, and then as a secretary of a party cell. In 1920, Iezhov received a promotion; he was appointed military commissar of the local Radiotelegraph School of the Red Army. In April 1921, Iezhov headed the Agitation and Propaganda Department of the Kremlin district committee of the RCP(b) in Kazan. In July, he was transferred to the Tatar regional party committee, where he held the same position. At the end of the year, he was appointed deputy executive secretary of the Regional Committee of the CPSU (*obkom*).

After 1922, Iezhov's career began to make impressive progress. From February 1922 to January 1926, he headed various regional committees of the Communist Party, including in Kyrgyzstan and Kazakhstan. In December 1925, as a delegate to the 14th congress of the CPSU, Iezhov met I. M. Moskvin, who headed the Organizational and Distribution Department of the CC CPSU. On January 7, 1926, Iezhov was sent to Moscow to take Marxism-Leninism courses at the CC CPSU. When he finished the courses, on July 16, 1927, Moskvin appointed him as his assistant. On December 16, 1929, Iezhov was transferred to the USSR People's Commissariat of Agriculture, where he served as deputy people's commissar of personnel. A mass campaign to eliminate "kulaks," part of Soviet collectivization policy, had just begun, and the People's Commissariat of Agriculture was to play an important role in it. Iezhov's work was highly appreciated, and he was even noticed by Stalin, with whom Iezhov met in November 1930.

In July 1930, at the 16th party congress, Iezhov was elected a candidate member of the Central Committee. On November 14, 1930, he received a new promotion and became head of the Distribution Department of the Central Committee. In December 1932, Stalin ordered the next systematic party purge. And in April 1933, he entrusted Iezhov with an extremely important and responsible task: Iezhov headed the Central "Purge Commission" and was responsible for "cleansing of the party ranks." During work in this commission, Iezhov received his first experience in planning and conducting large-scale cleansings.

On February 10, 1934, Iezhov was elected a member of the Central Committee, the CC

Orgburo, and the Central Commission for Party Control. On March 10, 1934, he became the head of the Industrial Department of the Central Committee, and the following year, he became a secretary of the Central Committee. At the same time, he served as the head of the Department of Planning, Trade, and Finance and the Political and Administrative Department of the CC CPSU. Also in 1934–1935, at the suggestion of Stalin, Iezhov headed the investigation of Kirov's murder and the Kremlin case, linking them with the activities of former oppositionists: **Zinoviev**, **Kamenev**, and **Trotsky**. This gave impetus to the "Kirov Stream" (the unofficial name of the mass repressions in Leningrad after the murder of Kirov), which became a rehearsal for the Great Purge. Iezhov was personally present at the execution of Zinoviev, Kamenev, and others, and kept the bullets with which they were killed as souvenirs on his desk.

On September 25, 1936, Stalin and Zhdanov, who were on leave, sent a telegram to the Politburo in which they ordered the immediate appointment of Iezhov as people's commissar of internal affairs of the USSR. The next day, Iezhov headed the Commissariat. At the same time, he retained all his party posts. Previously, no person other than Stalin was able to concentrate such power in their hands. The State Security Organs (Main Directorate of State Security of the USSR), the police, and auxiliary services (such as highways and fire departments) were all subordinated to Iezhov. In 1937, Iezhov was elected a deputy of the Supreme Soviet of the USSR, and on October 12, 1937, he was introduced to the Politburo of the Central Committee as a candidate member. This was the zenith of his career.

In his new post, Iezhov formed a "team" of people ready to carry out any orders and started to cleanse the state security agencies of Iagoda's people. He liquidated the Political Red Cross organization, which provided aid to political prisoners. On July 17, 1937, Iezhov was awarded the Order of Lenin "for outstanding achievements." On July 30, 1937, he signed NKVD Order No. 00447 "On Repression of Former Kulaks, Criminals, and Other Anti-Soviet Elements." The scale of the repressions was so enormous that judicial authorities could not cope. To ensure that demands could be met, a whole structure of extrajudicial repressive organs was created. Special NKVD troikas were created at republican and various regional levels. Usually, troikas included the chief of the territorial subdivision of NKVD (a chairman of the troika), the prosecutor of the republic, oblast or krai, and the Communist Party secretary of the corresponding regional level. Their work was supervised by the Commission of the NKVD and the prosecutor of the USSR. The commission consisted of two people: the people's commissar of internal affairs of the USSR (Iezhov) and the prosecutor of the USSR. All investigations were carried out "in a speedy and simplified way." The practice of distribution orders was introduced (*raznariadka*). In *raznariadkas,* the NKVD indicated how many people should be arrested and executed in each region.

Soviet propaganda started a campaign to glorify Iezhov. He was nicknamed the "Iron Commissar." Iezhov personally took part in interrogations and drew up the execution lists. The Red Army and Military Maritime Fleet leadership were virtually destroyed: three out of five marshals, thirteen of fifteen army commanders, eight out of nine admirals, fifty out of fifty-seven army corps commanders, and 154 out of 186 division commanders were purged. When the wider purge started, in 1937 alone more than 936,000 people were arrested and more than 353,000 were executed for counterrevolutionary crimes. In 1938, more than 638,000 people were arrested. By the end of 1938, more than 1.3 million people were imprisoned in gulags.

The NKVD apparatus, led by Iezhov, prepared large, falsified open political trials, including those of the "Parallel Anti-Soviet Trotskyist Center" (January 23–30, 1937), "Anti-Soviet Trotskyist military organization" (June 11, 1937), "Anti-Soviet Bloc of Rightists and Trotskyites," and against Old Bolsheviks who played prominent roles during the Russian Revolution of 1917, or in Lenin's government. In 1937–1938, Iezhov was one of the most powerful Soviet leaders, the fourth person in the country after Stalin, Molotov, and Voroshilov. At the same time, by 1938 he had become completely mired in drunkenness and debauchery. Steadily, Iezhov, who became famous for use of sexual violence against both women and men, ultimately enraged even Stalin. According to Khrushchev's memoirs, "Iezhov by this time literally lost his human appearance, he simply became an alcoholic. . . . He drank so much that he did not look like himself." After Stalin decided to end the campaign of terror, Iezhov's days were numbered.

On April 8, 1938, Iezhov was appointed people's commissar of water transport (concurrently). In the second half of 1938, **L. Beria** was appointed Iezhov's first deputy. With Stalin's approval, the process of transfer of responsibilities began. Beria's influence increased dramatically and Iezhov understood that this meant his downfall. On November 23, 1938, Iezhov wrote a letter of resignation to Stalin and admitted himself responsible for the sabotage activities of "enemies of the people." On November 25, he was fired from the post of people's commissar of internal affairs, and on March 21, 1939, he lost the posts of Central Committee secretary and was removed from the Politburo and Orgburo. On April 9, 1939, due to the reorganization of the People's Commissariat of Water Transport, he ceased to be people's commissar.

On April 10, 1939, Iezhov was arrested in the office of **G. Malenkov**. He was sent to the Sukhanovo special prison of the NKVD. The progress of his case was monitored personally by Beria and his confidant B. Kobulov. Iezhov was accused of "preparing a coup d'etat," "preparing terrorist acts against the leaders of the party and government," as well as of sexual promiscuity, including homosexuality. On February 3, 1940, the Military Collegium of the Supreme Court of the USSR found Iezhov guilty and sentenced him to capital punishment. The next day, he was executed in the building of the Military Collegium of the Supreme Court of the USSR. His relatives were told that he died in prison on September 14, 1942.

In 1988, the Collegium for Military Affairs of the Supreme Court of the USSR refused to rehabilitate Iezhov.

IGNATIEV, SEMEN DENISOVICH (1904–1983). Ignatiev was chairman of the Committee of the International Criminal Police Organization, commonly known as INTERPOL, in the USSR (since 1953), minister of state security of the USSR (1951–1953), member of the CPSU since 1926, member of the Central Auditing Commission of the CPSU (1939–1952), member of the Central Committee of the CPSU (1952–1953, 1953–1961), and a member of the Presidium of the Central Committee of the CPSU (1952–1953). He played an active role in Stalin's purges.

Semen Ignatiev was born in 1904 in the village of Karlovka, Kherson Governorate (now Ukraine), into a poor Ukrainian peasant family. From 1914 to 1919, he worked at a cotton gin plant in the city of Termez (Central Asia), where his parents had moved from Ukraine. In 1919, he joined the Komsomol, and by the end of the year, Ignatiev became the secretary of the Komsomol cell of the main depot of the Bukhara railway. In 1920, as an active Komsomol member, he was transferred first to the political department and later to the military department of the All-Bukhara Cheka (the All-Russian Extraordinary Commission). Ignatiev participated in the repressions against the members of the *Basmachi* movement (a decentralized Turkestani Muslim movement that undertook a lengthy uprising against Russian Imperial and Soviet rule). In 1922, Ignatiev became deputy head of the organizational department of the Central Committee of the Komsomol of Turkestan. In 1926, he joined the CPSU. From December 1929 to August 1931, he was the head of the mass sector of the Central Asian Bureau of the All-Union Central Council of Trade Unions.

In 1935, Ignatiev graduated from the Department of Aircraft Manufacturing Engineering with the Aviation Faculty of the Stalin Industrial Academy (Moscow), where he studied from August 1931. From October 1935 to October 1937, he assisted the head of the Industrial Department of the CC CPSU. From October 25, 1937, to March 7, 1943, he served as the first secretary of the regional committee of the Buriat-Mongol ASSR and the Ulan-Ude city committee of the CPSU.

During his term, he was elected a deputy of the Supreme Soviet of the USSR and BMASSR. From 1943 to 1950, Ignatiev pursued a successful administrative career in the central party apparatus. His career growth can be explained by the fact that Ignatiev became close to **G. Malenkov**. He also enjoyed the patronage of **N. Patolichev**. During these years, he served as party secretary of the Central Committee in Buriat ASSR, Bashkir ASSR, Belarusian SSR, and Uzbek SSR. Simultaneously he was head of the General Department of the CC CPSU.

From December 1950 to February 1952, Ignatiev led the Department of Party, Trade Union and Komsomol of the CC CPSU. It was the key department in charge of the appointment and relocation of the entire Soviet political elite and supervision of the entire Soviet nomenklatura. As part of the new position, Ignatiev was included in the special commission of the Central Committee, headed by Malenkov, which had to check the mutual complaints between the minister of state security **Viktor Abakumov** and deputy minister of the Ministry of Internal Affairs **Ivan Serov**. On July 11, 1951, shortly after the arrest of V. S. Abakumov, by special decree, Ignatiev was appointed a representative of the Central Committee in the Ministry of State Security (MGB). On August 9, 1951, on Malenkov's initiative, he became the head of the MGB of the USSR.

From May 29, 1952, he simultaneously headed the Security Department of the MGB (after the removal of the long-term chief of Stalin's security, Lieutenant General N. Vlasik), which provided security for Stalin and other members of the top party and state leadership. After 1952 and until 1961, he was a member of the Central Committee of the CPSU. In October 1952, he became a member of the Presidium of the Central Committee. During his tenure as head of the secret police, he carried out an extensive purge against Jews in the state security organs and helped to propagate antisemitism in the USSR. He targeted Jews in the Zionist conspiracy headed by the former minister Abakumov. Ignatiev personally "investigated" the "**Doctors' Plot**," the "Mingrelian case" (directed against **L. Beria**), and the "case of V. Abakumov" and his employees. He personally ordered the torture of the former minister of state security and former chief of the Main Security Directorate of the USSR Ministry of State Security. Also, according to some sources, he devised assassination plots against the former head of the 1917 provisional government, A. Kerensky, Yugoslav leader **Josip Broz Tito**, and the leaders of Russian émigré organizations in Germany and France. Ignatiev became the most dangerous rival of Beria in the final years of Stalin.

After Stalin's death in March 1953, the Ministry of State Security merged with the Ministry of Internal Affairs, headed by Beria. Ignatiev became a secretary of the CC CPSU. Beria looked for a means to demote Ignatiev, and in April 1953, he was removed from both his position in the Secretariat and the CC CPSU. Nevertheless, thanks to Malenkov's intervention, Ignatiev was not arrested. He was appointed first secretary of the Bashkir regional committee of the CPSU. After the arrest of Beria on July 7, 1953, Ignatiev was returned to the Central Committee. In 1957–1960, he was appointed as first secretary of the Tatar Regional Committee of the CPSU. In 1960, Ignatiev went into retirement and lived in Moscow. After his death on November 27, 1983, he was buried in Moscow.

IKRAMOV, AKMAL IKRAMOVICH (1898–1938). Ikramov was a Soviet state and party leader, one of the organizers and first secretary of the Central Committee of the Communist Party of Uzbekistan, a member of the special troika of the NKVD of the USSR. He was arrested and executed in 1938 as part of the Great Purge during the Stalin period.

Akmal Ikramov was born into an Uzbek peasant family in Tashkent. In February 1918, he joined the RCP(b). He first worked as deputy chairman of the Namangan Revolutionary Committee, then as a secretary of the Fergana and Syr-Darya regional committees of the RCP(b). He played a key role in the suppression of the counterrevolution against Bolshevik rule in Central Asia. From 1921 to 1922, he was a secretary of the Central Committee of the Communist Party of Turkestan. In 1922, he studied in Moscow at the Sverdlov Communist University. After graduation, Ikramov served in the Secretariat of the Tashkent regional party committee. In March 1925, he was appointed secretary of the Central Committee of the Communist Party of Uzbekistan.

In 1925, Ikramov became candidate member of the Central Committee of the CPSU(b), a position he retained until 1934. From 1929 to 1937, he was first secretary of the Central Committee of the Communist Party of Uzbekistan and the first secretary of the Tashkent City Committee. During this period, he participated in a special troika, created by the All-Union NKVD, and actively participated in the Stalinist repressions. In February 1937, he was a member of the Commission of the Plenum of the Central Committee preparing the trial of the Right Opposition leaders **Bukharin** and **Rykov** On September 20, 1937, Ikramov was arrested and accused of anti-Soviet, Trotskyist activities. He was sentenced to death and shot on March 13 (according to other sources, on March 15), 1938. On June 3, 1957, he was fully rehabilitated and reinstated in the party.

IUMASHEV, IVAN STEPANOVICH (1895–1972). Commander of the Black Sea and Pacific fleets, navy admiral (1943), commander-in-chief of the Soviet Navy (1947–1951), Hero of the Soviet Union (1945), and Soviet naval minister (1950–1951), Ivan Iumashev was born in Tiflis, the Russian Empire (now Tbilisi, Georgia), into the family of a railway employee. In 1912, he was drafted into the Imperial Russian Navy. In 1914, he graduated from the Jung School in Kronstadt, after which he served in the Baltic Fleet and sailed on the cruiser *Bogatyr* as the foreman of the first tower. After the February Revolution of 1917, Iumashev was elected chairman of the Sailors' Committee but soon retired from service due to illness. In February 1919, he voluntarily joined the "Workers' and Peasants' Red Fleet" and participated in the civil war on the ships of the Astrakhan-Caspian and Volga-Caspian military flotilla. He took part in the defense of Astrakhan.

From August 1920, Iumashev served in the Baltic Fleet. In August 1920, he was appointed commander of the *plutong* (artillery battery) on the battleship *Petropavlovsk* (renamed *Marat* on March 31, 1921). During the Kronstadt anti-Bolshevik uprising of sailors in March 1921, Iumashev refused to join the rebellious members of the Petropavlovsk crew and was arrested. After the suppression of the rebellion, he was released. From May 1921, he served as the second assistant commander on the battleship *Marat*. In 1924, Iumashev took part in the first long-distance cruise of the Soviet fleet: the passage from Arkhangelsk to Vladivostok on the patrol ship *Vorovsky*.

In February 1925, Iumashev graduated from Higher Special Courses for Naval Commanding Officers. After graduation, he served on the destroyers *Lenin* and *Voikov*. Later he was appointed second assistant to the commander of the battleship *Marat*.

In July 1926, he was transferred to the Black Sea Fleet, where he was appointed senior assistant to the commander of the cruiser *Comintern*. In February 1927, he was made commander of the destroyer *Dzerzhinsky*. In 1932, after graduation from the Special Courses for the Naval Command Staff, Iumashev became commander of the light cruiser *Profintern*. In 1934, he was made commander of a destroyer division. In 1935, Iumashev was awarded the rank of flagship of the second rank (corresponding to the rank of counter admiral). In September 1937, he was appointed chief of staff and, from January 1938, commander of the Black Sea Fleet. In April 1939, he was made flagship of the first rank.

From March 1939 to January 1947, Iumashev commanded the Pacific Fleet. He made a significant contribution to its development and strengthening, to the construction of naval bases, airfields, and coastal defense in the Far East. On May 31, 1943, he was awarded the military rank of admiral. During August–September 1945, the Pacific Fleet under his command successfully assisted the troops of the 1st and 2nd Far Eastern Fronts in defeating the Kwantung Army, and participated in the liberation of South Sakhalin and the Kuril Islands. On September 14, 1945, Iumashev was awarded the title of Hero of the Soviet Union, along with the Order of Lenin and the Gold Star medal.

In January 1947, Ivan Iumashev was appointed commander-in-chief of the USSR Naval Forces. In February 1950, he became Soviet naval minister and a member of the Bureau for Military-Industrial and Military Affairs of the Council of Ministers of the USSR. In early July 1951, during a meeting of the Main Military Council of the Navy, Stalin severely criticized the Soviet fleet. In his speech, he admitted that the USSR was seven to eight years behind the major maritime powers. Stalin was dissatisfied with Iumashev's performance as minister and also by the fact that the minister periodically indulged in alcoholic binges. In July 1951, Iumashev was removed from his ministerial post and appointed head of the Order of Lenin K. E. Voroshilov Naval Academy. In January 1957, the naval commander retired.

Iumashev died on September 2, 1972, and was buried in St. Petersburg.

IVANOV, VLADIMIR IVANOVICH (1893–1938). A Soviet party and statesman, first secretary of the Central Committee of the Communist Party of Uzbekistan (1925–1927), and first secretary of the Northern Regional Committee of the CPSU (1931–1937), Ivanov was purged in the last of the Moscow Show Trials, the Trial of the 21.

Vladimir Ivanov was born in Tula into the family of a blacksmith. In 1909–1910, he took part in the strikes of school students. By 1912, he was an activist of the student Social Democratic movement. In 1916, he was arrested for several days for participating in student revolutionary circles. In 1918, he graduated from the Medical Faculty of Moscow University. Concerning his formal party activities, he joined the RSDWP in 1915, and from February to July 1917, during the rule of the provisional government, he was secretary of the Khamovniki District Committee of the RSDWP in Moscow. During the October Revolution and into 1918, he was a member of the Military Revolutionary Committee and the Red Guards' headquarters of the Basmany District of Moscow. In 1917, Ivanov was also a member of the Presidium of the Moscow City Council.

In September–November 1919 during the Russian Civil War, Ivanov was appointed a member of the Revolutionary Military Council of the Fergana Front in the Turkestan Autonomous Soviet Socialist Republic. In 1920–1921, he was the executive secretary of the Iaroslavl Provincial Committee of the RCP(b). From 1921 to 1924, Ivanov served as the head of the Organizational Department of the Moscow Committee of the RCP(b). In May–October 1924, he was appointed chairman of the Moscow Control Commission of the RCP(b) and head of the Moscow Workers' and Peasants' Inspection. He was also a member of the Central Control Commission of the RCP(b) and candidate member of the Presidium of the Central Control Commission of the RCP(b) (1924–1925).

From October 1924, Ivanov served as a chairman of the Orgburo of the Central Committee of the All-Union Communist Party of Bolsheviks in the Uzbek SSR. In 1924–1925, he was the first secretary of the Provisional Organizational Bureau of the Communist Party of Uzbekistan and member of the Revolutionary Committee of the Uzbek SSR. From 1925 to 1927, he was the first secretary of the Central Committee of the Communist Party of Uzbekistan. From 1927 to 1931, Ivanov was second secretary of the North Caucasian Regional Committee of the CPSU. Later, from 1931 to 1937, he became the first secretary of the Northern Regional Committee of the CPSU. Ivanov was appointed a member of the Central Committee of the CPSU (1934–1937) and candidate member of the CC CPSU (1925–1934).

On November 1, 1937, he was arrested and accused of participation in the "Anti-Soviet Bloc of Rightists and Trotskyites." He pleaded guilty to organizing kulak uprisings in the Caucasus in 1928, sabotage, and treason. On March 13, 1938, he was sentenced to capital punishment. On March 15, 1938, he was executed in Moscow. He was posthumously rehabilitated in June 1959.

K

KAGANOVICH, LAZAR MOISEEVICH (1893–1991). A Soviet state and party leader and administrator, one of the main associates of Stalin, known for his harsh measures in the famine in Soviet Ukraine, the patron of the Moscow Metro, which bore his name for many years, and a prominent party and Politburo member throughout the time of Stalin, Kaganovich had two spells as party leader (first secretary of Ukraine) and was a secretary of the CC CPSU (1924–1925, 1928–1939), candidate member of the Politburo of the Central Committee of the CPSU (1926–1930), and member of the Politburo (Presidium) of the Central Committee (1930–1957).

Kaganovich was born into a Jewish peasant family in Kabany village, Radomyshl uezd, Kyiv Governorate, Russian Empire (later it was rernamed Dibrova, Polissia district, Kyiv region, Ukraine. (In 1999, the village was included in the Chernobyl Nuclear Power Plant Zone of Alienation.) He had twelve siblings, but only six of them reached adulthood. From the age of 14, he worked in Kyiv at various enterprises, shoe factories, and shoe stores. Deprived of many rights, the population of Jewish youth was a fertile environment for revolutionary agitation. Under the influence of agitation and following the example of his elder brother, Mikhail, who joined the ranks of the Bolsheviks in 1905, Lazar became a member of the RSDWP(b) at the end of 1911. In 1915 he was arrested and deported to his home village but soon illegally returned to Kyiv. In 1916, under a false name, he worked as a shoemaker at a shoe factory in Ekaterinoslav (later Dnipropetrovsk; today Dnipro, Ukraine), where he organized and headed the illegal Union of Shoemakers. He also served as a head of the district and a member of the Ekaterinoslav Committee of the Bolshevik party. Later, he led the Melitopol Shoemakers Union, as well as the parallel organization in Iuzovka (Stalino, modern Donetsk).

After the February Revolution of 1917, Kaganovich played an important role in the restoration of the Bolshevik organization in Iuzovka and was elected a deputy chairman of the Iuzovka Soviet. In Iuzovka, he met and became a mentor of the young Nikita Khrushchev. In May 1917, Lazar was drafted into the Russian Army but soon became a leader of the Bolshevik soldiers' organization in Saratov. Later, during the October Revolution, he led the uprising in Gomel (today Homiel, Belarus). In December 1917, Kaganovich became a delegate to the third All-Russian Congress of Workers', Soldiers', and Peasants Deputies' Soviets, which took place on January 23–31, 1918, in Tauride Palace, Petrograd. At the Congress of Soviets, he was elected to the All-Russian Central Executive Committee of the RSFSR. From January 1918, he was based in Petrograd. In spring 1918, together with other members of the All-Russian Central Executive Committee, he moved to the new capital, Moscow, where he became commissar of the Propaganda Department of the All-Russian Collegium for the organization of the Red Army. From June 1918 to September 1919, he stayed in Nizhny Novgorod, where he was an agitator for the Provincial Committee, head of the Agitation Department, and chairman of the Ispolkom (Executive Committee). During this period, he was also Kommunar of the Special Purpose Units (CHON) or "communist squads."

From September 1919 to September 1920, Kaganovich served as governor of the Voronezh gubernia. In September 1920, he was transferred to Central Asia and worked there as a member of the Turkestan Commission of the All-Russian Central Executive Committee and member of the Turkestan Bureau of the Central Committee of the RCP(b). Simultaneously, he became one of the leaders of the Revolutionary Military Council of the Turkestan Front and served as people's commissar of the workers' and peasants' inspection of the Turkestan Republic and chairman of the Tashkent City Council. In May 1922, Kaganovich was transferred to Moscow, where he headed the Organizational Bureau or Orgburo of the Secretariat. He rose very rapidly in the party hierarchy thereafter. In 1924, he became a member of the CC CPSU, and from 1924 to 1925 he served as a secretary of the Central Committee.

In 1924, after Lenin's death, an acute internal party struggle took place. It was very important for Stalin to secure the support of Ukraine, the largest Soviet republic after the RSFSR. In 1925, on Stalin's recommendation, Kaganovich, as one of his most trusted subordinates, was elected first secretary of the Central Committee of the Communist Party of Ukraine.

During this period, two main policies were implemented throughout Ukrainian Republic: the policy of "Ukrainization," the practice of promoting Ukrainian culture, language, and schools, and the struggle against "bourgeois and petty bourgeois nationalism." The main task of party leaders was to build up Ukrainian Communist cadres and to strengthen Soviet power in the territory of Soviet Ukraine. It was not an easy task to distinguish clearly between these two policies. Kaganovich clearly drifted toward the second course: he was merciless to everything that seemed to him to manifest Ukrainian nationalism. His truculent rule led to frequent conflicts with the chairman of the Council of People's Commissars of Ukraine, Vlas Chubar. Oleksandr Shumsky, a member of the CC CPU and the people's commissar of education of Ukraine, was another active opponent of Kaganovich. In 1926 he even made an appointment with Stalin and demanded Kaganovich's withdrawal from Ukraine. Although Stalin agreed with some of Shumsky's arguments, he simultaneously supported Kaganovich by sending a special letter to the Politburo of the CC CPU. The case ended with the resignation of Shumsky from the post of People's Commissariat for Education and his recall from the Ukrainian SSR. In 1928, nevertheless, due to numerous protests against Kaganovich's measures, Stalin felt obliged to transfer him to Moscow.

At the beginning of 1930, Kaganovich was appointed first secretary of the Moscow regional and then the City Party Committee. This same year, he became a full member of the Politburo of the CC CPSU (the only Jew in the Politburo after the removal of Trotsky, Zinoviev, and Kamenev). In 1929–1934, as a secretary of the Central Committee and head of the agricultural department of the Central Committee, Kaganovich directly supervised collectivization. In October 1932, he headed extraordinary commissions on increasing grain procurements in the North Caucasus. His commission introduced the practice of listing Stanitsas (a type of rural localities) that did not fulfill the grain procurement plan on the so-called "blackboards." In total, during the work of the Kaganovich's commission, 15 Stanitsas were listed on the "blackboards," and as a result, they were isolated and cut off from trade, leading to death by hunger for hundreds of people. Also, from November 1 to December 10, in the course of the fight against "sabotage," 16,864 "kulaks and anti-Soviet element" were arrested in the North Caucasian Territory.

The first half of the 1930s was the peak of Kaganovich's career. Along with Zhdanov, Molotov, Voroshilov, Mikoian, Malenkov, and Beria, he established himself as one of the most influential party leaders in the Soviet Union. Kaganovich was entrusted with a wide range of tasks: in addition to the agricultural sector and collectivization, he oversaw the reconstruction of Moscow. He headed the construction of the first stage of the Moscow Metro, which until 1955 was known as Metropoliten imeni L. M. Kaganovicha. During this period, he actively promoted N. S. Khrushchev as one of his protégés.

In 1937, during the February–March plenum of the CC CPSU, Kaganovich advocated for new repressions in Soviet society. During the Great Terror, he—along with other close associates of Stalin—was responsible for issuing a verdict for the so-called "Stalin's shooting lists " (the lists of extrajudicially accused persons). The signatures on the lists meant a guilty verdict: typically execution by shooting, by either an individual or a firing squad. The signature of Kaganovich is found on 189 lists. As a result, more than 19,000 people were convicted and shot. For his mercilessness, he was nicknamed "Iron Lazar." In 1937, Kaganovich made a number of trips to different regions of the USSR (Kyiv, Iaroslavl, Ivanovo, and the Western regions) to carry out purges among the party and the Soviet leadership.

In 1937, Lazar Kaganovich was appointed the people's commissar of heavy industry. Simultaneously, from August 1938, he served as deputy chairman of the Council of People's Commissars of the USSR. In 1939, Kaganovich was the people's commissar of the fuel industry. From October 12, 1939, to 1940, he served as people's commissar of the oil industry.

In 1941, at the beginning of the **Great Patriotic War** (1941–1945), Kaganovich was railways commissar. In 1942 he became a member of the **State Defense Committee** and later headed the political administration of the Transcaucasian front. On October 4, 1942, the command post of the Black Sea group of forces near Tuapse, where Kaganovich was located, was bombed. He was wounded by shrapnel in the arm. In 1943, he was awarded the title of hero of socialist labor. From 1944, he was appointed deputy chairman of the Soviet government. In 1947, Kaganovich became first secretary and member of the Politburo of the Central Committee of the Communist Party (Bolsheviks) of Ukraine, replacing Khrushchev, but this was a short-term phenomenon, and Khrushchev returned to the party post before the end of the year.

After the war, Stalin began to lose the confidence in Kaganovich, meeting him less often and no longer inviting him to his lengthy late-night meals. Kaganovich's career began to decline. After the 19th congress of the CC CPSU in 1952, Kaganovich was elected to the expanded Presidium of the Central Committee and even to the Bureau of the Central Committee but did not enter the group of "five" most trusted party leaders selected by Stalin.

After Stalin's death, Kaganovich was able to gain more influence for a short time. As one of the first deputy chairmen of the Council of Ministers of the USSR and a member of the Bureau of the Presidium of the Central Committee, he controlled several important ministries. He supported Khrushchev's and Malenkov's proposal to arrest and eliminate Beria. Later, he was engaged in the development of new pension legislation. After the adoption of this new legislation, all citizens of the USSR were able to receive a pension. In 1957, Khrushchev put an end to Kaganovich's career, and he was relieved of all official functions and was removed from the Politburo and the Central Committee as a member of the "anti-party Molotov-Malenkov group" that opposed de-Stalinization. In 1961, due to Khrushchev's efforts, Kaganovich, his former patron, was expelled from the Communist Party. Nevertheless, he held the rank of a personal pensioner of federal significance and enjoyed the privileges corresponding to this status.

On July 25, 1991, Lazar Kaganovich died at the age of ninety-seven, five months before the collapse of the USSR, the country he had served from the first days of its existence.

KAGANOVICH, MIKHAIL MOISEEVICH (1888–1941). A Soviet statesman and party leader, and the older brother of Lazar Kaganovich, Mikhail Kaganovich—like his more famous brother—was born in the village of Kabany, Radomysl district, Kyiv Governorate, Russian Empire. He received a primary education and was employed as a metalworker. In

1905, he joined the RSDWP(b). Because of his revolutionary activity, he was arrested several times. In 1917–1918, he was a member of the headquarters of the Red Guard detachments at the Unecha station (Chernihiv province). From 1918 to 1922, he was first appointed chairman of the Arzamas Military Revolutionary Committee, later serving as chairman of the Surazh Council (Smolensk province) and a secretary of the Vyksa district committee of the RCP(b). In 1923–1927, he was the chairman of the Nizhny Novgorod Governmental Council of National Economy. With the support of his younger brother (Lazar), he was transferred to Moscow.

From 1927 to 1934, Mikhail became a member of the Central Control Commission of the CPSU. During 1927–1930, he was a candidate member of the Presidium of the Central Control Commission of the CPSU and a member of the board of the People's Commissariat of the Workers' and Peasants' Inspection of the USSR. In 1930–1932, he was a member of the Presidium of the Central Control Commission of the CPSU. In 1931, he headed the Main Machine-Building Directorate. He also served as deputy chairman of the Supreme Economic Council of the USSR. From 1932 to 1936, Mikhail Kaganovich was deputy people's commissar of heavy industry of the USSR and became the closest employee of the commissar, Sergo Ordzhonikidze. From 1934, he was a member of the CC CPSU. In 1934–1939, he was a candidate member of the Organizational Bureau (Orgburo) of the CC CPSU. At the same time, in 1935–1936, he was the head of the Main Directorate of the Aviation Industry of the People's Commissariat for Heavy Industry. From October 15, 1937, to January 11, 1939, he headed the Defense Industry of the USSR.

On December 12, 1937, Mikhail Kaganovich was elected a deputy of the Supreme Soviet of the USSR. On January 11, 1939, the People's Commissariat of the Aviation Industry of the USSR was separated from the Defense Industry and placed under the command of Mikhail Kaganovich. On January 10, 1940, he was relieved of his post as people's commissar and appointed director of the Ordzhonikidze Aviation Plant in Kazan. In February 1941, at the 18th conference of the All-Union Communist Party), he was threatened with expulsion from the Communist Party. He committed suicide on July 1, 1941.

KALININ, MIKHAIL IVANOVICH (1875–1946). A Bolshevik revolutionary and a Soviet politician, member of the CC CPSU(b) (1919–1946), candidate member of the Politburo of the CC CPSU(b) (1919–1926), and member of the Politburo of the Central Committee (1926–1946), Kalinin served as head of state of the Russian Soviet Federative Socialist Republic and later of the Soviet Union (from 1919 to 1946) and was nicknamed the "All-Union Headman." In some ways a figurehead, Kalinin managed to survive the turbulence of the purges and was often seen at Stalin's side.

Mikhail Kalinin was born in Verkhniaia Troitsa, Tver province, Russian Empire into a Russian peasant family. He graduated from the elementary community (*Zemstvo*) school, after which he started to work for neighboring landowner D. P. Mordukhai-Boltovsky. In 1889, he was taken to St. Petersburg, where he worked for Mordukhai-Boltovsky as a lackey (manservant). This job allowed him to read many books from the owner's library. In 1893, he became an apprentice at St. Petersburg Ammunition Factory. In 1895, he started to work at the Putilov munitions factory as a turner. There, Kalinin worked ten hours a day and earned up to forty rubles per month, a reasonable salary at a time when a kilogram of the best beef cost twenty-five kopecks, and a loaf of bread three kopecks.

At the Putilov Plant, one of the largest factories in Russia, Kalinin took part in illegal revolutionary circles, and in July 1899, together with other members of the Marxist circle, he was arrested. After ten months in prison, he was exiled to Tiflis, Georgia. There he joined the Tiflis Social Democratic organization and became acquainted with Georgian revolutionary Koba (the future Stalin). In March 1901, he was arrested again and exiled to Revel (today, Tallinn, Estonia). He worked in Revel about a year as a turner at the Volta factory and organized an underground printing house. In 1902, Kalinin found employment in Tallinn railway workshops. He united Tallinn's various Marxist circles into a social democratic organization headed by the Central Workers' Circle. In January 1903, Kalinin was arrested and sent to the Kresty prison in St. Petersburg. In July 1903, he was again exiled to Revel. From 1904 to 1905, he served his exile in the Olonets province to the north (Karelia).

Kalinin took part in the Russian Revolution of 1905. During this period, he met Vladimir Lenin and made a pleasant impression on him. Kalinin was an ideal Bolshevik: peasant by birth and a factory worker by trade, he knew how to appeal to a crowd. He was also familiar with the theories of Karl Marx. In 1912, at the sixth conference of the RSDWP, he was designated a candidate for the Central Committee of the party and was introduced to its Russian Bureau. On January 8, 1916, he was arrested by the Petrograd secret police and imprisoned. At the end of the year, Kalinin was released from prison with subsequent deportation to eastern Siberia under the public supervision of the police, but he was able to escape and continued party work in Petrograd.

During the February Revolution, Kalinin was one of the leaders of the protests. He led a column of demonstrators to the Kresty prison. The protestors disarmed the guards, and all prisoners, including murderers, rapists, and robbers, were released. For several weeks Petrograd became a center of crime. In August 1917, Kalinin was elected a member of the Petrograd City Duma. He actively took part in the preparation of the October Revolution. In November 1917, after the revolution, the Petrograd City Duma elected Kalinin mayor of the city. After the dissolution of the Petrograd City Duma in August 1918, he headed the Commissariat of the Union of Communes of the Northern Region and the Petrograd Labor Commune. In 1919, after Iakov Sverdlov's death (March 1919), Kalinin, on Lenin's recommendation, was elected president of the All-Russian Central Executive Committee, the nominal head of state of Soviet Russia. The name of this post would be changed twice. First, in 1922, it became the chairman of the Central Executive Committee of the Congress of Soviets, and second, in 1938, it was changed to the chairman of the Presidium of the Supreme Soviet. For twenty-seven consecutive years, Kalinin nominally headed the USSR. In the 20th century, he was the formal head of the Russian (Soviet) state longer than any other leader.

During the civil war in Russia (1917–1922), Kalinin headed the "October Revolution" propaganda train. During five years, he made twelve voyages around the central regions of Russia, Ukraine, the North Caucasus, and to almost all fronts in the Russian Civil War. In 1919, after the defeat of N. Iudenich's army, he visited revolutionary Kronstadt. On March 1, 1921, on the eve of the Kronstadt Uprising, accompanied only by his wife, Kalinin once again arrived at the fortress hoping to end the unrest. However, when he tried to speak to the rebels, the sailors interrupted him, and he was forced to leave Kotlin Island.

In 1921–1922, after the famine in the Volga region, Kalinin personally visited the affected regions. From July 1921 to October 1922, he headed the Pomgol Central Commission (an abbreviation of the Russian term *Pomoshch golodaiushchim* or "Help for the Starving"). In 1924, after Lenin's death, he became an ally of Stalin and a member of his inner circle. From January 1926 to June 1946, Kalinin was a full member of the Politburo. On December 1, 1934, on the day of the assassination of **S. Kirov**, Kalinin signed a decree of the Central Executive Committee and the Council of People's Commissars of the USSR "On Amendments to the Existing Criminal Procedural Codes of the Union Republics." This decree essentially legalized mass repressions. Kalinin regularly signed execution lists, which were then sent to all members of the Politburo. He also signed an order to execute 25,700 Polish "nationalists and counterrevolutionaries." This execution became a part of the Katyn massacre. On January 17, 1938, during the first session of the Supreme Soviet of the USSR of the first convocation, Mikhail Kalinin was elected chairman of the Presidium of the Supreme Soviet of the USSR.

Despite his post, Kalinin was unable to protect his own family from Stalin's terror.

In October 1938, Iekaterina Lorberg, Kalinin's wife, was arrested on charges of being a "Trotskyist" (under the anti-terrorist law signed by Kalinin). She was tortured in Lefortovo Prison and sentenced to 15 years in prison. In June 1945, she was released after a personal request by Kalinin. During the **Great Patriotic War** (1941–1945), Kalinin continued to serve as a propagandist.

In 1946, Kalinin retired, and on June 3 he died of cancer in Moscow. He was one of the few Old Bolsheviks to survive the Stalinist purges.

KAMENEV, LEV BORISOVICH (LEO ROZENFELD) (1883–1936). Kamenev was a Russian revolutionary, one of the Old Bolsheviks, a Soviet politician, one of Lenin's oldest associates, chairman of the Moscow City Council (1918–1926), deputy chairman of the Council of People's Commissars of the Russian Soviet Federative Socialist Republic (Sovnarkom) (1922), chairman of the Council of Labor and Defense (STO) (1924–1926), member of the CPSU Central Committee (1917–1927), member of the CC CPSU Politburo (1919–1926), member of the Central Executive Committee, and chairman of the USSR Central Executive Committee.

Leo Rozenfeld was born into an Orthodox family in Moscow. His father, a baptized Jew, began as a railway worker on the Moscow-Kursk railway and subsequently became an engineer. His mother, who was Russian, graduated from the Bestuzhev Courses in St. Petersburg (the largest women's higher-education institution in Imperial Russia). Both parents were actively involved in the radical student movement in the 1870s. Leo had a younger brother, Nikolai Borisovich Rozenfeld, who was born in 1886 and later became a painter and graphic artist. In 1935, he was arrested and died in prison.

Rozenfeld graduated from the boys' Gymnasium in Tiflis (now Tbilisi), Georgia. During his studies in the Gymnasium, he became involved in a radical student movement. In 1901, he began studies at the Law Faculty of Moscow University. In this same year, he joined the Social Democratic Party, and from 1903, he was a member of the Bolshevik faction. On March 13, 1902, after participating in student demonstrations against Tsar Nikolai II, he was arrested and exiled to Tiflis.

In fall 1902, Kamenev visited Paris, where he made the acquaintance of Lenin. In 1903, he returned to Russia and became involved in underground work. During this period, he helped to organize a railroad strike in Tiflis. In 1903–1905, he propagated Bolshevik revolutionary ideas in Tiflis, Moscow, and St. Petersburg. In the winter of 1904, Lev Kamenev was once again arrested for membership of the RSDWP. He spent five months in prison, then returned to Tiflis (now called Tbilisi). In 1905, together with Stalin and others, he was a member of the so-called Caucasian Union Committee of the RSDWP.

In 1907, at the fifth congress of the RSDWP, Kamenev was elected to the Central Committee of the party and at the same time became part of the separate "Bolshevik Center" created by the Bolshevik faction. Kamenev led revolutionary work in the Caucasus, Moscow, and St. Petersburg. After the dissolution of the Second State Duma of the Russian Empire, Lev Kamenev remained in St. Petersburg as part of the Bolshevik core. In spring 1908, he was arrested and remained in prison until the summer, when he moved to Geneva and joined the editorial board of the newspaper *Proletary*. In 1908, 1912, and 1913, he represented the Bolsheviks at conferences on Lenin's behalf, wrote articles for the party press, and worked as a lecturer at the party school in Longjumeau (France). Kamenev was Lenin's main controversialist. He was not afraid to take an opposing view, and Lenin appreciated this quality. However, Lenin often became annoyed and quarreled with Kamenev.

In 1914, Kamenev took over as editor of the party newspaper, *Pravda*. In November 1914, he was arrested and exiled to the Turukhansk *krai* (Krasnoiarsk region in central Siberia) the following year. While in exile in Achinsk, Kamenev, together with several merchants, sent a telegram to the tsar's brother, Mikhail Romanov, welcoming his voluntary renunciation of the throne. Kamenev returned from exile after the February Revolution of

1917. Unlike Lenin, he supported the provisional government and thought that it could be useful in the fight against "the old Imperial regime." On the eve of the October Revolution, in *Novaia Zhizn* newspaper, edited by **Maksim Gorky**, Kamenev published an article together with **Zinoviev**. In this article, the authors presented arguments against Lenin's idea to seize power in Russia through an armed uprising. Lenin saw the editorial as a betrayal and suggested that his comrades-in-arms should be expelled from the party. But other Bolsheviks did not support such drastic action. At the end of October, Lev Kamenev, taking advantage of Lenin's absence, held a meeting of the Central Committee, at which he pushed through the decision to include representatives of other socialist parties in the new government.

During the October Revolution on October 25 (November 7), 1917, Kamenev was elected chairman of the All-Russian Central Executive Committee. After the revolution, he proposed to introduce the Mensheviks and members of Socialist Revolutionary Party into the coalition, but Lenin was opposed and insisted that the Central Committee of the RSDWP(b) remove Kamenev as a member. Kamenev resigned in response. His post was taken by **Iakov Sverdlov**. Lenin, however, was not willing to remove him permanently.

In November 1917, Kamenev became a member of the delegation sent to Brest-Litovsk to conclude a separate agreement with the Central Powers, by which Russia would withdraw from the First World War, abandoning its alliance with Britain and France. In January 1918, Kamenev headed the Soviet delegation to France, but the French government refused to recognize his authority. On March 24, 1918, on his way back to Russia, he was arrested by the Finnish authorities in the Aland Islands. On August 3, 1918, Kamenev was released in exchange for Finns arrested in Petrograd. From September 1918, Kamenev was a member of the Presidium of the All-Russian Central Executive Committee, and from October 1918 he was chairman of the Moscow Soviet, a post he held until May 1926.

In March 1919, Kamenev became a member of the Politburo of the Central Committee of the RCP(b). In May 1919, he was sent to Ukraine to bolster the grain procurement program. This mission provoked the Grigoriev rebellion against the Red Army (May 7–31, 1919). The collapse of the Southern Front and the successful advance of Denikin's White Guard Volunteer Army toward Moscow in the summer and autumn of 1919 were the indirect consequences of Kamenev's decisions made while he was in Ukraine.

On April 3, 1922, Kamenev proposed to appoint Stalin as general secretary of the Central Committee of the RCP(b). Since 1922, due to the illness of Lenin, Kamenev had chaired Politburo meetings. On September 14, 1922, Kamenev was appointed deputy chairman of the Council of People's Commissars (CPC) of the RSFSR and deputy chairman of the Council of Labor and Defense of the RSFSR. In December 1922, after the formation of the USSR, Kamenev became a member of the Presidium of the Central Executive Committee of the USSR. In 1923, he took up the post of deputy chairman of the Council of People's Commissars of the USSR and the Council of Labor and Defense of the USSR (1924–1926), as well as director of the Lenin Institute. Kamenev remained a consistent critic of granting broad rights to the Cheka.

At the end of 1922, together with Zinoviev and Stalin, he formed a ruling "triumvirate" (or *troika*) in the Communist Party directed against **L. D. Trotsky**. Once Stalin had profound disagreements on policy with the other two members of the triumvirate, embracing the New Economic Policy, Zimoviev became part of the so-called Left Opposition in the party. In 1925, Kamenev—together with Zinoviev and Lenin's widow, **N. Krupskaia**—formed an opposition to Stalin and **Bukharin**, and became one of the leaders of the so-called "new," or "Leningrad," and after 1926 the United Opposition.

Gradually, Stalin began to demote his rivals in the leadership. On January 16, 1926, Kamenev lost his posts in the CPC and the Council of Labor and Defense of the USSR and was given the role of people's commissar of foreign and internal trade of the USSR. On November 26, 1926, he was appointed plenipotentiary representative of the USSR in Italy.

Some historians believe that his appointment to Italy, ruled by the fascist Benito Mussolini, was a move to discredit Kamenev's revolutionary merits, one that could be used against him in later trials.

In October 1926, Kamenev was expelled from the Politburo. Other demotions followed: in April 1927, from the Presidium of the Central Executive Committee of the USSR; in October 1927, from the CC CPSU; and on November 28 from the Society of Old Bolsheviks. In December 1927, at the 15th congress of the CC CPSU, Kamenev was expelled from the party and deported to Kaluga. However, after making a statement and acknowledging his past mistakes, he was reinstated in the party in June 1928. In 1928–1929, he was the head of the Scientific and Technical Directorate of the Supreme Council of the National Economy of the USSR. In May 1929, he was appointed chairman of the Main Concession Committee at the Council of Peoples' Commissars of the USSR.

The return to acceptability was short-lived. In 1932, Kamenev was again expelled from the party and exiled, but in May 1933, he returned from exile and was reinstated. He was also appointed director of the Akademia publishing house. In January 1934, at the 17th congress of the CC CPSU, Kamenev was forced to make a public apology for his past actions and positions. In December 1934, after the assassination of **S. M. Kirov** in Leningrad, Kamenev was arrested. In early 1935, he was charged in connection with the "Kremlin Case" and was sentenced to five years in prison. In August 1936, Kamenev—together with Zinoviev, Kamenev, and fourteen others, mostly Old Bolsheviks—were put on trial, the so-called trial of the Sixteen (or the trial of the "Trotsky–Zinoviev Terrorist Center)." On August 24, he was sentenced to death and shot the next day.

Kamenev 's innocence was not established during the period of Khrushchev's Thaw, but in 1988 he was rehabilitated during the second wave of de-Stalinization, initiated by M. S. Gorbachev and his ideology secretary, Aleksandr Iakovlev.

KAMENEV, SERGEI SERGEEVICH (1881–1936). A Russian revolutionary and Soviet military leader, komandarm first rank (1935), Sergei Kamenev (not related to Lev Kamenev) was born into the family of a military engineer in Kyiv. In 1898, he graduated from the Vladimir Kiev Cadet Corps. On September 1 of the same year, he entered the elite Aleksandrovsky Military School in Moscow. He graduated from college third in his class. In 1900, he entered military service. From 1900 to 1904, he served as a battalion adjutant at the 165th Lutsk Infantry Regiment. On August 9, 1903, he was promoted to lieutenant. In 1907, Sergei Kamenev graduated from the Nikolaev Academy of the General Staff in St. Petersburg on the first category.

On May 7, 1907, he was promoted to Stabs-kapitan. From November 6, 1907, to November 7, 1909, Kamenev served in the 165th Lutsk Infantry Regiment. During this period, he became a teacher at the Kyiv military school, where he taught tactics and topography. From November 26, 1909, he worked as assistant senior adjutant of the staff of the Irkutsk Military District. From February 10, 1910, he was senior adjutant of the staff of the 2nd Cavalry Division. During his initial service as an infantry commander, he intensively studied cavalry affairs and participated in all cavalry maneuvers. From November 26, 1911, he was an assistant to the senior adjutant in the operational-mobilization department of the headquarters of the Vilna military district. On December 6, 1912, he was awarded the Order of St. Stanislaus of the third degree.

In the prewar period, Kamenev participated in numerous maneuvers and field trips, which significantly expanded his knowledge of military affairs, skills, and competence, essential for the position of general staff officer and commander. In 1914, he took part in an operational-level war game in Kyiv that simulated aspects of future warfare. Kamenev also studied in detail Russia's unsuccessful experience of the war with Japan in 1904–1905.

With the outbreak of the First World War, Captain Kamenev was sent to the front. He served as senior adjutant to the operational department of the 1st Army. In December 1915, he was promoted to colonel, and in March 1917 he was appointed commander of the 30th Poltava Infantry Regiment. During his service, he came across the pamphlet *Against the Current*, written by V. Lenin and **G. Zinoviev**, which he maintained "opened up new horizons" for him.[1]

In April 1918, Kamenev voluntarily joined the Red Army. He served as military commander of special "veil" detachment (*otriady zavesy*) in the Western Front. Such detachments were created on March 29, 1918 (after the signing of the Brest Peace Treaty), and had to cover the internal regions of Soviet Russia from a possible invasion of German troops. From June 1918, he served as commander of the 1st Vitebsk Infantry Division. With the support of **L. D. Trotsky**, Kamenev was promoted to the highest posts in the Red Army. In August 1918, he was appointed military officer of the Smolensk region. From August 1918 to July 1919, Sergei Kamenev served as commander of the Eastern Front troops. He led the Red Army's offensive on the Volga River and the Urals. Under his command, the Red Army conducted defensive and offensive operations against the armies of Admiral Kolchak. These operations clearly revealed his talent as a military commander. From July 8, 1919, to April 1924, he commanded the armed forces of the RSFSR. Under Kamenev's leadership, the final operations of the Russian Civil War, against the forces of Denikin and Wrangel, were carried out.

In 1920, Kamenev was awarded the Gold Combat Weapon with the decoration of the Order of the Red Banner. The same year, he developed a plan for an offensive operation against Poland during the Soviet–Polish war. However, the plan was not implemented, as it underestimated the strength of the enemy and was opposed by the command of the Southwestern Front, in particular by A. Iegorov and Stalin. In November 1920, Kamenev led operations to eliminate banditry and against counterrevolutionary uprisings in Karelia, Bukhara, Fergana, and Tambov. In Turkestan, he led the fight against members of Basmachi movement. During the course of this struggle, Kamenev's troops liquidated Enver Pasha, who under the slogans of Pan-Islamism tried to resist the Bolsheviks. In the summer of 1922, Kamenev received the Order of the Red Star of the first degree of the Bukhara People's Soviet Republic. In September 1922 he was awarded the Order of the Red Banner of the Khorezm People's Soviet Republic.

Kamenev was evaluated by his contemporaries and descendants in diverse ways. Ill-wishers spoke of him as "a man with a big mustache and little ability."[2] According to Trotsky, Kamenev "was overly optimistic and had strategic imagination, but at the same time he had a narrow outlook. Workers, Ukrainian peasants, and Cossacks, were unfamiliar to him. But he easily succumbed to the influence of the Communists. Kamenev was undoubtedly a capable military leader, with imagination and the ability to take risks, but he lacked depth and firmness. Lenin later became extremely disappointed in him and more than once very sharply criticized his reports."[3]

After the Civil War, Sergei Kamenev continued to work in the Red Army. He analyzed and rethought the experience of the First World War and the Civil War in his military-scientific works and lectures. He also participated in the development of new regulations for the Red Army. In March 1924, after the elimination of the post of commander in chief, he held numerous positions, including inspector of the Red Army, chief of staff of the Red Army, deputy commissar of the People's Commissariat for Military and Naval Affairs, chairman of the Revolutionary Military Council of the USSR, and chairman of the Frunze Military Academy. As head of the Air Defense Department of the Red Army, he made a significant contribution to improving the country's defense capability. Under his command, the air defense forces were reequipped with new equipment. Kamenev was also one of the founders of the famous OSOAVIAKhIM (a Soviet voluntary public organization that supported the army and the military industry—from 1951, its acronym was DOSAAF) and the chairman of the commission for large flights. He contributed to the organization of Arctic exploration as the chairman of the Government Commission of the Arctic. His last military rank in the Russian Imperial Army was colonel in the Red Army: army komandarm of the first rank. Five military leaders who served during the civil war under the command of Kamenev (**Voroshilov, Budenny, Blucher, Iegorov,** and **Tukhachevsky**) were awarded the higher rank of marshal.

In 1930, Sergei Kamenev joined the Communist Party. On August 25, 1936, he died of a heart attack. The urn with his ashes was buried in the Kremlin wall. Even though he died before the Great Terror, he posthumously was counted among the "enemies of the people." For several decades, his name and works were forgotten. Kamenev was rehabilitated after the twentieth party congress of the CC CPSU in 1956.

KHODZHAEV, FAYZULLA UBAYDULLAE-VICH (1896–1938). Khodzhaev was an Uzbek Soviet party leader and politician who served as the first head of the Bukhara People's Soviet Republic (which would later form part of the Uzbek Soviet Socialist Republic) and chairman of the Council of People's Commissars of the Uzbek SSR (1924–1937). He was executed during the Great Purge.

Fayzulla was born in Bukhara into a family of a wealthy Uzbek merchant. In 1907, the family left Bukhara for Russian Turkestan. In 1913, Fayzulla joined the Jadid movement (a movement of Muslim modernist reformers within the Russian Empire). In 1916–1920, he was one of the leaders of the Young Bukharians or Mladobukharians party (after 1917, he was a member of its illegal Central Committee), which was a part of the jadidist movement against the monarchical regime in the emirate. He organized a demonstration demanding a constitution and reforms and, after its dispersal, fled from Old Bukhara. Subsequently, Fayzulla worked in New Bukhara and Tashkent. One of his closest friends in the Young Bukharians party was the poet and historian Abdurauf Fitrat.

After the October Revolution in Russia, as a representative of the Revolutionary Committee, Fayzulla participated in the "Kolesovo events": an unsuccessful attempt to seize power in the Bukhara Emirate by Russian Bolsheviks and Young Bukharians in March 1918. After the defeat of the Kolesovsky campaign, Khodzhaev was sentenced to death by the emir government and fled to Turkestan.

On his way to Moscow, he was arrested by the government of Ataman Dutov and imprisoned in the Orenburg prison. Upon his release, he moved to Moscow. At the end of 1919, he arrived in Tashkent, where he organized a Bureau of Young Bukharians (revolutionaries). In Tashkent, he was the editor of the newspaper *Uchkun*. He was able to establish contacts with the revolutionary underground in Bukhara and supplied them with revolutionary literature. On September 20, 1920, during the Bukhara operation, the Young Bukharians, with the help of Soviet troops, achieved the overthrow of the emir. Shortly before these events, the twenty-four-year-old Khodzhaev was appointed chairman of the revolutionary committee, and in September 1920 he joined the RCP(b).

From September 1920 till December 1924, he headed the government of the Bukharan People's Soviet Republic and served as chairman of the Council of People's Nazirs until its integration into the Uzbek SSR. He also participated in the defeat of the rebel detachments in Uzbekistan. In 1922, he became a member of the Central Asian Bureau of the Central Committee of the CPSU(b). With the formation of the Uzbek SSR, he was appointed chairman of its Revolutionary Committee, and on February 17, 1925, by a resolution of the first Constituent Congress of Soviets of the Uzbek SSR, he was appointed chairman of the Council of People's Commissars of the Uzbek SSR and a member of the Presidium of the Central Executive Committee of the Uzbek SSR.

On May 21, 1925, the first session of the Central Executive Committee of the Soviet Union of the third convocation elected him one of the chairmen of the USSR Central Executive Committee. In the 1920s and 1930s, he was one of the leaders of the Uzbek SSR and Uzbek communist organizations but was never elected to the highest party bodies of the CC CPSU. On November 9, 1934, Khodzhaev became a member of the Political Commission of the Central Committee, which was aimed at combating "baisko-kulak resistance" (other members of the commission were **Kuibyshev** and **Ikramov**).

On June 17, 1937, after the seventh congress of the Communist Party(b) of the Uzbek SSR, he was dismissed from all government and party posts and expelled from the All-Union Communist Party. On July 9, Khodzhaev was proclaimed "an enemy of the people" and arrested in Tashkent. During interrogations, he was tortured and beaten. In March 1938, he was one of the party leaders accused at the Third Moscow Trial, together with **N. I. Bukharin, A. I. Rykov**, and other prominent Soviet communists. On March 13, 1938, he was found guilty of organizing a Trotskyist conspiracy aimed at overthrowing Soviet power in Uzbekistan, as well as in espionage for Germany, Japan, Poland, and the United States, and sentenced to death. He was shot at the Kommunarka training ground on March 15, 1938.

In 1965 he was fully rehabilitated and reinstated in the party as a victim of Stalinist repressions.

KHRULEV, ANDREI VASILEVICH (1892–1962). Khrulev was a Soviet military commander and statesman, the head of Main Intendant Directorate of the Red Army (1939–1941), deputy chief of the people's commissar of defense of the USSR, head of the Main Directorate of Logistics of the Red Army (1941), people's commissar of railways of the USSR (1942–1943), army general (1943), head of the Rear Services of the Soviet Army (1943–1950), and creator of the modern concept of the unified system of the Rear Services of the Armed Forces of the USSR.

Andrei Khrulev was born on September 30, 1892, into a poor peasant family in the village of Bolshaia Aleksandrovka, Iamburg district of the Petersburg province (now the Kingisepp district of the Leningrad region). His father, Vasily Vasilevich Khrulev, was a blacksmith. Before moving to the village, he worked for a long time at factories in St. Petersburg. He had a reputation as a hardworking and intelligent boy. In 1903, he successfully graduated from the zemstvo school, after which he moved to St. Petersburg. For eleven and a half years, he worked in the workshop of a goldsmith. Later, he graduated from evening general education courses. During these years, Andrei Khrulev developed contacts with members of the Bolshevik branch of the RSDWP. In 1912, during a police search, the newspaper *Pravda* was found among his belongings. Khrulev was arrested and jailed for six months. After imprisonment, he was expelled from Russia for two years and exiled in Estonia. After returning to St. Petersburg (from 1915 to 1917), he worked as a mechanic at the Okhtinsky gunpowder factory.

During the October Revolution of 1917, Khrulev took part in the storming of the Winter Palace and in the suppression of the anti-Bolshevik attacks by former Russian leader Aleksandr Kerensky and his military commander Piotr Krasnov. In February 1918, he was sent to the Mogilev province to carry out propaganda activities. In March of the same year, he returned to Petrograd and formally joined the Bolshevik Party. Until June he worked as a party organizer and chairman of the regional committee of the revolutionary guard. He was then appointed the secretary of the factory committee and a member of the Porokhovsky District Council. In August 1918, as a volunteer, he joined the Red Army and was assigned to the 1st Regiment in Petrograd.

At the end of 1919, Khrulev was sent to the south region of the country to fight Denikin's White forces. For his initiative and courage in the battles with Denikin's troops, he was awarded the Order of the Red Banner. In September 1920, he took part in the defeat of the troops of General P. Wrangel. In late 1920 to early 1921, he fought against the armed formations of Nestor Makhno in Ukraine. By that time, he already held the positions of assistant chief and then chief of the political department of the 11th Cavalry Division of Budenny's First Cavalry Army. He remained at the front until the end of the Civil War.

After the war he remained in military service and from May 1922, Khrulev served as chief of the political department and military commissar of the 14th Cavalry Division of the North Caucasus Military District. In October 1922, he became the military commissar of the 4th Cavalry Division, and from May 1924, the commander and commissar of the

44th Territorial Cavalry Regiment of the 3rd Cavalry Brigade.

From October 1924 to August 1925, Khrulev studied at the Higher Military-Political Courses, and after graduation he was appointed military commissar and head of the political department of the 10th Maikop Cavalry Division of the Moscow Military District. In December 1928, he became deputy head of the political department of the Moscow military district. In July 1930, by the decision of the Revolutionary Military Council of the USSR, Khrulev was appointed head of the Central Military-Financial Directorate of the Workers' and Peasants' Red Army for Military and Naval affairs. He was a success in this post and was able to create a sophisticated logistical system for the Red Army and to strengthen financial discipline in both the army and navy. In November 1935, he was awarded the title of corps commissioner (military rank of the highest military-political layer of the Workers' and Peasants' Red Army) and the honorary title of "Drummer of the Financial Front." However, in 1936 he was removed from his post and taken to the reserve. He was suspected of being involved in "the military conspiracy of Tukhachevsky and others."

In August 1936, Khrulev was appointed head of the Main Construction Directorate of the Armed Forces under the Soviet government. In May 1938, he became the head of the Military Construction Directorate of the Kyiv Special Military District. A year later, his managerial skills were recognized, and in October 1939, he became head of the Supply Department of the Red Army. After the beginning of the Winter War (the Soviet invasion of Finland, November 30, 1939–March 13, 1940) and the formation of the Northwestern Front, organizational weaknesses in the work of the rear were revealed. Khrulev decided to petition the people's commissar of defense for the creation of the Main Intendant Directorate of the Red Army. He became its head when it was founded in August 1940. In this same year, he was awarded the Order of Lenin and the military rank of lieutenant general of the intendant service for his outstanding services. Although, in a short time, many measures were taken to improve the work of the intendant service, Khrulev understood that without good theoretical training, it would be very difficult to manage the army's supplies. Therefore, immediately after the end of the Finnish War (a victory but one in which the Red Army incurred disproportionate losses), he began to study organization theory of rear services and supply logistics. In 1940, he read the works of professors F. Maksheev, K. Goretsky, and N. Yanushkevich. He also studied materials on the quartermaster supplies during the First World War, analyzed the experience of organizing the supply of the Red Army during the Civil War, and later took into account the difficult experience of the first months of the **Great Patriotic War** (1941–1945). Based on his studies, he developed a coherent system of organization and work of the rear in war conditions. In the first half of 1941, Khrulev organized a large-scale inventory of military property in the army. Under his leadership, new standards for clothing and food supply were developed.

In July 1941, Khrulev was appointed deputy people's commissar of defense of the USSR, and simultaneously, from August 1941, he became head of Main Directorate of the Rear Services of the Red Army. He managed the rear of the Red Army throughout the war. In November 1942, he was promoted to the rank of colonel-general of the intendant's service. From March 1942, he was also appointed people's commissar of railroads of the USSR. In September 1943, Khrulev was awarded the Order of Suvorov first class, and in November he was promoted to the military rank of general. With Khrulev's growing popularity and authority, the number of his "ill-wishers" grew. Among them was people's commissar of internal affairs **Lavrenty Beria**. Because of Beria's intrigues, Khrulev resigned from the post of people's commissar of railways but remained the head of the rear of the Red Army.

After the war, Khrulev continued to lead the rear of the Soviet army. From March 1946, he served as the rear of the armed forces and deputy minister of the armed forces of the USSR in charge of the rear (after 1950, deputy minister of war). In 1951–1953, he was deputy minister of the building-materials industry of the USSR. In October 1953, he was transferred to the reserve but continued to hold leading positions in the civil service. For his service, he was awarded two Orders of Lenin, four Orders of the Red Banner, and two Orders of Suvorov First Class.

Khrulev died on June 9, 1962, and was buried in the Kremlin Wall in Moscow. He was one of the initiators of the rehabilitation of military leaders who were repressed during the years of the Great Terror. His petitions for the rehabilitation of his former colleagues were submitted even before Stalin's death.

KHRUSHCHEV, NIKITA SERGEEVICH (1894–1971). Khrushchev was a Soviet politician, first secretary of the CC CPSU (1953–1964), chairman of the USSR Council of Ministers (1958–1964), chairman of the Bureau of the Central Committee of the CPSU for the RSFSR (1956–1964), Hero of the Soviet Union (1964), three-time Hero of Socialist Labor (1954, 1957, 1961), and member of the NKVD troika of the USSR in the Moscow region (July 10–30, 1937). The most prominent part of his career took place after the death of Stalin. He led the USSR during the Cold War, supported the early Soviet space program, initiated a process of "de-Stalinization," was responsible for suppression of a revolt in Hungary (1956), and approved the construction of the Berlin Wall (1961). He is one of three Soviet leaders who was removed from power, along with Mikhail Gorbachev and Georgy Malenkov. The period of Khrushchev's rule is often called the "Thaw."

Khrushchev was born in the village of Kalinovka, Kursk province (near the Ukrainian border), into a poor peasant family. His father, Sergei Nikanorovich, was a coal miner. He received his primary education at a parish school, where he studied for about two years. When he was nine years old, his father took him out of school and sent him to work in the field. In the early 1900s, his family moved to Iuzovka (Stalino, Donetsk), where Nikita, at the age of 14, began working at an engineering plant.

From 1912, he worked as a coal miner, a profession that exempted him from military service when war broke out in August 1914.

In 1918, he joined the Bolshevik Party and participated in the civil war. In 1918, he led a detachment of the Red Guard in Rutchenkovo; then he was appointed a political commissar of the 2nd Battalion of the 74th Regiment of the 9th Rifle Division of the Red Army on the Tsaritsyn front. In the summer of 1920, he graduated with honors from the party school of the political department of the 9th Army. In September 1920, he was appointed an instructor in the Political Department of the 9th Kuban Army. He took part in the war in Georgia. After the end of the Civil War, Khrushchev became an assistant director for political affairs for the Rutchenkovo mine in the Donbas region.

In 1922, Khrushchev became a student of the Rabfak (Soviet special educational institution, which prepared Soviet workers to enter higher education) of the Don Technical Institute in Iuzovka, where he became the party secretary. The same year he met Nina Kukharchuk, his future wife. In 1927, as a representative of Iuzovka, he was invited to the Congress of the All-Union Communist Party. During the congress he made the acquaintance of Stalin's "gray cardinal," **Lazar Kaganovich**. Kaganovich saw political potential in Khrushchev and contributed to his rapid career growth. In 1928, Khrushchev, with the help of Kaganovich, was promoted to the central apparatus of the Communist Party of Ukraine (CPU). To fulfill job requirements, he had to enter the Industrial Academy of Moscow (secondary education was not enough for an official at the republican level). In 1930, he became party secretary of the school and started to rise rapidly through the party ranks. In his memoirs, Khrushchev mentioned that his links with fellow Academy student Nadezhda Allilueva, Stalin's wife, attributed to his rapid rise.

In 1931–1932, on the recommendation of Kaganovich, Khrushchev became the head of the Bauman and Krasnopresnensky district committees in Moscow. In January 1932, he was appointed second secretary of the Moscow City Committee of the CC CPSU. In January 1934, he became the first secretary of the Moscow City Committee and second secretary of the Moscow Oblast Committee of the CPSU. In this post, Khrushchev supervised the construction of the Moscow metro and was awarded the Order of Lenin.

During the Great Purge, many of Khrushchev's comrades were arrested. In his memoirs, he wrote that almost everyone who worked with him was arrested.[4] Only three out of the thirty-eight leaders of the Moscow city and regional party organizations survived. But Khrushchev was unharmed. He assisted in the purge of many friends and colleagues in Moscow Oblast. In 1937, Khrushchev became a member of a "purge troika." In 1938, he became head of the Communist Party of Ukraine and a candidate member of the CC CPSU Politburo. A year later he became a full member of the latter. In these positions, he showed himself as a ruthless persecutor of so-called "enemies of the people." In 1939, after the Soviet invasion of eastern Poland, almost 120,000 people from Western Ukraine were repressed and expelled from their lands. Khrushchev also led the Russification in Ukraine.

During the **Great Patriotic War** (1941–1945), Khrushchev was a political commissar and member of the military councils of the Southwest, Stalingrad, South, Voronezh, and the first Ukrainian fronts. He fully supported Stalin's military decisions and was one of those responsible for the disastrous encirclement of the Red Army near Kyiv (1941) and in Kharkiv (1942). Stalin consulted with Khrushchev on the appointment or removal of different commanders from office (e.g., Andrei Ieremenko and Vasily Chuikov). Before a counteroffensive, Khrushchev traveled to the fronts, checked the combat readiness and morale of the troops, and personally interrogated the prisoners. On February 12, 1943, after the victory at Stalingrad, he was awarded the rank of lieutenant general. For participation in the Battle of Stalingrad and the Battle of the Kursk Salient, he received the Orders of Suvorov and Kutuzov. During the Victory Parade in Moscow, he was on the podium of Lenin's Mausoleum together with Stalin and the country's top leadership.

After the war, from August 1944 to December 1949, he served as first secretary of the CC CPU and chairman of the Council of People's Commissars of Ukraine. It was a hard period for Ukraine: its industry had been destroyed, and agriculture faced critical shortages. In 1946 drought struck the republic and caused famine. Khrushchev's task was to restore the destroyed economy and cities. Moreover, he also led a struggle against nationalists of the Ukrainian Insurgent Army (UPA) in western Ukraine. In February 1945, Khrushchev was awarded the Order of Merit for the Fatherland, first degree, "for the successful implementation of the agricultural plan." In early 1947, however, Khrushchev was removed from the post of first secretary of the Communist Party of Ukraine, though he retained his government post. At this time, he fell seriously ill with pneumonia. According to some sources, the real reason for his removal was due to his appeals to Stalin to aid Ukraine. His replacement as party leader was his mentor **Kaganovich**, a reassuring sign. At the end of the year, Khrushchev was reinstated in his party post. In December 16, 1949, he was recalled to Moscow and became a secretary of the CC CPSU and first secretary of the Moscow City Committee of the CPSU. In 1952, he was a member of the Presidium of the Central Committee and became a member of the leading "five" created by Stalin.

After Stalin's death, he headed the commission that organized the farewell ceremony and funeral. In the post-Stalin battle for power, Khrushchev allied with **Malenkov** against **Beria**. In June 26, 1953, Khrushchev was one of the initiators of Beria's arrest. On September 7, 1953, Khrushchev was elected the first secretary of the CC CPSU. It was an unexpected decision for the Soviet people, since during the years of Stalin's rule, Khrushchev was clearly seen as an unlikely leader from the ruling group. For some months, it was unclear who would emerge as the country's leader, even though the party leadership had been crucial in the past. But in 1955, Khrushchev organized the removal of Premier Malenkov and replaced him with **Nikolai Bulganin**. On February 25, 1956, during his speech at the twentieth congress of the CC CPSU, Khrushchev put forward the thesis that the war between capitalism and communism is not "fatally inevitable." At a closed session, Khrushchev made a report (so-called "secret speech") "On the Personality Cult of Stalin and Its Consequences (Mass Repressions)." As a result of this report, by the end of 1955, thousands of political prisoners had returned home from the gulag labor camps. Also, in 1961, following the twenty-second party congress, the city of Stalingrad was renamed Volgograd, and Stalin's remains were removed from Lenin's Mausoleum in Moscow's Red Square. Earlier, the Secret Speech triggered a wave of unrest in the countries of the Eastern Bloc, particularly in Poland (October 1956) and Hungary (October and November 1956). The latter was suppressed by a Soviet invasion.

In June 1957, Khrushchev (with the help and support of **Georgy Zhukov**) blocked a Malenkov-led coup and in March took over the premiership. The members of the Presidium seeking to reverse the move against Stalin's legacy were branded "the anti-party group"—consisting of **Molotov**, Malenkov, Kaganovich, and **Shepilov**—and removed from the Central Committee (later, in 1962, they were expelled from the party). The composition of the Presidium of the Central Committee was expanded to fifteen members, most of whom were supporters of Khrushchev. In October 1957, on the initiative of Khrushchev, Marshal Zhukov, who had supported him against his rivals, was removed from the Presidium of the Central Committee and relieved of his duties as minister of defense of the USSR. A possible reason for this decision was Khrushchev's fear of Zhukov's influence in the armed forces. After March 27, 1958, Khrushchev served as chairman of the USSR Council of Ministers, thereby combining party and state positions, which put an end to the principle of collegial leadership in the country.

Khrushchev remained in office until 1964, when he was removed by a KGB-engineered coup, which established a collective leadership under **Brezhnev**, **Kosygin**, and **Podgorny**. There were various reasons, linked to both his foreign and domestic policies. He was an erratic and controversial leader, but his period in power eased the tensions of the Stalin years. Ironically, it was a close associate and follower of Stalin who repudiated him and charted a new and more moderate direction.

The main initiators of Khrushchev's replacement were A. Shelepin, D. Poliansky, V. Semichastny, and Brezhnev. Within the Presidium, only **Mikoian** remained loyal to Khrushchev. Khrushchev signed a letter of resignation. He was released from party and state posts because "of old age and deteriorating health" and sent into retirement. Khrushchev settled in a dacha in the village not far from Moscow until his death in 1971.

Nikita Khrushchev and Stalin

KIROV, SERGEI MIRONOVICH (NÉE KOSTRIKOV) (1886–1934). A Russian revolutionary, Soviet statesman and politician, and a close personal friend of Stalin, Kirov was first secretary of the Leningrad Regional Committee of the All-Union Communist Party (Bolsheviks). His assassination was used as a pretext to start Stalin's first Great Purge.

Sergei Kostrikov was born in Urzhum, Viatka province (today Kirov Oblast in European Russia), where his parents arrived from the Perm province shortly before his birth. He had six siblings, but the first four children in the family died in infancy. In 1890, Sergei's father, who was an alcoholic, abandoned the family, and in 1994 his mother died from tuberculosis. His sisters were raised by their grandmother, and Sergei was sent to an orphanage. He graduated from the Urzhum city school. During his studies, he was repeatedly awarded with certificates and books. In 1901, after graduation, Sergei received a scholarship from wealthy Urzhum benefactors and began studies at Kazan industrial school. There, he also started to attend underground student and workers' circles.

In 1904, he completed his education with a first-degree award and was among the top five graduates of that year. In the same year, he moved to Siberia and began working as a draftsman at the Tomsk city government and enrolled in preparatory courses at the Tomsk Technological Institute. In Tomsk, in November 1904, he joined the RSDWP. His party alias was Serge. In 1905, he took part in a demonstration for the first time and was arrested by the police. After release from prison, he continued his participation in revolutionary activity. In July 1905, the Tomsk City Party Conference elected Kirov a member of the Tomsk Committee of the RSDWP. In October 1905, he organized a strike at the big Taiga station. In July 1906, he was arrested and imprisoned for a year and a half in the Tomsk fortress (prison). In 1908, Kostrikov became a professional revolutionary in Irkutsk and Novonikolaievsk. In 1909, he moved to Vladikavkaz and became an employee of the North Caucasian Kadet newspaper *Terek*, publishing articles under the pseudonym Sergei Mironov. In April 1912, he adopted the pseudonym "Kirov." He remained in Terek until March 1917.

According to the official version of Soviet history, Kirov's political views before 1917 were clear: he was a convinced Leninist. But according to some historians,[5] Kirov did not choose a "political platform" for a long time. He sympathized with the Mensheviks, supported the provisional government (he openly wrote about this in his articles), wrote for a Kadet newspaper, and only after the October Revolution of 1917 did he join the Bolsheviks.

In the spring of 1918, he was elected a member of the Terek Regional Council, and in July he participated in the fifth All-Russian Congress of Soviets as a guest. In November, he became a full delegate of the sixth All-Russian Congress of Soviets. From February 25, 1919, he was chairman of the Provisional Revolutionary Committee in Astrakhan and led the suppression of the "counterrevolutionary rebellion." More than four thousand people were killed. He fought for the Red Army in the Russian Civil War and became a member of the Revolutionary Military Council of the 11th Army that same year. On April 28, 1920, as part of this unit, he entered Baku and became a member of the Caucasian Bureau of the Central Committee of the RCP(b). In June 1920, he was appointed plenipotentiary of Soviet Russia in Georgia. In October 1920, he headed the Soviet delegation at the negotiations on a peace treaty with Poland in Riga.

In 1921, at the tenth congress of the RCP(b), he was elected a candidate member of the Central Committee. The same year, he became the first secretary of the Central Committee of the Communist Party of Azerbaijan. In April 1923, at the twelfth congress of the RCP(b), he was elected a member of its Central Committee. On January 8, 1926, Kirov was appointed first secretary of the Leningrad Provincial Committee (Regional Committee), the City Party Committee, and the Northwestern Bureau of the Central Committee of the CPSU. He also became a candidate member of the Politburo of the CC CPSU. As a member of the Central Committee, he was sent to Leningrad to conduct an ideological struggle against the Zinoviev opposition. From 1930, he was a full member of the Politburo of the CC CPSU and the Presidium of the All-Russian Central Executive Committee of the USSR. Despite enjoying Stalin's favor, Kirov remained an insignificant figure in the Politburo. He rarely visited Moscow and was absent from most Politburo meetings. All his attention was focused on Leningrad.

Kirov loved books and collected a huge personal library. In 1928, he met **Maksim Gorky** and supported his publishing endeavors. In 1933, together with the head of the GPU for the city of Leningrad F. Medved and party member I. Kodatsky, he became a member of the "troika" of the Leningrad region. In 1934, Kirov was awarded the Order of Lenin for outstanding services in the restoration and reconstruction of the oil industry. In this same year, he became a member of the Secretariat and a member of the Orgburo of the CC CPSU.

On the evening of December 1, 1934, Kirov, was shot by Leonid Nikolaev in a corridor of the Smolny Institute, where the Leningrad City Committee and the Regional Committee of the All-Union Communist Party of Bolsheviks were located. According to one version,[6] the personal life of Sergei Kirov was the reason for his murder. Nikolaiev was the husband of Milda Draule, with whom Kirov was having an affair. There was also speculation that Stalin himself had ordered the assassination as a pretext for a major purge of party personnel. To date, there is little foundation for this theory. A few hours after the murder, the Soviet authorities announced that Kirov had become a victim of conspirators—enemies of the people. On the same day, the Presidium of the Central Executive Committee of the USSR adopted a resolution "On Amendments to the Existing Criminal Procedure Codes of the Union Republics: On the Procedure for Conducting Cases on the Preparation or Commission of Terrorist Acts." Kirov's assassination gave impetus to massive repressions, known as the Great Terror (*see* **Great Purge of 1937–1938**), that lasted for several years.

In the Soviet period, Kirov's activities in Leningrad and his personality were mythologized. Cities, streets, enterprises, institutions, and collectives were named after Kirov. Soviet artists, sculptors, writers, poets, and filmmakers immortalized the memory of Kirov in numerous works. The former Viatka province still retains Kirov's name more than three decades after the end of the Soviet Union.

KIRPONOS, MIKHAIL PETROVICH (1892–1941). A Soviet military leader, colonel general (February 22, 1941), and Hero of the Soviet Union (March 21, 1940), Mikhail Petrovich Kirponos was born on January 12, 1892, in the town of Vertievka, Chernihiv province (currently Chernihiv Oblast of Ukraine) into an impoverished Ukrainian peasant family. For a year he studied at a parish school, followed by three years in a zemstvo school. In 1907, he took part in peasant unrest in the village of Vertievka, for which he was arrested for a short time. From 1909, he worked as a forester and watchman in Kursk province and, after 1912, in the former occupation in Mikhailovsky district of Chernihiv province.

In September 1915, he was drafted into the Russian Imperial Army. In 1915, after graduating from instructor courses at the Oranienbaum Officer Rifle School, he served in the 216th Reserve Infantry Regiment in the city of Kozlov (now Michurinsk, Tambov region). In 1917, he graduated from the military paramedical school. In August 1917, he served as a company paramedic of the 258th Olgopol Infantry Regiment on the Romanian Front. He was by this time an active supporter of the Bolsheviks and was elected the chairman of the soldiers' regimental committee. In January 1918, Kirponos was arrested for organizing fraternization with Austro-Hungarian soldiers of the enemy Central Powers at the front.

In March 1918, after demobilization, he joined the Red Army and became a member of the Bolshevik party. During the Civil War, he organized rebel detachments, who fought against the German invaders, Haidamaks, and White Guards in Ukraine. Soon he became chief of staff, assistant commander, and commander of the 22nd Ukrainian Rifle Regiment of the 44th Rifle Division. The regiment successfully fought against the White Guards in Zhytomyr, Berdichev, and Kyiv. The Revolutionary Military Council of the republic awarded Kirponos a Mauser. In July 1919, he was appointed assistant chief of the Divisional School of Red Commanders (*chervonykh starshyn*) of the 44th Rifle Division in Zhytomyr and Hlukhiv. In 1922, he graduated from this school as an external student.

In 1927, Kirponos graduated from the M. V. Frunze Military Academy and was appointed chief of staff of the 44th Rifle Division. From 1934 to 1939, he was chief of the Supreme Soviet of the Tatar Autonomous Republic Kazan

Military School. He took part in the Soviet–Finnish War of 1939–1940. In March 1940, by the decree of the Presidium of the Supreme Soviet of the USSR, Kirponos was awarded the title of Hero of the Soviet Union, the Order of Lenin as part of the award, and the Gold Star Medal for his skillful command and heroism shown in battles. In April 1940, he was commander of the 49th Rifle Corps, and in June of the same year, he was given command of the Leningrad Military District.

On January 14, 1941, he was appointed commander of the Kyiv Special Military District.

After the beginning of the **Great Patriotic War**, this district was transformed into the Southwestern Front, with Colonel General Kirponos as front commander. His frontline troops fought heavy defensive battles in Right-Bank Ukraine suffering defeats at the Battle of Brody in late June 1941, and the Battle of Uman (July–August 1941), in which he commanded the Southwestern Front. Defensive actions on important lines and directions were combined with counterattacks. For about two months, the front defended the Kyiv fortified area and retained its combat effectiveness while retreating to the Dnipro River. The front, which had no reserves, was unable to stop the offensive of Guderian's 2nd Panzer Group, redeployed from Moscow to the southern direction. By September 14, the 5th, 21st, 26th and 37th armies were surrounded. On September 20, 1941, the front commander Kirponos, chief of staff of the front V. Tupikov, and member of the Military Council of the Front M. Burmistenko were killed in action during the defense of Kyiv. Kirponos was buried nearby in a wood. In December 1943, the remains of Colonel-General Kirponos were reburied with military honors in Kyiv in the A. Fomin Botanical Garden. In 1957, his ashes were transferred to the Park of Eternal Glory.

KOLLONTAI, ALEKSANDRA MIKHAILOVNA (1872–1952). A Russian revolutionary, Soviet statesperson, and diplomat, Kollontai was envoy extraordinary and minister plenipotentiary of the USSR, people's commissar of social welfare in the first Soviet government (1917–1918), the first woman minister in Russian history, one of the first female ambassadors, and the only Bolshevik leader during the October Revolution, other than Stalin himself, to have survived the purges.

Aleksandra Domontovich was born in St. Petersburg into a wealthy noble family of Russian, Ukrainian, and Finnish ancestry. Her father, high-ranking general Mikhail Domontovich, was descended from a Ukrainian Cossack family, took part in the Russian–Turkish war of 1877–1878, and was the governor of Tarnovo (Bulgaria) in 1878–1879. Her mother, Aleksandra Massalin-Mravinskaia, was the daughter of a Finnish manufacturer. Aleksandra was educated at home. She spoke several foreign languages (English, German, French, Swedish, Norwegian, Finnish, and others) and was interested in literature and history. She was greatly influenced by her home teacher, M. Strakhova, who sympathized with the ideas of the 19th-century revolutionary group Narodnaia Volia. In 1890, 18-year-old Shura, as she was called growing up, was introduced to the empress and dined at the same table with the heir to the throne: the future Emperor Nikolai II.

In 1893, Aleksandra married a distant cousin, a graduate of the Military Engineering Academy, the impoverished officer Vladimir Kollontai. Her mother objected bitterly to this union. In 1894, Aleksandra bore a son, Mikhail. The young woman became interested in Marxist ideas and started to attend secret meetings organized by her new friend, Elena Dmitrievna Stasova, the closest friend of **Nadezhda Krupskaia** and Vladimir Ulianov (Lenin). In 1898, Aleksandra left her husband and son and traveled to Switzerland, where she entered the University of Zurich. On the advice of Professor Heinrich Herkner, in 1899 she went to England to study the English labor movement. In England she met the noted Fabians Sydney and Beatrice Webb.

In 1899, Kollontai became a member of the RSDWP. In 1901, she traveled to Geneva, where she met Georgy Plekhanov, the legendary "father" of Russian Marxism. In 1903, at the time of the split in the RSDWP between the Mensheviks under Iuly Martov and the

Bolsheviks under V. I. Lenin, Kollontai did not join either faction. In 1904, however, together with Plekhanov, she sided with the Bolsheviks. In 1905, on Bloody Sunday, as a Bolshevik agitator, she tried to dissuade workers from marching to the Winter Palace "to the tsar," but when this failed, she accompanied them. In November 1905, she met Lenin for the first time. During the Revolution of 1905, Kollontai initiated the creation of the Society for Mutual Aid to Women Workers. Kollontai's association with the Bolsheviks ended temporarily in 1906, when she rejected their boycott of the Duma elections, maintaining that it was still possible to wield some influence through the assembly.

In 1908, she went into exile in Germany, where she met leaders of the German communist party Rosa Luxemburg and Karl Liebknecht. The revolutionaries helped her to move to Sweden when Germany declared war on Russia, heralding the start of the First World War. For her active anti-militarist propaganda, in particular for the publication of an anti-war article in a Swedish magazine in November 1914, she was arrested by the Swedish police and deported from the country by personal decree of King Gustav V. Henceforth, Kollontai finally became closer to the Bolsheviks.

After the February Revolution of 1917, she returned to Russia and became a member of the Executive Committee of the Petrograd Soviet. On April 1917, she participated in the seventh conference of the RSDWP(b) and was one of the few delegates who fully supported Lenin's positions set forth in the April Theses. At the first All-Russian Congress of Soviets, she was elected a member of the Central Executive Committee from the Bolsheviks. During the period of "dual power" (March–November 1917), she propagated Bolshevism among soldiers and sailors, which provoked a response by the provisional government. Returning from a meeting of the left-wing anti-war Zimmerwald Association in Stockholm in July 1917, Kollontai was arrested by order of the provisional government.

During the sixth congress of the RSDWP(b) in 1917, she was elected in absentia (she was still under arrest) as one of the honorary chairpersons of the congress and a member of the party Central Committee. She became the first woman in the Bolshevik leadership, and as a feminist, she was prepared to delay demands for women's rights for the sake of the revolution and its success.

After the October Revolution of 1917, she was elected a member of the All-Russian Central Executive Committee and received the post people's commissar of social welfare in the first Soviet government. During the Civil War, Kollontai was sent to Ukraine, where she headed the People's Commissariat of Agitation and Propaganda of the Crimean Soviet Republic, as well as the political department of the Crimean Army. At the end of the war, she worked as the head of the women's department (*zhenotdel*) of the Central Committee of the RCP(b). The department fought for equal rights for women and men, struggled against illiteracy among the female population, and informed about new working conditions and family organization. On December 31, 1917, the first Russian/Soviet decree on the protection of mothers and infants was issued under her signature. Also, with Kollontai's participation, drafts of decrees on divorce, civil marriage, and maternity leave were prepared. She presented the idea of social education. Under her leadership, a system of nurseries and kindergartens was established in the new state. She also gave lectures at the Sverdlov Communist University (a school for activists in Moscow) and worked in the **Comintern**.

Gradually, she became an internal critic of the Communist Party. In March 1918, Kollontai supported the position of Nikolai Bukharin and the "left communists" and opposed the Brest Peace Treaty. In protest, she even resigned from the government. Together with Aleksandr Shliapnikov, a Russian communist revolutionary and a memoirist of the October Revolution of 1917, she headed the **Workers' Opposition** movement inside the Russian Communist Party. Kollontai also criticized the New Economic Policy proposed by Lenin in March 1921. She was among those who signed the so-called "Letter of the 22."

In early 1920s, Kollontai was appointed to various diplomatic positions abroad. This made her the world's third woman serving in diplomacy. Among the main reasons for her appointments were her strong ties with the European socialist movement and the experience of working as secretary of the International Women's Secretariat under the Comintern. Appointments to distant posts also prevented Kollontai from playing any further roles in opposition at home. From 1923, she first worked as an attaché to the Soviet commercial mission in Norway and later was appointed Soviet Envoy Extraordinaire and Plenipotentiary and Trade Representative in Norway. Her appointment contributed greatly to the political recognition of the USSR by Norway. Her efforts and work in Norway transformed the diplomatic mission into an embassy, and Alexandra Kollontai became Soviet ambassador extraordinaire and plenipotentiary to Norway. From 1926 till 1927, Kollontai was appointed as a Soviet representative in Mexico and was able to achieve some success in improving Soviet–Mexican relations. However, she was unable to withstand the hot climate, which negatively affected her heart, and was transferred back to Oslo.

In 1930–1945, Kollontai was first an envoy and then an ambassador to Sweden, and was also part of the Soviet delegation to the League of Nations. Her main task was to neutralize the influence of Nazi Germany in Scandinavia. In Sweden, Kollontai achieved a number of diplomatic victories. During the course of the Finnish campaign, she was instrumental in preventing a Swedish advance into the Soviet Union, and in 1944 Kollontai convinced Finland to withdraw from the war, significantly accelerating the advance of Soviet troops into Europe. Political ties with the Scandinavian world were in the capable hands of Kollontai, which was how she avoided Stalin's purges of 1937–1938. In addition, Stalin did not perceive Kollontai as a serious political opponent and was constantly making fun of her. In her turn, Aleksandra Mikhailovna fully supported Stalin's policies.

On the eve of the end of the Great Patriotic War, Kollontai suffered a stroke, which ended her political career. In mid-March 1945, the diplomat was brought from abroad to Moscow, where she began her rehabilitation. For the final seven years of her life, Kollontai used a wheelchair and lived in seclusion in her own apartment on Malaia Kaluzhskaia Street. Despite the partial paralysis of the body, she still performed the functions of a foreign policy consultant. Kollontai died on March 9, 1952, from a second heart attack.

KONEV, IVAN STEPANOVICH (1897–1973). commander of the 1st Ukrainian Front during the **Great Patriotic War**, marshal of the Soviet Union (1944), twice Hero of the Soviet Union (1944, 1945), chevalier of the Order of Victory (1945), and member of the CPSU Central Committee (1952–1973), Ivan Konev was born on December 28, 1897, in Lodeino Nikolsky Uezd of the Vologda province (today Podosinovsky district of the Kirov region), into a peasant family. His mother, Evdokya Stepanovna, died after giving birth to his sister Marya, and Ivan was raised by his aunt, Klavdya Ivanovna Mergasova. He graduated from parish school in 1906 and the Nikolo-Pushemskoye zemstvo school in 1912. From the age of 15, he worked as a seasonal worker at the timber exchanges in Podosinovets and Arkhangelsk. In May 1916, he was drafted into the Russian Imperial Army and participated in the First World War. Six months later, his father was drafted into the militia. Ivan graduated from the training artillery team and first served in the reserve heavy artillery brigade (Moscow); then in 1917 as a junior noncommissioned officer, Konev was sent to the Southwestern Front. He fought as part of the 2nd Separate Heavy Artillery Division of the 2nd Heavy Artillery Brigade. He was demobilized in January 1918.

In 1918, Konev joined the Bolshevik Party. He was elected as a district military commissar in the city of Nikolsk, Vologda province. Later, under **Kliment Voroshilov**'s command, he fought against units of the White Army, the Far Eastern Army, and Japanese interventionists in Transbaikalia and the Far East. From the Far Eastern army party organizations, he was elected a delegate to the tenth congress of the RCP(b). While traveling to Moscow, he became acquainted with Commissioner Aleksandr Bulyga, who later became better known as the writer Aleksandr Fadeiev. When they heard about the Kronstadt uprising, they both, along with other volunteers, went to Petrograd and took part in its suppression. After his return to Moscow, as a delegate of the congress, Konev was photographed in the Kremlin with Lenin.

After the end of the Civil War, from December 1922, he was appointed military commissar of the 17th Primorsky Rifle Corps. From August 1924, he became commissioner and head of the Political Department of the 17th Nizhny Novgorod Rifle Division. In 1926, he graduated from advanced training courses for higher command personnel at the Frunze Military Academy of the Red Army. The same year he was appointed commander and commissar of the 50th Rifle Regiment of the Nizhny Novgorod Rifle Division. From 1932 to 1934, he studied at the Special Group of the Frunze Military Academy. After graduation, he consistently commanded a regiment, division, corps, army, troops of the Trans-Baikal, and North Caucasian military districts. In August 1938, he was appointed commander of the reinforcement group of the Mongolian Army, which later was united with the rest of the Soviet troops in Mongolia. In September, when it became known as the 57th Special Corps. Konev became its first commander. In July 1938, he was awarded the rank of corps commander, and in March 1939, second rank army commander. In 1940, Konev was awarded the rank of lieutenant general and was appointed commander of the North Caucasian Military District.

After the beginning of the Great Patriotic War, Lieutenant General Konev was appointed commander of the 19th Army in the Vitebsk region. His troops fought near Vitebsk and took part in the battle for Smolensk, which was overrun by the German Army Group Center. On September 11, 1941, Konev was awarded the rank of colonel general, and was appointed commander of the Western Front. After his troops suffered a severe defeat at Viazma, commander Konev was demoted to deputy front commander. A special commission from the **State Defense Committee**, headed by **V. Molotov** and Voroshilov, arrived to investigate the causes of defeat and punish Konev.

G. Zhukov defended Konev, which saved him from a potential trial and execution.

In October 1941, Konev became commander of the Kalinin Front, participated in the Battle for Moscow, and conducted the Kalinin defensive operation and the Kalinin offensive operation. In January 1942, the name of Konev became closely associated with another major setback for Soviet troops, the Battle of Rzhev (January 8, 1942–March 31, 1943), a series of battles that had the goal of pushing the German Army Center further away from Moscow. From August 26, 1942, to February 27, 1943, he was again appointed commander of the Western Front, and participated in the infamous Operation Mars, a failed operation to parallel Operation Uranus further south that freed Stalingrad from the Germans and their allies. After leading the unsuccessful Zhizdrinsky operation, he was again removed from his post and was appointed to command the much less important Northwestern Front. However, the troops of this front suffered heavy losses during the Staraia Russa offensive operation (March 4–19, 1943).

In the spring of 1943, Konev was appointed commander of the Steppe Front, which made a significant contribution to the defeat of Hitler's troops during the Battle of Kursk. Konev's troops liberated Belgorod and Kharkiv. On October 20, 1943, Konev was appointed commander of the 2nd Ukrainian Front and conducted the Nizhnedneprovskaia, Korsun-Shevchenkovskaia, Kirovograd, and Uman-Botoshanskaia offensive operations. On March 26, 1944, the troops of the 2nd Ukrainian Front were the first to reach the state border of the USSR. On July 29, 1941, Konev was awarded the Hero of the Soviet Union with the Order of Lenin and the Gold Star medal, demonstrating his meteoric rise as a military commander following the earlier failures.

In February 1945, Konev's troops led the Lower Silesian operation, and in March, the Upper Silesian operation, achieving significant results in both. His armies performed brilliantly in the Berlin and Prague operations, the final battles of the Second World War in Europe. Together with marshals Zhukov and **K. Rokossovsky**, Konev is widely regarded as the leading commander of the Soviet Army. On June 1, 1945, Marshal Konev was awarded a second Gold Star medal.

After the war, from June 1945, Konev was appointed commander-in-chief of the Central Group of Forces in Austria and high commissioner for Austria. From July 1946, he was commander-in-chief of the ground forces and deputy minister of the armed forces of the USSR. In March 1950, he became chief inspector of the Soviet Army and deputy minister of war of the USSR. From November 1951, Konev became commander of the Carpathian Military District.

In 1953, Konev was chairman of the Special Judicial Presence that sentenced Beria to death. In May 1955, he was appointed the first deputy minister of defense of the USSR and commander-in-chief of the ground forces. In 1956–1960, Konev became the first deputy minister of defense of the USSR, and simultaneously from 1955 the commander-in-chief of the joint armed forces of the Warsaw Pact countries. In this capacity, he led the suppression of the 1956 Hungarian uprising.

On October 25, 1957, during the exclusion of Marshal Zhukov from the Central Committee of the party, Konev supported Khrushchev and other members of the Presidium. In August 1961–April 1962, during the Berlin Crisis that followed the erection of the Berlin Wall, Konev was commander-in-chief of the Group of Soviet Forces in Germany. On January 30, 1965, as part of a Soviet government delegation, he took part in the funeral of former British Prime Minister Winston Churchill.

Konev died of cancer on May 21, 1973, and is buried in Red Square near the Kremlin wall.

KOSIOR, STANISŁAW VIKENTYEVICH (1889–1939). A Soviet party leader and statesman, first secretary of the Communist Party of Ukraine, deputy prime minister of the USSR, member of the Politburo of the CC CPSU, member of the Central Executive Committee, Central Executive Committee of the USSR and its Presidium, and member of the Supreme Soviet of the Soviet Union (since 1937), Kosior was one of the active organizers and subsequent victim of the Stalinist repressions.

Stanislav Kosior was born in 1889 in the town of Vengruv, Sedlec province in the Russian Empire (now Poland) into a family of Polish factory workers. The family had five sons, four of whom became underground revolutionaries. After graduating from the Sulinsky factory primary school in 1902, Kosior took a job as a mechanic at the same factory. In November 1905, he took part in factory strikes. In 1907, he joined the RSDWP and from 1908 to 1911 headed its Sulina organization. In 1910, he created a football club, which served as a cover for underground work and gained popularity among the masses. Kosior was arrested four times in this period, and in 1911 he was exiled to the Iekaterinoslav province. From 1912 to 1914, he conducted underground work in Kharkiv, Kyiv, and Poltava. In the fall of 1914, he was among the organizers of the Kyiv Committee of the RSDWP(b), and after its failure, in 1915, he moved to Moscow. In this same year he was once again arrested and exiled to Irkutsk province for three years, though he did not serve a full term.

After the February Revolution, Kosior moved to Petrograd, where he worked in the party organization of the Narva-Peterhof region and was a member of the city's Bolshevik Committee in the Executive Commission. In October 1917, he was appointed commissioner of the Petrograd Military Revolutionary Committee. During the period of the Brest Peace Treaty, Kosior joined the "left communists" in opposing the negotiations with the Central Powers.

In 1918, Kosior was one of the organizers of the Communist Party of Ukraine. In March of this year, he was appointed the people's commissar of finance of Ukraine, and the following month he was a member of the Organizing Bureau of the first congress of the CP(b)U. In August 1918, he led underground party work in regions of Ukraine occupied by German troops. From November 1918 to February 1919, he was secretary of the underground Right Bank (Kyiv) Regional Committee of the CPU(b).

From May 1919 to December 1920, Kosior was secretary of the Central Committee of the Communist Party (Bolsheviks) of Ukraine (CC CPU). In July–December 1919, he also headed the Front Bureau of the CC CPU. In 1920, he commanded the Caucasian Army of Labor (Kavtrudarmia) and supervised the eviction of the Terek Cossacks from the Mountain Autonomous Soviet Socialist Republic. From 1922 to 1925, he was secretary of the Siberian Bureau of the Central Committee of the RCP(b). In 1924, he became a member of the CC CPSU. From 1925 to 1928, Kosior was a member of the Orgburo and a secretary of the CC CPSU. In January 1928, Kosior supervised the expulsion of **L. D. Trotsky** to Alma-Ata.

From 1928 to 1938, Kosior held the position of general (first) secretary of the CC CPU, replacing **Lazar Kaganovich**, who was recalled to Moscow. Kosior was an active supporter of Stalin's policies in Ukraine. Under Kosior's leadership, collectivization was carried out at an accelerated pace. He was one of the main culprits of the mass famine in Ukraine (1932–1933). Knowing about the impending famine, he sent calming reports to Moscow, though he was under great pressure to fulfill grain procurement quotas. In 1935, ironically, he received the Order of Lenin "for outstanding achievements in agriculture." In January 1938, he became deputy chairman of the Council of People's Commissars of the USSR and chairman of the Soviet Control Commission. During this period, Kosior was one of those who signed so-called Stalinist execution lists during the Great Purge. He personally signed five such documents.

On May 3, 1938, Kosior was stripped of all party posts and arrested. He was charged with belonging to the so-called "Polish Military Organization." On February 26, 1939, he was sentenced to death and executed the same day by **Vasily Blokhin**.

After Stalin's death, Kosior was rehabilitated by the Soviet government on March 14, 1956. On January 13, 2010, the Kyiv Court of Appeal in Ukraine recognized Kosior as one of the organizers of the "genocide in Ukraine in 1932–1933." He is depicted as such at the Museum of the Holodomor Memorial in Kyiv.

KOSYGIN, ALEKSEI NIKOLAEVICH (1904–1980). Kosygin was a Soviet statesperson and party leader, member of the Communist Party from 1927, candidate member of the Politburo of the CC CPSU (1946–1953, 1957–1960), deputy of the Supreme Soviet of the USSR (1946–1980), chairman of the Council of Ministers of the USSR (1964–1980), and two-time hero of socialist labor (1964, 1974). He was born in Saint Petersburg into a working-class Russian family. His father, Nikolai Ilich, worked as turner at the St. Petersburg mine and torpedo plant "Lesner." His mother, Matrona Aleksandrovna, died when he was a child.

At the age of 15, Aleksei, at that time a student of the Petrovsky Real School, voluntarily joined the Red Army. After three years of service, he returned to Petrograd and finished his studies. After graduation from a cooperative technical school, the young specialist went to Siberia to participate in the development of industrial cooperation. In October 1925, the Novosibirsk organization of the Communist Party accepted Kosygin as a candidate member of the party on a two-year term.

In 1928, on the initiative of the first secretary of the Siberian Regional Committee of the CPSU, **R. I. Eikhe**, Kosygin was invited to Novosibirsk, where he worked as the head of the planning department of the Siberian Regional Union of Consumer Cooperation. In 1930, on his return to Leningrad, Kosygin enrolled at the Leningrad Textile Institute, from which he graduated in 1935. Even before graduation, he started to work as a foreman at the Zheliabov Textile Factory. From 1937 to 1938, he was director of the Oktiabrskia factory in Leningrad.

In 1938, at the behest of **A. Zhdanov**, Kosygin was appointed head of the Industrial and Transport Department of the Leningrad Oblast Committee of the CPSU. During the same year, he became the chairman of the Leningrad City Executive Committee. On January 2, 1939, he headed the People's Commissariat of Light Industry.

On March 21, 1939, at the 18th CC CPSU congress, Kosygin was elected a member of the Central Committee and was appointed people's commissar of the textile industry of the USSR, a position he held until 1940. In April 1940, he was appointed deputy chairman of the Council of People's Commissars of the USSR and chairman of the Council on Consumer Goods under the Council of People's Commissars of the USSR.

During the **Great Patriotic War**, Kosygin served as chairman of the Council of People's Commissars of the RSFSR (1943–1946). In June 1941, Stalin appointed him deputy chairman of the Council for the Evacuation of Industrial Enterprises. Kosygin helped to lead a team of inspectors that evacuated more than 1,500 of the country's strategically important factories to the east. On October 25, 1941, he joined the committee dealing with the evacuation of food, raw materials, industrial goods, equipment for refrigerators, textile, clothing, tobacco factories and soap factories, raw tobacco and makhorka, soap, and soda from the frontline zone.

From January to July 1942, during the Leningrad Blockade, Kosygin was responsible for organizing food supplies for the besieged city. At the same time, he supervised the evacuation of civilians. Also, he headed the construction of an ice road ("Road of Life") and a pipeline across Lake Ladoga and participated in the work of local Soviet Party bodies and the Military Council of the Leningrad Front. On August 23, 1942, he was appointed commissioner of the Central Committee of the CC CPSU and the Council of People's Commissars of the USSR for procurement of local types of fuel. From June 23, 1943, he was chairman of the Council of People's Commissars of the RSFSR (from March 15, 1946, the Council of Ministers of the RSFSR). In 1944, he headed the Currency Committee, which included the ministers of foreign trade and finance, the State Control, and the chairman of the State Bank.

Stalin liked Kosygin and gave him a friendly nickname—"Kosyga" (scythe). After the war, Kosygin's career made further progress. In 1945, he was appointed chairman of the Operations Bureau of the Council of People's Commissars of the RSFSR and was involved in the work of the Special (Atomic) Committee (a body created in the USSR 14 days after the atomic bombing of Hiroshima and aimed to expedite the creation of nuclear weapons to maintain parity between the USSR and the United States).

On March 19, 1946, Kosygin served as deputy chairman of the Council of Ministers of the USSR and was elected a candidate member of the Politburo of the CC CPSU. During the famine of 1946–1947, he supervised the supply of food aid to the most affected regions. In February 1948, Kosygin was elected a member of the Politburo of the CC CPSU. From February 16 to December 28, 1948, he worked as minister of finance of the USSR and from December 1948 to March 1953, he was minister of light industry of the USSR. Simultaneously, from 1948 to 1953, Kosygin was appointed a member of the Bureau of the Council of Ministers of the USSR. On February 7, 1949, he also became chairman of the Bureau of Trade of the USSR (under the Council of Ministers of the USSR). In 1951, Kosygin headed a commission that considered the question of dissolving the Moscow Institute of Physics and Technology of Moscow State University. On October 16, 1952, he was elected a candidate member to the Presidium of the Central Committee of the CPSU.

Immediately after Stalin's death, during a large-scale reshuffle in the highest echelons of power, Kosygin lost his post as deputy chairman of the Council of Ministers of the USSR. He was also removed from the list of the candidates for membership in the Presidium of the Central Committee of the CPSU. From March 15 to August 24, 1953, Kosygin worked as minister of light and food industry of the USSR, and then from August 24, 1953, to February 23, 1954, minister of industrial consumer goods of the USSR. In December 1953 Kosygin was once again appointed deputy chairman of the Council of Ministers of the USSR, a term he served from February 1954 to December 1956. On December 25, 1956, he was appointed first deputy chairman of the State Economic Commission of the Council of Ministers of the USSR for the current planning of the national economy. On May 23, 1957, he was appointed first deputy chairman of the USSR State Planning Committee (Gosplan).

In 1957, he was approved as a member of the Main Military Council under the Defense Council of the USSR. In June 1957 he was elected a candidate member to the Presidium of the Central Committee of the CPSU.

In June 1957, **Khrushchev**'s personal support allowed Kosygin to return to the Presidium of the Central Committee (June 29, 1957–May 4, 1960). From March 20, 1959, to May 4, 1960, Kosygin was chairman of the USSR State Planning Committee. In 1959, he was a member of the Council of Defense of the USSR. On March 24, 1959, he was also appointed representative of the USSR in the Council for Mutual Economic Assistance (*Comecon*). On May 4, 1960, Kosygin was elected a member of the Presidium of the CC CPSU. In May 4, 1960, he became the first deputy chairman of the Council of Ministers of the USSR, thus combining party and government positions.

In October 1964, Kosygin supported the conspiracy that removed Khrushchev from office. From October 15, 1964, to October 23, 1980, he was chairman of the Council of Ministers of the USSR, with **L. I. Brezhnev** occupying the leading party role and amassing increasing power. Kosygin held this post for 16 years, the longest period of any holder of the role. In 1965 Kosygin initiated economic reforms in industry. He advocated the decentralization of the national economy and the greater independence of enterprises. The reforms began well but were not brought to their logical conclusion.

Kosygin was a brilliant diplomat who was able to quickly solve various international problems. With his direct participation, the Arab–Israeli conflicts of 1967 and 1973 were resolved. He helped to bring about an end to American bombing of Indochina in the early 1970s. His main diplomatic victory was the resolution of the long-standing Soviet–Chinese conflict. Thus, his career blossomed after the death of Stalin as he assumed one of the leading roles in the state.

In October 1980, Kosygin was hospitalized, and the same day he wrote a brief letter of resignation. He died on December 18, 1980.

KRESTINSKY, NIKOLAI NIKOLAEVICH (1883–1938). An Old Bolshevik, Soviet statesperson and politician, diplomat, member of the CPSU since 1903, member of the Politburo of the Central Committee of the RCP(b), member of the Organizational Bureau (Orgburo) of the Central Committee of the RCP(b), secretary of the Central Committee of the RCP(b), and member of the Central Committee of the Party, Krestinsky was born in Mogilev (today Mahiliou, Belarus) into the family of a teacher. In 1901, he graduated with a gold medal from the Vilna gymnasium and in 1907 from the Law Faculty of St. Petersburg University. After graduation he worked as an assistant and attorney at law. He became a member of the RSDWP in 1903, and formally joined the Bolshevik faction in 1905. From 1906, Krestinsky represented the Northwestern Regional Committee of the RSDWP in the Central Committee. He conducted party work in Vitebsk (Viciebsk), Kovno, Vilna (Vilnius), and St. Petersburg, and was arrested several times. In 1908–1914, he was a legal adviser to a number of trade unions and Social Democratic factions in the third and fourth State Dumas. In 1912, he was nominated for elections to the State Duma of the fourth convocation in the city of St. Petersburg.

After the February Revolution of 1917, Krestinsky became the chairman of the Ural regional committee and deputy chairman of the Iekaterinburg city committee of the RSDWP(b). In August 1917, at the sixth congress of the RSDWP(b), he was elected a member of the Central Committee. During the October Revolution of 1917, Krestinsky was appointed chairman of the Iekaterinburg Military Revolutionary Committee. He was an active participant in the struggle for the establishment of Soviet power in the Urals. He was a member of the Constituent Assembly on the Bolshevik list. In 1918, he was appointed member of the Board of the People's Commissariat of Finance of the RSFSR, deputy chief commissar of the People's Bank of the RSFSR, and commissioner of justice of the Petrograd Labor Commune and the Union of Communes of the Northern Region. During the conclusion of the Brest-Litovsk Peace

Treaty in 1918, he joined the "left communists" who wanted to continue the war against the Central Powers. On March 25, 1919, Krestinsky was elected to the first Politburo. Simultaneously, he became a member of the Central Committee's Secretariat and served as responsible secretary of the Central Committee until 1921. In 1920, during a discussion about the role of trade unions, together with L. Serebriakov and E. Preobrazhensky, he supported the platform of L. D. Trotsky. Because of this, during the tenth congress (1921), he was removed from the Central Committee and Politburo, vacating his post first for Molotov and then for Stalin.

In October 1921, he was appointed ambassador to Germany. During 1923–1926, Krestinsky supported the **Left Opposition** against Stalin. In 1927, however, he distanced himself from Trotsky. In 1930–1937, Krestinsky was deputy and first deputy people's commissar of foreign affairs of the USSR. From March to May 1937, he was the first deputy people's commissar of justice of the USSR.

During the Great Terror, he was arrested. Krestinsky was accused of having connections with Trotsky and with German intelligence, and of preparing terrorist acts against the party leadership. He was sentenced to death and shot on March 15, 1938. In July 1963 he was rehabilitated.

KRIUCHKOV, PIOTR PETROVICH (1889–1938). A lawyer, publisher, personal secretary, and attorney of the writer **Maksim Gorky**, director of the Gorky Museum, and one of the defendants of the Case of the Anti-Soviet "Bloc of Rights and Trotskyites," Piotr Kriuchkov was born in Perm. His father, Piotr Petrovich Kriuchkov, a native of St. Petersburg, graduated from the Kazan Veterinary Institute in 1887 and served as a city veterinarian. Before the revolution, Piotr's father was a magistrate, zemstvo chief (1903), and inspector of the Kazan Veterinary Institute. Piotr's mother, Maria Edmundovna (née Goebel), was the daughter of a Baltic German nobleman and French countess. Maria Edmundovna graduated from high school in Perm and received the title of city teacher of Russian and German. The Kriuchkov family had four children: a daughter and three sons.

Piotr Kriuchkov graduated from the Law Faculty of St. Petersburg University. For some time, he was an assistant to the attorney at law and served in the St. Petersburg city administration. Although he was not a revolutionary, he accepted the October Revolution (1917) and collaborated with the new government.

In early 1920s, Kriuchkov served as a representative of the Soviet trade office in Berlin for the book publishing society Kniga (Book). From 1927, he worked in the society "International Book," from where, with the assistance of actress Maria Andreieva, he was soon transferred to the state publishing house (Gosizdat). Kriuchkov collaborated with the GPU and with **G. Iagoda** personally.

For many years, Kriuchkov was the secretary of Maksim Gorky, whom he had known since 1918. As secretary, he was involved in organizing the publication of Gorky's works in the USSR and abroad, establishing meetings and contacts with various people and organizations. Gorky had complete faith in his secretary and highly appreciated Kriuchkov's business qualities, energy, speed, order, and organization. However, later, in Moscow, in 1931–1936, Kriuchkov was the organizer of the Soviet "golden cage" for Gorky—the provision of an impressive Moscow villa and constant manipulation through propaganda.

After Gorky's death (1936), Kriuchkov became a member of the "Commission for the Acceptance of Gorky's Literary Legacy and Correspondence" (formed by a resolution of the Politburo on June 18, 1936) and was appointed the first director of his archive. On February 14, 1937, by the decree of the Presidium of the Central Executive Committee of the USSR, he was approved as the director of the Gorky Museum in Moscow.

On October 5, 1937, Kriuchkov was arrested and prosecuted, along with twenty others, in the Third Moscow Trial. According to court materials, on behalf of Iagoda and along with doctors Lev Levin and Dmitry Pletnev, he had participated in a conspiracy to kill Gorky and his son. Kriuchkov and Levin were sentenced to death. Their personal property was confiscated. On March 15, 1938, Kriuchkov was executed at the Butovo training ground. In 1988, he was fully rehabilitated.

KRUGLOV, SERGEI NIKIFOROVICH (1907–1977).

A leader of the state security organs of the USSR, people's commissar (minister) of internal affairs of the USSR from 1945 to 1956, state security commissioner of the second rank (February 4, 1943), colonel general (July 9, 1945), member of the CPSU since December 1928, candidate member of the CC CPSU (1939–1952), member (1952–1956), and deputy of the Supreme Soviet of the USSR (1946–1958), Sergei Kruglov was born in a village in the Tver Governorate of the Russian Empire into a poor family of the local blacksmith. In 1924, he graduated from primary school. In June 1924, he became a secretary, and from December the chairman of the Nikiforovsky village council (Rzhevsky district, Tver province). In 1926–1928, he was a repair worker and a locksmith at the Vakhonino state farm in the same district. From 1928 to 1929, Kruglov was a member of the board and later a chairman of the board of the consumer society "Sozvezdie" (Tver province). In November 1929–December 1930, he served in the Red Army as a junior auto mechanic of the 3rd Tank Regiment in the Moscow Military District.

In 1934, Kruglov graduated from the Karl Liebknecht Institute in Moscow and in 1935 from the Japanese Department of the Soviet Institute of Eastern Cultures. He also studied in the History Department of the Institute of Red Professors but did not graduate. From December 1937, he was responsible organizer of the Department of Party Leading Bodies (ORPO) of the CC CPSU(b). He was fluent in English and Japanese.

In November 1938, Kruglov was appointed a special commissioner of the People's Commissariat of Internal Affairs. From February 1939 to February 1941, he served as deputy people's commissar of internal affairs of the USSR for personnel. Later, he became head of the Personnel Department of the NKVD of the USSR. From February 26 to July 31, 1941, and from April 26, 1943, to December 29, 1945, Kruglov was appointed first deputy, and from July 31, 1941, to April 26, 1943, deputy people's commissar of internal affairs of the USSR. During this period, GULAG and industrial departments of the NKVD were transferred to his jurisdiction. During the **Great Patriotic War**, Kruglov was sent to the front to organize a Blocking Detachment (*zagraditelnye otriady*) and strengthen discipline in the army. In July–October 1941, he was a member of the Military Council of the Reserve Front. Kruglov supervised arrests and executions in the army. In October 1941, he was appointed the commander of the 4th Sapper Army and the head of the 4th department of defensive work. In 1944–1945, he was in charge of mass deportations of the population, including Chechens and Ingushetians. For this operation he was awarded the Order of Suvorov of the first degree. These deportations were accompanied by violence against the population and mass executions of people (including children, women, and the elderly) without trial. In 1944, he carried out an operation against nationalist insurgents in the western regions of Ukraine. He also supervised the creation of "special prisons" for party activists. Kruglov organized the security of the Soviet delegation during the **Ialta** and **Potsdam** conferences and was awarded the Order of the British Empire and the American military award "the Legion of Merit."

In December 1945, Kruglov was appointed people's commissar of internal affairs of the USSR, and from March 1946 to March 1953, he carried the title of minister of internal affairs of the USSR. In 1939–1952, he was a candidate member, and in 1952–1956 he was a full member of the CC CPSU. In 1948, he organized the deportation of German population from the Kaliningrad region, the former East Prussia, annexed to the USSR after the end of the Second World War. As head of the minister of internal affairs of the USSR, Kruglov played a major role in providing the gulag prison labor for the Soviet nuclear program.

After Stalin's death, when the Ministry of Internal Affairs and the Ministry of State Security were united under the leadership of Beria, Kruglov was appointed first deputy of the minister of internal affairs. After Beria's arrest, on June 26, 1953, he became a minister. Until

March 13, 1954, when the KGB was separated from the Ministry of Internal Affairs, the entire punitive apparatus of the USSR was under Kruglov's jurisdiction.

N. S. Khrushchev decided not to leave such power in the hands of Beria's former subordinate, and on January 31, 1956, Kruglov was removed from the Ministry of Internal Affairs and transferred to the post of deputy minister of electric power-stations of the USSR. In July 1958, he was sent into retirement as an invalid. In 1959 he was deprived of his general's pension and evicted from an elite apartment. On June 6, 1960, he was expelled from the party for "gross violations of socialist legality." He spent the rest of his life in relative poverty. On July 6, 1977, he was reportedly hit by a train and died. Another source suggests he may have committed suicide.[7] He was buried in Moscow.

KRUPSKAIA, NADEZHDA KONSTANTINOVNA (1869-1939). Krupskaia was a Russian professional revolutionary, Soviet Party, public, and cultural figure, organizer and chief ideologist of Soviet education and communist education of youth, wife of the first chairman of the Council of People's Commissars of the USSR (Vladimir Ilich Lenin), doctor of pedagogical sciences, honorary member of the Academy of Sciences of the USSR (1931), member of the Presidium of the Supreme Soviet of the USSR, and member of the CC CPSU.

Nadezhda Krupskaia was born into impoverished noble family in St. Petersburg. Her father, Lieutenant Konstantin Ignatievich Krupski, a poor nobleman, retired officer, and collegiate assessor, participated in the Committee of Russian Officers and supported the participants of the Polish uprising of 1863. Her mother, Elizaveta Vasilevna Tistrova, daughter of mining engineer Vasily Ivanovich Tistrov, graduated from the Pavlovsk Military Orphanage Institute for Noble Maidens. In 1858, Elizaveta Vasilevna received a diploma of a home teacher and became the governess of three children of the landowner Rusanov in the Vilna province. The regiment, where the young officer Krupsky served, was in the neighborhood. Rusanov arranged parties, and at one such party Lieutenant Krupsky and Elizaveta Vasilevna met. Nadezhda was their only daughter. Nadezhda's father died at the age of forty-four from tuberculosis. Her mother, despite financial difficulties, assigned her daughter to the private Female Gymnasium of Princess A. A. Obolenskaia in St. Petersburg a (prestigious private girls' secondary school). According to one source,[8] Nadezhda graduated from gymnasium with a gold medal. But in her book *My Life*, Nadezhda wrote that it was always difficult and boring to study and difficult to understand material in the gymnasium.

After graduation, Nadezhda studied for a year at the Bestuzhev courses. During her studies, she joined students' revolutionary discussions and Marxist circles (*kruzhki*). From 1891 for five years (until her first arrest), she taught at a Sunday evening school and carried out propaganda among the workers. Nadezhda taught herself German in order to read Marx in the original. In 1894, a friend from one circle introduced her to Vladimir Ulianov (later known as Lenin). The future leader of the revolution was impressed by Nadezhda's faith in revolution and ability to convince others. Nadezhda, in turn, was impressed by his speeches. Together with him, she took part in the activities of the Union for the Struggle for the Liberation of the Working Class.

In December 1895, Lenin was arrested. Fellow revolutionaries instructed Krupskaia to communicate with him, visit him in prison, and send him books. On August 12, 1896, her house was searched, and she was arrested too. In March 1897, Krupskaia was released. In 1897, when Vladimir Ilich was arrested and exiled to Shushenskoe, he started to call Nadezhda his "fiancée" (this status allowed her to visit him). At the end of 1897, Krupskaia was exiled to Ufa. In order for her to be allowed to join him in Siberia, Ulianov proposed marriage. On July 10, 1898, Lenin and Krupskaia were married in a church. Their wedding rings were forged from copper pennies by exiled Finn Oscar Alexandrovich Engberg, who was once a jeweler's student (they did not wear them). Since Nadezhda Konstantinovna never parted with her mother, Elizaveta Vasilevna came to Siberia with her.

In 1898, Krupskaia joined the RSDWP. She was known under several party pseudonyms (Sablina, Lenina, N. K., Artamonova, Onegina, Ryba (fish), Lamprey, Rybkina, Sharko, Katia, Frey, Gallilei). Upon their release, the couple emigrated and settled in Munich, Germany. During this period, she became the secretary of the newspaper *Iskra* and participated in the preparation and holding of the congress of the RSDWP in London. In 1905, together with Lenin, she returned to Russia and became the secretary of the Central Committee. After the defeat of the Revolution of 1905 in Russia, they once again emigrated. Krupskaia worked as a teacher at the party school in Longjumeau near Paris. She became her husband's main assistant in all his endeavors, including as a personal secretary, assistant, and skillful text editor.

In the spring of 1917, Lenin and Krupskaia returned to Petrograd. She assisted Lenin before and during the October Revolution. After the victory of the October Revolution, Nadezhda Konstantinovna became a famous person in Soviet Russia. From 1917, Krupskaia was a member of the Vyborg District Council of Petrograd and the State Commission on Education and became an organizer of the Soviet preschool educational system. In 1920 she chaired the *Glavpolitprosvet* at the People's Committee of Education and initiated the creation of the "Friend of Children" society. She organized the proletarian youth movement and was involved in the creation of Komsomol and Pioneer movements.

Krupskaia is associated with the beginning of the development of the entire Soviet educational system. She formulated its fundamental premise: "School should not only teach, it should be the center of communist education." Krupskaia was awarded the academic degree of doctor of pedagogy. As an ideologist of Communist education, she criticized the pedagogical system developed by Anton Makarenko (after her speech at the Komsomol congress in May 1928 criticizing Makarenko, he was soon removed from the leadership of the Gorky colony). Krupskaia was also an activist of Soviet censorship and anti-religious propaganda. In the position of chairman of the *Glavpolitprosveta*, she sent out instructions for the removal of "ideologically harmful and obsolete literature" from public libraries. According to her instructions, Chekists had to be recruited for this task. On her order too, the works of Kant, Schopenhauer, Descartes, Leskov, Plato, and others were prohibited. Along with Trotsky, Krupskaia was considered one of the most powerful Bolshevik agitators, and the status of "Lenin's wife" began to denote not so much marital status as a state position.

From 1920, Lenin was increasingly ill and periodically lost consciousness. During such seizures, he appeared confused and disoriented, and his wife remained the only thread connecting the disabled leader with the outside world and Soviet power. Even during her husband's life, in 1922, Krupskaia had to face Stalin's rudeness. Allegedly, after this incident at the end of 1922, Lenin's "Letter to the Congress," his so-called will, appeared. In the testament Trotsky was called "the most capable in the Central Committee," and Bukharin "the favorite of the party." In the appendix drawn up in January 1923, Lenin stated directly that Stalin needed to be removed from the post of general secretary. In January 1924, when Lenin died, however, Stalin overcame at the helm and then successfully passed all competitors, and by the end of the 1930s, Lenin's will was declared to be a fake. Krupskaia was unable to exert much influence on the situation from the mid-1920s and gradually lost her exalted position in the state.

At the 14th congress of the All-Union Communist Party (Bolsheviks), which was held on December 18–31, 1925, in Moscow, Krupskaia supported the "new opposition"— **Grigory Zinoviev** and **Lev Kamenev**—in their struggle against Stalin, but later recognized this position as erroneous. In 1924, Krupskaia became a member of Central Control Commission of the CPSU, and in 1927 a member of the CC CPSU. In 1929, she was appointed deputy people's commissar of education of the RSFSR.

In the 1930s, she saw how persecutions began not only against "enemies of the people" but also against their children and tried to resist, but she was removed from her post and confined to library work. But even in this post, Krupskaya actively corresponded with pioneers and Soviet children. She initiated the opening of many museums in the USSR, including the Belinsky and Lermontov museums in Penza region. Until the end of her life, she remained a member of the Central Committee of the All-Union Communist Party of Bolsheviks, the All-Russian Central Executive Committee, and the Central Executive Committee of the USSR. In 1937, she was elected a deputy of the Supreme Soviet of the USSR of the first convocation. She also served as a member of the Presidium of the Supreme Soviet of the USSR. Nadezhda Konstantinova died suddenly on February 27, 1939, the day after her seventieth birthday.

KRYLENKO, NIKOLAI VASILEVICH (1885–1938). An Old Bolshevik, member of the Bolshevik Party since 1904, Soviet statesman and party leader, supreme commander-in-chief of the Russian Army after the October Revolution of 1917, candidate member of the Central Executive Committee of the USSR of the first through fourth convocations, member of the Central Control Commission of the CPSU in 1927–1934, and one of the organizers of mass repressions, Nikolai Krylenko was born in Bekhteievo, Sychyovsky Uezd, Smolensk Governorate, into the family of the populist revolutionary Vasily Abramovich, and his wife, Olga Aleksandrovna (née Tripetskaia). Vasily Abramovich, the son of a peasant, entered an underground student circle during his studies at St. Petersburg University and took part in the revolutionary student movement. For these activities he was expelled from the university and exiled to the village of Bekhteevka, Smolensk province. In 1890, Nikolai's family moved to Smolensk, where his father edited the opposition newspaper *Smolensky Vestnik*. In 1902, Nikolai's family moved first to Kielce, and then to Lublin, where his father worked as a tax collector.

At the age of ten, Nikolai began to study at the Lublin classical gymnasium, from which he graduated in 1903. This same year, he entered St. Petersburg University. While studying history and literature, he participated in student circles and took part in street demonstrations. In December 1904, Krylenko became a member of the Bolshevik Party. During the Russian Revolution of 1905, he was a member of the Bolshevik Committee of St. Petersburg. In 1906, Krylenko became an agitator for the Moscow committee of the RSDWP(b). In June 1906, he went abroad to Belgium and France for several months. In November, he returned to St. Petersburg, where he worked under the names "Renault," "Gurniak," and "Abramov." On June 5, 1907, he was arrested in St. Petersburg at the Creighton factory. After his release, he immediately left for Finland, where he took part in party work. Later he was arrested again. After serving a month in prison, on December 6, 1907, Krylenko was released for lack of evidence, and exiled to Lublin.

In the spring of 1909, Krylenko withdrew from party activities, finished his degree, and received a diploma. From 1911, he returned to Communist activity, working as an assistant editor for the Bolshevik newspapers *Zvezda* and *Pravda*. In 1911, Krylenko was sent to Krakow to meet Lenin. In 1912–1913, he served in the military as a volunteer in the 69th Ryazan Regiment. In 1913, he was discharged. On December 11, 1913, he was arrested again and exiled from St. Petersburg to Kharkiv for two years. During his exile, he earned a law degree. From Kharkiv, Krylenko and his wife emigrated first to Galicia and Vienna, later to Switzerland. In July 1915, by decision of the Central Committee of the party, N. V. Krylenko and his wife secretly returned to Russia and settled in Moscow. However, in November, both were arrested. Krylenko, as a draft dodger, was moved to Kharkiv, where he remained in prison until April 1916. After release, he was sent to the Southwestern Front.

After the February Revolution of 1917, he disseminated Bolshevik propaganda among soldiers, including the newspaper *Pravda*. He was elected chairman of the 11th Army's committee, and on May 3, he was delegated to Petrograd. In March 1917, Krylenko—together with N. I. Podvoisky, V. I. Nevsky, and other Bolsheviks—entered the military organization under the Petrograd Committee of the

RSDWP(b). In September–October 1917, the Bolsheviks, led by V. I. Lenin, began to intensively prepare for an armed seizure of power. On October 12, 1917, the Military Revolutionary Committee (MRC) was created in the Petrograd Soviet, including as members N. I. Podvoisky, V. A. Antonov-Ovseenko, N. V. Krylenko, and other leaders of the Bolshevik Party. Krylenko became one of the October uprising's leaders. At the Second All-Russian Congress of Soviets, he was elected to the first Soviet government as people's commissar and member of the Committee on Military and Naval Affairs (together with V. A. Antonov-Ovseenko and P. Ie. Dybenko). In November 1917, Krylenko was appointed commander in chief of the Soviet Army. His main task was to create the Armed Forces of the Soviet Republic. However, in the spring of 1918, according to Krylenko, due to "fundamental disagreements on the formation of the Red Army," he left the post and was transferred to the People's Commissariat of Justice of the RSFSR.

In the spring of 1918, Krylenko started organizing the work of the first revolutionary tribunals. He was a brilliant orator and polemicist and was fanatically devoted to the ideas of the revolution. He acted as the prosecutor in the trials of the English diplomat Bruce Lockhart, the provocateur Malinovsky, and left and right social revolutionaries, as well as in the cases of the former tsarist prosecutor Vipper, prison warden Bondar, Cheka employee Kosyrev, and many others. As Soviet prosecutor, he supported the accusation in all major counterrevolutionary and criminal cases of that time and earned a reputation as "the prosecutor of the proletarian revolution." The whole history of the formation of the organs of the Soviet prosecutor's office is inextricably linked with the name and activity of Krylenko. He was the author of the draft of the first Regulation on Prosecutor's Supervision. After the formation of the prosecutor's office, Krylenko was appointed to the post of senior assistant to the prosecutor of the Republic and simultaneously became deputy people's commissar of justice of the RSFSR. He held these positions until September 1928.

In 1931, Krylenko was appointed people's commissar of justice of RSFSR. He acted as a prosecutor at the main political trials, including the famous "Shakhty affair" (1928), the trial of the "Industrial Party" (1930), "the Trial of the Union Bureau of the Mensheviks" (1931), "the Glavtop Case," and "the Case of Polish Priests." In 1934, he was awarded the academic degree of doctor of state and legal sciences. From July 20, 1936, to January 15, 1938, Krylenko served as people's commissar of justice of the USSR. He actively fought against **Vyshinsky** and Vinokurov (chairman of the Supreme Court of the USSR) for influence in the system of judicial organs of the USSR. The result of this struggle was the victory of Vyshinsky's group and the prosecution of Krylenko and his supporters. In 1938, at the first session of the Supreme Soviet of the USSR of the first convocation, N. V. Krylenko was publicly criticized. On January 31, 1938, by order of the people's commissar of internal affairs of the USSR **Iezhov**, Krylenko was arrested and charged with connections with the right anti-Soviet organization, which was allegedly headed by Bukharin. On July 29, 1938, by the verdict of the Military Collegium of the Supreme Court of the USSR in the context of the case of "counterrevolutionary fascist-terrorist organization of climbers and tourists," Krylenko was shot by **Vasily Ulrich**. He was buried at the Kommunarka training ground.

On May 11, 1955, the USSR prosecutor general, R. A. Rudenko, sent a note on the rehabilitation of N. Krylenko to the CC CPSU. The Military Collegium of the USSR Supreme Court rehabilitated Krylenko on July 29, 1955. On October 7, 1955, by decision of the Party Control Commission, he was reinstated in the party.

KUBATKIN, PIOTR NIKOLAEVICH (1907–1950). An NKVD official who headed foreign intelligence as the head of the first Main Directorate of the USSR Ministry of State Security, lieutenant general, and deputy of the Supreme Soviet of the USSR of the first and second convocations, Piotr Kubatkin, a Russian by nationality, was born in the village of Kolberovsky, a coal mining region in Rostov province (today it is part of Luhansk region, Ukraine), into the family of a miner. In 1918, he graduated from a four-year primary rural school in the village of Orekhovo. From 1921 to 1927, he worked as a laborer in a Kolberovsky mine. In 1927–1929, he was involved in Komsomol activities.

In September 1929, Kubatkin was called up for military service and served in the border troops of the Joint State Political Directorate (OGPU). After demobilization in March 1932, he worked as an assistant to the operative officer of the Special Department of the Odessa Regional Department of the GPU. In 1934, he became deputy head of the Political Department. From 1935, Kubatkin headed the Frunzovsky District Branch of the People's Commissariat for Internal Affairs (NKVD) in Odesa Region. In March 1937, he began studies at the Central School of the NKVD of the USSR. On August 15, 1937, he graduated and started work in the central office of the Main Directorate of State Security of NKVD. In 1939, Kubatkin was appointed secretary of the Party Committee of the Directorate. In 1939–1941, he headed the State Security Department of the Moscow Region.

His career was facilitated by two circumstances: firstly, he had no pre-revolutionary party experience: he did not belong to any groups in Soviet political leadership, and did not take part in the "Red Terror" during the Civil War. Secondly, he was smart enough not to exhibit excessive "zeal" in the repression and therefore was able to "survive" both Iagoda and Iezhov's terms as leaders of Stalin's security service. In 1939, the "purges" in the Main Directorate apparatus began after the dismissal of Iezhov. Kubatkin avoided a thorough investigation of cases and did not consider appeals. Dozens of people ended up in Siberia or were executed because Kubatkin did not wish to peruse their personal files. On the other hand, he destroyed some documents discrediting a number of people from the new leadership of the NKVD since he did not want "high-profile cases" and "conflicts."

Soon after the outbreak of the German-Soviet war, when the threat of the blockade of Leningrad became a reality, Kubatkin was appointed head of the Leningrad Directorate of the NKVD (August 24, 1941). During the blockade, he launched a fierce struggle against those who expressed doubts about the actions of the party and the command. He also rooted out criminal elements and looters in the city, and exposed alleged spies and saboteurs. He coped with these problems with the help of specific measures. NKVD patrols shot on the spot violators of law and order or just suspicious citizens: for example, those who did not have documents or could not convincingly say where and why they were going. The practice of the death penalty for committing serious crimes was introduced. But very often people who happened to be near the scene of the incident were executed. All this could to some extent be justified by the military situation in the besieged city, but Kubatkin did not manage to eradicate prostitution, speculation, or serious crimes. There were also more complex problems that came with acute hunger—for example, cannibalism. The Criminal Code of the USSR did not contain an article on cannibalism. There were no trials for them. By the decision of Kubatkin, cannibals were taken out of the city and shot, and their bodies were dumped in Lake Ladoga.

In 1943, Kubatkin received the title of state security commissioner of the third rank. In September 1945, he was promoted to the post of the head of foreign intelligence (MGB first directorate) of the USSR. But on September 9 of the same year, he suddenly submitted a letter of resignation. Most likely, the reason was related to his health issues. He received the position of the head of the state security in Gorky region. In March 1949, he was dismissed. Kubatkin's health deteriorated, and he began to drink heavily. In July 1949, he was arrested and accused of "criminal non-reporting" about the activities of the arrested A. Kuznetsov, N. Voznesensky, and others allegedly involved in the **Leningrad affair**. Kubatkin refused to admit his guilt. In the fall of 1950, he was sentenced to twenty years in prison. But further investigations were extended 15 times, and a year later the case was finally revised. On October 27, 1950, the Military Collegium of the USSR Supreme Court sentenced Kubatkin to capital punishment. He was shot immediately. His mother, sister, wife, and son were arrested and imprisoned.

On March 17, 1954, his family members were rehabilitated, and two months later, on May 26, 1954, Kubatkin was also rehabilitated posthumously.

KUIBYSHEV, VALERIAN VLADIMIROVICH (1888–1935). A revolutionary, Soviet party and state leader, and one of the closest associates of and principal economic adviser to Stalin, Valerian Kuibyshev was born in Omsk into a Russian military family. His father, Vladimir Iakovlevich Kuibyshev, was a hereditary army man, a lieutenant colonel, and participant of the Russo-Japanese War of 1904–1905. His mother, Iulia Nikolaevna Kuibysheva (née Gladysheva), was a teacher. Soon after Valerian's birth, his family moved to the town of Kokchetav (now a city in northern Kazakhstan). In August 1898, ten-year-old Valerian returned to Omsk and was enrolled in the Siberian Cadet Corps. As the son of a military man, he received full government financial support. In 1903, Valerian became a member of the illegal Social Democratic circle. The first such circles had appeared in Omsk in 1896–1897. In the summer of 1904, while on vacation in Kokchetav, he received Social Democratic leaflets from Omsk and distributed them around the city. In 1904, at the age of 16, he joined the Russian Social Democratic Workers' Party (RSDWP).

In 1905, Kuibyshev graduated from the Omsk Cadet Corps and entered the St. Petersburg Military Medical Academy. In 1905, he organized the transportation and storage of weapons for workers' squads. In 1906, he was expelled from the academy for participating in a student strike and returned to Omsk, where he was elected a member of the local committee of the RSDWP. From March 1906, he conducted illegal revolutionary activities in Siberia, the Far East, the Volga region, and Ukraine. Kuibyshev was under constant police surveillance. He was arrested eight times and spent seven years in exile. From December 1914, he became a member of the Petrograd Committee of the RSDWP. In 1916, he was exiled to the Turukhansk region, but after the February Revolution of 1917, he was released.

In 1917, he became the leader of the Samara organization of the RSDWP and chaired both the Samara Revolutionary Committee and the provincial party committee. After the late 1917 elections, he was elected a member of the Constituent Assembly. In 1918, he was the chairman of the Samara Provincial Executive Committee. Kuibyshev criticized the conclusion of peace with Germany at Brest-Litovsk in March of this year. During the Russian Civil War, Kuibyshev chaired the revolutionary committee of Samara province and became a political commissar in the 1st and 4th Red Armies. From April 1919, he became a member of the Revolutionary Military Council of the Southern Group of the Eastern Front during the counteroffensive operation on the Eastern Front. In July 1919, together with S. Kirov, he led the defense of Astrakhan. From October 1919 to August 1920, Kuibyshev was deputy chairman of the All-Russian Central Executive Committee and the Central Committee of the RCP(b) for Turkestan affairs. At the same time, he was a member of the Revolutionary Military Council and headed the political administration of the Turkestan Front. In September 1920, he was appointed plenipotentiary in the Bukhara People's Soviet Republic. In December 1920, Kuibyshev became a member of the Presidium and head of the Economic Department of the All-Union Central Council of Trade Unions.

After the end of the Civil War, he held leading trade union posts. On March 13, 1921, by the decision of the RCP(b) Orgburo, Kuibyshev was sent to Samara as a representative of the Central Committee of the RCP(b). In April 1921, he became a member of the Presidium of the Supreme Council of the National Economy and from November the head of *Glavelektro*. At this post, he supervised practical implementation of the GOELRO plan (the first-ever Soviet plan for national economic recovery and development). In 1923–1926, Kuibyshev served as people's commissar of the Russian Federation and deputy chairman of the Council of People's Commissars of the Soviet Union and the Council of Labor and

Defense. In 1926, he chaired the Supreme Council of the National Economy. From 1927, he became a member of the Politburo of the CC CPSU. In November 1930, he was appointed chairman of the USSR State Planning Committee (Gosplan). Kuibyshev directly participated in developing the national economic plans of the first and second **Five-Year Plans**. From February 1934, he also chaired the Soviet Control Commission. He was one of Stalin's closest associates and his adviser on economic issues. Kuibyshev was one of the initiators of the first edition of the *Great Soviet Encyclopedia*.

On January 25, 1935, Kuibyshev died suddenly in his office. The official version of death was blockage by a thrombus of the right coronary artery of the heart. The body was cremated, and an urn with his ashes was interred in the Kremlin wall. In that same year, the city of Samara was renamed Kuibyshev in his honor, a name it retained until 1991, when it reassumed its original name.

KULIK, GRIGORY IVANOVICH (1890–1950). Kulik was a Soviet military commander and marshal of the Soviet Union, member of the CPSU (1917–1945), member of the CC CPSU (1939–1942), deputy people's commissar of defense of the USSR, and head of the Main Artillery Directorate of the Workers' and Peasants' Red Army, first rank commander.

Grigory Kulik was born in the village of Dudnikovo (now in the Poltava district of Ukraine) into a poor Ukrainian peasant family. He was the youngest of seven children. He graduated from the fourth grade of a rural school and was engaged in peasant labor in his parents' household. From November 1912, he served in the Russian Imperial Army. During the First World War, he received the rank of noncommissioned officer and commanded a platoon. He conducted revolutionary propaganda among soldiers and in June 1917 was arrested. After his release, he was transferred to the Romanian front. In October 1917, Kulik deserted and in November of the same year became a member of the RCP(b).

In November 1917, after returning from the front, he created a detachment of Red Guards in Poltava and fought against the *Haidamaks* and the Germans. As part of this detachment, he joined the 5th Red Army, commanded by **K. Voroshilov**. In March 1919, Kulik was appointed commissar of the Kharkiv province and head of the Kharkiv garrison and took part in the liquidation of several anti-Soviet rebellions. In particular, he led the suppression of Menshevik and Socialist Revolutionary Party uprisings in the cities of Belgorod, Sumy, and Kharkiv. In June 1920, he became chief of artillery in the **Budenny**'s First Cavalry Army. During the Civil War, Kulik was seriously wounded three times, lightly wounded twice, and shell-shocked twice. He participated in engagements against the troops of Denikin, Wrangel, and in the Soviet–Polish war (1919–1921). In 1921, he was awarded his second Order of the Red Banner. He received a third later in 1930, during commemoration of the anniversary of the defense of Tsaritsyn. After the end of the Civil War, Kulik remained in the army.

In 1924, Kulik graduated from the Higher Academic Courses for Command Staff and in 1932 from the Frunze Military Academy. From November 1932, he was appointed commander of the 3rd Rifle Corps. In 1936, under the pseudonym "General Cooper," Kulik, as a military adviser to the commander of the Madrid Front, took part in the Spanish Civil War. However, in May 1937, he returned to the USSR. From May 23 of the same year, at the suggestion of Stalin, he was appointed chief of the Main Artillery Directorate. Also, in March 1938–June 1941, he was a member of the Main Military Council of the Red Army. Kulik took part in hostilities against the Japanese at Khalkhin-Gol (1939) and in the Soviet–Finnish War (1939–1940). In March 1940, he received the Gold Star of the Hero of the Soviet Union.

At the beginning of the **Great Patriotic War** (1941–1945) Kulik was appointed deputy people's commissar of defense of the USSR for artillery. In June 1941, he was sent to the Western Front, but his unit was encircled, and he was fortunate to survive. In August–September 1941, he commanded the 54th Army on the Leningrad Front, which allowed Germans to break through to Lake Ladoga and later unsuccessfully tried to help the besieged Leningrad. On November 9, 1941, by personal order of Stalin, he was sent to Kerch to help the 51st Army. On November 12, Kulik was ordered to evacuate military equipment from Crimea, and on November 16, Kerch surrendered to the enemy. For these constant failures, Kulik was court-martialed and demoted to the rank of major-general.

On April 15, 1943, Kulik was repromoted to the rank of lieutenant general and appointed commander of the 4th Guards Army, which was part of the Steppe Military District. From October 1943, he worked at the Main Personnel Directorate. On November 3, 1944, he was awarded a fourth Order of the Red Banner, and on February 21, 1945, he was awarded the fourth Order of Lenin. His career had recovered. In January 1944, he was appointed deputy head of the Main Directorate for the formation and staffing of the Red Army. In the summer of 1945, he was appointed deputy commander of the Volga Military District. Yet on June 28, 1946, he was dismissed from his post and again demoted to the rank of major-general. The reason for this removal were his complaints and criticism of Nikolai Bulganin and Lavrenty Beria.

On January 11, 1947, Kulik was arrested. On August 24, 1950, he—together with the Hero of the Soviet Union Colonel-General V. Gordov—was found guilty of treason and sentenced to death. He was executed the same day.

On September 28, 1957, by a decree of the Presidium of the Supreme Soviet of the USSR, Kulik was posthumously restored to the rank of marshal and Hero of the Soviet Union.

KUN, BÉLA (BORN BÉLA KOHN) (1886–1938). A Hungarian Communist revolutionary and politician, one of the organizers of the Hungarian Communist Party, participant of the defense of Petrograd and the suppression of the Left SR revolt in Moscow (1918), people's commissar of foreign affairs and people's commissar of military affairs of the Hungarian Soviet Republic (1919), and a member of the Executive Committee of the International (1921), Béla Kohn was born in Szilágycseh, Transylvania, Kingdom of Hungary, the Austro-Hungarian Empire (today it is part of Romania). His father (Samu Kohn), an ethnic Jew, was a Transylvanian rural notary, and his mother Rosa Goldberger, also Jewish, converted to Calvinism (a religious Protestant minority in Catholic Hungary). Béla received his education at the Silvania Fogimnazium in Zilah and the famous Reformed kollegium (grammar school) in the city of Kolozsvar (now Cluj-Napoca, Romania). During his studies, he was awarded the prize for the best work in literature. After graduation from school, Béla studied at the Faculty of Law of Kolozsvar University. During his studies, Kun became acquainted with the activities of left-wing intellectuals in Budapest. In 1902, at the age of 16, he became a member of the Hungarian Social Democratic Party and participated in establishing the Transylvanian branch of the party. Also, he participated in the creation of Marxist student organizations. In 1904, Kun dropped out of university and started work as a journalist. In 1905, he led strikes at many industrial enterprises in Transylvania. In Kolozsvar, the strike led to bloody clashes with the police. For participating in strike activities, Kun was sentenced to thirty months in prison but served only 16. After his release in 1908, he took part in the leadership of the Social Democratic Party and the trade union movement in Kolozsvar. In 1913, he was elected a delegate to the party congress.

In 1914, with the outbreak of the First World War I, Kun was drafted into the army and sent to the front. In 1916, his unit surrendered to the Russians and was sent to a prisoner of war camp in the Urals. In February 1917, Kun joined the Bolshevik Party. He became one of the organizers of the Red Guard and recruited Hungarian and Romanian (mostly mercenaries) former prisoners of war into its ranks. During 1918, these Hungarian units under Kun's supervision, were used for punitive purposes. In July 1918, Kun's mercenaries were used during suppression of the Left SR uprising in Moscow and against peasant uprisings in the Saratov and Samara provinces. It is impossible to establish the exact number of those killed by Kun's troops, but the count was in the thousands. Kun participated in the executions of hostages and "class enemies" in Siberia and became known as one of the bloodiest Bolshevik executioners.

In November 1918, after meeting with Lenin, Kun departed for Budapest. Lenin instructed him to lead the Hungarian communists. He headed the Central Committee of the Hungarian Communist Party and on March 21, 1919, Hungary was proclaimed a Soviet republic. Bela Kun formally held the post of foreign affairs commissar, but de facto became the head of the country's government. He prohibited all opposition parties and closed all non-communist newspapers. He also organized the expropriation of all property of the bourgeoisie and landowners. Famine broke out in Hungary and people tried to leave the country. But Kun announced the death penalty for those trying to leave the "socialist fatherland." On June 24, 1919, Kun, following Lenin's demands, announced the beginning of the "Red Terror" in Hungary. Initially, 590 people were executed in Budapest. Matyas Rakosi was among Kun's assistants. Soon after the start of the terror, the offensive of the Romanian, French, and Czechoslovak troops began. The Bolsheviks were unable to provide Hungary with military assistance, and the Hungarian Soviet Republic fell. Kun fled to Soviet Russia.

In October 1920, during the Russian Civil War, Kun was appointed a member of the Revolutionary Military Council of the Southern Front. On November 16, 1920, the Crimean Revolutionary Committee was formed, with Kun as its leader. Together with R. Zemliachka, Iu. Piatakov, and other members of the Revolutionary Committee, he became the organizer of the Red Terror on the peninsula, and up to 120,000 people were executed in Crimea on his initiative.

In 1921, Kun became a member of the Executive Committee of the **Comintern**. In this post, he was sent by Trotsky to Germany, where he tried to start a communist uprising but failed. In 1921–1923, Kun was a member of the Uralburo in Iekaterinburg and head of the Agitprop department of the regional Bureau of the RCP(b). From July 1924, Kun was in charge of the Agitprop Department of the Executive Committee of the Comintern and was a member of the Central Committee of the Communist Party of Hungary. In April 1928, he was arrested in Vienna for revolutionary activities and was threatened with extradition to the Hungarian military regime (in Hungary, Kun was denounced as a war criminal and put on the international wanted list). He was released after two months and returned to Moscow.

In 1928, when Trotsky lost the struggle for power in the Kremlin, Stalin kept Kun at a distance. After 1933, when Hitler came to power in Germany, Kun began to create serious difficulties for Stalin. His presence in the USSR was one of the main arguments in favor of Hungary's alliance with Hitler. All Stalin's attempts to improve Soviet–Hungarian relations were thwarted as a result.

In 1937, during the Great Terror, Kun was arrested, accused of Trotskyism, and executed on August 29, 1938. In 1955, he was rehabilitated.

KUZNETSOV, ALEKSEI ALEKSANDROVICH (1905–1950). A member of the Communist Party from 1925, member of the Central Committee (1939–1949), member of the Organizing Bureau of the Central Committee (1946–1949), first secretary of the Leningrad Regional Committee of the CPSU and the City Party Committee (1945–1946), secretary of the Central Committee (1946–1949), and lieutenant general, Aleksei Kuznetsov was a protégé of Lieutenant General A. Zhdanov, one of the organizers of the defense of Leningrad, a member of the military councils of the Northern and Leningrad fronts and the Baltic Fleet during the **Great Patriotic War** (1941–1945). On his wife's side (Zinaida Voinova), Kuznetsov was a relative of **A. Kosygin**.

Kuznetsov, an ethnic Russian, was born in Borovichi (now Novgorod Oblast, Russia) into a worker's family. In 1922, he began his working career as a sorting worker at a sawmill in Borovichi. In 1924–1932, he held different posts in the Komsomol organization of Novgorod province and in Leningrad. In 1925, he became a member of the CPSU. From 1932, he performed party duties in

Leningrad and worked as an instructor of the Leningrad City Committee, and as a deputy secretary and secretary of the district party committees in Leningrad, and head of the regional committee department. In 1938, **A. Zhdanov** appointed Kuznetsov second secretary of the Leningrad City Committee of the CPSU. In this post, Kuznetsov joined a Special troika (NKVD) and participated in Stalin's repressions. In December 12, 1937, Kuznetsov was elected deputy of the Supreme Soviet of the USSR of the 1st and 2nd convocations and by 1939, he was a member of the CC CPSU.

During the **Great Patriotic War** (1941–1945), Kuznetsov was one of the organizers of the defense of Leningrad. He was appointed a deputy chairman of the Commission for the Defense of Leningrad, and chairman of the Commission for the Creation of Fortifications around Leningrad and the Food Commission. He was also a member of the military councils of the Baltic Fleet, Northern and Leningrad Fronts, and the 2nd Shock Army. In 1943, for his work during the siege, he was promoted to lieutenant general.

After the war, Kuznetsov was involved in the atomic project of the USSR. Because of his efforts and those of the director of the Radium Institute V. Khlopin, the institute received additional premises. In 1945–1946, Kuznetsov served as the first secretary of the Leningrad Regional Committee and the City Party Committee. From March 18, 1946, to March 6, 1949, he was a member of the Orgburo of the CC CPSU. Simultaneously, from March 18, 1946, to January 28, 1949, Kuznetsov served as a secretary of the Central Committee. In 1919–1949 he also headed the Personnel Department of the CC CPSU. In June 1947, Kuznetsov attended the Philosophical Discussion, organized by A. Zhdanov.

On August 13, 1949, Kuznetsov—together with M. Rodionov (chairman of the RSFSR Council of Ministers) and P. Popkov (first secretary of the Leningrad Regional Committee and the City Committee of the VKP[b])—was arrested on false accusations of misuse of the Soviet state budget for "unapproved business in Leningrad," which was labeled as anti-Soviet treason. Within the scope of the "**Leningrad case**," the leaders of the Leningrad Regional Committee of the All-Union Communist Party were accused of trying to form a Russian Communist Party to counterbalance the All-Union Party and begin a confrontation with the CC CPSU. On September 30, 1950, by the decision of the Military Collegium of the Supreme Court of the USSR, Kuznetsov was sentenced to death and was shot on October 1 of the same year.

On April 30, 1954, Kuznetsov was rehabilitated by the same body. On February 26, 1988, the Central Control Commission of the Communist Party of the Soviet Union restored Kuznetsov's Party membership.

KWIRING, EMANUEL IONOVICH (1888–1937). A Soviet statesman, representative of the Volga Germans, doctor of economics (1934), and an economist in the State Planning Committee (Gosplan), Emanuel Kwiring was born into a family of German colonists in Friesenthal, in the Samara Governorate of the Russian Empire (present-day Novolipovka, Saratov Oblast, Russia), where his father worked as a local clerk. In his early years, he became a socialist activist. His first acquaintance with Marxist ideology was derived from the local zemstvo doctor: a young Bulgarian student. In 1906, Kwiring obtained a job in a pharmacy in Saratov. There, he participated in the League of Assistance to the Trade Union. In 1912, he moved to the capital city and entered the St. Petersburg Polytechnic Institute, where he studied at the Department of Commercial Economics. In December 1912, Kwiring joined the staff of *Pravda* and became a member of the Bolshevik Party. In 1913–1914, he was elected a secretary of the Bolshevik faction in the Duma. In 1914, the tsarist authorities arrested Kwiring and sent him into exile in Iekaterinoslav (later Dnipropetrovsk, today Dnipro, Ukraine).

In Ukraine, Kwiring was an active participant in revolutionary activities. At the end of 1917, he headed the Iekaterinoslav Soviet of Workers' and Soldiers' Deputies and was responsible for the normalization of the situation in the city. Between 1917 and 1918, he served as chairman of the Iekaterinoslav committee of the RSDWP(b), chairman of the Iekaterinoslav Military Revolutionary Committee, and chairman of the Iekaterinoslav Soviet. Kwiring was an active participant in the creation of the Communist Party of Ukraine as an integral part of the unified RCP(b) and criticized the idea of creation of a separate Ukrainian Communist Party. Later, he was appointed chairman of the Supreme Soviet of the National Economy of the Ukrainian SSR and became a member of the Provisional Workers' and Peasants' Government of Ukraine. During peace talks in Riga (1920), which preceded the signing the Peace of Riga with Poland, Kwiring was a member of the Ukrainian delegation.

In 1923–1925, Kwiring was appointed the first secretary of the CC CPU. Subsequently, he was transferred to Rostov-on-the-Don. After Lenin's death in 1924, he supported **G. Zinoviev**, **L. Kamenev** and Stalin in their fight against **Trotsky**. Kwiring actively helped in the elimination of one of the main Ukrainian Trotskyists—**G. Rakovsky**. When the "New Opposition" of Zinoviev and Kamenev tried to change the balance of power within the party in their favor, they decided to win over Kwiring. In January 1925, Kwiring, who arrived with other Ukrainian Communists in Moscow at the Plenum of the Central Committee of the RCP, was invited to meet Zinoviev. At this meeting, they discussed the removal of Stalin from the post of general secretary. Kwiring remained silent about his agreement with Zinoviev and Kamenev. However, Stalin's associates became aware of the meeting on the following day. In April 1925, a plenum of the CC CPU organized a meeting of the Politburo, at which the question of Kwiring's removal from his post was discussed. On March 20, 1925, Kwiring tendered his resignation from the post of the first secretary of the Central Committee. Another reason for his resignation was the criticisms of the perceived passive implementation of Ukrainization under his leadership.

In 1927–1931, Kwiring served as deputy chairman of the State Planning Committee of the USSR (Gosplan) and deputy people's commissar of railways of the USSR. In 1934–1937, he became a director of the Economic Institute of the Communist Academy at the Central Executive Committee of the USSR.

On October 16, 1937, Kwirling was arrested. On November 26, 1937, he was sentenced to death by the Military Collegium of the Supreme Court of the USSR and shot the same day. His body was cremated in the Donskoi Monastery.

On March 14, 1956, he was rehabilitated by the Military Collegium of the USSR Supreme Court.

NOTES

1. See, for example, "Kamenev, Sergei Sergeievich," *Muzei istory Rossiiskogo kadetstva*, http://cadethistory.ru/kamenev-sergey-sergeevich.
2. A. V. Ganin, "Otsy-osnovateli RKKA," in *Povsednevnaya zhyzn genshtabistov pri Lenine i Trotskom* (Moscow: Kuchkovo pole, 2016), 111.
3. Ibid.
4. N. S. Khrushchev, *Vospominanya*, vol. 1 (Moscow, Moskovskie Novosti: 1999), http://lib.ru/MEMUARY/HRUSHEW/wospominaniya1.txt.
5. For example: Oleg Khlevnyuk, *Politbiuro: Mekhanizm politicheskoi vlasti v 1930-e gody* (Moscow: ROSSPEN, 1996), 120–21.
6. P. A. Sudoplatov, "Ubiystvo Kirova. Mify i politicheskiye spekulyatsii," in *Spetsoperatcii. Lubyankai Kreml 1930–1950 gody* (Moscow: OLMA-PRESS, 1997), www.lib.ru/POLITOLOG/SUDOPLATOW/specoperacii.txt_with-big-pictures.html.
7. Jeanne Vronskaya and Victor Chuguev, eds., *A Biographical Dictionary of the Soviet Union* (Munich: K. G. Saur, 1992), 375.
8. S. U. Manbekova, "Molodye gody," in *Naslednitsa: stranitsy zhyzni N.K.Krupskoi* (Leningrad: Lenizdat, 1990), 55.

L

LAZURKINA, DORA ABRAMOVNA (1884–1974). A professional revolutionary, Russian political activist, Old Bolshevik, devoted Leninist, longtime member of the RSDWP (1902), teacher, director of the preschool division of the People's Commissariat for Education (1918–1922), director of the Herzen State Pedagogical University, publicist, and memoirist, Dora Lazurkina used the nickname "Comrade Sonia."

She was born in Novozybkov, Chernigov province (currently in Briansk Oblast, Russia), into a Jewish family. Her father was a forester. At the age of nine, she entered the Novozybkovskaia women's gymnasium, from which she graduated with a gold medal. At the age of 15, she joined the local Social Democratic circle. N. Chernyshevsky's *What Is to Be Done?* and E. Voynich's *The Gadfly* were her favorite books. In 1900–1902, Lazurkina enrolled in the courses of Peter Lesgaft, a specialist in physical training, in St. Petersburg. During her studies, Dora became an active participant in student revolutionary circles and read Marx's *Capital* and Lenin's articles. She was engaged in propaganda work among the workers and distributed the newspaper *Iskra*.

In 1902, she joined the RSDWP and adopted the pseudonym Sonia. In May, she was arrested for preparing a May Day demonstration and spent eight months in prison. After her release, Lazurkina was exiled under police supervision to Novozybkov. She left her native town for Odesa, where she changed her name and became a professional revolutionary. In 1903, she was arrested and imprisoned again. Seven months later, she was released on bail without the right to return to the capital for a period of five years. In Odesa, she met Mikhail Semenovich Lazurkin (party pseudonym: Boris), a professional revolutionary and her future husband.

In 1904, after another release from arrest, Sonia left for Geneva, where she met Lenin for the first time. For eight months she lived in the Ulianovs' apartment. On January 10, 1905, just after the Bloody Sunday events in St. Petersburg, on Lenin's instructions, she returned first to St. Petersburg, and then to Odesa, where she became a liaison officer with the Foreign Bureau of the Central Committee of the RSDWP. She was arrested by the police and exiled to the Arkhangelsk province, from where she was able to escape. Between 1905 and 1907, she was arrested several times. After 1908, Lazurkina graduated from Frobel's Pedagogical Institute. After graduation, she began to engage in pedagogical work and campaigned to raise money for the Bolshevik press.

After the February Revolution of 1917, Lazurkina became a member of the Petrograd Committee of the RSDWP(b) and the Petrograd Central City Duma, and was elected a delegate to the seventh (April) All-Russian Conference of the RSDWP(b). Among her personal friends were such prominent party leaders as **N. Krupskaia, F. Dzerzhinsky, S. Kirov, G. Ordzhonikidze,** and **A. Lunacharsky.**

In December 1918, Lazurkina was transferred to the People's Commissariat of Education as the head of the Preschool Department.

In this post, she became a member of the State Commission on Public Education. In 1928, Lazurkina was appointed director of the Leningrad State Pedagogical Institute named after A. Herzen. In 1932–1934 she worked as deputy secretary of the Leningrad Party Control Commission. After Kirov's murder, she was expelled from the party but later was reinstated. In 1934–1937, she headed the Department of Schools of the Leningrad city committee of the CPSU.

On August 8, 1937, Lazurkina was arrested by the NKVD. Her husband was expelled from the party, arrested, and died under suspicious circumstances in a NKVD prison (he was shot by an investigator during the interrogation, and then thrown out into the street in order to fake a suicide). For "participation in a counterrevolutionary organization," she was initially sentenced to five years in exile, but on November 10, 1939, she was sentenced to eight years of forced labor camps. In 1955, she was released after spending a total of eighteen years in camps, prisons, and exile. The same year, she and her husband were rehabilitated. During the years of imprisonment, she became mentally ill. Until the end of her life, she suffered from nightmares about tortures and surveillance.

In 1956, Lazurkina became a state pensioner (*pensioner soyuznogo znacheniya*), and in the following year, the fiftieth anniversary of the revolution, she was awarded the Order of Lenin. In 1961, she was elected a delegate to the twenty-second congress of the CPSU. During the congress, Lazurkina supported the proposal to remove Stalin's body from the mausoleum. In her speech, she recounted that she had a dream in which Lenin told her he did not want to lie next to Stalin's body.

On January 24, 1974, exactly fifty years after the death of her revered Lenin, Dora Lazutkina died in Leningrad at the age of 90. She was buried in the Bogoslovskoe Cemetery in Leningrad (now St. Petersburg).

LENINGRAD AFFAIR. The Leningrad Affair (also known as the Leningrad Case) concerns a series of arrests in the late Stalin era, reportedly engineered by **G. Malenkov** and **L. Beria** against leading figures in the Leningrad party organization. These leaders were accused of a number of crimes, most specifically wishing to promote the city of Leningrad over the city of Moscow, wishing to glorify the survivors of the Siege of Leningrad, seeking to establish the city as the leading one of the RSFSR, and supporting the establishment of a Russian Communist Party as a rival to the CPSU. The initial catalyst appears to have been a trade fair held in January 1949, organized by the city's party leaders—Piotr Popkov and Aleksei Kuznetsov—and the head of the State Planning Committee of the USSR, **N. Voznesensky**. It resulted in the arrest of about two thousand leading figures from the Leningrad City and Oblast party committees, leading industrial managers, as well as members of the scientific and educational elite and their replacement with officials from Moscow. In addition to Voznesensky, chairman of the Russian government Mikhail Rodionov, Kuznetsov, Popkov, P. G. Lazutin, and Ia. F. Kapustin were executed on October 1, 1950, for taking funds from the state budget for the promotion of Leningrad, which was declared an act of treason. In the background to the case was the history of the party leadership in the city, which had been run by Stalin's rival, **G. Zinioviev**, until his demotion in 1926, the aftermath of the assassination of **S. Kirov**, which had started the **Great Terror**, and the prominence until his death in 1948 of **A. Zinoviev**. In short, Beria and Malenkov, with the assistance of **V. Abakumov** and the MGB, used the opportunity to remove some rivals. Those accused were rehabilitated after the twentieth party congress, but their gravesites were never uncovered. Moreover, the files relating to the trials have yet to be declassified by the Russian Federation, so there is much that is still unknown.

LEVIN, LEV GRIGOREVICH (1870–1938). A physician, doctor of medical sciences, professor, and consultant of the medical and sanitary administration of the Kremlin, Levin was the personal physician of many party and government leaders.

Lev Levin, nee Usher Gershevich Leib Levin, was born in Odesa into a Jewish family.

He graduated from the Natural Sciences Department of the Physics and Mathematics Faculty of Novorossisk University. In 1896, he also graduated from the Medical Faculty of the Moscow University. In 1896-1897, he worked as a doctor in clinics in Berlin and Paris. After his return to Russia, he was a doctor in Moscow. Between 1907 and 1919, Levin first worked as a factory doctor and later was transferred to the resort hospital of the People's Commissariat of Health of the RSFSR. For a short period, Levin served in the Red Army. From 1920, he worked in the Kremlin hospital as a physician-resident, head of the therapeutic department, and consultant of the Medical and Sanitary Department of the Kremlin. Simultaneously, he worked at the medical unit of the People's Commissariat for Internal Affairs (NKVD) of the USSR and was the attending physician of **F. Dzerzhinsky**, **V. Menzhinsky**, **G. Iagoda**, and other high-ranking officials. On February 17, 1937, Levin—together with the people's commissar of health (G. Kaminsky), the head of the Kremlin's *Lechsanupr* (I. Khodorovsky), and the doctor on duty (S. Mets)—signed a falsified medical report stating that the cause of death of **S. Ordzhonikidze** was heart paralysis.

On December 2, 1937, Lev Levin was arrested in connection with the case of the "Anti-Soviet Right Trotskyist bloc." He was accused of the murder of Menzhinsky, **V. Kuibyshev**, and **M. Gorky**. On March 13, 1938, Levin was sentenced to death and shot two days later. In September 1938, his son Vladimir (born 1903), a professor of the Moscow Institute of Law and assistant head of the second division of the Western People's Commissariat of Foreign Affairs of the USSR, was also arrested and shot on charges of involvement in the plot.

On February 4, 1988, Levin was rehabilitated for lack of corpus delicti.

LITVINOV, MAKSIM MAKSIMOVICH (1876-1951). Litvinov was a prominent Soviet diplomat and politician, people's commissar of foreign affairs of the USSR (1930-1939), member of the Central Executive Committee of the USSR of the second through seventh convocations, deputy of the Supreme Soviet of the USSR of the first and second convocations, member of the CC CPSU (1934-1941), representative of the USSR in the League of Nations (1934-1938), Soviet ambassador to the United States (1941-1943), and Soviet envoy to Cuba (1942-1943).

Meir Henoch Wallach, née Meir Henoch Wallach-Finkelstein, was born in Białystok, Grodno Governorate, the Russian Empire, into a merchant family and received a traditional Jewish upbringing. First, he studied at the *cheder* (a traditional elementary school teaching the basics of Judaism and the Hebrew language), then at the Bialystok real school, from which he graduated in 1893. After graduation, he joined the Russian army as a volunteer and for five years served in Baku as part of the 17th Caucasian Infantry Regiment. After retiring in 1898, he worked as an accountant in the city of Klintsy and a manager of a sugar factory in Kyiv.

In 1898, Wallach-Finkelstein became a member of the RSDWP and worked with the newspaper *Iskra*. He started to use the pseudonym Maksim Litvinov to help avoid arrest. But police also knew him as Papasha, Felix, Graf (Count), and Nic. In 1901, he was arrested and incarcerated in the Lukianovskaia prison in Kyiv. In August 1902, he supervised the escape of eleven Social Democrats ("Iskra-ists") from prison. After the escape, Litvinov emigrated to Switzerland and became a member of the administration of the Foreign League of Russian Revolutionary Social Democracy. He was responsible for the delivery of the newspaper *Iskra* to Russia. In 1903, he joined the Bolsheviks after the split in the RSDWP. He was an attendee at the second congress of the RSDWP, having met Lenin for the first time in the Reading Room of the British Museum in London.

In 1904, Litvinov returned to Russia and took part in the revolution of 1905. In October 1905, together with L. Krasin and **M. Gorky**, he organized the first legal Bolshevik newspaper *Novaia Zhizn* (editor N. Minsky) in St. Petersburg. In 1906, Litvinov emigrated again and based himself in Paris, though he traveled widely. Abroad, he was engaged in arms purchases posing as a foreign businessman and arranging their delivery to Russia. In 1908, he was arrested in France while using the name Meer Wallach and carrying banknotes that were traced to the bank robbery in Tiflis, Georgia, a year earlier. Later, the French government deported him to Britain, where he lived for the next eight years. In England, Litvinov was working in the International Socialist Bureau. In February 1915 in London, he spoke on behalf of the Central Committee of the RSDWP at a conference of socialists of the Entente countries. He condemned the First World War and was under an arrest warrant in several European countries.

In 1916, Litvinov married the writer Ivy Low, a British citizen of Hungarian Jewish background. The two had met in London. She returned with him to the USSR in 1918 and remained there for two decades after Litvinov's death.

After the October Revolution of 1917, Litvinov was appointed the Soviet government's plenipotentiary representative in Britain, though that country never accorded him official accreditation. Moreover, after the arrest of Bruce Lockhart, the head of the British diplomatic mission, in Moscow, Litvinov was detained by the British government in response as a hostage. In 1918, Litvinov was exchanged for Lockhart and returned to Moscow, where he joined the executive of the People's Commissariat for Foreign Affairs.

In December 1918, on Lenin's instructions, Litvinov was sent to Stockholm with Soviet peace proposals to the Entente powers (the so-called Litvinov Declaration). In 1919, he signed a peace treaty with Estonia. In March 1919, Litvinov participated in negotiations with the American representative, William Christian Bullitt, in Moscow. In November 1919, Litvinov left for Copenhagen, where he conducted negotiations with the British representative. As a result, on February 12, 1920, a British-Soviet prisoner exchange agreement was signed. In April–May 1922, together with Chicherin, Litvinov participated in the work of the Soviet delegation at the Genoa Conference. Then he headed the Soviet delegation to the international economic conference in the Hague. In December 1922, Litvinov chaired a conference on disarmament in Moscow, which was attended by representatives of Poland, Lithuania, Latvia, Estonia, and Finland. In 1923, he signed trade agreements on behalf of the Soviet Union with Norway and Germany.

In 1930, Stalin appointed Litvinov people's commissar of foreign affairs of the USSR. In this post he pursued a policy of collective security. Litvinov headed the Soviet delegations at the League of Nations conference on disarmament (1932) and the Peace Economic Conference in London (1933). In 1934–1938, he represented the USSR in the League of Nations. In 1934, Litvinov became a member of the CC CPSU, remaining until 1941. In 1935, Litvinov negotiated treaties of mutual assistance with France and Czechoslovakia. Consultations on the rapprochement between the USSR and Germany caused tension in relations between Litvinov and Stalin, and especially with Molotov. On May 3, 1939, Stalin replaced Litvinov—who was a Jew and a sincere opponent of an alliance with Nazi Germany—with Molotov. In February 1941, Litvinov was expelled from the CC CPSU.

Shortly after the German invasion of the Soviet Union (June 1941), Litvinov was appointed deputy people's commissar of foreign affairs and at the same time ambassador to the United States (until 1943). In 1942–1943, Litvinov was also the USSR's envoy to Cuba. He actively contributed to the conclusion of Lend-Lease Agreement between the Soviet Union and the United States (1942). In 1943, he was recalled to Moscow and in October participated in the Moscow Conference of the Council of Foreign Ministers of the United States, Great Britain, China (represented by its ambassador to the Soviet Union, Foo Ping-Sheung), and the USSR (the Big Four Conference). In September 1944, Litvinov negotiated an armistice with Finland. In June 1946, Litvinov was dismissed from his post as deputy minister for foreign affairs. At the end of 1951, he suffered a heart attack and died on December 31.

LIUBCHENKO, PANAS PETROVYCH (1897–1937). Liubchenko was a Ukrainian revolutionary and Soviet politician. From 1934 to 1937, he was chairman of the Council of People's Commissars of the Ukrainian SSR, the formal head of government.

Panas Liubchenko was born in Kaharlyk (Ukraine) into a peasant family. He graduated from the village school and from 1909 studied at the Kyiv military paramedical school. From 1913, he took part in the revolutionary movement and was a member of the left wing of the Ukrainian Socialist-Revolutionary Party. In 1914, he graduated from school and became a military paramedic. With the outbreak of the First World War, he served in the 33rd Ieletsky Infantry Regiment on the Southwest Front and was wounded twice. After recovering, he worked as a paramedic in Kyiv district military hospital. From 1916, he started to collaborate with the magazines *Socialistychna dumka* (*Socialist Thought*) and *Nashe slovo* (*Our Word*).

After the February Revolution of 1917, he became a member of the "Borotbists" party and became a member of Kyiv Council of Labor Deputies. Later, he was elected to the Ukrainian Central Rada (Central Committee). He belonged to the left faction, which advocated for the establishment of Soviet power in the Ukrainian lands and cooperation with the Russian Bolsheviks. In 1920, after the dissolution of the "Borotbists," Liubchenko joined the Communist Party of Ukraine. In 1920–1921, he served as deputy chief of the political department of the 2nd Cavalry Army. In 1921–1922, he was transferred to Chernihiv and Donetsk provincial executive committees. In 1922–1925, Liubchenko was appointed chairman of the All-Ukrainian Union of Agricultural Cooperation. In 1925–1927, he chaired the Kyiv District Executive Committee. In 1927–1934, he was appointed a secretary of the CC CPU and became a candidate member of its Politburo.

In 1930, he acted as a public prosecutor at "The Trial of the Union for the Liberation of Ukraine" (one of the show trials in the Soviet Union). Soon he began to play a leading role in the collectivization of the republic and in the confiscation of food from peasants (eventually such measures led to the famine of 1932–1933 in Ukraine). From April 28, 1934, to August 30, 1937, Liubchenko served as chairman of the Council of People's Commissars of the Ukrainian SSR. He was elected a delegate of the 15th, 16th, and 17th congresses of the CPSU. At the 17th congress, he was elected a candidate member of the CC CPSU. In 1935, he was awarded the Order of Lenin.

In August 1937, at the plenum of the Central Committee of the CPU, Liubchenko was unjustly accused of leading a counterrevolutionary nationalist organization in Ukraine. He denied all charges but believed he was about to be arrested. On August 30, 1937, he returned home, shot his wife, and then committed suicide. In 1965 he was rehabilitated.

LOPATIN, ANTON IVANOVICH (1897–1965). A Soviet military leader, commander of armies during the **Great Patriotic War**, general-lieutenant (1942), Hero of the Soviet Union (April 19, 1945), and member of the CPSU from 1919 to 1965, Anton Lopatin was born into a Russian peasant family in the village of Kamennaia, Brest district, Brest region (today it is in Belarus). In 1916–1917, he served in the Russian Imperial Army and fought on the Southwestern Front of the First World War. In August 1918, he joined the Red Army. During the Civil War, Lopatin served first as assistant commander and then as squadron commander of the 1st Cavalry Army. He fought against Denikin's and Wrangel's armies. In 1919, Lopatin became a member of the RSDWP(b). In 1920, he fought in the Soviet–Polish War. After the war, he continued to serve in the 21st Cavalry Regiment as squadron commander and the head of the regimental school.

In 1925–1927, Lopatin studied at the Leningrad Advanced Officer Training courses for command personnel. In 1929 he graduated from the assistant regimental commander training courses at the Leningrad Higher Cavalry School. From November 1931, Lopatin served as commander of a cavalry regiment. In July 1937, he was appointed commander of the 6th Cavalry Division. From September 1938, he worked as a tactics instructor in the cavalry courses of the Red Army. In July 1939, Lopatin was appointed inspector of the cavalry of the Trans-Baikal Military District. In June 1940, he served as acting deputy commander of the 15th Army of the Far Eastern Front. From November 1940, he became commander of the 31st Rifle Corps in the Kyiv Special Military District.

At the beginning of the Great Patriotic War (1941–1945), General-Major Lopatin was appointed commander of the 31st Rifle Corps, a part of the 5th Army of the Southwestern Front. He took part in the border battles in Ukraine, near Lutsk and the Battle of Kyiv (1941). From October 1941, Lopatin served as commander of the 37th Army of the Southern Front and took part in the Rostov offensive operation in 1941. In June–July 1942, he commanded the 9th Army of the Southwestern Front and fought in the Donbas and in the Don regions. In August–September 1942, Lopatin commanded the 62nd Army of the Stalingrad Front but was removed from his post by the front commander, **A. Ieremenko**.

After a short stay in the reserve of the Headquarters (Stavka of the Soviet Armed Forces), he was sent to the Northwestern Front. From October 1942, he commanded the 43rd Army, and from March 1943, the 11th Army on the Northwestern Front. In 1942 and 1943, he participated in the Battle of Demiansk. In September 1943, Lopatin became commander of the 20th Army of the Kalinin Front. From January to July 1944, he served as a deputy commander of the 43rd Army of the 1st Baltic Front and took part in the Belarusian offensive. In July 1944, Lopatin, at his own request, was appointed commander of the 13th Guards Rifle Corps of the same army and participated in the Belarusian, Baltic, Gumbinnen-Goldap, East Prussian, and Zemland offensive operations. On April 19, 1945, Lopatin was awarded the title Hero of the Soviet Union, the Order of Lenin, and the Gold Star medal. In July 1945, Lopatin was given command of the 2nd Separate Rifle Corps of the Trans-Baikal Front and took part in the Soviet–Japanese War of 1945.

After the war, in 1947, he graduated from the K. E. Voroshilov Military Academy of the General Staff of the Red Army. From 1947 and until his retirement in 1954, General-Lieutenant A. Lopatin occupied high-ranking posts in staffs of several military districts. In total, he was awarded three Orders of Lenin, three Orders of the Red Banner, two Orders of Kutuzov first class, and the Order of the Red Star medals. He died on April 9, 1965.

LUNACHARSKY, ANATOLY VASILEVICH (1875–1933). Lunacharsky was an active participant in the Revolution of 1905 and the October Revolution, Soviet politician, writer, translator, publicist, critic, art critic, playwright, essayist, journalist, the first Bolshevik Soviet people's commissar of education (Narkompros), and an academician of the Academy of Sciences of the USSR.

Anatoly Lunacharsky was born in Poltava, Russian Empire (today Ukraine). He was the illegitimate child of Aleksandr Ivanovich Antonov (1829–1885) and Aleksandra Iakovlevna Lunacharskaia, née Rostovtseva (1842–1914). Lunacharsky received the patronymic, surname, and rank of nobility from his stepfather, Vasily Fedorovich Lunacharsky. The difficult relations between his mother and stepfather had a dramatic effect on Anatoly.

In the 1890s, while studying at the First Male Gymnasium in Kyiv, Lunacharsky became interested in Marxist ideas of social democracy and joined the Society of Social Democrats. In 1892, he was included in an illegal educational Marxist center. At the age of 17, he wrote his debut article. In 1895, after graduating from the high school, he went to Switzerland, where he entered the University of Zurich. At this university, he studied philosophy (including the works of Karl Marx, Friedrich Engels, and French materialist philosophers) and natural sciences under the supervision of Richard Avenarius—a German-Swiss philosopher who formulated the radical positivist doctrine of "empirical criticism" or empirio-criticism. Lunacharsky was greatly influenced by Avenarius's positivist views. In Zurich, he met Rosa Luxemburg, Leo Jogiches, Maxim Kovalevsky, **Georgy Plekhanov**, and other Social Democrats.

In 1896–1898, Lunacharsky traveled through France and Italy. In 1898, he arrived in Moscow and became engaged in revolutionary activities. A year later, he was arrested and deported to Poltava. In 1900, he was arrested again and after a short imprisonment was sent into exile: first to Kaluga, and subsequently to

Vologda and Totma. In 1903, after the party split into Bolsheviks and Mensheviks, Lunacharsky committed himself to the former once it was clear there was no chance of reconciliation. In 1904, after the end of his exile, he moved to Kyiv, and then to Geneva, where he became a member of the editorial boards of the Bolshevik newspapers *Proletary* and *Vpered* (*Forward*).

In October 1905, Lunacharsky returned to Russia. In St. Petersburg, he collaborated with the Bolshevik newspaper *Novaia Zhizn* (*New Life*) and carried out propaganda among workers and students. In December, he was arrested but was able to flee abroad. In 1906–1908, he was the head of the art department of the magazine *Prosveshchenie* (*Education*). In 1908, Lunacharsky split with the Bolsheviks. In 1909—together with his brother-in-law Aleksandr Bogdanov, Grigory Aleksinsky, **Maksim Gorky**, and others—he became one of the organizers of the Social Democratic group *Vpered* and the Capri Party School, based on their sojourn on the island of this name. In 1913, he left the group due to group's transition from cultural and propaganda work to political activity.

After the February Revolution of 1917, Lunacharsky returned to Russia and joined the RSDWP(b). In late August–September 1917, he was elected a member of the Petrograd City Duma and chairman of its cultural and educational section. From October 1917 to 1929, he served as people's commissar of education. In this post, Lunacharsky became one of the organizers and theorists of the Soviet education system, higher and vocational education. During the first post-revolutionary months, he actively defended the preservation of Russia's historical and cultural heritage. In 1918–1922, Lunacharsky, as the representative of the Revolutionary Military Council, worked in the frontline regions. In 1919–1921, he became a member of the Central Auditing Commission of the RCP(b).

From 1927, Lunacharsky was involved in diplomatic work and served as the deputy head of the Soviet delegation at the disarmament conference (1927). He also headed the Soviet delegation to the League of Nations. From September 1929, he was the chairman of the Scientific Committee of the Central Executive Committee of the USSR. Lunacharsky was a supporter of the translation of the Russian language from Cyrillic to the Latin alphabet and considered such a transition inevitable. In 1929, the People's Commissariat of Education of the RSFSR formed a commission to develop the question of the romanization of the Russian alphabet. In the early 1930s, Lunacharsky served as director of the Institute of Russian Literature of the Academy of Sciences of the USSR and was one of the editors of the Literary Encyclopedia. He was personally acquainted with such famous foreign writers as Romain Rolland, Henri Barbusse, George Bernard Shaw, Bertolt Brecht, Karl Spitteler, H. G. Wells, and others.

In September 1933, Lunacharsky was appointed Soviet ambassador to Spain, but he died on his way to Spain in December 1933. His body was cremated, and an urn with his ashes was installed in the Kremlin Wall on Moscow's Red Square.

M

MAISKY, IVAN MIKHAILOVICH (NÉE IVAN LIAKHOVETSKY) (1884–1975). A Soviet diplomat, historian, politician, the Soviet Union's Ambassador to the United Kingdom before and during the Second World War (1932–1943), and full member of the USSR Academy of Sciences (November 30, 1946), Ivan Maisky was born in the town of Kirillov, Novgorod province, Russian Empire (now Vologda Oblast, Russia), into a Polish Jewish family. His father was a military doctor, later a doctor of medicine and scientist who came from the Kherson province (now Kherson, Ukraine). His mother was a teacher. Ivan first studied at the gymnasium in Cherepovets, and later, after his family moved to Omsk, he graduated from the city's gymnasium. After graduation, he studied at the Faculty of History and Philology of St. Petersburg University, but for participation in the student movement, he was excluded from the university and sent back to Omsk under police supervision. In exile, in 1903, he joined the RSDWP, Menshevik branch. During the revolution of 1905–1907, Maisky was a member of the Saratov Soviet of Workers' Deputies. In early January 1906, he was arrested and sent to exile in Tobolsk for two years.

In 1908, he emigrated first to Switzerland and later to Germany, where in 1912 he graduated from the Economics Department of the University of Munich. After graduation, he moved to England. During the First World War, he was a Menshevik Internationalist. He returned to Russia in May 1917 and worked as a member of the board at the Ministry of Labor with the provisional government. Maisky reacted negatively to the seizure of power by the Bolsheviks in October 1917. In November 1917, he was elected a member of the Central Committee of the Menshevik Party. In the summer of 1918, he was the minister of labor in the Committee of Members of the Constituent Assembly (*Komuch*) in the Samara government. Komuch was an anti-Bolshevik government, which was formed in Samara after the Czech Legion had occupied the city on June 8, 1918, and operated until 1922. Since the Menshevik Party refused to support this government, in September 1918 Maisky was expelled from the Menshevik Central Committee and from the party. Later, Maisky almost paid with his life for participation in Komuch. In 1922, he was brought to trial in connection with the "Trial of the Right SRs." Komuch was liquidated by the White leader, Admiral Aleksandr Kolchak, at the end of December 1918. Some of its members were arrested.

In 1919, Maisky was in Mongolia, where, as he later wrote, as a representative of the Irkutsk office of the Tsentrosoiuz, he conducted scientific expeditions and studied the economic system of this country and foreign trade prospects. In 1921, a report titled "Modern Mongolia: Report of the Mongolian Expedition Equipped by the Irkutsk Office of the All-Russian Union of Consumer Partnerships Tsentrosoiuz" was published in Irkutsk. Later in 1959, on the basis of this report, Maisky published the monograph *Mongolia on the Eve of the Revolution*.[1] After spending sixteen to seventeen months abroad, in September 1920, with the end of the Civil War in Transbaikalia and the outbreak of hostilities in Mongolia, the expedition returned to Russia.

In February 1921, the Siberian Bureau of the Central Committee was admitted to the RCP(b). Maisky joined the All-Russian Communist Party (b) and was appointed chairman of the newly formed Siberian State Planning Committee. In 1922, he was transferred to Moscow and held different diplomatic positions. First, he served as the head of the press department of the People's Commissariat for Foreign Affairs (NKID), and later he became an editor of *Zvezda* magazine. In 1922, he was a prosecution witness at the trial of the Socialist Revolutionaries. He also worked as a lecturer at the Communist University. During this period (1923–1925), he wrote several books on such topics as modern Germany, August Bebel, Ferdinand Lassalle, and David Lloyd George.

In 1925–1927, Maisky was an adviser to the press office of the USSR in London. After the severance of diplomatic relations with England in 1927, he served as adviser to the Soviet Embassy in Japan, where he worked until 1929. In 1929–1932, he was the plenipotentiary of the USSR in Finland. On January 21, 1932, he signed the Soviet–Finnish Non-Aggression Pact. He published a series of books under various pseudonyms. Under name I. Taigin, he published *England and the USSR* (1926) and *How an English Worker Lives* (1928). Maisky also published *Universal Strike and the Struggle of Miners in England* (1926) under the pseudonym M. James, *Finland* (1931) under the name V. Krylov, and *The Origin of Capitalist Japan* (1934) as V. Svetlov.

During 1932–1943, Maisky served as ambassador extraordinary and plenipotentiary to Great Britain. In February 1934, he conducted successful negotiations to lift the embargo on the import of Soviet goods to Britain and concluded a Temporary Trade Agreement between the USSR and Britain (February 16, 1934). From 1936 to 1939, Maisky was the Soviet envoy to the Committee of Non-Intervention during the Spanish Civil War and actively tried to prevent Western countries from aiding the troops of General F. Franco. In 1937–1939, he also served as Soviet representative in the League of Nations. On July 30, 1941, he signed the agreement on restoration of diplomatic relations between the USSR and the government in exile of the Polish Republic (better known as the "Maisky-Sikorsky" or "Sikorsky-Maisky" agreement).

In 1943, Maisky was unexpectedly removed from his post. Almost simultaneously, the USSR ambassador to the United States, **M. Litvinov**, was also recalled. According to British diplomats, these changes signaled that Stalin had decided to interact with his allies without intermediaries. He did not need such authoritative and independent personalities as Maisky and Litvinov in his negotiations. From 1943 to 1946, Maisky served as deputy minister of foreign affairs and chairman of the Inter-Allied Reparation Commission in Moscow. Maisky took part in the **Ialta** (1945) and **Potsdam** (1945) conferences of the so-called Big Three (USSR, United States, and Britain). In 1946, Maisky was dismissed from the diplomatic service, but at the same time, he was elected a full member of the USSR Academy of Sciences, at the Institute of History.

On February 19, 1953, he was arrested and charged with espionage for Britain and anti-Soviet activities. As Maisky himself later admitted, the arrests were part of Beria's attempt to collect incriminating material on Molotov. The death of Stalin and the fall of Beria did little to change the position of Maisky. In the summer of 1955, he was sentenced to six years in prison "for misconduct" but was immediately pardoned by the Supreme Soviet of the USSR. In 1960, he was rehabilitated. In 1966, he signed a letter from twenty-five cultural and scientific workers to the general secretary of the CPSU Central Committee **L. Brezhnev** opposing the rehabilitation of Stalin.

During the last years of his life, Maisky continued to work at the Institute of History of the Academy of Sciences of the USSR (in 1968, it was renamed the Institute of General History of the Academy of Sciences of the USSR). On Maisky's initiative, research groups for studying Spain and England were created at the Institute of History.

On September 3, 1975, Maisky died in Moscow at the age of 91.

MALENKOV, GEORGY MAKSIMILIANOVICH (1901–1988). A Soviet politician and party leader, Malenkov was Stalin's associate and was heavily involved in Stalin's purges. He was a member of the CC CPSU (1939–1957), candidate member of the Politburo of the Central Committee of the CPSU (1941–1946), member of the Politburo (Presidium) of the Central Committee (1946–1957), member of the Orgburo, CC CPSU (1939–1952), secretary of the CC CPSU (1939–1946, 1948–1953), deputy of the Supreme Soviet of the USSR (1938–1958), chairman of the Council of Ministers of the USSR (1953–1955), member of the so-called Anti-Party Group (those within the leadership of the Communist Party of the USSR who unsuccessfully attempted to remove Nikita Khrushchev as first secretary of the party in June 1957), and the de facto leader of the Soviet state from March 1953 to February 1955.

Georgy Malenkov was born in Orenburg in the Russian Empire. His father, Maksimilian Malenkov, was an employee in the railway department. During the 18th century, Malenkov's ancestors immigrated from Macedonia. They earned noble rank as a reward for their faithful services. Georgy's grandfather was a colonel, and the grandfather's brother was a rear admiral. His mother, on the other hand, was born into the family of a blacksmith. In 1919, Georgy graduated from a classical gymnasium and volunteered for the Red Army. In 1920, he joined the RSDWP(b) and worked as a political commissar of a propaganda train on the Eastern and Turkestan fronts.

After the end of the Civil War, Malenkov moved to Moscow and in 1921 entered Bauman Moscow State Technical University. He left his studies just before graduation in 1925 because he was invited to work as the technical secretary of the Organizational Bureau of the Central Committee of the All-Union Communist Party of Bolsheviks, where he soon proved to be an excellent worker. In 1930, **L. Kaganovich** promoted him to the post of the head of the Organizational Department of the Moscow Committee of the CPSU. In 1934–1939, Malenkov was appointed head of the Department of Party Leading Bodies of the Central Committee. In 1935–1936, after Stalin put forward the slogan "Cadres decide everything," Malenkov conducted a checking campaign and created registration cards for all members and candidates of the CPSU—in total about 2.5 million. On the basis of this collected card index, a grandiose centralized nomenclature personnel system was built. This system became Malenkov's main party specialty.

In the summer of 1937, on Stalin's behalf together with **N. Iezhov**, M. Frinovsky, **A. Mikoian**, and **L. Kaganovich**, Malenkov traveled to Belarus, Armenia, Georgia, Tajikistan, the Tatar Autonomous Soviet Socialist Republic, Novosibirsk Region, Sverdlovsk Region, and other areas to check the activities of local party organizations, the NKVD, and other state bodies during the Great Terror. Based on the results of these inspections, Malenkov prepared two reports, which played an important role in cutting down the mass repressions. In January 1938, at the Plenum of the Central Committee, Malenkov produced the report "On the Shortcomings of the Work of Party Organizations with the Exclusion of Communists from the CPSU(b)," and in August a report "On Excesses." Malenkov also played a major role in the downfall of Iezhov. He accused the latter and his department of the destruction of cadres loyal to the Communist Party. Together with Beria, he took part in the arrest of Iezhov (he was arrested in Malenkov's office). In 1939–1946 and 1948–1953, Malenkov was a secretary of the CC CPSU. Simultaneously, in 1939–1946, he led the Personnel Department of the Central Committee. From March 1939 to October 1952, he was a member of the Orgburo of the CPSU.

Before the start of the **Great Patriotic War** (1941–1943), Malenkov was in charge of the secret apparatus of the **Comintern**. During the war, he was appointed a member of the **State Defense Committee** (GKO) (June 1941–September 1945). In July–October 1941, he oversaw the formation of a new type of military formation: the Guards of Rocket Artillery

Units of the Red Army. On February 21, 1941, Malenkov became a candidate member of the Politburo, CC CPSU. As a member of the GKO, Malenkov visited crucial sectors of the Soviet–German front. He visited Leningrad in August 1941, Moscow in the fall of 1941, Stalingrad in August 1942, and the Western Front in early 1944. But his main duty was to equip the Red Army with combat aircraft, and he successfully coped with this important task. On September 30, 1943, by the decree of the Presidium of the Supreme Soviet of the USSR "for special services in the field of strengthening the production of aircraft and engines in difficult wartime conditions," Malenkov was awarded the title of hero of socialist labor with the Order of Lenin and the Hammer and Sickle gold medal. In the fall of 1944, during the Kremlin's meeting regarding the "Jewish problem," Malenkov spoke in favor of "increasing vigilance." After his speech, it became extremely difficult for Jews to obtain high posts. In 1943–1945, Malenkov became chairman of the Committee under the Council of People's Commissars of the USSR responsible for the restoration of the national economy in the areas liberated from the Nazi occupation, and from May 15, 1944, he simultaneously held the post of deputy chairman of the Council of People's Commissars.

After the war, Malenkov headed the committee for the dismantling of German industry. As a member of the Politburo and secretary of the CC CPSU, he dealt with issues of industry and agriculture, as well as issues of ideological work. He became the second-ranked person in the party after Stalin. From May 1946 to May 1947, Malenkov was appointed chief of the Soviet Missile Program and became a member of the Special Committee on the Use of Atomic Energy. In the fall of 1947, he participated in the work of the Cominform under the leadership of **A. Zhdanov**. After the split with Yugoslavia and Zhdanov's death, Malenkov took over the leadership of the entire "ideological policy" of the Central Committee. At the same time, he was entrusted with overseeing agriculture, a formidable task in the early postwar years.

In 1949–1950, Malenkov played one of the main prosecuting roles in the "Leningrad affair." More than two thousand people were arrested and several dozen were shot. In 1949–1952, he was also entrusted with running the case of the Jewish Anti-Fascist Committee and the ideological campaign to "fight rootless cosmopolitanism." In October 1952, at the 19th congress of the CPSU, Malenkov made a report on Stalin's behalf on new ideas on domestic and international politics. These ideas were developed in Stalin's subsequent pamphlet, *Economic Problems of Socialism in the USSR*. At the party plenum, Malenkov was elected a member of the Presidium (then new name for the former Politburo) of the CC CPSU.

After Stalin's death on March 5, 1953, Malenkov was elected chairman of the Council of Ministers of the USSR and secretary of the CC CPSU, and effectively the leader of the country. Later in March, during the first closed meeting of the Presidium of the Central Committee, he announced the need to "end the policy of the cult of the individual and move to collective leadership of the country." However, there was no significant reaction to Malenkov's proposal. In May 1953, on the initiative of Malenkov, a government resolution was adopted that eliminated the so-called "envelopes" with additional remuneration for party officials. In the summer of 1953, Malenkov proposed to significantly reduce taxes on peasants and cancel all past collective farm debts, and to increase the production of consumer goods, prioritizing light industry. In September 1953, he transferred control over the party apparatus to **Khrushchev**. Malenkov supported the struggle against **Beria** and initiated the process of de-Stalinization of society. But he was unable to prevent the growth of Khrushchev's influence once the latter had control over the party apparatus.

In 1955, Malenkov lost his post of chairman of the Council of Ministers and was demoted to deputy chairman. Khrushchev's policy prompted Malenkov to team up with Kaganovich and **V. Molotov** and to start a campaign against Khrushchev. At a meeting of the Presidium of the Central Committee, they opposed Khrushchev and received the support of the majority of the members of the highest party body. They were joined by **K. Voroshilov**, **N. Bulganin**, M. Pervukhin, M. Saburov, and **D. Shepilov**. However, Khrushchev's supporters were able to quickly convene a Central Committee Plenum, at which the "anti-party group" was defeated. In June 1957, Malenkov was removed from the Central Committee and transferred to the position of director of a power plant in Ust-Kamenogorsk. Later he was transferred to the thermal power plant in Ekibastuz, and in November 1961, he was expelled from the CPSU (unlike Molotov, he was not restored in his later years). In this same year, he retired. After 1973, he lived in Moscow until his death on January 14, 1988.

MALINOVSKY, RODION IAKOVLEVICH (1898–1967). A Soviet statesman and talented military leader, marshal of the Soviet Union (1944), twice Hero of the Soviet Union (1945, 1958), people's hero of Yugoslavia (1964), minister of defense of the USSR (1957–1967), and member of the CPSU Central Committee (1956–1967), Rodion Malinovsky was born in Odesa into a Ukrainian peasant family. In 1911, he graduated from the parish school in the village of Klishchevo (now Vinnitsa region, Ukraine). From 1911 to 1914, he worked as a farm laborer and worker. After the outbreak of the First World War, at the age of 15, he was enlisted as a volunteer in the machine-gun detachment of the 256th Elisavetgrad Infantry Regiment. In 1915, Malinovsky was awarded the Cross of St. George. In February 1916, he was sent to France as part of the Russian Expeditionary Corps. In 1919, he returned to Russia and voluntarily joined the Red Army. He fought against the White Army in Siberia and against the gangs of General Ungern in Transbaikalia.

After the end of the Civil War, Malinovsky remained in the army. In 1926, he became a member of the CPSU. From 1927 to 1930, he studied at the Frunze Military Academy. In January 1937–May 1938, Colonel Malinovsky was a military adviser during the Spanish Civil War, in support of the Republican government. Under the pseudonym "Colonel Malino," he organized military operations against Franco's rebel army. Due to his participation in the Spanish Civil War, he managed to escape the 1937 repressions inside the Red Army. For his service, he was awarded the Order of Lenin and the Order of the Red Banner and was promoted to major general. In 1939, he became a lecturer at the Frunze Military Academy. In March 1941, Malinovsky headed the 48th Rifle Corps in the Odesa Military District.

With the outbreak of the **Great Patriotic War** (1941–1945), the 48th Rifle Corps led by Malinovsky participated in heavy battles on the state border of the USSR. Due to the purges in the Red Army in 1937–1938, at the beginning of the war the Soviet Army experienced a shortage of competent officers. Malinovsky, with his knowledge and military experience, was a priceless asset. In August 1941, he was appointed first as chief of staff, then as commander of the 6th Army. From September 29 to November 4, 1941, he participated in the Donbas defensive operation. From December 1941 to July 1942, he commanded the Southern Front. On July 22, 1942, his troops left the city of Rostov-on-Don, evidently without waiting for an order from above. As a result, he saved the remaining troops of the Southern Front from encirclement, but at the same time he earned Stalin's disfavor. Immediately after the fall of Rostov, Stalin issued his famous order no. 227, "Not a Step Backward!" (July 28, 1942). The Southern Front was disbanded. In August 1942, Malinovsky was downgraded to commander of the 66th Army, which operated north of Stalingrad. From October 1942, he became deputy commander of the Voronezh Front and, in November 1942, commander of the 2nd Guards Army. During the Battle of Stalingrad, Malinovsky commanded the latter army, which played a very important role in the offensive at Stalingrad and took part in the urban warfare.

In the winter of 1942, Illarion Larin, Malinovsky's personal friend and member of the Military Council of his army, shot himself and left a note that ended with the words: "Long live Lenin!" Stalin started to suspect that this was a demarche and intended to get rid of Malinovsky. Khrushchev, who at this time was a member of the Military Council of the Stalingrad Front, stood up for Malinovsky and saved him from likely trial and death. Later, Malinovsky's army, in cooperation with other armies, stopped and then defeated Army Group Don of Field Marshal Erich von Manstein, which was trying to relieve General Friedrich Paulus's 6th Army trapped inside Stalingrad. Malinovsky's troops also liberated Rostov and Donbas (1943) and Right-Bank Ukraine. On April 10, 1944, they liberated Odesa. In May 1944, he was appointed commander of the 2nd Ukrainian Front.

Together with General **Tolbukhin**'s troops, Malinovsky's armies defeated the southern wing of the German front and were able to encircle twenty-two German divisions and the 3rd Romanian Army during the Jassy-Chisinau operation (August 20–29, 1944). During this operation Malinovsky demonstrated his military leadership talents. He took into account not only the operational-strategic but also the military-political factors associated with the need to separate Romania from Germany. Based on this, he decided to attack with the most powerful, crushing first strike and to break through the enemy's defenses in as short a time as possible. This well-thought-out strategy was brilliantly implemented. By August 23, 1944, the troops of the 3rd Ukrainian Front, in cooperation with the 2nd Ukrainian Army, closed the encirclement of a large enemy grouping in the Chisinau region. Moreover, there was a simultaneous encirclement and destruction of the enemy and the development of an offensive on external front in the direction of Ploesti and Bucharest. The whole operation lasted only five to six days. Romania was forced to surrender and declared war on Germany. During this operation, Malinovsky was slightly wounded. On October 9, 1944, he was awarded the title of marshal of the Soviet Union.

Troops of the 2nd Ukrainian Front under the command of Malinovsky liberated Romania, Hungary, Austria, and Czechoslovakia. In the spring of 1945, in cooperation with Tolbukhin's troops, Malinovsky successfully carried out the Vienna operation, which effectively eliminated the German front in Austria, and joined with the Allied troops. At the same time, the troops of the right wing of his front carried out the Banska Bystritskaia offensive operation in March 1945. Following the complete defeat of enemy troops in this operation, Malinovsky was awarded the highest Soviet military leader's order of "Victory."

After the end of the European campaigns of the Second World War in Austria and Czechoslovakia, Malinovsky was transferred to the Far East, where he took command over the Trans-Baikal Front, to lead the Soviet attack on the remaining troops of Imperial Japan. Under his command, the Soviet army, quite unexpectedly for the Japanese, broke through the Gobi Desert into the central part of Manchuria and encircled and completely defeated the Japanese troops. Malinovsky was awarded the title of Hero of the Soviet Union for this operation. For his military talents and the ability to conduct offensive operations, he received the nickname "General Forward."

After the war, Malinovsky headed the troops of the Trans-Baikal-Amur Military District, then was appointed commander-in-chief of the troops of the Far East. In 1956, Malinovsky became deputy minister of defense of the Soviet Union and commander-in-chief of the ground forces. In October 1957, he became minister of defense of the USSR, succeeding **G. Zhukov**, whose ambitions were feared by both Stalin and **Khrushchev**. As minister of defense, he supported the development of nuclear missile forces of strategic deterrence, but he did not see them as a war weapon. He made an important contribution to strengthening the combat power of the USSR and, at the same time, the strategic rearmament of the army.

Malinovsky wrote dozens of articles on the most topical issues of military development and military history. Numerous historical and memoir books were published under his editorship. In 1958, on his sixtieth birthday, Malinovsky was awarded a second Gold Star medal. During his service, he was awarded twelve orders in total, including five Orders of Lenin, the Order of Victory, three Orders of the Red Banner, and nine medals. He also received state awards from Hungary, Indonesia, China, North Korea, Morocco, Mexico, Mongolia, Romania, the United States, France, Czechoslovakia, and Yugoslavia.

Marshal Malinovsky hosted his twentieth and last parade of troops on Red Square on November 7, 1966. During this parade, he was already seriously ill. He died on March 31, 1967, and was buried in the Kremlin Wall.

MENZHINSKY, VIACHESLAV RUDOLFOVICH (Polish: **WIESŁAW MĘŻYŃSKI**) (1874–1934).

Menzhinsky was a Polish-Russian revolutionary, Soviet party leader, one of the leaders of the Soviet state security organs, people's commissar of finance of the RSFSR (1918), **F. Dzerzhinsky**'s successor in the post of the chairman of the Joint State Political Directorate—OGPU (1926–1934), and a prominent writer.

Viacheslav Menzhinsky was born in St. Petersburg, into a Polish noble family of the Orthodox faith. His grandfather was a choral singer. His father, Rudolf Ignatievich Menzhinsky (1835–1919), was a privy councilor and a graduate of St. Petersburg University. He worked as a history teacher at the most prestigious educational institutions of St. Petersburg, including Cadet Corps, Page Corps, Marynsky Institute, the women's boarding house Madame Truba, the Higher Women's Bestuzhev Courses, and the Roman Catholic Theological Academy. Viacheslav's mother, Maria Aleksandrovna Shakeieva, was a daughter of an inspector of the School of Cavalry Ensigns and Junkers. Menzhinsky had two sisters.

In the first grades of the sixth St. Petersburg gymnasium, Menzhinsky studied together with A. Kolchak, who later transferred to the Naval Cadet Corps. Viacheslav graduated from the gymnasium in 1893 with a gold medal and continued his studies at the Faculty of Law of St. Petersburg University. During his studies, he became familiar with the works of Marx. He started to participate in Marxist circles and was known as one of the best polemicists at student gatherings. In 1902, he joined the RSDWP. In 1905, he became a member of the military organization of the St. Petersburg Committee of the RSDWP. Later, he created and armed a detachment of militants in Iaroslavl. In 1906, Menzhinsky was arrested, but he was able to escape from Russia in the following year. Despite clear evidence of his criminal terrorist activities in Europe, he was not extradited to a Russian court.

From 1907, Menzhinsky lived in exile in Belgium, Switzerland (Zurich and Geneva), France, and the United States, and participated in the work of foreign organizations of the RSDWP. He also collaborated with the Bolshevik newspaper *Proletarian*. Together with the editorial office, he moved to France, where he attended lectures at the University of Paris and studied different languages. While in Paris, Menzhinsky became a member of the Vpered group. From 1915, he worked at the Crédit Lyonnais bank.

After the February Revolution of 1917, Menzhinsky returned to Russia and entered the Bureau of the Military Section of the Central Committee of the Bolshevik Party. In this post, he became one of the organizers of the Red Guard, Lenin's main force in his seizure of power during the October Revolution. Menzhinsky became a member of the Petrograd Military Revolutionary Committee (VRK) and was people's commissar of finance in the first Bolshevik government. In this position, he was engaged in the expropriation and nationalization of the property of the "bourgeoisie."

In the fall of 1919, Menzhinsky became a member of the Presidium of the All-Russian Extraordinary Commission (VChK or Cheka) and deputy chairman of the Special Department for Combating Counter-Revolution and Espionage in the Army and at the Front. He sanctioned mass extrajudicial executions of former officers of the Russian Empire who joined the Bolsheviks, executions of those officers who did not want to serve the Bolsheviks, and repressions against civilians in the frontline zone "for sympathy with the counter-revolution."

As the head of the Special Department, Menzhinsky bore some responsibility for the death of the poet Aleksandr Blok. In July 1921, the people's commissar of education asked Lenin to allow Blok to go abroad for treatment (he was seriously ill). Lenin asked Menzhinsky for his opinion. Menzhinsky opposed Blok's departure from Soviet Russia. While they were deciding what to do with Blok, the great poet died on August 7, 1921.

In the fall of 1923, Menzhinsky became first deputy chairman of the State Political Directorate (GPU). He initiated provocations against the Russian diaspora (operations "Trust," "Syndicate," and "Syndicate-2") and organized the abductions and murders of its prominent figures (in particular, Baron P. Wrangel, who was poisoned in 1928). He created false underground anti-Soviet organizations, and when many people tried to join them, they were arrested. Menzhinsky initiated the falsification of the first mass political trials: the Shakhtinsky case (1928), the case of the Industrial Party and the Labor Peasant Party (1929–1930), the case of the Union Bureau of Mensheviks (1931), the case of the party of Right Socialist Revolutionaries (1922, conducted on behalf of Cheka leader Dzerzhinsky), and cases of "nationalist" organizations in Belarus, Ukraine, and Georgia. Hundreds of innocent people were arrested and killed during these trials.

For his service to the state, Menzhinsky was twice elected to the Central Committee of the Bolshevik Party, and in 1924 he received the Order of the Red Banner. In 1929–1931, on his initiative, the operation "Spring"—directed against regular military personnel—was carried out. During 1930, thirty-one thousand officers and specialists were killed. On Menzhinsky's initiative, political isolators were created. During eight years of his tenure as the head of the OGPU, his department turned into a "state within a state," preserving and strengthening the OGPU as the "punishing sword" of the party.

During the last two years of his life, Menzhinsky was seriously ill. He died on May 10, 1934, from a heart attack, at the government dacha "Gorki-6." Later, at the political trials of 1937–1938, it was announced that Menzhinsky had been killed by **Iagoda** on the instructions of the "Right-Trotskyist bloc." The accusation cannot be corroborated, however. He was buried in the Kremlin Wall. Streets in Moscow, Briansk, and other cities in the former Soviet Union are still named after him.

MERKULOV, VSEVOLOD NIKOLAEVICH (1895–1953). Merkulov was a Soviet statesman and party leader, general of the army (1945), head of the Main Directorate of State Security of the USSR (1938–1941), people's commissar (minister) of state security of the USSR (1941, 1943–1946), and minister of state control of the USSR (1950–1953). He was also a writer, a playwright, and a member of **L. Beria**'s inner circle—having worked with him since the early 1920s and as a member of Beria's so-called "Georgian mafia."

Vsevolod Merkulov was born in the village of Zagatala (present-day Azerbaijan) into a noble family. His father was a captain in the Russian Imperial Army. His mother, Ketevan Nikolaievna, née Tsinamdzgvrishvili, was a noblewoman from a Georgian princely family. From early childhood, Vsevolod was fond of literary pursuits, but during his studies at the Tiflis men's gymnasium, he became interested in electrical engineering. His articles were even published in Odesa in a specialist magazine. In 1913, he graduated from the gymnasium with a gold medal and entered St. Petersburg University's Department of Physics and Mathematics. While studying at the university, Vsevolod also wrote several romantic stories that were published in literary magazines and received positive reviews.

In October 1916, after completing the third year of his university studies, he was drafted into the army. He served in Orenburg in a reserve regiment but later was promoted to ensign and transferred to Novocherkassk (Rostov region, Russia). From September to October 1917, he served in Rivne (Western Ukraine), and from October 1917 to January 1918, he was transferred to the 331st Orsk Regiment in the 4th Army of the Southwestern Front (near Lutsk, Western Ukraine). In January 1918, due to illness, he was evacuated to Tiflis to stay with relatives, and in March 1918, he was demobilized.

From September 1918 to September 1921, he worked as a clerk, then as a teacher at the Tiflis School for the Blind, where his mother was the director. In 1919, he joined the Sokol Society, where he took part in amateur performances. Merkulov joined the Bolshevik Party relatively late, in 1920. By this time, it became clear that Lenin's government would survive, so his choice was practical rather than ideological. In 1921–1931, Merkulov held various positions in the apparatus of the Transcaucasian and Georgian All-Russian Extraordinary Commission (Cheka) and State Political Directorate (GPU). In 1931, he was transferred to party work. In 1931–1934, he served as an assistant of Beria, the secretary of the Transcaucasian Regional Committee of the CPSU and first secretary of the Central Committee of the Communist Party of Georgia. Merkulov took part in organizing mass repressions. During these years, he became Beria's closest associate and confidant. He even wrote a brochure about Beria, *Faithful Son of the Party of Lenin-Stalin*, which endeared him to his patron and boosted his career.

In September 1938, he moved to Moscow and was awarded the special title of state security commissioner of the third rank (on the same day, Beria was awarded the special title of state security commissioner of the first rank). With the appointment of Beria as the head of the Main Directorate of State Security of the USSR (GUGB), Merkulov became his deputy. From October 26 to December 17, 1938, he headed the 3rd Department of the GUGB NKVD of the USSR. From December 17, 1938, to February 3, 1941, he was first deputy people's commissar of the NKVD and head of the Main Directorate of State Security (GUGB). From March 21, 1939, to August 23, 1946, Merkulov was a member of the CC CPSU. He supervised repressions of **N. Iezhov**'s cadres and their removal from the apparatus. He was considered to be one of the cruelest investigators of the NKVD, and personally supervised the torture of those under investigation. In the fall of 1939, he led an operation to "identify and isolate" harmful elements in Poland, and then conducted a massive purge in newly annexed Western Ukraine. In 1940, he was included in the "troika" that led the execution of Polish officers (Katyn massacre). In 1943–1944, Merkulov headed the USSR Government Commission to investigate the massacre, which led to the conclusion that it had been carried out by the Nazi invaders at a later date.

In November 1940, Merkulov, as part of the delegation led by Molotov, went to Berlin to conduct negotiations with the leaders of Nazi Germany. Together with other members of the delegation, he attended a luncheon at the Imperial Chancellery hosted by Hitler in honor of the Soviet delegation (Hitler himself was not present).

Merkulov was responsible for harsh measures in the Baltic States in 1940–1941, where mass arrests and deportations of the population to Siberia were carried out. From February to July 1941, and again in 1943–1946, he was appointed people's commissar (minister) for state security of the USSR. In June 1941, he gave an order to "cleanse" jails in Western Ukraine—as a result, about ten thousand people were shot—just prior to the arrival of the German Army. After the war, in May 1946, Merkulov was dismissed as minister of state security and replaced by **Abakumov**. The reported reason was his unsatisfactory work. He was also demoted to the rank of candidate member of the CC CPSU.

In 1946–1950, Merkulov worked in the Main Directorate of Soviet Property Abroad. In 1950, he was appointed as a minister of state control of the USSR. After Stalin's death, he went on leave "due to health reasons." Later he moved abroad (to the GDR) "on vacation." After his return, he was arrested on September 18, 1953. During the investigation, Merkulov was asked to give detailed evidence against L. Beria, V. Abakumov, and others, but he refused. On December 23, 1953, together with Beria and others, he was sentenced to death as an "English and American spy" and executed the same day.

MEZHLAUK, VALERY IVANOVICH (NÉE MARTIN JOHANNOVICH) (1893–1938). A Soviet government and party official and chairman of the State Planning Committee (Gosplan) (1934–1937), Mezhlauk was known for his caricature drawings made during various meetings.

Valery Mezhlauk was born in Kharkiv, Russian Empire (today, Ukraine). His father, Ivan Martinovich Mezhlauk (Meshlauk), was a Latvian teacher. He was educated at the University of Leipzig and before the Revolution of 1917, he was director of the Novokhopërsk men's gymnasium, where he taught Latin. Valery's mother, Rosa Schiller, was German and owned two tenement houses in Kharkiv. Valery had four brothers. His elder brother, Ivan, became a member of the RSDWP at an early stage. Valery followed his example, joining the party in 1907. In 1914, Mezhlauk graduated from Kharkiv University with a diploma in history and philology, and in 1917 he received a degree in jurisprudence from the same university. From 1913 to 1916, Mezhlauk was a lecturer at this institution.

In March 1917, Mezhlauk first joined the Menshevik Internationalist wing and later in July the Bolshevik faction of the Kharkiv united organization of the RSDWP. He participated in the creation of the Red Guard and the Kharkiv Socialist Youth Union. In 1917, he was elected to the Kharkiv Committee of the RSDWP(b), the Council of Workers' and Soldiers' Deputies, the All-Russian Revolutionary Committee, and the provincial General Staff for Combating Counter-Revolution. In February–March 1918, he was appointed people's commissar of finance of the Donetsk-Krivoi Rog (Krivyi Rih) Soviet Republic and a member of the regional committee of the CPU(b) of the Donbas and Donetsk military headquarters.

In September 1918–1920, he became a member of the Revolutionary Military Council (*Revvoensovet*) of the 5th Army of the Eastern Front, which in September 1918 participated in the capture of Kazan; the 10th Army of the Southern Front, which participated in the Tsaritsyn Defense of 1918–1919; the 14th Army of the same front, which fought in the Donbas with units of the Volunteer Army; the 2nd Army of the North Caucasian Front, and the 2nd Labor Railway Army in Voronezh. He also served as a member of the military council of the Tula fortified region. Simultaneously, in January–June 1919, Mezhlauk was appointed people's commissar of military and naval affairs of Ukraine (from February together with N. I. Podvoisky), then the deputy people's commissar. From March 1920, he was the leading figure of various railways: the Moscow-Baltic, Moscow-Kursk, and Northern. From 1921 to 1922, he served as deputy people's commissar of railways of the RSFSR.

In 1922–1924, he was a member of the Collegium of the People's Commissariat of the RSFSR-USSR, and in 1924–1931, he became a member of the Presidium of the Supreme Council of the National Economy of the USSR. Simultaneously, he served as chairman of the *Glavmetall* of the Supreme Council of the National Economy of the USSR (1926–1928) and deputy chairman of the Supreme Council of the National Economy of the USSR (1928–1931). In 1927, he became a candidate member and in 1934, a member of the CC CPSU.

Mezhlauk was one of the main theorists and organizers of the Soviet planning and distribution system, and author of the book *On Planned Work and Measures for Its Improvement*. Industrialization in the USSR was carried out under his leadership. In 1930, he also worked as a responsible editor of the newspaper *For Industrialization* (1930). In November 1931, Mezhlauk was appointed first deputy chairman of the State Planning Agency (Gosplan) and deputy chairman of the Council of People's Commissars of the USSR. At the same time, until February 1937, he was deputy chairman of the Council of Labor and Defense of the USSR and people's commissar of heavy industry of the USSR (February–October 1937). In August–October 1937, he was appointed people's commissar of mechanical engineering of the USSR. Mezhlauk participated in the development of the first, second, and third Five-Year Plans and in the creation and development of the production base of the aviation and tank industries.

Mezhlauk is perhaps best known for his caricature portraits painted during meetings of the Politburo of the Central Committee and the Presidium of the Supreme Council of the National Economy, at plenums of the Central Committee, party congresses, and so on. Among the most famous are portraits of **L. Kaganovich**, **S. Kosior**, **L. Kamenev**, **A. Mikoian**, **A. Rykov**, **K. Voroshilov**, **V. Kuibyshev**, **Iu. Piatakov**, **M. Tomsky**, and others. He was also an author of a number of works in the field of economics and planning.

On December 2, 1937, Mezhlauk was arrested on charges of treason, industrial sabotage, contacts with the German government, and heading a Latvian counterrevolutionary terrorist organization. On July 28, 1938, he was sentenced to death by the Military Collegium of the Supreme Court of the USSR and shot. His wife, Charna Markovna Mezhlauk (Maers-Mikhailova), was also arrested and exiled to Kolyma, where she died (she was mentioned in the camp memoirs of Evgenia Ginzburg). In 1956, Mezhlauk was rehabilitated.

MIKHOELS, SOLOMON (NÉE SHLOYME VOVSI) (1890–1948). Mikhoels was a Soviet Jewish actor and director of the Moscow State Jewish Theater, theater teacher, public figure, People's Artist of the USSR (1939), laureate of the Stalin Prize, second degree (1946), chevalier of the Order of Lenin (1939), and chairman of the Jewish Anti-Fascist Committee during the Second World War.

Solomon Mikhoels was born in Dünaburg (today Daugavpils, Latvia) into an Orthodox Jewish family. In 1903, he graduated from *Heder* (Jewish Primary Religious School for boys). According to his own recollections, only at the age of 13 did he start to receive a secular education and begin to learn the Russian language. In 1905–1908, he studied at the Riga Real School. During his studies, he participated in amateur performances and concerts. In 1911–1913, he studied at the Kyiv Commercial Institute (now the Kyiv National Economic University named after Vadym Hetman) but was expelled for participation in student unrest. From 1915 to 1918, he studied at the Faculty of Law of Petrograd University.

In 1918–1919, Solomon studied at Aleksandr Gransky's Jewish Chamber theater, and from 1919, he started to perform in it. In 1920, together with the theater, he moved to Moscow. In 1925, the studio was transformed into the Moscow State Jewish (Yiddish) Theater (*GOSET*). In 1928, Solomon's theater toured Germany, France, Belgium, the Netherlands, and Austria. In 1929, after A. Granovsky's decision not to return to the USSR, Mikhoels became the artistic director and chief director of the theater. In 1931, along with theatrical work, he started to teach at the theater's school (later the school was transformed into the Moscow State Jewish Theater School). In 1939, Mikhoels received the honorary title People's Artist of the USSR. He became very popular not only in the Soviet theatrical environment but also abroad. His popularity among the Jewish population, who saw him as their most significant representative, was used by the Soviet authorities for propaganda purposes: he was entrusted with various public posts.

In 1941, after the outbreak of the Second World War, Mikhoels together with the GOSET was evacuated to Tashkent. In February 1942, he became the first chairman of the Jewish Anti-Fascist Committee (JAC). Among the most prominent members of the JAC were Solomon Lozovsky (former Soviet vice-minister of foreign affairs and the head of the Soviet Information Bureau), Shakne Epshtein, Itzik Feffer, Ilia Ehrenburg, Solomon Bregman (deputy minister of state control), Aaron Katz (general of the Stalin Military Academy), Boris Shimeliovich (chief surgeon of the Red Army and director of Botkin Hospital), Shlomo Shleifer (chief rabbi of Moscow), Lina Stern (Soviet scientist, the first female full member of the Russian Academy of Sciences), Israel Fisanovich (Hero of the Soviet Union), and others. The committee was established on the initiative of the Soviet authorities as a propaganda tool and aimed to organize political and material support for the USSR. In this capacity, Mikhoels was allowed to visit the United States, Canada, Mexico, and Great Britain to seek financial support for the Soviet struggle against Nazi Germany. Mikhoels was able to receive aid from such famous people as Rabbi Stephen Wise, Albert Einstein, and Fiorello La Guardia; he raised millions of dollars for the Soviet Union.

In February 1944, Mikhoels, together with Fefer and Epstein, wrote a letter to Stalin with a request to consider the establishment of a Jewish autonomous region in Crimea. It never came to fruition. After the end of the war, Mikhoels was seen as a Jewish representative of the Soviet authorities. He was invited abroad to participate in international conferences but never again was he allowed to leave the USSR. In 1946, he was awarded the Stalin Prize. After the war, members of the JAC were trying to help Jews and to establish contact with Western Jewish organizations, hoping to organize humanitarian supplies to the USSR to help survivors. They also started the Black Book project, which aimed to collect material on Nazi crimes against the Jewish population on occupied territories. Stalin and Soviet authorities were not happy with the growing authority of the JAC and with their unauthorized activities.

On January 12, 1948, Mikhoels, together with a colleague, theatrical critic Vladimir Golubov (Potapov), were murdered in Minsk. After Stalin's death (1953), it was revealed that the world-famous theater director and Jewish public figure was killed by the USSR Ministry of State Security (MGB) on the direct orders of Stalin. The murder was disguised as a truck accident. The MGB officers who killed Mikhoels later received the highest state awards of the USSR: three were awarded the Order of the Patriotic War of the first degree, and one the Order of the Red Star; the direct head of the operation, Lavrenty Fomich Tsanava (head of the Belarusian MGB), received the Order of the Red Banner.

Mikhoels's death was followed by the closure of the JAC and arrest of most of its members. In July 1949, the GOSET theater was also closed and never restored. During the **Doctors' Plot** in early 1953, Mikhoels's second cousin, a military doctor, M. Vovsi, was also arrested.

MIKOIAN, ANASTAS IVANOVICH (1895–1978). One of the "Old Bolsheviks," Mikoian was a revolutionary, Soviet politician and party leader, party member of RSDWP from 1915, member of the Central Committee of the CPSU (1923), and member of the Politburo of the CC CPSU (1935–1966).

Anastas Mikoian was born into a poor Armenian peasant family in the village of Sanahin, Ielizavetpol Governorate, Russian Empire (currently in Armenia). At the age of nine, since he did not speak Russian and since in the Russian Empire education in all gymnasia was carried out in Russian, he was sent to the theological seminary in Tiflis. During his studies, Mikoian became interested in Bolshevik ideas. He read a lot and was influenced by works of Hakob Melik Hakobian (Raffi), Jean Jaurès, and Marx. In 1915, he joined the RSDWP (Bolshevik faction). In 1916, he graduated from the seminary and decided to continue his studies at the Higher Theological Academy in Echmiadzin (now Armenia). Mikoian never managed to graduate from the academy. The February Revolution began, and Mikoian became one of the ideological leaders and organizers of the revolutionary movement in Echmiadzin.

After the February Revolution, he carried out party propaganda work in Tiflis and Baku (by this time he had learned the Georgian and Azerbaijani languages). Some time later, he headed the Baku Bolshevik regional committee. In October 1917, after the October Revolution, Mikoian took part in the work of the first congress of Caucasian Bolshevik Organizations and was a member of the Presidium of the Baku Bolshevik Committee. He also worked as an editor of the newspapers *Sotsial-Demokrat* and *Izvestia*. In March 1918, he took an active part in suppressing the Ganja Uprising, an anti-Bolshevik rebellion that took place in Ganja, Azerbaijan. In the summer of 1918, during the battle with German-Turkish troops, he was the commissar of the Red Army brigade.

In 1918, after the temporary fall of the Soviet power in Baku, Mikoian led the underground city party committee. He tried to free arrested Baku Commissars but was arrested in Krasnovodsk and narrowly escaped being shot.

In February 1919, Mikoian was released, and in March he headed the Baku Bureau of the Caucasian Regional Committee of the RCP(b). He became one of the leaders of the revolutionary movement in the Caucasus. Having established contact with Moscow and Astrakhan, he organized the delivery of oil products to the Soviet Republic. In 1919, he advocated the independence of Azerbaijan and disagreed with many Armenian Communists on this issue. As a result, in Armenian circles he was called the "Muslim communist." In October 1919, he was summoned to Moscow, where he met V. Lenin for the first time and became a member of the

All-Russian Central Executive Committee. In Moscow, Mikoian participated in meetings of the Politburo and the Organizing Bureau of the Central Committee of the RCP(b). In Moscow, he joined the All-Russian Central Executive Committee.

In 1920, Mikoian returned to the Caucasus and was appointed to the post of an authorized Revolutionary Military Council and head of the Gubkom. For military services during the Civil War, Mikoian was awarded the Order of the Red Banner. In 1922–1924, he was appointed secretary of the Southeastern Department of the Central Committee of the RCP(b) in Rostov-on-Don. From 1922, he was a candidate of the Central Committee of the RCP(b), and in 1923 he became a full member. After Lenin's death, Mikoian supported Stalin. In 1924–1926, he served as secretary of the North Caucasian Regional Party Committee and member of the Revolutionary Military Council of the North Caucasian Military District. From July 23, 1926, on Stalin's recommendation, he became a candidate member of the Politburo, CC CPSU.

On August 14, 1926, Mikoian was appointed people's commissar of internal and foreign trade of the USSR (he was the youngest people's commissar). In this post, he oversaw trade of works of art from Soviet museums. On November 22, 1930, the People's Commissariat for Foreign and Internal Trade was divided into the People's Commissariat for Foreign Trade and the People's Commissariat for Supply. The latter was headed by Mikoian. On July 29, 1934, when the People's Commissariat for Supply was divided into the People's Commissariat for Internal Trade and the People's Commissariat for the Food Industry, Mikoian headed the latter. In 1935, he became a full member of the Politburo. In 1936, he visited the United States and got acquainted with the latest technologies in the food industry. After his return, he supervised the rapid development of the food industry (especially the meat industry) and introduced new products into the USSR. He also led a project on printing a cookbook (*The Book of Tasty and Healthy Food*), which encouraged home cooking and was printed in 1939. He also contributed greatly to the development of Soviet advertising. In 1938–1949, he was minister (people's commissar until 1946) of foreign trade. In 1938, he was elected to the Supreme Soviet of the Bashkir Autonomous Soviet Socialist Republic of the first convocation.

During the **Great Patriotic War** (1941–1945), Mikoian served as chairman of the Committee for Food and Clothing Supply of the Red Army. In 1942, a failed attempt was made to kill Mikoian by a deserting Red Army soldier. In 1942–1945, Mikoyan became a member of the USSR **State Defense Committee**. Simultaneously in 1943–1946, he was a member of the Committee of the Council of People's Commissars of the USSR for the restoration of the national economy in the areas liberated from the Nazi invaders. By the decree of the Presidium of the Supreme Soviet of the USSR of September 30, 1943, Mikoian was awarded the title of hero of socialist labor, as well as the Order of Lenin, and a "Hammer and Sickle" gold medal for special services in organizing the supply of food, fuel, and clothing to the Red Army in difficult wartime conditions during the Great Patriotic War.

In 1946–1955, Mikoian served as deputy chairman (in 1955–1964, first deputy chairman) of the Council of Ministers of the USSR. Simultaneously in 1946–1949, he was minister of foreign trade of the USSR. By the end of the 1940s, Stalin planned new purges. In 1949, Mikoian fell out of favor with Stalin, who decided to remove him from the posts of minister of trade and deputy chairman of the Council of Ministers. The situation was provoked by Mikoian's protests against the deportation of the Ingush and Chechens during the war. Mikoian along with **V. Molotov**, found himself in a vulnerable position. But Stalin died before he was able to put this plan into motion.

In 1953–1955, Mikoian was reappointed minister of trade of the USSR. After Stalin's death, he supported **N. Khrushchev** in his struggle for power. In 1956, he helped Khrushchev to write the Secret Speech and supported de-Stalinization. By 1957, Mikoian was considered one of Khrushchev's closest associates. On behalf of Khrushchev, Mikoian conducted negotiations with American politicians and discussed Soviet–Cuban cooperation with Fidel Castro.

In 1964–1965, Mikoian was appointed chairman of the Presidium of the Supreme Soviet of the USSR. In 1965, he stepped down but remained in the Presidium of the Supreme Soviet of the USSR until 1974. Mikoian started his career under Lenin and resigned under Brezhnev. After retirement, he lived in Moscow until his death on October 21, 1978. During his lifetime, he was awarded six Orders of Lenin, Orders of the October Revolution, and Orders of the Red Banner. He was the most notable Old Bolshevik to survive the Purges of 1937–1938.

MILIUTIN, VLADIMIR PAVLOVICH (1884– 1937). A Russian Bolshevik (from 1910) and Soviet politician, Miliutin was people's commissar of agriculture in the first Soviet government (1917), people's commissar and head of the Central Statistical Office of the USSR (1928–1930), member of the Central Committee of the RSDWP(b) (April 1917–March 1918), candidate member of the Central Committee of the RCP(b) (1920–1922), member of the Central Control Commission of the CPSU (b) (1924–1934), member of the All-Russian Central Executive Committee from June 1917, director of the Central Statistical Administration (1928), and an enthusiastic supporter of the first Five-Year Plan. He was also an author of many works on the economy, including *Agrarian Policy in the USSR* (1926) and *History of the Economic Development of the USSR* (1928).

Vladimir Miliutin was born into the family of rural teacher Pavel Viacheslavovich Miliutin in Kursk Governorate, Russian Empire. Vladimir's mother, Iulia Nikolaevna Iazykova, was a distant relative of the poet Nikolai Iazykov (1803–1846). In 1903, he graduated from the Kursk Real School and moved to St. Petersburg. In this same year, he entered the Law Faculty of St. Petersburg University and immediately began to participate in student organizations and the student revolutionary movement. In 1903, Miliutin joined the Russian Social Democratic Workers' Party (RSDWP)— first the Menshevik branch and, in 1910, the Bolshevik faction. He carried out party work in Kursk, Moscow, Orel, St. Petersburg, and Tula. He was repeatedly detained by the tsarist government for his constant revolutionary activity. Altogether, he was arrested eight times and spent about five years in prison. Twice he was exiled to the Vologda province in northwest Russia.

After the February Revolution of 1917, Miliutin became a member of the Saratov Committee of the RSDWP(b) and chairman of the Saratov Council of Workers' and Soldiers' Deputies. In April 1917, at the seventh All-Russian Party Conference, he was elected to the Central Committee of the RSDWP(b). In October 1917, Miliutin became a member of the Petrograd Military Revolutionary Committee and people's commissar of agriculture in the new Soviet government. After the October Revolution, he advocated for a coalition socialist government with the participation of Mensheviks and Socialist-Revolutionaries. Due to his disagreement with the policy of the Central Committee of the RSDWP(b), he resigned from the CC and his government post. Later, he admitted his mistake and was elected a member of the Constituent Assembly.

From November 1918 to March 1921, Miliutin served as deputy chairman of the Supreme Soviet of the National Economy. In 1921–1922, he was deputy chairman of the Economic Meeting of the Northwest Region. In 1922–1924, he was appointed the representative of the **Comintern** in Austria and the Balkans. In 1924–1928, he was a member of the Collegium of the People's Commissariat of the Workers' and Peasants' Inspection of the USSR. Simultaneously, in 1924–1934, he was a member of the Central Control Commission of the All-Union Communist Party of the Bolsheviks (VKP[b]). In 1925–1927, he also served as deputy chairman of the Communist Academy. From March 3, 1928, to January 23, 1930, he headed the Central Statistical Administration of the USSR. From December 1929 to April 1934, Miliutin served as deputy chairman of the USSR State Planning Committee (Gosplan). From April 1934, he was chairman of the Committee for the Management of Scientific and Educational Institutions of the Central Executive Committee of the Soviet Union.

On July 26, 1937, despite the fact that Miliutin had always been a loyal supporter of Stalin, he was arrested and convicted by the Military Collegium of the USSR Supreme Court on charges of participation in a counterrevolutionary terrorist organization. On October 29, 1937, he was sentenced to death and shot. On May 26, 1956, Miliutin was rehabilitated by a decision of the Military Collegium of the USSR Supreme Court.

MOLOTOV, VIACHESLAV MIKHAILOVICH (NÉE SKRIABIN) (1890–1986). A Russian revolutionary, Soviet politician and diplomat, and one of the Old Bolsheviks, Molotov was a protégé who was nicknamed "Stalin's Shadow." He was chairman of the Council of People's Commissars (1930–1941), people's commissar, minister of foreign affairs of the USSR (1939–1949 and 1953–1956), and hero of socialist labor (1943).

Viacheslav Skriabin was born in the village of Kukarka, Iaransk Uezd, Viatka Governorate, Russian Empire (present-day Sovetsk, in Kirov Oblast). His father, Mikhail Prokhorovich Skriabin, was a merchant. His mother, Anna Iakovlevna Nebogatikova, was also from a merchant family. In 1908, Viacheslav graduated from the Kazan Real School. Even before graduation, in 1906, he had joined the RSDWP(b). In 1909, he was arrested for participation in revolutionary activities and sent into exile in Vologda. In 1911, he was released. In 1911–1912, he studied at the St. Petersburg Polytechnic Institute but did not graduate. In 1912–1913, he became secretary of the editorial office of the newspaper *Pravda*. Around the same time, Skriabin met Iosif Dzhugashvili (Stalin). During the First World War, he was engaged in a wide variety of draft-evasion practices and lived under false names. From 1915, Skriabin started to use the party pseudonym Molotov ("hammer") on a regular basis. In this same year, he was again arrested for his party activity and deported to the Irkutsk province. In 1916, he was able to flee from his exile and return to the Russian capital, where he became a member of the Russian Bureau of the Central Committee of the RSDWP(b).

During the February Revolution (1917), Molotov spoke out against assistance to the provisional government. Stalin often called him Molotoshvili. During the October Revolution of 1917, Molotov was a member of the Petrograd Military Revolutionary Committee. In 1918–1920, he occupied various leading party posts in the Volga region. In the summer of 1919, while traveling on the propaganda steamer *Krasnaia Zvezda*, he met **Nadezhda Krupskaia** (he had encountered **V. Lenin** two years earlier). From 1920 to 1921, he was secretary of the Central Committee of the Communist Party of Ukraine. His party career flourished quickly. Already in 1920, Molotov became a candidate member and, in 1921, a member of the Central Committee. He also received full membership of the CC Orgburo. In March 1921, at the tenth party congress, Molotov was appointed responsible secretary of the Central Committee of the RCP(b) and became a candidate member of the Politburo. In 1922, the post of responsible secretary was renamed "general secretary" and transferred to Stalin. Molotov became the de facto second secretary.

After Lenin's death on January 21, 1924, Molotov was a member of the commission that organized Lenin's funeral. He became one of the most loyal supporters of Stalin and a leading figure in Stalin's "inner circle." Molotov backed Stalin in his struggle for power first against **L. Trotsky** and later against **L. Kamenev**, **G. Zinoviev**, and the so-called "Right Deviation" associated with Soviet party theoretician **N. Bukharin**. On January 1, 1926, under Stalin's patronage, Molotov was elected a member of the CPSU Politburo. From November 1928 to April 1929, Molotov headed the Moscow party organization, where he replaced N. Uglanov, one of the leaders of the "Right Deviation."

In 1930, Molotov was appointed chairman of the Council of People's Commissars of the USSR. He served in this capacity, the de facto head of government, until 1941, when he was replaced by Stalin, and served as his deputy. In the early 1930s, a permanent

Defense Commission was created under the Council of People's Commissars of the USSR (after 1937, it was renamed the Defense Committee). It was headed by Molotov until 1940. In 1937–1939, he served as chairman of the Economic Council (EcoSo) of the Soviet government. The period of Molotov's government leadership was one of high growth of the gross domestic product and the state's defense capability, industrialization, urbanization, and modernization. It was also a period of genuine mass enthusiasm during the first Five-Year Plan. During the First and Second Five-Year Plans, Molotov worked very enthusiastically, but he had some serious differences with his main assistants (the people's commissars), including **S. Ordzhonikidze**, the people's commissar of heavy industry of the USSR. In such conflict situations, Stalin almost always supported Molotov.

In 1931–1932, Molotov headed the campaign to collectivize agriculture and led the Extraordinary Commission for Grain Procurements in Ukraine. In December 1931, at a meeting of the Politburo of the CC CPSU, he discussed the extreme dissatisfaction with the implementation of the plan on the part of the peasantry and demanded to use "special measures" to increase it. Molotov personally signed the "Law of Three Spikelets," which was used during the famine of 1932–1933. Under this law, Soviet authorities increased penalties (the highest punishment was execution by shooting) for people who tried to appropriate kolkhoz property. Even those who collected the grains (or spikelets) left behind in the field were treated as enemies of the people and socialist rule. In 1936, Molotov, due to his opposition of the open trial against **L. Kamenev** and **G. Zinoviev**, nearly ended up in the dock himself. However, very soon he ceased to object to repressions and took an active part in organizing the mass terror of 1937–1938. Molotov signed the largest number of resolutions (372, which was much higher than the number signed by Stalin) related to repressions, as well as execution lists for those from the highest party and state apparatus.

On May 3, 1939, Molotov, while retaining the post of chairman of the USSR Council of People's Commissars, replaced **Maksim Litvinov** as people's commissar of foreign affairs. He began his new appointment by purging the people closest to Litvinov. A group of Litvinov's former employees was arrested the day after Molotov assumed office. At the same time, Molotov promoted a number of young diplomats, including **A. Gromyko**. On August 23, 1939, in the capacity of the people's commissar of foreign affairs, Molotov—together with the minister of foreign affairs of Nazi Germany, Joachim von Ribbentrop—signed the Soviet–German Non-Aggression Pact. This document is also known as the "Molotov-Ribbentrop Pact." Several secret articles—which defined the borders of Soviet and German spheres of influence across Poland, Latvia, Lithuania, Estonia, and Finland—were attached to the treaty.

On September 28, 1939, Molotov signed a new German–Soviet Frontier Treaty. As a result, the eastern parts of Poland with a predominantly Ukrainian and Belarusian population were annexed to the Ukrainian SSR and the Belarusian SSR, and the Vilnius region with the city of Vilna became part of the then independent Lithuania, annexed by the Soviet Union formally the following year. In mid-November 1940, Molotov visited Berlin. During the three-day stay, he had a meeting with Adolf Hitler and two official meetings with Joachim Ribbentrop. On April 5, 1941, he participated in signing the Treaty of Friendship and Non-Aggression with Yugoslavia (a day before the start of the German invasion of this country) and the Soviet–Japanese pact of neutrality. On May 6, 1941, Molotov was dismissed from the post of the head of the government. Stalin himself headed the Council of People's Commissars of the Soviet Union, and Molotov was appointed his deputy.

On June 22, 1941, Molotov, in the capacity of vice chairman of the Council of the People's Commissars and people's commissioner for foreign affairs, announced the German invasion on the radio. During the **Great Patriotic War** (1941–1945), Molotov served as deputy chairman of the **State Defense Committee**. In October 1941, during the Viazemskaia operation, Molotov was sent to the battle zone, his only trip to the front. In late May to early June 1942, Molotov visited Great Britain and the United States on a diplomatic mission. On May 26, 1942, together with British foreign minister Anthony Eden, he signed the Anglo–Soviet Treaty in London. In 1943–1945, Molotov took part in the **Tehran** (1943), **Ialta** (1945), and **Potsdam** (1945) conferences. In addition to diplomatic work, Viacheslav Molotov was responsible for the production of tanks, for which he later received the title of hero of socialist labor with the Order of Lenin and the Hammer and Sickle medal. In 1942, he also headed the Soviet "atomic project." On October 14, 1944, on Molotov's initiative, the Moscow State Institute of International Relations was founded on the basis of the Faculty of International Relations of Moscow State University.

After the end of the war, Molotov, as the head of Soviet foreign policy, often traveled abroad. He participated in the conference in San Francisco that created the United Nations Organization. In 1946, he also led Soviet delegations at most sessions of the Council of Foreign Ministers of the USSR, the United States, Great Britain, France, and China at the Paris Peace Conference, where he actively defended the territorial interests of Albania, Bulgaria, and Yugoslavia. On March 19, 1946, the Council of People's Commissars was transformed into the Council of Ministers, and Molotov became its first deputy chairman. In this capacity, he supervised education, science, and law enforcement. Molotov actively supported the idea of the creation of the state of Israel. He regularly participated in the work of the UN in the United States, and because of his implacable position, as well as the frequent use of the "veto" right, he was nicknamed "Mr. No" in diplomatic circles. He was widely regarded as a difficult and abrasive personality not only in his home country but also abroad.

From 1947 to 1949, Molotov headed Soviet foreign intelligence as chairman of the Information Committee under the USSR Council of Ministers. In 1949, he was a member of the Permanent Commission for open trials of former servicemen of the German army and German punitive bodies held responsible for atrocities against Soviet citizens during the German occupation of the Soviet Union. Molotov also took part in organizing trials of German and Japanese war criminals.

By the end of the 1940s, Molotov's power began to decline. On March 4, 1949, he was removed from the post of foreign minister (**A. Vyshinsky** replaced him), and his wife, Polina Zhemchuzhina (who was responsible for textiles in the Ministry of Light Industry), was arrested for treason in the same year. In October 1952, at the Plenum of the Central Committee, Stalin criticized both Molotov and **A. Mikoian**. Molotov's position looked precarious with another purge imminent. At the same time, official Soviet propaganda continued to portray Molotov as Stalin's closest associate. In 1952, in the alphabet book for elementary school children (Bukvar), portraits and biographies of Lenin, Stalin, and Molotov were included. The death of Stalin on March 5, 1953, probably saved Molotov's life, as well as that of his wife, who was released on the orders of **L. Beria**.

On this same day, Molotov was again appointed minister of foreign affairs and at the

Viacheslav Molotov

same time first deputy chairman of the Council of Ministers of the USSR. He supported the arrest of Beria and the removal of **G. Malenkov** from the post of chairman of the Council of Ministers of the USSR. In 1955, Molotov was appointed chairman of the commission for reviewing open trials and a closed trial of military leaders. Subsequently, Molotov and **Khrushchev** began to disagree on many issues. Molotov objected to the complete withdrawal of Soviet troops from Austria in 1955 and was skeptical about the normalization of relations with Yugoslavia. In 1957, Molotov led the so-called "Anti-Party Group" against Khrushchev. Teaming up with **L. Kaganovich** and G. Malenkov, Molotov attempted to remove Khrushchev. But Khrushchev's supporters were able to quickly organize the Central Committee Plenum, at which the "Anti-Party group" was defeated. On June 29, 1957, Molotov was removed from all posts "for belonging to the Anti-Party group" and removed from both the Presidium of the CPSU Central Committee and the CPSU Central Committee. In 1957, he was appointed USSR ambassador to Mongolia, but his term was short-lived because of his health problems. From 1960 to 1961, he headed the Soviet office at the headquarters of the UN International Atomic Energy Agency (IAEA) in Vienna. In mid-November 1961, Molotov was recalled from Vienna, removed from his post, and expelled from the party. On September 12, 1963, Molotov went into retirement.

Shortly before Molotov died on November 8, 1986, his party membership was restored.

NOTES

1. I. V. Kulganek, "I. M. Maisky—mongoloved, obshchestvenny deiatel (1884–1975)," in *Mongolica XIV* (St. Petersburg: Rossiiskaya Akademia Nauk, 2015), 6.

NAZI–SOVIET PACT. A nonaggression pact between Germany and the Soviet Union—also known as the Molotov-Ribbentrop pact or, less commonly, the Hitler-Stalin Pact—it was an intergovernmental agreement signed in Moscow on August 23, 1939, by the minister of foreign affairs of Germany, Ribbentrop, and the people's commissar of foreign affairs of the USSR, **V. Molotov.**

According to this pact, the parties pledged to refrain from attacking each other and to maintain neutrality if one of them became the object of hostilities by a third party. The parties also guaranteed the rejection of allied relations with other countries, which "directly or indirectly aimed at the other party."[1] The pact provided for the mutual exchange of information on issues affecting the interests of the other party. Also, Germany and the USSR were to resolve disputes exclusively by peaceful means. The pact was concluded for a period of ten years. If one of the countries did not warn about its termination a year before the expiration date, the contract was supposed to be extended for another five years.

The signing of this document (it was immediately published) became a sensation and testified about a radical turn in the foreign policy of the USSR and Germany. But the treaty itself was the standard diplomatic document of the time. For example, in 1934 Germany and Poland signed the "Declaration on the Non-Use of Force," which was actually an almost-identical nonaggression pact. In 1941, Japan and the USSR concluded the "Pact of Neutrality," and so on.

A distinctive feature of the treaty was the secret protocol that defined the borders of Soviet and German spheres of interest in eastern Europe between the parties in the event of "territorial and political reorganization." The protocol recognized the inclusion of Latvia, Estonia, Finland, the eastern regions of the Polish state, and Bessarabia in the sphere of interests of the USSR. Lithuania and the western part of Poland were included in the sphere of German interests. Rumors about the existence of an additional secret protocol emerged shortly after the signing of the pact. But its text was published only in 1948 from photocopies. In the USSR, the existence of the protocol was categorically denied. Molotov, who signed the Non-Aggression Pact and the secret protocol to it, denied its existence until his death in 1986. The original of the secret protocol was found in the archives of the Politburo of the Central Committee of the CPSU only in 1993.

On September 1, 1939, the day after the ratification of the treaty, Germany attacked Poland. In full accordance with the secret protocol, in 1939 German troops did not enter the eastern regions of Poland inhabited mainly by Belarusians and Ukrainians, as well as the territories of Latvia, Lithuania, and Estonia, which were subsequently occupied by Soviet troops. On September 17, 1939, Soviet troops entered the territory of the eastern regions of Poland. In 1939–1940, relying on left-wing political forces in these countries, Soviet leadership established control over Latvia, Lithuania, and Estonia. Also, after the **Soviet-Finnish War**, based on the agreed sphere of interests of the USSR, the Soviet state seized part of Karelia and territories adjacent to Leningrad.

As a result, in 1939–1940, Germany, confident in the inviolability of its eastern borders, avoided a war on two fronts, successively defeated Poland, France, and smaller European countries, and trained an army with two years of combat experience to attack the USSR in 1941. Moreover, the USSR supplied Germany with Soviet raw materials and food. The Soviet Union, having increased its territory at the expense of Poland, Romania, and the Baltic States, received time to reequip the army. On the other hand, the conclusion of a treaty with Hitler, as well as the ensuing military conflict with Finland and the exclusion of the USSR from the League of Nations, undermined the international authority of the Soviet Union as a real force capable of resisting Nazism. It provoked the strengthening of anti-Soviet tendencies in the West and complicated the participation of foreign communist parties in the anti-fascist movement, since at the direction of the **Comintern**, they stopped political and propaganda work against Nazi Germany. According to many historians, the main beneficiary of the pact was Nazi Germany.

In 2009, the European Parliament proclaimed August 23, the date of the signing of the Non-Aggression Pact between Germany and the Soviet Union, as European Day of Remembrance for Victims of Stalinism and Nazism.

NEW ECONOMIC POLICY (NEP). An economic policy proposed by **V. Lenin** in March 1921 and adopted first in Soviet Russia and later in the USSR, the NEP included a return to commodity-money relations, the abolition of enforced grain procurements (*prodrazvertka*), the introduction of *prodnalog* (food tax), freedom of trade, monetary reform (1922–1924), and the attraction of foreign capital. In 1928, Stalin announced the first **Five-Year Plan** for the development of the national economy of the USSR and renationalized much of the economy. This marked the end of the NEP. Legally, the NEP was terminated only on October 11, 1931, when a resolution on the complete ban on private trade in the USSR was adopted.

After the Russian Civil War of 1917–1921, the situation in the country was disastrous. Russia lost over a quarter of its national wealth and huge territories (Poland, Finland, Latvia, Estonia, Lithuania, western Belarus, the Volhynia region of western Ukraine, and Bessarabia). The policy of **War Communism** introduced in 1918 caused economic troubles, food shortages, and hardships. The volume of industrial and agricultural products decreased dramatically. The standard of living of the Russian population dropped sharply. Industrial output in 1920 had decreased by seven times in comparison with 1913. Many sectors of the Russian economy were completely destroyed. As a result, peasants engaged in mass protests. Uprisings covered Tambov region, Ukraine, the Don, the Kuban, the Volga region, and Siberia. Red Army units were sent to suppress these uprisings. Peasant revolts coupled with an insurrection of the Soviet sailors, soldiers, and civilians of the port city of Kronstadt against the Bolshevik government of the Russian SFSR in Spring 1921, caused a critical crisis for the Soviet regime. Socialism did not begin on a good note. The Soviet government had to respond to all these challenges. The NEP was an unexpected and powerful move.

There was no unity on the NEP within the Soviet leadership itself. Its methods were rejected or questioned by part of the leadership. Nevertheless, given the critical situation in the country, many party leaders considered that it was necessary to make a compromise with peasantry, Lenin at the forefront. The NEP was seen as a temporary admission of capitalist elements, such as freedom of trade and freedom of private enterprise, while creating the conditions for socialism. The main political goal was to relieve social tension and to strengthen the social base of Soviet power in a form of alliance between workers and peasants and to create a link between town and countryside. The economic goal of the NEP was to prevent further worsening of social life, extricate Soviet Russia from the crisis, and restore the economy. The social goal was to provide favorable conditions for building a socialist society, without waiting for the world revolution. In addition, NEP was aimed at restoring normal foreign policy ties and overcoming international isolation.

The decree of the All-Russian Central Executive Committee "On the Replacement of Food and Raw Materials Appropriation with a Tax in Kind" (the tax was supposed to become progressive), adopted on March 21, 1921, at the tenth party congress, initiated the transition from War Communism to the New Economic Policy. The introduction of the tax in kind did not become a single measure. In May 1921, the Bolsheviks had to legalize free trade, and with it the whole complex of commodity-money relations. In July of the same year, the Council of People's Commissars restored payments for rail and water transportation of goods and passengers, and in August, they were extended to postal services, telegraph services, and utilities. Part of the light and food industries, and most of the trade, passed into private hands. At the same time, the state continued to control heavy industry and transport. But state-owned enterprises also switched to market relations. They united into self-supporting trusts that had to sell their products on the market and existed based on cost accounting (*khozraschet*).

The main directions of the New Economic Policy included the following:

- Replacement of surplus appropriation with a tax in kind: The fixed food tax was much smaller (initially set at about 20 percent of the net product of peasant labor) and allowed peasants to have surplus products for sale;
- Introduction of free trade: Free trade allowed receiving income from the sale of goods and thus stimulated interest in production of goods. It also significantly intensified the development of commodity-money relations and exchange between town and country. But this policy caused disappointment among some party leaders. For example, at the Politiburo meeting on August 25, 1921, Trotsky pessimistically remarked that "the days of Soviet power are numbered";
- The transfer of small and medium-sized enterprises to private ownership: This measure stimulated production of industrial goods and greatly contributed to the rapid restoration of industry;
- Creation of commercial banks: Commercial banks were able to provide enterprises with loans.
- Formation of concessions and joint ventures with the participation of foreign firms: This measure did not have a significant impact, because economically developed foreign states were very suspicious of the Soviet country.
- Financial reform: This was a vitally important measure that allowed the government to stabilize commodity-money relations, eliminate inflation, and increase the role of the state as a guarantor of the New Economic Policy. By the early 1920s, banknotes issued by tsarist Russia, the Kerensky government of 1917, and the Soviet government were in circulation in the country. One ruble in 1913 corresponded in purchasing power to 28 million rubles in 1921. In November 1922, the first banknotes of the new Soviet currency (*chervontsy*) were put into circulation. Monetary reform also aimed to stabilize the monetary and credit relations of the USSR with other countries. A banking system was also developed, which included the State Bank, a network of cooperative banks, a Commercial and Industrial Bank, a Bank for Foreign Trade, and a network of local communal banks. Direct and indirect taxes were introduced (industrial, income, agricultural, excise taxes on consumer goods, local taxes), as well as payment for services (transport, communications, utilities, etc.).

As a result of the implementation of the NEP, industrial recovery began. Some successes were achieved in metallurgy and mechanical engineering. The devastation in railway transport was overcome. Overall, the peasantry greeted the NEP with great enthusiasm. However, the wealthier peasants were taxed at higher rates. Thus, on the one hand, the opportunity was provided to improve welfare, but on the other, there was no point in expanding the household. Although the well-being of peasants increased in comparison with the prewar level and the number of poor decreased, the number of rich peasants also decreased. Procurement of grain in 1924 was relatively successful, as the plan was fulfilled by 86 percent. The overstocking crisis was overcome. Bread prices stabilized. Overall, reform yielded a number of positive results, and by 1926 the food supply improved significantly. The revival of wholesale trade led to the emergence of a wide network of trade enterprises, fairs, as well as commodity exchanges (dominated by the Moscow Exchange), which operated under state control. In the 1920s, commercial credits financed approximately 85 percent of all sales of goods. In 1925, the share of private trade in wholesale was 40–80 percent.

Earlier such regulation in Europe was introduced only during wartime, but NEP became a system of state regulation of the industrial-agrarian economy in peacetime. Political power remained in the hands of the leadership of the RCP(b) and later CPSU, and the party became the only legal political force. The regime deployed harsh measures against opposition parties and priests of the Russian Orthodox Church. Nevertheless, debates regarding further ways of building socialism arose among the communists. The left opposition—led by **L. Trotsky**, **L. Kamenev**, and **G. Zinoviev**—was against the NEP, while the right wing of the party—headed by **N. Bukharin**, **A. Rykov**, and **M. Tomsky**—defended this policy as a path to socialism. The party apparatus, controlled by Stalin, supported NEP and gradually marginalized the left opposition, which was completely defeated by 1927. In 1925, the possibilities for the development of market relations in the countryside were expanded. Hired labor was allowed. However, the NEP was unable to provide the state with sufficient funds for further development of the economy and, above all, industrialization.

In the second half of the 1920s, the NEP entered a crisis period. In 1924–1926, the prewar level of production was reached, and the work of heavy industry was restored. But at the same time, the commodity and sales crisis intensified. Peasants refused to sell grain to the state because the state continued to raise the prices of industrial products. The correspondingly low price of agricultural goods created the "scissors crisis." The market was saturated with expensive goods, but the majority of the population could not afford to buy them. Also, in 1926 the procurement campaign ended in failure. In 1927, bread lines in the big cities appeared for the first time in several years. Moreover, the country's population grew faster than the gross grain harvest. As a result, the provision of grain per capita decreased from 584 kg in 1913 to 484 kg in 1928. The productivity of agricultural labor stagnated. Peasant labor remained predominantly manual. Only 15 percent of farms had agricultural machinery: seeders, reapers, threshers, and so on. However, industry was unable to provide the required modernization of agriculture since it was mainly a prewar industry and required modernization itself. Resources for modernization could be obtained in two ways: by intensifying the exploitation of labor or by the seizure of food resources from peasants.

The failure of grain procurements convinced Stalin and his supporters that the NEP model, which justified itself during a brief period in 1922–1925, was unable to ensure the country's sustainable development over the long term. For forced industrialization, bread was needed for a new industrial workforce moving from the villages to the towns. Stalin decided to get it by returning to a form of War Communism, this time accompanied by mass collectivization of households. Anti-speculation laws began to be actively used for the seizure of bread. Also, the serious grain procurement crisis of 1926–1928 saw the introduction of ration cards in 1928 and the adoption of some emergency measures to solve the food problem. Such "extraordinary measures" provided grain in 1928 but discouraged peasants from producing a surplus. Food production fell dramatically. In addition, a decline in trade and lack of funds led to a decrease in the production of industrial goods. Also, unemployment rose significantly, reaching 1.5 million by 1928.

Stalin's actions in 1928 caused an acute conflict in the leadership of the CPSU(b), which ended in the defeat of the "right opposition" and the victory of Stalin's supporters in 1929. In April 1929, the 16th conference of the CC CPSU adopted a draft of the first Five-Year Plan, which called for accelerated industrialization, collectivization, and cultural revolution. In August 1929, a rationing system was introduced in the USSR, and the market economy collapsed. In June 1929, the forced sale of "surplus" was legalized. Although this policy was not officially canceled, its ideology started to be criticized. Moreover, the following measures were employed:

- the rejection of free market and transition to state trade;
- the nationalization of private enterprises and commercial banks;
- the creation of agricultural collective enterprises, controlled by the state, instead of individual peasant farms; and
- the concentration of all funds in the hands of the state and industrialization according to a single state plan.

Legally, the NEP was terminated only on October 11, 1931, when a resolution on complete prohibition of private trade in the USSR was adopted. Mistakes and miscalculations of Soviet economists and politicians that led to the NEP crises can to some extent be explained by the novelty of the tasks set and the general cultural and economic situation in Russian society in the 1920s. The undoubted success of the NEP was the restoration of the destroyed economy, but since after the revolution the USSR lost many highly qualified personnel (economists, managers, production workers), the absence of skilled professionals produced the miscalculations and mistakes that brought an end to the NEP.

There has been much speculation concerning whether Lenin intended the NEP to be a temporary or more permanent policy. The Bolshevik's leader's premature death does not permit a definite answer. When Mikhail Gorbachev became general secretary of the CC CPSU, he praised the NEP and regarded it as the path correctly laid out by Lenin, but the anticipated longevity of the change of direction remains a matter for debate.

NOTES

1. See, for example, https://sourcebooks.fordham.edu/mod/1939pact.asp (accessed August 10, 2021).

ORAKHELASHVILI, MAMIA (RUSSIAN: IVAN) (1881–1937). A Georgian Bolshevik involved in the revolutionary movement in Russia and Georgia, Orakhelashvili was an RSDWP member since 1903, candidate member of the Central Committee CPSU (1923–1926), member of the CC CPSU (1926–1937), and member of the Central Executive Committee of the USSR of the first through sixth convocations.

Mamia Orakhelashvili was born in the Kutaisi Governorate, Imperial Russia (present-day Georgia), into a noble family. He graduated from the Kutaisi classical gymnasium and studied at the Medical Faculty of the University of Kharkiv. In 1903, he transferred to the Military Medical Academy in St. Petersburg. In 1903, he joined the RSDWP. In the same year, he was arrested for the first time for the participation in the student revolutionary movement. In the summer of 1906, he traveled to Paris and Geneva for medical treatment. Upon his return, he was arrested in the case of the Avlabar printing house (an underground printing house of the Caucasian Union Committee of the RSDWP).

After graduating from the academy in 1908, Orakhelashvili worked as a doctor in the Transcaspian region. In 1914–1917, he worked as a military doctor in the army of the Russian Empire. In 1917, he served as a chairman of the RSDWP(b) committee and chairman of the Council of Workers' and Soldiers' Deputies in Vladikavkaz. From October 1917 to May 1920, Mamia was a member of the Caucasian Regional Committee of the RSDWP(b), the chairman of the Central Committee of the Communist Party of Georgia, and a member of the Caucasian Bureau of the Central Committee of the RCP(b). After the establishment of the Soviet power in Georgia, he worked in various party posts: chairman of the Revolutionary Committee of Georgia, secretary of the Central Committee of the Communist Party (Bolsheviks) of Georgia, and deputy chairman of the Council of People's Commissars of Georgia. In December 1922, he was appointed chairman of the Council of People's Commissars of the Transcaucasian Socialist Federative Soviet Republic. From July 6, 1923, to May 21, 1925, Orakhelashvili was a deputy chairman of the Council of People's Commissars of the USSR.

In 1926–1929, he became the first secretary of the Transcaucasian Regional Committee of the CPSU(b). At the same time, he was executive editor of the newspaper *Zaria Vostoka*. In 1927–1930, he was a member of the editorial board of the *Great Soviet Encyclopedia* and *Pravda* newspaper. From January to November 1931, he served as the chairman of the Council of People's Commissars of the Transcaucasian Socialist Federative Soviet Republic. In 1932–1937, he became a deputy director of the Marx-Engels-Lenin Institute under the Central Committee of the CPSU.

In May 1937, Orakhelashvili was expelled from the Central Auditing Commission and from the party. In April of the same year, he was exiled to Astrakhan. On June 26, he was arrested. During interrogation, Orakhelashvili was harassed, beaten, and tortured and made false accusations against a significant number of people. Before his execution, Orakhelashvili shouted: "Long live Soviet power!" His daughter and wife were also arrested. He was rehabilitated on July 1, 1955.

ORDZHONIKIDZE, SERGO (GRIGORY) KONSTANTINOVICH (1886–1937). A Georgian Bolshevik and Soviet politician, one of the top leaders of the CPSU(b) and the Soviet state, and a close friend of Stalin, Grigory Ordzhonikidze was born in the village of Goresha, Kutaisi province, Russian Empire (now the Imereti region of western Georgia), into an impoverished Georgian noble family. Six weeks after his birth, Grigory's mother, Eupraxia Tavarashvili, died from a serious illness. In the spring of 1898, he graduated from a two-year school in the village of Kharagauli. That same year, his father, Kote Ordzhonikidze, died. In 1905, Grigory graduated from the paramedic school of the Mikhailovsky hospital in Tbilisi. In 1903 he joined the Bolshevik wing of the RSDWP. According to Ordzhonikidze's daughter, her father met Stalin in a revolutionary circle during this time. In 1907, he became a member of the Baku Committee of the RSDWP. In 1904, he was arrested for possession of illegal Communist literature but was soon released.

In 1905, Grigory was an active participant of the First Russian Revolution in Transcaucasia. In December 1905, he was arrested again and was jailed in the Sukhumi prison until May 1906, when he was released on bail. In August of the same year, with a false passport, he left for Germany. In early 1907, Ordzhonikidze returned to the Caucasus and settled in Baku. There he worked as a paramedic in the oil fields and actively participated in party activities. On May 1, he was arrested during a May Day demonstration and spent twenty-six days in prison—he was held under the pseudonym "Kuchishvili." In November 1907, Ordzhonikidze was arrested again on charges of banditry and spent eighteen months in the prisons of Baku and Sukhumi. In the Baku prison, Ordzhonikidze once again met the revolutionary "Koba," Iosif Dzhugashvili, the future Stalin. The weaker personality, "Sergo," soon fell under Koba's strong influence.

In February 1909, Ordzhonikidze was exiled to the Ienisei province, but in August escaped from exile, returned to Baku, and then left for Persia. He lived in Tehran and took part in the revolution that was taking place there at that time. At the end of 1910, "Sergo" went to Paris, and in the spring of 1911, he studied at the Leninist party school in Longjumeau (the first educational organization established by the RSDWP for training party cadres). In the summer of 1911, Lenin sent Ordzhonikidze to Russia to organize the All-Russian Party Conference. In January 1912, when the sixth conference of the RSDWP was held in Prague, Ordzhonikidze was a delegate and, together with Stalin, was elected to the Central Committee of the party. On April 14, 1912, Ordzhonikidze was arrested in St. Petersburg. After three years of imprisonment in the Shlisselburg Fortress, he was exiled to Iakutsk in eastern Siberia, where he worked as a doctor.

After the February Revolution, in June 1917, Ordzhonikidze returned to Petrograd and became a member of the local Bolshevik City Committee and the Executive Committee of the Petrograd Soviet. He actively participated in the October Revolution of 1917 and was included in the first composition of the All-Russian Extraordinary Commission (**Cheka**). During the Civil War, Ordzhonikidze was appointed the Bolsheviks' commissar in Tsaritsyn, South Russia, Ukraine, the North Caucasus, the Caspian Sea, Belarus, and Tiflis. In March 1920, he was appointed chairman of the North Caucasian Revolutionary Committee and chairman of the Caucasian Bureau of the Central Committee of the RCP(b). He was directly involved in the revolutionary overthrow of the governments in Azerbaijan, Armenia, and Georgia, and the creation of the Transcaucasian Socialist Federative Soviet Republic. In 1920–1921, Ordzhonikidze participated in the Bolshevik policy of systematic repressions against Cossacks of the Russian Empire and deportations of Terek Cossacks.

From February 1922 to September 1926, Ordzhonikidze served as the first secretary of the Transcaucasian Regional Committee of the RCP(b). In July–November 1926, he became a candidate member of the Politburo of the CC CPSU, and in September he was appointed the first secretary of the North Caucasian Regional Committee of the RCP(b). In November 1926, Stalin, now at the top of the Soviet Olympus after his victory over Trotsky and Zinoviev-Kamenev, transferred his old friend Sergo from the Caucasus to Moscow. In 1926–1930, Ordzhonikidze served as a chairman of the Central Control Commission of the CPSU, people's commissar of the workers' and peasants' inspection, and deputy chairman of the Council of People's Commissars of the USSR.

In 1930, Ordzhonikidze became a full member of the Politburo. In November 1930, he was appointed chairman of the Supreme Council of the National Economy of the USSR, and on January 5, 1932, he was transferred from this position to the post of people's commissar of heavy industry of the USSR. In this post, he oversaw numerous construction projects during the first Five-Year Plan. The powerful people's commissar managed to attract qualified specialists, including former oppositionists. Steadily, Ordzhonikidze became more critical of Stalin's policies, though he still considered the Soviet leader his friend. Gradually, relations between Stalin and Sergo deteriorated. In 1936, Ordzhonikidze's older brother Pavel was arrested. In January 1937, Ordzhonikidze's deputy, formerly a prominent Trotskyist, **G. Piatakov**, was executed on charges of conspiracy and sabotage. Stalin accused Ordzhonikidze of "overlooking" the conspiracy in his department. Tensions between Stalin and his former friend escalated. Ordzhonikidze secretly started to check his employees. On February 18, 1937, Ordzhonikidze shot himself. It was officially announced that he had died of a heart attack. During his career, he was awarded the Order of the Red Banner (1921) and Order of Lenin (1935).

ORLOV, ALEKSANDR MIKHAILOVICH (NÉE LEIBA LAZAREVICH FELDBIN) (1895–1973). Orlov was a Soviet intelligence officer, major of state security (1935), illegal resident in France, Austria, and Italy (1933–1937), and NKVD resident and adviser to the Republican government on security in Spain (1937–1938). He moved to the United States in July 1938.

Lev Lazarevich Feldbin was born in the town of Babruisk, in the Russian Empire (today, Belarus), into an Orthodox Jewish family. With the outbreak of the First World War, the family moved to Moscow, where Lev was admitted to the Lazarevsky Institute of Oriental Languages. After two semesters of studies, he then transferred to the Faculty of Law of Moscow University. In 1916, he was drafted into the Imperial Russian Army, where he served in the rear. After the February Revolution of 1917, he joined the RSDWP (Internationalists). With the outbreak of the civil war, he joined the Red Army and was enrolled in the Special Department of the 12th Army (military counterintelligence). Orlov became an active participant of the Red Terror in Kyiv. He participated in the disclosure of the counterrevolutionary organizations in Kyiv and personally led and directed sabotage operations in the territories controlled by the anti-communist White movement.

In May 1920, Orlov joined the Russian Communist Party (Bolsheviks) and the All-Russian Extraordinary Commission (Vcheka, later Cheka). In 1920–1921, he occupied different posts in the Arkhangelsk Cheka. In 1921, he left the Red Army and returned to Moscow to resume his studies at the Faculty of Law of Moscow University. In Moscow, he worked for several years under the supervision of Nikolai Krylenko at the Bolshevik Supreme Tribunal. In May 1924, after graduation from

Ordzhonikidze (left), with Stalin and Mikoian

the university, Lev Nikolsky (Orlov's official surname from 1920) received an invitation from his cousin Zinovy Katsnelson, a Soviet special services leader who headed the Economic Department of the State Political Directorate (GPU), to join the Soviet secret police as an officer of the Finance Department. In 1925, he headed the Border Guard unit of the Sukhumi garrison of the GPU Detachment of border troops in Transcaucasia.

In 1926, Lev Nikolsky started to work at the First Main Directorate (the organization responsible for foreign operations and intelligence activities). In subsequent years, he went on long- and short-term "business" trips to France, Germany, the United States, Italy, Austria, Czechoslovakia, Switzerland, Great Britain, Estonia, Sweden, and Denmark. From 1934, he worked with Kim Philby, a British intelligence officer and a double agent for the Soviet Union, and the Cambridge Group (the Cambridge Spy Ring). In 1932, Orlov, under the cover of a representative of "Lnoexport," was sent to the United States. The purpose of his trip was to establish relations with his relatives from Babruisk and receive a genuine American passport in the name of William Goldin, which would allow him to travel freely throughout Europe. He also explored the possibility of establishing, with the help of his Jewish relatives, Soviet intelligence networks in the United States. In October 1935, upon his return to the USSR, Orlov was appointed deputy head of the Transport Department of the Main Directorate of State Security of the People's Commissariat for Internal Affairs (NKVD). In December 1935, he was promoted to the rank of major of state security.

In 1936, with the outbreak of the Spanish Civil War, Orlov was sent to Spain as a resident and chief adviser on internal security and counterintelligence to the Republican government of Spain. He organized the Military Information Service (SIM), the secret service of the Spanish Republican Armed Forces, an analogue of the NKVD. During the course of the civil war, Orlov and his subordinate, Iosif Grigulevich, organized so-called "mobile groups." He authorized the use of torture in order to obtain confessions (beatings, mock executions, disorientation, and sensory-deprivation techniques) and allowed extrajudicial executions of suspects. SIM, established with the help of Orlov, held prisoners in its own clandestine prisons in Madrid and Barcelona, named "Checas" after the Soviet Cheka. The grim regime established in these prisons differed little from Stalin's gulag.

In 1937, Orlov headed the suppression of the anarchist movements in Catalonia. He allowed the use of combat gases during the "cleansing" operations in the mountainous regions. In June 1937, Orlov organized the kidnapping of Andreu Nin Perez, the leader of the Workers' Party of Marxist Unification (POUM), which was formed by a merger of the Trotskyist Communist Left of Spain (ICE) and the Workers and Peasants' Bloc (against **Trotsky**'s will). After torture, on Orlov's order, Nin was secretly killed. After these "successes," **N. Iezhov** instructed Orlov to create a sabotage school in Spain for training militant, partisan, and sabotage groups for operations behind enemy lines. Orlov also commanded the operation on the transfer of 510 tons of gold, corresponding to 72.6 percent of the total gold reserves of the Bank of Spain, from the Spanish gold reserves in Madrid to Moscow.

In the fall of 1936, many of those considered the founders of the Cheka were removed from their posts and executed. The Great Terror also affected diplomats. In 1937, the plenipotentiary representatives of the USSR in Madrid, Marcel Rosenberg and Leon Gaikis, were recalled to Moscow, arrested, and executed. In July 1937, rumors reached Orlov that his relative and patron Zinovy Katsnelson had been removed from all posts (by that time he was the deputy head of the gulag and the head of Dmitlag) and arrested. In June 1938, Orlov was ordered to come to Antwerp to meet with Sergey Spigelglas, who was acting head of the Soviet foreign intelligence service. Orlov understood that he could be the next victim of repression and decided to flee to the United States. He stole around $90,800 (approximately $1.5 million in 2014 prices) from the NKVD operational funds (according to other sources, up to $600,000) and—together with his wife (also a resident) and his daughter—departed secretly for France on July 13, 1938. On July 21, he arrived in Montreal (Canada) and then moved to the United States. To insure himself against possible problems, Orlov wrote a letter to Iezhov and Stalin, in which he threatened to disclose the Soviet agents to the Americans if he was touched. Since the U.S. president Roosevelt personally gave Orlov a guarantee of security, and Stalin did not want to spoil relations with the Americans, Orlov was not persecuted by the Soviet authorities. On August 13, 1938, Orlov sent a letter to L. D. Trotsky, warning him of a possible assassination attempt. Later it turned out that Trotsky considered Orlov's letter to be a hoax planted by the NKVD.

Orlov's defection caused a significant escalation of repressions among the leading cadres of Soviet intelligence. Many employees who had previously worked with Orlov were declared "enemies of the people" and repressed. Orlov lived a modest life in the United States without legal status. Only in April 1955 did the U.S. Congress pass a bill granting Orlov and his wife permanent residence and U.S. citizenship. From that time on, Orlov became a well-paid consultant to the CIA Counter-Intelligence Staff. He gave lectures to intelligence officers, who later received appointments to the Warsaw bloc countries. He also published several books.

In the early 1960s, **N. Khrushchev**, using the Soviet journalist and intelligence officer M. Feoktistov, tried to establish contacts with Orlov. He hoped that Orlov would return to the USSR and that he would be involved in the anti-Stalinist campaign. Orlov refused.

In 1973, Orlov died suddenly in Cleveland. An investigation of his death was conducted by the FBI, the results of which have not been made public to date.

P

PATOLICHEV, NIKOLAI SEMIONOVICH (1908–1989). Patolichev was a Soviet party leader and politician, member of the CPSU (from 1928), member of the CC CPSU (1941–1986, candidate member from 1939), candidate member of the Presidium of the CC CPSU (1952–1953), first secretary of the Central Committee of the Communist Party of Belarus (1950–1956), ambassador extraordinaire and plenipotentiary of the Soviet Union, minister of foreign trade of the USSR from 1958 to 1985, twice hero of socialist labor (1975, 1978), one of two holders (the second was D. Ustinov) of eleven Orders of Lenin, the highest award of the USSR, and holder of the Order of the October Revolution and Order of the Red Banner of Labor.

Nikolai Patolichev was born in the village of Zolino, Vladimir Governorate (now Volodarsky district, Nizhny Novgorod Oblast), into a large, poor family. His father, Semion Mikhailovich Patolichev (1883–1920), was a good friend of Stalin. During the Civil War (1918–1920), he commanded a squadron, a cavalry regiment, and a cavalry brigade of the 1st Cavalry Army. He was killed during the Polish–Soviet War in 1920. Nikolai, orphaned at the age of twelve, grew up in the family of his uncle.

In 1921, Nikolai labored at a factory in the village of Rastiapino (in 1929, it was renamed Dzerzhinsk), now in Nizhny Novgorod Oblast. In 1928, he graduated from the plant's professional technical school. The same year, he joined the All-Union Leninist Young Communist League (Komsomol). In 1929–1930, he was appointed the secretary of the Dzerzhinsky Regional Committee of the Komsomol. In 1930–1931, he became the secretary of the Varna regional committee of the Komsomol in Cheliabinsk region. In 1937, he graduated from the Military Chemical Academy of the Red Army, after which he was appointed as an assistant to the head of the chemical service of the 1st Moscow Proletariat Red Banner Rifle Division.

In 1938, Patolichev was sent as a special representative of the CC CPSU at the Iaroslavl rubber plant. In January 1939, he was promoted to the first secretary of the Iaroslavl City Committee and the Regional Committee of the CPSU, making him the youngest regional leader in the Soviet Union. In 1940, at an extraordinary Plenum of the CC CPSU, General A. Khrulev introduced Patolichev to Stalin, **K. Voroshilov**, and **S. Budenny**, who had been well acquainted with his father. This meeting likely played an important role in Nikolai's future career, since Patolichev entered Stalin's inner circle.

In October 1941, Patolichev headed the Iaroslavl City Defense Committee. By the beginning of the **Great Patriotic War** (1941–1945), the serial production of the important M-105 engine for military aviation was launched at Rybinsk Machine-Building Plant under Patolichev's leadership. Also, the economy of the region was reconstructed on a war footing. From January 1942 to March 1946, he was first secretary of the Cheliabinsk Regional Committee and the city's party committee. During the war, Cheliabinsk was the major industrial center for relocated Soviet manufacturing. In 1943, Patolichev pioneered the creation of the Ural Volunteer Tank Corps. Since Cheliabinsk became a major production site of Soviet KV and T-34 tanks in the Second World War, it was nicknamed *Tankograd* (the city of tanks). Thanks to Patolichev's efforts, the city's civilian machine-building plants promptly adapted to arms production. He was also responsible for the evacuated factories and plants. Around seven hundred industrial enterprises—more than half of those evacuated to the eastern regions of the country—were transferred to the area.

In 1946–1947, Patolichev was recalled to Moscow and was appointed a secretary of the CC CPSU, replacing **G. Malenkov**, who was temporarily out of favor. In March 1946, he became a member of the Orgburo of the CC CPSU. Simultaneously, he headed the Inspection Department of the party organs and served as a deputy chairman of the Council for Collective Farm Affairs under the Council of Ministers of the USSR. In May 1947, he was transferred to Ukraine and served there as a secretary of the Central Committee of the Communist Party of Ukraine for the next seven months. In 1947–1950, Patolichev was appointed first secretary of the Rostov Oblast Committee and City Party committee. From July 1950 to 1956, he was the first secretary of the Central Committee of the Communist Party of Belarus.

In 1956, Patolichev was appointed deputy minister of foreign affairs of the USSR. He had the rank of ambassador extraordinary and plenipotentiary. From August 1958 to September 1985, he headed the Ministry of Foreign Trade of the USSR. Under his leadership, the ministry achieved an 18-fold increase in the volume of foreign trade. In October 1985, Nikolai Patolichev retired (Boris Aristov replaced him in his post) and became a personal pensioner of federal significance. He died in Moscow on December 1, 1989.

PAVLOV, DMITRY GRIGOREVICH (1897–1941). A Soviet military leader, Hero of the Soviet Union (June 21, 1937), and general of the army (February 22, 1941), Pavlov commanded the Soviet Western Front during the initial stage of the German invasion in June 1941.

Dmitry Pavlov was born in the village of Voniukh, Kostroma governorate (now Kostroma region), into a family of poor Russian peasants. He finished four classes of a rural school and two grades of Sukhoverkhovsk professional school. Due to his family's lack of money, he was unable to finish his studies and started to work in the village.

After the outbreak of the First World War, he volunteered for the Imperial Russian Army. He first served as an ordinary soldier in the 120th Serpukhov Regiment, in the 5th Hussar, 20th Rifle Regiment, and the 202nd Reserve Regiment but was able to rise to the rank of senior noncommissioned officer. He took part in the hostilities against the Austro-German troops on the Southwestern Front during the Brusilov breakthrough. In 1916, he was wounded and was taken prisoner on the Stokhod River (now in Volyn Oblast, Ukraine). He was held captive in the Wittenberg prisoner of war camp in Germany. As a POW, he worked at a factory and in mines. On January 1, 1919, Pavlov was released from captivity and returned home. For some time, he worked in the Department of Social Security and Labor Protection of the Kologrievsky District Labor Committee.

On August 25, 1919, Pavlov was drafted into the Red Army and sent to the 56th Food Battalion. He served first as a Red Army soldier, and later as a food clerk in the food squads (*prodotriad*) in Levashovskaia and Klimovskaia volosts, where he was responsible for collecting the tax in kind. From November 1919 to May 1920, Pavlov was a cadet of the Kostroma Infantry Command courses. After graduation, he was sent to the 8th Red Cossacks Cavalry Division, where he served in a separate reserve division as a platoon commander of a hundred and a division commander. He fought on the Southwestern and Southern Fronts, and participated in the battles against the Revolutionary Insurrectionary Army of Ukraine, also known as the Black Army or simply as Makhnovtsi (after their leader Nestor Makhno).

In 1922, Pavlov graduated with honors from the 24th Omsk Infantry School. From

April 1922, he commanded a regiment of the 10th Cavalry Division (the regiment was stationed in Semipalatinsk, now Semey, Kazakhstan). From June 1922, he was appointed assistant commander of the 56th Cavalry Regiment of the 6th Altai Separate Cavalry Brigade and fought against the anti-Soviet armed detachment of A. Salnikov and A. Kaigorodov in the Barnaul district. In 1923, he was transferred to the Turkestan Front, where he fought against the Basmachi movement. In August 1923, he was transferred to the Eastern Bukhara and led operations against the bands of Ibrahim-Bek, Ala-Nazar, Barot, Hodman, and Hadji-Ali. From June 1924, Pavlov became assistant commander of the combat unit of the 48th and 47th Cavalry Regiments.

From October 1925 to June 1928, Pavlov studied at the Frunze Military Academy of the Red Army. Upon graduation, on July 1, 1928, he was appointed military commander of the 75th Cavalry Regiment of **Konstantin Rokossovsky**'s 5th Separate Kuban Cavalry Brigade. In 1929, he participated in the Sino-Soviet conflict. In March 1930, Pavlov was recalled to Moscow and continued his education at the Military Technical Academy. After graduation in 1931, he commanded various mechanized units in the Belarusian Military District. In 1936, Brigade Commander Pavlov was awarded the Order of Lenin.

During the Spanish Civil War, from October 1936 to June 1937, Pavlov along with other Soviet "military advisers" fought on the side of the Republican government. Under the pseudonym "De Pablo," he commanded a brigade of Soviet tanks. For his role in this war, he was awarded the title Hero of the Soviet Union. In November 1937, Pavlov headed the Directorate of Tank and Armored Car Troops of the Red Army. Simultaneously, from March 1938 to June 1941, he was a member of the Main Military Council of the Red Army. In 1939–1940, Pavlov took part in the Winter War (Soviet–Finnish War). In June 1940, Pavlov became commander of the Western Special Military District, which with the outbreak of the **Great Patriotic War** (1941–1945) was transformed into the Western Front. The troops of the Western Front suffered disastrous defeats during the first days of Operation Barbarossa in Western Belarus and in the Minsk region.

On June 30, 1941, Army General Pavlov was removed from his post and summoned to Moscow. From there he was sent to the front without a specific position, but in July, he was arrested. By a decree of the **State Defense Committee** of the USSR, on July 16, 1941, General of the Army Pavlov and a group of other military leaders were accused of cowardice, inaction, lack of discipline, the collapse of command and control of troops, and of surrendering warehouses and property to the enemy without a fight, in an unauthorized abandonment of combat positions. Their case was transferred to a military tribunal. By the verdict of the Military Collegium of the Supreme Court of the USSR, on July 22, 1941, Pavlov and a number of others were sentenced to death. and shot the same day. On March 21, 1947, by the decree of the Presidium of the Supreme Soviet of the USSR, Pavlov was stripped of the title of Hero of the Soviet Union and all other state awards.

In 1957, Pavlov and other generals convicted with him were rehabilitated posthumously.

PERVUKHIN, MIKHAIL GEORGIEVICH (1904–1978). A Soviet statesperson and political and military leader, Pervukhin was people's commissar (minister) of the chemical industry of the USSR (1942–1950), first deputy chairman of the Council of Ministers of the USSR (1955–1957), member of the Presidium of the CC CPSU (1952–1957), lieutenant general of the engineering and technical service, hero of socialist labor, and chairman of the State Commission during tests of "RDS-1" (the Soviet Union's first nuclear weapon test).

Mikhail Pervukhin was born in the village of Iuriuzansky Zavod, Ufa Governorate, Russian Empire into a Russian working-class family (his father was a blacksmith). In June 1919, he joined the All-Union Leninist Young Communist League (Komsomol) and took an active part in the creation of the Komsomol organization in the city of Zlatoust (Cheliabinsk region). In September 1919, he was admitted to the Communist Party. The same year, at the age of 15, he became a member of the Zlatoust city Commission on the Nationalization of bourgeoisie property. In October–November 1920, Pervukhin took part in the suppression of the peasant uprising in the Zlatoust region. From January to September 1921, he worked for the newspaper *Borba*. After graduating from the after-school lessons in May 1920, Pervukhin worked as an extracurricular instructor in the Iuriuzan District Department of Public Education.

During the Civil War, Pervukhin took part in the suppression of the anti-Bolshevik uprising in the city of Zlatoust and in the South Urals. For most of 1921, he was an executive secretary on the editorial board of the newspaper *Proletarskaia mysl* (Proletarian thought) and was a member of the Bureau of the Zlatoust Komsomol District Committee.

In 1922, Pervukhin was enrolled at the Moscow Institute of the National Economy, from which he graduated in October 1929 with a degree in electrical engineering. After graduation, he took up the position of engineer at Mosenergo (Moscow Energy). From May 1930 to February 1933, he was head of the electrical department of the Barrikady plant in Stalingrad. In February 1933, he was transferred to the Kashirskaia Power Plant, where he first served as chief engineer and, from May 1936, as director. In June 1937, Pervukhin was returned to Mosenergo, where he was appointed chief engineer and deputy chief of the enterprise. From September of the same year, he headed Glavenergo of the People's Commissariat of Heavy Industry. At the beginning of 1938, Pervukhin was first promoted to the post of deputy people's commissar, and later first deputy people's commissar of heavy industry. In January 1939, he was appointed people's commissar of electric power stations.

In March 1939, at the 18th congress of the CC CPSU, Pervukhin was elected to the party's Central Committee. From May 1940 until May 1944, he worked as deputy chairman of the Council of People's Commissars of the USSR and the chairman of the Council on Fuel and Electricity with the Soviet government. After the outbreak of war, on June 24, 1941, he was appointed deputy chairman of the Council for Evacuation. From August 2, 1941, Pervukhin became commissioner of the **State Defense Committee**'s Office of Military and Chemical protection of the Red Army. On February 26, 1942, he was appointed people's commissar of the chemical industry. In 1944, he was awarded the rank of lieutenant general of engineering and technical service. In February 1943, the USSR State Defense Committee reviewed and approved a program on scientific and technical research on the practical use of "intra-nuclear" energy. This program laid the foundation for the development of the first Soviet atomic bomb. Pervukhin became a curator of the atomic project on the part of the Council of People's Commissars of the USSR.

After the war, Pervukhin occupied the posts of deputy chairman of the Council of Ministers of the USSR and minister of the chemical industry of the USSR. His main task was to restore and develop one of the most important sectors of the Soviet Union's economy destroyed by the war. In August 1945, Pervukhin was included in the Special Committee, and on November 30 of the same year, he became the chairman of the Engineering and Technical Council under the Special Committee. On August 29, 1949, the first domestic nuclear charge was successfully tested. Pervukhin was the chairman of the State Commission on these tests. For the successful completion of trials, Pervukhin was awarded the title of hero of socialist labor.

In January 1950–February 1955, he was deputy chairman of the Council of Ministers of the USSR. In October 1952, during the 19th congress of the CPSU (the last one before Stalin's death), Pervukhin was inducted into the Presidium of the CPSU Central Committee. After Stalin's death, he was appointed minister of the combined Ministry of Power Plants and Electrical Industry. Between December 1953 and February 1955, Pervukhin chaired the Bureau for Energy, Chemical, and Timber industries under the Council of Ministers of the USSR. In February 1955–July 1957, he was promoted to first deputy chairman of the Council of Ministers. Simultaneously, from December 1956 to May 1957, he worked as chairman of the State Economic Commission of the Council of Ministers of the State Planning Committee of the USSR. In April 1957, Pervukhin was appointed minister of medium machine building (responsible for atomic weapons) of the USSR.

In 1956–1957, Pervukhin became close to the so-called "Anti-Party Group" headed by **G. Malenkov, L. Kaganovich,** and **V. Molotov.** Pervukhin supported them at a meeting of the Presidium of the CC CPSU when the group opposed **Khrushchev.** As a result of his participation in the group and following its demise, he was demoted to candidate member of the Presidium. In July 1957, he was downgraded further to the post of the chairman of the State Committee of the Council of Ministers of the USSR for Foreign Economic Relations. In February 1958, Pervukhin was appointed ambassador to the German Democratic Republic, and in October 1961 he was removed from the Central Committee of the CPSU. In 1963–1965, he was appointed head of the Energy and Electrification Department of the Council of the National Economy of the USSR. From 1965, he served as the head of the Department of Territorial Planning and Production Location. He was also a member of the board of the USSR State Planning Committee. He died on July 22, 1978.

PETROVSKY, HRYHORY IVANOVICH (1878–1958). An Old Bolshevik and Russian revolutionary, Petrovsky was the leader of the Bolshevik faction in the fourth State Duma of the Russian Empire, Soviet and Ukrainian party leader and statesman, head of the People's Commissariat of Internal Affairs of the RSFSR (1917–1918), chairman of the All-Ukrainian Revolutionary Committee (1919–1920), chairman of the All-Ukrainian Central Executive Committee (1919–1938) and the USSR Central Executive Committee (1922–1938), and one of the Soviet officials responsible for implementing Stalin's policies of collectivization and for the famine of 1932–1933 in Ukraine.

Hryhory Petrovsky was born in the village of Pechenihy, Kharkiv Governorate (now Kharkiv region, Ukraine), into the family of a tailor and a laundress. Hryhory's father died when he was three years old, and his mother, a widow with three children, was forced to move to Kharkiv. After two years of studies at the Kharkiv seminary, Grigory at the age of 11 started to work for a locomotive depot. At the age of 15, he moved to the Briansk Metallurgical Plant in Iekaterinoslav (later Dnipropetrovsk, currently Dnipro, Ukraine). He devoted himself to revolutionary ideas. In 1897, he joined the Iekaterinoslav Union of Struggle for the Liberation of the Working Class, and in 1898 he became a member of the RSDWP. In 1900 and 1903, he was arrested twice for his revolutionary activities. In 1905, during the first Russian Revolution, he became secretary of the Iekaterinoslav Soviet of Workers' Deputies and a member of the Strike Committee. In 1906, he spent a few months in Germany.

In 1912, Petrovsky, now working as a turner at the Mariupol plant "Providence," was elected a deputy to the Russian fourth State Duma as a Bolshevik representative of workers of the Iekaterinoslav Governorate. During his term as a deputy, Petrovsky gave about thirty speeches, some of which were prepared by Lenin. He touched upon a wide range of issues from improvement of working conditions for workers to the right of Ukrainians to use their own language. On May 20, 1913, Petrovsky delivered a speech in the Duma in which he pressed for opening Ukrainian schools with Ukrainian-language instruction. He also advocated the use of the Ukrainian language in court and in all administrative institutions in the territories inhabited by Ukrainians. His performances in the Duma were always memorable. In fact, Petrovsky was the only one in the Bolshevik faction capable of maintaining the "parliamentary dialogue" with the imperial government.

In November 1914, he was arrested, and in February 1915 he was exiled to the Turukhansk region in eastern Siberia. He was liberated by the Revolution of 1917 and became a commissioner of Iakutia (today Sakha) and a chairman of the local Civil Security Committee. In July 1917, he was sent to the Donbas region and became a member of the Iekaterinoslav Provincial Committee of the RSDWP(b) and chairman of its Bolshevik faction in the Provisional Council of the Russian Republic. From November 1917 to March 1919, Petrovsky was appointed people's commissar of interior affairs. In this post, he supervised the creation of the All-Russian Extraordinary Commission (Cheka) and the workers' and peasants' militia. In 1918, as a member of the Russian delegation, he took part in negotiations with the Germans that resulted in the Treaty of Brest-Litovsk. He personally signed Fania Kaplan's death sentence (regarding the attempted assassination of Lenin) and an official decree announcing the Red Terror. Between 1920 and 1923, he held important posts in the **Comintern**. During this period, Petrovsky focused on Moscow and completely rejected the ideas of Ukrainian national communists regarding the possibility of creating an independent Soviet Ukrainian state. On December 30, 1922, Petrovsky, as a representative from Ukraine, signed the Treaty on the Creation of the USSR and became the delegate of the Ukrainian SSR in the USSR Central Executive Committee. Also, until January 12, 1938, he was co-chairman of the USSR Central Executive Committee. In 1926, the city of Iekaterinoslav was renamed Dnipropetrovsk in his honor, a name it retained until May 2016, when it was renamed Dnipro.

At the end of October 1932, he was responsible for the implementation of grain procurements in the Donetsk region. Together with **L. Kaganovich**, Petrovsky became one of the main executors of Stalin's policies in Ukraine at the time of the famine of 1932–1933 known as Holodomor. On December 2, 1937, he was elected a deputy of the Council of the National Supreme Soviet of the USSR of the first convocation (1937–1946). At the same time, from January 17, 1938, to May 31, 1939, he was deputy chairman of the Presidium of the Supreme Soviet of the USSR. Unlike many other Old Bolsheviks, he escaped repression in the 1930s, but several of his relatives were less fortunate. His eldest son, Petro, who participated in the storming of the Winter Palace in 1917 and worked as an editor of the *Leningradskaia Pravda* newspaper, was arrested in 1938 and executed in 1941.

In 1939, Petrovsky was criticized, expelled from the Communist Party, and removed from all posts. In 1940, the director of the Museum of the Revolution, Fiodor Samoilov (formerly also a Bolshevik deputy of the fourth Duma), appointed him as his deputy for administrative, economic, and scientific affairs. Petrovsky worked there until his death in 1958.

He is buried in Moscow on Red Square near the Kremlin wall.

PIATAKOV, GEORGY (IURY) LEONIDOVICH (1890–1937). A revolutionary, anarchist (from 1905), terrorist, Bolshevik (from 1912), and member of the Left Opposition to Stalin, Piatakov was accused of conspiring with Trotsky. His party aliases were Kievsky, Lialin, Petro, and Iaponets (Japanese).

Georgy Piatakov was born in 1890 in a village near the Marynsky sugar factory (Kyiv province). His father, engineering technologist Leonid Timofeevich Piatakov, was a director at this factory. In 1902, Georgy became a student of the St. Catherine Realschule in Kyiv. In 1904, he joined a Social Democratic circle and in 1905 was expelled from the school for his activities. During the first Russian Revolution of 1905, he took an active part in the revolutionary movement in Kyiv and headed the circle of anarchists. In 1907, he graduated from Realschule as an external student and started his studies at the Department of Economy of the Law Faculty of St. Petersburg University. In 1910, after three years of studies, Georgy was expelled. That same year, he joined the RSDWP's Bolshevik faction. In April 1912, he was elected secretary of the Kyiv Committee of the RSDWP. He was arrested several times and spent a year and a half in exile in the Irkutsk province, in the village of Usole.

In October 1914, he escaped from exile and made his way to Switzerland via Japan and the United States. In 1915, together with **V. Lenin**, he became an editor of the *Kommunist* magazine. But shortly thereafter, Piatakov became Lenin's opponent. A disagreement arose between them over the right of nations to self-determination. Piatakov, unlike Lenin, advocated the total abolition of nations. Due to this disagreement, Piatakov left the editorial office of the magazine and immigrated to Stockholm. In 1916, he was expelled from Sweden and moved to Norway.

After the February Revolution, Piatakov returned to Russia. In April 1917, he became chairman of the Kyiv Committee of the RSDWP and actively opposed Lenin's April Theses advocating a takeover of power by the Soviets. In September 1917, he headed the Kyiv Soviet of Workers' and Soldiers' Deputies and the Military Revolutionary Committee. He sharply opposed the Ukrainian nationalists and stood for the transfer of power to the Soviets. Piatakov believed that the party should reject the "chauvinistic" idea of self-determination of nations, which "contradicts internationalism." During the October Revolution of 1917, Piatakov was summoned to Petrograd, where he participated in the seizure of the State Bank and was appointed its commissar.

From December 1917 until early March 1918, he served as chief commissioner of the State Bank. In 1918, he became one of the founders of the Communist Party (Bolsheviks) of Ukraine and Ukrainian Red Army. During the "Brest Discussion," concerning Russia's treaty with the Central Powers, he supported the positions of Left Communists and advocated a revolutionary war with Germany. Protesting the signing of the Brest Peace Treaty, he resigned from the government and went to Ukraine. During the Civil War, he fought in the "Red Cossacks" corps under the leadership of V. Primakov.

In July 1918, at the first congress of the CP(b)U, Piatakov was elected secretary of the Central Committee. In this post, he participated in the suppression of the uprising of the Left Socialist-Revolutionaries (Left-SRs). In November 1918, Piatakov became a member of the Ukrainian Revolutionary Military Council. From November 1918 to January 1919, he headed the Provisional Workers' and Peasants' Government of Ukraine, which was created by the Bolsheviks to fight S. Petliura's Directory of the Ukrainian National Republic. On January 24, Moscow replaced Piatakov with **Christian Rakovsky** (a Bulgarian socialist revolutionary and lifelong collaborator of Leon Trotsky). After that, Piatakov again headed the Secretariat of the Central Committee of the CPU(b), as well as the Military Revolutionary Tribunal.

In March 1919, Piatakov was a delegate at the eighth congress of the RCP(b). During the congress, he unsuccessfully opposed Lenin's position on national self-determination. In January–February 1920, Piatakov briefly led the military intelligence of the Red Army. Together with Rosalia Zemliachka (a Russian revolutionary, vice president of the Council of People's Commissars of the USSR, and the only woman to have served in a high governmental post during the Stalin era) and **Bela Kun**, he was one of the organizers of the Red Terror in Crimea (1920–1921). Terror was carried out during the Civil War against former soldiers and officers of the White Russians led by General Piotr Wrangel and civilians. At least fifty-six thousand people were executed in Crimea.

In 1920, Piatakov was given control over industries in Ukraine. From November 1920 to December 1921, he led the Central Directorate of the Donbas Coal Industry. During this period, he was an opponent of the **NEP**. In 1921–1923, he was a candidate member of the Central Committee of the RCP(b). In March 1922, he was appointed the deputy chairman of the State Planning Commission (Gosplan).

Piatakov was a friend of **E. Preobrazhensky** and supported his ideas. From 1923, he also became an active supporter of the Left Opposition. After Lenin's death, he sided with **L. Trotsky** against Stalin. In 1923–1927, he was a member of the CC CPSU, chairman of the Main Concession Committee (the Soviet government authority in charge of foreign concessions in the USSR) and at the same time deputy chairman of the Supreme Council of the National Economy of the USSR. Piatakov was one of the authors of the draft of the first Five-Year Plan and advocated the rapid industrialization of Ukraine.

At the 15th congress of the CC CPSU(b) (1927), as a supporter of Left Communist views and Trotsky's ideas, Piatakov was expelled from the party. In 1927, he was sent as a head of the trade mission of the USSR in France. In 1928, after declaring his withdrawal from the opposition and Trotskyism, he was reinstated in the party. In 1928, he was appointed deputy chairman of the State Bank of the USSR. In the Spring of 1929, he became a chairman of the board of the State Bank of the USSR. A year and a half later (in October 1930), failures in the first stage of the credit reform led to Piatakov's removal from the post.

In 1930, Piatakov was reelected a member of the CC CPSU and a member of the Presidium. In 1931–1932, he became a deputy chairman of the Supreme Council of the National Economy of the USSR and a chairman of the Vsekhimprom (All-Union Association of the Chemical Industry). In 1932–1934, he held the post of the deputy people's commissar of heavy industry of the USSR, and in 1934–1936, he was appointed first deputy people's commissar of heavy industry of the USSR.

Soon, Stalin launched his Great Terror against Old Bolsheviks. Sensing the danger, Piatakov began to drink heavily. On September 12, 1936, he was arrested on charges of anti-party and anti-Soviet activities. Piatakov was among the main defendants in the trial of the "Parallel Anti-Soviet Trotskyist Center," where he was accused of a joint conspiracy with Trotsky. Allegedly, their goal was to seize power in the USSR with the help of Nazi Germany in exchange for large territorial concessions at the expense of the Soviet Union. The prosecution provided "evidence" that Piatakov had secretly met with Trotsky in Norway, although the administration of the Oslo airfield confirmed that no foreign aircraft had arrived at the time of the supposed meeting with Trotsky. The accusation was among the most far-fetched of many such fabricated narratives.

On January 30, 1937, Piatakov was sentenced to death and executed. He was rehabilitated and reinstated in the party posthumously in 1988, during the Gorbachev era.

PLETNEV, DMITRY DMITRIEVICH (1871–1941). A Russian and Soviet medical scientist, professional doctor, and publicist, and a defendant at the Third Show Trial (March 1938), known as "The Trial of the Twenty-One," of the so-called "Bloc of Rightists and Trotskyites."

Dmitry Pletnev was born in 1871 in the Poltava Governorate (according to some sources in the Kharkiv Governorate), into the family of a landlord. the future scientist received an excellent education and became fluent in German and French. After graduating from high school, he entered the Faculty of Medicine of Kharkiv University. During the third year of his studies, he transferred to Moscow University, from which he graduated in 1895 with honors.

In 1896, Pletnev was appointed resident physician of the Novo-Ikaterininskaia hospital, where he worked under the guidance of A. Ostroumov, K. Pavlinov, V. Shervinsky, L. Golubinin, and A. Fokht. From 1900, he worked as an assistant to the Medical Faculty. In November 1906, Pletnev defended his dissertation on the origins of cardiac arrythmias and was elected an unsalaried lecturer at Moscow University. In 1907–1908, Pletnev visited leading clinics and laboratories in Germany, France, Switzerland, and the Austro-Hungarian Empire.

In 1911, together with other professors, Pletnev resigned from the university in protest over the actions of the minister of public education, Lev Kasso, who issued several circulars that destroyed the autonomy of the university. After his dismissal, Pletnev became a professor at the Guerrier Courses, Moscow Higher Courses for Women. He also joined the Constitutional Democratic Party (*Kadets*). In March 1917, he returned to Moscow University as a professor and director of the faculty's Therapeutic Clinic. Later, he became the director of the Hospital Therapeutic Clinic of the First Moscow State University.

In June 1929, Pletnev left the university, evidently as a result of a conflict with **Andrei Vyshinsky**, the then-rector. From the end of 1929, he worked as a consultant of the Medical and Sanitary Administration of the Kremlin, the Central Hospital of the Northern Railway, and the First Communist Hospital (now the Main Military Clinical Hospital, named after N. Burdenko). Between 1930 and 1937, he headed the Therapeutic Department at the Central Institute for Advanced Medical Studies. Simultaneously, from 1929, he was in charge of the Therapeutic Clinic of the Moscow Regional Clinical Institute. Pletnev was among the creators of Soviet cardiology. The scientist developed special methods to treat patients with heart failure. He published a methodological guide: *Fundamentals of the Therapy of Chronic Heart Failure* (1932). In 1933, he also organized and headed the Research Institute of Functional Diagnostics and Experimental Therapy. V. Lenin, **N. Krupskaia**, **I. Pavlov**, and many other Soviet party and state leaders were among Pletnev's patients. On January 5, 1933, Professor D. Pletnev was awarded the title of honored scientist of the RSFSR. In 1936, he published the main work of his life: the book *Heart Diseases*.

In 1937, Pletnev's career ended unexpectedly. On June 8, 1937, the newspaper *Pravda* published an article about Pletnev titled "Professor-Rapist, a Sadist." Subsequently, the NKVD fabricated a case against him. Pletnev was arrested and jailed in the Lubianka internal prison. On July 18, he was sentenced to two years of probation. In December 1937, Pletnev was arrested again in a new trumped-up case against the anti-Soviet Right-Trotskyist Bloc (headed by **Bukharin**). Along with other doctors, he was accused of the murder of **V. Kuibyshev** and **M. Gorky**. In 1938 he acted as a defendant at the Third Moscow Trial. Pletnev became one of three defendants at the trial who managed to avoid being shot that year. He was sentenced to twenty-five years in jail with confiscation of property. On September 11, 1941, during the offensive of the Wehrmacht troops, Pletnev, together with other political prisoners, was executed by the NKVD in the Medvedevsky forest near Orel. This mass execution became known as the Medvedev Forest Massacre.

Pletnev was rehabilitated in 1985.

PODGORNY, NIKOLAI VIKTOROVICH (1903–1983). Podgorny was a Soviet statesman and party leader, second secretary of the Communist Party of Ukraine (1953), chairman of the Presidium of the Supreme Soviet of the USSR (1965–1977), deputy of the Supreme Soviet of the USSR (1954–1979), member of the CC CPSU (1956–1981), member of the Presidium/Politburo of the CC CPSU (1960–1977), and two-time hero of socialist labor.

Nikolai Podgorny (Ukrainian: Mykola Pidhorny) was born in the town of Karlivka, Poltava Governorate, Russian Empire, into a Ukrainian working-class family. From 1917, he worked as a locksmith's apprentice and was employed in mechanical workshops. The same year, Podgorny became one of the organizers of the local branch of the All-Union Leninist Young Communist League (Komsomol). Between 1921 and 1923, he served as a secretary of the Karlivsky district Committee of the Komsomol.

In 1923–1926, Podgorny studied at the workers' faculty of the Kyiv Polytechnic Institute. In 1930, he joined the CPSU. In 1931, he graduated from Kyiv Technological Institute of Food Industry. After graduation, he started to work in the sugar industry in Ukraine, first as an engineer and later as deputy chief engineer and chief engineer. In 1939, Podgorny was promoted to deputy people's commissar of the food industry of Ukrainian SSR. In 1940–1942, he was appointed deputy people's commissar of the food industry of the USSR. But by **A. Mikoian**'s order, he was removed from office for deception: Podgorny had reported that he personally supervised the evacuation of one of the sugar factories in the Voronezh region, but in reality, since the factory was under enemy fire, Podgorny did not come near the factory.

In 1942, Podgorny was appointed director of the Moscow Technological Institute of the Food Industry. In 1944, after the liberation of Ukrainian territory from German troops, he served as deputy people's commissar of the food industry of the Ukrainian SSR. In Ukraine, he took an active part in the establishment of Soviet institutions, and in organizing food supply and food industry enterprises.

In 1946–1950, Podgorny served as Permanent Representative of the Council of Ministers of the Ukrainian SSR under the Council of Ministers of the USSR. From 1950 to 1953, he became first secretary of the Kharkiv Oblast Party Committee. Simultaneously, in 1952–1956, he was a member of the Central Auditing Commission of the CPSU. In 1953, Podgorny was appointed second secretary of the CC CPU, and from 1957 to 1963, he served as the first secretary of the Ukrainian party apparatus.

In 1960, Podgorny became a member of the Politburo. On October 30, 1961, speaking at the twenty-second congress of the CPSU, on behalf of the delegation of the Communist Party of Ukraine, he supported the proposal to remove the sarcophagus with Stalin's body from the mausoleum during this final phase of **N. Khrushchev**'s de-Stalinization campaign. From June 21, 1963, to December 6, 1965, Podgorny served as secretary of the CC CPSU and supervised light industry. Even though Podgorny was N. Khrushchev's protégé and his career grew rapidly during the latter's leadership, he took an active part in preparing a conspiracy against the Soviet leader. In 1964, after Khrushchev's dismissal, Podgorny became a member of the ruling **Brezhnev-Kosygin**-Podgorny triumvirate. During the period of so-called collective leadership, Podgorny, along with A. Kosygin, became one of the most influential members of the Politburo.

On December 9, 1965, Podgorny replaced A. Mikoian, who had reached retirement age, in the post of chairman of the Presidium of the Supreme Soviet of the USSR, the ceremonial president of the country. He remained in this post until June 16, 1977. The power of the Supreme Soviet and its Presidium were expanded during Podgorny's tenure and this allowed him to strengthen his positions in the Politburo. As the formal head of the Soviet state, he was actively involved in diplomatic work and repeatedly traveled abroad with official visits. At the time of his resignation in 1977, Podgorny was considered by Western Sovietologists to the second most influential member of the Politburo after Brezhnev.

On May 24, 1977, the Politburo made the unanimous decision to remove Podgorny from office. On June 16, 1977, he resigned from the post of chairman of the Presidium of the Supreme Soviet of the USSR and retired. After his resignation, Podgorny was widely criticized in the Soviet press.

On January 11, 1983, Podgorny died in Moscow.

PODVOISKY, NIKOLAI ILICH (1880–1948). A Russian revolutionary, Bolshevik, Soviet political and military leader, and people's commissar of military affairs (November 1917–March 1918), Nikolai Podvoisky was born in Kunochevsk village, Chernihiv province (Ukraine), into the family of a rural priest-teacher. After graduating from theological school, he entered the Chernihiv Theological Seminary. In 1901, he enrolled at the Demidov Law Lyceum (Iaroslavl). During this same year, he joined the RSDWP. After the party split during the second congress of the RSDWP, he sided with the Bolsheviks. In 1904–1905, Podvoisky became chairman of the Bolshevik Student Committee and a member of the Northern Committee of the RSDWP.

During the first Russian Revolution (1905), Podvoisky became one of the leaders of the Ivanovo-Voznesensk Soviet of Workers' Delegates and led the textile workers' strike. He also organized workers' fighting squads in Iaroslavl. In October 1905, during a demonstration, Podvoisky was brutally beaten by the Black Hundreds and received severe wounds. In 1906, after several arrests, he emigrated first to Germany and later to Switzerland.

After his return to Russia in 1907, he worked in the illegal Bolshevik organizations in St. Petersburg, Kostroma, and Baku. In 1907–1908, he was one of the leaders of the legal Zerno party publishing house in the Russian capital. In 1910–1914, he helped to publish the newspapers *Zvezda* and *Pravda*. In 1915–1916, he was the editor of the magazine *Insurance Questions* and headed the financial commission of the Russian Bureau of the Central Committee of the RSDWP(b). In November 1916, Podvoisky was arrested and sentenced to exile in Siberia, but he was released during the February Revolution.

In March 1917, Podvoisky became a member of the Petrograd Committee of the RSDWP(b), a deputy of the Petrograd Soviet, and an organizer of the Red Guards. He also headed the Military Organization under the Central Committee of the RSDWP(b). In October, he was appointed chairman of the Petrograd Military Revolutionary Committee. From November 1917 to March 1918, he held the post of people's commissar of military affairs. At the same time, from January 1918, he was chairman of the All-Russian Collegium for the

Organization and Formation of the Red Army. As people's commissar of military affairs, Podvoisky directly supervised the demobilization and dissolution of the Imperial Russian Army and the formation of the Red Army. He also participated in the reorganization of the Russian War Ministry and the system of military educational institutions.

In March 1918, Podvoisky left the post of people's commissar of military affairs and entered the Revolutionary Military Council. During the Civil War, he planned military operations of the Red Army, which led to numerous tactical victories. In January 1919, he also took up the post of people's commissar of military affairs of the Ukrainian SSR. In October, he became a member of the Revolutionary Military Council of the 7th Army of the Western Front, and in January 1920, of the 10th Army of the Caucasian Front.

In 1920, Podvoisky became chairman of the Supreme Council of Physical Culture. He believed that systematic sport activities and physical training helped the needs of the Red Army. He considered the formation of the Red Sport International (*Sportintern*)—an international sports organization that potentially could become an ideological counterweight to the Olympic Games—but was not given time to put the idea into fruition. In 1923, he was replaced by N. Semashko, who became the chairman of the Supreme Council of Physical Culture. By 1926, he also lost control over *Sportintern*.

In 1924, Podvoisky became a member of the Central Control Commission of the CPSU. He worked in the Commission on the History of the October Revolution and the RCP(b). In 1927, he consulted **S. Eisenstein** during his work on film *October* and had a cameo role in this celebratory dramatization of the October Revolution of 1917. In 1935, Podvoisky retired for health reasons but remained engaged in propaganda, literary, and journalistic pursuits. In October 1941, as the German Army advanced into Russia, he volunteered to dig trenches near Moscow. He also supplied troops with literature and carried out propaganda work among them.

In 1945, he was awarded the medals "For Victory over Germany in the **Great Patriotic War** of 1941–1945" and "For Valiant Labor in the Great Patriotic War of 1941–1945."

Podvoisky died on July 28, 1948.

POSTYSHEV, PAVEL PETROVICH (1887–1939). A Soviet political and party leader, party propagandist, and publicist, Postyshev is considered to be one of the principal architects of the famine of 1932–1933 in Ukraine, one of the organizers but also a victim of Stalinist repressions, and the initiator of the creation of the Soviet secular holiday "New Year" instead of Christmas (1935).

Pavel Postyshev was born in the city of Ivanovo-Voznesensk (now Ivanovo), Vladimir Governorate, Russian Empire, into a working-class family. He had a limited primary education (in fact, he was almost illiterate) and started to work at the age of nine. In his early youth, he became interested in communist ideas, and in 1900 he began to participate in workers' circles. In 1904, Pavel joined the RSDWP (Bolshevik). He was an active participant in the first Russian Revolution (1905) and the famous Ivanovo strike. In 1906, he was elected a member of the board of the trade union of cotton printers and member of the Ivanovo city committee of the RSDWP. In November 1907, he organized a one-day protest strike against the dispersal of the State Duma and was arrested. In April 1908, Postyshev was arrested again, and in 1912, he was sent to exile in the Irkutsk province. In 1914–1917, he became a member of the Irkutsk Bureau of the RSDWP.

In August 1917, Postyshev was elected deputy chairman of the Irkutsk Council. In December 1917, he served as a member of the Military Revolutionary Committee and supervised the work of the Central Bureau of Trade Unions. In 1918, Postyshev became the chairman of the Revolutionary Tribunal and a member of *Tsentrosibir* (Central Executive Committee of Siberian Soviets). In 1919, during the Russian Civil War, he participated in the partisan movement and served as a commissar in the detachment of Ivan Shevchuk. Between 1920 and 1922, he served as a commissioner of the Central Committee of the RCP(b) in the Far Eastern Republic (FER). Simultaneously, he was a member of the Military Council, first of the Amur Military District, later of the Eastern Front of the FER. He was also chairman of the Baikal Provincial Executive Committee and a participant in the Volochaev battles. In April 1922, he was appointed Regional commissar of the FER in Verkhneudinsk.

In 1923, Postyshev was transferred to work in Kyiv, where in 1925 he became secretary of the Kyiv provincial committee (then district committee) of the CPU. In 1925, he became a candidate member and then from 1927 a member of the Orgburo, of the CC CPSU. In November 1926, he was appointed secretary of the Kharkiv District Committee and the Central Committee of the CPU. Until 1934, Kharkiv was the capital of the Ukrainian SSR. In 1930–1933, he became a secretary of the CC CPSU and head of the Organizational-Instructor Department of the CC CPSU. In November 1932, during the famine period, he was sent first to the Lower Volga region (*Povolzhye*) and later to Ukraine (together with **L. Kaganovich**), as a specially authorized representative of the Central Committee and the Soviet government. On January 24, 1933, Postyshev was appointed second secretary of the CC CPU with plenipotentiary powers while concomitantly holding the position of first secretary of Kharkiv City and Oblast party organizations.

He was responsible for carrying out emergency measures to fulfill the plan on grain procurements. Postyshev insisted on declaring the Ukrainian SSR a "zone of continuous collectivization" and issued instructions on measures for *dekulakization*. He did not take any measures to localize the beginning of the famine. Moreover, he authorized the use of units of the Red Army to suppress unrest in the starving areas. His main assistants in the controlling grain procurements were: V. Balitsky, **S. Kosior**, and I. Iakir. In 1933, he also participated in the party purge in Ukraine in which he accused some well-known Ukrainians of nationalism. For his "achieved results," Postyshev was promoted to candidate member of the Politburo in 1934.

Such rapid career growth for an illiterate person who was unfamiliar with Ukrainian realities could be explained both by Postyshev's cruelty and ability to carry out any decisions of the leadership of the Soviet state. In Ukraine, he created his own cult of personality. Streets, squares, power plants, factories, and even the central radio of the Ukrainian SSR were named after him. Postyshev's portraits on the streets and in offices were more common than Stalin's. Anyone who dared to contradict him or his wife, who took a major post in Kyiv, ended up with dismissal from work or even imprisonment.

When Postyshev tried to expose Kaganovich as the "enemy of the people," however, he was harshly criticized and lost his post. He was transferred to the Kuibyshev region as the first secretary of the regional committee. Postyshev himself thought that the reason for his dismissal was the fact that he did not carry out the purges in Ukraine ruthlessly enough. Thus, he started a new wave of mass arrests in Kuibyshev. The level of arrests was so high that a special commission from Moscow, which was headed by L. Mekhlis, found out that as a result of Postyshev's extensive hunt for "enemies of the people," the Kuibyshev regional organization of the CPSU(b) had practically been eradicated. Postyshev was once again harshly criticized in the Central Committee and the Politburo.

In February 1938, Postyshev was accused of being a Trotskyist, removed from all posts, and arrested. On February 26, 1939, he was shot in Kuibyshev. He was rehabilitated in 1956. At the twentieth congress of the CC CPSU, **N. Khrushchev** called him "a real Leninist." In January 2010, the Ukrainian Court of Appeal accused Postyshev, along with other Soviet leaders, of organizing a manmade famine (Holodomor) in 1932–1933. His portrait, as one of the famine's perpetrators, adorns the entrance of the Famine Memorial in Kyiv.

POTSDAM CONFERENCE. Also known as the Berlin Conference, it was attended by government leaders of the Soviet Union (Stalin), United States (Truman), and Great Britain

(Churchill), which took place between July 17 and August 2, 1945, in Potsdam, one of the suburbs of occupied Berlin. Following a British general election, Churchill was replaced by Clement Atlee on July 28. The conference also included each country's foreign minister, as well as military leaders and translators. The Potsdam meeting was intended to expand on the decisions made at Ialta earlier in the year and the main focus was the future of Germany, which was to be divided into four zones of Allied occupation (France was granted an occupation zone even though French leader Charles De Gaulle was not invited to the Conference). The Soviet side had proposed the creation of a provisional German government, but United States and Britain countered that there could be several German administrative branches operating under the Control Council for Germany. The proposal, however, was eventually rejected too. The Allies anticipated the complete dismantling of the German state and those industries that could be used for military purposes. Nazi organizations and their affiliates were to be dissolved and rendered incapable of any revival (the SS, SD, Gestapo, and others). Nazi leaders were to be put on trial. The heads of the three states also signed an agreement on reparations, both from the individual occupation zones, with the Soviet side also having the right to obtain addition supplies from the Western zones of occupation.

The conference affixed the Polish-German border at the Oder-(Western) Neisse Line, meaning that the territories of East and West Prussia, Silesia, and most of Pomerania were to be ceded, mostly to Poland, but also the city of Koenigsberg and surrounding region were to be transferred to the Soviet Union. For Stalin, the key result was the retention of territories of eastern Poland annexed in September 1939, as well as the Baltic States, and the Bessarabian and Bukovinian territories of Romania, all annexed in 1940. German populations living in the ceded territories, as well as in Czechoslovakia and Hungary, were to be removed westward as soon as possible. The leaders also decided to divide up the German fleet and cargo ships between United States, the USSR, and Great Britain. From the Soviet perspective, the Western powers betrayed the Soviet side four years later when they decided to form a West German state from their occupation zones, and the NATO military alliance shortly thereafter. In contrast to the meetings at Tehran and Ialta, the Potsdam Conference was notable for the acrimony and disagreements between the Western leaders on the one hand and Stalin on the other. For example, the Western Allies refused the Soviet demand for reparations as impossible to fulfill but did agree that the Soviets could exact reparations from the U.S. and British occupation zones, which contained Germany's main industrial zones. They agreed also on the creation of a Council of Foreign Ministers, the complete denazification of Germany, and the transfer of the city of Koenigsberg and surrounding region to the Soviet Union. The Americans detonated the first atomic bomb about a week after the conference started. Though Stalin was informed of the fact, he did not react strongly. The Western Allies gave Japan the choice between unconditional surrender or complete devastation, and two bombs were dropped on Hiroshima and Nagasaki just a few days after the conference ended, on August 6 and 9, respectively,

PREOBRAZHENSKY, IEVGENY ALEKSEEVICH (1886–1937). A Russian revolutionary, one of the leaders of the Russian and international communist movement, an Old Bolshevik, and a Soviet economist, publicist, and sociologist, Preobrazhensky authored the book *New Economy* and coauthored (together with **N. Bukharin**) *The ABC of Communism* (1919), a popular exposition of the program of the RCP(b). He was directly involved in the murder of Emperor Nikolai II and his family.

Ievgeny Preobrazhensky was born in the town of Bolkhov, Orel Governorate, Russian Empire, into the family of an Orthodox priest. He first studied at his father's parish school and then, in 1895–1897, at the Bolkhov city school. Between 1897 and 1905, he was enrolled at Orel classical male gymnasium. As a child, he seemed to have some religious leanings, but at the age of 14 he abandoned his belief in God and became interested in politics and rationalist philosophy. The change brought him into a conflict with his father.

In 1901–1902, Preobrazhensky became acquainted with illegal literature and gradually became more militant. Between 1903–1904, he became a member of the Social Democratic troika in the Orel classical male gymnasium, which acted as a cell of the Orel Committee of the RSDWP. He conducted social democratic propaganda among students of various educational institutions and kept illegal literature. In February 1904, the Orel Committee of the RSDWP accepted Preobrazhensky as a member and assigned him to the group of propagandists.

In April–May 1905, Preobrazhensky headed students' general strikes and rallies in Orel. By this time, he had become an avid Bolshevik. In October 1905, Preobrazhensky participated in the fight against counterrevolutionary pogroms in Orel. In October–November 1905, he worked as party propagandist at one of the Briansk factories. In November–December 1905, Preobrazhensky was a responsible propagandist of the Presnensky District Committee of the RSDWP in Moscow and participated in the Moscow uprising in December 1905. In March 1906, he was arrested in Perm and spent five months in prison.

In August 1906, he led party work in Iekaterinburg, Cheliabinsk, and Ufa. The Perm Committee of the RSDWP sent him to St. Petersburg to purchase automatic pistols for its combat squad, but he was arrested en route at the Kazan Station in Moscow. After his release from prison in 1907, Preobrazhensky became a member of the Ural Regional Committee of the RSDWP and led party work in the South Urals. As a delegate of the Ural committee, he attended the third conference of the RSDWP (1907), where he met V. Lenin. In March 1908, Preobrazhensky was arrested again. In the fall of 1909, he was sentenced to exile but in 1911 managed to escape.

In 1911–1912, he was employed by the legal Marxist newspaper *Obskaia Zhizn* in the city of Novo-Nikolaevsk (now Novosibirsk) and was a member of the Novo-Nikolaevsk committee of the RSDWP. In the fall of 1912, he was arrested again and exiled. In 1915, the tsarist authorities allowed Preobrazhensky to move from his place of exile to the city of Irkutsk. Between 1915 and 1917, he conducted party work in Irkutsk and Chita and became a member of the Irkutsk Committee of the party. In April 1917, he was elected a delegate to the first All-Russian Congress of Soviets of Workers' and Soldiers' Deputies in Petrograd. After the October Revolution (1917), he participated in the establishment of Soviet power in Zlatoust and the Zlatoust mountain district.

During the Civil War (1918–1920), Preobrazhensky was a candidate member of the Ural Regional Committee of the Russian Communist Party (Bolsheviks) and a member of the editorial board of the newspaper *Uralsky Rabochy*. As president of the Presidium of the Ural Regional Committee, Preobrazhensky was directly involved in the killing of former tsar Nikolai II and his family; their execution happened under his watch. As a delegate from the Bolshevik faction to the All-Russian Congress of Soviets of Workers, Peasants, Red Army and Cossack Deputies (1918), he participated in the suppression of the Left SR uprising in Moscow and was slightly wounded.

In January–August 1918, Preobrazhensky joined the Left Communists group. Between the end of 1920 and the spring of 1921, during the trade-union debate (a political discussion inside the Bolshevik party on the role of the trade unions in RSFSR), Preobrazhensky—together with **N. Bukharin** and others—formed a "buffer group" that advocated for the reconciliation of all factions and groups. In April–June 1920, Preobrazhenskyy became the first head of the Agitation and Propaganda Department of the Central Committee of the RCP(b) (*Agitprop*).

In 1921–1924, he was appointed chairman of the Finance Committee of the Central Committee of the RCP(b) and the Council of People's Commissars (SNK) of the Russian Socialist Federal Soviet Republic (RSFSR). Simultaneously, in 1921, he served as chairman of the Main Directorate of vocational schools and higher educational institutions of the People's Commissariat of Education of the RSFSR. After March 1921, he strongly opposed the **NEP** and developed his own plan for industrialization.

In 1923, Preobrazhensky joined the Left

Opposition. He was one of the initiators and authors of the "Statement of 46." In 1927, he was expelled from the party and from the Society of Old Bolsheviks. In January 1928, he was exiled from Moscow to the Kazakh city of Uralsk, where he worked in the planning bodies. During 1928–1930, he worked at the State Planning Committee of the Tatar Autonomous Soviet Socialist Republic.

After the beginning of industrialization in the USSR, Preobrazhensky supported Stalin. In July 1929, together with **K. Radek** and **I. Smilga**, Preobrazhensky sent a letter to the CC CPSU declaring an ideological and organizational break with the opposition. In January 1930, he was restored to membership in the CPSU and appointed deputy chairman of the Nizhny Novgorod Regional Planning Committee.

Between 1932 and 1933, he became a member of the Board of the People's Commissariat of Light Industry of the USSR. After he personally saw the results of Stalin's policy in the countryside, Preobrazhensky again turned from a conditional ally into a convinced enemy of Stalin's policies. Together with I. Smirnov, he created an underground opposition organization. In 1933–1936, Preobrazhensky was appointed deputy chairman of the Central Planning and Finance Department of the People's Commissariat of Grain and Livestock Farms of the USSR. In 1936, he was again expelled from the CPSU.

In the winter of 1936, Preobrazhensky was arrested on charges of creation and leading of the "Young Trotskyist Center" and participation in a counterrevolutionary terrorist organization. On July 13, 1937, he was sentenced to death by the Military Collegium of the USSR Supreme Court and executed.

He was posthumously rehabilitated on December 22, 1988, by the Plenum of the Supreme Court of the USSR.

RADEK, KARL BERNGARDOVICH (NÉE KAROL SOBELSOHN) (1885–1939). Radek was a Marxist, an international revolutionary, leader of the international Social Democratic and Communist movement, Soviet politician, writer, journalist, publicist, diplomat, literary critic, member of the Central Committee of the RCP(b) (1919–1924), and member of the Executive Committee of the **Comintern** (1920–1924).

Karol Sobelsohn was born in Lemberg, the Austro-Hungarian Empire (now Lviv, Ukraine) into a Jewish Litvak family. His father, who was a postal worker, died when Karol was only five years old. He spent his childhood and youth in Tarnow (now in Poland), where his mother worked as a teacher. In 1902, he graduated from a Polish gymnasium as an external student. He received further education at the Faculty of History at the University of Krakow. He also studied in Leipzig and Bern.

At the age of 14, Karol entered socialist circles and conducted propaganda among workers. For these activities, he was twice expelled from the gymnasium. In 1902, he became a member of the Polish Social Democratic Party of Galicia and Cieszyn Silesia. In 1904, he joined the Social Democracy of the Kingdom of Poland and Lithuania (SDKPiL). In 1905, Radek illegally arrived in Warsaw, where he participated in the 1905 Revolution. Together with J. Tyszka, Rosa Luxemburg, J. Markhlevski, and others, he worked as an editor of the newspaper *Tribuna*. In 1906, he was arrested and spent six months in prison. During his imprisonment, he intensively studied Russian.

In the spring of 1907, Radek was arrested again, and in the winter of the same year he was exiled to Austria. In 1908, he became an active leader of the left wing of the German Social Democratic movement. Due to the conflict with R. Luxemburg, he was later expelled from the party. He also collaborated with the German Social Democratic press and published numerous articles. Radek also attended lectures on Chinese history at the University of Leipzig and on international politics at the seminary of Karl Lamprecht (a German historian, who used interdisciplinary methods and focus on broad social, environmental, and even psychological questions in history). During this period, Radek acquired wide contacts in the social democratic movement in Europe. At the beginning of the First World War, he supported an internationalist position and was forced to move to Switzerland, where he participated in conferences of left-wing Socialists. During this period, he became close to the Bolsheviks and moved to their camp.

In April 1917, Radek became a member of the overseas mission of the RSDWP(b) in Stockholm. He was one of the organizers of Lenin's return to Russia from Switzerland in a "sealed carriage" and accompanied him on his way through Germany. In November 1917, Radek headed the Department of External Relations of the All-Russian Central Executive Committee, and in December, he participated in negotiations with the Germans in Brest-Litovsk. In 1918, he was one of the leaders of Left Communists who opposed the signing of a peace treaty with Germany. After the start of the November Revolution in Germany, he became one of the leaders of the Communist Party of Germany and represented the interests of the **Comintern** in that country. In February 1919, Radek was briefly arrested. In 1919–1924, he became a member of the Central Committee of the RCP(b). Simultaneously, he was a member of the Executive Committee of the Comintern. During this period, Radek maintained contacts with the left (pro-communist) faction of the Poale Zion party (a movement of Marxist–Zionist Jewish workers founded in various cities of Poland, Europe, and the Russian Empire at the beginning of the 20th century), which sought to join the Comintern.

During the Polish-Soviet War (1920), Radek became a member of the Polish Revolutionary Committee, created as the future Communist government of Poland. In July–September, he was at the front. In October 1920, he entered Germany illegally, where he aimed to organize a "united front" of communists and social democrats. In January 1922, on behalf of the People's Commissariat for Foreign Trade, he conducted secret negotiations in Berlin with the commander of the Reichswehr, General Hans von Seeckt, and tried to obtain German military assistance for Soviet Russia. In April 1922, he led the Comintern delegation at the congress of the three internationals.

In May 1923, Radek returned to Germany. In June 1923, he advocated for an alliance of communists with German nationalists (even National Socialists) in the struggle against a common enemy: "bourgeois democracy." In October 1923, he was supposed to participate in the leadership of a planned uprising in Hamburg, but it broke out before his arrival and ended in failure.

After his return to the Soviet Union, Radek took part in a party discussion on the side of the Trotskyist opposition. In 1924, at the fifth congress of the Comintern, he defended the tactics of a "united front," but after the victory of **G. Zinoviev**'s position on this issue, Radek left his post in the Comintern. In 1925–1927, he was appointed rector of the Moscow Sun Yat-sen Communist University of the Toilers of China (a Comintern school that operated from 1925 to 1930) and served as a member of the editorial board of the *Bolshaia Sovetskaia Entsiklopedia* (*Great Soviet Encyclopedia*).

In 1927, at the 15th congress of the CPSU, together with seventy-five other active participants of the Left Opposition, Radek was expelled from the party. From January 1928 to May 1929, he was sent into exile to Tobolsk, and few months later he was transferred to Tomsk. Soon he announced his break with Trotskyism and started negotiations with the Soviet authorities. In May 1929, he was returned from exile. On July 6, Radek—together with **E. Preobrazhensky** and **I. Smilga**—published a letter of repentance, in which he stated that he regretted his opposition activities. Subsequently, he declared himself a supporter of Stalin (who at that time had adopted several ideas of the "Trotskyists"). In 1930, Radek was again admitted to the CPSU. He worked as the head of the International Information Department of the CC CPSU. In 1929, he informed the Joint State Political Directorate (OGPU) that Iakov Blumkin (a Left Socialist-Revolutionary, Bolshevik, and an agent of the Cheka and State Political Directorate [GPU]) had delivered a letter from **L. Trotsky** to him.

In 1934–1936, Radek became a member of the editorial board of the newspaper *Izvestia*, where he worked under the leadership of **N. Bukharin**. In 1935, Radek became a member of the Constitutional Commission of the Central Executive Committee of the USSR and, together with Bukharin, wrote the draft of the so-called Stalin Constitution (1936). In August 1936, during the first "Show Trials," Radek supported the severe punishment of Zinoviev and **L. Kamenev**.

In October 1936, Radek was arrested and accused of treason. He confessed only after two and a half months of interrogation. Reportedly, he decided to cooperate with the investigation after a meeting with Stalin, who, in exchange for a promise to save his life, demanded that Radek incriminate himself and others (including Bukharin). On January 23–30, 1937, during the trial, Radek was accused of being a member of the "Parallel Anti-Soviet Trotskyist Center." He actively cooperated with the prosecution at the trial and received a sentence of ten years in labor camps. On May 19, 1939, nevertheless, he was executed at the direction of the NKVD leadership in a labor camp.

In 1988, Radek was reinstated in the party and rehabilitated by the USSR Supreme Court.

RAKOVSKY, CHRISTIAN (NÉE KRASTYO GEORGIEV STANCHEV) (1873–1941). A Bulgarian socialist revolutionary, Bolshevik, Soviet political and diplomat, and member of the revolutionary movements in the Balkans, France, Germany, Russia, and Ukraine, Christian Rakovsky was born in the town of Kotel, in the Ottoman Empire (now Bulgaria) into a Bulgarian family. He was the grandson of the famous revolutionary Georgy Rakovsky. Despite the fact that he was an ethnic Bulgarian, he also had a Romanian passport. He studied at a Bulgarian gymnasium but was expelled twice (in 1886 and 1890) for revolutionary agitation. In 1887, he changed his name, Krastyo ("cross" in the Bulgarian language) Stanchev, to Christian Rakovsky. In 1889, he declared himself a devout Marxist.

In 1890, Rakovsky emigrated to Geneva (Switzerland), where he entered the Medical Faculty of Geneva University. In this city, through Russian emigrants, he became acquainted with the Russian Social Democratic movement. In particular, he became close to the founder of the Marxist movement in the Russian Empire, **Georgy Plekhanov**. Rakovsky took part in organizing the International Congress of Socialist Students in Geneva. In 1893, as a delegate from Bulgaria, he attended the Socialist International Congress in Zurich. He collaborated with the first Bulgarian Marxist magazine, *Den'*, and the Social Democratic newspapers *Rabotnik* and *Drugar* (*Tovarishch*). According to Rakovsky's autobiography, his hatred for Russian tsarism intensified at this time.

In the fall of 1893, Rakovsky entered the Medical School in Berlin, but due to his close ties with revolutionaries from Russia, he was expelled from there within six months. In Germany, Rakovsky collaborated with Wilhelm Liebknecht at *Vorwärts* (the main newspaper of the German Social Democrats). In 1896, he graduated from the Medical Faculty of the University of Montpellier in France, where he received a doctorate of medicine. In 1897, he moved to Russia and married Elizaveta Riabova (she died in childbirth five years later). From the fall of 1898 to spring 1899, he served in the Romanian army.

After the split of the RSDWP into Bolsheviks and Mensheviks in 1903, Rakovsky took an intermediate position and tried to reconcile the two groups. Between 1903 and 1917, along with **M. Gorky**, he served as a link between the Bolsheviks, with whom he sympathized in terms of economic program, and the Mensheviks, in whose activities he found positive political moments. In addition to the Russian revolutionaries, Rakovsky for some time worked with Rosa Luxemburg in Geneva.

After completing his studies in France, Rakovsky arrived in St. Petersburg, where he offered his services in coordinating the work of Marxist circles in Russia and abroad, visiting Miliukov and Struve. But soon he was expelled from the country and left for Paris. In 1900–1902 he once again visited the Russian capital, and in 1902 he returned to France.

Although Rakovsky's revolutionary activities during this period extended to most European countries, his main focus was on the Balkans (primarily Bulgaria and Romania), where he aimed to organize Socialist movements. For propaganda purposes, he founded the left-wing Romanian newspaper *Sotsial-Demokrat* and a number of Bulgarian Marxist periodicals in Geneva. In 1907–1914, he was a member of the International Socialist Bureau (the permanent organization of the Second International).

After his return to Romania, Rakovsky settled in Dobruja, where he worked as an ordinary doctor. In 1913, **L. Trotsky** visited him. Rakovsky became one of the founders of the Romanian Social Democratic Party (PSDR). During the First World War, Rakovsky supported the left wing of international social democracy and condemned the imperialist nature of the war. In September 1915, he, along with other left socialists, was one of the organizers of the anti-war international socialist Zimmerwald Conference.

In August 1916, after Romania entered the war on the side of the Entente, Rakovsky was arrested on charges of spreading defeatism and espionage for Austria and Germany. He was imprisoned until May 1, 1917, when he was liberated by Russian Army. After release, he immediately left for Russia. During the attempt to overthrow the government and arrest leading Bolsheviks led by General Lavr Kornilov, Rakovsky was hidden by the Bolshevik organization at the Sestroretsk tool plant. From there, he first moved to Kronstadt and later to Stockholm, where he remained during the October Revolution of 1917.

In November 1917, Rakovsky joined the RSDWP(b) and led party work in Odesa and Petrograd. In early January 1918, Rakovsky was appointed as an organizer-commissar of the Council of People's Commissars of the RSFSR. He spent some time in Sevastopol and organized an expedition to the Danube against the Romanian authorities, who had already occupied Bessarabia. Later, he was sent to Odesa, where he headed the "Supreme Autonomous Collegium for Combating Counter-Revolution in Romania and Ukraine" (the local unit of the All-Russian Extraordinary Commission). He also became a member of the Rumcherod (a self-proclaimed and short-lived organ of Soviet power in the southwestern part of Russian Empire that functioned during May 1917–May 1918). From Odesa, Rakovsky was sent to Mykolaiv, Crimea, and Iekaterinoslav, then to Poltava and Kharkiv. In April 1918, Rakovsky, along with Stalin and Manuilsky, went to Kursk to conduct peace negotiations with the Ukrainian Central Rada. But in Kursk, the delegates received a message about Skoropadsky's coup in Kyiv, ending the leadership of the Rada. The new government invited the Bolshevik delegation to come to Kyiv to negotiate.

In September 1918, Rakovsky was sent on a diplomatic mission to Germany, but soon—together with the Soviet ambassador in Berlin (Ioffe), **Bukharin**, and other comrades—he was expelled from Germany. As the Soviet delegation exited Germany, it learned the news about the November revolution in Berlin. Rakovsky tried to return to Berlin but was detained by the German military authorities and sent to Smolensk.

After his return, he became one of the organizers of Soviet power in Ukraine. From January 1919 to July 1923, Rakovsky served as the chairman of the Council of People's Commissars (Ukraine) and the people's commissar of foreign affairs of the Ukrainian SSR. Simultaneously, from January 1919 to May 1920, he was appointed the people's commissar of internal affairs. From 1919 to 1927, Rakovsky was a member of the Central Committee of the RCP(b). In 1919–1920, he was a member of the CC Orgburo. From December 17, 1919, to February 19, 1920, Rakovsky headed the All-Ukrainian Revolutionary Committee (at that time the highest legislative and executive body of power of the Ukrainian SSR). During this time, he was the supreme political leader in the republic. In 1922, as part of the Soviet delegation, Rakovsky took part in the work of the Genoa Conference.

In 1923, Rakovsky joined Trotsky's Left Opposition. At the twelfth congress of the RCP(b), he decisively opposed Stalin's nationality policy. In July 1923, Rakovsky was removed from the post of the chairman of the Council of People's Commissars of Ukraine and sent as the Soviet Ambassador to Britain. From October 1925 to October 1927, he served as a trade representative, then plenipotentiary in France. In 1927, he was removed from all posts and expelled from the Central Committee. At the 15th congress of the All-Union Communist Party (Bolsheviks), he was expelled from the party. At a special meeting at the OGPU, he was sentenced to four years of exile and was sent to Kostanay in Kazakhstan. In 1931, he was exiled to Barnaul in the Altai region of Siberia.

In 1935, Rakovsky announced that he had ended all links with the opposition and was allowed to return to Moscow. In November 1935, he was restored to party membership. But in 1936, he was again expelled from the party. On January 27, 1937, he was arrested based on **N. Iezhov**'s special message to Stalin. In March 1938, he was a defendant at the trial in the case of the "Anti-Soviet Trotskyist bloc." On March 13, 1938, he was sentenced to twenty years in prison with confiscation of property. He began to serve his punishment in Orel Prison. On September 11, 1941, however, Rakovsky, along with S. Bessonov and **Pletnev**, was shot in Medvedev forest.

On February 4, 1988, by order of the Plenum of the Supreme Court of the USSR, he was rehabilitated, and on June 21, 1988, he was reinstated in the party.

RIUTIN, MARTEMIAN NIKITICH (1890–1937). An Old Bolshevik, Soviet politician, candidate member of the CC CPSU (1927–1930), and the leader of the "Union of Marxist-Leninists," a pro-peasant political faction organized against Stalin, Martemian Riutin was born into a peasant family in the village of Verkhne-Riutino, Irkutsk Oblast, Siberia, Russian Empire. His father, Nikita Pavlovich Riutin, was a village carpenter. Martemian's first teachers were the exiled settlers Vinogradov and Perepelitsin, who taught him how to read and write. When an elementary school was opened in a neighboring village, Martemian became the best student in it. The exiled Social Democrat B. Markovin helped Riutin to enter the Irkutsk Teachers' Seminary. The beginning of his studies coincided with the First Russian Revolution (1905). Riutin regularly attended political rallies along with other seminarians, but he did not join any revolutionary organization. In 1908, he graduated from the Irkutsk Teachers' Seminary. After graduation, he worked as a teacher in the village of Shivera, where he became acquainted with Marxist literature, namely the works of Lenin, K. Marx, F. Engels, A. Bebel, and K. Kautsky. In 1912, he created a Marxist circle. In October 1914, Riutin joined the Bolshevik Party.

After the outbreak of the First World War, Riutin was mobilized into the army, and after graduating from the Irkutsk School of Praporshchik (a junior officer rank in Imperial Russia), he was sent to Harbin (now in China) to serve in the 618 Tomsk squad. In the army, Riutin conducted revolutionary propaganda among the soldiers. In March 1917, he approached a line of soldiers and announced the February Revolution and the fall of the tsarist regime. He was elected to the Harbin Soviet of Workers' and Soldiers' Deputies and became a chairman of the Harbin Committee of the RSDWP(b). He also edited the journal *Borba* (*Struggle*). He made an unsuccessful attempt to establish Soviet power in the city. On November 27, the Chinese authorities demanded the expulsion of the revolutionary-minded 618 and 559 military infantry brigades, as well as personally the Bolsheviks Riutin and Slavin from the city. In December 1917, due to the persecution by the Chinese authorities, Riutin fled to Irkutsk.

In the spring and summer of 1918, with the beginning of foreign intervention and the revolt of the Czechoslovak Legion, the situation in Siberia became more complicated. The Bolshevik organizations were forced to go into an illegal position. Riutin headed one of the most successful partisan detachments in the Baikal region. After the liberation of Novonikolaevsk by the Red Army, Riutin worked in the political department of the 5th Army. In 1919, he was appointed chairman of the Irkutsk Provincial Executive Committee and member of the Novonikolaevsk Revolutionary Committee. In March 1920, he was elected chairman of the Presidium of the Irkutsk Provincial Party Committee and a delegate to the tenth congress of the RCP(b). With other delegates, he took part in the suppression of the Kronstadt rebellion (March 1–18, 1921).

In 1922, Riutin was transferred to the Southeastern Bureau of the Central Committee of the RCP(b) and was made secretary of the Dagestan Regional Party Committee. In March 1924, he headed the Propaganda Department of the Moscow Committee of the RCP(b). In 1925, he was appointed secretary of the Krasnopresnensky District Party Committee. During 1924–1927, Riutin actively supported Stalin in his struggle against **L. Trotsky** and the Left Opposition. In December 1927, at the 15th congress of the CPSU, Riutin demanded organizational and ideological surrender from the Left Opposition. At the congress he was elected a candidate member of the Central Committee.

In 1928, Riutin sharply changed his attitude toward Stalin and his entourage. In the fall of 1928, he was appointed deputy editor of the newspaper *Krasnaia Zvezda* (*Red Star*). In 1929, he became the Central Committee commissioner for collectivization in Kazakhstan and Eastern Siberia. He was sent to his native village in Siberia to report on the progress of collectivization. But instead of progress, he witnessed the side effects of forced collectivization: violence, widespread famine, and mass deportation. Upon his return, Riutin, like many other party leaders, disputed Stalin's policy of rapid collectivization in the countryside and his methods of industrialization. He also opposed the intensification of repressions against kulaks and the better-off middle peasants. Riutin supported the ideas of Right Opposition and headed the pro-peasant political faction dissatisfied with Stalin's policy. In January 1930, he published an article in *Krasnaia Zvezda* in which he criticized the implementation and methods of collectivization.

In March 1930, Riutin, on the personal decision of Stalin, was removed from his post at *Krasnaia Zvezda*. In fact, he was promoted to chairman of the board of the *Soyuzkino* (state All-Union Film and Photo Association) and a member of the Presidium of the Council of National Economy. In reality, however, in this post he could no longer directly influence political decision-making. On September 20, 1930, Riutin was invited for an "interrogation" at the Central Control Commission of the CPSU. Members of the Presidium of the Central Control Commission, E. Iaroslavsky and M. Shkiriatov, questioned him. On October 5, 1930, at a Politburo meeting chaired by **V. Molotov**, a decision was made to expel Riutin from the party "for treacherous double-dealing and an attempt at underground propaganda of right-wing opportunist views." In October, he was excluded from the party and dismissed from his post.

On November 13, 1930, Riutin was arrested on charges of counterrevolutionary agitation and spent several months in Butyrka prison. During interrogations, Riutin firmly denied his guilt. On January 17, 1931, the Special Council of the Joint State Political Directorate declared the accusations against Riutin unconfirmed, and he was released.

After his release, he worked as an economist at the Soiuzelektro enterprise. In 1932, Riutin gathered around him a group of like-minded friends (V. Kaiurov, M. Ivanov, P. Galkin, G. Rokhkin, and several other Old Bolsheviks), and together they organized the "Union of Marxist-Leninists." In March 1932, Riutin prepared a two-hundred-page document titled "Stalin and the Crisis of the Proletarian Dictatorship." In May 1932, he prepared an appeal "to all members of the CPSU(b)," in which he accused Stalin of usurping power and abandoning Lenin's ideas. During summer and early fall, the so-called "Riutin Platform," which aimed to unite "right" and "left" communists, secretly circulated these documents among party members. The organizational meeting, during which the creation of the "Union of Marxist-Leninists" was proclaimed, took place on August 21, 1932, near Moscow. In addition to non-party Riutin, fourteen communists from Moscow and Kharkiv attended. The existence of the "Union" ended on September 14, 1932.

On September 22, 1932, Riutin was arrested. He was extremely courageous during interrogations and took all the blame on himself. He confessed that he stood at the head of the organization and singlehandedly wrote the entire platform. Riutin was tortured and blackmailed. He signed all the required confessions and "repentance" that were demanded of him. On October 11, 1932, he was sentenced to ten years in prison on charges of participating in a counterrevolutionary right-wing organization. All Riutin's associates received from five to ten years in prison. He was detained first in the Suzdal political isolator, then in the Verkhneuralsk political isolator.

In the summer of 1936, Riutin was dispatched to Moscow. In October, the new people's commissar of internal affairs, **N. Iezhov**, ordered a new investigation into the case of Riutin. Despite cruel torture and promises to give him freedom, Riutin refused to answer the investigator's questions and to sign some "interrogation protocols" that had been prepared in advance. On November 4, 1936, he made a statement to the Central Executive Committee of the USSR, categorically denying his involvement in terrorism and stating that he would not "apologize and ask for forgiveness" in the event of a death sentence. On January 10, 1937, at a closed trial that lasted only forty minutes, he was sentenced to death. When asked about his guilt, he said that he "did not want to give an answer, and generally refuses to give any evidence on the merits of the charges against him." The same day he was executed.

His wife and both sons were killed in Stalin's prisons. Only his daughter, Liubov, who was tortured by the NKVD and imprisoned in camps, survived the terror.

On June 13, 1988, Riutin was posthumously rehabilitated.

RODIONOV, MIKHAIL IVANOVICH (1907–1950). A Soviet statesperson, chairman of the Council of Ministers of the Russian SFSR (1946–1949), and victim of Stalin's postwar purges, Rodionov was executed in the aftermath of the Leningrad Affair.

Mikhail Rodionov was born in the village of Ratunino, Makaryevsky Uezd (Nizhny Novgorod Governorate), Russian Empire (now Lyskovsky district, Russia), into a large middle-income peasant family (*seredniak*). At the age of eight, Mikhail started his studies at a rural school. From the age of 10, he helped his parents with the housework, and during the summer he worked for wealthy fellow villagers or landowners. In 1921, after leaving the parental home, he continued his studies at the commune school at the village of Lyskovo. After graduation, he studied at the Lyskovo Pedagogical College and received the diploma of a public-school teacher.

During 1927–1930, Rodionov worked as secretary at the Kislovsky volost Committee of the Komsomol and as a political education inspector of the Lyskovsky Regional Department of Public Education. In 1929, he joined the CPSU. In 1930, he was transferred to the Nizhny Novgorod District Department of Public Education. In 1930–1931, he served as head of the Bor (Nizhny Novgorod Oblast) Pedagogical College. From 1931 to 1935, he headed the Department of Culture, Agitation and Propaganda and served as deputy secretary of the Borsky District Committee of the CPSU.

In December 1935, Rodionov was elected first secretary of the Ivanovo district (now the Kostroma region) Committee of the CPSU. In 1938, he headed Gorky Regional Department of Public Education. In 1938–1939, he served as the third secretary of the Gorky Oblast Committee of the CPSU. In 1939–1940, Rodionov was appointed chairman of the Gorky Regional Executive Committee. From February 1940 till March 1946, he became the first secretary of the Gorky Oblast and City committee of CPSU. Simultaneously, from 1941 to 1943, he served as a chairman of the Gorky Defense Committee. During the **Great Patriotic War** (1941–1945), Rodionov was appointed commissioner of the **State Defense Committee** and was responsible for the production of combat vehicles and ammunition in the Gorky Oblast. He also served first as a member of the Military Council of the Moscow Military District, and later, of the Gorky Military District. He was involved in organizing and formation of military units which were sent to the front. He often visited military units and maintained close contact with military divisions and units at the front. On his initiative, delegations of Gorky residents repeatedly went to the front with gifts for soldiers. For exemplary fulfillment of his tasks during the wartime, he was awarded two Orders of Lenin, the Order of the Red Banner of Labor, the Order of the Patriotic War of the first degree, and many medals.

In March 1946, Rodionov was appointed chairman of the Council of Ministers of the RSFSR and a member of the CC Orgburo. But in spring 1949, he was dismissed from office, removed from the Orgburo, and sent to study at the Academy of Social Sciences under the auspices of the CC CPSU. He did not finish his studies because in the summer of the same year, he was arrested in the so-called Leningrad Affair. Along with other defendants, he was charged with "creating an anti-party group, carrying out sabotage and subversive work against the party and the state, separatism, treason, violation of state plans and economic crimes." The All-Russian Wholesale Fair, held January 10–20, 1949, in Leningrad, served as a pretext for fabricating false accusations. Rodionov was found guilty and executed on October 1, 1950. His wife and eldest daughter were also arrested and sent to a labor camp.

Rodionov and his family members were rehabilitated in 1954 after Stalin's death.

ROSENGOLTS, ARKADY PAVLOVICH (1889–1938).

Soviet statesman and military leader, commissar of foreign trade of the USSR, and a defendant at the Moscow Trial of the Twenty-One (1938), Arkady Rozengolts was born in Vitebsk, Russian Empire (today Viciebsk, Belarus), into a Jewish family. His father, Faivel (Pavel) Nakhimovich Rozengolts, was a merchant-gunsmith. Already in 1905, at the age of 16, Arkady joined the Bolshevik faction of the RSDWP and became involved in revolutionary activities. After graduation from the Vitebsk gymnasium, he continued his studies at the Kyiv Commercial Institute, from which he successfully graduated in 1914. During his stay in Kyiv, Arkady continued to be involved in revolutionary activities. Between 1914 and 1915, Arkady worked as an insurance agent in Iekaterinoslav and Moscow.

During the February Revolution of 1917, Rosengolts took an active part in the armed uprising in Moscow. After the revolution, he was elected a member of the Executive Committee of the Moscow Soviet of People's Deputies (*Mossovet*), Moscow Revolutionary Military Committee, and a candidate member of the Central Headquarters of the Red Guard. From 1918, he became a member of the Revolutionary Military Council of the RSFSR (*Revvoyensoviet*) and a member of the Revolutionary Military Councils of several armies on the Eastern and Western fronts. During this period, he worked very closely with **L. Trotsky**.

In March 1919, during the eighth congress of the RCP(b), Rosengolts countered the "military opposition" a group of delegates of the eighth congress, mainly left-wing communists, who advocated the preservation of partisan methods of army management and warfare and opposed the formation of a regular army. The "military opposition" included A. Kamensky, **V. Smirnov**, G. Safarov, **G. Piatakov**, A. Bubnov, Ie. Iaroslavsky, V. Sorin, **K. Voroshilov**, P. Goloshchekin, A. Miasnikov, R. Zemliachka, and others. In 1920, Rozengolts was awarded the Order of the Red Banner of the RSFSR.

After demobilization in 1920, Rozengolts was appointed to the People's Commissariat of Railways of the RSFSR. In 1922, he was a member of the Collegium of the People's Commissariat of Finance of the RSFSR. During his tenure, he conducted secret cooperation negotiations between the Red Army and the Reichswehr (the German armed forces). In 1923–1924, he headed the Main Directorate of the Air Fleet (Vozdukhoflot) under the Council of People's Commissars of the USSR, and simultaneously he served as a deputy people's commissar.

In 1925, Rozengolts was appointed adviser to the Plenipotentiary Representation of the USSR in Great Britain and Chargé d'Affaires of the USSR in Great Britain (he replaced L. Krasin who was in poor health). In this post, he was engaged in espionage activities. These activities ultimately led to the deterioration of diplomatic relations between the USSR and Great Britain. In 1927, diplomatic relations between two countries were interrupted when the British accused the Soviet Trade Mission in London of spying.

In 1927–1930, Rozengolts became acting deputy people's commissar of the Workers' and Peasants' Inspection (Rabkrin). On November 22, 1930, he was appointed people's commissar of foreign trade. Also, between 1927 and 1934, Rozengolts was a member of the Central Control Commission of the CPSU. Simultaneously, from July 1930 to February 1932, he was a member of the Presidium of the Central Control Commission. In April 1933, he received the Order of Lenin for exceptional personal merits and outstanding work in the organization and management of foreign trade of the USSR. In 1934, Rozengolts was elected a candidate member of the CC CPSU.

After the outbreak of Stalin's great repressions, in June 1937, Rozengolts was dismissed from his office. On October 7, 1937, he was arrested, and along with **N. Bukharin**, **A. Rykov**, and other Soviet officials, he became one of the defendants of the Third Moscow Trial. During the trial, he was accused of attempting to assassinate Lenin and Stalin, and engaging in espionage, and sabotage. On March 13, 1938, he was executed at the Kommunarka training ground. His wife, Zoia Aleksandrovna, was also arrested and shot. His elder son, Valery, suffered incarceration but avoided execution.

In 1988, Rosengolts was rehabilitated during Gorbachev's de-Stalinization campaign.

RUDZUTAKS, JĀNIS (YAN) (1887–1938). Rudzutaks was a revolutionary, Soviet statesperson, party and trade union leader, member of the Central Executive Committee of the USSR of the first through seventh convocations, member of the CC CPSU (1920–1937), member of the Politburo of the CC CPSU (1926–1932), candidate member of the Politburo of the CC CPSU (1923–1926, 1934–1937), member of the Orgburo of the CC CPSU (1921–1922, 1923–1924), secretary of the CC CPSU (1923–1924), and people's commissar of transportation (1924–1934).

Janis Rudzutaks was born in the Kuldiga district, Courland Governorate (now Saldus municipality, Latvia), into the family of a Latvian farmworker. He finished two grades of parish school, and in 1904, he moved to Riga and became a factory worker. In 1905, he became a member of the RSDWP (Bolshevik faction). In 1906, he joined the Riga Committee of the RSDWP, and in 1907, he headed the Vindavskaia Party organization. For his revolutionary activities, Janis was arrested, and in 1909, a military court sentenced him to 15 years of hard labor (later the term was reduced to 10 years). He served his sentence in Riga Central prison, and later he was transferred to Butyrka prison in Moscow.

After his release, during the February Revolution of 1917, Rudzutaks was appointed a secretary of the All-Russian Central Council of the Trade Union of Textile Workers. He also became a member of Presidium of the Moscow Council of Trade Unions. During the October Revolution of 1917, he participated in street battles in Moscow. Between 1917 and 1920, he served as chairman of the Moscow Oblast Council of the National Economy. From March 1918 to October 1924, he was also a member of the Presidium of the All-Union Central Council of Trade Unions, and simultaneously between 1920 and 1921, he served as general secretary of the All-Union Central Council of Trade Unions. In 1919, he was also appointed chairman of the Main Directorate of Water Transport of the People's Commissariat of Railways of the RSFSR. From October 1919, Rudzutaks was a member of the Turkestan Commission of the All-Russian Central Executive Committee and the Council of People's Commissars of the RSFSR.

In 1920–1921, Rudzutaks served in various positions, including chairman of the Central Committee of the Trade Union of Transport Workers, the Turkestan Commission of the All-Russian Central Executive Committee, and the Council of People's Commissars of the RSFSR. Between March and October 1921, he was chairman of the Turkestan Bureau of the Central Committee of the RCP(b). In 1921, he participated in the so-called "discussions about trade unions." During these discussions, he supported Lenin's stance against **L. Trotsky** and **N. Bukharin**. According to **N. Krupskaia**, Lenin liked Rudzutaks and even considered him to be suitable for the post of general secretary.

In 1922, Rudzutaks was a member of the Soviet delegation at the Genoa Conference. Between 1922 and 1924, he was appointed chairman of the Central Asian Bureau of the Central Committee of the RCP(b). Simultaneously, in 1923–1924, he was secretary of the CC RCP(b). After Lenin's death, he became a Stalin loyalist. In 1927, during the October Plenum of the CC CPSU, he proposed Stalin for the post of general secretary. Between 1924 and 1930, Rudzutaks served as people's commissar of railways of the USSR (he replaced **F. Dzerzhinsky** in this post). From 1926 to 1937, he was deputy chairman of the Council of People's Commissars of the Soviet Union and the Council of Labor and Defense. From 1928, he also served as the chairman of the Committee for the Chemicalization of the National Economy under the Council of People's Commissars of the USSR. In 1930, he initiated a decree of the Council of People's Commissars of the USSR on the removal of bells from all churches. In his opinion, this step could help to compensate for the lack of metal necessary for minting coins. In 1932–1934, Rudzutaks served as chairman of the Central Control Commission of the CPSU and people's commissar of the Rabkrin of the USSR.

In May 1937, Rudzutaks was suddenly expelled from the Politburo and Central Committee. On May 25, 1937, he was arrested by the NKVD. According to the allegations, he headed an anti-Soviet nationalist Latvian organization, was engaged in sabotage, and was a spy for foreign intelligence services. He was sentenced to death and executed on July 28, 1938.

In 1955, Rudzutaks was posthumously rehabilitated, cleared of all charges, and reinstated in the party. His case was cited by **N. Khrushchev** in his speech to the twentieth CC CPSU congress in 1956 as an example of unjustified arrests and executions.

RYKOV, ALEKSEI IVANOVICH (1881–1938). Rykov was a Russian revolutionary, Soviet politician, the first people's commissar of internal affairs of the RSFSR (1917), people's commissar of posts and telegraph of the USSR (1931–1936), chairman of the Council of People's Commissars of the USSR (1924–1930), chairman of the Supreme Council of the National Economy of the RSFSR (1918–1921, 1923), chairman of the Supreme Council of the National Economy of the USSR (1923–1924), and a member of the CC CPSU Politburo (1922–1930).

Aleksei Rykov was born into a Russian peasant family in Saratov. He graduated from the Saratov classical gymnasium. At this time, Saratov was an "exile city." Many political prisoners (mainly workers and students) were exiled to the city, and revolutionary circles flourished there. While still in the gymnasium, Aleksei started to study *Das Kapital* and became carried away by Karl Marx's ideas. Also, Nikolai Rakitnikov, the leader of the Socialist Revolutionary Party, had a significant impact on him. In 1898, Rykov joined the RSDWP and became actively involved in the party work of illegal circles. On the eve of his final exams, a search was conducted in the Rykovs' house. Although nothing was found, Aleksei received a reduced assessment for behavior and could not enter prestigious universities.

In 1900, he started his studies at the Faculty of Law at Kazan University, the same faculty where Lenin had previously studied. During his studies, he entered the local committee of the Social Democratic Party and started to work in the student committee. In 1901, he was expelled from the university for participation in the revolutionary movement, arrested, and spent nine months in prison. After release, he was exiled to Saratov, where in 1902 he organized the May Day demonstration. The demonstration was dispersed by the police and the Black-Hundreds ultranationalist movement. In 1903, he became a professional revolutionary and was forced to go underground. The same year in Geneva he met with Lenin for the first time. Two months later, with a fake passport, he returned to Russia and started to work in the Northern Committee of the RSDWP in Iaroslavl and Kostroma provinces. Later, he worked in the party committees in Nizhny Novgorod and Moscow. From June 1904, Rykov was on the "permanent wanted list" of the tsarist Okhrana and was arrested eight times.

Rykov played an active role in the Russian Revolution of 1905. In March 1905, he was delegated to the third congress of the Bolshevik Party in London. Subsequently, he became a constant member of the party's Central Committee. After the third congress, he headed the St. Petersburg Committee. In 1906, he was exiled to Pinega, Arkhangelsk province, but was able to flee from his place of exile. In 1910–1911, Rykov went into exile in France. In August 1911, he returned to Russia. In Moscow, he was arrested and exiled again to the Arkhangelsk province. In 1912, Rykov was released due to an amnesty of prisoners. After release, he went to Moscow and recommenced his revolutionary pursuits. In November of the same year, he was arrested again and exiled to the Narym Territory. In 1915, Rykov tried to escape but was arrested and returned to his place of exile.

After the February Revolution of 1917, Rykov returned from exile. In May, he was elected a member of the Presidium and deputy chairman of the Moscow Council of Workers' Deputies. In July, at the First All-Russian Congress of Soviets, he was elected a candidate member of the All-Russian Central Executive Committee. In August, he was elected a member of the Central Committee of the Party. Although Rykov opposed Lenin's April Theses and believed that there were no prerequisites for a socialist revolution in Russia and the impetus for the revolution should be from the more industrialized West, he became an active organizer of the October Revolution of 1917.

After the Revolution, Rykov was appointed people's commissar of internal affairs in the first Soviet government (the Council of People's Commissars). His first decree was titled "On the Workers' Militia." He also signed a decree "On the Transfer of Private Real Estate to the Jurisdiction of Cities." This decree initiated the beginning of mass resettlement of representatives of the urban lower class to the apartments of wealthy citizens and officials. Rykov—along with **L. Kamenev, G. Zinoviev**, and others—supported the idea of including representatives of the Socialist-Revolutionaries and Mensheviks into the government. The Bolshevik Party's Central Committee condemned their position and demanded that they abandon it. Consequently, they resigned from the Central Committee and from the government. After his resignation, Rykov started to work in the Moscow City Council (*Mossovet*), dealing with food supply to the city of Moscow. Later, he became a member of the board of the RSFSR People's Commissariat of Food.

Between April 1918 and May 1921, Rykov was appointed chairman of the Supreme Council of National Economy. From 1919, he became a member of the Politburo of the Central Committee of the RCP(b). From 1921 to 1923, he served as deputy chairman of the Council of People's Commissars. In 1923, he was elected a member of the Politburo of the CC CPSU. On July 6, 1923, he was appointed chairman of the Supreme Economic Council of the USSR and deputy chairman of the Council of People's Commissars and the Council of Labor and Defense of the USSR. Since Lenin, who was the chairman of the Council of People's Commissars, was seriously ill, the leadership of the government was concentrated in Rykov's hands. In January 1924, he himself suffered a heart attack.

After Lenin's death, Rykov supported Stalin, **G. Zinoviev**, and **L. Kamenev** in their struggle against **L. Trotsky**, and later he supported Stalin against Zinoviev and Kamenev once the triumvirate dissolved. On February 2, 1924, he was appointed chairman of the Council of People's Commissars of the USSR and chairman of the Council of People's Commissars of the RSFSR (i.e., he headed both governments). As head of state, Rykov abolished the prohibition of alcohol in December 1924 (Rykov himself drank a lot and was even treated for drunkenness in Germany). Vodka that appeared on sale after his decree was named "rykovka."

In 1928–1929, Rykov opposed the budget increase in the Union Republics, the cancellation of the New Economic Policy (NEP), as well as the sudden switch to rapid industrialization and collectivization. He emphasized the need to implement the NEP on the basis of cooperation between workers and peasants. In April 1929, at the Central Committee Plenum, Rykov was sharply criticized for his affiliation with the Right Opposition (the term given to the supporters of the NEP in the internal power struggle). He was forced to admit that he was "wrong," and a year later, along with **M. Kalinin** and **A. Ienukidze**, he signed a decree on the fight against kulaks. On December 19, 1930, Rykov was removed from the post of chairman of the Council of People's Commissars of the USSR, and on December 21, 1930, he was removed from the Politburo. In January 30, 1931, Rykov was appointed people's commissar for posts and telegraphs of the USSR.

In March 1937, Rykov was expelled from the Communist Party and arrested. At the Trial of the Twenty-One, Rykov—along with Bukharin, **N. Krestinsky, C. Rakovsky, G. Iagoda**, and others—were accused of treason (the "Anti-Soviet Bloc of Rights and Trotskyites"). On March 15, 1937, he was executed.

In 1988, Rykov was rehabilitated. In June of the same year, he was posthumously reinstated into the party.

S

SAPRONOV, TIMOFEI VLADIMIROVICH (1887–1937). A Russian revolutionary, an Old Bolshevik, and one of the leaders of the Left Opposition, Timofei Sapronov was born in the village of Mostaushka, Tula Governorate, the Russian Empire, into an impoverished Russian peasant family. The family had eight children. At the age of seven he entered the village school. At the age of eight he started to work as shepherd. Later, as a 12-year-old boy, he was taken by a local landowner (Countess Levshina) to St. Petersburg. In his childhood he liked to read about the "lives of the saints" and appeared to have a religious leaning. In St. Petersburg, together with Countess Levshina, he visited numerous churches, monasteries, and "holy graves." Before long, Timofei befriended the countess's doorman, Malinin, who supplied the young boy with revolutionary literature and became his mentor. During the winter of 1900–1901, Timofei witnessed numerous student demonstrations and their clashes with the police in St. Petersburg. Timofey developed an interest in revolutionary ideas, which shook his faith in God. For a year, the boy worked as a servant in exchange for room and food, but after this period he requested payment for his labor, and the countess dismissed him from service.

After his return, Sapronov worked as a house painter. In 1905, he went to Moscow and found himself in the whirlpool of the Revolution. He was unfamiliar with the goals and objectives of different political parties, most of which had been founded recently, but revolutionary literature, mass demonstrations, and rallies transformed him ideologically. After the failure of the revolution, he began to comprehend political events and joined the group of workers-Bolsheviks from Abrikosov's and Ding's manufacturing companies. The group soon disbanded, but Sapronov continued his revolutionary activities. Left to his own devices, he tried to organize professional unions and party circles among construction workers. In 1912, he became a member of the Bolshevik faction of the RSDWP. Just before the outbreak of the First World War, he managed to legalize the builders' union, which adopted a strong anti-war stance. In 1916, Sapronov was mobilized into the army, but he was released due to illness. During the war he lived and worked illegally in Moscow, Leningrad, Saratov, Nizhny Novgorod, and Tula. He worked in the governing bodies of the party organizations of these cities and actively participated in organizing factory committees, rural, volost, and district councils and party cells.

After the October Revolution of 1917 and until the end of 1919, he was chairman of the Moscow Oblast Executive Committee. In 1920, after the liberation of Kharkiv from Denikin's troops, he was appointed chairman of the Kharkiv Oblast Revolutionary and Executive Committee. He took part also in organizing Soviet governing bodies in Moscow, Petrograd, Kharkov, and Samara oblasts. In 1921, he became deputy chairman of the Supreme Council of National Economy. He also served as the secretary of the Urals Bureau of the Central Committee of the RCP, a member of the Central Committee of the RCP

(1922–1923), chairman of the Small Council of People's Commissars, and a member of the All-Russian Central Executive Committee and its Presidium, and worked in a number of other central and local party economic and professional bodies. In 1922, he was a member of the Russian delegation at the Genoa Conference. Between 1923 and 1924, he was appointed chairman of the Presidium and secretary of the All-Union Central Council of Trade Unions. From 1925, he worked as a member of the board of the Main Concession Committee.

In 1920–1921, Sapronov became one of the leaders of the Group of Democratic Centralism (Detsysty). Many group members belonged to the "Left Communist" faction or to the "military opposition. Democratic centralism opposed "bureaucratic centralism"—the bureaucratization of party and Soviet bodies. Since Sapronov held numerous posts in the party apparatus, he knew how it worked and started to actively criticize it. In 1923, the Detsysty supported **L. Trotsky** and became an integral part of the Left Opposition. Sapronov shared many ideas of the Left Opposition but fully rejected their idea of reforming the CPSU. He also thought that Trotsky was not radical enough. Thus, in 1926, together with **V. Smirnov**, Sapronov formed his own group, the so-called "group of fifteen" (also known as the "Sapronov group"). In December 1927, by a resolution of the 15th congress, Sapronov, together with thirty members of the "Trotskyist-Zinovievist" opposition, was expelled from the party. In 1928, he was exiled to the Crimean ASSR. Little is known about Sapronov's life after exile, other than that he was severely ill.

In 1932, he was arrested again and imprisoned. On September 28, 1937, he was sentenced to death and executed the same day.

He was rehabilitated on March 28, 1990.

SERGE, VICTOR (NÉE VICTOR LVOVICH KIBALCHICH) (1890–1947). A Russian and French-speaking writer, poet, historian, revolutionary Marxist, journalist, member of the Communist Party, and a prominent figure in the **Comintern**, Victor Kibalchich was born in Brussels into a family of revolutionary emigrants from Russia. Before emigration, his father, Lev (Leonid) Ivanovich Kibalchich, was an infantry trooper of the Imperial Horse Guards from Kyiv and supported the Narodniks (Populist) movement (Narodnichestvo). His mother, Vera Frolova (née Pederowska), was a Polish noblewoman. In his early teens, the family traveled through England, France, Switzerland, and Belgium. According to Kibalchich, his parents wandered through Europe "in search of cheap place for living and good libraries." Victor was educated by his father and refused to go to university. In 1903, he read Louis Blanc's *History of the French Revolution*. He also became acquainted with P. Kropotkin's views. He was impressed with these authors and became interested in socialism and anarchism.

In 1905, his parents split, and Victor started to work and live on his own. He first worked as a photographer's assistant and later as clerk, draftsman, and central heating technician. He joined the Young Socialist movement but was very quickly disappointed with it. After breaking with the socialists, Victor, together with his friends Raymond Callemin and Jean de Boe, became increasingly involved in anarchism. Victor even spent some time in the anarchist commune in the forest near Brussels. In 1908, he started to write his first articles. Under the pseudonym "Le Retif" (the Restive One), he wrote for the anarchist newspaper *Le Revolte*. In 1909, he left Brussels, moved to Lille, and later settled in Paris. In the French capital, he started to collaborate with the anarchist newspaper *L'Anarchie* (which had been established in April 1905 by Albert Libertad). In 1910, he became the editor of *L'Anarchie*. In France, he drew close to the famous Jules Bonnot, leader of a criminal anarchist organization called "the Bonnot Gang." In 1911, Kibalchich was arrested for his involvement with the gang, and in 1913, he was sentenced to five years in prison. He was imprisoned in the Melun prison on an island in the Seine, forty kilometers from Marne.

Kibalchich was still in prison when the First World War started. He was released from prison, and in 1916 he moved to Barcelona (Spain was neutral during the war). In Barcelona, he started to use the pen name Victor

Serge. Under this pseudonym, he wrote articles for the anarchist newspaper *Tierra y Libertad*. In 1917 (after the February Revolution in Russia), Victor returned to France, intending to travel onward to Russia, but he was arrested by French authorities. In 1919, the French government exchanged him for a French officer detained by the Petrograd Cheka and sent him to Russia.

In the USSR, Kibalchich was welcomed by famous writer **Maksim Gorky**. He decided to join the CPSU(b) and worked in the Third International, which was then headed by **G. Zinoviev**. Between 1921 and 1926, he worked illegally in Germany and Austria. His main task was to help to prepare revolutions there. In 1926, after the failure of revolutions, he was transferred back to Leningrad (Petrograd had been renamed after Lenin in 1925). In 1923, Victor joined the anti-Stalinist Left Opposition. In 1928, he was expelled from the party for his political views and briefly arrested. In 1933, he was arrested again and exiled to Orenburg. Only because he was an internationally recognized writer and his novels were highly praised by André Gide and Romain Rolland was he able to avoid death during the Great Terror. In 1935, during his visit to the USSR, Rolland personally asked Stalin to allow Serge to leave the USSR. Moreover, Serge's friends, representatives of the European left intelligentsia and workers' movements, launched a broad campaign for his release. As a result, in April 1936, Serge was expelled with his family to Belgium (the French government did not allow Victor Serge to enter France). Soon, the Soviet authorities revoked his Soviet citizenship. In Orenburg, Serge had written his novels *The Doomed* and *The Tempest* and a book of poems titled *The Resistance*, but when he left the USSR, all the manuscripts were confiscated. Later he was only able to recover poems from memory.

From Brussels, Serge criticized the repressive Soviet government under Stalin. He considered it his duty to make public information about the real situation in the USSR. In a letter to Trotsky on May 27, 1936, he wrote about the need to launch a public campaign in order to save political prisoners, opponents of the Stalinist regime, and to draw attention to the suppression of freedom of thought and speech in the Soviet Union. In his works, he described the Soviet repressive system (as it had developed by 1936): from prisons and concentration camps to the destruction of freedom of movement through a passport system. In the mid-1930s, the nature and scale of the punitive system created in the "state of workers and peasants" was almost unknown abroad. Victor Serge was among the first who comprehensively characterized the Soviet state system and repressive mechanisms of its functioning. Some information mentioned in his works, in particular information about political prisoners—their life and struggle in special political prisons (political isolators) and exile—were and remain unique. In the pamphlet *From Lenin to Stalin*, published in 1937, Serge explained that the entire policy of the ruling bureaucracy in the USSR was "determined by fear and panic. Keeping in fear the disenfranchised population, the system herself is gripped by constant anxiety."[1] These observations provide one of the most compelling descriptions of the period of Great Terror in the USSR.

In 1940, Serge, together with his son Vladimir, fled from the German occupation of Belgium to Marseille. From there he emigrated to Mexico, where he continued his literary activity. He died of a heart attack in Mexico City on November 17, 1947, his premature death hastened by his periods of imprisonment.

SERGEEV, FEDOR ANDREEVICH (1883–1921). A Bolshevik revolutionary, Soviet political, state and party leader, member of the RSDWP(b) from 1901, and founder and head of the Donetsk-Krivoi Rog Soviet Republic, Sergeev was a close friend of **Sergei Kirov** and Stalin.

Fedor Sergeev was born in the village of Glebovo, Kursk Governorate, the Russian Empire (now Fatezhsky district, Kursk region, the Russian Federation). His father, Andrei Arefevich Sergeev, was a state peasant who became a construction contractor. Fedor spent his childhood and youth in Iekaterinoslav (Dnipro, Ukraine). He entered a private preparatory school there, and in 1892, he entered the Iekaterinoslav (realschule). In 1901, after graduation, he became a student at the Mechanical Department of the Moscow Imperial Technical School. During his studies, he became interested in revolutionary ideas, joined the RSDWP, and took the nickname "Artem." For participation in a student demonstration in February 1902, he was arrested and imprisoned. In the fall of 1902, Artem left Russia and continued his education abroad. Between 1902 and 1903, he was a student at the Russian Higher School of Social Sciences in Paris, organized by M. Kovalevsky (a famous Russian jurist, sociologist, historian, and ethnographer). While in Paris, he studied socioeconomic sciences, technology, strategy, and military affairs. He was greatly impressed by Lenin's lectures, "Marxist Views on Agrarian Question in Europe and in Russia," when the future Soviet leader came to Paris from London in February 1903. Sergeev also became close to the family of the famous scientist I. Mechnikov.

In April 1903, Sergeev returned to Russia and began illegal revolutionary activities in the Donbas. In the village of Fedorovka, in Iekaterinoslav province, he organized the first peasant Social Democratic organization in the region and coordinated its May Day strike. Later, he worked as an assistant driver in Iekaterinoslav and conducted propaganda work among railway workers and miners. In 1904, he was sent to proselytize revolutionary propaganda in Mykolaiv, where in November of the same year he was arrested. At the beginning of 1905, after release from the tsarist prison, Artem, by the decision of the party (Bolsheviks), went to Kharkiv, where he created a revolutionary group called "Vpered" (Forward). In November–December 1905, Kharkiv proletarians were preparing for an armed uprising. For this purpose, workers' squads were created, and Artem organized daily military training for them. In December 1905, he led the armed uprising in Kharkiv. Between 1905 and 1907, he took an active part in the events of Russian Revolution in Ukraine and the Urals. In March 1907, he was arrested again and in September 1909 was sentenced to exile for life in eastern Siberia. In the summer of 1910, he fled through Japan, Korea, and China to Australia. On his way to Australia, he lived in Harbin, Nagasaki, Hong Kong, and Shanghai.

In Australia, Artem headed the Union of Russian émigré workers. Along with fellow Australian factory workers, they fought for their rights. The union established a Russian newspaper called *Australian Echo*. Artem regularly spoke at rallies about the need to fight against capitalism for a better life of the working class. For organizing unsanctioned rallies, he was arrested and incarcerated in Brisbane prison.

After the February Revolution of 1917, he returned to Russia through Vladivostok. In July 1917, he arrived in Kharkiv and soon headed the Bolshevik faction of the Kharkiv Council. Later, he was elected secretary of the bureau of the Donetsk Regional Committee of the RSDWP(b), then the secretary of the Kharkiv Regional Bureau of the Metalworkers' Trade Union. In August, he was elected a delegate to the sixth congress of the RSDWP(b), where he was elected a member of the Presidium and became a member of the Central Committee. In October, he was one of the organizers of the armed uprising in Kharkiv and the Donets basin region. In November 1917, Artem was elected chairman of the Executive Committee of the Kharkiv Council and the Provincial Military Revolutionary Committee. In December, at the first All-Ukrainian Congress of Soviets, he was elected a member of the Secretariat and the Central Executive Committee of the Ukrainian SSR.

Artem was a strong supporter of the idea of Donetsk autonomy, and in 1918 he founded the Donetsk-Krivoy Rog (Krivyi Rih) Soviet Republic. On February 14, he was elected chairman of the Council of People's Commissars (Sovnarkom) and people's commissar of the national economy, then people's commissar of foreign affairs of this largely unrecognized republic. He was also one of the organizers of the Ukrainian Central Military-Revolutionary Committee, which resisted the Central Rada, Ataman Kaledin's Cossacks, and the Austro-German troops. He also organized the First Donetsk Army (the field army of the Donets-Krivoy Rog Soviet Republic during the Russian Civil War), which in 1918 was integrated into the Red Army headed by **K. Voroshilov**.

In March 1918, Artem de facto resigned from his government post due to the military intervention on the territory of the Republic, and its later unification with the Soviet Ukraine. In April, he participated in the Tsaritsyn campaign to evacuate the Republic's government and troops to the territory of the RSFSR. At the beginning of June, he was sent to the North Caucasus to establish supply routes, visiting Armavir, Maikop, Vladikavkaz, and Tuapse. At the end of August, he was again sent to Ukraine, where he became chairman of the All-Ukrainian Central Military Revolutionary Committee and participated in preparation of an uprising. In November, he headed the Military Department of the Provisional Workers' and Peasants' Government of Ukraine. On January 16, 1919, after the resignation of **G. Piatakov**, Artem was elected chairman of the government, but on January 24, he gave up the post to **H. Rakovsky**, who had been sent from Moscow. On January 28, when Soviet power was restored, Artem was appointed people's commissar of Soviet agitation and propaganda in Ukraine. In the summer of 1919, as chairman of the Donetsk Provincial Executive Committee, Artem was one of the active participants and leaders of the struggle against the troops of General A. Denikin in the Donbas. After the end of the Civil War, he took part in the restoration of Donbas coal mines.

In 1919–1910, Artem served as an extraordinary representative of the Central Committee of the RCP(b) and the All-Russian Central Executive Committee at the Bashkir Military Revolutionary Committee of the Bashkir Autonomous Soviet Socialist Republic (BASSR). Simultaneously, from mid-December 1919 to June 1920, he was chairman of the Society for Aid to Bashkiria (*Bashkiropomoshch* was a commission in the Bashkir Military Revolutionary Committee for the social security of the population of the Bashkir Republic). In January 1920, he participated in the so-called "January conflict" between *Bashrevkom*, the Government of the Bashkir ASSR, *Bashobkom*, the first secretary of the Bashkir regional branch of the Communist Party of the Soviet Union, and the centralized government bodies of the RSFSR. In February–March 1920, as a representative of the Cheka, he led the suppression of the "Pitchfork Uprising" of 1920, also known as "Black Eagle Uprising" (a peasant uprising against the Soviet policy of **War Communism**). He also countered the Bashkir national movement and helped to deprive the Bashkir Republic of political and economic autonomy. The brutal suppression of the uprisings and looting of the population led to tragic consequences and mass famine among the population in 1921–1922 (known as the "Great Hunger"), when, according to incomplete data, 650,000 people died.

In April 1920, Artem was again elected chairman of the Donetsk Provincial Executive Committee. His main task was to restore coal mines in the basin. From March 1919 to March 1920, he was a candidate member of the Central Committee of the RCP(b). At the ninth and tenth congresses of the RCP(b), he was elected a full member of the Central Committee. From November to December 1920, he served as executive secretary of the Moscow Committee of the RCP(b), then chairman of the Central Committee of the All-Russian Union of Miners, and as a member of the All-Russian Central Executive Committee.

In 1921, during the test of the *Aerowagon*, Fedor Sergeev died. He was buried in Red Square in Moscow in a mass grave. His son, Artem Fedorovich Sergeev, was raised by Stalin. Until the age of sixteen, the boy (Stalin called him "Tomik," which stood for "Triumph of Marxism and Communism") grew up in the Stalin family. Later he graduated from an artillery school, became one of the founders of the antiaircraft missile forces of the USSR, and participated in the **Great Patriotic War**. He remained a devoted Stalinist throughout his life.

SEROV, IVAN ALEKSANDROVICH (1905–1990). Serov was head of the Workers' and Peasants' Militia of the NKVD of the USSR (1939), people's commissar of internal affairs of the Ukrainian SSR (1939–1941), deputy people's commissar (minister) of internal affairs of the USSR (1941–1947), first deputy minister of internal affairs of the USSR (1947–1954), the head of the KGB (March 1954–December 1958), head of the GRU (1958 and 1963), general of the Soviet Army (August 8, 1955, demoted to major general on April 12, 1963), and Hero of the Soviet Union (May 29, 1945, stripped of the title on March 12, 1963).

Ivan Serov was born in the village of Afimskoe, Vologda Governorate, the Russian Empire, into a family of Russian peasants. In 1916, he graduated from the village's elementary school and entered junior high school in the town of Kadnikov. While at school, he joined the All-Union Leninist Young Communist League (Komsomol). In 1925, he became a candidate member of the RCP(b). In this same year, he enrolled in the Red Army. Between August 1925 and August 1928, he studied at the Leningrad Infantry School. In June 1926, he was accepted as a member of the CPSU.

From August 1928, Serov served in the 66th Infantry Regiment of the 22nd Infantry Division as a platoon commander. In 1931, he graduated from the Artillery Officers' School of Leningrad. In September 1931, he was appointed battery commander of the 6th Artillery Regiment in the North Caucasian Military District. From March 1934, he served as assistant chief of staff of the regiment, then as chief of staff of an artillery regiment in the 24th Rifle Division. In 1935, Serov studied at the Military Engineering Academy of the Red Army, before being transferred in May 1936 to the Higher Academic Courses in Frunze Military Academy. After graduating in 1939, he was transferred to the People's Commissariat for Internal Affairs (NKVD). After **N. Iezhov**'s displacement in November 1938, the new people's commissar of internal affairs, **L. Beria**, launched a new wave of purges. Many vacancies opened in the NKVD. The lack of personnel was compensated by Komsomol activists, university graduates, and students of military academies. Artillery Major Serov was one of them. In February 1939, he was appointed head of the Main Directorate of the Workers' and Peasants' Militia of the NKVD of the USSR. From July 29, 1939, he was transferred to the post of deputy head of the Main Directorate of State Security of the NKVD of the USSR. He also headed the Second (secret-political) Department.

On September 2, 1939, Serov became the people's commissar of internal affairs of the Ukrainian SSR. In this post, he took part in implementation of the Secret Protocol to the Molotov-Ribbentrop Pact: annexation of Western Ukraine and its integration into the Soviet Union (as part of the Ukrainian SSR). He also participated in negotiating the terms of surrender of the Polish troops in Lviv during the Red Army's Polish campaign. Between May 1940 and May 1941, Serov served as a member of the Central Committee of the CPU and member of the Politburo of the CC CPU. During this period, Serov became close with the future marshal **G. Zhukov**, who commanded the Kyiv Special Military District in the second half of 1940. In Ukraine, he also made the acquaintance of its party leader, **N. Khrushchev**.

From February to July 1941, Serov became the first deputy people's commissar of state security of the USSR. Between July 1941 and February 1947, he served as deputy people's commissar (from March 1946, minister of internal affairs) of the USSR. Simultaneously, during the **Great Patriotic War** (1941–1945), he headed the rear services of the Moscow zone (October 1941–February 1942). By the decision of the **State Defense Committee** of the USSR of October 8, 1941, he was appointed the head of the group of "five," created for the mining and destruction of important objects in Moscow in the event of the surrender of the city. Stalin ordered him to remain in occupied Moscow, if necessary, as an illegal resident of the NKVD. In 1942, Serov also was a member of the State Defense Committee's commission for organizing the defense of the North Caucasus. He was one of organizers of the deportation of the Chechens, Ingush, Volga Germans, Kalmyks, Crimean Tatars, and people from the Baltic States. For these tasks, he received the Order of Suvorov first degree and the Order of the Red Banner. At the same time, in January–June 1945, Serov was deputy commander of the 1st Belarusian Front and an NKVD commissioner at the front. From August 1941, he also served as a member of the Military Council of the Air Force of the People's Commissariat of Defense of the USSR.

During the war, Serov carried out many tasks of the State Defense Committee of the USSR and Stalin's personal tasks. He visited besieged Leningrad and the heavily bombarded city of Stalingrad. In August 1943, he organized Stalin's three-day trip to the front and personally accompanied him. He was one of the organizers of the partisan movement and Destruction Battalions in the USSR and one of the senior figures in SMERSH (an umbrella organization for three independent counterintelligence agencies in the Red Army). In 1944, he was also appointed NKVD's adviser to the Ministry of Public Security of Poland and led the arrests of the commanders of Polish Home Army (*Armia Krajowa*). Between June 1945 and November 1946, Serov was also the deputy chief of the Soviet military administration in Germany and NKVD commissioner of the Group of Soviet Occupation Forces in Germany. He led the formation of the state security organs in the Soviet zone of occupation (i.e., the Stasi, the East German secret police), and carried out arrests of leaders of the Communist Party of Germany deemed a threat to Stalin.

In 1946, Serov was appointed a member of the Special Committee on Jet Engineering under the Council of Ministers of the USSR (Second Main Directorate). He played a key role in finding German specialists from socalled "missile programs" and in restoration of missile production in Germany. In November 1946, he also organized the transfer of German scientists and engineers to the USSR. From February 1947 to March 1954, Serov was the first deputy minister of internal affairs of the USSR. In March–June 1952, he supervised the construction of the Volga-Don Canal, for which he was awarded the Order of Lenin on September 19, 1952. On March 6, 1953, during Stalin's funeral, he was responsible for ensuring order in Moscow. On March 11, 1953, after the creation of a united USSR Ministry of Internal Affairs under the leadership of **L. Beria**, he was reappointed as first deputy minister. Serov became one of the few leaders of the USSR Ministry of Internal Affairs involved in Beria's overthrow. According to **Zhukov**'s memoirs, during Beria's arrest in June 1953, Serov was instructed to personally arrest Beria's bodyguard.[2]

In March 1954, Serov was appointed the first chairman of the Committee of the State Security under the Council of Ministers of the USSR (KGB). He became one of the closest associates of **Khrushchev**. He was one of the initiators of the mass rehabilitation of victims of Stalinist repression. On March 19, 1954, along with the prosecutor general, the ministers of internal affairs, and justices of the USSR, he sent a memorandum to the Presidium of the Central Committee of the CPSU on the mass review of cases convicted of "counterrevolutionary crimes."

During the Hungarian Revolution of 1956, which occurred in part as a response to the de-Stalinization campaign in the Soviet Union, Serov played a key role in suppression of the uprising: he led arrests of participants, organized deportations of Hungarians, and coordinated the creation of new security agencies in Hungary. During the June and October 1957 Plenums of the CC CPSU, Serov played an important role and helped Khrushchev to maintain his power. On December 10, 1958, he headed the Main Intelligence Directorate of the USSR (GRU). He was also appointed a deputy chief of the general staff of the armed forces of the USSR. During his tenure, he was an important player during the Cuban Missile Crisis of 1962.

On February 2, 1963, Serov was dismissed from GRU due to "loss of vigilance" (GRU Colonel Oleg Penkovsky had been exposed as a double agent of American and British intelligence). In February 1963, he was appointed assistant commander of the troops of the Turkestan Military District, where he was responsible for military educational institutions. On March 7, 1963, he was demoted to major general, and on March 12, he was stripped of the title of Hero of the Soviet Union "for blunting political vigilance." In August 1963, he was appointed assistant commander of the Volga Military District. In April 1965, he was expelled from the CPSU and dismissed.

He died on July 1, 1990, at the Central Military Clinical Hospital named after A. Vishnevsky in Krasnogorsk.

SHAKHTY TRIAL OF 1928. At the beginning of 1928, as Stalin was consolidating power across the Soviet Union, the OGPU began to uncover plots and conspiracies. One of the earliest was the Shakhty Trial, which took place from May 18 to July 6, in a special office of the Supreme Court of the USSR, chaired by **A. Vyshinsky**, and with the participation of the state prosecutor, **N. Krylenko**. The accused were fifty-three engineers and technicians employed in the Donbas coal industry, specifically at the Shakhty coal mine. The context was Stain's wish to intensify industrial development against the wishes of the Right Opposition led by **Nikolai Bukharin** and **Aleksei Rykov**, and to use the trial as a means to intimidate those who objected. Stalin took a personal interest in the trial, which set a precedent for others that followed. Those on trial were accused of working for foreign agents and of sabotaging equipment, weakening Soviet industry, and preparing the way for foreign intervention into the Soviet Union. The accusations were farfetched. Nevertheless, the sentences were harsh, and five of the accused were executed by shooting; forty received prison sentences of one to ten years; four were released conditionally; and four were exonerated. The trial led to further removal of "harmful influences" in other factories and enterprises.

SHAPOSHNIKOV, BORIS MIKHAILOVICH (1882–1945). A Russian and Soviet military leader, talented military theorist, chief of the staff of the Red Army, and marshal of the Soviet Union (1940), Boris Shaposhnikov was born at Zlatoust, near Cheliabinsk (in the Russian Urals). His father, Mikhail Petrovich, who had Orenburg Cossack origins, served as a private employee. His mother, Pelageia Kuzminichna, worked as a teacher. Boris earned his early education at the Krasnoufim industrial school. In 1899, he graduated from Perm Real School (Realschule). In 1900–1901, he worked as a clerk at a state-owned wine warehouse in Belebei, where he had moved with his parents.

Since military education was free of charge in the Russian Empire, Boris decided to pursue a military career. In 1901, he entered the Moscow Military School, from which he graduated with the rank of *Podporuchnik* (second lieutenant) in 1903. After graduation, he was sent to the First Turkestan Infantry Battalion. In 1907, he continued his education in the General Staff Academy in St. Petersburg. At the academy, he studied together with P. Wrangel, one of the future leaders of the White Army during the Civil War. In 1910, Shaposhnikov graduated from the academy with honors and in the rank of staff captain.

After graduation from the academy, Shaposhnikov served in the 1st Turkestan Rifle Regiment. In 1912, he was transferred to Częstochowa as senior adjutant of the headquarters of the 14th Cavalry Division of the Warsaw Military District. From August 1914, Shaposhnikov participated in the First World War as an adjutant of the headquarters of the 14th Cavalry Division (14th Army Corps) on the Southwestern Front. He participated in the Battle of Galicia (1914) and received a head wound near Sochaczew in 1915. In September 1917, Shaposhnikov was promoted to the rank of colonel and commanded the 16th Mingrelian Grenadier Regiment. He was awarded with crosses of Anna, Stanislav, and Vladimir with swords and bows—six orders in total.

In 1917, Shaposhnikov fully supported the October Revolution. In May 1918, he was one of the first officers of the Russian Imperial Army to join the new Red Army. On May 22, he was appointed assistant chief of the Operations Directorate of the Headquarters of the Supreme Military Council. During September–October 1918, he headed the Intelligence Department of the Headquarters of the Revolutionary Military Council. During 1919, he successively held various command positions and was promoted to the rank of chief of operations directorate of the field headquarters of the Revolutionary Military Council. In the fall of 1919, Shaposhnikov took an active part in the development of the counteroffensive operation against the troops of General A. Denikin. In 1920, he participated in the Polish-Soviet War and in the defeat of the tsarist ex-officer

Baron P. Wrangel in Crimea. During the Civil War, Shaposhnikov also developed most of the major directives, orders, and instructions for fronts and armies. In 1921, he was awarded the Order of the Red Banner.

After the end of the Civil War, in 1921, Shaposhnikov became first deputy chief of staff of the army's general staff. In 1923, he published the book *Cavalry*, in which he summarized the experience of combat use of this type of troops during the First World War and the Civil War. In 1924, he also published the military-historical work *On the Vistula* about the Soviet–Polish War. Between 1925 and 1927, he commanded the Leningrad Military District. In May 1927, he was transferred to the Moscow Military Districts. Between 1927 and 1929, he published an important three-volume military theory book, *The Brain of the Army (Mozg Army)*. In 1928–1931, he was chief of staff of the Red Army. In 1930, he joined the CPSU. In July 1931, he was appointed commander of the Volga Military District. Between 1932 and 1935, Shaposhnikov served as the head and military commissar of the M. V. Frunze Military Academy. In June 1935, he was awarded the title of professor and, in September of the same year, the military rank of commander of the first rank. On May 5, 1937, he again headed the general staff. From 1937 to 1945, Shaposhnikov was elected a deputy of the Supreme Soviet of the USSR of the first convocation, from the Moscow region. On March 21, 1939, he became a candidate member of the CC CPSU.

Shaposhnikov was one of the few "military specialists" (*voyienspetsy*) who managed not only to avoid Stalin's Great Purge of the Red Army but also to become his trusted military assistant. Despite his background in the tsarist army, he was able to win Stalin's great respect and built a successful career. In May 1940, Shaposhnikov was awarded the military rank of marshal of the Soviet Union. This rank, which was created in 1935, was the highest military rank in the army. The first Soviet marshals were Vasily Blucher, **Semen Budenny**, **Kliment Voroshilov**, **Aleksandr Iegorov**, and **Mikhail Tukhachevsky**. After Stalin's purges, only three of them remained alive by the end of the 1930s. In 1940, **Semen Timoshenko**, **Grigory Kulik**, and Shaposhnikov received their marshal stars.

In August 1940, Shaposhnikov was appointed deputy people's commissar of defense of the USSR. In this new post, he oversaw the construction of fortified areas and developed new methods of combat training of troops and operational training for command personnel. He also initiated the development of new methods of conducting military exercises and maneuvers. Finally, he improved the work of the Red Army Headquarters and general staff. Shaposhnikov paid special attention to the improvement of strategic leadership and establishment of uninterrupted control at all levels of the Red Army.

After the outbreak of the Great Patriotic War, from June 23 to July 16, 1941, Shaposhnikov worked in the Council for Evacuation at the Council of People's Commissars of the USSR. On July 10, he became a member of the Supreme Command Headquarters. On July 29, 1941, he was again appointed chief of the general staff of the Red Army. In this post, he participated in the development of proposals for the preparation and conduct of the Red Army's counteroffensive during the winter of 1941–1942. Shaposhnikov also participated in the development of the general staff's proposals for the implementation of the Smolensk defensive battle (July 10–September 10, 1941), the counteroffensive near Moscow (December 1941–January 1942), and the general offensive of the Red Army (January–April 1942). On May 11, 1942, due to health issues, Shaposhnikov was replaced by **A. M. Vasilevsky**. From May 1942 to June 1943, Shaposhnikov served as a deputy people's commissar of defense of the USSR. In June 1943, he was appointed chief of the Military Academy of the General Staff.

He died of a serious illness on March 26, 1945, forty-four days before the Allied forces' victory in Europe.

SHARANGOVICH, VASILY FOMICH (1897–1938). A Belarusian politician, second secretary of the Central Committee of the Communist Party of Belarus (1930–1934), member of the Party Control Committee (1934–1937), and first secretary of the Central Committee of the Communist Party of Belarus (1937), Vasily Sharangovich was born in the village of Kochany, Miadzel District, Minsk region (now in Belarus), into a peasant family. He graduated from a rural school in his native village and continued his studies at the Miadzel school. After school, he worked as a handyman, a locksmith, and an assistant driver. In December 1917, he joined the RSDWP(b). In 1918, during the occupation of Belarus by the troops of German Kaiser Wilhelm, he was arrested. After his release, he moved to Soviet Russia and volunteered for the Red Army. In 1919, after the outbreak of the Soviet–Polish war, he was sent to conduct clandestine activities in Minsk province. With a fake passport, he crossed the front line and traveled 75 kilometers on foot. On January 28, 1920, he organized the first congress of partisans of Minsk province. On April 5, 1920, the second congress of the Minsk region's partisans took place in the village of Mikhnovichi. In 1920, he was arrested by Polish authorities and sentenced to death. Later, he was transferred to a prison in Poznan, where his death sentence was commuted to twenty years of penal labor. In 1921, the Soviet authorities obtained his release in exchange for two Polish engineers.

Between 1921 and 1923, Sharangovich worked in the judicial system of the Belarusian Soviet Socialist Republic (BSSR). In 1923–1924, he served as a senior assistant to the prosecutor of the Republic. In 1924–1929, he was appointed an executive secretary of the Belarusian Council of Trade Unions. Simultaneously, from 1925, he served as a member of the Central Committee of the Communist Party of Belarus (CPB). In 1926, he was transferred to Siberia, where he headed the Organizational Department of the Novosibirsk Regional Trade Union Council (*Kraisouprof*). In 1929, he was appointed the first secretary of the Irkutsk Regional Committee of the CPSU. Between October 1930 and February 1934, after transferring to the Belarusian SSR, Sharangovich served as the second secretary of the CC CPB. For his clandestine activities and struggle during the Soviet–Polish War, he was awarded the Order of the Red Banner and an honorary weapon.

In 1934, Sharangovich was elected a member of the Party Control Commission (PCC) within the CC CPSU and PCC commissioner for Kazakhstan. In 1936, he served as the second secretary of the Kharkiv Oblast Committee of the CPU. In March 1937, Sharangovich was appointed the first secretary of the Central Committee of the Communist Party of the BSSR, the first ethnic Belarusian to lead the republican party. In this post, he led mass repressions in the republic. According to some sources, in 1937, he sent an encrypted message to Moscow, in which he proposed to execute 3,000 people for their counterrevolutionary activities and to expel 9,800 people from the BSSR.[3]

On July 17, 1937, Sharangovich was arrested and accused of participation in the Anti-Soviet "Bloc of Rightists and Trotskyites." On March 4, after interrogation, Sharangovich fully admitted his guilt (including the participation in organizing and preparing a terrorist act against **K. Voroshilov** in 1936). On March 13, 1938, he was found guilty and executed two days later.

On January 19, 1957, Sharangovich was rehabilitated. In 1958, he was reinstated into the party.

SHCHADENKO, EFIM AFANASEVICH (1885–1951). A Soviet politician, military leader, colonel general (1942), member of the RSDWP(b) (1904), member of the Central Control Commission (1930–1934), member of the CC CPSU (1939–1941), candidate member of the CC CPSU(b) (from 1941), and deputy of the Supreme Soviet of the USSR of the first convocation (1937–1946), Shchadenko was one of Stalin's associates who was involved in mass repressions in the Red Army.

Efim Shchadenko was born in the village of Kamenskaia (now the town of Kamensk-Shakhtinsky, Rostov Oblast) into a family of Ukrainian laborers. For two years he studied in a parish school. After school, he worked as a tailor and lived in different cities, including Rostov-on-Don, Baku, and Piatigorsk. In

1904, he became interested in revolutionary activities. In Piatigorsk he joined the Russian Social Democratic Labour Party (RSDWP). During the Russian Revolution of 1905, he lived in Baku, where he organized a strike that lasted about two months. In the fall of 1906, Shchadenko moved to Vladikavkaz, where he also worked as a tailor. In Vladikavkaz, he established underground Bolshevik circles in tailors' workshops and in the 81st Infantry Apsheron Regiment. He also organized the Igla (Needle) Union, which regularly held strikes. In 1907, Igla held a massive May Day meeting, during which a huge fight between its participants and the Black Hundreds (Chernosotentsy) broke out. Shchadenko, as an organizer of the meeting, was threatened with arrest and forced to leave for Kamenskaia. After his departure, the revolutionary circles fell apart. On August 20, 1907, Shchadenko helped to organize a strike of shoemakers in Kamenskaia, but it was dispersed by the authorities. Its organizers, including Shchadenko, were arrested but soon released due to lack of evidence. Shchadenko then organized the first Kamenskoe tailors' partnership, which operated on the principle of a commune. As a result, four private workshops went broke. The police closed the Kamenskaia tailors' partnership, and Shchadenko left the town.

In 1913, Shchadenko was arrested and sentenced to two years in prison for his revolutionary activities. In August 1914, soldiers of the Reserve Dragoon Cavalry division located near the prison dispersed the prison guards and freed the prisoners. During this event, Shchadenko got acquainted with a noncommissioned officer, **S. Budenny**, who served in the battalion. Shchadenko returned to his hometown, and in February 1917, he became chairman of the Kamensk Committee of the RSDWP(b). During the October Revolution of 1917, as a delegate to the second All-Russian Congress of Soviets of Workers' and Soldiers' Deputies, he was sent to Petrograd. Upon his return to Kamenskaia, he organized detachments of the Red Guard and participated in the defeat of the counterrevolutionary centers on the Don River. In January 1918, he was elected a member of the Don Military Revolutionary Committee (*Revvoyensoveta*). In May–June 1918, Shchadenko's detachment of the Red Guard participated in the defense of Tsaritsyn. During these battles, Shchadenko was wounded in the arm and shoulder.

On August 16, 1918, Shchadenko was appointed commissar of all armies of the Tsaritsyn Front. During the next five months, he led the formation of the Gromoslavsky Infantry Regiment, the Regiment of Poor Peasants, forty-eight Marching Battalions, twelve squadrons, twenty-three machine-gun teams, and eight batteries, as well as the First Donetsk-Morozov Division. Between November 1918 and January 1919, he was appointed Special commissioner of the Revolutionary Military Council of the 10th Army. From January 28 to June 15, 1919, he served as a member of the Revolutionary Military Council of the Ukrainian Front and deputy people's commissar of military affairs of Ukraine. In November 1919–July 1920, he was a member of the Revolutionary Military Council of the 1st Cavalry Army. Between July 16 and October 8, 1920, he was appointed a member of the Revolutionary Military Council of the 2nd Cavalry Army. Since Shchadenko participated in almost all the major battles of the Red Army during the Russian Civil War, and fought against Denikin's, Petliura's and Wrangel's troops, he earned lasting fame. During this period, he also became a close friend and ally of both Budenny and **K. Voroshilov**.

After the Civil War, Shchadenko completed two courses at the M. V. Frunze Military Academy. On April 10, 1922, for his participation in the battles, he was awarded the Order of the Red Banner, at the behest of Stalin and Voroshilov. Around the same time, Shchadenko had surgery to have his kidney removed. Health issues prevented him from completing his studies at the academy. On April 1, 1924, he was appointed political inspector of the Red Army Cavalry. In this position, he took part in the military reform of 1924–1925. In the late 1920s, Shchadenko's career came to a standstill. On September 1, 1926, he was sent on long-term leave for health reasons. In January 1927, he was transferred to the Main Directorate of the Red Army. He continued his medical treatment and was even treated in Germany, but nothing helped him. During his illness, he wrote a book about the history of the 1st Cavalry Army, which was never published.

In March 1930, Shchadenko was appointed political assistant to the director of the M. V. Frunze Military Academy. In the post, he showed fanatical devotion to Stalin and to Communist ideology. He became extremely paranoid and was obsessed with strengthening "class vigilance" and identifying "class enemies" who, in his deep conviction, were present in great numbers in the academy. Being practically uneducated (although he was constantly trying to educate himself), he was treated with suspicion, mockery, and even malice by those who had an education, especially former officers who had served previously in the Imperial Russian Army (military specialists). Shchadenko came to hate even his former fellow soldiers who were lucky to graduate from the academy. A great opportunity to take revenge on them came during the high-profile "Case Vesna" (a case organized by the OGPU in 1930–1931 against Soviet Red Army officers and civilians, who had served earlier in the Imperial Russian Army or White Army). In 1930, as a result of Shchadenko's accusations, fifteen people from the academy were arrested. Two of them immediately testified against the commander of the Leningrad Military District, **M. Tukhachevsky**.

On February 23, 1935, Shchadenko, together with Budenny and Voroshilov, was awarded the Order of Lenin as one "of the organizers and leaders of the First Cavalry Army." On November 28, 1935, he received the rank of corps commissar. On the one hand, the title was prestigious. On the other hand, Voroshilov and Budenny, with whom he was once on an equal footing in the Revolutionary Military Council of the First Cavalry Army, became marshals of the Soviet Union. Moreover, Shchadenko did not consider Budenny as an authority at all. He was very proud that he was in the leadership of the academy during the period when Budenny studied there (1930–1932). According to Shchadenko's colleges, he became extremely rude and unreasonably harsh toward students and even the teaching staff of the academy. He wrote numerous denunciations. Ultimately, Shchadenko was fired from the academy. Even though during this period, he should have been more concerned with the possible collapse of his own career, he was more obsessed with the possible arrest of Tukhachevsky (after the arrest of the deputy commander of the troops of the Leningrad military district, V. Primakov, in August 1936, the arrest of Tukhachevsky was quite realistic).

In December 1936, Shchadenko was appointed deputy commander for political affairs and head of the Political Administration of the Kharkiv Military District. In May 1937, he was transferred to the Kyiv Military District. Although he did not stay at this post for long, he became an active participant in the repressions. On November 23, 1937, he was appointed deputy people's commissar of defense of the USSR and head of the Command-and-Control Administration of the Red Army. Since Stalin needed his trusted man to control the personnel in the army, he personally appointed Shchadenko to this post. Simultaneously, from March 1938 to July 1940, the latter served on the Main Military Council of the Red Army.

After the outbreak of the **Great Patriotic War** (1941–1945), from August 8, 1941, to May 20, 1943, Shchadenko served as the deputy people's commissar of defense of the USSR and the head of the Main Directorate for the formation and staffing of the Red Army (*Glavupraform*). Between September 26 and October 20, 1943, he was appointed a member of the Military Council of the Southern Front, and after that, he was transferred to the 4th Ukrainian Front. He participated in the Donbas and Melitopol offensive operations. In 1944, he was transferred to the Main Political Directorate of the Red Army.

He died on September 6, 1951, and was buried in Moscow.

SHOW TRIALS (1936–1938). The Show Trials were a public spectacle by which Stalin eliminated his perceived enemies within the party and the NKVD. They took place in the House of Unions in Moscow in three stages, following the assassination of **S. Kirov** in December 1934 and the mass arrests and executions that followed. The cases were concocted by **N. Iezhov**, who became the head of the NKVD after the first trial, while the prosecutor-general was **A. Vyshinsky** and the presiding judge was **V. Ulrikh**. The first trial, held between August 19 and 24, 1936, featured **L. Kamenev** and **G. Zinoviev**, who had already been tried previously and given five-year prison sentences. They were accused, along with the absent **L. Trotsky**, of attempting to assassinate Stalin in league with foreign powers, as part of a "Trotskyite-Zinovievite Terrorist Center," along with fourteen others. Kamenev and Zinoviev had been subjected to harsh prison conditions and received threats to their families. Their confessions were given on the assurance that they and their families would be spared. After the trial, they were executed, along with all the other defendants.

The second trial, held on January 23–30, 1937, focused on a "Parallel Anti-Soviet Trotskyist Center" and featured **K. Radek, Iu. Piatakov, G. Sokolnikov**, and fourteen others. Thirteen were executed, while Radek managed to evade death briefly by implicating others. That paved the way for other trials. The first—that of military leaders headed by General **M. Tukhachevsky**—was not a show trial, as it was held in a secret military tribunal, but it was a pivotal occasion that led to the deaths of the Red Army's senior military officers and preceded a general purge of the Red Army. Finally, in March 1938, the Trial of the Twenty-One accused **N. Bukharin** of attempts to kill Lenin and Stalin, as well as poisoning the writer **M. Gorky**. Also on the dock were the former chairman of the Council of People's Commissars (**A. Rykov**), **C. Rakovsky, N. Krestinsky**, and **G. Iagoda**; the organizer of the first Moscow trial, Bukharin's testimony was ambivalent, an admission of general guilt but denial of specific crimes, and underlined his wish to preserve his family. Alongside Bukharin were the former head of government (**A. Rykov**) and **G. Iagoda**, the former NKVD leader whose role had been taken over by Iezhov. Nineteen of the accused were executed, and the remaining two were killed in prison by 1941. The trials were ostensibly an effort to convince international observers that the cases were genuine. Initially, this plan appeared to work, but the Bukharin trial raised many questions, as observers began to recognize the absurdity of the accusations. The accused were subject to abuse during the hearings, particularly by Vyshinsky, who berated them with vicious rhetoric and slanders.

SHVERNIK, NIKOLAI MIKHAILOVICH (1888–1970). Shvernik was a Soviet politician, member of the Central Executive Committee (1927–1938) and the Presidium of the Central Executive Committee of the USSR (1935–1938), deputy of the Supreme Soviet of the USSR (1937–1966), chairman of the Presidium of the Supreme Soviet of the USSR (1946–1953), member of the Presidium (Politburo) of the CC CPSU (1952–1953 and 1957–1966), and hero of socialist labor (1958).

Nikolai Shvernik was born in St. Petersburg into a large working-class family. He graduated from a parish school and continued his education in vocational school. From 1903, he started to work as a turner at an electromechanical plant. On January 9, 1905, he became an eyewitness to the tragic events of the "Bloody Sunday." The tragedy enhanced his interest in politics, and soon he joined the RSDWP. Initially, he supported the Mensheviks, but he switched shortly thereafter to the Bolshevik faction.

In 1910–1911, Shvernik was elected a board member of the Union of Metalworkers in St. Petersburg. In 1913, he left St. Petersburg and worked in Tula, Samara, and Saratov. At the age of twenty-one, he became a member of the St. Petersburg Party Committee. In 1913, in order to avoid arrest, he left the capital city and for a short time worked in Tula. After his return to St. Petersburg, he got a job at Erickson's plant and resumed anti-government propaganda. He was arrested for revolutionary activities and exiled to Tula. In the spring of 1915, together with his wife, he was exiled to Samara, where he established contact with the Bolsheviks and led revolutionary work and anti-war agitation there. In February 1917, he was exiled to Saratov.

After the February Revolution (1917), Shvernik returned to Samara, where he was elected chairman of the Trubochny district Party Committee, chairman of the board of the plant's Trade Union, and a member of the Presidium of the Executive Committee of the City Council. Also, he led party work in the trade unions. In October 1917, he became chairman of the All-Russian Committee of Artillery Plant Workers and a member of the Board of Artillery Plants. During the October Revolution of 1917, he was elected as chairman of the Samara Soviet. In June 1918, he fought against the Czechoslovak Legion (White Czechs as they were called in the Bolshevik press), which were defending Samara together with the White Army. Between July and October 1918, he served as the military commissar of the 2nd Simbirsk Rifle Regiment of the 1st Combined Simbirsk Division. His Division overthrew the Committee of Members of the Constituent Assembly (an anti-Bolshevik government that operated in Samara during the Russian Civil War of 1917–1922). From October 1918, Shvernin was transferred to the Main Artillery Directorate. In April 1919, he became the chairman of the Samara City Executive Committee. In 1919–1921, he worked in senior positions in the army supply system in the Caucasus.

In 1923, Shvernik was appointed deputy chairman of All-Union Commission for the Fight against Illegal Alcohol, Cocaine, and Gambling. In 1923, he was elected a member of the Central Control Commission of the Communist Party, and in 1924, he became a member of the Presidium of the Central Control Commission of the RCP(b). From February 1924 to December 1925, he was people's commissar of the Workers' and Peasants' Inspectorate of the RSFSR (Rabkrin). At the 14th party congress in December 1925, Shvernik was elected a member of the Central Committee. In 1925–1926, he worked as a secretary of the Leningrad Regional Committee and the Northwestern Bureau of the Central Committee of the CPSU. From April 9, 1926, to April 16, 1927, he was appointed secretary of the CC CPSU and at the same time a member of the Orgburo.

In March 1927, he was released from work in the Secretariat and the Orgburo and sent to the Urals to work as the secretary of the Ural regional party committee. In this post, he proved to be a consistent supporter of industrialization. In 1929, after return to Moscow, he was appointed chairman of the Central Committee of the Metalworkers' Trade Union. After the 16th congress of the CPSU, on July 13, 1930, he was elected a member of the Central Committee Organizing Bureau (until March 18, 1946) and a candidate member of the Central Committee Secretariat (until January 26, 1934). After this period, his work was closely associated with the trade unions. In 1930, he was elected the first secretary of the All-Union Central Council of Trade Unions. He served in this post until March 1944.

During his tenure, Shvernik did not protect the interests of the workers, but forced them to obey all decisions of the party and government. Many of his initiatives rendered the working conditions of the Soviet people more difficult. Collective agreements were canceled, an employment record book was introduced, additional payment for overtime work was canceled, and the working day was sharply increased from eight hours to ten to twelve hours. Also, the list of dangerous jobs was significantly reduced. As a result, women and teenagers from the age of 16 were sent to work in hazardous conditions and take night shifts. Shvernik eliminated from the legislation such concepts as "occupational diseases" and "industrial injury." Safety requirements were dropped dramatically. Shvernik introduced these measures to increase production and to cut budget expenditures. His actions ran counter to the Constitution of the USSR and caused significant limitation of social and legal guarantees and rights of the Soviet workers. Shvernik also approved the creation of the "State Labor Reserves"—the system of forced labor of youths from the age of 14. During the **Great Patriotic War**, he had an opportunity to significantly improve the nutrition of the workers but did nothing in order to resolve this issue. He completely ignored the fact that workers lived in dugouts and barracks without basic amenities. Ironically, the All-Union

Central Council of Trade Unions was one of the richest organizations in the USSR, and Shvernik himself received an annual salary of one hundred rubles per month.

Between 1937 and 1946, Shvernik became a deputy of the Supreme Soviet of the USSR and headed its upper chamber: the Council of Nationalities. At the same time, he was a member of the Moscow "NKVD troika." He personally approved arrests and exile for twenty thousand "kulaks" and fifty thousand "enemies of the people." Shvernik's signature was found under dozens of "execution lists" sent by the NKVD to the members of the CC CPSU for the approval. Also, from November 2, 1942, to June 9, 1951, Shvernik was appointed chairman of the Extraordinary State Commission for the establishment and investigation of the atrocities of the German fascist invaders and their collaborators and the damage they caused to citizens, collective farms, public organizations, state enterprises, and institutions of the USSR. Along with the authentic task of disclosing Nazi crimes, this commission was engaged in unlawful activities. For example, on the instructions of the Politburo, Shvernik and his colleagues falsified data on the circumstances of execution of Polish officers in Katyn. Some information on the activities of the Polish and Ukrainian rebels, the Baltic "Forest Brothers," and the Cossack volunteers who served in the Wehrmacht, were also falsified. These falsifications resulted in trials and executions of innocent people. During the war, Shvernik also headed the Evacuation Council and was responsible for evacuation of Soviet industry to the eastern regions of the USSR. He initiated the creation of the Anglo-Soviet Trade Union Committee, the main task of which was to unite the efforts of the trade unions of the two countries against Germany. He participated in preparation of the conference, which laid the foundation for the creation of the World Federation of Trade Unions.

In 1946, Shvernik replaced **M. Kalinin** in the post of the chairman of the Presidium of the Supreme Soviet of the USSR (the formal head of state). In this post, on March 26, 1947, he signed a decree initiated by Stalin on abolition of the death penalty. On January 12, 1950, he signed a new decree on its restoration. Shvernik headed the committee for organizing celebration events of Stalin's official seventieth birthday (December 21, 1949). He proposed to establish the Order of Stalin, but the idea was not supported by Stalin himself. Also, he proposed to award Stalin with a second star of the Hero of the Soviet Union and the Order of Victory, but the Soviet leader refused to accept these accolades. When the Politburo was transformed into the Presidium of the Central Committee, Shvernik was elected a member of the Presidium and served in this post from October 16, 1952, to March 5, 1953.

After Stalin's death, Shvernik lost his main party and state posts. In December 1953, he became a member of the Special Judicial Presence of the Supreme Court of the USSR, during **L. Beria**'s trial. Shvernik supported **Khrushchev** in his struggle for power, and when the latter emerged victorious, in February 1956, he was appointed chairman of the Party Control Committee under the CC CPSU. He served there until November 1962. In 1957, he once again became a member of the Presidium of the Central Committee. From November 1962 to March 1966, he headed the party commission under the CC CPSU for the rehabilitation of victims of political repression (the so-called Shvernik Commission). The representatives of the CPSU (members of this commission) were responsible for checking criminal cases and reviewing decisions of the courts. Members of the Shvernik Commission conducted interrogations of witnesses and suspects; they gave direct instructions to the court, the prosecutor's office, the KGB, and the Ministry of Internal Affairs; and their activities exceeded their legal mandate. The commission decided who should be considered a victim of repression and who should be punished for crimes. Many "loyal Leninists" who actually committed crimes were rehabilitated by the commission. At the same time, Shvernik and his colleagues "cleaned up" the archives and destroyed incriminating materials that could expose information about the crimes of the CPSU leadership. He also destroyed compromising evidence on himself.

Also, Shvernik headed the Government Commission for the Reburial of Stalin. According to one account,[4] Shvernik shed tears during the reburial ceremony.

After the twenty-third congress of the CPSU in 1966, Shvernik retired. On December 24, 1970, he died and was buried in Red Square in Moscow.

SMILGA, IVAR TENISOVICH (1892–1938). An Old Bolshevik, Soviet political, state, and party leader, economist, member of the Left Opposition, member of the Party Central Committee (1917–1920, 1925–1927), and candidate member of the Central Committee of the RCP (1920–1921) and CPSU (1922–1923, 1924–1925), Ivar Smilga was born in Aloja (modern Latvia) into the family of a forester. His father, Tenis Smilga, was a revolutionary. In 1906, Tenis participated in the revolutionary activities in Latvia and was shot by soldiers during the riots. Even though Ivar was only 14 years old at the time his father was killed, he decided to join the revolutionary movement to fight the tsarist regime. In January 1907, he joined the RSDWP. In this same year, he was arrested for the first time for participation in a May Day demonstration.

In 1910, Ivar arrived in Moscow and entered the Faculty of Law at Moscow University. A year later, he was expelled for participation in students' demonstrations. In 1915, he was exiled to Siberia for illegal propaganda activities. After the February Revolution of 1917, he was released under the general amnesty and returned to Petrograd. In April 1917, he was elected to the Central Committee of the RSDWP and sent to Finland to conduct Bolshevik activities. On Lenin's instructions, Smilga organized the Finnish Red Guard and served as the chairman of the Regional Executive Committee of the army, navy, and workers of Finland. He took an active part in the preparation of the October Revolution in Petrograd. On the day of the uprising, he organized the transfer of troops loyal to the Bolsheviks from Finland to Petrograd. These troops took part in the storming of the Winter Palace and later in the suppression of the Junker mutiny. On November 1–3, 1917, Smilga's detachments were transferred to Moscow, where they took part in the street battles against troops loyal to the provisional government.

Between the end of 1917 and into 1918, Smilga served as a representative of the RSFSR in Finland. He was one of the main organizers of the revolutionary movement in Finland and participated in the Bolsheviks' attempt to seize power in the country. After the defeat of the Finnish revolution in 1918, he returned to Petrograd. From 1918 until 1921 during the Civil War, Smilga was a member of the Revolutionary Military Council of a number of fronts, including the North Ural-Siberian Front, the Eastern Front, the Southeastern Front, the Caucasian Front, the Western Front, the Southern Front, and the Crimean Front. On May 31, 1919, he was appointed head of the Political Administration of the Revolutionary Military Council (*Revvoiensoveta*) and supervised the work of all commissars in the Red Army. It is notable that commissars were responsible for monitoring the work of military experts (*voienspetzov*—former officers of the Imperial Army) and for extermination of "counterrevolutionary elements" in the front-line zones. Since Smilga coordinated their activities at the central level, he was personally responsible for the Red Terror in the Red Army. Smilga led the suppression of peasant uprisings in a number of regions, in particular the Vioshenskaia Uprising (the Upper-Don Anti-Bolshevik rebellion). He also took part in the battles against the troops of Aleksei Kaledin, Anton Denikin, and insurgent groups in Caucasus, the Urals, and Siberia. Smilga held this post until January 1921.

Since Smilga was one of Lenin's confidants, in subsequent years he held high positions in the party hierarchy. In 1921–1923, he served a member of the Presidium and a head of the Main Directorate for Fuel of the Supreme Soviet of the National Economy of the RSFSR. In 1923, he became a deputy chairman of the State Planning Committee of the USSR (Gosplan) and one of the main assistants of G. Krzhizhanovsky (chief of Gosplan). In 1923, he taught at the Moscow Mining Academy. Between 1924 and 1927, he was director of the Moscow Institute of National

Economy and gave lectures on the economic policy of the USSR.

After Lenin's death, Smilga supported **Trotsky**, although he objected to the creation of labor armies. In 1927, as a leader and active member of the Left Opposition, he was removed from all posts, expelled from the CPSU, and sent into exile. Three years later, he abandoned the Trotskyist opposition and returned to Moscow. After his return, he was reinstated in the party and received the post of deputy chairman of Gosplan of the USSR.

After **Kirov**'s assassination on December 1, 1934, arrests of Old Bolsheviks began. On January 1, 1935, Smilga was arrested. On January 10, 1937, by the Military Collegium of the Supreme Court of the USSR, he was accused of "participation in a Trotskyist counterrevolutionary terrorist organization" and sentenced to death. He was shot the same day. His body was cremated, and his ashes were buried in one of the common graves of the Donskoi cemetery. His wife, Nadezhda Poluian, a party member since 1915, was arrested after her husband and shot in Karelia in November 1937. Almost all her relatives, with rare exceptions, also became victims of Stalinist terror. Their daughter, Tatiana Smilga, was arrested in 1939. She was convicted of "counterrevolutionary agitation" and spent fourteen years in prisons, camps, and exile.

In April 1987, Ivar Smilga was rehabilitated.

SMIRNOV, VLADIMIR MIKHAILOVICH (1887–1937).

A Russian revolutionary, one of the leaders of the Bolshevik armed uprising in Moscow (1917), people's commissar of Trade and Industry of the RSFSR (1918), and member of the Left Opposition, Smirnov was a close associate of **Nikolai Bukharin**.

Vladimir Smirnov was born in Moscow into a family of middle-class background. He graduated from the Faculty of Law of Moscow University and worked in zemstvo institutions and in archives. He was an active participant of the Revolution of 1905. In 1907, together with other members of the Marxist circle (V. Obolensky, D. Bogolepov, V. Firsov, and others), he became a member of the RSDWP (Bolshevik faction). Later he became an agitator for the Moscow Committee of the RSDWP. He also worked for the newspaper *Nash Put'* (*Our Way*) and the magazine *Spartak*.

In 1914, Smirnov was drafted into the Russian Imperial army and served in the rank of *praporshchik* (a junior officer rank) in the 61st Artillery Brigade on the Western Front. After the February Revolution of 1917, Smirnov was transferred to Moscow, where he became a member of the editorial board of the newspaper *Sotsial-Demokrat*. He also became a member of the Moscow Committee of the RSDWP(b) and was elected as a delegate to the sixth congress of the party.

During the October Revolution of 1917, Smirnov was one of the leaders of the armed uprising and a member of the Military Revolutionary Committee in Moscow. On October 28, he was elected a member of the Combat Headquarters of the Moscow Military Revolutionary Committee. In November, he was transferred to Petrograd. In 1918, he was appointed people's commissar of industry and trade of the RSFSR. During February–March 1918, he was a member of the Revolutionary Defense Committee of Petrograd. In 1918, after the emergence of the "Left Communists," a faction within the Russian Communist Party (initially headed by Bukharin) that opposed the signing of the Brest-Litovsk Peace treaty with Imperial Germany (March 1918), Smirnov joined it and resigned from all party posts. In 1919, he opposed the bureaucratization of the party and Soviet institutions and monopolization of political power in the party (the dictatorship of the party). Together with other Old Bolsheviks (Valerian Obolensky-Ossinsky and **Timofei Sapronov**), Smirnov founded the Group of Democratic Centralism (the Decists or Decemists).

About the same time, he became the main spokesperson of the Military Opposition. On March 20, 1919, during the first meeting of the military section of the party congress, Smirnov gave a speech on the use of former tsarist officers (military specialists or *spetzy*) and political commissars in the Red Army. In this speech, he did not oppose the use of former tsarist officers, but he opposed **Trotsky**'s ideas on readoption of the military discipline of bourgeois armies. The mass enlistment of the peasantry into Red Army had created concerns on how to build and maintain discipline among the peasant recruits. The question of discipline elicited a debate. Smirnov supported collegial rule within the military, and his speech during the party congress contained certain criticisms of the army. From his point of view, discipline in the new army had to be created by the methods of political education, which could help to bring class consciousness to the level of mass discipline. Most of the military delegates disagreed with the collegial approach outlined by Smirnov and his ideas were heavily criticized during the third meeting of the military section. In 1920, at the ninth party congress, Smirnov also opposed Trotsky over the militarization of labor (introduction of the universal labor duty for peasants through mobilization).

Between 1921 and 1927, Smirnov served in various posts. During this period, he was a member of the Board of the Council of Labor and Defense, chairman of the Financial Commission of the Supreme Soviet of the National Economy, a member of the Presidium of the State Planning Committee (Gosplan), and a member of the Board of the Central Statistical Administration of the USSR. Simultaneously, between 1924 and 1926, he was a member of the editorial boards of the newspapers *Pravda* and *Ekonomicheskaia Zhizn*. In 1923, some leaders of the *Decists* joined Trotsky's Left Opposition. On October 15, 1923, Smirnov along with other leaders of the *Decists* signed the "Declaration of the Forty-Six," which criticized the economic and political failures of the Communist Party. In 1926, Smirnov together with Sapronov formed their own group, the "Group of 15," which joined the United Opposition headed by Trotsky, **G. Zinoviev**, and **L. Kamenev**.

In December 1927, at the 15th party congress, Smirnov was expelled from the party. On December 31 of this year, he was arrested and sentenced to a three-year exile to the Ural Region. He served his exile in Berezovo, where he lived in an apartment with a Joint State Political Directorate (OGPU) informant named "Kolchak." At the beginning of 1930, Smirnov was sentenced to three years in prison and was sent to a special political isolator in Suzdal. On November 10, 1932, his term of imprisonment was extended for two more years. On November 4, 1934, he was exiled for three years to the West Siberian Territory, to the city of Gorno-Altaysk.

After Kirov's murder (December 1, 1934), a criminal case was fabricated against the leaders of the so-called "counterrevolutionary *Decist* organization of Sapronov and Smirnov." In March 1935, Smirnov was arrested again, and, by the decision of the Special Meeting at the People's Commissariat for Internal Affairs of the USSR (NKVD), he was sentenced to a further three years of imprisonment.

At the beginning of 1937, Smirnov sent letters to the people's commissar of internal affairs (**N. Iezhov**) and the USSR prosecutor (**A. Vyshinsky**), in which he protested his imprisonment. On April 20, he was convoyed to Moscow, and on May 26, 1937, the Military Collegium of the Supreme Court of the USSR, chaired by **V. Ulrikh**, sentenced him to death for participating in a counterrevolutionary terrorist organization. The same day Smirnov was shot. At the trial, Smirnov pleaded not guilty and denied charges of counterrevolutionary activity.

On November 16, 1960, by the decision of the Plenum of the Supreme Court of the USSR, Smirnov was partially rehabilitated. He was fully rehabilitated in 1990.

SOCIALISM IN ONE COUNTRY. The theory that it was plausible to build a complete socialist society in the USSR, without the victory of the revolution in more advanced industrial countries. This theory was put forth by Stalin and **Nikolai Bukharin** in 1924 and became the official doctrine of the state after the 14th congress of the CPSU in 1925.

In January 1924, when V. Lenin died, a struggle for power in the party elite began. Stalin and **L. Trotsky** had their own views on the further development of the country. Even before 1917, Trotsky was a supporter of the idea of the "permanent revolution." He believed that "a socialist revolution begins on the national arena, develops on the international arena and ends on the world arena."⁵ From his point of view, there was no other way to fulfill and complete the construction of socialism in Russia and later in the USSR, than through the international revolution and until the final triumph of the new society across the entire planet. Stalin and Bukharin's concept was (from their point of view) further development of Leninism and had the advantage of expediency and patriotism, particularly after the earlier failure of revolutions in Germany and Hungary, and the failure of the Poles in 1920 to embrace the idea of a workers' state. The predominance of Stalin's idea was established when Trotsky was exiled to Central Asia in 1927 and expelled from the Soviet Union in 1929. The theory was convenient for the interwar period, allowing the country to develop economically even though lacking strong allies and partners.

SOKOLNIKOV, GRIGORY IAKOVLEVICH (NÉE HIRSCH BRILLIANT OR GIRSH YANKELEVICH BRILLIANT) (1888–1939).

Sokolnikov was an Old Bolshevik revolutionary; economist; Soviet politician; member of the Central Executive Committee of the USSR of the first, second, and seventh convocations; member of the Central Committee of the RSDWP (1917–1919 and 1922–1930); member of the first Politburo of the Central Committee of the RSDWP(b) (October 1917); candidate member of the Politburo of the CC CPSU (1924–1925); and candidate member of the CC CPSU (1930–1936).

Hirsch Brilliant was born in Romny, Poltava Governorate (today, Sumy Oblast, Ukraine), into a Jewish family. His father, Yankel Brilliant, was a doctor, collegiate councilor (a civil rank of sixth class in the Russian Empire), and the owner of a pharmacy. His mother, Fania Rosenthal, was the daughter of a merchant of the first guild. Hirsch moved to Moscow as a teenager and graduated from the Fifth Moscow Classical Gymnasium. He was well educated and spoke six languages. After graduation, he studied at the Faculty of Law of Moscow University. From 1903, Hirsch started to participate in the revolutionary movement. He joined the Bolshevik faction of the RSDWP in 1905 and dropped out of university to devote himself to revolutionary activities. He was an active participant in the events of 1905. In December 1905, he took part in the Moscow uprising. During the revolution, which reached a peak at the end of that year, he worked as a party propagandist in the Gorodsky district. He also was a member of the Sokolniki District Committee of the RSDWP and the Military-Technical Bureau under the Moscow Party Committee.

In the fall of 1906, together with **N. Bukharin**, with whom he was acquainted from their gymnasium, Sokolnikov unified the gymnasia circles in Moscow into a single social democratic organization of students. At the end of 1907, Sokolnikov was arrested, and in February 1909, he was sentenced to lifelong exile in Siberia. He was sent to the village of Rybnoi, in Ienisei province. Six weeks after his arrival in the place of exile, he managed to escape from Siberia and traveled via Moscow to Paris, which he made his home. While in France, he studied at the Faculty of Law of the Sorbonne University, from which he graduated in 1914. He also worked as a journalist in the newspaper *For the Party* and headed the workers' club Proletarian. After the outbreak of the First World War, he moved to Switzerland. There, he organized the bureau of foreign groups of Bolshevik party members and worked in the Swiss Social Democratic Party. He also collaborated with the Menshevik newspaper *Nashe Slovo*. Like others in the party, Sokolnikov had a negative attitude toward the First World War. In April 1917, after the February Revolution—together with **V. Lenin**, **G. Zinoviev**, **A. Kollontai**, and others—he returned to Russia, crossing Germany to Sweden in a "sealed carriage," and continuing by train through Finland to Petrograd.

Very quickly after his return to Russia, Sokolnikov became one of the leaders of the Moscow Bolsheviks and made up a new program for the Bolshevik Party. He sharply criticized the provisional government, Mensheviks, and Socialist-Revolutionaries. He thought that only Social Democrats-Internationalists were close to the Bolsheviks. At the sixth congress of the RSDWP(b) (July–August 1917),

Sokolnikov was elected a member of the Central Committee of the party. He also became a member of the political bureau of the Central Committee of the Bolshevik Party, a member of the Executive Committee (Ispolkom) of the Petrograd Soviet of Workers' and Soldiers' Deputies, and a member of the All-Russian Central Executive Committee of Soviets.

After the Bolsheviks seized power, Sokolnikov became a member of the new Central Executive Committee and held various government positions. In October, Sokolnikov—along with Lenin, Zinoviev, **L. Kamenev**, **L. Trotsky**, Stalin, and **A. Bubnov**—became a member of the first "Political Bureau" (Politburo). In November 1917, he led the nationalization of banks and supervised the creation of country's new banking system. In addition, Sokolnikov was included in the delegation that was sent to Brest-Litovsk to sign a truce with Germany. On March 3, 1918, he replaced Trotsky as head of the delegation and personally signed the final version of the Treaty of Brest-Litovsk on behalf of Soviet Russia (although he did not want to sign the surrender). Between May and June 1918, Sokolnikov served as a member of the Presidium of the Supreme Soviet of the National Economy (VSNKh) and worked for the newspaper **Pravda**. In June 1918, Sokolnikov conducted negotiations on economic and legal issues of the Treaty of Brest-Litovsk in Berlin.

From 1918 and almost until the end of the Civil War, Sokolnikov was on the front line. He was appointed a member of the Revolutionary Military Council of the 2nd and 9th Armies of the Southern Front. He had a negative attitude toward the policy of "decossackization," which aimed to exterminate the Cossacks. He supported the Red Cossack commander (former military sergeant major) Filip Mironov. He was also a consistent opponent of *partisanshchina* and supported the use of military specialists (*voienspetzy*). In 1919–1920, he served as commander of the 8th Army on the Turkestan Front. He was also appointed as chairman of the Turkestan Commission of the All-Russian Central Executive Committee and the Council of People's Commissars of the Soviet Union. In addition, Sokolnikov was chairman of the Turkburo of the CC CPSU. He had full military, civil, and judicial power in Turkestan and led the struggle against local nationalists, the Basmachi movement, and White troops. In early 1921, during a discussion about the role of trade unions, he supported the line of Trotsky and **N. Bukharin**.

In the fall of 1921, Sokolnikov was appointed a member of the Collegium of the People's Commissariat of Finance. In this post, he was responsible for introduction of the New Economic Policy (NEP). In 1922, Sokolnikov became deputy people's commissar of finance, but de facto he headed this department (the people's commissar, **Nikolai Krestinsky**, was also the plenipotentiary representative of the RSFSR in Germany and was constantly in Berlin). During this period, the country was going through a financial crisis—a period of uncontrollable, spiraling inflation. By 1921, the ruble had depreciated fifty thousand times compared to the prewar period, and the average prices of goods had increased more than 97,000 times. In the summer of 1922, Sokolnikov participated in the Hague Conference, an international finance conference at which capitalist states raised claims for compensation for previously owned industries that the Soviet government had nationalized. The main Soviet representative was **M. Litvinov**. In 1922–1924, Sokolnikov led monetary reform. He was a strong supporter of the creation of a stable currency and argued against the state monopoly of foreign trade. He also considered the Soviet economy to be part of the world economy.

In the fall of 1922, Sokolnikov officially became the people's commissar of finance of the RSFSR. In July 1923, after the formation of the People's Commissariat of Finance of the USSR, he headed this institution and served in this post until January 1926. During his tenure, a stable currency—the "gold banknotes" or "*chervonets*"—was introduced in the USSR. In the spring of 1924, treasury bills came into circulation. Steadily, the Soviet *chervonets* began to enter foreign markets. From April 1, 1924, the chervonets was quoted on the New York Stock Exchange. In 1925, the Soviet *chervonets* was officially quoted on other stock exchanges, including those of Austria,

Turkey, Italy, China, Estonia, Latvia, and Lithuania. Also, under Sokolnikov's supervision, a system of banking institutions was created in the USSR. State credit operations were introduced with short-term and long-term loans. Further, natural taxation was eliminated, and a system of taxes and revenues was created. Additionally, state insurance (*Gosstrakh*) and state labor savings banks were created, state and local budgets were differentiated, and norms of Soviet budget law were introduced. Thus, a more stable financial system was created in the USSR with significant input from Sokolnikov.

In June 1924, he became a candidate member of the Politburo of the Communist Party. In 1925–1926, however, he joined the new opposition led by Kamenev and Zinoviev, who had ended their triumvirate with Stalin. Sokolnikov advocated for collective leadership and expressed doubts about the need to preserve the post of general secretary of the Central Committee of the CPSU, held by Stalin. On 5 September 1925, Sokolnikov, together with Zinoviev, Kamenev, and **N. Krupskaia**, signed the "Platform of the Four" against Stalin's leadership. On January 16, 1926, Sokolnikov was dismissed from the post of people's commissar of finance and was appointed deputy chairman of Gosplan.

In 1927, Sokolnikov became a member of the "United Left Opposition" and was expelled from the party. In summer 1927, he broke with Trotskyism. In December 1927, he was reelected as a member of the Central Committee. During the Plenum of the Central Committee in July 1928, he still hoped to remove Stalin from the post of general secretary of the Central Committee. In 1928–1929, he was appointed chairman of the board of the USSR Oil Syndicate. In 1929, he became the Soviet ambassador to Great Britain, a difficult position given his lack of English. In March 1933, Sokolnikov became a member of the Collegium of the People's Commissariat of Foreign Affairs. Between May 1933 and June 1934, he served as a deputy people's commissar of foreign affairs of the USSR. From May 1935, he was the first deputy commissar of the wood industry of the USSR.

On July 26, 1936, Sokolnikov was arrested in the case of the "Parallel Anti-Soviet Trotskyist Center" (Second Moscow Show Trial), removed from the Central Committee, and expelled from the party. On January 30, 1937, he was sentenced to ten years in prison. According to the official statement, on May 21, 1939, Sokolnikov was assassinated in a prison by other convicts. However, an investigation carried out by the CC CPSU and the KGB in 1956–1961 showed that the murder of Sokolnikov (like that of **Karl Radek** two days earlier) was carried out under the leadership of the senior NKVD operative **P. Kubatkin**, on the instructions of **Lavrenty Beria** and Stalin personally.

On June 12, 1988, Sokolnikov was posthumously rehabilitated by the Plenum of the Supreme Court of the USSR. On December 16 of the same year, he was reinstated in the CPSU.

SOKOLOVSKY, VASILY DANILOVICH (1887–1968). A Soviet military leader who was one of the key Soviet military commanders during the Great Patriotic War (1941–1945), marshal of the Soviet Union (July 3, 1946), Hero of the Soviet Union (1945), and member of CC CPSU (1952–1961), Vasily Sokolovsky was born in the village of Kozliki, Bialystok district, Grodno province (now Poland), into a Belarusian peasant family. In 1905, he graduated from a parish school and started to work as a day laborer. In 1912, he graduated with honors from the two-year teachers' school. During the First World War, in 1915, he worked for several months on construction of defensive lines. In 1918, after graduation from the Nevelsk Teachers' Seminary, he worked as a teacher in a rural school. In this same year, he voluntarily joined the Red Army and participated in the Civil War.

In May 1918, Vasily graduated from the First Moscow military instructor courses and was sent to the Eastern Front as a company commander of the 2nd Ural Regiment. In June 1918, he was appointed a chief of battalion headquarters and instructor of the Red Guard detachment. In September 1918, he became acting regiment commander. Between

October 1918 to June 1919, he studied at the General Staff Academy of the Red Army. He was among the first intake of students, who joined the academy. Sokolovsky was pulled out of his studies and placed at the disposal of the Revolutionary Military Council of the 10th Army (on the Tsaritsyn and Caucasian fronts). From June to December 1919, Sokolovsky served as a senior assistant to the chief of staff and an interim brigade commander of the 32nd Infantry Division of the Southern Front. In 1921, he finally graduated from the General Staff Academy of the Red Army (he was among top three graduates) and after graduation held various command and staff positions.

Between October 1921 and April 1922, Sokolovsky worked as assistant to the head of the operational department of the Turkestan front. From April 1922, he was appointed as the chief of staff of the 2nd Turkestan Rifle Division and the Fergana Army Group. In May 1924, he became commander of the 2nd Turkestan Rifle Division and the Fergana Army Group. In this capacity, he fought against the Basmachi movement. In August 1924, Sokolovsky was appointed the chief of staff of the 14th Infantry Division of the Moscow Military District. From October 1926 to July 1930, he served as chief of staff of the 9th Rifle Corps in the North Caucasian Military District.

In 1928, Sokolovsky graduated from the Higher Academic Courses of the Frunze Military Academy of the Red Army. In January 1929, he was made chief of staff of the 5th Rifle Corps (the Belarusian Military District). From July 1930 to January 1935, he commanded the 43rd Infantry Division of the Belarusian Military District. Until May 1935, he served as the deputy chief of staff of the Volga Military District. In 1931, Sokolovsky joined the CPSU. From May 1935 to April 1938, he served as the chief of staff of the Ural Military District. Between April 1938 and February 1941, he was chief of staff of the Moscow Military District. From February to June 1941, Sokolovsky was the second deputy chief of the general staff of the Red Army.

After the outbreak of the **Great Patriotic War**, he was appointed the first deputy chief of the general staff of the Red Army. From July 1941, he served as the chief of staff of the Western Front. In this post, he was able to organize engineering work at the front lines and in the depths of the defense, and helped to coordinate the actions of the Soviet army during the Battle of Smolensk (July 1941). Further, he actively participated in planning, preparing, and conducting counteroffensive (December 5, 1941–January 7, 1942) and offensive (January 7–March 30, 1942) operations during the Battle of Moscow's Rzhev-Viazemskaia strategic offensive operation (January 8–April 20, 1941). In February 1943, Sokolovsky was appointed commander of the Western Front. Under his command, Soviet troops, in cooperation with other fronts, conducted the Rzhev-Viazma Offensive (1943), Orel (Operation Kutuzov) counteroffensive, part of the Kursk Strategic Offensive Operation in July–August 1943, and the second Battle of Smolensk (August 7–October 2, 1943). Praised for his successful leadership of the Rzhev-Viazma Offensive, Sokolovsky was awarded the Order of Suvorov, first class. During the Smolensk operation, on August 27, 1943, he was awarded the military rank of "general of the army," and after the successful completion of the operation, he was awarded a second Order of Suvorov, first class.

But not all his campaigns were successful. For failures during the Orsha and Vitebsk offensive operations in April 1944, Sokolovsky was removed from the post of front commander. In April 1944, he was made the chief of staff of the 1st Ukrainian Front. From April 1945 to June 1946, he served as the deputy commander of the 1st Belarusian Front. In these positions, he made a significant contribution to the planning, preparation, and implementation of the Lviv-Sandomierz Offensive (mid-July–August 1944), the Vistula-Oder Offensive (January–February 1945), and the Battle of Berlin (April–May 1945). For the successful conduct of the Vistula-Oder operation, he was awarded his third Order of Suvorov, first class. For skillful leadership during these military operations and personal courage, on May 29, 1945, Sokolovsky was awarded the title of Hero of the Soviet Union.

After the war, in March 1946, General Sokolovsky was made the commander-in-chief of the group of Soviet occupation forces in Germany and commander-in-chief of the Soviet military administration. Simultaneously, he was a member of the Control Council in Germany. Under his leadership, the **Berlin Blockade** (June 24, 1948–May 12, 1949) was launched and implemented, but ultimately failed to achieve its objectives (either to push the Western powers out of West Berlin or to prevent their establishing of a common currency in the western zones of Germany). In June 1946, Sokolovsky was awarded the title of marshal of the Soviet Union. In March 1949, he was appointed the first deputy minister of the armed forces of the USSR (from February 1950, the first deputy minister of war of the USSR). On June 16, 1952, he became the chief of the general staff and the first deputy minister of war of the USSR (from March 1953, deputy minister of defense). Sokolovsky used his knowledge of combat and practical experience to improve the structure of the Soviet armed forces. In 1960, he became the inspector of the Group of Inspectors General of the Ministry of Defense of the Soviet Union. Between 1952 and 1961, he was a member of the CC CPSU.

Sokolovsky was the author of a number of military historical and military theoretical works. He became widely known for his books *Military Strategy* (1962) and *The Defeat of the German-Fascist Troops Near Moscow* (1964). He was elected a deputy of the Supreme Soviet of the USSR of the second through seventh convocations (1946–1968). On May 8, 1965, he became an honorary citizen of Berlin (he was stripped of his honorary title on September 29, 1992). On March 24, 1965, he signed a letter to the Presidium of the Central Committee of the CPSU on awarding Moscow the title of Hero City. He also actively supported the idea of creating the Tomb of the Unknown Soldier in the capital and initiated the creation of the monument to the "Soldier-Liberator" in Treptow Park in Berlin

Marshal Sokolovsky died on May 10, 1968. The urn with his ashes was buried in the Kremlin wall necropolis on Red Square in Moscow.

STAKHANOV, ALEKSEI GRIGORIEVICH (1906–1977). A Soviet coal miner in the Donbas region who became the founder of the Stakhanov movement, and hero of socialist labor (1970), Aleksei Stakhanov was born in the village of Lugovaia, Orel Governorate, Russian Empire, into a poor peasant family. From early childhood, he worked as a farm laborer and a shepherd. For three years he studied at a rural school but never graduated. In his early career, when he was asked about his level of education, Aleksei usually responded that he was illiterate. In 1927, he moved to Irmino (Luhansk Oblast, Ukraine) and worked there at the Tsentralnaia-Irmino coal mine. He hoped to earn money, buy a horse, and return to his native village, but after some time he decided to stay on at the mine. In 1933, he began to work as a jackhammer operator. In 1935, he graduated from mining courses at his place of work.

In the 1930s, during the decade of rapid industrialization, the Soviet Union was swept by a fever of so-called "socialist emulation." In 1933, the Second Five-Year Plan began. By that time, it became clear that huge funds invested in Soviet industry had not yielded profit or financial gain. One of the reasons for this was the lack of qualified specialists. The Soviet economy began to struggle in meeting its assigned targets. Under these circumstances, the party leadership was looking for ways to intensify workforce productivity. Ordinary workers were encouraged to set labor records for the sake of a common bright future and in the hope of building communism.

On August 31, 1935, Donbas miner Stakhanov was reported to have set a record by mining 102 tons of coal in five hours and forty-five minutes, exceeding the daily quota by fourteen times (the daily quota was seven tons). Although Stakhanov's record was actually set by a team of five people and became possible only due to preliminary preparations and reorganization of the usual labor duties, it was recorded as a "personal" record. The idea to separate the tasks between different workers occurred to Stakhanov. According to his suggestion, the miner had to be engaged only in cutting coal activity, and the workers who had to work with him had to strengthen the vault of the mine and carry out other tasks. Stakhanov's idea was readily supported by the local party organizer, Konstantin Petrov, who decided to organize/stage the record-breaking feat. Stakhanov was allowed to try a new method of extraction. Petrov carefully prepared for the event: he chose the most coal-rich area, assigned two timbermen and two coal haulers to Stakhanov's brigade, and even went down the mine personally to control the working process and to help illuminate the working space. The editor of the local newspaper, who was supposed to record the historical event, was also invited to the mine. Usually, the coal mined during the shift was to be divided among the whole brigade. But this time, the record that exceeded the norm by fourteen times was awarded solely to Stakhanov (in reality Stakhanov and his assistants fulfilled less than three norms per person). In September, after his record was broken by N. Izotov (who had set the original record three years earlier), Stakhanov set a new record of 227 tons.

After the record, Stakhanov was admitted to the party and awarded the Order of Lenin. On September 1, the mine party committee decided to display Stakhanov's portrait on the mine's honor board and to pay him a bonus in the amount of a monthly salary (220 rubles). On September 3, he received a completely furnished and equipped apartment with a telephone (which was rare at that time). In addition, Stakhanov was provided with a personal horse-drawn carriage (*britzka*) with a coachman. His fame escalated. In September, the party newspaper *Pravda* published an article titled "The Record of the Miner Stakhanov," and a few months later the American newsmagazine *Time* placed his portrait on the cover.

Stakhanov's record became a symbol of Soviet record-breaking, symbolizing the drive to communism, and remained a part of Soviet propaganda for years to come. Using Stakhanov as an example, the Kremlin demonstrated that in the Soviet state, workers also could legally enrich themselves. Additionally, Stakhanov became an example of upward social mobility: an ordinary worker could advance directly from the mine into the ranks of the country's political elite. In 1936, Stakhanov was transferred to Moscow, where he was settled in a house on the embankment (a luxury residence for the Soviet elite) and provided with a personal car.

Stakhanov's record gave birth to the "Stakhanovite movement," which spread throughout Soviet industry and was supported and led by the Communist Party. On November 17, 1935, the All-Union Stakhanovite Conference took place at the Kremlin. At the beginning of the conference, the leader of the CC CPSU, Stalin, delivered his famous speech: "Life has become better, comrades. Life has become more fun. And when life is fun, work is good. . . . If our life was bad, unsightly, unhappy, then we would not have any Stakhanov movement." The terrible irony of the phrase lies in the fact that it was iterated on the eve of a new wave of repressions. At some point, the Stakhanovite movement helped to improve productivity in the Soviet industries. However, many problems occurred during this campaign. Soviet industrial enterprises began to demand new achievements from individual workers. This "continuous stakhanovization" gave rise to mass disorganization and damaged coal mines, and provoked decline in the overall quality of products. In some cases, this led to full collapse of production. Technical and organizational problems were evaluated as political sabotage. As a result, another wave of repression swept across the country.

Achieving his record did not bring happiness to Stakhanov's life. The fame, material benefits, and general attention became a heavy burden. Initially, his career developed quite well. In 1936–1941, he studied at the Industrial Academy in Moscow. In 1937, he was elected a deputy of the Supreme Soviet of the USSR. In 1941–1942 he was appointed the head of mine No. 31 in Karaganda. Between 1943 and 1957, he led socialist competition in the People's Commissariat of the Coal Industry of the USSR in Moscow. But steadily, Stakhanov became a chronic alcoholic.

Four years after the death of Stalin, in 1957, Stakhanov, at the direction of N. S.

Khrushchev, was transferred back to the Donetsk region. Stakhanov's family refused to follow him into "exile" and remained in Moscow. Stakhanov's dependence on alcohol increased as a result. Until 1959 he was deputy manager of the "Chistiakovantratsit" trust. In 1959, he was appointed assistant to the chief engineer of the mine department of the "Torezantratsit" trust. In 1974 he retired.

Stakhanov died in a psychiatric hospital, where he was treated for the consequences of chronic alcoholism (multiple sclerosis with partial memory loss, and delirium tremens). On November 5, 1977, he slipped on an apple skin, hit his head, and died without regaining consciousness. He was buried at the city cemetery in the city of Torez, Donetsk region. During his life, he was awarded two Orders of Lenin, an Order of the Red Banner of Labor, the "Hammer and Sickle" gold medal, and numerous other medals. His fame was fleeting, but his exploit was mentioned by Mikhail Gorbachev shortly after he was elected general secretary on the fiftieth anniversary of Stakhanov's feat, August 31, 1985.

Aleksei Stakhanov

STALINGRAD, BATTLE OF. A pivotal battle of the Second World War (**Great Patriotic War**) that brought the first major defeat of the German Army on Soviet soil. It took place from July 17, 1942, to February 2, 1943. The German Army Group South was split into two (armies A and B), and penetrated Soviet defenses before advancing to the Don River. By late July, the German 6th Army under General Friedrich von Paulus arrived at the Volga River north of Stalingrad backed by General Hermann Hoth's 4th Panzer Army in the southwest. They faced the Soviet 62nd and 64th armies and began a war of attrition over the next two months. Eventually, the struggle reached an impasse, with the Germans controlling most of the city but unable to capture it outright. In the meantime, General **A. M. Vasilevsky** concocted a plan for a counterattack (Operation Uranus) targeting the weaker Italian and Romanian troops. The attack started on November 19 as the Southwestern Front (**N. F. Vatutin**) and Stalingrad Front (A. I. Ieremenko) broke through the defenses to the north and south with the two armies joining up some forty kilometers west of the city, trapping the 6th Army inside the city. German attempts to rescue von Paulus, including one by General Manstein, were repelled, and on February 2, 1943, von Paulus surrendered to the Army of the Don Front led by **K. Rokossovsky**. German losses, dead or captured, exceeded 600,000, including twenty-four generals. Soviet losses were also very high, about double those of the defeated Germans. The battle was a psychological turning point both of the German-Soviet war and the Second World War, the first major defeat for Adolf Hitler, and the end of German expansion in the east.

STATE DEFENSE COMMITTEE. The State Defense Committee (GKO) was the highest organ of state power in the USSR during the **Great Patriotic War**. It was authorized on June 30, 1941, by a decree of the Supreme Soviet of the USSR together with the Council of Ministers and the CC CPSU, under the leadership of Stalin. Run by the latter and his closest associates, it had more flexibility to meet than formal Soviet organs. It had control over economic, military, and political measures with the task of mobilizing all resources for victory over the enemy. Modeled on a similar entity formed during the Russian Civil War, the GKO coordinated the war effort, made rapid decisions. In its early months, the GKO was concerned with evacuation of major factories, transport, and organizing of military fronts. By 1942, its chief concern was the direction of the military economy, including the creation of new fuel and metallurgical bases to compensate for the losses incurred on the southern front. By 1943, as the front moved westward, and the Soviet armies achieved significant victories, the chief task of the GKO was the restoration of the economy of the liberated territories. It was dissolved on September 4, 1945, (after the surrender of Japan) and its functions transferred to the Council of Ministers of the USSR.

SUSLOV, MIKHAIL ANDREEVICH (1902–1982). One of the Party's chief ideologists, member of the Politburo of the CC CPSU (1952–1953, 1955–1982), and secretary of the CPSU (1947–1982).

Mikhail Suslov was born into a peasant family in the village of Shakhovskoe, Saratov province (now Ulianovsk Oblast). His family was very poor, and his father worked part-time in the oil fields in Azerbaijan. As a child, Suslov was very energetic. At the age of 14, he organized a group of artisans and moved to Arkhangelsk. Soon his family joined him. After the October Revolution of 1917, Mikhail and his family returned to their native village.

After moving back to Shakhovskoe, Mikhail's father, Andrei, joined the Bolsheviks and became involved in party work. In 1918, at the age of 16, Mikhail also started to participate in political activities in the region. In 1918, he was a member of a Committee of Poor Peasants. In February 1920, he joined the Komsomol, and in 1921, he became a full party member of the RCP(b). The regional Komsomol organization sent him to study at the Prechistensky Rabfak (*rabochy fakultet*, "workers' faculty") in Moscow. From 1924 to 1928, Mikhail studied at Plekhanov Moscow Institute of the National Economy. Between 1929 and 1931, Mikhail was a graduate student at the Communist Academy. Simultaneously, he taught Political Economy at Moscow State University and the Industrial Academy.

In 1931, Suslov was transferred to the apparatus of the Central Control Commission of the CPSU and the People's Commissariat of the Workers' and Peasants' Inspectorate (Rabkrin). As an inspector of the Central Control Commission, he headed the commission responsible for purging the party in the Urals and Chernihiv regions. In 1934, he started to work at the People's Control Commission. In 1936–1937, Suslov studied at the Economic Institute of Red Professors. After graduation, he served in the Rostov Oblast Committee of the CPSU. On March 5, 1938, he was made second secretary of the same committee.

Between February 1939 and November 1944, Suslov was first secretary of the Ordzhonikidze (Stavropol) Regional Committee of the CPSU. In 1941–1943, he also was a member of the Military Council of the Northern Group of Forces of the North Caucasian Front. During the Nazi occupation of the Stavropol region, he organized and led the Stavropol Krai Headquarters of the Partisan (guerrilla) movement. After the liberation of the region from the German troops, he led the purge and arrests of so-called collaborators (very often those who did not join the partisan detachments were called "collaborators"). He also participated in the deportation of the Karachais (Operation Seagull, was the forced resettlement of the Karachai population to Central Asia in November 1943).

At the end of 1944, Suslov was transferred to Vilnius. On November 14, 1944, he was made chairman of the Bureau of the CC CPSU in the restored Lithuanian SSR. Under his leadership, the bureau performed purges and fought against detachments of Forest Brothers (a guerrilla movement against the Soviet regime). Suslov also led Soviet deportations from Lithuania in the early postwar years.

In 1946, Suslov was transferred to the apparatus of the CC CPSU in Moscow. On April 13, he headed the International Department of the CPSU and on May 24, 1947, he was appointed secretary of the CC CPSU. According to the archive of A. Iakovlev, who led the de-Stalinization campaign during Gorbachev's leadership of the USSR, on November 26, 1946, Suslov sent a note to Stalin, in which he made an accusation against the Jewish Anti-Fascist Committee.[6] This note catalyzed the start of investigation against this organization. As a result, 140 people were falsely accused of espionage and treason, twenty-three of them were killed, and twenty people spent up to twenty-five years in prison.

Between 1949 and 1951, Suslov was editor-in-chief of *Pravda* newspaper. During the 19th congress of the CPSU (the last under Stalin's leadership), he was elected to the Presidium of the CPSU. After Stalin's death (March 5, 1953), he was removed from Presidium. On April 16, he once again headed the International Department of the party. In this post he oversaw relations with foreign communist parties. On July 12, 1955, Suslov was reelected to the Presidium. From this time and until his death, Suslov played a huge role in the leadership of the Central Committee and the USSR.

After Stalin's death, Suslov actively supported **N. Khrushchev**. In June 1957, during the attempt to remove Khrushchev from the post of the first secretary, Suslov supported him. However, later Suslov played a crucial role in Khrushchev's removal. In 1964, he chaired the meeting of the October Plenum of the Central Committee of the CPSU, which relieved Nikita Khrushchev of both posts: first secretary of the Central Committee of the CPSU and chairman of the USSR Council of Ministers.

Under **Leonid Brezhnev**, Suslov became the second person in the Party and the main ideologist of the CPSU. During the Brezhnev era, Suslov influenced education, culture, and ideology in the country. He rigidly supported the ideas of the orthodox Marxism and rejected any deviation from this ideology. He was responsible for the persecution of the intelligentsia, the arrests of dissidents, and the exile of A. Solzhenitsyn and A. Sakharov. The last high-profile event in Suslov's biography is the Soviet Union invasion of Afghanistan in December 1979. Suslov was one of the leaders of the Politburo who made the decision to invade, along with the military officers. Suslov was pedantic and ascetic. He wore galoshes and old-fashioned suits. After his trips abroad, he immediately returned the remaining foreign currency to the party treasury. During his lengthy career, Suslov was awarded five Orders of Lenin, the Order of the October Revolution, the Order of the Great Patriotic War of the first degree, medals, and foreign awards, including the Order of Klement Gottwald (Czechoslovakia, 1977).

Mikhail Suslov died on January 25, 1982. He was buried on Red Square near the Kremlin wall next to the grave of Stalin. Soon after his death, Brezhnev also died, thus ending an era of what can be termed neo-Stalinism.

SVERDLOV, IAKOV MIKHAILOVICH (1885–1919). Sverdlov was an Old Bolshevik, professional revolutionary, one of the key leaders of the October Revolution (1917), party administrator, member of the Central Committee of the RSDWP(b) and RCP(b), chairman of the All-Russian Central Executive Committee (1917–1919), member of the editorial board of the *Pravda* newspaper, and one of the closest associates of Vladimir Lenin.

Iakov Sverdlov was born in Nizhny Novgorod into a Jewish family. His father, Mikhail (or Moishe) Izrailevich Sverdlov, was an engraver and also owned printing workshops. To pay for his children's education (in total he had eight children), he had an underground job forging various documents and stamps for revolutionaries. His forgeries were of very good quality. Iakov's mother, Elizaveta Solomonova, died in 1900, and his father married for the second time. Before his second marriage, he converted with his family to the Russian Orthodox Church. **Maksim Gorky**, who lived in Nizhny Novgorod in those years, was a frequent guest of the Sverdlov family.

Iakov finished four classes of the Nizhny Novgorod men's gymnasium. After his mother's death, Iakov and his brothers were forced to drop out the school due to financial problems. He became an apprentice pharmacist. In 1901, he joined the RSDWP and became a professional revolutionary. He distributed illegal literature, raised funds for the party, and organized an underground printing house. After the split of the Social Democratic Party at the second congress of the RSDWP in 1903, he joined the Bolshevik faction. During the First Russian Revolution of 1905, Sverdlov headed the work of the Bolsheviks in Iekaterinburg and Perm, and spent some of his time in the Moscow and St. Petersburg party organizations. Between 1901 and 1911, he was repeatedly arrested, imprisoned, and exiled. In the tsarist prisons, he was actively engaged in self-education.

After the sixth (Prague) All-Russian Conference of the RSDWP in 1912, Sverdlov was included in the Central Committee in absentia and elected to the Russian Bureau of the Central Committee of the RSDWP. In December 1912, he escaped from exile and settled down in St. Petersburg, where he became one of the leaders of the newspaper *Pravda* and the Bolshevik faction of the fourth State Duma. In 1913, he was arrested again and deported to the Turukhansk Territory (now part of the Krasnoiarsk Krai), where he met Joseph Stalin.

After the February Revolution of 1917, Sverdlov returned to Petrograd where he took an active part in disseminating Bolshevik propaganda. In April, he met Lenin for the first time. The same month, Sverdlov was sent to the Urals (Iekaterinburg) to oversee party activity there. In June, he returned to Petrograd and took an active part in the preparation for the October Revolution. He controlled the organizational bureau of the Central Committee. Together with **F. Dzerzhinsky**, he headed the Central Committee's Military Commission. In the fall of 1917, during preparation for the uprising, Sverdlov was responsible for the recruitment of people for the revolutionary committee.

At the end of November 1917, with the Bolsheviks now in power, he was elected chairman of the All-Russian Central Executive Committee (de jure he became the head of state of the Russian SFSR), continuing to remain secretary of the Central Committee of the RSDWP(b). Sverdlov became one of four leaders (along with Lenin, Trotsky, and Stalin) to address urgent issues in newly emerged country. Very soon, Sverdlov emerged, at least on paper, as the second most prominent person in the state after Lenin and concentrated colossal power in his hands. He was engaged in the selection process of party cadres for key posts.

Sverdlov strongly supported the decision of the Council of People's Commissars to conclude the Treaty of Brest-Litovsk in March 1918, which pulled Russia out of the First World War, with significant loss of its European territories. In 1918, he was chairman of the Commission that drafted the first Constitution of the RSFSR. In July 1918, he was one of the leaders of the suppression of the Left SRs in Moscow following their uprising. According to Trotsky, Sverdlov played an important role in the decision regarding the execution of the Romanov family in this same month. He initiated the creation of the School of Agitators and Instructors at the All-Russian Central Executive Committee and participated in the preparation of the first congress of the Communist International. After the attempted assassination of Lenin on August 30, 1918, Sverdlov headed the party and the state until Lenin's recovery. It was at the suggestion of Sverdlov that a decree on the Red Terror was adopted. He was also one of the initiators of the policy to eliminate the Cossacks. At the beginning of 1919, he took part in the work of the Congresses of the Soviets of Latvia, Lithuania, Belarus, and Ukraine.

On March 16, 1919, Sverdlov died suddenly. According to the official version of events, he died of either typhus or most likely influenza (the Kremlin's doctors diagnosed him with the Spanish Flu). According to another, uncorroborated, version, he was fatally beaten by workers during his political visit to the Ukraine and Orel. He was buried in the Kremlin wall in Moscow.

NOTES

1. Victor Serge, *From Lenin to Stalin* (New York: Pioneer Publishers, 1937), 59.
2. Evgenii Zhyrnov, "Iz vospominaniy marshala G. K. Zhukova," *Kommersant Vlast*, no. 24 (June 23, 2008): 10.
3. Irina Romanova, "'Kvoty perevypolneny': Strashnye arkhivnye dokumenty o 1937-m v Belarusi," *Nasha Niva*, April 23, 2019, https://history.nashaniva.com/?c=Ir&i=201497&lang=ru.
4. Viktor Ignatenko, "Vtorye pokhorony vozhdia," *Pravo vybora* 158, no. 3 (March 25–February 10, 2013), www.irkutsk.izbirkom.ru/etc/p5_158.pdf.
5. L. D. Trotsky, *K istorii russkoy revolyutsii* (Moscow: Politizdat, 1990), 286.
6. Aleksandr Iakovlev, "Dokument no 4. Zapiska A. N. Iakovleva, V. A. Medvedeva, V. M. Chebrikova, A. I. Lukianova, G. P. Razumovskogo, B. K. Pugo, V. A. Kriuchkova, V. I. Boldina, G. L. Smirnova v TsK KPSS 'Ob antikonstitutsionnoi praktike nachala 30-40h i nachala 50h godov,'" in *V tseliakh vosstanovlenya istoricheskoi i sotsialnoi spravedlivosti: A.N. Iakovlev i reabilitatsya zhertv politicheskikh repressy. 1988–1991*, www.mat.univie.ac.at/~neretin/1937/Iakovlev.html.

T

TEHRAN CONFERENCE. The first conference of the Allied leaders in the Second World War took place in Tehran, Iran, from November 28 to December 1, 1943. It included Stalin, U.S. president Franklin D. Roosevelt, and British prime minister Winston Churchill, along with diplomatic advisers and foreign ministers. The conference sought to decide the question about a second front on the European continent, a long-standing demand of Stalin to relieve pressure on the Soviet Union. Earlier, at a meeting in Quebec the previous August, the two Western Allies had devised a plan for Operation Overlord, which would begin around May 1, 1944. Though Roosevelt adhered to that plan, Churchill suggested an alternative attack on the Balkans (what he described as the "soft underbelly" of Europe. The Allied leaders concurred that the result of the war must be the unconditional surrender of Germany. The leaders agreed that at the end of the war, all forces should be removed from Iran, and materials provided as well as loans for rebuilding the Iranian economy. One of the social events at this first meeting of the three leaders was Churchill's birthday celebration (his 69th), at which he presented a sword to Stalin to mark the defense of the city of Stalingrad. In addition to the three leaders, attendees at the Tehran Conference included **V. Molotov**, Sir Archibald Clark Kerr, Harry Hopkins, W. Averell Harriman, and Anthony Eden.

TER-PETROSIAN, SIMON ARSHAKI (1882–1922). Ter-Petrosian was an Old Bolshevik; professional revolutionary; one of the organizers of underground printing houses and money expropriations as well as the transportation of weapons and literature; the organizer of the Bolshevik underground in the Caucasus and southern Russia (1918–1920); and an early companion to Stalin. Lenin characterized him as "a man of absolutely exceptional devotion, courage and energy."[1]

Simon Ter-Petrosian was born in Gori, Tiflis Governorate, the Russian Empire (now Georgia). His father was a wealthy Armenian contractor. His mother was Georgian. Simon had four siblings. At the age of seven he started to study at an Armenian school, and at the age of 11 he was transferred to a local city school. In 1898, Simon was expelled from school for bad behavior during the Law of God lesson. After his expulsion, he left for Tiflis,

Tehran Conference

where his aunt lived. Soon, he had to return to Gori due to his father's financial problems and his mother's illness. After his mother's death, Simon, together with his sisters, moved to Tiflis.

In his childhood, Simon became a close friend and then an ally of Stalin, who helped him to learn Russian (Stalin's mother was a friend of Simon's father). Under Stalin's influence, he became acquainted with Marxism. In 1901, Simon joined the RSDWP and received the underground name "Kamo." In 1903, he became a member of the Caucasian Union Committee of the RSDWP. Kamo was responsible for organizing the work of underground printing houses, money "expropriations," and delivery of propaganda literature and weapons from abroad.

In November 1903, Kamo was arrested for the first time. After nine months of incarceration, he was able to escape from prison. In 1904, he joined the Bolsheviks. In 1905, he actively participated in the revolutionary events. In December 1905, he was wounded, beaten, and arrested during the uprising in Tiflis. After spending two and a half months in prison, he once again managed to escape. He also helped to organize the escape of thirty-two prisoners from the Metekhi castle (a historic neighborhood of Tiblisi). In 1906, on the instructions of a combat group linked to the Central Committee of the RSDWP, he visited St. Petersburg, Finland, Sweden, and Germany and organized the delivery of weapons purchased by the Bolsheviks abroad to Russia (a ship with these weapons sank along the way from Bulgaria). In 1907, under the name of Prince Dadiani, he traveled to Finland, where he visited Lenin. At the end of this trip, Kamo returned to Tiflis with weapons and explosives. On June 13, 1907, he participated in the sensational Tiflis Bank Robbery, organized by Stalin.

In August 1907, Kamo left for Berlin. On November 9, 1907, the German police searched his Berlin apartment, where they found a large number of weapons, as well as a double-bottomed suitcase filled with explosives, and revolutionary literature. Kamo was arrested. He skillfully feigned insanity and insensitivity to pain and was able to puzzle the best doctors in Europe. According to the results of the examination carried out by German doctors after his arrest, he was declared insane. At the end of 1909, as an incurable patient, he was extradited to Russia, taken to Tiflis, and placed in prison, and then in a hospital. In August 1911, he escaped from the Tiflis Psychiatric Hospital. With the fame derived from his "adventures," Kamo received acclaim from the well-known German socialist Karl Liebknecht and many socialist newspapers, who started to refer to him as "the hero of the revolution."

After his escape, Kamo traveled to Paris and visited Lenin, who supplied him with money. From Paris he went to Constantinople, and from there to Bulgaria. While trying to return to the Caucasus, he was arrested by the Turkish authorities, but he managed to convince them that he was a Turkish agent. In 1912, he returned to Russia and made an attempt to arrange the expropriation of the money post. But the robbery attempt failed; Kamo was wounded, arrested, and again placed in the Metekhi castle. He was sentenced to death, but his sentence was commuted by an amnesty on the occasion of the Romanov Tercentenary (1913) to twenty years in prison. From 1915, he was serving his sentence in Kharkov prison (today Kharkiv, Ukraine).

Kamo was released from prison during the February Revolution of 1917. After his release, he first went to Moscow, then to Petrograd. He worked in the Baku Council and, after the end of the year, in the All-Russian Extraordinary Commission (Cheka). In Moscow, he also trained a battlegroup to fight in Denikin's rear. In the fall of 1919, he delivered weapons and money to Baku for an underground party organization and partisans of the North Caucasus. In January 1920, Kamo was arrested in Tbilisi by the Menshevik government and exiled. In April 1920, he took an active part in preparation of an armed uprising in Baku. In May 1920, he studied at the General Staff Academy in Moscow. In 1921, Kamo worked in the People's Commissariat for Foreign Trade of the RSFSR (Vneshtorg). In the following year, he was transferred to the People's Commissariat of Finance of Georgia.

On July 14, 1922, Kamo was involved in a road accident. A truck hit him while he was cycling in Tiflis. Suffering from a severe head injury, he was taken by the truck driver to the nearest hospital, the Mikhailovskaia, where he died a few hours later. There was some suspicion that his death was not an accident but a political murder that was ordered by Stalin personally.

TIMOSHENKO, SEMEN KONSTANTINOVICH (1895–1970).

Timoshenko was a Soviet military commander, marshal of the Soviet Union (1940), twice Hero of the Soviet Union (1940, 1965), Chevalier of the Order of Victory (1945), people's commissar of defense of the USSR (May 1940–July 1941), member of the Presidium of the Supreme Soviet of the USSR (1938–1940), member of the CC CPSU(b) (1939–1952), member of the CC CPU (1938–1940), deputy of the Supreme Soviet of the Ukrainian SSR of the first convocation (1938–1947), and candidate member of the CC CPSU (1952–1970).

Semen Timoshenko was born in the village of Orman, Bessarabia Governorate, in the Russian Empire (today Furmanivka, Odesa Oblast, Ukraine), into a large family of Ukrainian peasants. Semen was the youngest child in the family and had sixteen siblings. He graduated from the village school and worked as a farm laborer. In addition to Russian and Ukrainian, Timoshenko spoke the Moldovan dialect of the Romanian language.

In December 1914, Timoshenko was drafted into the Russian Imperial Army. In 1915, he graduated from Oranienbaum Machine Gun School and received the rank of *wachtmeister*. During the First World War, he served as a machine gunner on the Southwestern and Western Fronts. For his bravery, he was awarded the Cross of Saint George of the second, third, and fourth class. He was arrested after he struck an officer, but the February Revolution of 1917 saved him from a trial.

In 1918, Timoshenko joined the Red Army. He first commanded a platoon, then a squadron. In August 1918, he headed a cavalry regiment during the defense of Tsaritsyn. There he met Stalin (for whom the city would be renamed in 1925) and **K. Voroshilov** for the first time. In November 1918, Timoshenko was appointed commander of the 2nd Cavalry Brigade. In 1919, he became a member of the RCP(b). Between November 1919 and October 1921, he commanded the cavalry division of the 1st Cavalry Army under **S. Budenny** and Voroshilov. During this period, he became the closest associate of Budenny. In the 1st Cavalry Army, Timoshenko fought against White Army generals A. Shkuro, K. Mamontov, A. Denikin, and P. Wrangel. He also fought against the troops of N. Makhno and Polish troops headed by Josef Pilsudski. During the Civil War, Timoshenko was wounded five times but never left the front line. He was awarded three Orders of the Red Banner and the Honorary Revolutionary Weapon (it was awarded to senior commanders for exceptional combat achievement). He received the final one for participation in the Polish-Soviet War, in particular for the battles during the withdrawal of the 1st Cavalry Army from encirclement in Belarus.

Between 1922 and 1927, Timoshenko studied military-academic courses for the highest command personnel of the Red Army. In mid-January 1928, he led the 3rd Cavalry Corps. In 1930, he graduated from the Higher Military-Political Course of the N. G. Tolmachev Military-Political Academy. In August 1933, he was appointed deputy commander of the Red Army in the Belarusian SSR. In 1935, he was transferred to Kyiv, in 1937 to the North Caucasus, and in 1938 to Kyiv again. On February 8, 1939, he was appointed *komandarm* first rank. In 1939 he headed the troops of the entire western border region.

Timoshenko was able to survive the Great Purge due to his close and friendly relationship with Stalin. According to some sources, in 1935, when he became the deputy commander of the Kyiv Military District, the head of the NKVD. **N. Iezhov** included Timoshenko on the "blacklist." Timoshenko, who was sent to Italy in September 1935 as an observer of military drills, was suspected of espionage. But Stalin "saved" Timoshenko, who also evaded the purge of military officers in 1937.

During the Soviet invasion of Poland, between September 17 and October 2, 1939, Timoshenko commanded the Ukrainian Front. Under his leadership, Soviet troops captured Lviv, the main city in Western Ukraine. In 1939–1940, during the Soviet–Finnish War, he commanded the Northwestern Front. Under his leadership, Soviet troops succeeded in breaking through the Mannerheim Line after earlier setbacks under Voroshilov. On March 13, 1940, thanks to this successful operation, the USSR signed a peace treaty with Finland on its own terms. On March 21, 1940, Timoshenko was awarded with the title of Hero of the Soviet Union and with the award of the Order of Lenin and the Gold Star medal.

From May 7, 1940, to July 19, 1941, Timoshenko was people's commissar of defense of the USSR and a marshal of the Soviet Union. In this post, he tried to reorganize troops, improve their combat training, supervise technical reequipment, and train of new personnel (which was much needed due to a significant increase in the size of the army). Due to the outbreak of the **Great Patriotic War**, this reorganization was not fully completed. After the German invasion of the USSR, Marshal Timoshenko headed the Headquarters of the Supreme High Command (Stavka), which was formed on June 23, 1941, and included Stalin, **G. Zhukov**, **V. Molotov**, Voroshilov, Budenny, and N. Kuznetsov. Timoshenko failed to take effective measures to repel Hitler's aggression, and in July 1941, Stalin replaced him as people's commissar of defense and Stavka's chairman. On July 19, the Headquarters of the Supreme High Command was created under Stalin's command.

Until September 1941, Timoshenko remained the deputy people's commissar of defense of the USSR. Between July 2 and September 1941, Timoshenko was appointed commander of the Western Front. On July 10, he simultaneously headed the high command of the Soviet troops of the Western Direction Troops (he remained the commander-in-chief until the abolition of the high command on September 10, 1941). Between September 1941 and 1943, he commanded the Western, Southwestern, Stalingrad, and Northwestern Fronts. From March 1943 and until May 1945, he was a representative of the Stavka of the Soviet Armed Forces. In the fall of 1941, under Timoshenko's leadership, a Soviet counteroffensive was planned and carried out near Rostov-on-Don. As a representative of the Stavka, Timoshenko took an active part in the development and implementation of a number of important strategic operations of the Soviet troops. Freed from the burden of personal responsibility, Timoshenko turned out to be much more useful for the army. In a collegial discussion of offensive operations, the marshal's ideas turned out to be very useful. On June 4, 1945, Timoshenko was awarded the Order of Victory.

After the end of the war, for another fifteen years Timoshenko commanded various military districts and was appointed inspector-general of the Ministry of Defense of the USSR (mostly an honorary position). In 1965, on his seventieth anniversary, Timoshenko received his second star of Hero of the Soviet Union

Semen Timoshenko (left) with General G. K. Zhukov

"for services to the Motherland and the Armed Forces of the USSR." Timoshenko refused to write his memoirs because he believed that no one would publish the truth.

Timoshenko died on March 31, 1970. He was buried on Red Square in the Kremlin Wall.

TITO (JOSIP BROZ) (1892–1980). A Yugoslav communist revolutionary, politician, statesman, and military and party leader, Tito was head of the Communist Party of Yugoslavia (later the League of Communists of Yugoslavia) (1937–1980) and head of Yugoslavia from 1945 until his death in 1980—serving as both prime minister (1944–1963) and president (later president for life) (1953–1980), as leader of Yugoslav Partisans (1941–1945), and as marshal of Yugoslavia.

Josip Broz was born in the village of Kumrovec in the northern Croatian region of the Kingdom of Croatia-Slavonia, the Austro-Hungarian Empire (today Croatia). He was baptized in the Roman Catholic Church at birth. The father of the future Yugoslav leader, Franjo (Franz) Broz, was a Croat. Josip's mother, Maria Broz, née Javeršek, was Slovenian. Josip completed only four years of school, and throughout his life, his writing contained many grammatical errors. But at the same time, he had an extraordinary talent for studying foreign languages. At the end of his life, he spoke Serbo-Croatian, German, Czech, and Russian.

After school, Josip Tito worked at the family farm. As a child, Josip dreamed of becoming a tailor. He retained his passion for beautiful and elegant clothes throughout his life. His mother wanted him to become a priest, and his father wanted him to emigrate to the United States. However, the family was unable to raise money for a ticket to the United States, and 15-year-old Josip went to the city of Sisak in central Croatia, where he worked as a waiter. He did not like this job, and he decided to train as a locksmith. In September 1910, Josip completed his studies, became a qualified locksmith, and moved to Zagreb. In Zagreb, he joined the Metalworkers' Union and the Social Democratic Party of Croatia and Slavonia. At the end of 1911, in search of work, Tito moved to the Czech region of the Austro-Hungarian Empire, where he worked at Škoda plant in Pilsen. Later he also worked in Germany and Austria.

In May 1913, Broz was drafted into the Austro-Hungarian army. After the outbreak of the First World War (August 1914), Tito fought in the Serbian Campaign. In early January 1915, his regiment was transferred to Galicia on the Eastern Front. In the spring of 1915, in a battle on the Dniester, Josip was seriously wounded and captured by Russians. After falling into captivity, Broz spent thirteen months in Svyazhsk, Russia. In a camp hospital, located in the building of the Svyazhsk Assumption Cathedral, he was treated for pneumonia and typhus. During his stay in the hospital, with the help of two local schoolgirls, he learned the Russian language.

In mid-1916, Josip Broz recovered from pneumonia. The Russian authorities encouraged him to join the Serbian Volunteer Corps formed from prisoners, but he refused. He was transferred to a labor camp for prisoners of war (POW) in the city of Ardatov, Simbirsk province (now the Republic of Mordovia), where he worked at the mill. At the end of 1916, Broz was transferred to Kungur (a town in the southeast of Perm Krai) POW camp. There, he made his first contacts with Bolshevik workers and read Lenin's works.

In May, after the February Revolution of 1917, he was transferred to work at a station near Perm. From there he decided to flee to Petrograd. In the latter city, he was able to get a job at the Putilov munitions plant. Together with his fellow workers, Broz took part in the July Days demonstration against the provisional government. According to Broz himself, at that time he was not a faithful supporter of the Bolsheviks and simply participated in the demonstrations along with everyone else. After the failure of the protests, he fled to Finland but was captured by Russian police. By that time, Broz was fluent in Russian (he even spoke the Viatka dialect), so he was mistaken for a Russian and imprisoned in the Peter and Paul Fortress. Three weeks later, his identity was established, and he was sent to Kungur. Near Iekaterinburg, Josip managed to escape, and by the end of October 1917, he arrived in

Omsk. There, Broz joined the international detachment of the Red Guard, in which he served for several months. In the winter of 1917, he joined the Yugoslav section of the RSDWP(b). In 1918, Broz's detachment was defeated in a battle at Marianovka station, and the future Yugoslav leader fled to the village of Aleksandrovskoe near Omsk, where he hid for about a year. At the end of 1919, the village was occupied by the Red Army. At the end of 1920, Broz—together with his Russian wife, Pelageia Belousova—left Russia and went to the newly established Kingdom of Serbs, Croats, and Slovenes.

Upon his return, Broz became a member of the Communist Party of Yugoslavia (Komunistička partija Jugoslavije [KPJ]). In 1921, KPJ was declared illegal under the Yugoslav State Security Act. After the arrest of the KPJ leadership in January 1922, Broz started to work illegally for the party. While working as a party agitator, Broz received the nickname "Tito." Between 1925 and 1926, he worked at the shipyard in Kraljevica on the Adriatic coast. There he created and led the Communist Party organization. In 1926, he returned to Zagreb, where he became involved in the trade union movement. In 1927, he joined the KPJ's Committee in Zagreb. Since the Soviet authorities supported Broz, he rose rapidly in the ranks of the KPJ to the position of deputy of the Politburo of the KPJ Central Committee and headed the Croatian and Slovenian committees. In August 1928, Tito was arrested and accused of disseminating Communist propaganda. On February 21, 1929, he was sentenced to five years and seven months of hard labor. After his release in 1934, he immediately left Yugoslavia and returned to his revolutionary activities.

Between 1934 and 1936, Tito worked in the **Comintern** in Moscow. During this time, he also served as the director of the Publishing House of Foreign Workers in the USSR. In June 1935, he briefly met Stalin for the first time. In September 1936, the Comintern appointed Tito the organizational secretary of the KPJ in Moscow. One month later, he moved to Vienna. After the outbreak of the Spanish Civil War, in early December 1936, Tito was sent to Yugoslavia to recruit volunteers for the International Brigades to fight against the Francoists. In December 1937, he returned to Yugoslavia. During 1937–1938, Stalin purged the KPJ leadership. Most of Tito's associates, as well as his former and future spouses (Pelageia and Anna), were under suspicion of espionage. But Tito himself managed to survive Stalin's terror. In August 1937, after the arrest of Milan Gorkić (the general secretary of the KPJ), Tito took over the leadership of the KPJ. Between August 1938 and January 1939 and September to November 1939, he visited Moscow several times. In October 1940, Tito's status as general secretary of the KPJ was consolidated at the fifth underground party conference in Zagreb.

After Nazi Germany invaded Yugoslavia in 1941, the Communists were among the first to organize resistance. On July 4, 1941, Tito headed the Yugoslav Partisans (the National Liberation Army). Tito's Partisans were considered to be the most effective anti-Axis guerilla force in Europe during the Second World War. In 1944, around 650,000 partisans were organized in four field armies and fifty-two divisions. They were engaged in both guerilla and conventional warfare. The main goal was to liberate Yugoslavia from German invaders and to establish a multiethnic federal state. During the first months after the invasion, Tito's Partisans tried to cooperate with the Chetnik detachments during the war against the occupiers. In August–September, partisans and Chetniks conducted a number of joint operations. In September, Tito met Draža Mihailović, the leader of the Chetniks (the Chetnik Detachments of the Yugoslav Army—a Yugoslav, royalist, and Serbian nationalist movement and guerrilla force). However, ideological contradictions destroyed this shaky alliance. The Chetniks adopted a policy of collaboration with the occupying forces for almost all of the war, and they used terror tactics against Croats, Bosniaks, the Yugoslav Partisans, and their supporters. The Yugoslav government in exile broke off relations with Mihailović and recognized Tito as the supreme commander. The Americans and British both provided military assistance to the Yugoslav Partisans. On

May 25, 1944, German forces launched an operation (Operation Rösselsprung) aimed at capturing and killing Partisan leader Marshal Tito, but the operation failed.

On April 5, 1945, Tito signed an agreement with Stalin that allowed temporary entry of Soviet troops into the territory of Yugoslavia. Tito included into this agreement an important requirement: that the Soviet army would leave Yugoslavia once its "operational task" was completed. Together with units of the Red Army, Tito's Partisans liberated the country. For his role in the victory over the Axis powers in the fall of 1945, Tito became the last (excluding the later canceled award to **L. Brezhnev**) recipient of the Order of Victory.

On November 29, 1945, the Socialist Federal Republic of Yugoslavia (SFR Yugoslavia or simply Yugoslavia) was proclaimed, and Tito became its prime minister and minister of foreign affairs. Under his leadership, Yugoslavia started to pursue its own economic, internal, and foreign policy, but the country's objectives did not align with the interests of the Soviet Union and its Eastern Bloc allies. Steadily, Yugoslav relations with the USSR started to worsen (the conflict started to grow during the summer of 1947, when the United States intensified its support for western Europe). Finally, in 1948, the Tito-Stalin split occurred. One of the reasons for the split was the role of ideology. Yugoslavia claimed its own path to socialism, which deviated from the Marxist-Leninist line. Tito also overtly supported the uprising of the Greek Communists against the government, against Stalin's wishes. In addition, Tito did not want to give up on his territorial and political ambitions in the Balkans, in particular his expansionist foreign policy toward his country's neighbors (especially Albania). At some point Stalin's and Tito's interests clashed. On June 29, 1948, the Soviet press published a resolution of the Communist Information Bureau (Cominform) in which Yugoslav leaders were accused of deviating from the Marxist-Leninist line. Interstate and interparty ties with the USSR were broken. A propaganda campaign was launched from Moscow aimed at discrediting the Yugoslav leadership. During this period, Yugoslavia became closer to the United States and other NATO countries. The United States delivered a significant number of aircraft, tanks, and other weapons to Yugoslavia. Yugoslavia signed the Balkan Pact of 1953 (also called the Treaty of Friendship and Cooperation) with Greece and Turkey against Soviet expansion in the Balkans. Though Stalin had expected Tito to be overthrown, his subjects remained loyal to him.

In 1953, Tito was elected president of the country. He held the post until the end of his life. Under Khrushchev, who visited Yugoslavia in 1955, Soviet–Yugoslav relations were restored. In 1956, Tito approved the invasion of Soviet troops in Hungary, but in 1968 he condemned the invasion of Czechoslovakia by Warsaw Pact forces. In 1980, Tito fell seriously ill. In January he underwent an amputation of his left leg, but this did not improve his condition. He lay in a coma for over one hundred days.

Tito died in Ljubljana on May 4, 1980. He was buried in Belgrade, in the mausoleum "House of Flowers."

TOLBUKHIN, FEDOR IVANOVICH (1894–1949). A Soviet military commander, marshal of the Soviet Union (1944), Hero of the Soviet Union (1965, posthumously), chevalier of the Order of Victory (1945), People's Hero of Yugoslavia (1945), and Hero of the People's Republic of Bulgaria (1979, posthumously), Fedor Tolbukhin was born in the village of Androniki, 30 kilometers from Iaroslavl (Iaroslavl Province, the Russian Empire), into a large, prosperous Russian peasant family. His father, Ivan Feodorovich, traded forage in St. Petersburg. Fedor started his education at the parish school in Androniky and continued it in Davydkovo Zemstvo School. After the death of his father in 1907, he and his siblings were raised by his uncle Aleksandr, who was a merchant in St. Petersburg. Later, Fedor graduated from the Trading School of Tsarevich Aleksei, and in 1912, he was admitted to the St. Petersburg Imperial Commercial College. Simultaneously, from 1911, Fedor worked as an accountant in the commercial partnership "Klochkov and K."

In December 1914, after the outbreak of the First World War, Tobulkhin was drafted into the Russian Imperial Army. He was deployed as a motorcyclist and driver at the headquarters of the 6th Infantry Division and in the 22nd Infantry Regiment on the Northwestern Front. In 1915, he graduated from the Oranienbaum School of *Praporshchiki* (a junior officer rank in Imperial Russia) and was assigned to the 22nd Marching Reserve Brigade in Zhytomyr (now in Ukraine). From September 1915, he took part in battles on the Southwestern Front. Already during the First World War, Tolbukhin showed himself to be a talented commander. He participated in the Brusilov Offensive of 1916 against the Austro-Hungarian armies, which was initially quite successful. For his military achievements, he was awarded the Orders of St. Anne and St. Stanislav.

After the February Revolution of 1917, Tolbukhin was elected secretary, then chairman of the Soldiers' Committees. In March 1918, he was demobilized and worked in the 7th Military Road Detachment. After the beginning of the Civil War, in August 1918, Tolbukhin joined the Red Army. In 1919, he graduated from special courses at the headquarters of the Western Front and served at the headquarters of the 56th Infantry Division of the 7th Army on the Northern and Western Fronts. In December 1920, he was appointed chief of staff of the division. In this capacity, he took part in the Battle of Petrograd and fought against the troops of General N. Iudenich. He also participated in the Polish-Soviet War. In 1921, Tolbukhin took part in the suppression of the Kronstadt and East Karelian uprisings. For his participation in the Civil War, he was awarded the Order of the Red Banner.

After the Civil War, Tolbukhin continued his military career. In 1927 and 1929, he received advanced training for senior command personnel at the Frunze Military Academy. Between November 1930 and 1932, he served as chief of staff of the 1st Rifle Corps of the Leningrad Military District. In June 1934, he graduated from the Frunze Military Academy. From January 1935, he was appointed chief of staff of the 19th Rifle Corps of the Leningrad Military District. From September 1937, he became commander of the 72nd Infantry Division of the Kyiv Military District. In July 1938, he was appointed chief of staff of the Transcaucasian Military District.

Just two weeks after Germany's invasion of the USSR in June 1941, Major General Tolbukhin received an unusual order to plan and prepare a joint Anglo-Soviet invasion of Iran (Operation Countenance). It was necessary to prevent Germany from using Iran's oil and transport infrastructure against the USSR and Britain. The multipronged coordinated invasion started on August 25, 1941. In total, three Soviet armies (the 44th, 47th, and 53rd), with about one thousand tanks and several hundred aircraft, took part in the operation. The Iranians did not have time to organize resistance. The Shah of Iran, Reza Pahlavi, was forced to conclude a truce with Great Britain and the USSR. On September 15, 1941, the allies entered Tehran and took Iran under complete control. The Shah abdicated in favor of his son. Tolbukhin's operation was very successful and was conducted with minimal losses (forty soldiers and three aircraft). After the end of the operation, Tolbukhin negotiated the deployment of a contingent of the Soviet troops in large Iranian cities. The Red Army remained in Iran until May 1946 and was able to safeguard the so-called "Persian Corridor": a supply route through Iran into Soviet Azerbaijan, by which British aid and American Lend-Lease supplies were transferred to the USSR.

Around the same time, Tolbukhin developed the Crimean Operation. On December 28, 1941, Soviet troops started a powerful offensive and were able to recapture Kerch and Feodosia. The Kerch Peninsula was completely under the Red Army's control. The Germans withdrew part of their troops from Sevastopol, and Tolbukhin decided to gain a foothold in the recaptured positions. But the representative of the headquarters, Lev Mekhlis, demanded a Soviet attack. Tolbukhin refused, and he was removed from his post. Mekhlis's orders led to disaster. In May 1942, Soviet troops were defeated, with about 160,000 casualties and soldiers taken prisoner. Crimea and Sevastopol were lost for two years. The eight-month-long campaign to conquer the Crimea Peninsula is considered to be one of the bloodiest battles on the Eastern Front during the Second World War.

After Crimea, Tolbukhin was transferred to Stalingrad, where he commanded the 57th Army. His army blocked the German 4th Panzer Army in the southwest of the city. During the German attack, Tolbukhin paid special attention to the operational deployment of troops. His strategy was very successful. After months of difficult battles, he was still able to preserve the army's combat capability, and with the beginning of the counteroffensive, his troops actively participated in the destruction of the encircled enemy grouping. One of his important qualities was his calmness. It helped him make strategically important and correct decisions. For his achievements at the Battle of Stalingrad, Tolbukhin was awarded the Order of Suvorov first degree.

In January 1943, he was promoted to the rank of lieutenant general, and in September to general of the army. From February to March 1943, he was commander of the 68th Army on the Northwestern Front. From March 1943, Tolbukhin became commander of the Southern Front (on October 20, 1943, it was reorganized into the 4th Ukrainian Front) and, from May 1944, the 3rd Ukrainian Front. He led the troops during the liberation of Donbas, southern Ukraine, Crimea, Yugoslavia, Romania, Bulgaria, Hungary, and Austria. On September 12, 1944, when Soviet troops approached the western border of the Soviet Union, Tolbukhin was promoted to marshal of the Soviet Union. In September 1944, he was appointed the chairman of the Allied Control Commission in Bulgaria. On April 26, 1945, he was awarded the Order of Victory—the highest Soviet military order awarded only to generals and marshals for successfully conducting combat operations involving one or more army groups during the Second World War. On July 19, 1945, Tolbukhin, on behalf of the Soviet government, presented the Order of Victory to King Michael of Romania.

After the war, from July 1945, Marshal Tolbukhin was the commander-in-chief of the southern group of forces on the territory of Romania and Bulgaria. This group of forces was created to counter possible Turkish military actions in the Balkans (it was disbanded in February 1947). In December 1946, as part of the Soviet delegation, he participated in the Slavic congress. In January 1947, he was appointed commander of the Transcaucasian Military District. Tolbukhin also served as a deputy of the Supreme Soviet of the USSR (1946–1949).

Tolbukhin died of diabetes on October 17, 1949, in Moscow. He was cremated, and the urn with his ashes was buried in the Kremlin wall on Red Square.

TOMSKY, MIKHAIL PAVLOVICH (NÉE MIKHAIL PAVLOVICH IEFREMOV) (1880–1936). A Bolshevik; professional revolutionary; Soviet party leader; trade unionist; full member of the 11th, 12th, 13th, 14th, and 15th Politburo, and member of the CC CPSU, Tomsky was an ally of **Nikolai Bukharin** and **Aleksei Rykov**.

Mikhail Iefremov was born in Kolpino, St. Petersburg Governorate, into a lower-middle-class urban family. He graduated from the primary city school and started to work at various industrial enterprises of St. Petersburg. In the fall of 1904, he joined the Bolsheviks. He was an active participant of the Revolution of 1905. Also in 1905, Mikhail organized the Council of Workers' Deputies in Reval (now Tallinn, Estonia). In January 1906, he was arrested. After four months of imprisonment, he was deported to the Narym Krai (Tomsk) but was able to escape. Later he adopted the pseudonym Tomsky (naming himself after the city of his exile).

In August 1906, Tomsky arrived in St. Petersburg, where he was involved in party and trade union work. He became president of the Union of Engravers and Chromolithographers. In January 1907, he was elected to the St. Petersburg Committee of the RSDWP, and in spring he became a delegate to the fifth (London) congress of the RSDWP. At the congress he fully supported Lenin's ideas. In May 1909, he took part in the Paris meeting of the expanded editorial board of the illegal Bolshevik newspaper *Proletary*. The Central

Committee decided to send Tomsky from Paris to Moscow. In August 1909, he arrived in Moscow and organized a secret printing house, which printed the newspaper *Rabochee Znamia*. In December, he was arrested again. In November 1911, Tomsky was sentenced to five years of hard labor. In the spring of 1916, he was exiled to a settlement in the Kirensk district of the Irkutsk province.

After the February Revolution of 1917, in mid-April, Tomsky arrived in Petrograd and became a member of the new Petrograd Committee of the RSDWP(b). In July, he was transferred to Moscow, where he worked in the commission for elections to district councils. In the fall he became an editor of the magazine of the Moscow Union of Metalworkers, *Metallist*. During the October armed uprising in Moscow, the Moscow Military Revolutionary Committee sent Tomsky to Petrograd. On October 29, he had a meeting with Lenin, who promised to aid the Moscow Bolsheviks. In December 1917, Tomsky was elected chairman of the Moscow Council of Trade Unions.

In March 1919, Tomsky became a member of the Central Committee of the RCP(b). Between 1922 and 1930, he was a member of the Politburo. In 1920–1921 and 1924–1925, he was also a candidate member of the Orgburo of the CC CPSU. In 1925, together with Stalin, **Bukharin**, and **Rykov**, Tomsky opposed the "United Opposition" led by **Trotsky**, **Zinoviev**, and **Kamenev**. In January–February 1929, Tomsky, together with Bukharin and Rykov, opposed the cancellation of the **New Economic Policy** and the start of forced industrialization and collectivization. In April 1929, during the Central Committee Plenum, Stalin declared this position the "Right Opposition." The plenum decided to dismiss Tomsky from the post of chairman of the All-Russian Central Council of Trade Unions.

In 1930, Tomsky was removed from the Politburo, although he remained a member of the CC CPSU (from 1934, he was a candidate member). Henceforth, he did not take an active part in political life. In 1929, he was appointed chairman of the All-Union Association of the Chemical Industry, as well as deputy chairman of the Supreme Council of the National Economy of the USSR. From April 11, 1932, he worked as head of the United State Publishing House.

In August 1936, during the First Moscow trial (its official name was the "Trial of the Anti-Soviet United Trotskyite-Zinoviev Center"), Zinoviev and Kamenev unexpectedly began to testify about the involvement of Tomsky, Rykov, and Bukharin in counter-revolutionary activities. On August 22, 1936, **A. Vyshinsky** announced that the Prosecutor's Office had started an investigation into the activities of these persons. After the news about this investigation was published in the newspaper *Pravda*, Tomsky committed suicide by shooting himself at his dacha in the village of Bolshevo near Moscow. Before committing suicide, he wrote a letter to Stalin in which he stated that he had never taken part in any plots against the CPSU.

In late 1930s, the entire Tomsky family was repressed. His wife, Maria Ivanovna, was sentenced to ten years of confinement, and died in 1956 in Siberia. His eldest sons, Mikhail Mikhailovich and Viktor Mikhailovich, were arrested and shot. The youngest son, Iury Mikhailovich (1921–1997), received ten years in prison and nine years in exile, but ultimately survived.

TRILISSER, MIKHAIL ABRAMOVICH (NÉE MEIER ABRAMOVICH TRILISSER) (1883–1940). A professional revolutionary, one of the leaders of the Soviet state security organs, organizer of the foreign intelligence service, and Soviet chief of the Foreign Department of the Cheka, Meier Trilisser was born in Astrakhan into a large Jewish family. His father was a shoemaker. At the age of 10, he started to attend the city real school. After graduation in 1900, he went to Odesa to enter the university. In 1901, Trilisser joined the RSDWP and became a professional revolutionary. According to some sources, Lenin's brother D. Ulianov and R. Zemliachka, who created the Iskra organization in Odesa in 1901, played an important role in Trilisser's passion for revolutionary ideas. In this same year, he was arrested by the tsarist authorities and sent under police supervision to Astrakhan.

During the first Russian Revolution of 1905, Trilisser organized Bolshevik military organizations and led revolutionary propaganda in Kazan, St. Petersburg, and Finland. He was elected a member of the St. Petersburg Committee of the RSDWP(b). He was responsible for identification of police spies among the Bolshevik emigrants. In 1906, he was one of the organizers of the First Conference of the Military and Combat Organizations of the RSDWP in Tammerfors (now Tampere), Finland. The conference that was held in November 1906 supported the creation of an all-Russian military-combat organization and the total subordination of all military-combat work to the political leadership of party-wide organizations. In 1906, Trilisser received financial support from the Japanese envoy in Stockholm to buy weapons for the Bolsheviks and for anti-government agitation in Russia. He was associated with Finnish radical nationalists (the Finnish Active Resistance Party) who practiced terrorism and armed robberies to achieve their political goals. In 1907, Trilisser was arrested again. In 1910, he was sentenced to eight years of hard labor, but before completing this term, in November 1914, he was exiled to Siberia.

After the February Revolution of 1917, Trilisser was released and moved to Irkutsk. In Irkutsk, he worked as an editor of the social democratic newspaper *Voice of the Social-Democrat* and then in the military organization of the Irkutsk Bolshevik Committee. After the October Revolution, he became a member of the Central Executive Committee of Siberian Soviets (*Tsentrosibir*) and a member of the Military Revolutionary Committee of Siberia and Transbaikalia. From February 1918, he chaired the counterintelligence apparatus of the Revolutionary Investigative Commission at the Irkutsk Provincial Military Revolutionary Committee, which existed for several weeks until the government's decision to organize a local Cheka. In this capacity, he organized the fight against the anti-Bolshevik movement in Siberia.

Until 1921, Trilisser worked underground in Blagoveshchensk and organized a network of intelligence and secret communications of the Bolsheviks in the Far East. He also created a large agent network and supplied Moscow with information about Japanese actions and plans for White Army formations. After the departure of the Japanese troops, he became secretary of the Amur Regional Committee of the RCP(b), chairman of the Amur Regional Revolutionary Committee, and editor of the newspaper *Amurskaia Pravda*. In 1921, after the formation of the Far Eastern Republic, he was appointed its emissary in the Amur Region and a member of the State Political Guard, which performed counterintelligence tasks. He created the first special encryption service in the Soviet Far East for communication with Moscow and began to form a web of agents.

In February 1921, Trilisser took part in the work of the tenth congress of the RCP(b) in Moscow, and **Feliks Dzerzhinsky** offered him a job in the central apparatus of the **All-Russian Extraordinary Commission (Cheka)**. Dzerzhinsky wanted to establish a foreign intelligence system in the countries of Western and Eastern Europe. Trilisser accepted this offer, although he himself wanted to tackle the eastern region (China, Korea, Japan, and Mongolia). From December 1921, he worked as an assistant to the head of the Foreign Department (FD). At the same time, he was the head of the Far Eastern Department of the Executive Committee of the **Comintern**. In the Comintern he was involved in organizing revolutionary propaganda in Mongolia, China, and neighboring countries. In March 1922, he was appointed head of the GPU (the State Political Directorate) Foreign Department instead of S. Mogilevsky, who was sent to the Caucasus.

On December 19, 1922, by the decision of the Organizing Bureau of the Executive Committee of the Communist International (ECCI), Trilisser was included in the Permanent Illegal Commission of the Executive Committee of the Comintern, together with I. Piatnitsky, G. Eberlein, and E. Prukhniak. During this period, Trilisser was responsible for organizing the entire system of external (overseas) intelligence of the Cheka-GPU, establishing the work of residencies and selecting Soviet intelligence personnel. In each Soviet embassy, representative office, and trade mission, the residence network was organized. These networks were responsible for recruiting agents. Trilisser traveled abroad, where he arranged residencies and kept direct contacts with his agents. He helped to organize the "Trust" operation and played an important role in arrest and execution of British super-spy Sidney Reilly.

In 1925, Dzerzhinsky, who was also a chairman of the Supreme Council of the National Economy of the USSR, set the Foreign Department the task of obtaining economic, scientific, and technical information about achievements in foreign countries. In 1926, the Economic Division was organized at the FD OGPU. Dzerzhinsky and **V. Menzhinsky**, who oversaw intelligence, highly valued the work of Trilisser, and in 1926 he was appointed deputy head of the OGPU. Simultaneously, he headed foreign intelligence until October 1929, when he accused **G. Iagoda** of "indulging the rightists" (so-called "Trilisser fever"). Iagoda understood that Trilisser was a dangerous enemy and engineered his removal through the Central Committee.

After a series of failures in intelligence and the appearance of defectors in overseas residencies, in December 1930, Stalin transferred Trilisser to the Workers' and Peasants' Inspectorate (Rabkrin), in which he worked from 1930 to 1934. At the 17th congress of the CC CPSU in 1934, he was elected a member of the Soviet Control Commission for the Far Eastern Territory under the Council of People's Commissars of the USSR. In 1935–1938, he served as a member of the Presidium and a candidate member of the Secretariat of the Executive Committee of the Comintern, where he worked under the name Mikhail Aleksandrovich Moskvin.

On November 23, 1938, Trilisser was removed from all posts, expelled from the CPSU, and arrested. He was sentenced to death by the Military Collegium of the Supreme Court. On February 2, 1940, he was shot in Kommunarka, the NKVD execution site in Moscow Oblast. In 1957 he was rehabilitated.

TROTSKY, LEON/LEV (NÉE LEV DAVIDOVICH BRONSTEIN) (1879–1940). Trotsky was a Russian revolutionary, Soviet politician, one of the organizers and leaders of the October Revolution of 1917, one of the founders of the Red Army, one of the founders and ideologist of the **Comintern**, people's commissar of foreign affairs in the first Soviet government, people's commissar of military and naval affairs (1918–1925), the chairman of the Revolutionary Military Council of the RSFSR (then the USSR) from 1923, the leader of the "Left Opposition," and a member of the Politburo of the CC CPSU (1919–1926).

Lev Bronstein was born near village Ianovka, Kherson Governorate, in the Russian Empire (present-day Bereslavka, Kirovohrad Oblast in central Ukraine), into a wealthy Jewish family. His parents, David Leontevich (1843–1922) and Anna Lvovna Bronstein (née Zhivotovskaia), were wealthy farmers and grain merchants from a large Jewish community. At the age of seven, Lev attended a Jewish religious school, which he did not finish. Between 1889 and 1895, he studied at the St. Paul's School in Odesa, where he received an excellent education in different disciplines. According to Bronstein himself, after school he spoke Russian, Ukrainian, French, English, and German. Anton Gamow, the father of the famous Russian–American theoretical physicist and cosmologist Georgy Gamow, was among his teachers.

In 1896, Lev moved to Mykolaiv (Nikolaev), where he studied at the city's Realschule. Upon his graduation, Bronstein began to attend lectures at the Faculty of Mathematics of Odesa University. But very quickly, he became interested in revolutionary ideas and lost interest in his studies. First, he became interested in the Narodnik (Populist) movement, later in socialist ideas. At the university he met radical, revolutionary-minded youth and took part in the creation of the "South Russian Workers' Union." After one year of studies, Lev left the university and got a job at a shipyard in Mykolaiv. This post gave him a perfect opportunity to carry out revolutionary agitation among the workers. Steadily he started to read Karl Marx's works and subsequently became a fanatical adherent of Marxism (though initially he did not support this ideology). Bronstein firmly believed in internationalism, which was one of Marx's central tenets: "The workers have no Fatherland." He did not feel himself Russian or Jewish, and he did not feel either love or hate toward any nation. He believed that all nations were only material for the world revolution.

On January 28, 1898, Bronstein was arrested for the first time and spent two years in Odesa prison. There he was greatly impressed by the warden, Nikolai Trotsky, who held in obedience some one thousand prisoners, other guards, and the head of the prison. He became a role model for Lev, who later chose the surname "Trotsky" as his new pseudonym in his fake passport. Lev was sentenced to four years of exile in Eastern Siberia. Between 1900 and 1902, he lived in Irkutsk. There he worked as a clerk for a Siberian merchant and collaborated with the Irkutsk newspaper *Vostochnoe Obozrenie* (Eastern Review). Bronstein's works were published in Europe and attracted the attention of the leaders of the RSDWP. In the fall of 1902, they helped to arrange his escape from Siberia. Local Marxists handed him a new passport, in which Lev wrote his new surname, "Trotsky." In August 1902, Trotsky left his wife and two daughters in Siberia and fled abroad.

In October 1902, he arrived in London and immediately established contact with the leaders of the RSDWP. Lenin highly appreciated Trotsky's abilities and energy and proposed that he work at the editorial office of *Iskra* (*The "Spark"*), the political newspaper of Russian socialist emigrants established as the official organ of the RSDWP. During that period, Trotsky strongly supported Lenin's policies and even received the nickname "Lenin's truncheon." But such harmony did not last long. Already in 1903, he sided with the Mensheviks and began to accuse Lenin of promoting policies that would lead to a dictatorship. But his relations with leaders of the Mensheviks were also problematic, and in 1904, Trotsky started to advocate for the unification of the two factions (Bolsheviks and Mensheviks). This idea caused great political disagreement. As a result, Trotsky proclaimed himself a "non-factional" member of the RSDWP.

When revolution broke out 1905, Trotsky returned to St. Petersburg and, in October 1905, took an active part in the work of the Petersburg Soviet, becoming one of its three co-chairmen. He also worked as an editor of the newspaper *Izvestiia*. Throughout this period, Trotsky, together with Aleksandr Parvus (Israel Gelfand), developed the theory of the so-called "permanent (continuous) revolution." The theory postulated that revolution in Russia could only succeed if accompanied by revolutions in the more advanced industrial countries of Europe. By 1905, Trotsky had shown himself to be an outstanding leader, organizer, orator, and publicist. His revolutionary activities soon saw him imprisoned again. At the end of 1906, Trotsky was sentenced to exile in Siberia and deprived of all civil rights, but in February 1907, he was able to flee abroad.

Between 1907 and 1917, Trotsky lived in exile in Europe and the United States. In 1908, he moved to Vienna (then capital of the Austro-Hungarian Empire, now Austria), where he published the non-factional Social Democratic newspaper *Pravda*. In 1912, on Lenin's initiative, the Bolsheviks started to publish a newspaper with the same name in St. Petersburg. On April 23, 1912, the last issue of the Vienna newspaper was published. It was the period of the most serious disagreements between Lenin and Trotsky. In his telegrams and letters, Lenin insulted Trotsky and called him "*podlets iz podleisov*" (scoundrel of scoundrels) and "*iudushka*" ("Judas"/traitor). At the end of August 1912, a "unification" conference of the Social Democratic factions, organized and chaired by Trotsky, took place in Vienna. During this conference, Trotsky, without success, tried to unite the warring factions ("the August Bloc").

Between 1912 and 1913, Trotsky worked as war correspondent for the newspaper *Kievskaia Mysl* (*Kyivan Thought*) and covered events of the Balkan Wars. Later, during the Soviet era, Trotsky's collection of the war articles was republished as a six-volume collection under the title *The Balkans and the Balkan War* (1926). For Trotsky, the experience earned during this time helped to prepare him for the revolutionary year of 1917. In 1914, after the outbreak of the First World War, Trotsky and his family fled from Vienna to

Zurich, Switzerland. There he wrote a brochure titled "War and the International," which criticized the Social Democratic parties in Western Europe for supporting their governments in this war and claimed that "after the war, the Federal Republic of Europe—the United States of Europe—should be re-created not by diplomats, but by the proletariat." During the war, Trotsky also lived in France. In Paris, he joined the editorial office of the left socialist newspaper *Nashe Slovo* (*Our Word*).

In 1915, Trotsky participated in the Zimmerwald Socialist Conference, the first of three international conferences organized by antimilitarist socialist parties from countries that were originally neutral during the First World War. In 1916, the French authorities exiled Trotsky to Spain for his anti-war propaganda. In Spain, he was arrested and deported to the United States. The revolutionary did not expect a quick change of power in the Russian Empire and anticipated staying in New York City for a lengthy period. From January 1917, Trotsky worked for several socialist-oriented Russian-language newspapers. Trotsky studied the U.S. statistics of that period, and this information led him to the belief that America would play a decisive role in postwar world development. He also was active in politics: his speeches at rallies and "political banquets" were very successful. In addition, he gathered a group of supporters from among the members of the Socialist Party around him and took part in the creation of the newspaper *Class Struggle*.

Trotsky left the United States after the February Revolution, when the amnesty for political emigrants was announced in Russia. He welcomed the revolution as the beginning of the world's "permanent revolution." On his way to Russia, Trotsky was interned by the British naval authorities in the Canadian city of Halifax and was accused of receiving "German money" for the purpose of overthrowing the provisional government. He was imprisoned in Amherst Internment Camp in Nova Scotia. Lenin actively contributed to his release.[2] Despite past political differences, Lenin defended Trotsky in *Pravda*. In his April address "To the Soldiers and Sailors," as well as in the text "Against the Pogromists," Lenin also wrote that the arrest of "Comrade" Trotsky proved the powerlessness of the provisional government against England and France. After the new intervention of the Petrograd Soviet, Minister Pavel Miliukov was forced to turn to the British authorities with an official request for the release of Trotsky's group. On April 20, the detainees received permission to proceed further. Lenin's intervention was not the only reason for Trotsky's release, but it was an important factor. While in the camp, Trotsky successfully continued his propaganda work among German prisoners of war.

On May 17, Trotsky reached Russia and, within a few months, became the informal leader of the "Mezhraiontsy" (the Russian Social Democratic Labor Party [Internationalists]), who advocated the creation of a single Russian Social Democratic Workers' Party and opposed the provisional government. In April 1917, Trotsky supported Lenin's April Theses, in particular the idea of an immediate transition to a "socialist revolution." Trotsky became one of the chief propagandists among soldiers and sailors. He paid special attention to the Kronstadt sailors, among whom were a lot of anarchists.

In June 1917, at the First All-Russian Congress of Soviets of Workers' and Soldiers' Deputies, he was elected to its permanent body: the All-Russian Central Executive Committee (VTsIK). During the July Days (July 16–20), Trotsky supported the Bolsheviks, who helped to organize spontaneous armed demonstrations by soldiers, sailors, and industrial workers against the Russian provisional government, though Lenin felt the moment was premature for a full-scale revolution. The provisional government blamed the Bolshevik Party for organizing the violence during the July Days and arrested many of its leaders. Lenin managed to escape and flew to Finland. According to one source, Trotsky was arrested by the provisional government and spent a month in a prison,[3] but according to another,[4] in 1917, he did not appear on the list of those Bolsheviks whom the provisional government had designated for arrest. In August 1917, Trotsky together with a group of "Mezhraiontsy" was admitted in absentia to the Bolshevik Party and was elected to its governing body, the Central Committee of the RSDWP(b).

In September 1917, Trotsky was elected chairman of the Petrograd Soviet of Workers' and Soldiers' Deputies. He also was elected to the Pre-Parliament (Provisional Council of the Russian Republic), became a delegate to the second Congress of Soviets, and (after the October Revolution) was elected to the Russian Constituent Assembly. In Lenin's absence, the role of the leader of the Bolsheviks passed to Trotsky. In October, Trotsky, as chairman of the Petrograd Soviet, formed the Petrograd Military Revolutionary Committee, which consisted mainly of Bolsheviks and Left Socialist Revolutionaries. The main pretext for the formation of the Military Revolutionary Committee was a possible German offensive against Petrograd, or a repetition of the Kornilov putsch.

The Military Revolutionary Committee became the main body for the preparation of an armed uprising. Immediately after its formation, it began propaganda activities aimed to encourage units of the Petrograd garrison to support them. On October 16, Trotsky ordered the distribution of five thousand rifles to soldiers. Between October 21 and 23, the Bolsheviks held a series of rallies among wavering soldiers. Trotsky's oratorical skills greatly helped the Bolsheviks to win over the vacillating parts of the garrison to their side. Trotsky organized the defense of Petrograd from the attack of Cossacks of General Piotr Krasnov and other troops, who still supported the overthrown provisional government. In practice, Trotsky was one of the main leaders of the October Revolution. Trotsky also supported Lenin in the struggle against plans to create a coalition government of all socialist parties. He supported the establishment of a one-party dictatorship, the prohibition of non-Bolshevik media, and the use of mass terror against political opponents and untrustworthy groups.

After the Bolshevik victory, Trotsky entered the first Soviet government as the people's commissar of foreign affairs (a position without honor, he believed, and a completely unnecessary post). After taking up his position, Trotsky did not consider it necessary to develop a long-term foreign policy program for the Republic, since he was sure that the revolution would sweep away all borders, and there would be no more need for diplomats. Nevertheless, he had a meeting with former Foreign Ministry officials and said that the new government still needed these employees to remain at their posts. He also asked them to translate into foreign languages and send out to the leaders of foreign states the "Decree on Peace" adopted by the Congress of Soviets. In addition, Trotsky expressed a desire to review all secret treaties signed during the past five years. The ministry officials refused to cooperate with the new government and claimed that the texts of agreements with the allies were in different departments, and Trotsky had to find them himself. After his unsuccessful visit, Trotsky never returned to the Foreign Ministry building. Some former Russian diplomats who decided to stay at the ministry—including Dolivo-Dobrovolsky, Petrov, Voznesensky, and Polevanov, together with Nikolai Markin, Trotsky's close associate—organized translations and publication of secret documents. Already in December, the bulk of the classified documents were published in periodicals.

In this post, Trotsky unsuccessfully tried to achieve recognition of the Bolshevik government by the Entente states. In January, he headed the Bolshevik delegation during negotiations on the Treaty of Brest-Litovsk (a separate peace treaty signed on March 3, 1918, between the new Bolshevik government and the Central Powers—the German Empire, the Austria-Hungarian Empire, Bulgaria, and the Ottoman Empire). In the belief that the "world revolution" would begin soon, Trotsky tried to drag out negotiations. This strategy led to a sharp tightening of German demands. Trotsky wanted to declare the end of the war and at the same time to refuse to conclude peace (the tactics of "no war, no peace"). On February 9 (January 28), 1918, he announced the withdrawal of Russia from the war and gave an order for the general demobilization of the army, which was later canceled by Lenin. Trotsky's actions led to disorganization on the fronts and contributed to the success of the German offensive that began on February 18. Lenin, who initially advocated for the immediate signing of the agreement with Germany, managed to convince his fellow party members to accept the German conditions. Even though Germany put forward additional demands, the Central Committee of the RSDWP(b), from which Lenin threatened to resign if his demands were not met, voted to agree to sign the "obscene peace."

In March 1918, Trotsky, who had no military education and had never served in the army himself, was appointed to several key military positions in the newly formed Soviet Republic. He became chairman of the Supreme Military Council of the RSFSR and people's commissar of military and naval affairs of the RSFSR. Simultaneously, from September, he served as a chairman of the Revolutionary Military Council. In these posts, Trotsky became one of the key founders and the first commander-in-chief of the Workers' and Peasants' Red Army (RKKA).

Before the summer of 1918, the Red Army existed mostly on paper and was very small (due to the then-existing principles of voluntary recruitment), was poorly controlled, and had low combat readiness. Trotsky took up the formation of a new Red Army by taking tough measures. He supported the idea of universal conscription and abolition of the election of commanders, formed the institution of political commissars in military units, and through repressive measures introduced strict discipline among the troops. He ordered the imprisonment and execution of all disciplinary offenders and deserters, not even sparing those who were Bolsheviks. Trotsky's Red Army practiced the tactic that became a part of the Soviet campaign of political repression and mass killings, known as the "Red Terror." On Trotsky's initiative, the Red Army began to involve officers of the former Imperial Army (military experts or *voienspetzy*). In order to achieve their loyalty, on September 5, 1918, the people's commissar signed an order to take members of the families of military experts hostage.

In August 1918, Trotsky gave an order to create a personal armored train for his own usage. "Trotsky's train" allowed him to move quickly along the fronts of the Civil War. For two and a half years, he basically lived in it and became the true "military leader" of Bolshevism. Largely thanks to the people's commissar's train, Trotsky was able to take an active part in the formation of the Red Army and its first victories. As a result, he firmly consolidated power and his position in the highest layers of the Bolshevik party-state hierarchy. In addition to military affairs, he worked closely with Lenin on issues of domestic and foreign policy. When the **Comintern** was created in 1919, Trotsky became the author of its manifesto. He also became increasingly interested in economic questions.

On March 25, 1919, the Central Committee decided to reestablish the Politburo and appointed Trotsky, Lenin, Stalin, **L. Kamenev**, and **N. Krestinsky** its first members. Trotsky remained in this post until October 23, 1927. By the beginning of 1920, the Red Army under the leadership of Trotsky had managed to achieve decisive success in the Civil War. During the revolution and the Civil War, Trotsky became de facto the second person in the state. The Bolsheviks' powerful propaganda machine, of which he was a founder, endowed him with the heroic halo of "the leader of the victorious Red Army." By the end of the Civil War, his popularity and influence reached its climax, and a cult of his personality began to take a shape.

In January 1920, he headed the 1st Labor Army. On March 20, 1920, Trotsky was appointed the people's commissar of railways of the RSFSR. In this post, Trotsky established himself as a zealous supporter of the militarization of national economy. Between the end of 1920 and the spring of 1921, during the trade-union debate—a political discussion inside the Bolshevik party on the role of the trade unions in RSFSR—Trotsky advocated the general militarization of all industries and the working class. Lenin sharply criticized Trotsky, and this debate split the party into several factions. The Central Committee was split between Lenin's and Trotsky's supporters. In March 1921, during the tenth party congress, Lenin's faction won, and a secret resolution on "party unity," which banned factional activity, was adopted.

Later Stalin would use this resolution against Trotsky. At the end of the congress, Trotsky gave the order to suppress the Kronstadt rebellion. He also approved chemical warfare by gas shells and balloons in case of continuation of resistance. In 1922, Trotsky developed a scheme to confiscate the vast wealth of the Orthodox Church. The decree ordering the requisition of church objects containing jewels and other valuables that could be exchanged for hard currency was signed.

In 1922, Trotsky again became close to Lenin. But Lenin's health worsened, and a struggle for power flared up among the leaders of the Bolsheviks. At first, it seemed that Stalin, who did not have oratorical talent, had no chance in the fight against the world-famous "demon of revolution." Trotsky considered his leadership in the party to be a decided affair and did not think that Stalin—an "outstanding mediocrity"—could bypass him. But after Lenin's death, the bitter struggle between Trotsky and Stalin for leadership ended in Trotsky's defeat. On January 18, 1924 (just a few days before Lenin's death), the 16th party conference accused Trotsky of organizing factional activity. Trotsky's views (so-called Trotskyism) were declared a "petty-bourgeois deviation." In February 1924, the commission organized by the "troika" (Zinoviev-Kamenev-Stalin) identified "collapse" in the army. Under the pretext of strengthening the army's leadership, many of Trotsky's opponents, including **K. Voroshilov**, were appointed to top posts. During 1924, Trotsky gradually lost control of the army.

In May 1924, at the 16th congress of the Russian Communist Party, Trotsky was criticized once more. It was the first public confrontation between "troika" and Trotsky's Left Opposition. In January 1925, the Politburo removed Trotsky from the post of people's commissar and appointed him chairman of the Electrotechnical Committee. In October 1926, he was removed from the Politburo and the CC CPSU. In January 1928, he was expelled from the party and exiled to Almaty, Kazakhstan. In January 1929, he was accused of anti-Soviet activities and by decision of the Politburo was expelled from the USSR. Initially, he went to Turkey. In 1932, he was stripped of his Soviet citizenship.

Between 1929 and 1933, Trotsky, together with his wife and eldest son, Lev Sedov, lived in the Princes' Islands (Sea of Marmara, Turkey). In 1933, he moved to France, and in 1935, to Norway but without any semblance of permanence given the reluctance of the respective governments to harbor such a well-known revolutionary. At the end of 1936, he left Europe and settled in the Coyoacán area of Mexico City at the home of famous painters Diego Rivera and Frida Kahlo. Later, he moved to a fortified and heavily guarded villa. Trotsky continued to conduct active political and journalistic activities. In 1938, he and his supporters organized the Fourth International, which was supposed to become a revolutionary socialist international organization opposing both capitalism and Stalinism. In 1938, Trotsky's eldest son, Lev Sedov, died in a hospital in Paris.

On May 24, 1940, Soviet Special Services organized an attempt to murder Trotsky. His house was shelled, but he survived a raid. The group of terrorists was led by the Mexican artist and communist José (David) Alfaro Siqueiros. But during a second attempt, on August 20, 1940, Trotsky was mortally wounded by Spanish-born NKVD agent Ramón Mercader, who attacked him with an ice pick. Trotsky died on August 21. He was cremated and buried in the courtyard of his home in Coyoacán.

During the last years of his life, Trotsky worked on the second volume of the book *Stalin*, where he developed the hypothesis that Stalin had poisoned Lenin.

Trotsky was rehabilitated on June 16, 2001, by the General Prosecutor's Office of the Russian Federation, much later than most of his fellow revolutionaries.

TSUKERMAN, VLADIMIR MOISEEVICH (1891–1937). A Soviet orientologist-practitioner, diplomat in Central Asia and Iran, head of the Middle Eastern and First Eastern Departments, recipient of the Order of the Red Banner of Labor, and one of the defendants in the "Kremlin case," Vladimir Tsukerman was born in Simferopol, Crimea, into a Jewish family. Despite the fact that he only received a secondary education, he was able to build a prominent diplomatic career. First, he was appointed acting plenipotentiary representative of the RSFSR in the Bukhara Khanate. In 1920, he became deputy head of the Department of Foreign Relations of the Turkestan Commission of the All-Russian Central Executive Committee and the Council of People's Commissars of the RSFSR (from August, acting head of the department). Simultaneously, until 1921, he served as deputy commissioner of the People's Commissariat for Foreign Affairs of the RSFSR in Central Asia. From December 1920 and into 1921, Tsukerman was chairman of the Extraordinary Investigative Commission for the investigation of the case of the Khorezm Representative Office of the Turkestan Autonomous Soviet Socialist Republic in the city of Khiva. Tsukerman was a member of the Presidium of the Middle East section of the All-Russian Scientific Association for Oriental Studies, which was created on December 13, 1921, at the People's Commissariat of Nationalities. He also headed the First Eastern Department of the People's Commissariat for Foreign Affairs of the USSR.

On May 17, 1937, Tsukerman was arrested and charged with espionage. On August 20, 1937, Tsukerman's name was included on the Stalinist execution list. He was sentenced to death by Stalin, **Molotov**, **Kosior**, **Voroshilov**, and **Kaganovich**. On August 22, 1937, the verdict was formally approved at a meeting by the Military Collegium of the Supreme Court of the USSR. Tsukerman was executed the same day. He was rehabilitated posthumously on May 9, 1957.

TUKHACHEVSKY, MIKHAIL NIKOLAYEVICH (1893–1937). A Soviet military leader, military theorist, and marshal of the Soviet Union (1935), Mikhail Tukhachevsky was born in Aleksandrovskoe, Safonovsky District, Smolensk Governorate (today, Smolensk Oblast, Russia). His father, Nikolai Nikolaevich Tukhachevsky, was an impoverished Smolensk hereditary nobleman, and his mother, Mavra Petrovna Milokhova, was a peasant woman. Tukhachevsky had eight siblings. Since his childhood, Mikhail had dreamed of a military career. In 1912, after graduating from the 1st Moscow Cadet Corps, he entered the Aleksandrovsk Military School.

In July 1914, after the outbreak of the First World War, he joined the Semenovsky Regiment. As a part of the 1st Guards Division, he took part in battles with the Austrians and Germans on the Western Front. He participated in the Lublin, Ivangorod, and Lomzhinsky operations. He was wounded, and for his heroism, he was awarded five orders of various degrees over a six-month period. In February 1915, near the town of Kolno in Poland, he was taken prisoner by the Imperial German Army. After four unsuccessful attempts to escape, he was sent to a concentration camp in Ingolstadt (Bavaria), where he met Charles de Gaulle. In September 1917, he made a fifth escape attempt and was successful. In October, he returned to Russia through France, England, Norway, and Sweden and returned to his regiment.

In March 1918, Tukhachevsky voluntarily joined the Red Army and worked in the Military Department of the All-Russian Central Executive Committee. He joined the RCP(b) in the early spring of 1918 and was appointed military commissar of the Moscow region of defense. On June 26 of the same year, he was appointed commander of the 1st Army of the Eastern Front. From January 1919, he was transferred to the Southern Front, where he was appointed assistant front commander and commander of the 8th Army. In April 1919, Tukhachevsky was appointed commander of the 5th Army, which took part in the counteroffensive operations on the Eastern Front, in Zlatoust and Cheliabinsk, and helped to liberate the Urals and Siberia from the troops of Aleksandr Kolchak. During these operations, Tukhachevsky demonstrated outstanding organizational skills and military talent. His army played an important role in the defeat of the White Guard troops. In 1920, during the Polish-Soviet War, he commanded the Western Front, which was defeated by the Poles during the Battle of Warsaw.

Toward the end of the civil war, Tukhachevsky headed the 7th Army, and in March 1921 his troops suppressed the uprising in Kronstadt. He was also sent to put down the Tambov Rebellion. During this operation, Tukhachevsky received permission from Antonov-Ovseenko's commission to use chemical weapons (poison gas) against Tambov peasants, which led to very heavy casualties among civilians. Even his companions in arms noted the exceptional cruelty of the military leader. Tukhachevsky announced that total war, scorched-earth tactics, and summary execution were to be used against recalcitrant peasants. Around fifty thousand people, including nearly one thousand children, were imprisoned in concentration camps.

After the war, Tukhachevsky headed the Academy of the General Staff, which under his leadership was renamed the Military Academy of the Red Army. At the beginning of 1922, he was appointed commander of the Western Front. In April 1924, the Western Front was transformed into the Western Military District, and Tukhachevsky became the assistant chief and military commissar of the Red Army Headquarters. From July 1924, he was deputy chief of staff of the Red Army, and at the same time, from October 1, 1924, he was chief director of the Military Academy of the Red Army for strategy. After the death of **M. Frunze**, Tukhachevsky was appointed chief of staff of the Red Army and a member of the Revolutionary Military Council. He took part in the military reform of 1924–1925. From May 1928, he was commander of the Leningrad Military District. In 1931, Tukhachevsky became deputy people's commissar of military and naval affairs and chairman of the Revolutionary Military Council of the USSR and chief of armaments of the Red Army. In 1934, he was appointed deputy people's commissar of defense and, in April 1936, first deputy people's commissar of defense and head of the Combat Training Directorate. He was one of the initiators of the creation of a number of military academies. As a military leader and theorist, he paid attention to the nature of a future war. He also worked on development of the military doctrine of the Soviet Union. Tukhachevsky took part in the work of the commission (chaired by **K. Voroshilov**) at the military department of the *Great Soviet Encyclopedia*. He was a member of the editorial boards of several military scientific journals and wrote more than forty military theoretical works.

In 1933, Tukhachevsky was awarded the Order of Lenin, and in 1935, he was made a marshal of the Soviet Union (he was one of the first five Soviet marshals). His reforms in the armed forces and his views on preparing the army for a future war were met with resistance and opposition in the People's Commissariat of Defense. For various reasons, other marshals—including Voroshilov and **S. Budenny**—and commanders **P. Dybenko** and I. Belov disliked him. In turn, a number of military leaders (Ia. Gamarnik, P. Uborevich, I. Iakir, and others) developed a critical attitude toward Voroshilov's activities at the post of people's commissar of defense. However, Stalin sided with Voroshilov, and on May 11, 1937, Tukhachevsky was transferred to the post of commander of the Volga Military District.

On May 22, 1937, Marshal Tukhachevsky was detained on false charges of conspiracy with Nazi Germany against the current leadership of the USSR. By a court's decision on June 12, 1937, Tukhachevsky was found guilty and sentenced to death. From the courtroom, Tukhachevsky and other defendants were taken to the basement of the Military Collegium building and shot. A wave of mass repressions in the Red Army began. Tukhachevsky's wife and brothers were shot. His daughter and three sisters were sent to the gulag. His mother died in exile.

On January 31, 1957, marshal of the Soviet Union Mikhail Nikolaevich Tukhachevsky was rehabilitated by the decision of the Military Collegium of the Supreme Court of the USSR.

NOTES

1. V. I. Lenin, "V Revvoensovet respubliki," in *Leninskiy sbornik XXXV* (OGIZ: Gosudarstvennoe izdanie politicheskoy literatury, 1945), 73, http://nlr.ru/domplekhanova/dep/artupload/dp/article/RA3722/NA35944.pdf.
2. See, for example, Yu. Felshtinsky and G. Chernyavsky, "Novoye vozvrashcheniye v Rossiyu. Mezhrayonnaya gruppa," in *Lev Trotsky. Kniga 1. Revolyutsioner. 1879–1917* (Moscow: Tsentrpoligraf, 2012).
3. Ian D. Thatcher, *Trotsky* (London: Routledge, 2002), 83.
4. "Stenogrammy Sudov vremeni," 23. "Trotsky," *Tsentr Kurginyana*, accessed September 1, 2021, www.kurginyan.ru/publ.shtml?cmd=add&cat=3&id=133.

U

UGLANOV, NIKOLAI ALEKSANDROVICH (1886–1937). A prominent Bolshevik and Moscow party boss who was closely associated with **Nikolai Bukharin** and the so-called "Right Deviation," Nikolai Uglanov was born in the village of Feodoritskoe, Iaroslavl Governorate, into a Russian peasant family. He graduated from a village school, and from 1898 he started to work as an apprentice in a warehouse. Later, he followed his father and worked in St. Petersburg. In 1903, he joined the Social Democratic movement. He was an active participant in the Russian Revolution of 1905. In 1907, Uglanov joined the Bolshevik faction of the RSDWP.

Between 1908 and 1911, Uglanov carried out his military service and rose to the rank of noncommissioned officer. After demobilization, he lived in St. Petersburg and worked as a salesman. He also worked in trade unions and the magazine *Salesman's Bulletin* (*Vestnik prikazchika*), where he published articles under the pseudonym *Nikolai Ugriumy* (Gloomy). As a Bolshevik, he took part in meetings and demonstrations. In 1912, he was appointed chairman of the trade union of trade and industrial employees of St. Petersburg. On November 23, 1913, Uglanov was arrested for his revolutionary and propaganda activities but was soon released.

In 1914, with the outbreak of the First World War, Uglanov was inducted into the Imperial Army and sent to the front. He fought near Warsaw and was badly wounded. He was treated in a hospital in Moscow, where he met the prominent Bolshevik **V. M. Molotov**. After leaving the hospital, he deserted from the army and lived illegally in Petrograd. Soon he was arrested, and in the summer of 1916, he was sent to a reserve regiment in Petrograd.

Uglanov was an active participant of the February and October revolutions of 1917. After the February Revolution, he worked at the trade union. He met Lenin for the first time in the summer. After the October Revolution of 1917, he became one of the organizers of the Red Guard in Petrograd. He was also engaged in the formation of the apparatus of the Council of People's Commissars and food squads. For some time, he worked at the Petrograd Food Committee. From 1918, he was a member of the Petrograd Committee of the RCP(b). In the summer of 1919, Uglanov was elected a member of the Petrograd Committee of Bolsheviks.

Uglanov participated in the Civil War. Between 1919 and 1920, he served as the commissar at the 55th rifle division (Karelian front), which fought against the troops of White General **N. Iudenich**. In 1920, Uglanov was appointed the secretary of the Petrograd Union of Soviet Employees. On February 21, 1921, he became the secretary of the Petrograd Provincial Party Committee. In the spring of 1921, as an assistant to the military commissar of the Northern Group of Forces of the Red Army, he took part in the suppression of the Kronstadt uprising, for which he was awarded the Order of the Red Banner.

Between February 1922 and September 1924, Uglanov worked as the secretary of the Nizhny Novgorod Provincial Committee of the All-Union Communist Party of Bolsheviks. Simultaneously, from September 1924 to November 1928, he served as first secretary of the Moscow City and Regional Committees of the CPSU and a member of the Orgburo of the Central Committee. At the 14th party congress, he was elected a candidate member of the Politburo of the CC CPSU. At this time, he became an active supporter of the anti-Stalinist "right" opposition headed by N. Bukharin. He studied at the Industrial Academy (one of his fellow students was **N. Khrushchev**), where he led a group of "right-wingers." Uglanov supported the **NEP** and believed that it was necessary to develop not only heavy but also light industry. In July 1928, at the Plenum of the CC CPSU, Uglanov—together with N. Bukharin, **A. Rykov**, and **M. Tomsky**—opposed the introduction of industrialization and forced collectivization, and the use of extreme measures against peasants. In October 1928, when Bukharin was on vacation, a plenum of the Moscow Committee was held, at which Stalin accused the first secretary of "right deviation." Uglanov and his supporters found themselves in a minority. In November 1928, the Moscow party organization was defeated. Almost all its members, including Uglanov, lost their posts. Molotov was elected the new first secretary.

In 1928–1930, Uglanov served as the people's commissar of labor of the USSR. At the end of 1929, he publicly admitted his mistakes and withdrew his support from the leaders of the "Right Opposition." In 1930, the Party Board of the Central Control Commission of the All-Union Communist Party of Bolsheviks issued him a warning concerning his allegiances. In 1930, Uglanov headed the Astrakhan State Fish Trust. He sent a letter to the Central Committee in which he recognized Stalin as "the leader of the party, a staunch and faithful follower of Lenin." In February 1932, he was returned to Moscow and received the post of head of the Main Directorate of Light Industry of the People's Commissariat for Heavy Engineering of the USSR. Yet once in the city, he reestablished contacts with his supporters in the right-wing opposition. While discussing the situation in the party and the country with them, he concluded that the leadership of the CPSU, headed by Stalin, was unable to overcome the enormous difficulties in the economic and political life of the country. In October 1932, he was dismissed from work and in 1933 expelled from the party. He was accused of conducting "counterrevolutionary" activities and supporting the so-called Union of Marxist-Leninists (**Riutin**'s group). He was unemployed for several months.

On February 17, 1933, Uglanov was arrested in connection with the case of the "Bukharin school"—the case of the "anti-party counterrevolutionary right group." After writing several letters to Stalin, on April 16, 1933, he was released. In May, he headed the Obrybtrest (Tobolsk). On March 10, 1934, he was reinstated in the party.

On August 23, 1936, however, Uglanov was once again expelled from the CPSU and arrested. On May 31, 1937, on the order of the Military Collegium of the Supreme Court of the USSR he was sentenced to death and shot on the same day.

He was rehabilitated by the Plenum of the Supreme Court of the USSR on July 18, 1989.

ULRIKH, VASILY VASILIEVICH (1889–1951). An army military lawyer (November 20, 1935), colonel-general of justice (March 11, 1943), a senior judge of the USSR during Stalin's era, who served as the presiding judge at many of the major show trials during the Great Purges, Vasily Ulrikh was born in Riga, Latvia, in the Russian Empire. His father was a Latvian revolutionary of Baltic German descent, and his mother came from a Russian noble family. Due to his father's revolutionary activities, the family was exiled to Irkutsk for five years. In 1909, Vasily graduated from a real school in Riga. He joined the revolutionary movement in 1908 while still at school. In 1910, he became a member of RSDWP(b). In 1914, Vasily graduated from the commercial department of the Riga Polytechnical Institute. In 1915, he was drafted into Russian Imperial Army and sent to the front.

In the spring of 1918, Ulrikh took up a position in the All-Russian Extraordinary Commission (Cheka). He participated in the development of special operations. In 1919, he was appointed commissar of the headquarters of the internal security forces. Later he headed the Special Department of the naval forces of the Black and Azov seas. He also served as deputy head of the Counterintelligence Department of the Secret Operations Directorate of the State Political Directorate (GPU) (later the Joint State Political Directorate—OGPU).

In 1920, Ulrikh's military-judicial career began. He was appointed the first chairman of the military tribunal of the internal security troops of the NKVD of the republic (VOKhR). At the end of 1920, he was appointed a member of the Collegium of the Revolutionary Military Tribunal of the Republic. In 1921, Ulrikh became a chairman of the Military Collegium of the Supreme Court of the RSFSR. In 1926, he was appointed chairman of the Military Collegium of the Supreme Court of the USSR and deputy chairman of the Supreme Court of the USSR (in theory, such a combination of positions was not allowed by law). In 1926–1948, he headed the system of military tribunals of the USSR, which consisted of three branches: military tribunals of the Red Army, military tribunals of the navy, and military tribunals of the NKVD troops. Basically, he was not subordinate to the chairman of the Supreme Court of the USSR and was directly linked to the Politburo of the CC CPSU. He was very active in the struggle for power in the system of judicial authorities.

Ulrikh served as the presiding judge at many major show trials of the Great Purges, including the cases of the "Anti-Soviet United Trotskyist-Zinoviev bloc" (August 19–24, 1936), "the Parallel Anti-Soviet Center" (January 23–30, 1937), the trial of **Tukhachevsky** and others (June 11, 1937), the trial of the "Anti-Soviet Right-Trotskyist Bloc" (March 2–13, 1938), the trial of General A. Vlasov (July 30–31, 1946), and others. In 1935, Ulrikh presided over **Kirov**'s murder trial, during which he sentenced to death a whole group of people not involved in the murder, but who were familiar with some of its circumstances. Almost all these cases were completely fabricated and aimed to physically eliminate Stalin's political opponents. Ulrikh did not hesitate to sentence all defendants to death. In some cases, Ulrikh coordinated the court's verdict with Stalin and **L. Kaganovich** beforehand (e.g., before Tukhachevsky's trial). In the 1930–1940s, Ulrich was a member of a special closed Politburo commission on court cases. The commission approved all death sentences in the USSR. From time to time, Ulrikh personally executed alleged convicts. For example, he shot the people's commissar of justice **Nikolai Krylenko**. On December 12, 1937, he was elected a deputy of the Council of Nationalities of the Supreme Soviet of the USSR of the first convocation from the Komi ASSR. After the Second World War, Ulrikh presided during the early trials of the Zhdanovshchina, a period of enforced cultural uniformity in the early post–Second World War years (see **A. Zhdanov**)

In 1948, by decision of the Politburo, Ulrikh was dismissed from the post of chairman of the Military Collegium and deputy chairman of the Supreme Court of the USSR on charges of malpractice of employees of his office. He headed the higher military law courses at the Military Law Academy.

In 1951, Ulrich died of a heart attack and was buried at the Novodevichy Cemetery in Moscow.

V

VANNIKOV, BORIS LVOVICH (1897–1962). One of the main organizers of the Soviet atomic bomb project, and three-time hero of socialist labor of the Soviet Union, Boris Vannikov was born in Baku into a Jewish family of an oil worker. After graduation from elementary school, he worked in the oilfields, then on road construction, and as a locksmith at a factory. In 1918, he graduated from the Baku Polytechnical School. In 1916, he joined the Socialist Revolutionary Party (SRs), but left it the following year. In 1918–1919, Vannikov served in the Red Army, and in 1919, he became a member of the RSDWP's Bolshevik faction. He participated in the Civil War in the Caucasus. Between 1919 and 1920, he worked underground in Baku, and then in Tiflis. In 1920, he started to work for the senior inspector of the People's Commissariat of Workers' and Peasants' Inspection (Rabkrin).

In 1920, he moved to Moscow, where he occupied different positions. In 1924, he was appointed deputy head of the economic inspection of the Rabkrin of the RSFSR. After graduating from the Bauman Moscow State Technical University in 1926, he became director of the machine-building plant in Liubertsy. Later, he headed the machine-building plant in Perm. In 1933, he was appointed director of the Tula Arms Factory. Henceforth, his entire career would be associated with the production of weapons. From December 1936 to January 1937, Vannikov headed the Main Artillery and Tank Directorate of the People's Commissariat of Defense Industry of the USSR. In December 1937, he was appointed deputy commissar of armaments of the USSR. From January 1939 to June 1941, Vannikov was people's commissar of armaments of the USSR. From 1939, he was a member of the CC CPSU.

In early June 1941 (two and a half weeks before the outbreak of the **Great Patriotic War**), Vannikov was unexpectedly removed from his post and arrested. Until August 1941, he was imprisoned in the internal prison of the NKVD. Shortly before his release, he was asked to prepare a note for Stalin and to describe his views regarding the possibility of development of weapon production during wartime. After discussing his ideas with Stalin, Vannikov was provided with a special certificate stating that he had been arrested due to a misunderstanding and was considered fully rehabilitated. In the document, it was also indicated that by decree of the CC CPSU and the Soviet government, he was appointed deputy people's commissar of armaments of the USSR and had to immediately begin to fulfill his duties. Under Vannikov's leadership, the Soviet ammunition industry was able to increase its production capacity and to create new field, antiaircraft, and anti-tank artillery systems, mortars, and new models of small arms. During the war, the Soviet ammunition industry produced more than 1 billion sets of ammunition. On June 3, 1942, by the decree of the Presidium of the Supreme Soviet of the USSR, Vannikov was awarded the title of hero of socialist labor with the Order of Lenin and the Hammer and Sickle gold medal (in 1949 and 1954 he was awarded this title again).

From 1945 to 1953, Vannikov headed the First Main Directorate of the Council of People's Commissars of the USSR (which was responsible for the Soviet atomic project). He played an important role in the creation of the Soviet atomic bomb and in the production of nuclear weapons, serving as Beria's deputy in the Special Committee of the atomic project. Together with N. Borisov and A. Alikhanov, Vannikov developed a draft resolution of the Council of People's Commissars of the USSR on the creation of Laboratory No. 3 of the Academy of Sciences of the USSR (now the Institute for Theoretical and Experimental Physics). In 1947, Vannikov initiated the creation of a network of special faculties at several universities, which prepared specialists specifically for the atomic project. He oversaw their work together with I. Kurchatov. By the end of 1947, Vannikov became seriously ill (he worked in close proximity to the reactors). In 1951 and 1953, he was awarded the Stalin Prize. In 1953–1958, he worked as first deputy minister of medium machine building of the USSR (the ministry oversaw the production of atomic weapons).

In 1958 Vannikov retired. He died on February 22, 1962, in Moscow. The urn with his ashes was buried in the Kremlin Wall on Red Square.

VASILEV, ALEKSANDR FILIPPOVICH (1902–1984). Vasilev was a Soviet military intelligence officer, military diplomat, personnel officer of the Main Intelligence Directorate of the general staff of the Red Army, and Stalin's personal secretary-assistant on military-diplomatic cooperation with Soviet allies during the Second World War. He was the USSR's representative in the UN Military Staff Committee and was appointed lieutenant general (1944). During his career, he was awarded the Order of Lenin, three Orders of the Red Banner, the Order of Kutuzov, the Order of the Red Star, and others.

Aleksandr Vasilev was born in the village of Staroe Riakhino of the Novgorod Governorate into a Russian peasant family. In 1912, he graduated from a rural school, and in 1917 from higher school. On June 1, 1920, he joined the Red Army and participated in the Civil War. In 1920–1921, he fought in Ukraine against the troops of P. Wrangel and N. Makhno. In 1922, he was sent to Petrograd, where he studied at the 1st Leningrad Military School "Red October." In 1925, he became a member of the Leningrad city party organization of the RCP(b). In September 1926, he became a platoon "red commander" (*kraskom*). In May 1932, he was transferred to the Main Directorate of the Red Army. In March 1933, Vasilev was appointed assistant chief of the first sector of the sixth division of the headquarters of the Belarusian Military District.

In 1937, Vasilev graduated from the Special Faculty of the Frunze Military Academy. He received a diploma of a military intelligence officer and diplomat. He was proficient in several languages. In addition to his native Russian language, he was also fluent in Ukrainian, Belarusian, and Polish. At the Special Faculty, in addition to military regional studies and special disciplines, he studied German and English. In September–December 1937, he started his career at the Intelligence Directorate of the Red Army: the Intelligence Directorate of the general staff of the Red Army. He was promoted to major and from December 1937 to May 1939 he served as a head of the tenth department. From May 1939 to August 1940, he was made deputy chief of the directorate for military districts and communications. Simultaneously, in May–July 1939, he headed the fourth department of the Intelligence Directorate of the general staff of the Red Army. From August 1940 to June 1941, he was affiliated with the central apparatus of the Intelligence Directorate. In 1939, Vasilev participated in the campaign of the Red Army in Western Ukraine and Western Belarus (the eastern Polish territories allocated to the USSR in the Nazi Soviet Pact). In the autumn of the same year, he took part in hostilities against Finland in the Soviet–Finnish war of 1939–1940.

Just before the outbreak of the Great Patriotic War, in May–June 1941, Vasilev was appointed chief of the Intelligence Department of the headquarters of the Southern Front. There, he led operational tactical military intelligence operations in the rear of the Wehrmacht and established his own intelligence network. After the German invasion, he retreated along with the Red Army units to the east. Later, he was demoted and transferred to the post of deputy chief of staff of the Northern Group of Forces of the Transcaucasian Front.

In the summer of 1943, by Stalin's personal order, Vasilev was appointed Soviet military representative to the Allied forces in Italy, where, through the official military-diplomatic line, he established contact with the commander of the United Allied Forces, Dwight Eisenhower. On February 23, together with the governor general of Algeria and general of the army, Georges Catroux, Vasilev hosted the military parade dedicated to the twenty-fifth anniversary of formation of the Red Army. From the summer of 1943, he worked at the headquarters of the Anglo-American Allied Forces, monitoring the landing of an expeditionary force on the island of Sicily and the coast of Italy. From November 1944 to April 1945, he was head of the Soviet Military Mission in Great Britain.

By Stalin's order, Vasilev, together with **A. Gromyko**, was included in the Soviet delegation that participated in the International Conference in San Francisco, where from April to June 1945 as a military expert he worked on the development of the UN Charter. In July–September 1945, he was appointed chief of the special group of the Soviet Military Administration in Germany. From September 1947 to January 1950, he served as a representative of the USSR in the UN Military Staff Committee. In April 1950, he led the Foreign Relations Directorate of the Ministry of Defense of the USSR.

After Stalin's death, Vasilev was dismissed. After retirement, he was no longer involved in work in the Main Intelligence Directorate of the general staff of the USSR Armed Forces. He died in 1984 and was buried in Moscow at the Kuntsevo cemetery.

VASILEVSKY, ALEKSANDR MIKHAILOVICH (1895–1977).
Vasilevsky was a Soviet commander, marshal of the Soviet Union (1943), chief of the general staff of the Soviet Armed Forces (1942–1945), member of the Supreme Command Headquarters, commander-in-chief of the High Command of Soviet Forces in the Far East, minister of the armed forces of the USSR, minister of war of the USSR, member of the Central Committee of the CPSU (1952–1961), two-time Hero of the Soviet Union (1944, 1945), and chevalier of two Orders of Victory (1944 and 1945) and eight Orders of Lenin (1942, 1944, 1945, 1945, 1955, 1965, 1970, and 1975).

Aleksandr Vasilevsky was born in Novaia Golchikha, Kostroma Governorate, into a large Russian family. His father was a clergyman-psalmist who later became a priest. Both his mother and father were *Edinovertsy* (Russian Old Believers who became a part of the normative Orthodox Church system). In 1909, Aleksandr graduated from the Kineshma Theological School and entered the Kostroma Theological Seminary, from which he graduated in January 1915. The diploma of the seminary allowed him to continue his education in a secular educational institution.

In 1915, Vasilevsky volunteered to join the Russian Imperial Army, and in February he began his studies at the Alekseevskoe military school. In May 1915, he completed a four-month crash course and received the rank of *praporshchik* (a junior rank officer). From June to September 1915, he served in a reserve battalion in Iaroslavl province and Zhytomyr (now in Ukraine). In September 1915, he was sent to the 409th Infantry Novokhopersk Regiment on the Southwestern Front. At the end of April, he received his first award: the Order of St. Anne of the fourth degree with the inscription "For Bravery." In May 1916, he took part in the Brusilov Offensive into Austrian territory. In 1917, he served as battalion commander of the 409th Infantry Novokhopersk Regiment on the Southwestern and Romanian fronts.

According to Vasilevsky's autobiography,[1] after the February Revolution, some confusion was felt in the army. The "Military Revolutionary Committee of the Front" that emerged in those days, as well as most of the committees created in the armies, corps, and divisions, were entirely in the hands of the Socialist-Revolutionaries and Mensheviks. However, the growth of Bolshevik influence was also gradually felt, especially among ordinary soldiers. A significant part of the cadre officers was pro-monarchist and did not want any revolution in the country. Another part of the officers, especially those who had joined the army during the war, began to support the soldiers' position. Gradually, Vasilevsky also began to support anti-monarchist sentiments, condemn the war, and distrust the provisional government. In November 1917, Vasilevsky ended his military career in the Russian Imperial Army. He was not interested in politics and simply wanted to take up farming. Until June 1918, he helped his parents and was engaged in agriculture. From June to August 1918, he worked as a general education instructor in the Ugletskaia volost of Kostroma province.

From September 1918, Vasilevsky worked as a teacher in elementary schools in the villages of Verkhove, Tula Province. In April 1919, he was drafted into the Red Army and sent to the 4th Reserve Battalion as a platoon instructor. A month later, he was appointed commander of a detachment whose task was to assist in the emergency Soviet policy of *prodrazverstka*. In October 1919, Vasilevsky took command of a regiment. In December 1919, he was sent to the Western Front and was appointed deputy regimental commander of the 429th Infantry Regiment. In 1920, he participated in the Polish-Soviet War.

After the Civil War, from 1920, Vasilevsky served as assistant commander of the 142nd Infantry Regiment. Over the next ten years, he commanded all three regiments of the 48th Tver Rifle Division and headed the divisional school for junior commanders. In 1927, he graduated from the "Vystrel" course (an officer rifle-tactical training course of the Soviet Armed Forces).

In 1936, Vasilevsky entered the newly opened Academy of the General Staff of the Red Army (he was one of the first 137 students). In 1937, he graduated from the academy with honors. From October 1937 to May 1940, he worked on the general staff of the Armed Forces of the USSR. In 1938, he became a member of the CPSU. In 1939, Vasilevsky was appointed deputy commander of the Operations Directorate of the general staff. He was responsible for planning operations of the Soviet–Finnish Winter War of 1939–1940. In the spring of 1940, after the signing of the Moscow peace treaty, he headed the Soviet commission on the demarcation of the new Soviet–Finnish border. In May 1940, Vasilevsky was appointed first deputy chief of the Operations Directorate and was promoted to division commander. On November 9, 1940, as part of the Soviet delegation headed by **V. Molotov**, he participated in Soviet–German negotiations in Berlin to divide further the areas under occupation by the German and Soviet armies.

On August 1, 1941, Major-General Vasilevsky was appointed chief of the Operations Directorate of the general staff and deputy chief of the general staff. When the general staff was partially evacuated from Moscow in October 1941, Vasilevsky remained in the capital with his task force. During the Battle of Moscow, from October 5 to October 10, he was a member of the group of the State Defense Committee representatives. Vasilevsky played one of the key roles in organizing the defense of Moscow and counteroffensive. In April 1942, he was appointed first deputy chief of the general staff, and in June he was promoted to chief of staff. Simultaneously, from October 1942 he served as deputy people's commissar of defense of the USSR. As a representative of the Headquarters of the Supreme High Command, Vasilevsky took part in the preparation and conduct of many battles and operations of the **Great Patriotic War**. In the summer and autumn of 1942, Vasilevsky was at the front near Stalingrad. He planned and prepared the Soviet counteroffensive at Stalingrad named Operation Uranus.

On February 16, 1943, Vasilevsky was promoted to the rank of marshal of the Soviet Union. On behalf of the Supreme Command Headquarters, Vasilevsky coordinated the Voronezh and Steppe Fronts during the Battle of Kursk. He supervised planning and implementation of operations during the liberation of Donbas, Right-Bank Ukraine, and Crimea. On April 10, 1944, on the day of liberation of Odesa, he was awarded the Order of Victory.

This order was the second to be awarded (**G. Zhukov** received the first one). During the Belarusian Strategic Offensive Operation (Operation Bagration), Vasilevsky coordinated the 1st Baltic, 3rd Belarusian, and 2nd Baltic Fronts. After the Soviet troops entered the Baltic States, he became responsible for all Baltic fronts. On July 29, 1944, Vasilevsky was made a Hero of the Soviet Union with the award of the Order of Lenin and the Gold Star medal. In February 1945, he became a member of the Headquarters of the Supreme Command and after the East Prussian Operation, which entailed campaigns in Königsberg and other parts of the region, Vasilevsky was awarded his second Order of Victory. In June 1945, Vasilevsky was appointed commander-in-chief of the Soviet troops in the Far East. Under his leadership, the Manchurian Strategic Offensive Operation against the remnants of the Imperial Japanese army was prepared and successfully carried out.

In the postwar period in 1946–1948, Vasilevsky served as chief of the general staff. In 1948, he became first deputy minister of the armed forces of the USSR, and on March 24, 1949, he assumed the post of minister of the armed forces of the USSR (from February 26, 1950, the post was renamed "minister of war of the USSR"). On March 16, 1953, Vasilevsky was again appointed first deputy minister of defense of the USSR. In December 1957, he retired due to illness. From January 1959, Vasilevsky served as a general inspector of the Ministry of Defense.

Aleksandr Vasilevsky died on December 5, 1977. The urn with his ashes was buried in the Kremlin Wall on Red Square.

VINOGRADOV, VLADISLAV PETROVICH (1899–1962). A Soviet military leader; public figure; participant in the First World War, Civil War, and the Great Patriotic War; lieutenant general of the Quartermaster Corps; and nominal head of the Red Army-dominated Allied Commission for Romania, Vladislav Vinogradov was born in the village of Kuznetsovo, Kazan province (now the Republic of Mari El, Russia). His father, Petr Vinogradov, was an ethnic Mari. After graduating from the Kazan Theological Seminary in 1897, he married Vera Grigorevna Galbanskaia (Vladislav's mother was from an old priestly family) and became a priest. In 1907, after the death of Vladislav's father, the family moved to Cheboksary, where he entered the Cheboksary Religious School. In 1916, Vinogradov studied short-term courses at the Kazan Military School. After graduation, as a junior officer he served in the 94th Infantry Spare Regiment in Kazan. In 1917, he was sent to the 163rd Regiment on the Southwestern Front.

After the October Revolution of 1917, Vinogradov was demobilized and returned to Cheboksary. In early 1918, his mother died. In February of the same year, he started to work first as a clerk and then as a military instructor at the Military Division of the District Soviets. In 1920, Vinogradov commanded the Cheboksary battalion and then the Regimental District. Simultaneously, he worked as an assistant to the Chuvash regional military commissioner. In 1921–1922, during the period of famine in Chuvashia, Vinogradov helped to evacuate starving people to Turkestan. In his free time, he was the captain of the Cheboksary football team. In 1921, at the Chuvash regional military registration and enlistment office, a regional Council of Physical Education was created. Vinogradov, who promoted mass physical culture in Chuvashia, was appointed the chairman of a newly created organization.

In 1927–1930, Vinogradov was a student of the Rear and Supply Faculty of the Frunze Military Academy. After graduation, he occupied a leading post at the headquarters of the Moscow Military District and the general staff of the Red Army. He also headed the Supply Department at the Military Logistics Academy. In August 1940, Vinogradov was appointed deputy chief of staff for logistics of the Western Special Military District.

In December 1941, now with the rank of colonel, he was appointed deputy commander of the Western Front and then, from 1944, rear deputy commander of the 3rd Belarusian Front. At the end of 1941, he was made major general and then, in March 1943, lieutenant general. From September 1944 to March 1945, he was deputy chairman of the Allied Control

Commission in Romania. In September 1944, Vinogradov took part in the negotiations on the conclusion of an armistice with Romania.

After the war, from May 31, 1946, until July 3, 1948, Vinogradov worked as deputy minister of railways of the USSR. Subsequently, he was made rear chief of staff of the Armed Forces of the USSR. In 1949, he was appointed deputy head for scientific and educational work at the Military Academy of Logistics and Supply.

After retirement, Vinogradov made a significant contribution to the development of chess in the Soviet Union. He headed the chess federations of both the USSR and the RSFSR. He wrote a number of articles on chess theory and was an editor of collection of works on the history of chess in the USSR.

Vinogradov died on April 13, 1962, in Moscow. For his service in the Soviet Army, Vladislav Vinogradov was awarded the Order of Lenin, four Orders of the Red Banner, the Orders of Suvorov, Kutuzov, Bohdan Khmelnytsky, Patriotic War I degree, the "Crown of Romania," and others.

VLASIK, NIKOLAI SIDOROVICH (1896–1967). A Soviet security officer, Vlasik was head of Joseph Stalin's personal security (1931–1952) and a lieutenant general (1945).

Nikolai Vlasik was born in the village of Bobynichi, Grodno Governorate, in the Russian Empire (now in Belarus), into a poor Belarusian peasant family. At the age of three, he became an orphan. He graduated from a rural parish school. He started work at the age of 13, initially as a laborer for a landowner and, subsequently, as a digger on the railway and a laborer at a paper mill in Iekaterinoslav.

During the First World War, in March 1915, Vlasik was drafted into the Russian Imperial Army. During the war, he received the St. George Cross. During the October Revolution, Vlasik was a member of a platoon that supported the Bolsheviks. In November 1917, he started to work in the Moscow militia. In 1918, he joined the Red Army and participated in the defense of Tsaritsyn during the Civil War. In November of the same year, he joined the RCP(b). In September 1919, Vlasik was transferred to the **Cheka** under the direct supervision of **F. Dzerzhinsky**. On November 1, 1926, he was made senior commissioner of the operative branch of the Joint State Political Directorate of the USSR (OGPU), whose main task included the protection of the leaders of the party and state.

In 1927, Vlasik headed the special personal protective service in the Kremlin and became the de facto head of Stalin's security. This post became a turning point in his career. From 1931, Vlasik became Stalin's personal bodyguard. The official name of his position was constantly changing, but in fact, he guarded Stalin for twenty-five years. Remaining in the shadow of the leader, he ensured Stalin's safety around the clock, living in a room next to him. He also organized food and matters of daily existence for Stalin's entire family. After the death of Stalin's wife, **N. Allilueva**, he became a teacher of Stalin's children and a butler. In the fall of 1941, Vlasik was sent to Kuibyshev to monitor the government's move there. Later he was responsible for the protection of Stalin's residences while the Soviet leader was at the summits with U.S. and British leaders in **Tehran**, **Ialta**, and **Potsdam**.

In May 1952, Vlasik was removed from the post of chief of Stalin's security and sent to the Ural city of Asbest, where he was made the deputy chief of the Bazhenov Correctional Labour Camp. Colonel Nikolai Novik replaced him as head of security.

At the beginning of December 1952, Vlasik was arrested on charges related to the case of saboteur-doctors (**Doctors' Plot**). On December 16, he was expelled from the party. On January 17, 1953, the Military Collegium of the Supreme Court of the USSR found him guilty of abusing his power and embezzlement and sentenced Vlasik to ten years of exile. He was stripped of his general's rank and all state awards. Under the amnesty on March 27, 1953, Vlasik's exile term was reduced to five years. He was sent in exile to Krasnoiarsk. On December 15, 1956, by a decree of the Presidium of the Supreme Soviet of the USSR, Vlasik was pardoned with the removal of his criminal record, but he was not reinstated in military rank and awards. In the year 2000, the sentence against him was annulled, completing his rehabilitation more than three decades after his death.

After returning from exile, Vlasik lived in Moscow. He died on June 18, 1967, in Moscow from lung cancer. He was buried at the New Donskoi cemetery.

VOROSHILOV, KLIMENT IEFREMOVICH (KLIM VOROSHILOV) (1881–1969). Voroshilov was a party and military leader, close friend of Stalin, one of the original five marshals of the Soviet Union, people's commissar of defense (1925–1940), chairman of the Presidium of the Supreme Soviet (1953–1960), twice Hero of the Soviet Union (1956 and 1968), Hero of Socialist Labor (1960), and Hero of the Mongolian People's Republic (1957).

Kliment Voroshilov was born in the village of Verkhnee, Bakhmut uezd, Iekaterinoslav Governorate, Russian Empire (now Luhansk Oblast, Ukraine), into a Russian family. His father was a railroad worker and mother a day laborer. At the age of seven, Klim took a position tending sheep. In 1893–1895, he attended a zemstvo school. In 1896, he started work at the Iurievsky metallurgical plant in the city of Alchevsk. There, Voroshilov joined a social democratic circle and took part in a strike, for which he was arrested and fired from the plant. In 1903, he returned to Luhansk and obtained a job at the Hartmann steam locomotive plant. In that same year, he joined the Bolshevik faction of the RSDWP. In 1904, he became the leader of the Luhansk Bolshevik Committee. In December 1905, after being released from prison, he was elected chairman of the Luhansk Soviet. He organized workers' strikes and led the creation of military squads. In 1906, Voroshilov met Lenin and Stalin. The Bolshevik leaders made a strong impression on the young worker. But the sentiment was not reciprocated, as Lenin called him "the village boy" and "balalaika." In 1906 and 1907, Voroshilov was elected a delegate to the fourth and fifth congresses of the RSDWP(b). In 1908–1917, he conducted underground party work in Baku, Petrograd, and Tsaritsyn. During this period, he was repeatedly arrested and exiled. After the outbreak of the First World War, he managed to evade the draft and continued to disseminate Bolshevik propaganda.

After the February Revolution of 1917, Voroshilov was made a member of the Petrograd Soviet of Workers' and Soldiers' Deputies, a delegate to the seventh (April) All-Russian Conference, and the sixth congress of the RSDWP(b). In March, he was appointed chairman of the Luhansk Committee of the Bolsheviks and by August, he also headed the Luhansk Council and the City Duma. In November 1917, during the days of the October Revolution, Voroshilov was commissar of the Petrograd Military Revolutionary Committee. Together with **F. Dzerzhinsky**, he helped to organize the All-Russian Extraordinary Commission (VChK—Cheka). In early March 1918, Voroshilov organized the 1st Luhansk Socialist Detachment, which defended the city of Kharkiv from German–Austrian troops.

In July–August 1918, he commanded the Tsaritsyn Group of Forces. He became close to Stalin during the defense of Tsaritsyn, and this fact played a decisive role in Voroshilov's career. In August–September, he was a member of the Military Council of the North Caucasus Military District, and in September–October, he was appointed an assistant commander and a member of the Revolutionary Military Council of the Southern Front. In October–December 1918, Voroshilov commanded the 10th Army. In November 1918, he was introduced to the provisional government of Ukraine, and in January 1919, he was appointed people's commissar of internal affairs of Ukraine. In May, he commanded the troops of the Kharkiv Military District. In October 1919, he headed the 61st Infantry Division. Between November 1919 and March 1921, he served as a member of the Revolutionary Military Council of the 1st Cavalry Army. In March 1921, he took part in the suppression of the Kronstadt uprising.

In 1921–1924, Voroshilov was made a member of the Southeastern Bureau of the Central Committee of the RCP(b) and commander of the troops of the North Caucasus Military District. Later, in 1924–1925, he was placed in command of the troops of the Moscow Military District. He also served as a member of the Revolutionary Military Council of the USSR. After Lenin's death, he was appointed a member of the commission for organizing the funeral.

From November 1925 to June 1934, Voroshilov served as people's commissar of military and naval affairs and chairman of the Revolutionary Military Council of the USSR. During the 1930s, he took part in repressions against military personnel. From June 1934 to May 1940, he was appointed people's commissar of defense of the USSR. Simultaneously, from 1938, he became chairman of the Main Military Council. In 1935, he was made a marshal of the Soviet Union. In August 1939, Voroshilov headed the Soviet delegation during military negotiations between the USSR, Great Britain, and France, which proved fruitless.

Under Voroshilov's leadership, significant work was carried out on development of the armed forces of the Soviet Union, their technical reequipment, personnel training, and education. However, he underestimated the role of new technologies, and this caused significant damage to the combat readiness of the Red Army and affected the results of the Soviet–Finnish war of 1939–1940. For his mistakes in May 1940, Voroshilov was removed from the post of people's commissar of defense of the USSR (he was replaced by **S. Timoshenko**) and was appointed deputy chairman of the Council of People's Commissars (Sovnarkom) and chairman of the Defense Committee of the Sovnarkom.

During the Great Patriotic War, Voroshilov was a member of the State Defense Committee and the Headquarters of the Supreme Command. In July–August 1941, he was appointed commander-in-chief of the northwestern strategic direction. In September, he was made commander of the Leningrad Front. In September–November 1942, Voroshilov was commander-in-chief of the partisan movement. In January 1943, as a representative of the Headquarters of the Supreme High Command, Voroshilov, together with **G. Zhukov**, coordinated the troops of the Leningrad and Volkhov Fronts during the Operation "Iskra," which aimed to break the Wehrmacht's siege of Leningrad. Together with **A. Vasilevsky**, Voroshilov cordinated the actions of the 4th Ukrainian Front and the Separate Primorsky Army during the Crimean operation of 1944. In 1943, Voroshilov took part in the **Tehran Conference** of the leaders of the USSR, United States, and Britain.

In 1945–1947, after the end of the Second World War, Voroshilov was appointed chairman of the Allied Control Commission in Hungary. In 1946, he became deputy chairman of the Council of Ministers of the USSR. After Stalin's death, he remained in the government, joined the group of **N. Khrushchev**, and headed the Presidium of the Supreme Soviet of the USSR.

In 1961, Voroshilov wrote an address to the twenty-second congress of the CPSU in which he admitted his mistakes and his participation in the period of repressions. Marshal of the USSR Voroshilov died on December 2, 1969. He was buried in Moscow on Red Square near the Kremlin wall.

Voroshilov was the recipient of many awards during his career: twice Hero of the Soviet Union and Hero of Socialist Labor, eight Orders of Lenin, six Orders of the Red Banner, the Order of Suvorov first class, medals of the USSR, and medals of foreign states.

Kliment Voroshilov

VOZNESENSKY, NIKOLAI ALEKSEEVICH (1903–1950). Voznesensky was a Soviet politician, economist, member of the RCP(b) (1919), doctor of economics (1935), an economic planner who oversaw the running of the Gosplan during the Great Patriotic War (1941–1945), member of the CC CPSU (b) (1939–1949), candidate member of the Politburo of the CC CPSU(b) (1941–1947), member of the Politburo of the CC CPSU(b) (1947–1949), deputy of the Supreme Soviet of the USSR of the second convocation, academician of the USSR Academy of Sciences (1943), and laureate of the Stalin Prize, first degree (1947).

Nikolai Voznesensky was born in the village of Teploe, Tula Gubernorate, in the Russian Empire, into the family of an employee of the forestry office. His elder brother, Aleksandr Voznesensky, also became a famous Soviet economist. Nikolai began his career at a young age as a carpenter's apprentice and a printing house worker. In 1919–1920, he headed the Komsomol organization of the Chernsky district. In 1920, he was transferred to the Tula Provincial Committee of the Komsomol, where he headed the Planning and Financial Department. In 1925, he became editor-in-chief of the Tula regional newspaper *Molodoi Kommunar*.

In 1921–1924, Voznesenky studied at the Sverdlov Communist University, after which he was sent to the Donbas. In 1924–1926, he headed the Department of Agitation and Propaganda of the Ienakievo District Party Committee and served as a secretary of the Party Committee of the Ienakievo Metallurgical Plant. In 1927–1928, he was made deputy head of the Agitation and Propaganda Department of the Artemovsk District Party Committee. Between 1928 and 1931, Voznesensky studied at the Economic Institute of the Red Professors. After graduation, from 1931 to 1934, he worked as a lecturer at this university. At the same time, in 1932–1934, he was first a senior inspector and later head of the Planning and Accounting group at the Central Control Commission of the CPSU affiliated with the Workers' and Peasants' Inspection of the USSR. In 1934, he headed the planning and accounting group of the People's Control Commission of the Council of People's Commissars of the USSR. Between 1934 and 1939, he was a member of the People's Control Commission. In February 1934, he was made a representative of the People's Control Commission in the Donetsk region. In 1935–1937, Voznesensky served as chairman of the Leningrad City Planning Commission and deputy chairman of the Executive Committee of the Leningrad City Council.

In November 1937, Voznesensky was appointed deputy chairman of the State Planning Committee (Gosplan). From January 19, 1938, to March 10, 1941, and from December 8, 1942, to March 5, 1949, he held the position of Gosplan chairman. On April 4, 1939, Voznesensky was made deputy and then, from March 10, 1941, first deputy chairman of the Council of People's Commissars of the USSR. In 1938–1950, he served as a deputy of the Supreme Soviet of the RSFSR. During the Great Patriotic War (1942–1945), he was a member of the State Defense Committee, and in 1943, he was also made a member of the Committee of the Council of People's Commissars of the USSR dealing with economic rehabilitation and restoration of the liberated territories. In 1943, he became an academician of the USSR Academy of Sciences.

After the war, Voznesensky was included in the Special Committee under the State Defense Committee. With the help of the Gosplan employees, he collected significant material on the Soviet economy, which was presented in the monograph *The Military Economy of the USSR during the Patriotic War*. The manuscript was edited personally by Stalin. The book was published in 1947 and became a major scientific event. In 1948, Voznesensky was awarded the first degree Stalin Prize for this book. But in the following year, the book was withdrawn from libraries as an anti-Marxist publication, and on October 27, its author was arrested during the so-called **Leningrad Affair**.

On September 30, 1950, Voznesensky was found guilty of treason and sentenced to death. An hour after the verdict was pronounced, he was executed. His brother and sister were also shot. He was rehabilitated on April 30, 1954.

VYSHINSKY, ANDREI IANUARIEVICH (1883–1954). Prosecutor of the RSFSR (1931), prosecutor of the USSR (1935), and leader of the Soviet delegation at the Nuremberg Trials (1945-1946), Andrei Vyshinsky was born on December 10, 1883, in Odesa, in the Russian Empire. His father was descended from old Polish nobility and was a specialist in pharmaceutical products. His mother was a music teacher. Shortly after the birth of Andrei Ianuarievich, the family moved to Baku, where Andrei completed the first stage of his education. In 1901, he attended the Law Faculty of Kyiv University, but completed his studies only in 1913 because of his activities in student protests. Reportedly, his actions precluded him from a career in law at this stage of his life. In March 1902, he was dismissed from university without the right to return and placed under police supervision. He returned to Baku, where he joined the Menshevik wing of the RSDWP.

Further arrests followed between 1906 and 1908, and in the latter year he spent time in Bailov prison in Tblisi, where he met Stalin and possibly shared the same cell for some time. After his university graduation in 1913, he was a teacher of Russian literature, geography, and Latin in a private school in Baku, and began to practice as a lawyer. In 1915-1917 he served as an assistant to an attorney in Moscow district, P. N. Maliantovich.

Following the February Revolution of 1917 (March 8-12 in the contemporary calendar), Vyshinsky was appointed police commissioner of the Iakimansky District, and among his duties was a quest to search for and arrest "the German spy, Lenin." In 1920, he left the Mensheviks and formally joined the Bolshevik Party. In 1920-1921, he taught at Moscow State University and became dean of the Faculty of Economics at the Plekhanov Institute of National Economy. From 1923 to 1925, he took on the role of prosecutor of the Criminal Justice Board of the USSR Supreme Court, his first leading role in this capacity at the age of 40. In 1925-1928, he was rector of Moscow State University.

As Stalin consolidated his power, Vyshinsky took on ever-more-important roles. He chaired the trials of this period, such as the **Shakhty Trial** (1928) and the Trial of the Industrial Party (1930), and helped to create the atmosphere of suspicion and enemy intrusions into state life. He was also involved in education, and from 1928 to 1931 was a board member of the People's Commissariat of Education of the Russian SFSR. Vyshinsky was appointed prosecutor of the RSFSR on May 11, 1931, and shortly thereafter deputy chairman of the Commissariat of Justice of the RSFSR. In June 1933, he was promoted to deputy prosecutor of the USSR and the prosecutor from March 1935 to May 1939, thus covering the main period of the three Stalin Purge Trials in Moscow, over which he presided. In 1936, he received the degree of doctor of law.

Vyshinsky also set the tone for the trials with his inflammatory and incriminating remarks. Historians have described these trials in a number of ways: as a drama, based on near or complete fabrications, weaving stories so fantastic that they defied belief, and based on class principles rather than the validity of any individual case. The objectives were, however, quite simple: to ensure that the accused made private confessions while under interrogation by the NKVD, then publicly during the trial, incriminating numerous associates in their testimonies. In essence, the victims were accused of spying; treachery, plots to kill Stalin and his associates; plots to overthrow the Soviet Union in collusion with Poland, Britain, Germany, Japan, and other countries; and above all close ties with Stalin's enemies, principally **L. Trotsky**, but also other old Bolsheviks such as **G. Zinoviev**, **L. Kamenev**, and **N. Bukharin**. Aside from Trotsky, who by then was a resident of Mexico, the other formerly prominent figures had all been placed under arrest. Vyshinsky, along with the commissar of internal affairs for the later trials, **N. Iezhov**, was a member of the NKVD commission investigating espionage cases.

Those tried received a variety of severe sentences: the main leaders were sentenced to death, while lesser ones received lengthy prison sentences. Vyshinsky's venom in court may have been a result of fears that his Menshevik past could be used against him, particularly by **L. Beria**. In 1937, he led the case against Soviet military officers, and particularly **M. Tukhachevsky**, who was executed on June 12, based on charges drawn up by Vyshinsky and Iezhov. Several thousand officers were shot as a result of the trial, which was based on false evidence, like the preceding public court cases.

At the same time, Vyshinsky held other important roles in the Soviet administration, including director of the Institute of Law of the Soviet Academy of Sciences, and executive editor of the journal *Sovetskoe gosudarstvo i pravo* (*Soviet State and Law*), a position he retained until February 1950. In late May 1939, he was appointed deputy chairman of the Soviet government with responsibility for science, education, and legal organs dealing with criminal cases. He continued to wield considerable authority during the war years but declined toward the end of that period. He was a member of the Soviet delegation that signed an agreement with Britain on joint actions against Germany, and on June 14, 1943, he took on the role of extraordinary ambassador and plenipotentiary of the Soviet Union. He was also an important figure at the Conference of Foreign Ministers of the Allied powers (United States, Soviet Union, and Britain) in Moscow in October 1943, as well as at the **Ialta Conference** of Allied leaders F. D. Roosevelt, W. S. Churchill, and Stalin in February 1945, and at **Potsdam** later in the same year.

Ironically, Vyshinsky was the leader of the Soviet delegation at the Nuremberg Trials between 1945 and 1947, when the major Nazi leaders who were captured by Allied forces were put on trial. He was now dealing with genuine crimes against humanity. He also was prominent in most of the key political events that followed such as the division of Germany and the Paris Peace Conference. Between 1949 and 1953, he was Soviet foreign minister. Upon Stalin's death, this position was taken up by **V. Molotov** (his second stint), and Vyshinsky became the USSR ambassador to the United Nations in New York, where he resided at the time of his death from a heart attack on November 22, 1954, leaving behind his wife, Kara Mikhailova (1884–1973), and daughter, Zinaida (1909–1991), also a lawyer by training. He can be regarded retrospectively as one of the most loyal and sycophantic Stalinist officials, who was prepared to adopt the most ruthless measures against those considered the enemies of Stalin. Like Stalin himself, he is buried in the Kremlin wall.

NOTES

1. Aleksandr Vasilevsky, "Pervye shagi v borbe za Sovety," in *Delo vsey moey zhyzni* (Moscow: Politizdat, 1978), http://militera.lib.ru/memo/russian/vasilevsky/index.html.

W

WAR COMMUNISM. An internal policy of Soviet Russia, carried out during the Civil War, in 1918–1921. With the help of War Communism, the Bolsheviks solved two problems: they introduced elements of Communist relations (which meant, first of all, free labor and consumption), and they concentrated in their hands all the resources necessary for waging a civil war and fighting the intervention. Nationalization of all industries, the introduction of *Glavkism* (strict centralized management), *prodrazverstka* (requisition of grain and other agricultural products from peasants at nominal fixed prices according to specified quotas), state control of foreign trade, prohibition of strikes, obligatory labor duty for nonworking classes (*trudovaia povinnost*), centralized distribution and rationing of food and most commodities in urban centers, and a ban on private enterprise were the main policies introduced by War Communism.

With the victory of the October Revolution, the new government launched programs for quick and risky transformations. However, the outbreak of the Civil War and extreme exhaustion of resources forced the government to seek quick solutions to the problems. As a result, the policy of War Communism was implemented. The Bolsheviks borrowed some elements of this system from Imperial Russia (the grain *razverstka* introduced in 1916 during the First World War) and the government of A. Kerensky. Interestingly, the Bolsheviks took radical measures to create "Communist" relations in Russia, where, even according to the theories of Marxism, there were no economic prerequisites. The state took over the management of all economic and social relations, which led to the growth of the bureaucracy. The policy of War Communism was initiated formally during the eighth congress of the Russian Communist Party, which was held in Moscow on March 18–23, 1919, though most of its practices were in place by then.

Nationalization of all industries and the introduction of strict centralized management became one of the major characteristics of War Communism. The first nationalizations were launched under the provisional government. In June–July 1917, the "flight of capital" from Russia began. Among the first to leave the country were foreign entrepreneurs. They were followed by domestic industrialists. The question arose of how to deal with enterprises that were left without owners and managers. A. Smirnov's Likinskaya manufactory became the first company to be nationalized. From the summer of 1918 to the summer of 1919, the entire large-scale industry (enterprises with five hundred or more employees) was nationalized. By November 1918, already 9,542 enterprises were in the hands of the Soviet state. From the summer of 1919, the rate of nationalization increased dramatically. By the beginning of 1921, more than 250,000 enterprises, including medium and small industrial businesses, had passed into state ownership. By the end of the War Communist period, nationalization was generally completed. The decision to nationalize small-scale industry, adopted in November 1920, was not fully implemented due to the transition to the **New Economic Policy** (NEP) in the spring of 1921.

Glavkism, the centralization of industrial management of nationalized enterprises, was introduced by the Supreme Soviet of the National Economy, which was created on December 2, 1917. N. Osinsky (V. Obolensky) became the first head (chairman of the presidium) of this organization. During the Civil War, it was headed by **A. Rykov**. The Supreme Soviet of the National Economy managed enterprises through a system of main committees (*glavkov*), the maximum number of which reached forty-nine by the summer of 1920 (Glavruda, Glavtextil, Glavkrakhmal, Glavkozha, Glavgvozd, etc.). The enterprises were directly subordinate to the main committees, and the latter to the presidium of the Supreme Soviet of the National Economy. The mediators in the sphere of economic management were abolished. According to the orders of the central administration, the enterprises received raw materials and semifinished products and returned the manufactured products. Glavkizm was also extended to the management of transport, agriculture, construction, and procurement. The policy became an integral part of War Communism.

Prodrazverstka, food appropriation, also became one of the most important components of War Communism. It allowed the Soviet state to survive during a food crisis. At first, the Bolsheviks continued the grain monopoly proposed by the provisional government and the surplus appropriation system introduced by the tsarist government. On May 9, 1918, a decree confirming the state monopoly on the grain trade (introduced by the provisional government) and prohibiting private trade in grain was issued. On May 13, 1918, a decree of the All-Russian Central Executive Committee and the Council of People's Commissars, "on granting the people's food commissioner extraordinary powers to fight the village bourgeoisie, hiding and speculating grain reserves," established the main provisions of the food dictatorship. The purpose of the food dictatorship was the centralized procurement and distribution of food, suppression of the resistance of the *kulaks*, and the fight against *meshochniks*, or "people with bags." The People's Commissariat for Food received unlimited powers in the procurement of food.

The food dictatorship, declared in May 1918, reached a logical conclusion. On January 11, 1919, a decree of the Sovnarkom introduced *prodrazverstka* throughout Soviet Russia. It was later extended to Ukraine, Belarus, Turkestan, and Siberia. To ensure the fulfillment of the policy, food detachments from workers were sent to the villages. *Prodrazverstka* was the actual confiscation of almost the whole amount of grain and other products from the peasants. For the personal and economic needs of the peasants, the food detachments left a minimum quota. Initially, *prodrazverstka* covered only the collection of grain and grain fodder. But during the campaign of 1919–1920, it also encompassed potatoes and meat, and by the end of 1920, almost all agricultural products. The food confiscation system made it possible to solve the problem of the planned supply of food to the army, towns, and cities. It also helped to provide industry with the required minimum of raw materials. At the same time, *prodrazverstka* undermined the productive forces in the countryside, enormously damaged the agricultural sector, and provoked the 1920–1921 peasant uprisings (Makhnovist movement, the Antonov uprising, the West Siberian uprising, and hundreds of smaller uprisings). The rebels, with the support of wider strata of the population, put forward demands for freedom of trade, the end of *prodrazverstka*, and the elimination of the Bolshevik dictatorship. Labor revolts gripped Petrograd, Moscow, and other cities. In March 1921, the most serious event, the Kronstadt uprising, occurred. The participants of this revolt supported the principle of Soviet power but opposed the Bolsheviks and their policies.

In the face of widespread popular uprisings, the tenth congress of the RCP(b) decided to abolish *prodrazverstka* and replace it with a flat food tax. Peasants had to pay the tax but could sell the rest of the food. These decisions ended War Communism and launched a series of measures known as the New Economic Policy.

State control of foreign trade was also a part of War Communism. At the end of December 1917, foreign trade was placed under control of the People's Commissariat of Trade and Industry, and in April 1918 a state monopoly was declared. The merchant fleet was nationalized.

Also, an in-kind and egalitarian wage system was introduced. Workers and employees of state enterprises and institutions received a salary in food rations and consumer goods according to an equalization principle (*uravnilovka*), without taking into account the qualifications, quantity, and quality of products.

Additionally, obligatory labor duty was introduced. This duty was first declared by the third All-Russian Congress of Soviets and included in the constitution of the RSFSR in 1918. Later, it was included in the labor code adopted in December 1918. The main slogan of this policy, "He who does not work, neither shall he eat," was actually a New Testament aphorism originally found in the Second Epistle of Paul the Apostle and later cited by John Smith (an English soldier, explorer, colonial governor, and Admiral of New England) in the early 1600s. According to this policy, all able-bodied citizens of Russia from 16 to 50 years of age were obliged to engage in socially useful work; otherwise, they were forced to do it. A network of labor concentration camps was deployed. Wages in such concentration camps were paid in accordance with rates established by the respective trade union. The All-Russian Extraordinary Commission (Cheka) and, from the beginning of 1920, the Main Committee on General Labor Conscription (*Glavkomtrud,* created and headed by **F. Dzerzhinsky**) controlled the execution of the obligatory duties. Decrees adopted by the Council of People's Commissars on April 12, 1919, and April 27, 1920, prohibited unauthorized transition to a new job and absenteeism. Severe labor discipline was established. The system of unpaid work on weekends and holidays (*subbotniki*) became widespread. At the beginning of 1920, even some units of the Workers' and Peasants' Red Army were temporarily transformed into labor armies. They retained military organization and discipline but were working for the national economy.

As a result, instead of the unprecedented growth of labor productivity, War Communism brought a sharp decline. In 1920, labor productivity decreased, partly as a result of widespread malnutrition, to 18 percent of the prewar level. Whereas before the revolution the average worker consumed 3,820 calories per day, already in 1919, this figure had dropped to 2,680. This was not enough to support heavy physical labor. By 1921, industrial output had decreased threefold, and the number of industrial workers had fallen by 50 percent. At the same time, the bureaucratic apparatus (the staff of the Supreme Council of the National Economy) had grown from 318 people to 30,000. The situation in Petrograd, one of the major Russian cities and the former capital, became especially difficult. The population of the city during the Civil War decreased from 2.3 million people to 799,000, and the number of workers decreased by five times. Equally dramatic was the decline in agriculture. Grain production in 1920 fell in comparison with the prewar period by half. A black market emerged in Russia. The course adopted by Bolsheviks also led to hyperinflation. The experiment with organizing labor armies in 1920–1921 also completely failed. Mass desertion from labor armies was widespread.

War Communism helped the Soviet government turn the general situation in its favor during a period of civil conflict. But overall, such a policy destroyed production ties and aggravated the government's relations with the broad masses of the population. The economy was not rebuilt but rather began to fall apart even faster. As a result, War Communism was replaced by the New Economic Policy.

Z

ZAKOVSKY, LEONID MIKHAILOVICH (NÉE HENRIKS ŠTUBIS) (1894–1938). Zakovsky was a Latvian Bolshevik, Soviet politician, leader of the Soviet state security agencies, and commissar first class of state (the second rank in the NKVD). He was also people's commissar of internal affairs of the Belarusian SSR (1934), head of the NKVD of the Leningrad and Moscow regions, a member of the special troika of the NKVD of the USSR, and one of the key organizers of the Great Terror and mass executions at the regional level.

Henriks was born on the *khutor* (single-homestead settlement) Rudbarzhi of the Courland Governorate, in the Russian Empire (now Latvia), into a poor Latvian family. His father was a forester. In 1902, he entered elementary school, then studied for two years at the Liepāja city school, but in 1909, he was expelled for participating in the May Day demonstration. A safe house of the Liepāja RSDWP organization was organized in the Zakovsky family abode. Leonid worked in copper-tin workshops. In 1912, he started work as a cabin boy on the steamer *Kursk* and visited the United States, Brazil, and Argentina.

In 1913, Leonid joined the Bolshevik faction of the RSDWP. He was arrested several times. In 1913, the Kurland provincial gendarme administration characterized H. Štubis (Zakovsky) as politically unreliable member of the Liepāja group of anarchists. In 1914, he was exiled for three years to the Olonets Governorate. From January 1917, he lived in Petrograd. He was an active participant in the July Days uprising and the October Revolution (1917). With a detachment of sailors, Leonid participated in the seizure of the city telephone exchange. After the Revolution, Zakovsky became one of the founders of the All-Russian Extraordinary Commission (Cheka). In March 1918, he was made special commissioner of the Presidium of the Cheka on the Western, Southern, and Eastern fronts. He headed special detachments that carried out the suppression of anti-Soviet uprisings in Astrakhan, Saratov, Kazan, and other regions. Later, he headed the Special Department of the Caspian–Caucasian Front and the Information Department of the Special Department of the Moscow Cheka.

In 1921–1925, Zakovsky was the chairman of the Podolsk and Odesa city departments of the GPU (State Political Directorate) and the GPU representative in Ukraine and Moldova. He was involved in the murders and robberies of defectors and misappropriation of contraband, which eventually led him to a conflict with the political leadership of Ukraine. But he escaped any serious punishment and was promoted and transferred to Siberia, where by that time his fellow Latvian **R. Eikhe** had become the first secretary of the regional executive committee of the Soviets.

In 1926, Zakovsky was made plenipotentiary representative of the OGPU in Siberia and headed the Special Department of the Siberian Military District. In 1928, during Stalin's trip to Siberia, Zakovsky ensured his safety. Together with R. Eikhe, Zakovsky became one of the main organizers of collectivization in Siberia, where the party faced active resistance from "kulaks." He also was one of the initiators of the creation of the gulag system. From 1928, Zakovsky was the chairman of the troika of the plenipotentiary representation of the OGPU in Siberia.

In 1929–1930, the OGPU troika prosecuted 16,553 people, 4,762 of whom were executed, 8,576 people sent to camps, and others exiled. Zakovsky personally signed execution lists. By August 1930 Zakovsky was the OGPU's plenipotentiary representative in the West Siberian Territory. In March 1930, he led the suppression of the Muromtsevo peasant uprising. In the spring of 1931, Zakovsky came up with a proposal for the intra-regional expulsion of forty thousand peasant households. His proposal was approved by the Decree of the Bureau of the West Siberian Regional Committee of the CPSU(b) "On the Elimination of the Kulaks as a Class." As a result, 52,091 dispossessed families were deported within the region.

From April 10, 1932, Zakovsky was made the OGPU's plenipotentiary representative in the Belarusian SSR and head of the Special Department of the Belarusian Military District. In July–December 1934, he was people's commissar of internal affairs of the Belarusian SSR. In this post, he fabricated an extensive case against the "counterrevolutionary insurgent and espionage-sabotage organization Belarusian National Center." But already in December 1934, just after **S. Kirov**'s assassination, Zakovsky was transferred to Leningrad. In just one month, from February to March 1935, on the orders of Zakovsky (with **A. Zhdanov**'s approval), 11,702 people were deported from Leningrad to remote areas of Siberia and the Russian North. Zakovsky became a member of the Leningrad regional troika of the NKVD and personally participated in interrogations, torture, and executions. According to rough estimates, between 1934 and 1938, about eighty-five thousand people were executed in Leningrad, and hundreds of thousands were sent to camps and exile, where the majority died (the so-called "Kirov Stream"). On December 12, 1937, Zakovsky was elected a deputy of the Council of the Supreme Soviet of the Soviet Union of the first convocation from the Leningrad region.

In January 1938, he was appointed **Iezhov**'s deputy and headed the Moscow Regional Directorate of the NKVD. Although he headed the Moscow Directorate for only two months, this period was the peak of repression in Moscow. Zakovsky fabricated the case of the "Latvian National Center." In February–March 1938, he organized an "extermination action" against persons belonging to different national diasporas in Moscow (Poles, Germans, Balts, and others). He established a plan for the execution of 1,000–1,200 people per month. The executions were carried out at the Butovo Shooting Range near Moscow. Minors and even pregnant women were executed there. At the beginning of 1938, Zakovsky was one of the organizers of the trial against a group of **N. Bukharin**'s supporters.

In April 1938, Zakovsky was unexpectedly removed from all his posts, dismissed from the NKVD, expelled from the party, and arrested. He was charged with creating a "Latvian counterrevolutionary organization in the NKVD and with espionage for Germany, Poland, and England." The real reason for Zakovsky's arrest was Iezhov's decision to replace some executioners. In addition, the scale of the repressions in Moscow, ordered by Zakovsky, frightened city residents too much, and complaints about the abnormal situation in the city poured into the Central Committee. Finally, by the spring of 1938, Stalin had become disillusioned with Iezhov and his people.

According to official data, Leonid Zakovsky was executed on August 29, 1938. He has never been rehabilitated.

ZAVENIAGIN, AVRAAMY PAVLOVICH (1901–1956). Zaveniagin was one of the main organizers of Soviet industry ("marshal of the Soviet industry"), metallurgical engineer, founder of the Norilsk Mining and Metallurgical Combine and the city of Norilsk, lieutenant general (1945), deputy minister of internal affairs of the USSR (1941–1950), minister of medium machine building of the USSR, deputy chairman of the Council of Ministers of the USSR (since 1955), twice hero of socialist labor (1949 and 1954), winner of the Stalin Prize (1951), and curator of Soviet metallurgy and the Soviet atomic project.

Avraamy Zaveniagin was born at the Uzlovaia station of the Tula region into a large family of a railway worker. In 1912, he entered the Skopino Realschule, from which he graduated in 1919. In November 1917, he became a member of the CPSU(b). In 1919, Zaveniagin, by then editor of the Riazan newspaper *Izvestiia*, was appointed head of the Political Department of the Riazan Infantry Division, which fought in the Donbas during the civil war. In 1919–1920, he was elected a member of the All-Ukrainian Central Executive Committee. The young party member was responsible for mobilization of the population to fight against Admiral A. Kolchak, the leader of the White armies. During the offensive of White General A. Denikin, he formed an infantry division and headed its political department. He participated in battles against local gangs and headed the revolutionary committee in the city of Starobelsk. Between June 1922 and September 1923, Zaveniagin was the executive secretary of the district committee of the CPSU in the city of Iuzovka (later Stalino, currently Donetsk).

In 1923, party leadership sent Zaveniagin to Moscow, where he became vice-rector for administrative and economic affairs and at the same time a student of blast-furnace production in the Moscow Mining Academy. In 1930, after the academy was divided into six independent universities, he became the first rector of the Moscow Institute of Steel and Alloys (MISiS) and also headed the State Institute for the Design of Metallurgical Plants (*Gipromez*) in Leningrad. In January–August 1933, Zaveniagin was appointed director of the Dneprovsky metallurgical plant in Kamensky (from 1936 to 2016, the city was called Dniprodzerzhinsk, Ukraine; its current name is Kamianske). He managed not only to revive the metallurgical plant but also to make it number one in the country among the enterprises of ferrous metallurgy. In 1933–1937, he was director of the Magnitogorsk Metallurgical Combine. After a brief spell as deputy people's commissar of heavy industry, in 1938, Zaveniagin headed the construction of the Norilsk Mining and Metallurgical Combine (Norillag). By the end of 1939, it employed more than 19,000 prisoners.

In 1941, he was appointed deputy people's commissar of internal affairs of the USSR. In 1945, he became one of the organizers of the First Main Directorate under the Council of Ministers of the USSR. He was responsible for the creation, formation, and development of the atomic uranium hydrogen industry in the USSR. For these purposes, in mid-May 1945, Zaveniagin headed a group of specialists that was sent to occupied Germany. German equipment, more than one hundred tons of uranium, as well as a large group of world-famous scientists—metallurgists, chemists, and physicists—were brought from Germany to the USSR. This brought the Soviet Union a year closer to its first nuclear weapon test.

In 1953, Zaveniagin was made deputy minister of medium machine building (atomic weapons) of the USSR. In 1955, he became deputy chairman of the Council of Ministers of the USSR and minister of medium machine building. On December 31, 1956, he died suddenly from a heart attack. He was cremated, and an urn with his ashes was placed in the Kremlin wall.

ZHDANOV, ANDREI ALEKSANDROVICH (1896–1948). Zhdanov was an ideologue of **Socialist Realism**, member of the CC CPSU, candidate member of the Politburo of the CC CPSU (1935), full member (1939), secretary of the CC CPSU (from 1934), a member of the Orgburo CC CPSU, colonel general (June 18, 1944), and the founder of the Zhdanov Doctrine, which became Soviet cultural policy. He was believed to be the successor-in-waiting to Stalin, but he died prematurely.

Andrei Zhdanov was born in Mariupol, Iekaterinoslav Governorate, in the Russian Empire (now Ukraine). Andrei's maternal grandfather, Pavel Ivanovich Platonov-Gorsky, was the rector of the Moscow Theological Academy. His father, Aleksandr Zhdanov, was an associate professor at the same academy. Aleksandr became one of the first researchers of the apocalypse in Russia and the creator of a series of lectures on the history of the Old Testament. He also became interested in the ideas of Marxism and social democracy. Because of these views, he was expelled from the academy. From 1893, he held the post of inspector of public schools in the Iekaterinoslav Governorate. Aleksandr Zhdanov became the first teacher of his son Andrei and had a great influence on him.

After his father's death, the family—Andrei's mother, he, and his three sisters (Anna, Tatiana, and Elena)—moved to the Tver Governorate. In 1915, Andrei Zhdanov graduated from the Tver Realschule, and in 1916, he entered Moscow Agricultural Institute. From 1912, he was a member of the Social Democratic circles, and in 1915, he joined the RSDWP(b). In July 1916, he was drafted into the army and enlisted in the preparatory training battalion in Tsaritsyn. Later he was sent to the 3rd Tiflis School of Warrant Officers, from which he graduated with that status. From February 1917, he served in the 139th Infantry Reserve Regiment in the city of Shadrinsk, Perm Governorate, where he conducted Bolshevik propaganda among the soldiers. In August 1917, during the period of the provisional government in Russia, he was made chairman of the Shadrinsky Committee of the RSDWP(b). In January–April 1918 (before the city was occupied by the White Army), he was deputy chairman of the executive committee of the Shadrinsk Soviet of Workers' and Soldiers' Deputies and was the editor of the local newspaper *Peasant and Worker*.

In 1918, Zhdanov became a member of the Russian Communist Party (RCP(b). From the summer of 1918, he served as a political worker in the Red Army. He held the post of inspector of the propaganda bureau of the Ural District Military Registration and Enlistment Office. He was also an employee of the Political Department of the 3rd Army and headed the Cultural and Educational Department of the Ufa Provincial Military Registration and Enlistment Office. Subsequently, he worked at the Political Department of the 5th Army of the Eastern Front. Zhdanov also held numerous party posts in Tver and Nizhny Novgorod. In May 1919, he returned to Tver and headed the organizational and agitational department of the Provincial Military Registration and Enlistment Office. In 1922, he was made chairman of the Tver Provincial Executive Committee.

Between 1924 and 1934, he served as first secretary of the Nizhny Novgorod (after 1932, it was renamed Gorky) Provincial Committee (after 1929, the Regional Committee) of the CPSU. During this period, Stalin began to pay more attention to Zhdanov. In 1925, Zhdanov was made a candidate and then, two years later, a member of the CC CPSU.

In the mid-1930s, Zhdanov entered the top leadership of the USSR and became one of Stalin's confidants. He participated in the development and implementation of the ideological policy of the party and was one of the developers of the new party course, which partially rehabilitated the Russian pre-revolutionary historical and cultural heritage.

On February 10, 1934, Zhdanov was transferred to Moscow and appointed the secretary of the Central Committee responsible for ideology. He also became a member of the Orgburo of the CC CPSU. He held these positions until the end of his life. In 1934, he also helped to organize the First Congress of Soviet Writers, where the principles of Socialist Realism were formulated. He headed the CC Commission to prepare a history textbook for elementary schools. By the 1930s, Zhdanov had become an influential party ideologist and coauthor (together with Stalin and Kirov) of comments on the basic principles of studying and teaching history (published in 1936).

After **S. Kirov**'s assassination, in December 1934, Zhdanov was made first secretary of the Leningrad Regional Committee and City Committee of the CPSU. In 1935, he became a member of the Military Council of the Leningrad Military District. Zhdanov was one of the main organizers of political repressions in Leningrad and other regions. In the fall of 1937, he initiated the purges in the Bashkir Party organization. During the Great Terror, Zhdanov became one of the members of the Politburo of the Central Committee who approved the so-called execution lists. He personally signed 176 execution lists (by comparison, Stalin signed 357).

In 1938, Zhdanov became a member of the Main Military Council of the Soviet Navy. From July 15, 1938, to June 20, 1947, he also served as chairman of the Supreme Soviet of the RSFSR. From 1939 and until his death, he was a member of the Politburo, CC CPSU. In 1939–1940, Zhdanov headed the Department of Propaganda and Agitation of the CC CPSU. Simultaneously, in 1939–1940, he was a member of the Military Council of the Northwestern Front during the Soviet–Finnish War.

During the **Great Patriotic War** (1941–1945), from June 23, 1941, Zhdanov held the post of permanent adviser at the Headquarters of the Supreme High Command. He was also a member of the Military Councils of the Northwest Direction (July–August 1941) and the Leningrad Front (August 1941–August 1944). He was one of the organizers of the defense of Leningrad during the blockade. In 1944–1947, he was Soviet representative at the Allied Control Commission in Finland, which monitored the observance of the terms of the armistice agreement between the USSR and Finland.

By the mid-1940s, Zhdanov had promoted a number of his supporters from the Leningrad party organization to the highest party and state posts (in 1949–1952, most of them were repressed and executed within the scope of the fabricated **Leningrad Affair**). The "Leningraders" advocated the rehabilitation of Russian patriotism in the USSR, rejection of discriminatory policies toward the RSFSR within the Union, greater influence for the Russian republic within the Soviet Union, and creation of the Central Committee Bureau for the RSFSR and the Russian Communist Party. With the support of Zhdanov, on January 13, 1944, the Leningrad City Executive Committee returned the historical names of twenty streets, avenues, and squares in Leningrad.

In 1946, with the outbreak of the Cold War, Zhdanov, on behalf of Stalin, led an ideological campaign that aimed to tighten party control over the creative intelligentsia and to intensify propaganda of the ideas of Soviet patriotism. The same year, he developed the "Zhdanov Doctrine," which soon became Soviet cultural policy. According to this doctrine, Soviet writers, poets, artists, actors, directors, and intelligentsia in general had to adapt their works to the party line. In the late 1940s, Zhdanov started to criticize the poets of the Russian Silver Age. In June 1947, on behalf of the Central Committee, Zhdanov led philosophical discussions on these issues. In 1947, on his initiative, the journal *Problems of Philosophy* was established, and the Publishing House of Foreign Literature was founded. In February 1948, Zhdanov started the so-called antiformalism campaign: a campaign of criticism and persecution against many prominent Soviet composers such as Dmitry Shostakovich, Sergei Prokofiev, Aram Khachaturian, and dozens of others. He also led a campaign against "cosmopolitanism" and "servility to the West."

In 1946–1948, a sharp struggle between two groups (**L. Beria** and **G. Malenkov** on the one hand and Zhdanov and his supporters on the other) started. Many historians believe that, in 1948, Zhdanov's position in the internal party confrontation, as well as Stalin's attitude toward him, significantly deteriorated. Zhdanov was known to be a heavy drinker, which brought him serious health problems.

Zhdanov died on August 31, 1948, from a heart attack in the sanatorium of the Central Committee of the CPSU, where he was treated for cardiovascular disease. His death gave impetus to the beginning of the so-called **Doctors' Plot**. Zhdanov was buried near the Kremlin wall in Moscow.

Andrei Zhdanov with Joseph Stalin

ZHUKOV, GEORGY KONSTANTINOVICH (1896–1974). Zhukov was a Soviet military commander, marshal of the Soviet Union (1943), four-time Hero of the Soviet Union (1939, 1944, 1945, 1956), holder of two Orders of Victory (1944, 1945) and six Orders of Lenin (1936, 1939, 1945, 1956, 1966, 1971), and minister of defense of the USSR (1955–1957). He was nicknamed "Marshal of Victory" for his role in the **Great Patriotic War**.

Georgy Zhukov was born in the village of Strelkovka, Kaluga Governorate, in the Russian Empire into a peasant family. After graduating from the parish school, Georgy was sent to Moscow to the home of his maternal uncle, Mikhail Artemevich Pilikhin, to study the fur business. During his work in his uncle's furrier shop, he tried to continue his education and enrolled in evening courses at the city school, from which he graduated in 1911.

In 1915, Zhukov was drafted into Russian Imperial Army. He served in the cavalry and rose to the rank of noncommissioned officer. He fought bravely and was awarded two St. George's Crosses. In the summer of 1916, Zhukov was seriously wounded, and his hearing was damaged. In the fall of 1918, he joined the Red Army, and on March 1, 1919, he became a member of the RCP(b). During the Civil War, he commanded a platoon and squadron, and fought on the Eastern, Western, and Southern fronts against the Ural Cossacks near Tsaritsyn, and the troops of Denikin and Wrangel. For his part in the suppression of the Tambov Rebellion of 1920–1921, Zhukov received his first Order of the Red Banner. At the end of May 1923, Zhukov took command of the 39th Regiment of the 7th Samara Cavalry Division. In 1924, he was sent to the Higher Cavalry School.

In 1925, after completing the Cavalry Advanced Training Courses for Command Personnel in Leningrad, Zhukov commanded the 42nd Cavalry Regiment. From 1926 to 1931, he taught military preconscription training at the Belarusian State University. In 1929, he graduated from the training courses for the highest command personnel of the Red Army in Moscow. The future famous military leaders **K. Rokossovsky**, I. Baghramyan, **A. Ieremenko**, and other Red commanders studied in these courses with Zhukov. From May 1930 to February 1931, Zhukov commanded the 2nd Brigade in the 7th Samara Cavalry Division headed by Rokossovsky. In February 1931, he was appointed assistant to **S. Budenny**, who was an inspector of the Red Army. From March 1933, he commanded the 4th Cavalry Division in Belarus, then the 3rd and 6th Cavalry Corps. For his skillful leadership, on August 16, 1936, Zhukov received the Order of Lenin. In 1937, he became the commander of the 3rd Cavalry Corps. In June 1938, he was promoted to deputy commander of the Belarusian Special Military District.

In the summer of 1939, Zhukov was appointed commander of the 57th Special Corps, and later he headed the 1st Army Group of Soviet Forces in Mongolia. On July 31, 1939, he was made Komkor (Corps commander). On August 29, 1939, he led a successful operation on the Khalkhin-Gol River (in Mongolia), which resulted in the defeat of the Japanese Sixth Army. As a result, Zhukov received his first star of the Hero of the Soviet Union and the star of the Hero of the Mongolian People's Republic. During this operation, Zhukov for the first time widely used tanks in counterattacks.

On June 7, 1940, Zhukov was appointed commander of the troops of the Kyiv Special Military District. From June 28 to July 4, 1940, he took part in the Soviet occupation of Bessarabia and Northern Bukovina, which were annexed from Romania by the USSR. In January 1941, he took part in two bilateral military operational-strategic games on maps. Both games were held in three stages, at each of which, the participants, in accordance with the tasks, made decisions and prepared in writing directives, combat orders, operational reports and other official documents. During the first simulation, which took place from January 2 to 6, 1941, he commanded the Western forces, which attacked Eastern forces (front commander D. G. Pavlov) from the territory of East Prussia and Poland. According to the conditions of the game, the Eastern forces had approximately one and a half times superiority in forces (and in tanks, almost threefold). Zhukov would later describe these exercises to be very similar to the actual German invasion of the USSR five months later. During the second simulation, which took place from January 8 to 11, 1941, Zhukov commanded the Eastern forces (Southwestern

Front), which repulsed the attack of Western, Southwestern, and Southern forces on the territory stretching from Brest to the Black Sea. The second game ended with a "strategic victory" of Zhukov's Eastern forces.

Following the results of the war games, in January 1941, Zhukov became chief of the general staff and at the same time deputy people's commissar of defense. During the Great Patriotic War, from June 23, 1941, he was a member of the Headquarters of the Supreme Command. From July 30 to September 10, 1941, he commanded the Reserve Front forces, which successfully carried out the first offensive operation in the Ielnia region. Later he commanded the troops of Leningrad, Western, 1st Ukrainian, and 1st Belarusian Fronts. From August 26, 1942, to June 1945, he also served as first deputy people's commissar of defense and deputy supreme commander-in-chief. During the war, he organized the defense of Leningrad, Moscow, and Stalingrad. Under Zhukov's command, the troops of the Leningrad Front, together with the Baltic Fleet, stopped the offensive of Army Group North near Leningrad in September 1941. Under his command, the troops of the Western Front defeated the troops of Army Group Center near Moscow, preventing the occupation of the Soviet capital. Zhukov coordinated the actions of the fronts near Rzhev (Operation Mars, 1942) which ended in failure, during the breakthrough of the Leningrad blockade (Operation Iskra, 1943), and during the Battle of the Kursk Salient (Summer 1943). The victories at Korsun-Shevchenkovsky and the liberation of the Right-Bank Ukraine are also associated with the name of Zhukov.

On January 18, 1943, the general of the army, Zhukov, was made "marshal of the Soviet Union" with the award of the special distinction "Marshal's Star." He became the first marshal to be appointed during the years of the Great Patriotic War. Twice during the war years Zhukov was awarded the highest commander's order "Victory." At the end of the war, troops under his command (1st Belarusian Front) were advancing to Berlin and were the first to reach the city. After its fall, and the suicide of Adolf Hitler (April 30), Zhukov was instructed to formally accept Germany's unconditional surrender on the night of May 8–9, 1945. On June 24, 1945, Marshal Zhukov, as a commander-in-chief, participated in the historic Victory Parade on Red Square in Moscow. Marshal **K. Rokossovsky** commanded the parade. On September 7, 1945, the Berlin Victory Parade was held by the Allies in Berlin near the Reichstag building and Brandenburg Gate. About five thousand troops from the Soviet Union, the United States, the United Kingdom, and France took part in the parade. Marshal Zhukov was the Soviet senior officer present at the parade.

In June 1945, the 1st Belarusian Front was renamed into the Group of Soviet Occupation Forces in Germany. Marshal Zhukov became the commander-in-chief of these forces. He also headed the Soviet military administration in Germany organized the same month. From March 21 to June 9, 1946, he was made commander-in-chief of the ground forces and deputy minister of the armed forces of the USSR. On June 9, 1946, in connection with the so-called "trophy case" (valuables collected during victories), Zhukov was removed from the post of commander-in-chief of the ground forces and deputy minister of the USSR armed forces, and appointed commander of the Odesa Military District. At the Plenum of the CC CPSU in February 1947, he was removed from the list of candidates for membership in the Central Committee of the CPSU. On February 4, 1948, Zhukov was transferred from the post of commander of the Odesa Military District to the post of commander of the Urals Military District. These measures suggest that Stalin was concerned by the marshal's growing power and influence and had him demoted to less senior posts. At the 19th party congress in October 1952, however, Zhukov was again elected a candidate member of the Central Committee.

After Stalin's death in 1953, at the request of **L. Beria**, Zhukov was appointed the first deputy minister of defense of the USSR (**N. Bulganin** became minister of defense). In 1954, Zhukov was instructed to prepare and conduct exercises under the code name "Snezhok" ("Snowball") with the use of an aerial detonation of a 40-kt RDS-4 nuclear bomb at the Totskoe nuclear exercise (Orenburg Oblast). On September 14, 1954, at least forty-five thousand soldiers took part in the exercises. Both military personnel and residents of the surrounding settlements were exposed to radioactive radiation. Information about these exercises was classified during the Soviet period.

From February 9, 1955, to October 26, 1957, Zhukov was the minister of defense of the USSR. During October 23–November 9, 1956, Zhukov played a key role in suppression of the anti-Communist uprising in Hungary. On December 1, 1956, Marshal Zhukov was awarded the title of Hero of the Soviet Union for the fourth time and received his fourth Gold Star medal and the Order of Lenin. Until December 18, 1981, he was the first and only four-time Hero of the Soviet Union (in 1981, **Leonid Brezhnev** received that status during his personality cult).

In June 1957, at the Plenum of the CC CPSU, Zhukov—together with the chairman of the KGB of the USSR, the general of the army (**I. Serov**), and others—actively supported **N. Khrushchev** in the fight against the so-called "anti-party group of **Molotov, Malenkov, Kaganovich,** and **Shepilov**." But on October 29, 1957, the Plenum ruled that Zhukov "violated the Leninist, party principles of leadership of the Armed Forces, [and] pursued a policy of curtailing the work of party organizations, political agencies and the Military Councils." By the same decree, Zhukov was removed from the Presidium and the CC CPSU. On February 27, 1958, by a decree of the Council of Ministers of the USSR, Zhukov was dismissed with the right to wear military uniforms. Zhukov was the only marshal of the Soviet Union who, after his resignation, was not enrolled in the Group of Inspectors General of the Ministry of Defense of the Soviet Union, which included all the prominent commander-heroes of the Great Patriotic War.

After Khrushchev's resignation (1964), on May 8, 1965, Zhukov was invited to the Kremlin Palace of Congresses for a solemn meeting dedicated to the twentieth anniversary of victory. Zhukov prepared and, with considerable difficulties, published his memoirs, *Memories and Reflections.*

He died on June 18, 1974. His ashes, contrary to Zhukov's last will to be buried in the ground and despite the family's requests, were buried in the Red Square in the Kremlin wall.

Georgy Zhukov

ZINOVIEV, GRIGORY IEVSEEVICH (NÉE OVSEI-GERSHON ARONOVICH RADOMYSLSKY) (1883–1936). Zinoviev was an Old Bolshevik and close colleague of Lenin, one of the seven members of the first Politburo (founded in 1917), candidate member of the Politburo of the Central Committee of the RCP(b) (1919–1921), member of the Politburo of the Central Committee of the Party (1921–1926), and member of the Orgburo of the Central Committee of the RCP(b) (1923–1924). After Lenin's death, he was one of the main candidates for leadership in the party. An active participant in the internal party struggle of the 1920s.

Grigory was born in Ielizavetgrad, Russian Empire (now Kropyvnytsky, Kirovohrad Oblast, Ukraine), into a wealthy Jewish family.

He was educated at home under the guidance of his father, Aaron Radomyslsky, who was the owner of a dairy farm. In his youth, he became interested in philosophy, politics, and world history, and in 1901, he joined the RSDWP. In 1902, after being persecuted by the police for organizing workers' strikes in Novorossiysk, he emigrated to Berlin, then lived in Paris and Bern, where in 1903 he met V. I. Lenin. From 1903 until the fall of the Russian Empire in February 1917, he was one of the most prominent Bolsheviks, and was one of Lenin's closest associates who worked with him both in Russia and abroad.

At the second congress of the RSDWP in 1903, Zinoviev supported Lenin's position and joined the Bolsheviks. Later he returned to his homeland, where he carried out active propaganda work on the territory of Ukraine. In 1904, due to an illness, he left the country again. He enrolled in the Chemistry Department of the University of Bern, Switzerland, but interrupted his studies to participate in the Russian Revolution of 1905. After his return to Russia, he was elected a member of the St. Petersburg City Committee of the RSDWP. Due to new arrests of radicals, he returned to Bern and enrolled this time at the Faculty of Law. In March 1906, he was again in St. Petersburg. At the fifth RSDWP congress in London, he was elected to the Central Committee (he received the most votes after Lenin). He became one of the editors of the clandestine newspapers *Sotsial-Demokrat* and *Vpered* (*Forward*). In 1908, Zinoviev was arrested, but after three months he was released due to an illness. Together with Lenin, he left Russia and emigrated to Austria.

Forced immigration lasted until 1917. After the February Revolution, in April, Zinoviev together with Lenin, Krupskaia and several other people, made a risky journey in a sealed train carriage to Russia across German-occupied Europe to Sweden, and then Finland. In Russia he joined the editorial board of *Pravda* and supported Lenin's April Theses. With the end of the dual power, Zinoviev, together with Lenin, hid in a hut in Razliv just outside Petrograd after the failure of the July Days protests in July. At the sixth party congress, Zinoviev was elected to the Central Committee, receiving only one vote less than Lenin.

In October, during a closed meeting of the Bolshevik Central Committee, together with **Lev Kamenev**, Zinoviev opposed Lenin's resolution on an armed uprising and voted against the overthrow of the provisional government, considering it premature. Moreover, Zinoviev and Kamenev also demonstrated their opposition to the majority of the members of the Central Committee members. By their open letter in the Menshevik organ *Novaia Zhizn* (*New Life*), they revealed to the government the intentions of the Bolsheviks and Left Socialist-Revolutionaries. Lenin considered these actions of Zinoviev and Kamenev treacherous and wanted to expel them from the party. However, Lenin himself published open letters in newspapers calling for the October coup and soon reconsidered his opinion.

After the seizure of power by the Bolsheviks in Petrograd, a serious split quickly emerged within the Bolshevik leadership: the workers' committees demanded the creation of a single socialist body of power that would not include Vladimir Lenin and **Leon Trotsky**. Zinoviev, Kamenev, and their supporters—V. Nogin and **A. Rykov**—hastened to take advantage of such sentiments. The group supported the stated demands, and at first, it seemed that Zinoviev's supporters would prevail, but Lenin and **Trotsky** soon managed to regain control. The next day, Zinoviev and his supporters left the Central Committee. In response, Lenin called his former comrades traitors and deserters. It seemed that Zinoviev's political career had come to an end. But the Bolsheviks lacked competent and experienced leaders, and Zinoviev returned to politics. Until the spring of 1918, he led the Petrograd Bolshevik Council, then served as chairman of the Council of People's Commissars of the Petrograd Commune, head of the Council of People's Commissars of the Union of Communes of the northern region, and even chairman of the Main Committee of the Revolutionary Defense of Petrograd.

Still, ideological clashes between Zinoviev and Lenin continued. In addition, Zinoviev spoke out against the plan to move the country's capital to Moscow. Nevertheless, he supported Lenin's position regarding the signing of the Brest-Litovsk Treaty with Germany and Austria-Hungary in 1918 and was able to regain trust of the chairman of the Council of People's Commissars. On March 8, 1918, Zinoviev was returned to the Central Committee. After the murders of M. Uritsky and V. Volodarsky in the summer of 2018, Zinoviev opposed Lenin's idea to start the so-called "Red Terror." Thus, some tensions remained between the two old comrades.

During the civil war and after it, however, Zinoviev was one of the main organizers of the "Red Terror" against the Petrograd intelligentsia and the former nobility. He was nicknamed "Grishka the Third" (after Grigory Otrepiev and Grigory Rasputin). From March 1919 to 1926, he was chairman of the Executive Committee of the Communist International (**Comintern**). During his presidency in the Comintern, he encouraged factional squabbles and was the first to introduce the term *social fascism* in the context of the social democratic parties of Western Europe. From 1921 to 1926, Zinoviev was a member of the Politburo.

Zinoviev played an important role in the rise of Stalin. It was he who suggested to appoint Stalin the general secretary of the Central Committee of the RCP(b). At the eleventh party congress in 1923, Zinoviev, together with Kamenev and Stalin, presented a political report to the Central Committee. At that time, the so-called "Kamenev-Zinoviev-Stalin troika" unified against Trotsky. However, in December 1925, at the 14th congress of the All-Union Communist Party, Zinoviev, supported by Kamenev and the Leningrad delegation, spoke out on behalf of the "new opposition" against Stalin's group (**Molotov**, **Rykov**, **Bukharin**, etc.). In 1926, Zinoviev was removed from the leadership of the Leningrad City Council and the Executive Committee of the Comintern. Additionally, by the decision of the plenum of the Central Committee, he was removed from the Politburo. In 1927, because of his union with Trotsky, Zinoviev was also removed from the Central Committee, expelled from the party and from the Society of Old Bolsheviks, and exiled. His supporters were also punished.

In 1928, after repenting his "deviations" from the party line, as dictated by Stalin, Zinoviev was reinstated in the party and was appointed rector of Kazan University. He was engaged in literary and journalistic activities. In October 1932, he was again expelled (for failure to inform on oppositionist party members of the so-called **Riutin Platform**) from the party, arrested and sentenced to four years of exile in Kostanai (Kazakhstan). In exile, he translated Adolf Hitler's *Mein Kampf* into Russian. In 1933, by decision of the Politburo, he was reinstated in the CPSU and appointed to work in the *Tsentrosoiuz*. In February 1934, he was even invited to the 16th party congress, where he once again recanted his views.

On December 16, 1934, after **Kirov**'s death and start of the Great Purge, Zinoviev was arrested again, expelled from the party, and sentenced to ten years in prison. In August 1936, Zinoviev was put on trial again. In the case of the first Moscow Show Trial, the "Trial of the Sixteen (the "Trotskyite-Zinoviev Terrorist

Zinoviev (right), with Stalin, Rykov, and Kamenev

Center"), he was sentenced to death. On August 26, Zinoviev was executed. His execution paved the way for the mass arrests and executions of the Great Purge of 1937-1938. **Iagoda**, who was present at the execution, took the bullets that killed Zinoviev and Kamenev to his home. Later, bullets were seized during a search after Iagoda's arrest and ended up in **Iezhov**'s house, from where they were seized when Iezhov himself was arrested.

In 1988, Zinoviev was rehabilitated during M. Gorbachev's de-Stalinization campaign.

ZORIN, VALERIAN ALEKSANDROVICH (1902-1986). A Soviet diplomat, deputy minister of foreign affairs of USSR (1947-1955), and member of the Central Committee of the CPSU (1961-1971), Valerian Zorin was born in in Novocherkassk into the family of a schoolteacher. He graduated from the Novocherkassk Realschule. In 1922, he joined the RCP(b). Between 1922 and 1932, Zorin worked in the Moscow Committee and the Central Committee of the Komsomol. In 1935, he graduated from the Higher Communist Institute of Education. From 1935, he occupied various party positions. Between 1939 and 1941, he served as deputy director of the Moscow Pedagogical Institute. In 1941, Zorin joined the People's Commissariat of Foreign Affairs of the USSR, where he held different positions including assistant secretary general of the People's Commissariat for Foreign Affairs, assistant to the head of the IV European Department, assistant deputy people's commissar of foreign affairs and head of the IV European Department. Between 1945 and 1947, he was appointed the USSR's ambassador to Czechoslovakia. He was one of the most influential of Stalin's officials in the country. In fact, he personally supervised the activities of the government of Czechoslovakia.

From March 1947 to November 1955, Zorin served as deputy minister of foreign affairs of the USSR. He would hold this post again twice: in 1956-1960 and 1963-1965. In 1949-1952, he headed the Information Committee under the USSR Ministry of Foreign Affairs, which was part of Soviet foreign intelligence. Also, between 1952 and 1953, he served as permanent representative of the USSR to the United Nations and in the UN Security Council. In 1955-1956, Zorin was the first Soviet ambassador to the Federal Republic of Germany. In February 1956, he was elected candidate member of the CC CPSU. In 1960-1963, he again represented the USSR at the UN. During this period, the most famous episode in his biography occurred. On October 25, 1962, during the Cuban missile crisis, Zorin participated in an emergency meeting of the UN Security Council, during which he had an engaging confrontation with Adlai Stevenson, who served as the U.S. Ambassador to the United Nations. In 1961, he was elected to the CC CPSU. From 1965 to 1971, Zorin served as the Soviet ambassador extraordinary and plenipotentiary of the USSR to France. Between 1971 and 1986, he was an ambassador on special missions at the Ministry of Foreign Affairs of the Soviet Union. He died in Moscow on January 14, 1986.

ZUBAREV, PROKOPY (1886-1938). Prokopy Zubarev was born in the village of Zubari, Kotelnichsky Uezd, Viatka Governorate, in Kirov Oblast, Russia. From 1901 to 1905, he studied at the Viatka Agricultural Technical School. In 1904, he became a member of the RSDWP(b). From 1904 to 1908, Zubarev was involved in party, agitation, and propaganda work. From 1909 to 1915, he held several positions in the Ufa Governorate, including as an accountant and instructor for cooperation in the Ufa provincial zemstvo. In 1915, he was drafted into the Russian Imperial Army, where he served until 1917.

In 1918, Zubarev returned to Ufa, where he served as commissioner (*komissar*), chairman of the Ufa Provincial Food Committee, and chairman of the Executive Committee of the Ufa Provincial Council. From July 1922 to December 1923, Zubarev was deputy chairman of the Council of People's Commissars and deputy chairman of the Economic Council of People's Commissars of the Bashkir ASSR. From 1924, he transferred to the Urals, where he served as the executive secretary of the Kurgan regional committee of Communist Party. In 1929-1930, he was chairman of the

Organizing Committee of the Presidium of the All-Russian Central Executive Committee for the northern outskirts, chairman of the Executive Committee of the Urals Regional Council, as well as the second secretary of the Urals Regional Committee of the party. From 1931 to March 1934, Zubarev was employed by the People's Commissariat of Agriculture of the USSR. In March 1937, he was appointed deputy people's commissar of agriculture of the RSFSR. He lived in Moscow in the famous "House on the Embankment." Many residents of this house were arrested and executed during Stalin's Great Purge.

On March 15, 1937, to follow suit, Zubarev was arrested. He was one of the accused in the case of the Anti-Soviet "Bloc of Rightists and Trotskyites," also known as the Trial of the Twenty-One (the last of the three public Moscow Trials). On March 13, 1938, by the decision of the Military Collegium of the Supreme Court of the USSR, he was found guilty and sentenced to death. On March 15, 1938, Zubarev was executed at the Kommunarka training ground.

In June 1965, he was rehabilitated by the decision of the Military Collegium Supreme Court of the Soviet Union.

ZVEREV, ARSENY GRIGOREVICH (1900–1969). People's commissar of finance (renamed as ministry in 1946) (1938–1960, with a break in 1948), candidate member of the Politburo of the CPSU (1952–1953), and general state counselor of the Financial Service (1948), Arseny Zverev was born into a poor working-class family in the village of Negodievo. In addition to Arseny, there were twelve other children. Eight of his brothers and sisters became members of the Communist Party. Arseny's father was literate and believed that Arseny should be educated. In 1912, he graduated from school and started to work at the Vysokovskaia Textile Factory. At the end of 1916, more than five thousand workers, including Zverev, went on strike at the factory. After the end of the strike, he lost his job and was forced to return home.

After the February Revolution of 1917, Zverev moved to Moscow, where he got a position at the Trekhgornaia Manufacturing Plant. In 1919, he joined the RCP(b) and volunteered to join the Red Army. In 1920, he graduated from a Cavalry School in Orenburg and became a Red commander. During the Civil War, Zverev fought against the detachments of Sapozhkov and Antonov. After demobilization, in 1922–1923, he worked as a food inspector. In 1924, he became a financial agent in the Moscow Provincial Financial Department. In 1924–1925, he studied at the Central Courses of the People's Commissariat of Finance.

In 1925, Zverev was transferred to Klin (Moscow Oblast) as deputy head of the Financial Department. He also served as chairman of the Klin district of the Executive Committee until 1929. From 1929 to 1930, he headed the Tax Department of the regional Financial Department of the Western region, and also headed the Briansk district Financial Department. Zverev had a negative attitude toward the **New Economic Policy** (NEP), and until the end of his life, he was an enthusiastic supporter of collectivization. Between 1930 and 1933, he studied at the Moscow Institute of Finance and Economics (now the Financial University under the Government of the Russian Federation). At the same time, he was the secretary of the party organization of the institute. In 1932, Zverev, while still a student, became the head of the Bauman Regional Financial Department of Moscow. While working there, he met with the people's commissar of finance, **G. Grinko**.

In 1936, Zverev was elected chairman of the Molotov District Council of Moscow and then, in 1937, first secretary of the District Committee of the RCP(b). Zverev's career took shape at a time of repressions and intense struggle within the Soviet elites. Many employees of the People's Commissariat of Finance and other financial institutions were repressed. But Zverev's career took a turn for the better, and it was Stalin who played the main role in his success. In 1937, Zverev was appointed deputy people's commissar of finance. After **V. Chubar**, who served as people's commissar of finance, was arrested and executed, Zverev was appointed people's commissar. After the renaming of the People's

Commissariats into Ministries in 1946, Zverev became the first Soviet minister of finance.

Stalin's choice of new people's commissar of finance was most likely influenced by the Zverev's adherence to principles. He earned a reputation as a harsh and outspoken critic of the shortcomings of the Soviet financial system early in his career. His philosophy of a socialist economy boiled down to the fact that enterprises should maintain an austerity regime and product losses should be eliminated, and he regarded overspending on wages as a violation of state discipline. Zverev paid special attention to the selection of new personnel. He began his reforms at the People's Commissariat of Finance of the USSR with the reorganization of its structure. Three main departments were formed: state insurance, financial control, and labor savings banks, as well as several directorates (budget, foreign exchange, state revenue, state loans, taxes, economic planning, etc.).

Zverev became the people's commissar of finance in a difficult period: the process of industrialization was underway, and the amount of funds needed for the defense industry was constantly growing. Soviet industrialization relied on internal sources, and not external, as was the case before 1917. Since Zverev relied exclusively on internal sources of financing, a regular issue of state internal loans was organized, with the loans distributed among the population. At Stalin's suggestion, Zverev paid great attention to increasing the country's gold reserves. He proposed to put 50 percent of all mined gold in the treasury and not touch this reserve under any circumstances, while the other 50 percent was used to cover necessary expenses. Stalin approved the order and considered the gold put in the treasury to be absolutely inviolable.

Under Zverev's leadership, the Soviet financial system was quickly rebuilt for military needs during the difficult years of the **Great Patriotic War**. Even in the tempestuous war years, Zverev did not change his principles in managing public finances and paid great attention to the creation of reserves. Under the leadership of Zverev, the People's Commissariat was evacuated from Moscow to Kazan.

One of his most important measures after the war was the 1947 monetary reform. The reasons for the reform were a sharp increase in government spending on defense during the war, a decline in retail trade, and increased inflation. The reform was of a confiscatory nature. The State Bank of the USSR exchanged old rubles for new ones at a ratio of 10:1. The metal coins were not subject to exchange and were accepted at par value. The deposits of the population, the size of which did not exceed three thousand rubles, were not subject to revaluation. Preparations for the reform started already during the war. The monetary reform made it possible to abolish the rationing system, helped to lower the prices of essential goods, and helped to reduce the amount of money held by the population. Many ordinary Soviet citizens viewed the reform as fair, as money obtained illegally during the war was confiscated.

In 1948 for a period of ten months, Zverev was removed from his post, made deputy minister of finance of the USSR, and replaced by **A. Kosygin**. But in December 1948, he was once again made the minister. In addition to the ministry post, Zverev simultaneously headed the Monetary Committee of the Council of Ministers of the USSR. During the Great Patriotic War, he worked in the State Staff Commission under the Council of Ministers of the USSR. Over the period 1939–1961, he was a member of the Central Committee of the party and a delegate to many party congresses. From 1937 to 1962, Zverev was a deputy of the Supreme Soviet of the USSR. At the 19th congress of the CPSU in 1952, the last one during Stalin's lifetime, he was elected a candidate member of the Presidium of the CC CPSU. For several decades he was a deputy of Moscow Council.

After Stalin's death, Zverev retained the post of minister of finance but immediately lost his membership in the reorganized Presidium of the CC CPSU. He had quite difficult relations with **N. Khrushchev**. In 1961, Zverev retired because of disagreements with Khrushchev, who was preparing a monetary reform of his own. Having become a pensioner of union significance, Zverev could not sit idle, however. He became a lecturer and professor-consultant at the All-Union Correspondence Financial Institute, created on his initiative (today the institute is part of the Financial University under the Government of the Russian Federation). In the last years of his life, Zverev defended his doctoral dissertation, which was devoted to the national income of the USSR. Zverev is remembered as "Stalin's Iron People's Commissar" and the first professional Soviet financier who relied solely on a planned economy.

Zverev died on July 27, 1969, and was buried at Novodevichy Cemetery in Moscow.

Bibliography

BOOKS

Applebaum, Anne. *Red Famine: Stalin's War on Ukraine.* New York: Doubleday, 2017.

Baberowski, Jörg. *Scorched Earth: Stalin's Reign of Terror.* New Haven, CT: Yale University Press, 2016.

Beria, S. *Beria, My Father: Inside Stalin's Kremlin.* London: Duckworth, 2003.

Bolton, Kerry. *Stalin: The Enduring Legacy.* London: Black House, 2012.

Boobbyer, Philip. *The Stalin Era.* London: Routledge, 2000.

Brackman, Roman, *The Secret File of Joseph Stalin: A Hidden Life.* London: Frank Cass, 2001.

Butler, Susan. *My Dear Mr. Stalin: The Complete Correspondence of Franklin D. Roosevelt and Joseph V. Stalin.* New Haven, CT: Yale University Press, 2008.

Cunningham, Kevin. *Joseph Stalin and the Soviet Union.* Greensboro, NC: M. Reynolds, 2006.

Dallin, Aleksandr, and F. I. Firsov. *Dimitrov and Stalin, 1934–1943: Letters from the Soviet Archives.* New Haven, CT: Yale University Press, 2000.

Daushvili, A. *Story of Soso Djugashvili.* N.p.: Tbilisi, 2000.

Davies, Sarah, and James R. Harris. *Stalin: A New History.* Cambridge: Cambridge University Press, 2005.

———. *Stalin's World. Dictating the Soviet Order.* New Haven, CT: Yale University Press, 2014.

Fiehn, Terry, and Chris Corin. *Communist Russia Under Lenin and Stalin.* London: Hodder Education, 2008.

Fitzpatrick, Sheila. *On Stalin's Team: The Years of Living Dangerously in Soviet Politics.* Princeton, NJ: Princeton University Press, 2015.

Getty, J. Arch, Oleg V. Naumov, and Benjamin Sher. *The Road to Terror: Stalin and the Self Destruction of the Bolsheviks, 1932–1939.* Updated and abridged ed. New Haven, CT: Yale University Press, 2010.

Gorbachevsky, B., and Stuart Britton. *Generalissimo Stalin: The Myth of Stalin as a Great Military Strategist: A Red Army Veteran Reflects on Stalin's Wartime Leadership.* Solihull: Helion & Company, 2014.

Gorlizki, Yoram, and O. V. Khlevniuk. *Cold Peace: Stalin and the Soviet Ruling Circle, 1945–1953.* Oxford: Oxford University Press, 2004.

Gorodetsky, Gabriel, ed. *The Maisky Diaries: Red Ambassador to the Court of St. James, 1932–1943.* New Haven, CT: Yale University Press, 2015.

———. *Grand Delusion: Stalin and the German Invasion of Russia.* New Haven, CT: Yale University Press, 1999.

Gregory, Paul R. *Terror by Quota: State Security from Lenin to Stalin (an Archival Study).* New Haven, CT: Yale University Press. 2009.

Grey, Ian. *Stalin.* N.p.: New Word City, 2017.

Harris, Jonathan. *Party Leadership under Stalin and Khrushchev: Party Officials and the Soviet State, 1948–1964.* Lanham, MD: Lexington Books, 2021.

Hasanli, Jamil. *Stalin and the Turkish Crisis of the Cold War, 1945–1953.* Lanham, MD: Rowman & Littlefield, 2011.

Hasegawa, Tsuyoshi. *Racing the Enemy: Stalin, Truman, and the Surrender of Japan.* Cambridge: Belknap Press, 2006.

Hoffman, David. *Stalinism: The Essential Readings.* Hoboken, NJ: Blackwell, 2003.

———. *Stalinist Values: The Cultural Norms of Soviet Modernity, 1917–1941.* Ithaca, NY: Cornell University Press, 2003.

Kerrigan, Michael. *Stalin: Man of Steel or Mass Murderer?* London: Amber Books, 2018.

Khlevniuk, O. V. *Master of the House: Stalin and His Inner Circle.* New Haven, CT: Yale University Press, 2009.

———. *Stalin: New Biography of a Dictator.* New Haven, CT: Yale University Press, 2015.

Kotkin, Stephen. *Stalin: Paradoxes of Power.* Volume 1. New York: Penguin Press, 2014.

———. *Stalin: Waiting for Hitler, 1929–1941.* Volume 2. London: Allen Lane, 2017.

Kowalsky, Daniel. *Stalin and the Spanish Civil War.* New York: Columbia University Press, 2008.

Kun, Miklós. *Stalin: An Unknown Portrait.* Budapest: Central European University Press, 2003.

Kuromiya, Hiroaki. *Stalin.* Harlow, England: Pearson/Longman, 2005.

Lukacs, John. *June 1941.* New Haven, CT: Yale University Press, 2006.

McCauley, Martin. *Stalin and Stalinism.* 4th edition. Abingdon, UK: Routledge, 2019.

McCollum, Sean. *Joseph Stalin.* New York: Franklin Watts, 2010.

McDermott, Kevin. *Stalin: Revolutionary in an Era of War.* Houndmills, Basingstoke, Hampshire, UK: Palgrave Macmillan, 2006.

McKenna, Tony. *The Dictator, the Revolution, the Machine: A Political Account of Joseph Stalin.* Eastbourne, England: Sussex Academic Press, 2016.

McLaughlin, Barry, and Kevin McDermott. *Stalin's Terror: High Politics and Mass Repression in the Soviet Union.* Houndmills, Basingstoke, Hampshire, UK: Palgrave Macmillan, 2003.

McMeekin, Sean. *Stalin's War: A New History of World War II.* New York: Basic Books, 2021.

Medvedev, Zhores A., and Roy A. Medvedev. *The Unknown Stalin.* London: I.B. Tauris, 2003.

Mosier, John. *Deathride: Hitler vs. Stalin: The Eastern Front, 1941–1945.* 1st Simon & Schuster hardcover edition. New York: Simon & Schuster, 2010.

Murphy, David E. *What Stalin Knew: The Enigma of Barbarossa.* New Haven, CT: Yale University Press, 2005.

Naimark, Norman M. *Stalin and the Fate of Europe: The Postwar Struggle for Sovereignty.* Cambridge: Belknap Press, 2019.

———. *Stalin's Genocides.* Princeton, NJ: Princeton University Press, 2010.

Pisch, Anita. *The Personality Cult of Stalin in Soviet Posters, 1929–1953: Archetypes, Inventions and Fabrications.* Canberra: Australian National University Press, 2016.

Plamper, Jan. *The Stalin Cult. A Study in the Alchemy of Power.* New Haven, CT: Yale University Press, 2012.

Pons, Silvio. *Stalin and the Inevitable War: 1936–1941.* London: Frank Cass, 2002.

Rayfield, Donald. *Stalin and His Hangmen: The Tyrant and Those Who Killed for Him.* New York: Random House, 2005.

Read, Christopher. *Stalin: From the Caucasus to the Kremlin.* London: Routledge, 2017.

———. *The Stalin Years: A Reader.* New York: Palgrave Macmillan, 2003.

Rees E. A., ed. *The Nature of Stalin's Dictatorship: The Politburo, 1924–1953.* Basingstoke, UK: Palgrave Macmillan, 2004.

Reynolds, David, and Vladimir Pechatnov. *The Kremlin Letters: Stalin's Wartime Correspondence with Churchill and Roosevelt.* New Haven, CT: Yale University Press, 2019.

Rieber, Alfred J. *Stalin and the Struggle for Supremacy in Eurasia.* Cambridge: Cambridge University Press, 2015.

Roberts, Geoffrey. *Stalin's Wars. From World War to Cold War, 1939–1953.* New Haven, CT: Yale University Press, 2008.

Rubenstein, Joshua. *The Last Days of Stalin.* New Haven, CT: Yale University Press, 2016.

Rubenstein, Joshua, and Vladimir P. Naumov. *Stalin's Secret Pogrom: The Postwar Inquisition of the Jewish Anti-Fascist Committee.* Translated by Laura Esther Wolfson. New Haven, CT: Yale University Press, 2005.

Sebag Montefiore, Simon. *Stalin: The Court of the Red Tsar*. London: Weidenfeld & Nicholson, 2003.

———. *Young Stalin*. Toronto: McArthur, 2007.

Service, Robert. *Stalin: A Biography*. First Harvard University Press paperback edition. Cambridge: Belknap Press, 2006.

Shearer, David R. *Policing Stalin's Socialism. Repression and Social Order in the Soviet Union, 1924–1953*. New Haven, CT: Yale University Press, 2009.

Shearer, David R., and Vladimir Khaustov. *Stalin and the Lubianka*. New Haven, CT: Yale University Press, 2015.

Snyder, Timothy, and Ray Brandon. *Stalin and Europe: Imitation and Domination, 1928–1953*. Oxford: Oxford University Press, 2014.

Sobanet, Andrew. *Generation Stalin: French Writers, the Fatherland, and the Cult of Personality*. Bloomington: Indiana University Press, 2018.

Stalin, Joseph, L. M. Kaganovich, and R. W. Davies. *The Stalin-Kaganovich Correspondence, 1931–36*. New Haven, CT: Yale University Press, 2003.

Sullivan, Rosemary. *Stalin's Daughter: The Extraordinary and Tumultuous Life of Svetlana Allilueva*. New York: HarperCollins, 2015.

Suny, Ronald G. *Stalin: Passage to Revolution*. Princeton, NJ: Princeton University Press, 2020.

van Ree, Erik. *The Political Thought of Joseph Stalin: A Study in Twentieth-Century Revolutionary Patriotism*. London: RoutledgeCurzon, 2002.

Viola, Lynne. *Stalinist Perpetrators on Trial: Scenes from the Great Terror in Soviet Ukraine*. New York: Oxford University Press, 2017.

Volkogonov, Dmitri. *Stalin: Triumph and Tragedy*. New York: Grove Weidenfeld, 1991.

Weeks, Albert Loren. *Assured Victory: How "Stalin the Great" Won the War but Lost the Peace*. Santa Barbara, CA: Praeger, 2011.

———. *Stalin's Other War: Soviet Grand Strategy, 1939–1941*. Lanham, MD: Rowman & Littlefield, 2002.

Wood, Alan. *Stalin and Stalinism*. 2nd edition. London: Routledge, 2005.

Zuehlke, Jeffrey. *Joseph Stalin*. Minneapolis, MN: Twenty-First Century Books, 2006.

ARTICLES

Andrew, Christopher, and Julie Elkner. "Stalin and Foreign Intelligence." *Totalitarian Movements and Political Religions* 4, no. 1 (Summer 2003): 69–94.

Azadovsky, Konstantin, and Boris Egorov. "From Anti-Westernism to Anti-Semitism: Stalin and the Impact of the 'Anti-Cosmopolitan' Campaigns on Soviet Culture." *Journal of Cold War Studies* 4, no. 1 (2002): 66–80.

Baron, Nick. "Stalinist Planning as Political Practice: Control and Repression on the Soviet Periphery, 1935–38." *Europe-Asia Studies* 56, no. 3 (2004): 439–62.

Bauman, Zygmunt. "Stalin." *Cultural Studies/Critical Methodologies* 4, no. 1 (2004): 3–11.

Biskupski, M. B. B. "Roosevelt, Stalin, and Poland." *The Polish Review* 61, no. 1 (2016): 93–100.

Brandenberger, David. "Stalin, the Leningrad Affair, and the Limits of Russocentrism." *Russian Review* 63, no. 2 (2004): 241–55.

Brooks, Jeffrey. "Stalin's Politics of Obligation." *Totalitarian Movements and Political Religions* 4, no. 1 (Summer 2003): 47–68.

Bunce, Robin. "Lenin's Successor." *Modern History Review* 16, no. 1 (September 2004): 79.

Cavendish, Richard. "Death of Joseph Stalin: March 5th, 1953." *History Today* 53, no. 3 (2003): 55–56.

Chubariyan, Aleksandr, and Vladimir O. Pechatnov. "Molotov 'the Liberal': Stalin's 1945 Criticism of His Deputy." *Cold War History* 1, no. 1 (2000): 129–41.

Etty, John. "Lenin's Wonderful Georgian." *History Review* 49 (September 2004): 36–41.

Fitzpatrick, Sheila. "Culture and Politics under Stalin: A Reappraisal." *Slavic Review* 35, no. 2 (1976): 211–31.

———. "Politics as Practice: Thoughts on a New Soviet Political History." *Kritika* 5, no. 1 (Winter 2004): 27–54.

Förster, Jürgen, and Evan Mawdsley. "Hitler and Stalin in Perspective: Secret Speeches on the Eve of Barbarossa." *War in History* 11, no. 1 (2004): 61–103.

Getty, J. Arch. "Excesses Are Not Permitted: Mass Terror and Stalinist Governance in the Late 1930s." *Russian Review* 51, no. 1 (2002): 113–38.

Gidadhubli, R. G. "Looking Back on Stalin." *Economic and Political Weekly* 38, no. 16 (April 19–25, 2003): 1554–55.

Gorlizki, Yoram. "Ordinary Socialism: The Council of Ministers and the Soviet Patrimonial State, 1946–1953." *Journal of Modern History* 74, no. 4 (2002): 699–736.

———. "Stalin's Cabinet: The Politburo and Decision Making in the Post-War Years." *Europe-Asia Studies* 53, no. 2 (2001): 291–312.

Gregory, Paul R., and Andrei Markevich. "Creating Soviet Industry: The House That Stalin Built." *Slavic Review* 61, no. 4 (2002): 787–814.

Harris, James. "Was Stalin a Weak Dictator?" *The Journal of Modern History* 75, no. 2 (June 2003): 375–86.

Haslam, Jonathan. "Stalin and the German Invasion of Russia 1941: A Failure of Reasons of State?" *International Affairs* 76, no. 1 (January 2000): 133–39

Hauner, Milan L. "Stalin's Big-Fleet Program." *Naval War College Review* 57, no. 2 (2004): 87–120.

Himmer, Robert. "First Impressions Matter: Stalin's Initial Encounter with Lenin, Tammefors 1905." *Revolutionary Russia* 14, no. 2 (2001): 73–84.

Kneen, Peter. "De-Stalinization under Stalin? The Case of Science." *Journal of Communist Studies and Transition Politics* 16, no. 4 (December 2000): 107–26.

Kotkin, Stephen. "When Stalin Faced Hitler: Who Fooled Whom?" *Foreign Affairs* 96, no. 6 (November–December 2017): 48.

Kuromiya, Hiroaki. "Stalin and His Era." *The Historical Journal* 50, no. 3 (September 2007): 711–24.

Lang, Sean. "Stalin." *Modern History Review* 16, no. 1 (September 2004): 34–35.

———. "Terror under Stalin." *Modern History Review* 14, no. 3 (February 2003): 1215.

Lenoe, Matt. "Did Stalin Kill Kirov and Does It Matter?" *Journal of Modern History* 74, no. 3 (June 2002): 352–80.

Lynch, Michael. "The Roles of Lenin and Stalin in the Russian Revolution." *History Review* 34 (March 2000): 29–33.

Madievski, Samson. "The Doctors' Plot." *Midstream* 49, no. 6 (September/October 2003): 9–13.

Malashenko, Yevgeny Ivanovich. "Wartime Strategic Direction of Soviet Armed Forces: Historical Lessons." *Military Thought* 12, no. 4 (2003): 183–93.

Marples, David R., and Veranika Laputska. "Kurapaty: Belarus' Continuing Debates." *Slavic Review* 79, no. 3 (Fall 2020): 521–43.

Mawdsley, Evan. "Crossing the Rubicon: Soviet Plans for Offensive War 1940–1941." *International History Review* 25, no. 4 (2003): 818–65.

McDermott, Kevin. "Archives, Power and the 'Cultural Turn': Reflections on Stalin and Stalinism." *Totalitarian Movements and Political Religions* 5, no. 1 (2004): 5–24.

Medvedev, Zhores A. "The Puzzle of Stalin's Death." *Russian Social Science Review* 45, no. 1 (2004): 83–97.

———. "Stalin and the Atomic Gulag." *Spokesman*, no. 69 (2000): 91–111.

Meyer, Gerald. "Grover Furr on 'Joseph Stalin: Revisionist Biography': A Response." *Science & Society* 82, no. 4 (October 2018): 576–81.

Montefiore, Simon Sebag. "History and Biography." *History Today* 54, no. 3 (2004): 30–31.

Moraitis, George. "The Ghost in the Biographer's Machine." *Annual of Psychoanalysis* 31 (2003): 97–106.

Murphy, Mike. "Stalin Lives." *Weekly Standard* 8, no. 34 (May 12, 2003): 16–17.

Nordling, Carl O. "Stalin's Insistent Endeavors at Conquering Finland." *Journal of Slavic Military History* 16, no. 1 (2003): 137–57.

Pohl, J. Otto. "Stalin's Ethnic Cleansing of the Crimean Tartars and Their Struggle for Rehabilitation, 1944–1985." *Ukrainian Quarterly* 60, nos. 1–2 (Spring–Summer 2004): 33–56.

———. "Stalin's Genocide against the 'Repressed Peoples.'" *Journal of Genocide Research* 2, no. 2 (2000): 267–94.

Potapenko, Vladimir. "From the Time of Troubles to the Present Day." *Russian Politics and Law* 38, no. 1 (January/February 2000): 84–96.

Pringle, Robert W. "Modernization of Terror: The Transformation of Stalin's NKVD, 1934–1941." *International Journal of Intelligence and Counterintelligence* 17, no. 1 (Spring 2004): 113–23.

Rappaport, Helen. "Stalin and the Photographer." *History Today* 51, no. 6 (2001): 12–20.

Reed-Purvis, Julian. "The Party That Ate Itself." *History Review* 40 (September 2001): 13–18.

Rees, E. A. "The Great Terror: Suicide or Murder?" *Russian Review* 59, no. 3 (July 2000): 446–50.

Rees, Simon. "Historians Are Still Trying to Sort Out the Dark Private Life and Strange Death of Josef Stalin." *Military History* 20, no. 4 (2003): 18–22.

Rieber, Alfred J. "Stalin, Man of the Borderlands." *American Historical Review* 106, no. 5 (December 2001): 1651–91.

Roberts, Geoffrey. "Josef Stalin." *History Review* 47 (December 2003): 47–50.

Ryan, Karen. "The Devil You Know: Postmodern Reconsiderations of Stalin." *Mosaic: An Interdisciplinary Critical Journal* 36, no. 3 (September 2003): 87–111.

Sandle, Mark. "Stalin: Did He Preserve or Destroy Bolshevism?" *Modern History Review* 13, no. 4 (2002): 16–19.

Service, Robert. "Stalinism and the Soviet State Order." *Totalitarian Movements and Political Religions* 4, no. 1 (Summer 2003): 7–23.

Smith, Michael G. "Stalin's Martyrs: The Tragic Romance of the Russian Revolution." *Totalitarian Movements and Political Religions* 4, no. 1 (Summer 2003): 95–126.

Staerck, Gillian. "The Death of Stalin, 9 [sic] March 1953." *Modern History Review* 12, no. 4 (April 2001): 34–35.

———. "Joseph Stalin and Life in the Soviet Union 1924–53." *Modern History Review* 13, no. 3 (February 2002): 1.

Strobel, Warren P. "Why Stalin Thought the U.S. Would Stay Out." *U.S. News and World Report* 128, no. 24 (June 19, 2000): 34–35.

Swain, Geoffrey. "Lenin, Tyrant or Saviour? Trotsky, Bukharin or Stalin: Who Could Best Claim to Be Heir to All That Lenin Stood for, Good or Bad?" *Modern History Review* 16, no. 1 (September 2004): 2–6.

———. "Stalin's Foreign Policy 1928–1941." *Modern History Review* 15, no. 3 (2004): 12–16.

———. "Stalin's Rise to Power." *Modern History Review* 14, no. 3 (2003): 3–7.

Thatcher, Ian D. "Nazism and Stalinism." *History Review* 45 (March 2003): 8–13.

———. "Stalin and Stalinism: A Review Article." *Europe-Asia Studies* 56, no. 6 (September 2004): 907–32.

Todorov, Tzvetan. "Stalin Close Up." Translated by Karine Zbinden. *Totalitarian Movements and Political Religions* 5, no. 1 (2004): 94–111.

van Ree, Erik. "Stalin as Writer and Thinker." *Kritika* 3, no. 4 (2002): 699–714.

———. "Stalin's Bolshevism: The Year of the Revolution." *Revolutionary Russia* 13, no. 1 (2000): 29–54.

Veidlinger, Jeffrey. "Soviet Jewry as a Diaspora Nationality: The 'Black Years' Reconsidered." *East European Jewish Affairs* 33, no. 1 (2003): 4–29.

Ward, Chris. "What Is History? The Case of Late Stalinism." *Rethinking History* 8, no. 3 (2004): 439–58.

Wingrove, Paul. "The Mystery of Stalin." *History Today* 53, no. 3 (2003): 18–20.

Zhukov, Yuri M., and Roya Talibova. "Stalin's Terror and the Long-Term Political Effects of Mass Repression." *Journal of Peace Research* 55, no. 2 (2018): 267–83.

Zubkova, Elena. "The Soviet Regime and Soviet Society in the Postwar Years: Innovations and Conservatism, 1945–1953." *Journal of Modern European History* 2, no. 1 (2004): 134–52.

Index

Note: Bold numbers refer to dictionary entries

Abakumov, Viktor Semenovich, **13–14**, 19, 44, 86, 128, 143
Aleksandr II (tsar), 1
Allilue, Iosif, 15
Alliluev, Fedor Sergeevich, **14**
Alliluev, Sergei Iakovlevich, xviii, **14**
Allilueva, Nadezhda Sergeevna, xix, xxi, **14–15**, 80, 101
Allilueva, Svetlana Iosifovna, **15–16**
Andreev, Andrei Andreevich, **16**
April Theses, xix, 107, 169, 189, 232, 267
Azerbaijan, Azeris, 17, 41, 104, 142, 146, 159, 216, 226

Bagirov, Mir Dzhafar, 18
Baku, xviii, xix, 1–2, 14, 18, 19, 41, 79, 80, 104, 129, 146, 158, 172, 200–201, 220, 243, 249, 252
Balkan Pact (1953), 225
Batitsky, P. F., 19
Bazhanov, Boris Georgievich, **17**
Benediktov, Ivan Aleksandrovich, 15
Beria, Lavrenty Pavlovich, xxi–xxiii, 8, **17–19**, 21, 26, 41, 86, 90, 142; arrest and execution of, 13, 42, 102, 110, 115, 136, 138, 152, 197, 205; after death of Stalin, 45, 86, 91, 102, 115, 151, 265; in Great Patriotic War, 18, 100, 123; as NKVD leader, 6, 13, 22, 31, 85, 128, 137, 196, 211, 252; as party leader in Georgia, 41, 143; in postwar years (1946–53), 19, 86, 128, 136, 197, 244, 263
Berman, Boris Davydovich, **19–20**
Berman, Matvei Davydovich, **20**
Bliukher, Vasily Konstantinovich, **20–21**, 37
Blokhin, Vasily Mikhailovich, **21–22**, 111

Bolshevik Party, Bolsheviks. *See* Russian Social Democratic Workers' Party (RSDWP)
Brest–Litovsk Treaty, xix, 24, 33–34, 46, 95, 113–14, 121, 168, 179–80, 207, 210, 218, 233, 268
Brezhnev, Leonid Ilich, **22–23**, 217, 225, 266; death of, 217; as leader of USSR, 8, 66, 73, 103, 113, 172; and removal of Khrushchev, 103
Britain, British, xxii, 3, 7, 34, 62, 72–73, 95, 130, 145, 160, 182, 224, 230, 232, 252; at Ialta Conference, 7, 78, 136, 248; at Potsdam Conference, 136, 174–75, 248; relations with Soviet Union (Soviet Russia), 34, 130, 136, 151, 186, 211, 226, 245, 253; and Tehran Conference, 219, 246, 250
Briukhanov, Nikolai Pavlovich, **22–24**, 70
Bubnov, Andrei Sergeevich, **24**, 186, 210
Budenny, Semen Mikhailovich, **24–25**, 47, 68, 98, 163, 199, 201–202, 221–22, 237, 264
Bukharin, Nikolai Ivanovich, xx, xxi, 2, 4, **25–27**, 76, 81, 117, 176, 182, 187, 203, 207, 209–10, 227, 239, 252, 260, 268; and the *ABC of Communism*, 175; arrest, trial, and execution of, 20, 33, 67, 76, 87, 99, 180, 186, 189, 203, 228; and Brest Treaty, 107; and New Economic Policy, 4, 228; and Right Opposition, 16, 24, 39, 95, 119, 149, 156, 171, 198, 240; and Socialism in One Country, 208
Bulganin, Nikolai Aleksandrovich, **27–29**, 102, 123, 139, 265

Charkviani, Christopher, xvii
Chechnia, Chechens, 69; deportation of, by Stalin, xxii, 18, 115, 147, 196
Cheka (Extraordinary Committee to Combat Sabotage and Counter-Revolution), 18, 20, 27, **31**, 41, 49, 75, 85, 95, 141, 143, 159–61, 168, 193, 195, 220, 228–29, 240, 248–49, 257, 259. *See also* GPU, OGPU, NKVD
Cherniakhovsky, Ivan Danilovich, **31–32**
Chernov, Mikhail Aleksandrovich, **32–33**
Chicherin, Boris (brother of Georgy), 33
Chicherin, Boris (uncle of Georgy), 34
Chicherin, Georgy Vasilyevich, **33–34**, 130
Churchill, Winston S., 7, 78, 110, 174–75, 219, 253
Communist International (Comintern), xx, 4, 17, 27, 34, **39**, 42–43, 52, 70, 74, 107–108, 124, 137, 148, 154, 168, 179–80, 192, 218, 224, 229–30, 234, 268

Dagestan, Dagestanis, 69, 183
The Death of Stalin (movie), 8
Denikin, Anton, 3, 46, 68, 79, 81, 97, 122, 195, 198, 206, 221, 261, 264
Doctors' Plot, xxiii, 8, 13, 19, **44–45**, 86, 146, 248, 263
Dzhaparidze, P. A., xviii

Eiderman, Robert Petrovich, xxi

Famines, 124 (1921–22), 26, 93, 195, 247 (1932–33), 5, 16, 33, 35–36, 57, 89, 111, 131, 150, 167–68, 173–74, 184 (1946–47), 58, 102, 112
Fedorov, G. F., xix
Finansovaia Gazeta, 17
Five-Year Plans, **56–58**, 122, 144, 148, 150, 154, 157, 159, 169, 213, 220

Gegechkori, Nina Teymurazovna, 19
Georgia, Georgians, xvii, 1, 16, 18, 41, 87, 92, 94, 101, 104, 130, 142–43, 157–59, 219
Germany, Germans, xxii, 19–20, 26, 34, 41–42, 57, 77, 86, 107–108, 114, 135, 158, 179, 181, 193, 209, 223–24, 269; Berlin Blockade in, xxiii; and Brest–Litovsk Treaty, 121, 169, 180, 207, 210, 234, 268; in Great Patriotic War, 13, 41, 62, 140, 226; occupation of after Second World War, 36, 38, 66, 69, 78, 110, 175, 197, 213, 245, 253, 261, 265; and Pact with USSR, 6, 143, 150, 153–54; relations with USSR in interwar period, 33, 68, 124, 130, 180, 182; relations with USSR in postwar period (West Germany), 73; Tehran Conference and, 219
Gorbachev, Mikhail Sergeevich, 6, 16, 23, 27, 31, 73, 96, 101, 157, 170, 187, 216, 269
GPU (State Political Directorate), 31, 49, 75–76, 105, 114, 120, 142–43, 160, 180, 229, 241, 259. *See also* Cheka, OGPU
Great Patriotic War (Second World War, 1941–45), xxii, 7, 57, 61, **65–66**, 147, 185, 204; battle of Stalingrad. *See* Stalingrad, Battle of; NKVD in, 13; restoration of commemorations of, by V. Putin, 7–8; Soviet aircraft in, 78; Soviet military leaders in, 21, 25, 32, 36–37, 65, 69, 81, 100, 106, 108–109, 131–32, 139, 165, 211–12, 222, 244, 246–47, 250, 264–66; Soviet political leaders in, 28, 42, 72, 91, 94, 102, 112, 114–15, 122, 124–25, 137, 147, 150, 163, 185, 196, 199, 202, 204, 251, 263, 271; Soviet losses in, 62; Soviet victory in, xxiii; State Defense Committee in, 215–16
Great Purge (1937–38), xxi, 6, 21, 24, 28, 31, 41, 53, 57, **66–68**, 76, 82, 86, 91, 98, 101–103, 105, 111, 124, 128, 137, 161, 170, 193, 199, 221, 240–41, 259, 262, 268–69. *See also* Show Trials

Hitler, Adolf, 8, 77, 143; appointed German Chancellor, 43, 124; and Great Patriotic War, 215; meetings with Molotov, 150, 154; suicide of, 66, 265

Iagoda, Genrik, xxi, 21, 27, **75–77**, 84, 114, 129, 230, 296; arrest and execution of, 22, 84, 189, 203, 269; dismissal as head of Internal Affairs, xxi, 6, 20, 120, 260; as head of NKVD during Great Purge, 22, 31, 120, 142, 252, 269
Iakir, Iona, Emmanuilovich, xxi, 22, 47, 174, 237
Iakovlev, Aleksandr Nikolaevich (politician), 6, 96, 216

INDEX

Iakovlev, Aleksandr Sergeevich (aeronautical engineer), **77-78**
Ialta Conference, 7-8, 18, 61, 66, 72, **78-79**, 136, 151, 175, 248, 253
Iezhov, Nikolai, Ivanovich, xxi, 16, 21-22, **82-85**, 143; arrest and execution of, 18, 20, 22, 137, 269; and Iezovshchina, xxi, 21, 27, 31, **66-68**, 70, 76, 119-20, 160-61, 182, 184, 221, 203, 208, 253, 260. See also Great Purge
Ikramov, Akmal Ikramovich, xxi, **86-87**, 98
Industrial Party, xx, 119, 142, 252
Iskra (newspaper), xvii
Iumashov, Ivan Stepanovich, **87-88**
Ivanov, Vladimir Ivanovich, **88**

Japan, Japanese, 7, 21, 29, 37, 51, 66, 78, 108, 151, 229, 247, 264
Jewish Anti-Fascist Committee (League), xxiii, 8, 13, 138, 145, 216. See also Mikhoels, Solomon

Kaganovich, Lazar Moiseevich, 5, 17, 26, **89-91**, 101, 137, 144; and Anti-Party Group, 23, 29, 103, 138-39, 152, 167, 266; and Famine of 1932-33, 168, 174; and Moscow metro, 28; as party leader of Ukraine, 102; and Soviet leadership, 76, 111, 236, 241; and succession question, 19
Kaganovich, Mikhail Moiseevich, **91-92**
Kalinin, Mikhail Ivanovich, xvii, xxii, 18, 80, **92-94**, 189, 205
Kamenev, Lev Borisovich, xix, 6, 24, **94-96**, 144, 210, 234; arrest, trial, and execution of, 67, 76, 84, 150, 180, 203, 228, 252, 269; and October Revolution, 4, 267; and triumvirate with Stalin and Zinoviev, xx, 3-4, 189, 235, 268; and United (Left) Opposition, 4, 26, 55, 81, 90, 117, 126, 149, 156, 159, 208, 211, 228, 268
Kamenev, Sergei Sergeevich, **96-98**
Katyn massacre, 18, 22, 93, 143, 205
Khodzhaev, Fayzulla, **98-99**
Khrulev, Andrei Vasilevich, **99-101**, 163
Khrushchev, Nikita Sergeevich, 27-29, 85, **101-103**, 240; and Anti-Party Group, 23, 72, 110, 113, 116, 137, 139-40, 152, 167, 197, 217, 266; in Great Patriotic War, 82, 139; and Kaganovich, 89-90; secret speech at 20th Party Congress, 19, 22, 53, 72, 174, 188, 197; as Soviet leader, 3, 8, 23, 27, 31, 38, 58, 73, 96, 157, 172, 217, 225, 271; and succession question after Stalin's death, 19, 138, 147, 205, 250; as Ukrainian party leader, xxi, 91, 196, 214-15
Kirilina, Alla, 6
Kirov, Sergei Mironovich, 17, **103-105**, 121, 127, 193; assassination of, xxi, 5-6, 68, 76, 84, 93, 96, 128, 203, 207-208, 241, 260, 262, 268
Kirponos, Mikhail Petrovich, **105-106**
Knight, Amy, 6
Kollontai, Aleksandra Mikhailovna, 45-46, **106-108**, 209
Konev, Ivan Stepanovich, 7, **108-10**
Korean War, 19
Kork, Avgust Ivanovich, xxi
Kosior, Stanislaw Vikentyevich, 55, **110-11**, 144, 174, 236
Kosygin, Aleksei Nikolaevich, 23, 73, 103, **111-12**, 172, 271
Krestinsky, Nikolai Nikolaevich, **113-14**, 189, 203, 210, 234
Kriuchkov, Piotr Petrovich, **114-15**
Kronstadt Uprising, 24, 46, 87, 93, 109
Kruglov, Sergei Nikiforovich, 19, **115-16**
Krupskaia, Nadezhda, Konstantinova, 95, 106, **116-18**, 127, 149, 171, 187, 211, 267
Krylenko, Nikolai, Vasilevich, **118-19**, 160, 198
Kubatkin, Piotr Nikolaevich, **119-21**, 211
Kuibyshev, Valerian, Vladimirovich, 35, 76, 98, **121-22**, 129, 144, 171
Kuibyshev (city, region), 16, 67, 174, 248
Kulik, Grigory Ivanovich, **122-23**, 199
Kun, Béla, **123-24**, 169
Kuznetsov, Aleksei Aleksandrovich, 19, 120, **124-25**, 128, 222, 228
Kwiring, Emanuel Ionovich, **125-26**
Kyiv Special Military District, xxi, 62, 106, 196, 264

Lazarkina, Dora Abramovna, **127-28**
Left Opposition, 24, 26, 31, 95, 114, 156, 168-69, 177, 180, 182-83, 191-93, 206-8, 211, 230, 235. See also United Opposition, Trotsky, Leon Davidovich; Kamenev, Lev Borisovich; Zinoviev, Grigory Ievseevich

INDEX

Lenin, Vladimir Ilich, xvii, xviii, xix, xx, 1–5, 8, 14–16, 17, 26, 39, 42, 46, 48, 54–55, 58, 65, 79, 84, 93–95, 97, 102, 106, 109, 116–18, 124, 127–30, 141–42, 146, 148–49, 151, 158, 167–68, 171, 176, 179, 183, 187, 194, 203, 209, 217–20, 223, 227–28, 239–40, 249–50, 252, 266–68; and April Theses, 169, 189, 232, 267; attempted assassination of, 168, 218; illness and death of, 49, 76, 80, 90, 93, 117, 126, 147, 149, 169, 189, 207–208, 235, 266; Letter to the Congress of (Testament), 3, 117; marriage of, 109; Mausoleum of, 103; and New Economic Policy, 154, 157; and October Revolution of 1917, 119, 141, 206, 210, 267; and RSDWP split (1902), 106–107; and Stalin, 117, 184; and Trotsky, 231–35

Leningrad (city), xix, 2, 6, 14, 17, 32, 34, 36, 43, 48, 58, 61–62, 64–65, 75, 80, 82–83, 88, 92–94, 96, 99, 104–106, 111, 113–14, 116, 118, 125, 127–29, 133, 141, 148, 154, 158, 172, 176, 181, 188, 191, 193, 198, 203, 217–18, 220, 225, 227, 229, 231, 239, 260–61, 267–68; assassination of Kirov in, 5, 68, 84, 96, 105, 128; Leningrad Affair in, 8, 14, 19, 63, 120–21, 125, **128**, 138, 185, 251, 263; Leningrad Front during war, 112, 122, 124, 250, 263, 265; Military District of, 199, 202, 226, 237, 262; party organization of, 4–5; siege of, during war, 7, 66, 112, 120, 122, 124–25, 138, 197, 250, 263, 265

Leningrad Affair, 13–14, 19, 63, 120, **128**, 138, 185, 251, 263

Leningrad Higher Cavalry School, 81, 131

The Lessons of October, 4

Levin, Lev Grigorevich, 114, **128–29**

"Liquidation of kulaks as a class," 4–5, 22, 83, 90, 184, 189, 259–60

Litvinov, Maksim Maksimovich, xxi, **129–30**, 210; appointed Commissar of Foreign Affairs, 34, 130; dismissal of, as Commissar of Foreign Affairs, 150; as Soviet Ambassador to USA, 72, 136

Liubchenko, Panas, Petrovych, **130–31**

Lopatin, Anton Ivanovich, **131–32**

Lunacharsky, Anatoly Vasilevich, 24, 127, **132–33**

Luzhkov, Genrik, 21

MacArthur, Douglas, 7

Maisky, Ivan Mikhailovich, xxii, **135–37**

Malenkov, xxii, 71, 86, **137–39**; and Anti-Party Group, 19, 23, 29, 91, 103, 152, 167, 266; and the Doctors' Plot, 44–45; and the Great Purge, 85; and Leningrad Affair, 128; in Soviet leadership, 90, 164, 263; and succession question after Stalin's death, 86, 91, 102, 152

Malinovsky, Rodion Iakovlevich, **139–41**

Mao ZeDong, 8, 37

Marxism and the National Question, 2

Mensheviks, xviii, 18, 32, 34, 68, 95, 104, 106, 119, 122, 133, 135, 142, 144, 148, 181, 189, 203, 209, 220, 231, 246, 252, 267

Menzhinsky, Viacheslav Rudolfovich, 76, 129, **141–42**, 230

Merkulov, Vsevolod Nikolaevich, 13, **142–43**

Mesame Dasi group, xvii

Meshketian Turks, 18

Meyendorf, Baron Aleksandr, 34

Meyendorf, Zhorzhina, 33

Mezhlauk, Valery Ivanovich, **143–45**

Mikhoels, Solomon, 8, 13, **145–46**

Mikoian, Anastas Ivanovich, 137, 144, **146–48**; in postwar years, 103, 151, 172; in Stalin leadership (1930s), 90

Miliutin, Vladimir Pavlovich, **148–49**

Molotov, Viacheslav Mikhailovich, xxi, 19, 53, 84, 90, 114, 136, 147, 184, **149–52**, 239–40, 268; and Anti-Party Group (1957), 23, 29, 91, 103, 138–39, 167, 266; as Foreign Minister, 71–72, 130, 143, 253; and the Great Patriotic War, 6, 109, 219, 222; and the Great Purge, 47, 236; and letters to Stalin, 5; and Nazi–Soviet Pact, xxii, 153, 196, 246; and the Ukrainian famine (Holodomor), 36

Molotov–Ribbentrop Pact. *See* Nazi–Soviet Pact

Nazi–Soviet Pact, xxii, 78, 150, **153–54**, 196

New Economic Policy, 4, 26, 35, 39, 56, 95, 107, **154–57**, 189, 210, 228, 256–57, 270

Nikolaev, Leonid, 5, 105

NKVD (People's Commissariat of Internal Affairs), 5–6, 20–22, 27, 52, 63, 115, 119–20, 129, 143, 159–60, 195–96, 259–60; creation of, 27, 31; in Great Patriotic War,

7, 67, 115, 171, 196–97; military purge by, 47, 241; purge of, 6; troikas of, 52–53, 68, 86–87, 101, 125, 205; under Beria, xxii, 6, 13, 18–19, 22, 196, 230, 235; under Iagoda, 22, 75–77, 202, 208, 211; under Iezhov, xxi, 22, 36, 41, 51, 84–85, 128, 137–38, 171, 181, 185, 188, 202–203, 221, 252. *See also* Cheka, GPU, OGPU
Nogin, Viktor Pavlovich, xix, 267
Nuremberg Trials, 6, 252–53

October Revolution, xix, 4, 24, 34–35, 39, 45, 48, 59, 70, 75, 88–89, 93, 95, 99, 106–107, 113–14, 117, 132, 141, 149, 159, 169, 173, 182, 187, 189, 198, 201, 204, 206–207, 217–18, 230, 233, 239, 248–49, 255, 259–60
OGPU (Joint State Political Directorate), 13, 18, 20, 22, 27, 31, 49, 56, 75–76, 120, 141–42, 180, 182, 198, 202, 208, 230, 241, 248, 259. *See also* Cheka, GPU, NKVD
Orakhelashvili, Mamia, **157–58**
Ordzhonikidze, Sergo, xix, xxi, 49, 92, 127, 129, 150, **158–59**
Orlov, Aleksandr Mikhailovich, **159–61**

Patolichev, Nikolai Semionovich, 86, **163–64**
Pavlov, Dmitry Grigorevich, **164–65**, 264
Pervukhin, Mikhail Georgievich, 139, **165–67**
Petrovsky, Hryhory Ivanovich, **167–68**
Piatakov, Georgy Leonidovich, xxi, 24, 124, 144, **168–70**, 186, 195; arrest and execution of, 159, 203
Peters, Lana. *See* Allilueva, Svetlana Iosifovna
Petrograd. *See* Leningrad
Pletnev, Dmitry Dmitrievich, 114, **170–71**, 183
Podgorny, Nikolai, Viktorovich, 23, 103, **171–72**
Podvoisky, Nikolai Ilich, 118–19, 144, **172–73**
Postyshev, Pavel Petrovich, 16, **173–74**
Potsdam Conference, xxiii, 72, 115, **174–75**, 248, 253
Preobrazhensky, Ievgeny Alekseevich, 26, 114, 169, **175–77**, 180
Primakov, Vitaly Markovich, xxi, 169, 202
Putin, Vladimir Vladimirovich, 8
Putna, Vitovt Kazimirovich, xxi

Pravda, xix, xx, 2, 26–27, 45, 62, 65, 94, 99, 118, 125, 149, 158, 171–72, 208, 210, 214, 217–18, 228, 231–32, 267

Questions of Leninism, xx

Radek, Karl Berngardovich, xxi, 177, **179–81**, 203, 211
Rakovsky, Christian, xxi, 126, 169, **181–83**, 195, 203
Right Opposition, 16, 20, 24, 26–27, 31, 39, 87, 157, 184, 189, 198, 228, 240. *See also* Bukharin, Nikolai Ivanovich; Rykov, Aleksei Ivanovich; Tomsky, Mikhail Pavlovich
Riutin, Martemian Nikitich, xx, **183–85**, 240, 268
Riutin Platform. *See* Riutin, Martemian Nikitich
Rodionov, Mikhail Ivanovich, 19, 125, 128, **185–86**
Rokossovsky, Konstantin Konstantinovich, 7, 32, 66, 215, 264–65
Roosevelt, Franklin D., 7–8, 78–79, 161, 219, 253
Rosengolts, Arkady Pavlovich, **186–87**
Rudzutaks, Janis, 25, **187–88**
Russian Social Democratic Workers' Party (RSDWP), xviii, 2, 14, 17, 20, 21, 23, 24, 26–27, 34–36, 48, 55, 58, 59, 61, 65, 74, 75, 80, 83, 88–89, 92, 94–95, 99, 104, 106, 110, 113, 117–19, 121, 126–27, 129–31, 133, 135, 137, 141, 144, 146, 148–49, 157–58, 160, 167–69, 172–73, 176, 182–83, 186–88, 191, 193–94, 200–201, 203, 206–207, 209, 217–18, 220, 224, 227–29, 231, 233–34, 239–40, 243, 249, 252, 259, 262, 267, 269; Second Congress and split of (1903), 1, 106–107, 129, 181, 217, 231, 267; Fourth Congress of (Stockholm, 1906), xviii, 2, 58, 249; Fifth Congress of (London, 1907), xviii, 23, 48, 58, 94, 117, 227, 249, 267; Sixth Conference of (1912), 93, 158, 217–18; Sixth Congress of (1917), 107, 113, 194, 209–10, 249; Seventh All-Russian Conference of (1917), xix, 107, 127, 148.
Russo–Japanese War, 1, 25, 71, 121–22, 132, 140

Rykov, Aleksei Ivanovich, xxi, 76, 144, **188–89**, 256, 267; arrest, trial, and execution of, 16, 25, 33, 67, 87, 99, 186, 198, 203, 228; and Right Opposition, 4, 26–27, 156, 227–28, 240, 268

St. Petersburg. *See* Leningrad
Sapronov, Timofei Vladimirovich, **191–92**, 207–208
Serebriakov, Leonid Petrovich, xxi, 114
Serge, Victor, **192–93**
Sergeev, Fedor Andreevich, **193–95**
Serov, Ivan Aleksandrovich, 86, **195–98**, 266
Shakhty trial, xx, 119, **198**, 252
Shaposhnikov, Boris Mikhailovich, **198–99**
Sharangovich, Vasily Fomich, **199–200**
Shchadenko, Efim Afanasevich, **200–202**
Shliapnikov, A. G., 3
Show Trials, 6, 22, 33, 88, 131, 180, **202–203**, 240–41. *See also* Great Purge
Show Trials, xxi, 6, 22, 27, 33, 88, 131, 180, **202–203**, 240–41
Shvernik, Nikolai Mikhailovich, **203–206**
Singh, Bragesh, 15
Smilga, Ivar Tenisovich, xix, 177, 180, **206–207**
Smirnov, Vladimir Mikhailovich, 56, 177, 186, 192, **207–208**
Socialism in One Country, 4, 39, **208–209**
Sokolnikov, Grigory, Iakovlevich, xxi, 24, 203, **209–11**
Sokolovsky, Vasily Danilovich, **211–13**
Soviet–Finnish Non-Aggression Pact (1932), 136
Soviet–Finnish War. *See* Winter War
Soviet–German Treaty of Friendship and Borders (1939), xxii
Soviet–Japanese Neutrality Pact (1941), xxii, 150
Spanish Civil War, Spain, Spanish, xxi, 68, 122, 133, 136, 139 159–61, 165, 192, 224, 232
Stakhanov, Aleksei, **213–15**
Stakhanovite movement, xxi, 57, 214
Stalin, Iakov, 2, 15
Stalin, Iosif Vissarionovich, career of, 1–9; chronology of, xvii–xxiii; family of, xvii, 14–16
Stalin, Vasily, 15

Stalingrad (city), 56–58, 166; Battle of (1942–43), 7, 36–39, 62, 66, 82, 102–103, 109, 132, 138–40, 197, **215**, 219, 222, 227, 246, 265; in Russian Civil War, 3, 14, 25, 46, 79, 101, 122, 144, 159, 195, 201, 212, 248–49, 262, 264
State Defense Committee, 7, 18, 28, 66, 91, 109, 137, 147, 150, 165–66, 185, 196–97, **215–16**, 246, 250–51
Sudoplatov, P.A., xxi–xxii
Suslov, Mikhail Andreevich, **216–17**
Svanidze, Iekaterina (Kato), xviii, 2, 15
Svanidze, Ivan, 15
Sverdlov, Iakov Mikhailovich, xix, 19, 75, 95, **217–18**; death of, 93

Tehran Conference, xxii, 7, 72, 151, 175, **219**, 248, 250
Ter-Petrosian, Simon Arshaki, xvii, 14, **219–20**
Tiflis Theological Seminary, xvii
Timoshenko, Semen, Konstantinovich, 199, **221–23**, 250
Tito (Josip Broz), 19, 29, 43, 86, **223–25**; rift with Stalin, 19, 43
Tolbukhin, Fedor Ivanovich, **225–27**
Tomsky, Mikhail Pavlovich, 4, 144, **227–28**; and Right Opposition, 26–27, 156, 240
Trilisser, Mikhail Abramovich, **228–30**
Trotsky, Leon Davidovich, xix, 26, 34, 49, 60, 90, 114, 117, 124, 155, 160, 169, 180–81, 186–87, 217–18, **230–35**, 252, 267; assassination of, xxii, 161; and Civil War, 3; expulsion from USSR, 111, 209; and Great Purge of 1937–38, 6, 70, 76, 96, 170, 193, 203; and October Revolution, xix, 2, 4, 210, 218, 233; and Permanent Revolution theory, 39, 208–209; and Red Army, 97, 207–208, 233–34; and triumvirate against T., 4, 16, 95, 126, 149, 169, 189, 235, 268; and United (Left) Opposition, 4, 24, 26, 55, 81, 114, 156, 159, 168, 182–83, 192, 207–208, 228, 235
Truman, Harry S., 8, 174
Tsaritsyn, *see* Stalingrad
Tsukerman, Vladimir Moiseevich, **235–36**
Tukhachevsky, Mikhail Nikolaievich, xxi, 199, 202, **236–37**; arrest, trial, and execution of, 21–22, 25, 47, 80, 100, 202–203, 241, 252–53; in Russian Civil War, 46, 98; in war with Poland

Uborevich, Ieronim Petrovich, xxi, 22, 47, 237
Uglanov, Nikolai Aleksandrovich, 149, **239–40**
Ulrikh, Vasily, 203, 208, **240–41**
United Opposition, 4, 55, 81, 95, 208, 228

Vannikov, Boris Lvovich, **243–44**
Vasilev, Aleksandr Filippovich, **244–45**
Vasilevsky, Aleksandr Mikhailovich, xxii, 199, 215, **245–47**, 250
Vinogradov, Vladislav Petrovich, 44, 183, **247–48**
Vlasik, Nikolai Sidorovich, xxiii, 45, 86, **248–49**
Volgograd, *see* Stalingrad
Voroshilov, Kliment Iefremovich, xxii, 15, 28, 62, 144, 163, 235, **249–50**; and Anti-Party Group, 139; in Great Patriotic War, 109, 199, 222; and Great Purge, 200, 236–37; appointed Marshal of the Soviet Union, 199, 202; in Russian Civil War, 79, 98, 108, 122, 186, 195, 201, 221, 249; in Soviet leadership, 84–85, 90; in Winter War, 222
Voznesensky, Nikolai Alekseevich, 19, 120, 128, 233, **251**
Vyshinsky, Andrei, 119, 151, 170, **251–53**; and Show Trials, 6, 68, 198, 203, 208, 228

Wallenberg, Raoul, 13
War Communism, 4–5, 56, 62, 154–56, 195, **255–57**

Warsaw Pact, 69, 225
Winter War, 1939–40 (USSR and Finland), xxii, 37, 100, 106, 122, 153, 165, 222, 244, 246, 250, 263

Zakovsky, Leonid Mikhailovich, **259–60**
Zaveniagin, Avraamy Pavlovich, **260–61**
Zhdanov, Andrei Aleksandrovich, 84, 125, **261–63**; and Cominform, 138; and cultural uniformity, 241; death of, 19, 44, 128; power base in Leningrad, 90, 111, 125
Zhdanov, Iury, 15
Zhukov, Georgy, 6–7, 28, **263–66**; and Anti-Party Group, 103; arrest of Beria by, 19; as Defense Minister, 8, 140; fall from power, 110; in Great Patriotic War, 63, 66, 109, 196, 222, 247, 250
Zinoviev, Grigory Ievseevich, xix, 3, 17, 74, 90, 97, 180, 189, 209, **266–69**; arrest, trial, and execution of, xxi, 6, 67, 76, 84, 96, 150, 203, 241, 252; and Comintern, 39, 193; and October Revolution, 4, 95, 210; in triumvirate with Stalin and Kamenev, xx, 95, 126, 189, 235; and United Opposition with Trotsky and Kamenev, 4, 24, 26, 55, 81, 95, 104, 117, 149, 156, 159, 180, 192, 208, 211, 228
Zorin, Valerian Aleksandrovich, **269**
Zubarev, Prokopy, **269–70**
Zverev, Arseny Grigorevich, **270–72**
Zvezda (newspaper), 2, 65, 118, 136, 172

About the Authors

Alla Hurska was born and raised in the city of Rivne, Ukraine. Initially focusing on international relations, Alla studied in Ukraine, Poland, Germany, and Spain. Currently she is a graduate student in history at the University of Alberta (Edmonton, Canada).

Alla is an associate fellow with the International Centre for Policy Studies (Kyiv) and an analyst with the Jamestown Foundation (Washington, DC, US). She is a team member of the Defence and Security Foresight Group (European NATO team, University of Waterloo), and a graduate fellow of the North American and Arctic Defence and Security Network (Trent University, School for the Study of Canada).

Alla's main areas of research are geoeconomic and geopolitical issues in the post-Soviet area, including the Arctic region and geopolitics of gas and oil. She is also interested in the role of Russian propaganda campaigns in influencing public opinion and decision-making in post-Soviet countries. Alla's articles and expert comments have been published by international think tanks, research institutions, and news outlets, including the Jamestown Foundation (Washington, DC), Center for European Policy Analysis (Washington, DC), Diplomaatia (Estonia), ICPS (Ukraine), *Kyiv Post* (Ukraine), Barcelona Centre for International Affairs (CIDOB), the Autonomous University of Barcelona, *El Periódico de Catalunya* (Spain), and *El Confidencial* (Spain). She also coauthored a peer-reviewed article titled "Russia's Private Military Contractors: Cause for Worry?" published in *Canadian Military Journal*.

Dr. David R. Marples is distinguished university professor and was chair, Department of History and Classics, University of Alberta (2014–2019). He teaches Russian and East European history. He holds a PhD in economic and social history from the University of Sheffield (1985). At the University of Alberta, where he has been employed since 1991, he received a McCalla Professorship in 1998, the Faculty of Arts Prize for Full Professors in 1999, the J. Gordin Kaplan Award for Excellence in Research in 2003, a Killam Annual Professorship in 2005–2006, and the University Cup, the university's highest honor, in 2008. He has held several major awards from the Social Sciences and Humanities Research Council of Canada (SSHRC), most recently for the topic "History, Memory, and World War II in Belarus."

Dr. Marples has served as a consultant on current affairs in Belarus, Ukraine, and Russia to a wide array of government and nongovernment organizations, including the U.S. Department of State, the U.S. Embassy in Minsk, the UK Embassy in Minsk, the Foreign and Commonwealth Office of the United Kingdom, the Department of National Defence (Canada), the Department of Foreign Affairs and International Trade (Canada), as well as Voice of America and RFE/RL. He is a member of the advisory board on Belarus for the German Marshall Fund of the United States. He is a former associate editor of *Nationalities Papers* and *Canadian Slavonic Papers* and serves on the editorial boards of those two journals as well as several other, mainly European-based, journals. In 2014, he was a visiting fellow at the Center for Slavic and Eurasian Studies, Hokkaido University, Japan.

Dr. Marples has authored sixteen single-authored books and four edited books on various topics, including twentieth-century Russia, Stalinism, contemporary Belarus, contemporary Ukraine, and the Chernobyl disaster. His recent books include *Understanding Ukraine and Belarus* (Bristol: E-nternational Relations, 2020), *Our Glorious Past: Lukashenka's Belarus and the Great Patriotic War* (Stuttgart, Germany: Ibidem Verlag, 2014), *Russia in the 20th Century: The Quest for Stability* (London: Routledge, 2011), *Heroes and Villains: Creating National History in Contemporary Ukraine* (Budapest: Central European University Press, 2008), and *The Collapse of the Soviet Union, 1985–1991* (London: Longman, 2004). He has written more than 120 scholarly articles in refereed journals, and his speaking engagements have included the universities of Toronto, London, Tokyo, Western Australia, the Lazarski University in Warsaw, Poland, and in the United States, Harvard University, Stanford University, University of California at Berkeley, Ohio State University, and others.

www.ingramcontent.com/pod-product-compliance
Lightning Source LLC
Chambersburg PA
CBHW080935300426
44115CB00017B/2822